Fundamentals of Geography

Fundamentals of Geography

EARL B. SHAW

Professor of Geography
Assumption College
Worcester, Massachusetts

John Wiley & Sons, Inc., New York · London · Sydney

Library of Congress Catalog Card Number: 65-19475
Printed in the United States of America

By Earl B. Shaw

Anglo-America

World Economic Geography

Principles of Human Geography
  (with the late Ellsworth Huntington)

Preface

Fundamentals of Geography presents a sequence and an analysis of topics which I have used, with certain deviations, for many years of teaching classes starting the study of geography.

I believe that students should initially be introduced to (1) the meaning of and relationships between the physical and cultural environment; (2) the influences of the physical environment upon man and his activities; and (3) the changes that man has made upon that environment. Such an introduction is contained in the first chapter.

To provide a better understanding of the all-important physical environment, the ten following chapters contain descriptions of physical factors and of their relationships with man. These factors include location, climate, land forms, water bodies, vegetation, soils, and minerals.

Although the student should gain considerable knowledge of the earth by studying physical geographic factors and their distribution, he needs to know more about the world. Some of this additional knowledge may be gained through a study of five chapters emphasizing a regional and economic approach. Geographers stress several advantages for a study of the world by a regional approach. (1) It may give a better understanding of a large unit by a systematic examination of parts showing considerable similarity; (2) Dividing the earth into regions may be a good method of organizing factual material about the world, its people, and their activities; and (3) By the use of regional techniques, regions of like characteristics throughout the world can be compared and contrasted.

The climatic base is chosen for the regional section because no geographic factor influences man more than climate. There are important climatic effects upon his health, his clothing, his shelter, and his food; and in spite of the great decline in the number of agricultural workers employed in Western farming, more people throughout the world work in agriculture than in any other industry.

The five regional chapters are followed by three that stress the geography of manufacturing, trade, and population. An understanding of these topics is fundamental to any beginning course in geography.

Finally, I believe that students beginning the study of college geography should know something about the ways in which geography influences the large number of political problems that face today's world. For this reason the final chapter provides a brief introduction to political geography.

In order to stimulate further research, useful references are listed at the conclusion of each chapter. All references are chosen from magazines and books well known and easily available to American geographers. Questions based upon materials found in the text, as well as ones based upon listed references, are included. These offer opportunity for student review of major topics and study beyond the text itself.

Illustrations have been chosen for two main purposes: to emphasize topics described in the text and to add information that otherwise cannot be included. Attention is called to the black and white regional maps. Most students need to see a regional map before they can (1) understand the size and shape of a region; and (2) learn its location with reference to other regions and to the world as a whole.

The Appendix consists of ten world maps, which show distribution of important agricultural crops and domestic animals. These maps became available in September 1964, when a revision of *A Graphic Summary of World Agriculture: 1949* was issued by the United States Department of Agriculture. The original maps had no markings for latitude and longitude, but because students beginning the study of geography need mathematical orientation, a few coordinates have been added.

At the back of the book, four colored foldout world maps show precipitation, climates, soil groups, and vegetation regions. These are more comprehensive and detailed than the black and white maps of precipitation, soils, and vegetation appearing in the text. The colored map of the Köppen-Geiger system of climate classification gives the student a chance to compare this system with Trewartha's system, used in the regional maps in Chapters 12 through 16. I have included several questions designed to encourage such comparisons.

I am indebted to many persons for ideas, information, and illustrations; I have borrowed from colleagues, former teachers, students, government agencies, and business firms. To all who have contributed, I am extremely grateful.

EARL B. SHAW

Worcester, Massachusetts

April 1965

Frontispiece: Steel Plant at an Indiana Harbor
(Courtesy Youngstown Sheet and Tube Company)

Contents

Color Plates at End of Book

Part One

Introduction to Human and Physical Geography

Chapter One

Earth and Man Relationships

People in different parts of the world vary greatly in physical appearance, dress, manners, and ideals. They eat different kinds of food, build houses that range from grass huts to skyscrapers, and enjoy pleasures as diverse as skiing and cock fights. They differ especially in their ways of work and the kinds of occupations by which they earn a living. A stock broker can hardly live in the same way as a herder of llamas. Differences in language, government, education, and religion are conspicuous. Then, too, some people, such as West Europeans may be active and inventive. Others, such as the Papuans of New Guinea (Fig. 1–1), may be so inactive that they rarely do anything differently from their ancestors. Some of these differences are biological; people are born with a certain complexion. Others are cultural; people have invented certain tools and worked out certain ideas in some places and not in others. Still other differences result from contrasts in the physical environment. People can mine copper only where copper ore is in the ground.

Many of these differences are the subject matter of geography. The geographer's problem is to find out not only how all sorts of human conditions are distributed over the earth's surface but also why they are distributed in that particular fashion. He finds that in many cases the distribution is directly connected with physical features such as mountains, rivers, rainfall, or forests. In others, distribution depends upon human factors, such as density of population, stage of civilization, or the physical and mental capacities that people inherit from their ancestors. Even where human conditions are directly responsible for the distribution of certain types of man's activity, further study may show that indirectly the geographical environment[1] has much to do with the situation.

Hence geography emphasizes the nature and distribution of the relationships[2] between geographical environment and human activities and qualities.

HOW GEOGRAPHY MAY BE STUDIED

The science of geography may be studied in many ways. One way is to think of the subject as a series of problems or questions for which answers may be found. Some problems are large and complex, like the problem of how much the progress of a given people is due to the geographical conditions under which they live. For example, why are there primitive hunters in the forests of the Upper Amazon, unprogressive cattle raisers in the African Sudan, and highly civilized manufacturing and commercial people in southern Honshu?

The geographic approach to problems of this

[1] Broadly speaking the geographic environment includes the physical and the cultural environments. Among the physical items are location, land forms, climate, water bodies, soils, minerals, plants, and animals. The cultural environment refers to man-made features such as houses, factories, schools, roads, planted crops, and so forth. Thus, where man has changed the physical environment, the changed landscape becomes the cultural environment; and together the physical environment and the cultural environment make up the whole of the geographic environment. Geographers also use the terms physical and cultural to distinguish between natural and man-made landscapes.

[2] A clearer understanding of the geographic approach may be gained if relationships among elements of the physical environment are examined before relationships between the physical and cultural environments are sought. For example, it is not enough to study the relationships between the tribes of the Upper Amazon and their isolated environment. It should also be known why there is such a heavy rainfall; how the vegetation is related to the climate; how the climate and vegetation influence the character of the soils; and how the land forms influence the degree of flooding and drainage.

Fig. 1-1   An Assembly of New Guinea Natives. A meeting has been called by an Australian official to settle an infringement of a minor native tabu. The officer will probably issue a public rebuke to the offending member of the clan. Under old tribal conditions, this minor offense could have caused bloodshed and the development of a long-standing feud. Today, improved transport permits frequent visits to New Guinea hamlets by Australian officials, and such quarrels are settled by peaceful action in public assembly. (*Australian News and Information Bureau*)

kind may be facilitated by solving many smaller problems first—problems such as the effects of location, climate, vegetation, soils, land forms, and distance from the oceans upon man's food, clothing, shelter, tools, occupations, health, and energy.

Two simple questions and answers will illustrate. (1) Why is winter school attendance uncertain in northern New England? In northern New England, during almost every winter, schools and colleges are closed for a day or more simply because the deep snow cripples transportation so much that students and faculty cannot arrive at their classes. (2) Why does a baseball pitcher's curve ball work better in New York than in Denver? The curve ball works better in a sea-level location like New York than in the mile-high city of Denver because the lighter air of Denver offers less friction than the heavier air of the port city; thus, the baseball's course is more nearly straight in the highland city.

In spite of the large number of both simple and complex problems in geography, most of them can be classified under a few main headings; and all of these are likely to show some

TABLE 1-1 The Elements of Human Geography

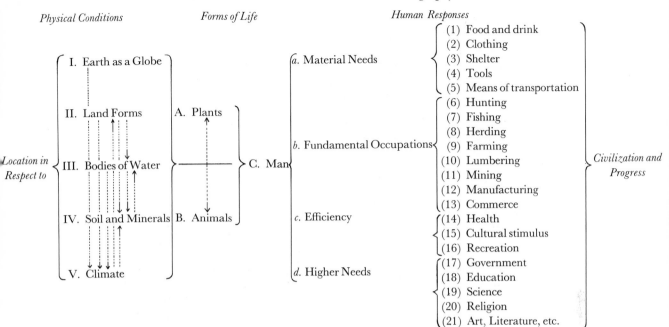

The arrows and their dotted extensions indicate the chief ways in which the physical conditions influence one another. Climate, for example, is influenced by the earth's spherical shape, by the form of the land, and by bodies of water such as oceans. It in turn influences the form of, the earth's surface, the quality of the soil, and the nature of mineral deposits. It also influences bodies of water, but this relationship and certain others are omitted to avoid crowding.

Courtesy of Ellsworth Huntington and Earl B. Shaw,
Principles of Human Geography, John Wiley & Sons, 1951.

relationship to the geographic environment (Table 1–1). A few illustrations of such relationships between major factors of the physical environment may be helpful at this point.

Location on the Earth as a Globe. Location on a rotating, globe-shaped earth is more important than many realize. It gives any one object practically the same weight everywhere. The earth's rotation gives day and night; and the middle latitude seasons, with all of their many influences, arise from the fact that the earth not only rotates, but also has an inclined axis and revolves about the sun.

On a rotating globe, such as the earth, the primary method of defining location is by latitude and longitude. Latitude, or distance north and south of the equator, is especially important because it largely determines, barring high elevation above sea level, whether a place is hot, warm, cool, or cold. The location of Russia, most of it in high latitudes, with a long northern border fronting the Arctic, and an equally long border fronting the Arctic, and an equally long

southern border near the middle of the world's largest land mass, Eurasia, is probably the most significant fact in the country's geography.

Land Forms. Relief features of the earth may be divided into a few major classes: (1) continents and ocean basins, with their various sizes and shapes, and the many islands appearing at the surface of the oceans which separate the continental masses; (2) major relief divisions of the continents such as mountains, plateaus, and plains; (3) minor subdivisions which include the minute forms of relief found in large sections of plains, plateaus, and mountains.

To illustrate man's adjustments to these classes of relief features, the following examples may be cited. Obviously, the location of a place on the periphery of a large continent is likely to give it far different climate, soil, and vegetation from that of a place located toward the interior of a great land mass; and a man living in a high mountainous region will of necessity employ different techniques in providing food from those

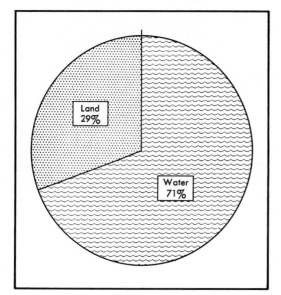

Fig. 1–2   Proportions of Land and Sea. The sea covers approximately 71 per cent of the earth's surface.

practiced by an agriculturist living on plains of nearly level land at lower elevations. Finally, road building on a marshy plain may be much more expensive than that on a slightly rolling surface with much better drainage.

Water Bodies. The more than 70 per cent of the earth's surface that is covered by oceans, seas, rivers, and lakes (Fig. 1–2) exerts a great influence upon man and his activities. Oceans separate continents from each other, and this separation has helped bring about differences in various forms of life upon the continents. For example, water has isolated Australia from other continents for so long that the movement of animals from other huge land masses has been stopped for millions of years. Species and genera have evolved in other continents while Australia remained apart; and thus most of the fauna of other lands are represented neither by living nor by fossil species. In fact, the water barrier which cut off Australia from animal immigrants from other countries was formed at the beginning of the Age of Mammals—before many prominent varieties of the world's fauna, cats, swine, horses, cattle, sheep, and rabbits, had originated. Thus these animals are not indigenous to Australia; and the island continent possessed mammals of only the most primitive

types when discovered by the European civilization.

But if water prevented passage of animals between Asia and Australia, it did not stop man's movement from continent to continent when he had invented ships capable of crossing oceans. Such ships moving across uncharted seas enabled him to inaugurate the Great Age of Discovery.

In the historic past, before the air and atomic ages, great stretches of water have given protection to man. For example, the English Channel protected Britain during many of her early wars. The shallow waters of the Zuyder Zee have provided a challenge to the Dutch who have reclaimed thousands of acres for the production of much needed agricultural crops (Fig. 1–3). Great rivers have carried soils to form the wide alluvial plains; these plains may support millions of farmers, such as those who live on the plain of China's Hwang Ho. Rivers like the Colorado, the Indus, and the Nile provide irrigation water for millions of people living on the dry lands of the earth. Salt- and fresh-water fisheries contribute an important element of diet to many of the world's people. To millions of Japanese, such waters make possible an annual per capita consumption of approximately 100 pounds of fish.

Soils and Minerals. A large part of the world's wealth comes from the soil. The soils of the United States Corn Belt were enriched by Pleistocene glaciation during a period when North American climates were much colder than they are today. As the ice sheet moved south, it leveled the land, mixed the soils, and even transported soils from what is now Canada into what is now Midwestern United States (Fig. 1–4).

After the Pleistocene ice receded, prairie grasses became established on much of what is now the Corn Belt, and this vegetation further enriched the soil. Today, prairie-earth and chernozem soils, relatively level land, ample well distributed rainfall, and hot summers, all combine to make the Corn Belt one of the world's richest and most diversified agricultural regions.

Mineral wealth, as well as soil, is of vast importance. Iron ores from Labrador, from the Lake Superior Region, from Venezuela, from

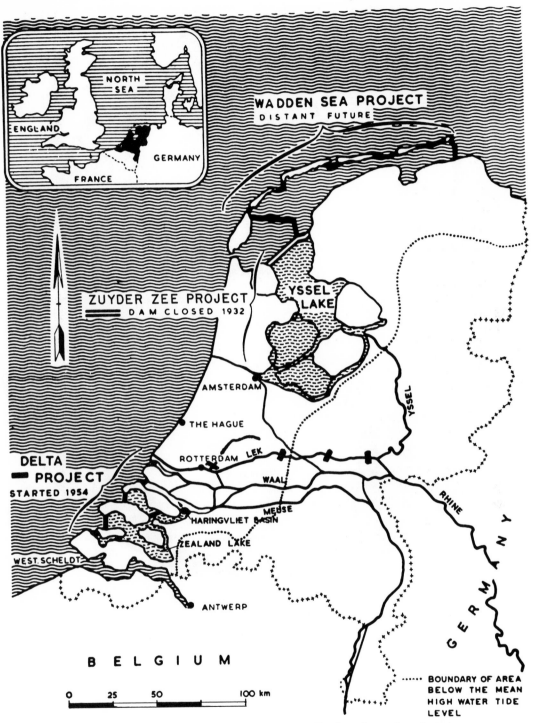

Fig. 1–3 The Dutch Call it Coastline Shortening. The three dam projects shown in the drawing show one completed, the Zuyder Zee Project; one in the dam-building stage, the Delta Project; and the third on the drawing board for completion in the future, the Wadden Sea Project. All this dam building will not only shorten the coastline; but more important it will make the country much safer from sea attack. As a result of the Dutch success in accepting the challenge of the North Sea, six out of ten Dutchmen live and work in safety below sea level. (*Courtesy Netherlands Information Service*)

Fig. 1–4   Northern Hemisphere Glaciation. White sections show lands covered with ice during the glacial ages. Arrows indicate generalized direction of flow of the ice. Shorelines are shown as they were when sea level was 300 feet lower than at present. (*C. R. Longwell and R. F. Flint,* Introduction to Physical Geology, *2d ed., John Wiley & Sons, 1962*)

Sweden, from Liberia, and from many other countries keep steel mills running in the United States and elsewhere.

The ownership and control of Atacama nitrates brought on the war of the 1880's between Chile on one side and Bolivia and Peru on the other. As a result of this war, Bolivia lost a former outlet to the Pacific, and Chile gained mineral resources that supported government expenses for nearly half a century.

Finally, the atomic age leans heavily upon uranium. For many years, the United States procured the mineral from foreign sources such as the Congo and Canada; but at present, discoveries of large local supplies, especially in the Four Corners Region of the West, have made the country self-sufficient.

Climate. Climate depends much upon location; it is greatly influenced by land forms and water bodies and influences them in return. It also plays a great part in determining the character of soils. The difference between the desert climate of the Peruvian coast and the wet climate of the forested headwaters of the Amazon in eastern Peru is influenced greatly by the Andean Cordillera. The sand dunes of Mongolia are a result of a desert climate; the "Black Earth" region of the Ukraine owes its rich soil partly to a climate too dry for trees but good for grass; the infertile laterites of wet tropical regions show what happens to soil in a warm moist climate.

Climate also affects the character of plants and animals in different regions. It permits oranges and bananas to grow in Costa Rica and wheat in Minnesota. Man's energy is also influenced by climate. The Costa Rican planter on the Caribbean Lowlands cannot work as hard for long periods of time as the Minnesota farmer. In the far North and South, not only does climate limit food supply, but also the steady cold makes consistent progress difficult. In the Amazon Basin, on the other hand, a hot, damp climate hampers progress by favoring malaria and other deadly diseases. In countries such as England, where temperatures are relatively mild, where cyclonic storms bring adequate well distributed precipitation for food production as well as variability in the weather, the climate surely has contributed significantly to the progress of civilization.

The Forms of Life

Plants. It is almost impossible to think of climate, soils, minerals, water bodies, land forms, and location without thinking of plants. The location of Greenland reminds one of its 90 per cent ice cover and the small sections of coastal fringe supporting a primitive and sparse plant life. When land forms are considered, the word "plain" may bring to mind broad acres of rich crops, while the word "mountain" may suggest rugged terrain supporting a natural forest cover rather than fields of grain.

Even in bodies of water, plants influence man through minute forms which are eaten by fish. Thus plants support an enormous tonnage of fish life. There is little reason for thinking of soil except as it enables corn, wheat, or grass, for example, to grow richly as in the United States Corn Belt, whereas in other regions such as sandy parts of Cape Cod, it makes the land scarcely worth cultivating.

Scientists have known for years that some

(A)   (B)

Fig. 1–5   Mineral Indicating Plants. The plant to the left (A) is a specimen of *Astragalus thompsonae,* or Thompson's loco, an indicator of selenium and uranium in Utah; the one to the right (B) is *Eriogonum ovalifolium,* or silver plant, used as an indicator of silver veins in Montana. The tape in the foreground, unrolled to about 12 inches, gives an orientation as to size. (*Helen L. Cannon and the U.S. Geological Survey*)

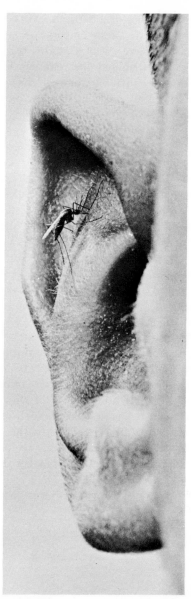

Fig. 1–6   Anopheles Mosquito Inserting its Proboscis into a Man's Ear. Today, the female anopheles mosquito is at war with 140 nations (only the female transmits malaria). Through the loss of countless productive man-hours, she retards world progress and causes an economic loss which staggers the imagination. Moreover, it is estimated that in India alone, malaria was the direct cause of death of 30 million persons over a period of three decades. (*Park Davis & Co.*)

trient and normally in a more soluble state near copper deposits, that nourishes the flower. Again, a few species of locoweed seem to prefer uranium-bearing areas. Although the locoweed doesn't really thrive on uranium, it does absorb large amounts of selenium, an element usually found in association with uranium. Prospectors call the California poppy, locoweed, and other plants showing an affinity for certain minerals "indicator plants" (Fig. 1–5).

Animals. Animals influence man in many ways. If the horse or ox had never been tamed, the prairies might have remained uncultivated. In most parts of Europe and America it would have been almost impossible to get rid of grass in cultivated fields if there had been no animals to draw the plow. Without sheep not only would our food supply be diminished, but we would lose fine natural fiber for warm winter clothing. Even before he learned to weave wool, man protected himself from the cold with fur, and that too is derived from animals. Even more important in our daily lives are cows, which give us the most nearly perfect of all foods— milk. Hens lay billions of eggs every year and add materially to man's food supply. In sections of Central Africa, the tsetse fly not only kills horses and cattle, but it also transmits to man a terrible wasting disease, and in most tropical regions the malarial mosquito (Fig. 1–6) continually brings sickness and helps to make its victims inefficient. Even in the United States, animals are harmful as well as helpful. The common fly brings dangerous maladies; and not only does the rat consume millions of dollars worth of grain each year, it also spreads disease.

It should be fairly obvious from the comments above that location, land forms, water bodies, soils, minerals, climate, plants, and animals all influence man in various ways. These include man's attempts to supply his material needs, his work at various occupations, his desire for and attainment of what may be called higher needs, and also the efficiency with which he accomplishes these fundamental aims.

Of course, the degree with which man achieves these aims successfully varies with differing physical conditions. Progress is also influenced by factors other than those of the physical environment, factors such as biologic inheritance, the stage of culture that has been

plants grow, and in fact thrive in areas where there is a higher than average concentration of certain minerals. The California poppy, for instance, grows larger and thicker in regions where there is a concentration of copper. Of course, it may be phosphate, a good plant nu-

reached by a group of people, and other non-geographic influences. Thus, while the physical environment is important in man's progress toward a higher civilization, it is only one of several elements which contribute to the desired goal.

MAN'S ROLE IN CHANGING THE FACE OF THE EARTH[3]

While man's activities are greatly influenced by the earth on which he lives, he is capable of making, has made, and will continue to make significant changes on the face of that earth. It may be useful to cite a few examples showing how man has altered the various features of his physical environment.

.   **Climate.** About thirty-five years ago Robert De Courcy Ward wrote an article entitled "How Far Can Man Control His Climate."[4] The gist of his findings may be summed up in his closing sentence: "We are lords of every specimen of air which we can bottle up and imprison in our laboratories. . . . In the open we are practically powerless."

Today, most scientists consider this statement too pessimistic. In an article, "Modifying Weather on a Large Scale," Science, October 31, 1958, H. Wexler suggests that the average energy absorbed by the earth's surface can be increased significantly by large scale blackening of light colored deserts and the polar ice caps; he goes on to say that the return of infrared radiation to space can be reduced by the formation of ice clouds—clouds which can be developed in the cheapest and most effective way by the application of nuclear energy.

Again, at a Buenos Aires meeting in November 1963, scientists making plans for the International Hydrological Decade to begin in 1965

were in general agreement that rain making would be easy by 1975. At this same conference mention was also made of new methods to conserve moisture by (1) covering reservoirs with a thin impermeable chemical that will lessen the evaporation of water; (2) covering plant leaves with wax to slow down water consumption; and (3) spreading a bituminous substance that retains humidity over soil.

Although success in these changes may not become widespread for a few more years, man already has changed climates by the removal of forests and by the planting of forests, by the cultivation of the land, by the building of reservoirs, by the drainage of lakes; by building towns, and by the invention and use of various devices for the control of frost. And since the late 1950's man has been building and equipping stations at or near the South Pole, where he stays with temperatures reaching lower than 100 degrees below zero (Fahrenheit). True, during his stay he has not yet changed the polar climate, but his inventive genius makes it possible to live and carry on scientific work in one of the world's most trying climates (Fig. 1–7).

If the future holds as much potential for the adjustment to weather and for weather controls as now seems possible, vast unused areas may be added to present agricultural land by only slight changes in precipitation and temperature; and hurricanes may be diverted or their force lessened by separating them into small storms before an enormous amount of energy gathers in one storm. Finally, a rather disturbing question arises about man's mastery of these and other weather controls. If he is able to use such knowledge as a weapon in cold or hot wars —if he can injure enemy agricultural production, hinder enemy commerce, and slow down enemy industry—will all this be good or bad for the world as a whole. In short, in learning to upset nature's present weather and climate balance, will man make conditions better or worse for future generations.

Water Bodies. The Dutch have made great progress in decreasing the earth's sea surface and increasing the world land area. A ninth century traveler found half of what is now the Netherlands to be salt water and mud flats, the other half a waste of sand, moors, and heath land. People along the foggy northern shores

---

[3] For a good description of man-made changes and of the men who have made significant contributions to the study of these changes, see *Man's Role in Changing the Face of the Earth*, An International Symposium under the co-chairmanship of Carl O. Sauer, Marston Bates, and Lewis Mumford, and edited by William L. Thomas, Jr., University of Chicago Press, 1956, xxxviii and 1193 pp.

[4] Ward, Robert De Courcy, "How Far Can Man Control His Climate," *The Scientific Monthly*, January 1930, vol. XXX, pp. 5–18.

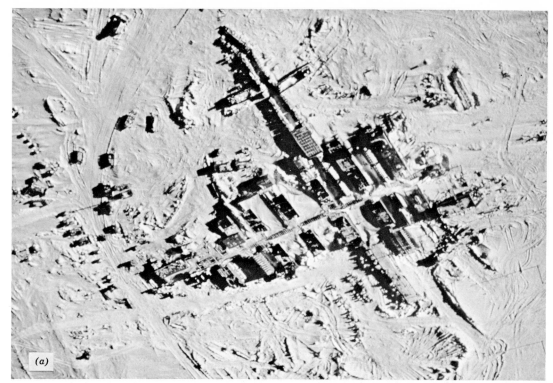

Fig. 1–7   Contrast in Antarctic Expeditions. Little America (*a*) is located about 40 miles northeast of Admiral Byrd's old camps near the Bay of Whales. The largest U.S. scienific station in Antarctica during the IGY, it was operative from 1956 through 1958.

Captain Falcon Scott's 1902 camp (*b*) housed the entire Scott expedition. It is immediately adjacent to the present large U.S. facility on McMurdo Sound. Since the camp picture was taken, the New Zealand Antarctic Society has restored the Scott building and other Antarctic sites of historic significance. (*a*) *Official U.S. Navy Photograph;* (*b*) *Paul Dalrymple, U.S. Army Natick Laboratories*)

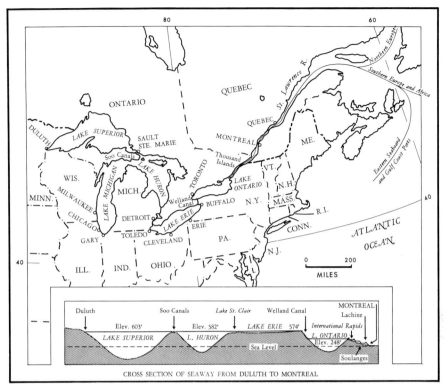

Fig. 1–8   The Great Lakes-St. Lawrence Seaway. The greatest problems in seaway improvement occurred in the 182-mile stretch between Lake Ontario and Montreal, where rapids have always made river navigation hazardous. Here, old canals have been deepened, and new canals and locks have been constructed to a depth of at least 27 feet. Power facilities have been added capable of an electrical output several times that of the Colorado River's Hoover Dam.

built *terpen,* or mounds, on which they were able to keep their huts and a few cattle above the tides (see Fig. 1–3).

Soon they began to enclose damp pastures with artificial embankments to keep out the water and to permit improvement of the land. As this process continued through the centuries, more and more land, protected by dikes, replaced marsh and water. However, these additions were not made without interruption. During the stormy years of the late Middle Ages, many hard won fields were lost to the sea; and even as recently as January 1953, high tides and onshore winds broke Zeeland's dikes and inundated more than 400,000 acres. But the Dutch never give up. They still block the tides and push back the ocean; and by 1958 about half of the Netherlands was protected by dikes, and approximately 60 per cent of the population, 7 million people, were living below sea level.

Man has also made significant changes in water bodies through building canals such as the Panama, the Suez, and the Soo. He has made seaports of inland cities like Chicago, Cleveland, Milwaukee, Toledo, and Detroit by deepening parts of the St. Lawrence river; by building canals and locks around falls and rapids in the St. Lawrence and among the Great Lakes; and by improving port facilities in these cities (Fig. 1–8).

Every year newspaper and magazine articles are written about the possibility of deepening Bering Strait to encourage the movement of warm ocean currents into the Arctic Ocean. Results are pictured as raising the temperatures of the tundra shores of the bordering lands many degrees F. This project may be attempted some day. Costs of the change in water temperatures would be far less than the United States annual expenditures for military defense.

Other man-made changes include the alteration of coastlines; for example, man has developed the Intra-Coastal Canal along the United States Atlantic and Gulf Coast; moreover, he has altered aquatic life by eliminating most of the sea lamprey in the American Great Lakes; he has drained coastal marsh lands; cut through river meanders and built dams and reservoirs to control floods; and increased the quantity and improved the quality of ground water as well as surface water.

In connection with man's changes of and within water bodies, mention should be made of the havoc that may occur because of man's persistence in exploiting only selected species of aquatic life. In short, throwing ocean flora and fauna out of balance may be worse than doing the same thing among flora and fauna on land because life in the ocean is harder for man to control.

Soils. Not all of man's changes in soils can be classified as beneficial to humanity. In the southern United States, soils have been depleted by an emphasis upon one crop farming with money crops such as cotton and tobacco. In the Appalachian country, hill lands have been cropped carelessly, and soils have been removed by erosion. In the Palouse country of the Northwest, excessive cropping to wheat has damaged the naturally rich volcanic earth; in the Great Plains and in the Intermontane Plateaus, over grazing has changed vegetative cover and soils for the worse.

But much of man's work with soils has resulted in improvement. Commercial fertilizers now improve soil fertility and soil structure. In countries such as Lebanon, man has built soil terraces and increased crop production enormously. What a contrast there is between man's building terraces in Lebanon and in building the Egyptian pyramids. Both enterprises consumed millions of man hours of work. In Lebanon the work increased man's food supply significantly. In Egypt, the work satisfied the vanity of a few despotic rulers.

In the Western Hemisphere, California for instance, terracing on some of the rolling lands also takes place. But here soil conservation includes many other practices such as irrigation, drainage, alkali reclamation, limiting erosion, levelling of land, blasting of hardpan, subsoiling, application of such soil amendments as lime or gypsum, the use of organic matter and organic fertilizers, and the use of commercial fertilizers. Recently commercial fertilizers have been applied to forest crops as well as to agricultural lands in the United States.

Minerals and Power Resources. Man's work in changing the earth's minerals and power resources is probably as great as his work with soils. In many places he has altered the landscape by strip mining coal, by sinking deep shafts for metallic minerals, by boring wells for petroleum and natural gas, and by mining various ores from huge open pits. He has fashioned towns, cities, and routes of transport with minerals made into bricks, cement, asphalt, rails, and so forth. Many of the means of transportation which appear on the face of the earth were made from minerals formerly within the earth. In one case he has produced synthetic rubber from petroleum and natural gas—rubber that appears on the millions of cars carrying man and his commercial products. And finally, he is now producing synthetic minerals—for example the synthetic diamonds used in industry; and he uses various minerals in producing the atomic bombs, which may remove him from what is left of the face of the earth.

Land Forms. Although man's changes in the earth's land forms are far less significant than the natural growth of mountain ranges, the peneplanation of upland regions, or the invasion of the continents by ice and transgression seas, man has made a definite impression on the earth's face in several areas. He has tunneled through the Alps, the Rockies, and the Andes to quicken communication through these obstacles. He has cut waterways through the Isthmus of Suez, the Isthmus of Panama, and many other of the earth's land constrictions. He has tied together the great rivers of Germany, the Weser, the Rhine, the Elbe, and the Oder by a series of canals. At present with the great power of nuclear energy, man may literally remove mountains if they become too serious an obstacle for his progress (Fig. 1–9).

Plants. One of man's greatest changes on the face of the earth has come in the alteration of plant life. Even primitive man has been active in this change, most of it destructive. Man-made fires have removed thousands of square miles of

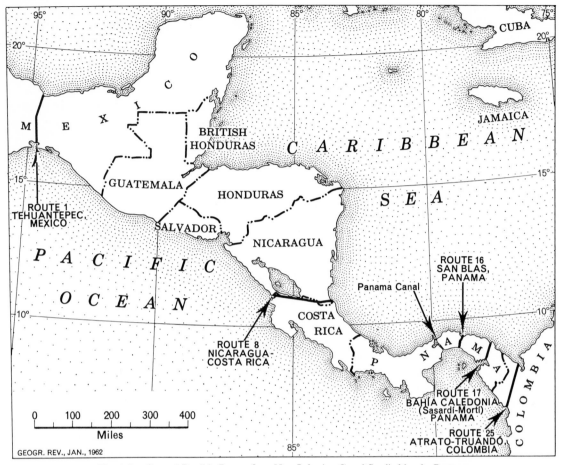

Fig. 1–9. Several Possible Routes for a New Isthmian Canal Studied by the Panama Canal Company. The cost of nuclear excavation of a sea-level canal along the Sasardi-Morti route is estimated at less than half the expense of one excavated by conventional engineering methods. No safety problem is regarded as serious enough to make the nuclear project unfeasible. But political problems may delay it or make it impossible. (*W. N. Hess and* Geographical Review, *Jan. 1962*)

forest; in the Philippines about 18 per cent of the total area is covered by grass as a result of shifting cultivation and fires.

Again, fires have been used on grass land to remove dead coarse grasses and to allow new grass to profit by the period of heaviest precipitation. But fires started to improve the quality of grass may invade the surrounding forests. Such fires play an important part in their influence upon African plant life. All over the southern part of Sudan, parts of Ethiopia, and the Lake Plateau, grass is burned every year. This practice kills many trees, and those that remain may be stunted in their growth.

Africa is not the only continent where a care-

less forest policy has been employed. In North America, the United States went through three major steps in handling the national forest policy. In an anxiety to make the land livable and productive, (1) uncontrolled exploitation was permitted; land was cleared quickly to make room for farms and towns; then to supply wood for these farms and towns, trees were cut so rapidly to provide for farm, home, and population expansion that (2) it became necessary to import forest resources to fulfill domestic needs. At last (3) the nation now practices scientific forestry, and once more has achieved self-sufficiency in tree products. Forest management at present stresses such progressive steps as fire protection; tree farming; a tax system which encourages treating forests as crops rather than considering them as minerals to be mined; disease and insect control; and selective cutting.

Great progress has been made in each of these practices. A pertinent comment may be made on selective cutting. In the past, owners of forest lands were likely to remove the better trees first, because of the quality and quantity of the wood. Of course, this left inferior trees to reproduce, thus lowering the overall quality of the lumber stand. Now forest companies are using the superior trees to propagate a new race of taller, straight, healthier trees with greater wood content; and the inferior trees are removed to give the better trees greater opportunity to grow and reproduce. In time this practice should change radically the character and productiveness of the world's commercial forests.

Some of man's greatest changes in the face of the earth have come through his replacement of natural plant life with hybrids. These include improved varieties of cereals such as corn, wheat, and rice; citrus fruits such as oranges, grapefruit, and lemons; fibers, including cotton and flax; gums, among which rubber is important; and many other plants. Truly, man has achieved progress in plant breeding.

Animals. Man's improvements on animal life have kept pace with his progress in plant breeding. Wild sheep have been replaced by the Merino, famous for a heavy growth of wool; by the Shropshire, well known for the large quantity of mutton on its carcass; and by the Tasmanian sheep, one of the best dual purpose animals—useful for both meat and wool.

Again, man no longer depends upon the wild boar for his bacon and animal fats; instead he breeds a great variety of swine which provide pork in huge quantities. To name but a few of the many breeds developed in the last few centuries there are the Poland China, the Chester White, the Tamworth, the Duroc Jersey, and the Hampshire.

Finally some of man's greatest accomplishments in the domestication of animals have come in the cattle industry. Milk has been improved in quantity and quality with the development of such breeds as the Guernsey, the Jersey, the Brown Swiss, and the Holstein. Meat

production has been aided with the addition of the Hereford, the Shorthorn, and the Angus.

One of the most recent advances in cattle breeding occurred in the United States. King Ranch, in Texas, has developed a breed of cattle, the Santa Gertrudis, which holds considerable promise for cattle raisers on tropical grazing lands. When the English Shorthorn or Durham is crossed with the Indian Zebu or Brahman, the resulting strain retains many of the best qualities of both parents. The offspring from these parents inherits fairly good meat and milk production from the Durham mother and great resistance to tropical heat, diseases, and insect pests from the Indian father.

In the first part of the chapter, stress is placed upon the influences of the earth upon man's activities, with earth the dominant factor. In the latter part, emphasis is placed upon man's changes of the earth, with man the dominant element. Both conditions belong in the study of human geography; and both reciprocal relationships may be found in the same area or region. Greenland may serve as a good example.

In northern Greenland, man's anxiety over the defense of Anglo-America has encouraged him to change the physical landscape by building an anchor for the DEW line—Distant Early Warning service (Fig. 1–10). Here not only has man's inventive genius given him equipment to survive a harsh climate; but his ingenuity has created devices such as radar to detect coming enemy attack. Here political relations have made precautions seem necessary. Here man's inability to get along with man receives precedence over the earth environment in the building of structures to change that environment. However, earth environment still shows an influence upon man's choice of a strategic defense location.

In southern Greenland, changes in the earth environment, not man-made, are the overpowering influence in changing man's occupations. The North Atlantic Ocean bathing Greenland's southwest coast began to grow warmer in the 1920's. This encouraged a poleward movement of seals and a northward migration of cod. Prior to the 20th century, the seal was a dominant factor in Greenland's economy. It was a source of food, clothing, oil for light and heat, and bone for implements. Sealing was a subsistence occupation, that is it pro-

Fig 1–10 Dye 2, One of the Dew Line East Stations. Dye 2, located just south of the Arctic Circle in Greenland, has an elevation of 7650 feet above sea level. The building is 133 feet wide and 144 feet long and represents the most modern Arctic construction. Built during the period 1959–1961, the camp is normally elevated 20 feet above the snow surface; but if more snow accumulates around the base it may be elevated further by two 350-ton hydraulic jacks placed on each of eight pairs of columns which support the building. The top of the radome is about 150 feet above the snow surface. The large antenna within the radome is for tracking any objects coming over the stations; and the large antennas on the sides are for lateral communication. The camp has a winter complement of about 25 people, which includes both United States and Danish citizens; during the summer the number may increase to nearly one hundred. (*Donald Houge, U.S. Army Natick Laboratories*)

vided the hunter with so many of his necessities that he needed little contact with the commercial world. Now the seal has moved away from Greenland's major centers of population.

The present day emphasis upon cod fishing differs from the former sealing economy; commercial fishing requires a different set of tools and techniques from those employed in catching seals; and since the fisherman cannot live directly from the cod as he did from the seal— now he sells his catch of fish—he has learned about a money economy.

Thus, because of the changing sea environment, man has completely changed his economy. Here earth, not man, seems uppermost in changing man's activities.

QUESTIONS, EXERCISES, AND PROBLEMS

1. With examples taken from the text, show how each feature of the physical environment influences man and his activities. Work out the exercise with examples other than those in the book.
2. With examples taken from the text, show how man has changed significantly each feature of the physical environment. Work out the exercise with examples other than those in the book.
3. Identify the following authors by emphasizing their

contributions to the literature dealing with man's role in changing the face of the earth: George Perkins Marsh, Alexander Ivanovich Woeikof, Nathaniel Southgate Shaler, Paul Vidal de la Blache, Jean Brunhes, Albert Demangeon, Marion Isabel Newbigin.

4. Comment on the following statement: "The story of man's role in changing the face of the earth begins with the invention of fire-making and the domestication of plants and animals; continues through his trade, warfare, migrations, and the spread of transportation facilities, fields, and settlements; and culminates in the development of modern mining and manufacturing."

SELECTED REFERENCES

Bjorklund, E. M., "Ideology and Culture Exemplified in Southwestern Michigan," *Annals of the Association of American Geographers,* July 1964, pp. 227–241.

Cannon, Helen L., "Botanical Prospecting for Ore Deposits," *Science,* September 2, 1960, pp. 591–598.

Douglas, William O., and Hare, Clyde, "Banks Island: Eskimo Life on the Polar Sea," *National Geographic,* May 1964, pp. 702–735.

Fonaroff, L. Schuyler, "Malaria Geography: Problems and Potentials for the Profession," *Professional Geographer,* November 1963, pp. 1–7.

Hess, W. N., "New Horizons in Resource Development, the Role of Nuclear Explosions," *Geographical Review,* January 1962, pp. 1–25.

Isaac, Erich, "The Act and the Covenant, the Impact of Religion on the Landscape," *Landscape,* Winter 1961–1962, pp. 12–17.

Jackson, J. B., "The Four Corners Country," *Landscape,* Fall 1960, pp. 20–26.

James, Preston E., editor, *New Viewpoints in Geography,* Twenty-Ninth Yearbook of the National Council for the Social Studies, 1959.

Leopold, Luna B., "Water and the Southwest," *Landscape,* Fall 1960, pp. 27–31.

Meigs, Peveril, "Some Geographical Factors in the Peloponnesian War," *Geographical Review,* July 1961, pp. 370–381.

Moore, W. G., *A Dictionary of Geography,* Penguin Books, 1958.

Nelson, Howard J., "Walled Cities of the United States," *Annals of the Association of American Geographers,* March 1961, pp. 1–23.

Sauer, Carl O., "Homestead and Community on the Middle Border," *Landscape,* Fall, 1962, pp. 3–7.

Schultz, Harald, "Indians of the Amazon Darkness," *National Geographic,* May 1964, pp. 736–758.

Shaw, Earl B., "Geography and Baseball," *Journal of Geography,* Feb. 1963, pp. 74–76.

Stamp, L. Dudley, editor, *A Glossary of Geographical Terms,* John Wiley and Sons, 1961.

Thomas, William L., Jr., editor, *Man's Role in Changing the Face of the Earth,* University of Chicago Press, 1956.

Thralls, Zoe A., "Geography: Its Nature and Function," *The Teaching of Geography,* Ch. 1, pp. 1–18, Appleton-Century-Crofts, 1958.

Udall, Stewart L., *The Quiet Crisis,* Holt, Rinehart, and Winston, 1963.

Wagner, Philip I., "Natural and Artificial Zonation in a Vegetation Cover: Chiapas, Mexico," *Geographical Review,* April 1962, pp. 253–74.

Whittemore, K. T., "The Supplementary Geographical Reading Materials," *Professional Geographer,* Sept. 1961, pp. 5–10.

Wilmsen, Edwin N., "The House and the Navaho," *Landscape,* Fall 1960, pp. 15–19.

Chapter Two

The Earth's Location, Form, and Motions

The earth is an oblate spheroid,[1] that is a sphere flattened at the poles and bulging at the equator. As a result of polar flattening and equatorial bulging, the earth's diameter from pole to pole is about 7900 miles or about 27 miles less than that at the equator. The spheroid's circumference is approximately 25,000 miles.

The earth revolves about the sun once in 365 days, 5 hours, 48 minutes, and 46 seconds. It rotates on its axis once in approximately 24 hours. The average distance of the earth from the sun as it moves around its orbit is about 93 million miles. When the earth is in perihelion, closest to the sun, the mileage is about 91 million; when it is in aphelion, farthest from the sun, it is about 94 million miles away (Fig. 2–1).

The Human Significance of the Earth's Location, Form, and Motions. The qualities which the earth possesses by reason of being a rotating spheroidal planet revolving around the sun have an incalculable influence upon human affairs. If the earth were altered in shape even a little, if it rotated or revolved more slowly, or if it were composed of different materials, the development of plants, animals, and man would have been correspondingly altered.

For example, if the earth were nearer the sun, the world would receive more heat, and a year would be shorter. If it were farther from the sun, there would be less heat, and the year

would be longer. A change in the inclination of the earth's axis would alter seasons in middle and high latitudes. If there were no inclination, there would be no seasons; if there were less inclination, there would be less difference between summer and winter; if there were a greater inclination of the axis, there would be a more significant difference between winter and summer. If the earth were to rotate on its axis once every twelve hours, think of the consequent alteration in the length of day and night and in the number of days in a year.

Suppose that the earth rotated from east to west instead of from west to east as it does. The sun, moon, and stars would rise in the west and set in the east. Wouldn't that seem queer? Surely enough has been said to show that *plants, animals, and man are adapted to a globe with a definite shape, size, location, and set of motions.*

Proofs of the Earth's Shape and Motions. A few proofs of the earth's approximately spherical shape may be noted: (1) During an eclipse of the moon, the earth's shadow is circular. This phenomenon gives evidence of the earth's shape, because a sphere is the only geometrical solid that at all angles would develop a circular shadow; (2) the hull of a distant receding ship disappears before the sails, the masts, the smokestacks, or the smoke. Conversely when a distant ship moves into port, the smoke, smokestacks, masts, or sails may be seen before the hull; (3) the most spectacular proof of the earth's spherical shape comes through photographs taken from planes thousands of feet in the air and from rockets soaring hundreds of miles into space.

Proof of the earth's rotation may be seen in the rising and setting of the sun, moon, and planets and in their daily movement across the sky. Another evidence of rotation is the course of a ball dropped from a great height. Barring a

[1] Studies during the geophysical year, 1959, show that the spheroid is 50 feet higher than formerly assumed at the North Pole; 25 feet lower in the northern middle latitudes; 50 feet lower at the South Pole; 25 feet higher in the southern middle latitudes. However, these minor computation changes do not eliminate polar flattening nor do they make the earth pear-shaped. They merely show the earth a little bit lop-sided or asymmetrical causing a slight modification of the oblate spheroidal shape. For further information see Anastasia Van Burkalow, "What Shall We Teach About the Earth's Shape?" *Journal of Geography,* May 1960, pp. 229–34.

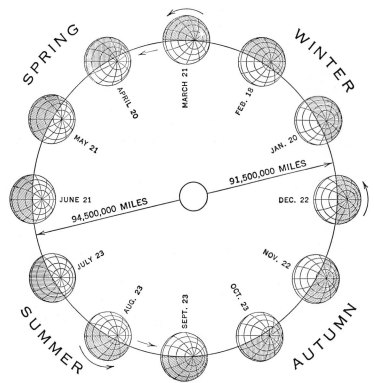

Fig. 2–1   The Seasons and Length of Day and Night in the Northern Hemisphere. The circle in the center represents the sun, shown smaller than the earth although actually thousands of times larger. The North Pole is aimed in the same direction throughout the year, but the zone within the Arctic Circle is completely in sunlight June 21, completely in darkness December 22, and except at the pole, has about 12 hours of daylight and darkness on March 21 and September 23. Note that the sun is closer to the earth in winter than in summer. However, the effect is almost negligible in the amount of heat received.

slight deflection due to the varying density of different parts of the earth, a plumb line suspended from a lofty structure such as the Eiffel Tower in Paris points straight toward the earth's center. If a ball be dropped from the point of suspension, it will not strike the earth at the point toward which the plumb line is directed, but an inch or more to the east. During the few seconds while the ball is falling, both ball and earth move eastward by rotation. The ball falls, perfectly straight, but because it starts at a point outside the earth's surface, it has an eastward motion greater than that of the point on the surface below it.

A third proof of earth rotation came with the Foucault pendulum, which proved not only that the earth rotates but that the rotation is from west to east. In the year 1851, a French

scientist by the name of Foucault (foo-ko′) suspended a pendulum by a wire 200 feet long from the top of the Pantheon in Paris. The pendulum was set swinging in a north-south line. As the swinging continued, its direction of vibration apparently changed slightly from east of north to west of south. When kept swinging long enough, it appeared to continue changing until it swung along a northeast-southwest line, then an east-west line, and so on until it had completed the entire circle of directions.

Rotation on the earth's axis determines the positions of the North and South Poles and that of the equator; and latitude may be defined as location with reference to the equator.

Revolution of the earth around its orbit can also be proved by several bits of evidence. If the earth did not revolve about the sun, the stars would be in the same part of the sky each night. This is not the case, for there is a slight change in positions of the stars from night to night, sufficient to make a complete change of stars in the sky in six months and to bring them back to the first position in one year.

Further proof of earth revolution may be seen by the occurrence of the seasons in the middle and high latitudes. If the earth should stop revolving in its orbit, but continue to rotate on its axis, the vertical ray of the sun would reach the earth at the same place during the entire year. The sun would rise day after day at the same time in the same direction for all places on the same parallel. It would have the same noon altitude day after day. It would always set at the same time and in the same direction. There would be no change in the length of day and length of night for any one latitude. With no change in amount of sunshine, there could be no change of season anywhere.

The change from the high sun at noon in June, in the Northern Hemisphere, to the low sun at noon in December proves that the earth's axis is inclined to the plane of the earth's orbit instead of being vertical. Because of this tipping, the two tropics—Cancer in the Northern Hemisphere and Capricorn in the Southern Hemisphere—are 23½ degrees from the equator. In the same way the two polar circles—the Arctic Circle in the north and the Antarctic Circle in the south—are 23½ degrees from the poles.

Latitude

As previously indicated, latitude implies location with reference to the equator. Imaginary circular lines parallel to the equator on a globe are called parallels of latitude. They are numbered and the numbers are preceded by the terms North or South, depending upon whether the parallels lie north or south of the equator.

There is a clear relationship between the position of the noonday sun and the latitude of any place on the earth's surface (Figs. 2–2 and 2–3). Wherever one may be, the number of degrees of an arc from the zenith (directly overhead) to the noonday sun is always equal to the number of degrees of latitude between the observer's position and the part of the earth where the sun's rays are falling vertically at noon. The noonday sun's rays fall vertically (1) over the equator, 0°

latitude, on March 21 and September 21, the dates of the equinoxes; (2) on the Tropic of Cancer, 23½° North on June 21, which is the summer solstice of the northern hemisphere; (3) and on the Tropic of Capricorn, 23½° South on December 21, which is the winter solstice of the northern hemisphere. The Nautical Almanac, available from the Superintendent of Documents, Government Printing Office, Washington, D.C. gives the parallels of latitude on which the sun is directly overhead at noon on all other days of the year.

Another principle associated with latitude provides important geographic information. If the latitude of a place is known, one may learn the zenith distance of the noonday sun by applying the following rule. Wherever one may be, the zenith distance of the noonday sun is equal to the same number of degrees on an arc in the sky as the number of degrees of latitude between the observer and the place where the sun's rays are falling vertically at noon.

The terms high, low, and middle latitudes are used frequently by geographers. The names arise because low numbers are used for places near the equator, high numbers for places near the poles, and medium sized numbers for those places between the equator and the poles. The highest latitude a place may have is 90°, found at the North and South Poles. The lowest latitude, 0° appears at the equator. Generally speaking, areas lying between 0° and 30° North or South are called low latitudes; those between 30° and 60° North or South are termed middle latitudes; and regions located between 60° and the poles are considered high latitudes.

Probably the most important relationship between latitude and man is latitude's influence upon climate; for latitude influences (1) the altitude of the noonday sun and (2) the length of daylight and darkness, the two most important climatic influences any place may have. And just as latitude influences climate, so too does climate influence vegetation and soils. Thus, latitude exerts a significant control, directly or indirectly, upon man's sources of food, shelter, and clothing.

Longitude and Time

Whereas the latitude of a place is always north or south of, or on, the equator, the longitude of

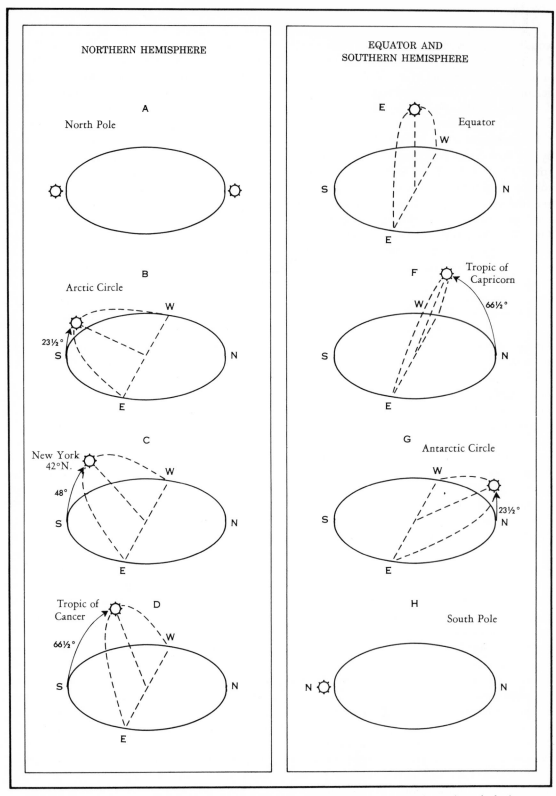

Fig. 2–2 Path of the Sun at Different Latitudes, September Equinox. Notice that the *noonday* sun is on the horizon at the poles; 23½ degrees above the horizon at the Arctic Circle; 42 degrees above the horizon at New York; 66½ degrees above the horizon on the Tropic of Cancer; directly overhead, 90 degrees above the horizon, at the equator; 66½ degrees above the horizon at the Tropic of Capricorn; and 23½ degrees above the horizon at the Antarctic Circle. What are the corresponding zenith distances in degrees?

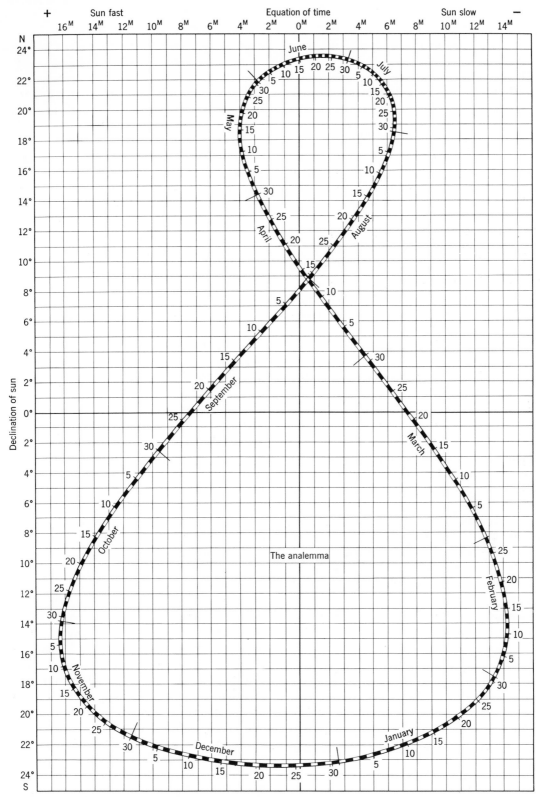

Fig. 2–3 The Analemma. The word analemma, derived from the Greek *analemma* meaning sundial, refers to a diagram with a shape slightly resembling the figure eight, drawn on many terrestrial globes. Its function is to give a graphic picture of continuing changes (1) in the apparent declination of the sun and (2) in the equation of time throughout the year. For a good detailed explanation and a well illustrated description of the device, see Erwin Raisz, "The Analemma," *The Journal of Geography*, vol. 40, pp. 90–97. *A. N. Strahler*, Physical Geography, *2d ed., John Wiley & Sons, 1962*)

a place is always east or west of, or on, the prime meridian.[2]

The prime meridian may be compared to a centrally located north-south trending city avenue crossed by an east-west street at right angles. Numbers on the east-west street extending west of the north-south major artery will be preceded by the term *West* because this portion of the east-west street lies west of the north-south artery; and numbers extending east of the north-south major artery will be preceded by the term *East*.

The prime meridian and other meridians are imaginary north-south lines extending from the north pole to the south pole on a globe. The name meridian comes from the words *medius*, meaning middle, and *dies*, meaning day; and a meridian of longitude joins all places having noon by the sun at the same time.

The highest longitude a place may have is 180°, and the lowest is 0°. Locations west of the prime meridian (0°) and between it and 180° have West Longitude, and those east of the prime meridian and between it and 180° have East Longitude. Since all meridians converge at the poles, there is no longitude there.

Time is measured by the rotation of the earth on its axis, a rotation which carries a place through 360° of a circle. A degree of circular measure consists of 60 minutes; and each minute is made up of 60 seconds. These degrees, minutes, and seconds are arcs of circumference, not time divisions. The time necessary for one rotation of the earth is approximately 24 hours. Each hour is divided into 60 minutes, and each minute into 60 seconds.

Difference in longitude brings a difference in time. A difference of 360 degrees of longitude makes a difference of 24 hours of time; a difference of 15 longitude degrees corresponds to a difference of one hour in time; and a difference of one longitude degree corresponds to a difference of four minutes in time.

The fact that the earth rotates from west to east is also important to consider in gaining the proper concept of longitude and time. When the sun has reached its greatest daily height at Greenwich at noon, an hour has already passed since it attained the highest point 15 longitude degrees east of Greenwich. However, another hour must elapse before the meridian 15 degrees West of Greenwich will move east far enough to experience the noonday sun (Fig. 2–4).

In the United States, the meridian of Boston will pass under the sun before the one at Chicago, and hence Boston will have its noon first; later, the meridian at Denver and the one at San Francisco will pass under the sun's influence, and as a consequence, noon will come to Denver about an hour later than to Chicago, and San Francisco's midday will be delayed still another hour. Thus meridians of longitude help to explain human activities that are related to conditions of time. Man's times of arising in the morning, of going to bed at night, of eating, of working, of playing, and of countless other activities are all related to the earth's rotation, to differences in longitude, and to the differing times when various meridians come into and go out of the light of the sun (Fig. 2–5).

Before rail, telegraph, and telephone lines became common, people in the United States used local sun time. However, in 1883, the United States railroads began using four standards[3] of time to take the place of 53 standards previously used. These four time belts use the sun time of the 75th, 90th, 105th, and 120th meridians of West Longitude, and are known by the names of Eastern, Central, Mountain, and Pacific Time.

Change in time from one belt to the other takes place not on the standard meridian, but at approximately 7½° from the reference line. Boundaries of each belt are somewhat irregular, with limits placed where change of time will

---

[2] Choice of the equator as a line of reference for determining the latitude of a place became nearly universal long before the choice of a reference line for longitude received wide acceptance. For many years, before improvements in transportation made the world relatively small, several countries chose the meridian passing through a capital city as a line of reference for measuring east-west distances. When world contacts became easier and quicker, talk of one reference line useful for measuring east-west distances for all countries brought forth the choice of the so-called prime meridian at Greenwich. Now most states count longitude from the north-south line which passes through the center of the base of the telescope in the Greenwich astronomical observatory near London. The adoption is not entirely universal, however, and world maps of longitude and time show where other time reference lines are used.

[3] Standard time is the civil time established by law or by general use over a region or country.

entail the least inconvenience. The telegraph, telephone, and radio sometimes cause people to use the time of some other belt than their own. The Stock Exchange in Chicago, for example, finds it convenient to be open at just the same hours as those of the New York Stock Exchange.

How Travelers Gain or Lose Time. On a journey around the world a traveler seems to gain or lose 24 hours of time. For example, in 1519 the explorer Magellan left Spain with five ships to make the first voyage round the world. When his sole surviving vessel reached Spain three years later, the crew could not understand why their reckonings made the date September 6, while the people at home said it was September 7. No mistake could be found in the ship's records, and the travelers were much puzzled

until Paoli Sarpi told them that during their adventurous voyage they had lost a day by going west around the world with the sun. If they had gone east, they would have gained a day, and would have recorded the date of their return as September 8.

This is the explanation. Suppose that a traveler leaves London on Monday at noon and travels west 15° of longitude each day. Since 15° corresponds to a difference of an hour of time, the sun at the second noon will reach the zenith an hour later than at London. Therefore at noon by the sun on Tuesday, the traveler's watch, with London time, will say 1 P.M. If he sets it back an hour his day will be 25 hours instead of 24. If he keeps on around the world, he will traverse 360° of longitude and change his watch by one hour 24 times. Whether he travels

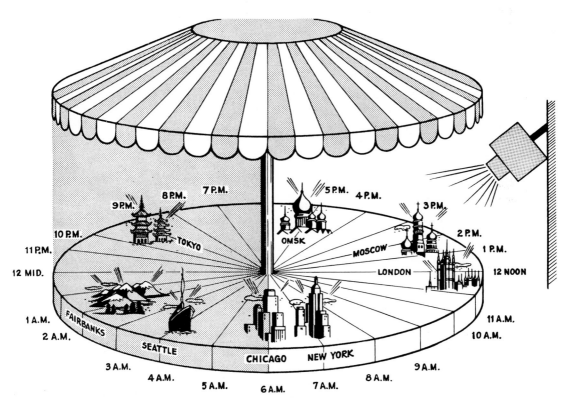

Fig. 2–4 The Rotation of the Earth on its Axis. The rotation of the earth on its axis may be compared to a merry-go-round, or carousel, that makes one complete turn every twenty-four hours. In one hour's time, the carousel, representing the earth, turns through 15 degrees of longitude. The spotlight, at the right of the merry-go-round, may be compared to the sun shining on part of the earth at all times. As any place on the carousel, representing the earth, turns toward the spotlight (the sun) that place has sunrise. As the place turns away from the sun, sunset occurs. The side facing the sun is in the daylight; the side facing away from the sun lies in the darkness. (*American Airlines and Air Education News*)

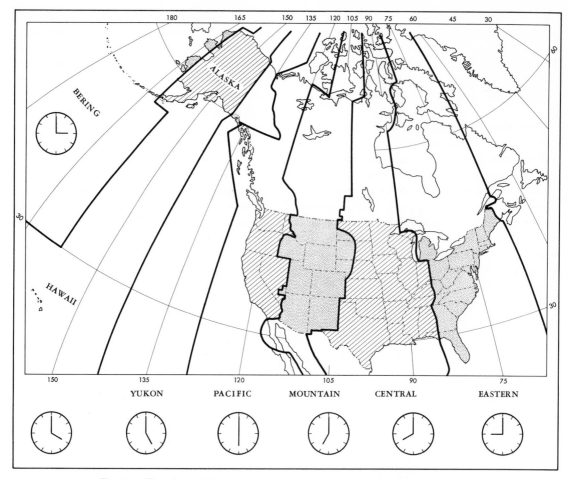

Fig. 2–5   Time Belts of the United States. Ideally, time belts should extend 7½ on either side of the meridian passing through them; but it is more advantageous for time zones to conform to state, county, or physiographic boundaries. The Standard Time Act provides a single standard for Alaska, based on the 150th meridian W., but this time is observed only in central Alaska. Pacific time is observed in the S.E.; Yukon time in another portion of the coastal area; and Bering time along the west coast and in the Aleutian Islands. Hawaii standard time is based on the same meridian as that of central Alaska. (*T. E. Payne, and E. W. Martin,* Standard Time, *Interstate Commerce Commission, May 1963*)

slowly or rapidly the amount of time required for the sun to catch up with him will be the same for any given number of degrees, and when he gets back to London he will seem to have lost an entire day. In order to make his calendar like that of people at home, he must drop one date, just as Magellan's men dropped September 7.

In traveling east, the days are shortened instead of lengthened, and the watch must be set ahead instead of back. The interval from one noon to another is less than 24 hours, and the days pass more rapidly than at home. So when the traveler reaches home, his reckoning will be one day ahead of that of the people there. He must set his calendar one day back, and repeat one date.

Where Dates Are Changed. Whichever way one travels around the world, the date must be changed somewhere. It was thought best to change the day near the 180th meridian, for this lies almost wholly in the ocean, and comparatively few people cross it. For convenience the actual International Date Line departs slightly from the 180th meridian, for the Fiji and Chatham Islands prefer to have the same day as New Zealand; and the people on the Aleutian Islands wish to conform with the rest of Alaska. Whenever a ship or plane crosses this line it adjusts its time, that is, drops the next day if bound west, or adds a day if bound east[4] (Fig. 2–6).

Time Zones and the Air Age. A clear concept of time and its meaning is essential for planning in the air age, much more so in fact than in the steamship and railroad age. When it took several days to cross the Atlantic by fast steamer, a difference of 5 hours was of little consequence. The traveler could merely move his watch ahead or back after a night's sleep. With airliners crossing the Atlantic in a few hours, a 5-hour difference in time is of real significance. It means that communities are much closer to one another in travel time and that differences in clock time are accentuated.

Daylight-Saving Time. The practice of using daylight-saving time takes advantage of the fact that more hours of daylight occur in middle latitudes during summer than in winter. Although noon is approximately halfway between sunrise and sunset, people in manufacturing districts normally get up at an hour closer to noon than the hour at which they retire. In spite of the difference in time of sunrise with the season of the year, prior to the establishment of daylight-saving time, work in the factories continued to commence at the clock hour of 7 or 8 and in stores and banks at the clock hour of 9 or 10.

During the war periods, the United States government ruled in favor of daylight saving largely for the following reasons: When a person rises an hour earlier in the long daylight of summer, he can easily complete his regular routine work and play by sunlight and normally be ready to retire at nightfall or shortly thereafter; thus he is likely to conserve more electricity used for artificial lighting than was possible under the pre-war schedule of rising an hour later. Conservation of electricity means more saving of fuel used in producing electric power. More-

over, the longer period of light after completion of work in the factory or store leaves opportunity for more hours of daylight work in home gardens, which were important food sources during the war years. Since World War II, the

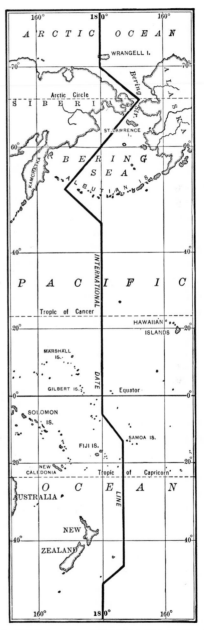

Fig. 2–6 The International Date Line. Note the Line's eastward bulge to permit all eastern Siberia to have the same time; the western bulge to allow similar time throughout the Aleutian Islands; and finally the eastern bulge to permit certain island groups in the vicinity of New Zealand to conform with New Zealand time.

[4] For example, in crossing the *Line* on Tuesday at 11 A.M. going from San Francisco to Tokyo, the time becomes Wednesday 11 A.M. west of the *Line*. Again, in crossing the *Line* on Tuesday at 11 A.M. going from Tokyo to San Francisco, the day becomes Monday, 11 A.M. east of the *Line*.

use of daylight-saving time has continued in many parts of the United States during the summer.

THE SEASONS

Basic Causes for the Seasons

The seasons (see Fig. 2–1) play such an important part in the life of man that it is of interest to understand their causes. Seasonal changes in high and middle latitudes are due to (1) the degree of inclination of the earth's axis to the plane of the earth's orbit; (2) the parallelism of the earth's axis at one position on the earth's orbit to itself at any previous position on the earth's pathway around the sun; (3) rotation of the earth on its axis; (4) revolution of the earth about the sun.

Remove any one of the four causes listed above, and the seasons would no longer exist. With any suitable equipment, such as a season apparatus that shows earth movements and positions in relation to the sun, try an experiment in which one of the four causes is removed, and you will soon see the truth of the preceding statement.

The basic causes for the seasons also determine four factors that significantly influence man and his activities: (1) differences in length of day and night, (2) differences in the relative distance traversed by the sun's rays in the atmosphere, (3) the varying slant of the sun's noonday rays, and (4) the varying distance of the earth from the sun. Each of these factors will receive a brief analysis.

How Daylight and Night Vary in Length. The cause of variations in length of daylight and night is illustrated in Fig. 2–1. This figure represents the distribution of sunlight in the Northern Hemisphere during each month of the year. Sizes of earth, sun, and orbit are not represented in accurate proportion because the sun is so much larger than the earth and so far from it that an accurate scale drawing would not be feasible in a book of this size. In Fig. 2–1 the North Pole is the only one seen, and the earth is revolving around the sun in the direction shown by the dates and inner arrows. It rotates in the same direction, that is, counterclockwise, as shown by the outer arrows.

At the spring equinox, March 21, the sunlight barely reaches the North Pole. Hence at the pole the sun is seen on the horizon. There it remains throughout the 24 hours swinging around the horizon through 360°; but not seeming to rise higher or to sink lower. Except at the poles all parts of the earth at this date have a day and night of about equal length. Therefore this date is called the equinox, for the name means "equal night." There is another equinox about September 22.

Now look at the diagrams for April, May, and June. At the Pole, the sun is considerably above the horizon. In spite of the earth's rotation, it remains visible at all times, so that there is no night. Day after day it appears at a slowly increasing height. If its path were traced in the heavens, it would form a flat spiral mounting slowly upward until it reaches its highest point about June 21. Then the sun ceases to rise in the heavens and seems to stand still before it begins to descend. Hence June 21 is called the solstice, or the standing still of the sun.

One may work out the length of days at different latitudes and seasons. On July 23, about five-sixths of the Arctic Circle is in the sunlight at any one moment. Therefore a miner at the great bend of the Yukon sees the sun five-sixths of the time, or about 20 hours. During the night of only four hours, the sun is so near the horizon that there is light enough for work all the time. During so brief a night, the earth has little chance to cool off. Hence even in high latitudes mid-summer days may be warm if there is no ice or snow to be melted. That is why lichens, flowers, and grass grow beyond the Arctic Circle.

Now see how daylight and darkness compare at latitude 45° North, the approximate location of St. Paul, Minnesota, for the month of July. In Fig. 2–1, approximately 4½ out of the 12 divisions into which the meridians divide the 45th parallel are in darkness. Since each division represents 30 degrees of longitude, the dark part of the circle contains about 135° and the light part approximately 225°. As 15° of longitude corresponds to an hour of time, the night makes up only nine hours in comparison to a daylight period of fifteen hours.

The Relative Distance Traversed by the Sun's Rays in the Atmosphere. At sunrise or sunset, even on the hottest day, it is possible,

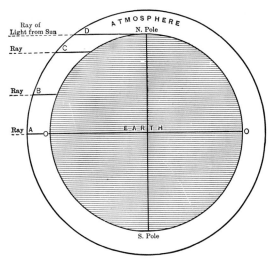

Fig. 2–7   Effect of the Atmosphere on the Strength of Sunlight.

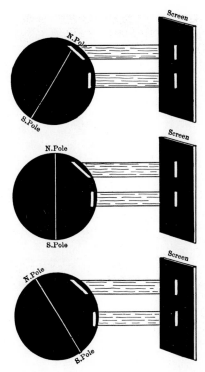

Fig. 2–8   Effect of Latitude and of Tilting of the Earth's Axis on the Area Warmed by a Given Amount of Sunlight.

though not advisable, to look directly at the sun. At noon, however, this is impossible. The reason for the contrast is that the air itself intercepts much light and heat, while the dust and moisture contained in the air intercept still more. At sunrise or sunset the rays of light reach the eye after passing through much more air than at noon, as may be seen in Fig. 2–7, where the solid horizontal line at D is three or four times as long as the one at A. Hence much less heat reaches the earth's surface when the sun is low. In polar latitudes the sun never rises high, and such regions are never hot at any season. In middle latitudes, the sun is low during part of the year and high at other times, and here pronounced seasons of warm and cool weather occur. In equatorial latitudes, where the sun is always high, the weather is warm at all times and marked seasonal temperature contrasts are unknown. Here the diurnal temperature variations are greater than the annual, and night has been called the winter of the tropics.

The Varying Slant of the Sun's Noonday Rays. In Fig. 2–8 the middle globe shows the earth at the equinoxes, March 21 and September 21. The noonday sun, which is far away to the right, is so situated that its rays are vertical at the equator. A screen with two rectangular holes of the same size has been placed between the sun and the earth. The same amount of sun-

light falls through each hole and warms a spot on the earth's surface. The spot at the equator, however, is much smaller than the one between 50° and 60° North. This difference in size is due to the fact that at the equator the noonday rays fall vertically, and hence cover the smallest possible space, while toward the poles the sun's rays fall aslant and are spread over an area twice as large as at the equator. Since the amount of heat is the same in both cases, a square mile, for instance, receives twice as much heat at the equator as a square mile in the other position. This simple illustration shows that the sun gives most heat where its noonday rays are vertical and least where they are most slanting.

The upper globe (Fig. 2–8) shows the conditions at the June solstice. Since the sun's rays are then vertical at noon at the Tropic of Cancer, the sun is also quite high in the heavens in the United States, and there a given amount of light and heat is concentrated in a relatively small area. In winter, on the contrary, the noonday sun is vertical at the Tropic of Capricorn, 47° south of the summer position, as the lower globe shows. Therefore, in all parts of the

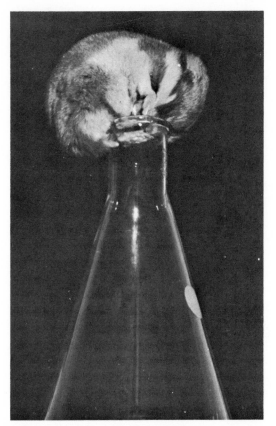

Fig. 2–9   Hibernating Hamster. This hibernating hamster has been placed on the top of a flask to show the typical position of hibernation. All evidence indicates that hibernation has been developed through evolution to permit the animal to escape from an unfavorable environment. At least 5 of the 18 living orders of mammals contain species which hibernate. The optimum environmental temperature for hibernation in most mammals is about 40 F, and the hibernator's temperature is very close to this. Folklore to the contrary, bears do not enter the deeply hibernating state. They often retire to dens during the winter and remain curled in a ball for long periods, but Hock and others have shown that their body temperature does not drop below 91 F, and they are ready to wake up at once and amble drowsily away. (*Courtesy Dr. Charles P. Lyman and the Department of Anatomy, Harvard Medical School*)

United States light falls at a considerable slant, a given quantity is spread over a larger area than in summer, and the heating effect is less.

The Influence of Earth Distance from the Sun. In January the earth is about 3 million miles nearer the sun than in July. But occurrence (1) of the cold season of the northern hemisphere when the earth is nearest the sun and (2) the warm season when the sun is farthest from the earth are facts which suggest that this

variation in distance makes little difference in the amount of sun's heat received by the earth. In fact this change in distance between the two bodies is a minor influence upon earth heating and cooling when compared with the angle of the sun's rays and the length of day (see Figs. 2–1 and 2–8).

Responses to the Seasons

Plants and Animals. In the whole realm of nature, few conditions of the environment equal the seasons in their effect upon life. One of the most obvious results is the revival of vegetation in the spring and its return to a barren state of dormancy in the winter. It is hard to realize the significance of this change unless one lives where there is almost complete uniformity at all times, as in the equatorial rainforest. Equally important is the effect of the seasons upon the production of seeds, fruits, tubers, and many of the devices by which plants store up either food or water. Without this seasonal storage, man and many animals, ranging from rodents to birds, insects, and worms, would be unable to find food.

In the middle latitudes all sorts of grains, nuts, root crops, and fruits owe their origin primarily to the necessity of storing food during one season so that the plant may have something upon which to make a start when the period of unfavorable weather is ended and the season of growth has come. In parts of the low latitudes, where there is plenty of warmth and moisture at all times, edible seeds and fruits are rare. In such places plants grow so fast that many of them can easily reproduce themselves by mere spores such as those of the fern or by the vegetative growth of shoots as in the banana. In oceans, where the contrast between one season and another is reduced to slight proportions, no seed plants have evolved. What few there are have come back to the water from the land. It is enough for the water plant to send out spores —mere unclothed cells. They do not have to endure the rigors of a long cold or dry season. Nor is it necessary that they grow as fast as possible in order to make the most of the time when the weather is favorable. Hence it is not necessary that a small plant be packed away with its main organs already developed. Nor is a store of food needed to insure it a good start. This may be one reason why plant life of the ocean has remained at a low level, while that of the lands through the stimulus of variety, and especially of the seasons, has become highly diverse and progressive.

Among animals the effect of the seasons is as marked as among plants. Hibernation of rodents and insects, migrations of birds and fish, growth and shedding of winter hair or fur, molting of birds, and putting on fat at the approach of winter are all responses to the change of seasons (Fig. 2–9). These and similar changes have much importance to man. Wool, fur, lard, and bacon fat are articles which animals produce seasonally in order to protect themselves from winter. In warm countries sheep's wool may deteriorate to hair.

Effect of Length of Daylight on Seed and Crop Production. An important effect of length of daylight is seen in the production of seeds. For many species of plants, a certain definite duration of daylight is necessary if flowers and seeds are to be produced. In such cases, although temperature, moisture, and intensity of light all have a marked effect on size, shape, and vigor of stems and leaves, they do not have much effect on time of flowering. This may depend almost wholly on length of the period of light. For example, plants such as the radish usually blossom only when the period of light is long. For that reason many common vegetables of the middle latitudes will not produce seeds in the tropics, where daylight never lasts much more than 12 hours. On the other hand, when such plants are grown in a greenhouse during the short days of winter, they can be made to blossom by subjecting them to electric light during part of the night.

Length of daylight (Fig. 2–10) has an important bearing on temperature and thus upon crop production. In high latitudes, earth and

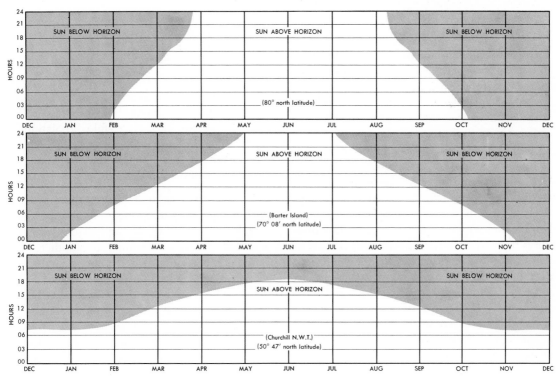

Fig. 2–10 Number of Hours Sun is above or below the Horizon. The vertical lines represent the 21st day of the month. The 24-hour day and the 24-hour night are important factors in the geography of lands north of the Arctic Circle, as shown at 80° north latitude and at Barter Island. In lands south of the Arctic Circle, such as Churchill, daylight and darkness periods are always less than 24 hours. (*Courtesy United States Air Force, from AFM 105–5,* Weather for Aircrews, *Sept. 1, 1962*)

air become very cold during the long winter nights. If snow falls, practically none melts during the short days. It may accumulate so that even the long days of summer cannot melt all of it, and hence no crops can be grown. On the other hand, where little of the summer's heat is used in melting snow, long days cause air to become warm in spite of the low position of the sun. Hence in Siberia, Canada, and Scandinavia, grain and vegetables can be raised as far north as the Arctic Circle. Sometimes steady growth throughout most of the 24 hours causes high yields of such crops as potatoes.

Physiological Reactions of Man to the Seasons. Among men, the influence of seasons is no less than among plants and animals. One of the best known seasonal effects is the variation in health from winter to summer. In climates such as those of northern United States and western Europe, the death rate is systematically lowest at the end of summer and highest late in winter. Certain diseases, however, such as digestive troubles, show an opposite variation, being most numerous and most likely to be fatal in summer.

Response of Human Activities to the Seasons. The majority of human activities show some variation according to seasons. With farming this is preeminently true. In the middle latitudes, a farmer who has few livestock has little to do during the winter. If snow lies on the ground or the soil is frozen, time often hangs heavily on his hands. In summer, on the contrary, in spite of long days the farmer is busy, and his work often piles up ahead of him. With students and most people who are engaged in literary and scientific pursuits, quite the opposite is true. In winter, when daylight is short in the middle and high latitudes, they often pore over books from morning until midnight. In summer, when long warm days are less conducive to study, they frequently vacation for weeks or months. Between farmers and students are people upon whom seasons have almost every degree of effect. The railroad man, manufacturer, banker, carpenter, and hardware merchant all have busy seasons and slack seasons at regular times of the year. Moreover, the nature of their work varies from season to season. Health and recreation vary similarly, for people generally have the best health in the summer and autumn. Games such as hockey are confined largely to winter, and games such as baseball are featured only in the summer. The difficulty is not to find examples of seasonal variations, but to find activities upon which seasons have no effect. And all these seasonal activities depend directly or indirectly upon differences in weather arising from the inclination of the earth's axis to the plane of its orbit, revolution of the earth around the sun, rotation of the earth on its axis, and parallelism of the earth's axis to itself at any previous position on the earth's orbit.

How the Seasons Have Helped to Civilize Mankind. Without seasons man might never have become civilized. When early man began to rely on his mind instead of on physical strength, one of his first important ideas was to store food for seasons of scarcity. As long as he lived by hunting, storing was relatively unimportant; but if he gathered nuts, it was important; and as soon as he relied mainly on farming, he could not live unless he stored up food in summer to last him through the winter. In regions with strong seasonal changes, storing of food was far more necessary than in warm regions with no real winter or dry season. Moreover, the strong contrast between the seasons stimulates him not only to store up food but also to make new inventions. In every stage of life those people are most successful who plan intelligently for the future that lies months or even years ahead of them. Seasons have been among the chief incentives to this kind of foresight.

Local Influences of Time and Season. Even within the limits of a single city or township, people's responses to day and night or to seasons vary from one locality to another. The hours of meals, shopping, recreation, and going to bed differ similarly according to whether a given section is inhabited mainly by day laborers, factory workers, clerks, or professional people. Another variation is seen in the hours at which most automobiles are in use and automobile accidents are most numerous. The theater district may be crowded when the factory district is empty. The geographical distribution of the police varies from hour to hour, day to day, and season to season according to whether people are going to work, to school, to stores for shopping, back to their homes, or to places of recreation. Whether houses are occupied or un-occupied varies widely in different seasons, for in certain sections the houses are almost vacant in summer, whereas in others, such as the sea-shore or any kind of summer resort, they are empty in winter. Certain businesses and certain kinds of street corners are especially busy at certain seasons because they sell soft drinks and ice cream, or do some other business that is more in demand at one time of year than at an-other. Distribution of crime, accidents, crowds, police, and places of recreation within any given community varies greatly from summer to win-ter. So, too, does the number of hours worked by the average person per day. In a section inhab-ited by farmers, day laborers, carpenters, and masons the hours of work per week are far greater in summer than in winter. The study of this sort of local diversification is called micro-geography.

MAPPING THE EARTH

In order to understand better the location, form, and motions of the earth, the geographer has used globes and maps to represent all or parts of the earth's surface. In fact, globes and maps are the main tools of the geographer.

The best representation of the earth is a globe, for it provides a model with the same spherical shape as that of the earth. Here all the earth's surface features can be represented correctly as to area, shape, scale, and direction. Areas may be shown in their proper size-relation to each other; shapes of earth features appear correctly; scale is the same all over the globe; and the com-pass direction from any point to any other point may be kept true. These space relationships can be displayed on a globe diagrammatically by the grid pattern made by the meridians of longi-tude and the parallels of latitude. Parallels of latitude appear as parallel circles spaced equally and becoming shorter and shorter in circumfer-ence toward the poles. The equator has twice the circumference of parallel 60° North or South. The meridians are half circles, crossing the par-allels at right angles and converging at the poles. These half circles spread apart at the equator, where the distance separating each of them is twice that occurring on parallel 60° North or South.

In spite of all the advantages of a globe for showing the true form of the earth, there are certain disadvantages that have encouraged the substitution of maps for showing the location and distribution of the earth features. One weakness of the universal use of globes is the fact that they can't be transported and dis-played as easily as maps. Probably this is the most important handicap.

Map Projections

The verb *"to project"* means literally *"to throw forward."* Thus a map projection throws forward the surface of a sphere upon a plane surface in somewhat the same manner that a motion pic-ture projector throws an image on the screen or a professional draftsman draws a three-dimen-sional solid object upon a two-dimensional plane surface. Although even the simplest pro-jections are the result of complex mathematical formulas, the map maker is likely to base his computations upon the idea of throwing for-ward the surface of the globe upon a plane sur-face.

Centuries ago the Greeks told a story about a great giant Antaeus who was the son of the sea god Poseidon and of the land goddess Gaea. As long as the giant kept in close touch with his parents, he was an invincible wrestler. So too, as long as the map maker who is wrestling with mathematical formulas keeps them in close touch with the globe his maps will retain more and more of the characteristics of the globe. That is an objective for which all geographers strive.

The map maker's first problem is to draw the grid system of a globe on a plane surface. He can then plot points of known latitude and longitude on the grid and connect these points to show the outlines of the continents, islands, seas, rivers, and other surface features. Ways of drawing a map grid are numerous, and each has its characteristic pattern known as a map projection. Such a projection may be defined as a systematic drawing of lines representing par-allels and meridians on a plane surface, either for the whole earth or for some portion of it.

In transferring earth features from the curved surface of a globe to the plane surface of a map, there is bound to be distortion. If you doubt this, take the skin off an orange in four quarters,

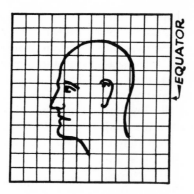

Normal Head *(a)*

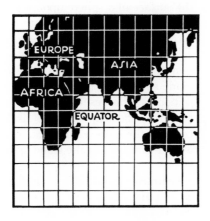

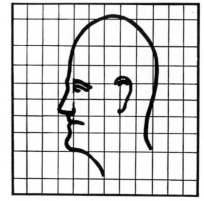

Mercator Projection *(b)*

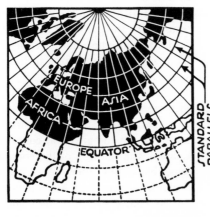

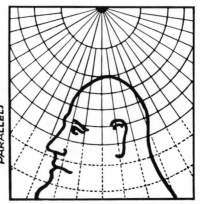

Conic Projection *(c)*

spread them out flat, and note that the only place each quarter contacts another is at the center. Thus some parts of the globe surface will have to be stretched more than other parts when transferred to a map; and no single map projection can equal the globe's correct representation of area, direction, scale, and shape. Some maps may lack truth in all of these quali-

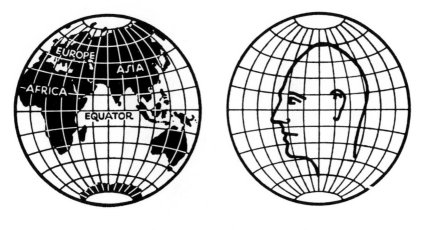

Equal Area Projection *(d)*

Pictorial Projection *(e)*

Fig. 2–11 Maps are Liars. In each map projection shown, the distortion is comparable to the distortion of the head to the right of the map. Directions may be taken accurately from the Mercator projection (*b*), but distances are correct only at the equator, and hence areas are greatly distorted, increasingly so toward the poles. The conic projection (*c*) gives distances, directions, and areas with fair accuracy for regions as large as the United States. Only a limited north-south area can be covered; therefore, only part of the head shows. The equal-area projection (*d*) gives true proportions of land surfaces by distorting the squares increasingly as they go out from the center, thus correcting the perspective. Relative directions are inaccurate. The pictorial projection (*e*) imitates a photograph of a globe. It is inaccurate in all respects, but it helps greatly to give an idea of the earth "in the round," with any desired point as center of the map. (*adapted from Otis P. Starkey and* New York Times Magazine)

ties. Usually, however, the purpose for which the map is made will influence a decision as to what qualities or quality to sacrifice and what ones or one to retain. In every map some truth or truths must be sacrificed (Figs. 2–11 and 2–12).

The grid pattern chosen for the map may give clues to the distortion of the globe surface because the globe grid will be changed in (1) the spacing of the lines; (2) their shapes; or (3) the angles at which they cross each other, or in all of these changes.

For example, if on a map the spacing of the parallels is unequal, the north-south scale is also unequal, being larger where the parallels are far apart and smaller where parallels are closer

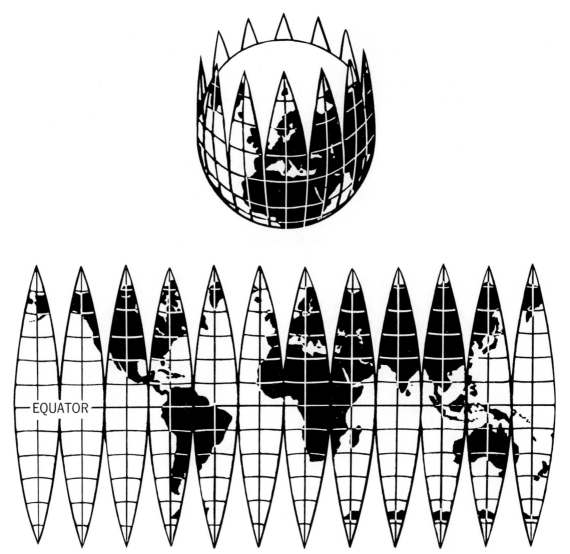

Fig. 2–12 Removing the Surface of a Globe. The map above results when the globe is peeled like an orange. As the segments are flattened out the continents and oceans split up and fall away from one another. All of this emphasizes the fact that transferring a globe surface to a map cannot be done without distortion somewhere. (*adapted from Otis P. Starkey and* New York Times Magazine)

together. Thus truth of scale is not achieved on such a projection. On a globe, however, a degree of latitude is essentially the same in length—about 69 miles—everywhere, and scale is constant north, south, east, and west.

The Mercator projection illustrates this distortion of scale. Although all projections are drawn according to mathematical formulas, the philosophy of the Mercator projection suggests a cylinder wrapped around the globe touching it everywhere at the equator. Lines are drawn

from the center of the globe to the cylinder through points to be located. When such a cylinder is slit and laid flat, the whole earth appears as a single map with only one break between the hemispheres. Both meridians and parallels are straight lines. Hence a given point of the compass is always in the same direction on all parts of the map, which is not true where the meridians or parallels are curved. Truth of direction makes the Mercator map advantageous to navigators and suggests a reason for its continued use. But this advantage is offset by the fact that on a true Mercator projection the poles cannot possibly be represented and high latitudes are exaggerated so extremely that they are usually omitted or arbitrarily reduced in size. On a Mercator map Greenland, 840,000 square miles and in high latitudes, is shown as large as the continent of South America, 6,860,-000 square miles in low latitudes.

When the geographer is more interested in correct relative size of earth features than he is in their shape, he may choose what is called an equal area projection for a study of aerial distribution. He may decrease the north-south scale and compensate for this change by a corresponding increase in east-west dimensions on the same part of the map. For example, a square two inches by two inches has the same area as a rectangle four inches by one inch, although the shape of the latter figure will be broader and shorter. Thus the map maker may retain correct relative size by accepting distortion of shape. This situation may be seen on the Mollweide and Goode homolographic projections.

Finally the cartographer can ignore the custom of making the upper part of the map north and instead place that direction at the center of the projection as it appears on the Lambert Azimuthal Equal Area projection. With the choice of such a projection he can show the grouping of lands of the northern hemisphere around the Arctic Ocean just as well as they appear on the globe. In this example the map maker sacrifices the customary orientation of directions on the map in order to emphasize relationships between this northern ocean and the surrounding continents.

We have cited only three examples of map projections although there are scores of them in use. In all of these, the cartographer will fail to include truth of area, shape, angle, and scale as they appear on the globe, for he cannot retain all truths appearing on a curved surface when he attempts to transfer that surface to a plane. Some distortion will be necessary; and it is literally true that all maps are liars in certain respects.

Topographic Maps. Maps can be used for hundreds of purposes including those showing distribution of all geographic features listed on Table 1–1 in Chapter 1. Since man lives and carries on most of his activities upon the earth's surface, especially on the land forms, some space should be devoted to the ways in which differences in topography may be shown on maps (Fig. 2–13). Contrasts in relief may be distinguished by such devices as color, shading, and contours. All geographers should understand the latter method of showing relief features because it is widely used throughout the world in detailed studies of relatively small areas.

In the United States, the Geological Survey has been making topographic maps since 1882. Under the general plan adopted, the country is divided into quadrangles bounded by parallels of latitude and meridians of longitude. These quadrangles are mapped on different scales, the scale selected for each map being that which is best adapted in general use for the development of the country; and consequently, although the maps are nearly uniform in size, the areas that they represent are of different sizes. Scale is shown at the bottom of the map graphically, and fractionally. For example, the scale of 1/62,500 means that 1 unit on the map (such as 1 inch, 1 foot, or 1 meter) represents 62,500 units on the earth's surface.

Topographic maps of the United States may be divided into three general classes: (1) maps of areas with problems of great public importance—for example, relating to mineral development, irrigation, or reclamation of swamp areas—are made with considerable detail on a scale of a half mile to the inch or larger and a contour interval of 1 to 100 feet depending upon the relief of the area mapped; (2) maps of areas with problems of average importance—such as most of the Mississippi Valley and its tributary valleys—are made on a scale of a mile to the inch and a contour interval of 10 to 100 feet; (3) maps of areas with problems of minor importance—such as mountain and desert regions of Arizona, New Mexico, or Nevada—are made with a scale of 2 to 4 miles to the inch and with a contour interval of 20 to 250 feet.

Relief is shown by contour lines (a contour line represents an imaginary line on the ground, every part of which is at the same altitude above sea level). Such a line could be drawn at any level, but in practice only the contours at certain regular intervals of altitude are shown. The datum or zero of altitude is mean sea level. In other words, the 20 foot contour line would be the shore line if the sea were to rise 20 feet. Contour lines show the shape of hills, mountains, and valleys as well as their altitude. Successive contour lines that are far apart on the map indicate a gentle slope, lines that are close together

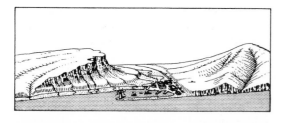

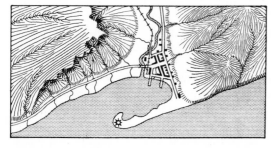

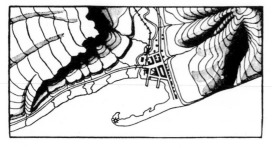

indicate a steep slope, and lines that run together indicate a cliff.

The contour interval, or the vertical distance in feet between one contour and the next, is stated at the bottom of each map. This interval differs according to the topography of the area mapped; in a flat country it may be as small as 1 foot; in a mountainous region it may be as great as 250 feet. In order that the contours may be read more easily, certain contour lines, every fourth or fifth, are made heavier than the others and are accompanied by figures showing altitude. The heights of many points— such as road intersections, summits, surfaces of lakes, and benchmarks—are also given on the map in figures, which show altitudes to the nearest foot.

The features shown on topographic maps may be arranged in three groups: (1) water, including seas, lakes, rivers, canals, swamps, and other bodies of water; (2) relief, including mountains, hills, valleys, and other features of the land surface; (3) works of man, such as towns, cities, roads, railroads, and boundaries. The symbols used to represent these features are usually shown and explained on the back or at the bottom of the map.

Each quadrangle is designated by the name of a city, town, or prominent natural feature within it, and on the margins of the map are printed the names of adjoining quadrangles of which maps have been published.

The aerial camera is now being used in connection with topographic mapping. By use of a stereoscopic plotting apparatus, aerial photographs are utilized in the making of regular

Fig. 2–13 Various Way to Show Relief. The sketch shown in the upper drawing represents a river valley that lies between two hills. In the foreground is the sea with a bay that is partly enclosed by a hooked sand bar. On each side of the valley is a terrace into which small streams have cut narrow gullies. The hill on the right has a rounded summit and gently sloping spurs separated by ravines. The spurs are truncated at their lower ends by a sea cliff. The hill at the left terminates abruptly at the valley in a steep scarp, from which it slopes gradually away and forms an inclined tableland that is traversed by a few shallow gullies. In the second drawing from the top, relief is shown by hachures; in the middle illustrations contours are used to show relief; in the fourth map, hachures and contours are combined; and in the bottom drawing, plastic shading and contours are combined. (*Courtesy E. Raisz*)

topographic maps that show relief as well as drainage and culture.

Hachures. As previously indicated, the earth's topographic features may be shown by hachures and by color as well as by contours. The preparation of hachure maps involves the use of shading or lines to show relief. Such lines are drawn short and close together to designate steep slopes; long and far apart to show gently rolling land; and lines may be omitted entirely to indicate level plains. Hachures do not give the specific information about surface features found on contour maps, but they provide a general idea of the land forms.

Color. Color is widely used on physical maps to denote differences in elevation. A widely accepted color scheme for altitude contrasts starts with greens for lowlands, followed with yellows, browns, and reds for various gradations at higher levels. Color may also be used to draw contrast between (1) political entities, (2) lands of heavy precipitation and desert country, (3) cold latitudes and warm ones, (4) rain forests and savannas, (5) pedalfer and pedocal soils, and (6) many other geographic features. Finally color may provide better legibility and attractiveness, two important goals in mapping both the physical and the man-made geographic environment.

Progress in World Mapping. Dr. Edward B. Espinshade, editor of Goode's Atlas, states well the great value of the map to the geographer: (1) it may be used as a base on which to record data; (2) as an analytic device to discover possible relationships between phenomena; (3) as a medium to present spatial relationships of earth phenomena; and (4) to reduce the landscape patterns to a size that is more manageable and that permits one to visualize the whole more readily.

With the great multitude of maps available in almost every conceivable size, shape, or form to serve the purposes listed above, it is difficult to realize that probably not more than a quarter of the earth's surface can be considered adequately mapped. Furthermore, with the increasing complexity of civilization and the growing demands upon resources, increasingly detailed special maps are needed showing the distribution of soils, population, land utiliza-

tion, and other physical, social, and economic phenomena. Despite the fact that much remains to be done, the progress being made is encouraging.

QUESTIONS, EXERCISES, AND PROBLEMS

1. Identify the following:

Equator	Parallel
Prime Meridian	Meridian
Arctic Circle	High, Low, and Middle
Antarctic Circle	Latitudes
Tropic of Cancer	Perihelion
Tropic of Capricorn	Aphelion
Latitude of North Pole	Revolution of Earth
Latitude of South Pole	Causes for the Middle
Rotation of Earth	Latitude Seasons
Daylight-Saving Time	International Date Line
Mercator Projection	Map Scale
Map Projections	Methods of Showing
Contour Line	Relief
Topographic Map	Contour Interval
Equinox	Zenith
Latitude	Solstice
Longitude	

2. Give proofs of the earth's shape and motions. Give the zenith distance of the noonday sun at your home city on the June solstice; the December solstice; the March equinox; and the September equinox.

3. Where may United States topographic maps be purchased? Which way do contours curve in crossing a stream?

4. An aircraft over the Pacific Ocean radios its position as Lat. 45° N, Long. 150° E, at 10 P.M. on April 25. The message is received almost immediately at Sitka, Alaska (approximate Lat. 60° N. Long. 135° W). What day and time is it in Sitka when the message is received?

5. Give several examples of how plants and animals respond to the seasons. Give illustrations of how length of daylight influences seed and crop production. What physiological responses to the seasons does man show? Indicate several responses in human activities to middle and high latitude seasons. Comment on the influences of seasons upon the progress of civilization.

SELECTED REFERENCES

Anderzhon, M. L., "Geographic Concepts in the Space Age," *Journal of Geography*, Jan. 1961, pp. 32–35.

Chamberlin, Wellman, *The Round Earth on Flat Paper*, National Geographic Society, Washington, D. C.

Forsyth, Elaine, *Map Reading*, National Council for Geographic Education, Publications Center, Illinois State Normal University, Normal, Illinois.

Greenwood, David, *Mapping,* University of Chicago Press, 1964.

Harris, Ruby M., *Handbook of Map and Globe Usage,* Rand McNally, 1959.

Harrison, Lucia C., *Sun, Earth, Time, and Man,* Rand McNally, 1960.

Headquarters, Department of the Army, *Map Reading,* Field Manual, FM 21–26, 1960.

Ives, Ronald L., "Longitude Degree Length at Various Latitudes," *Journal of Geography,* May 1964, pp. 205–10.

Jenks, G. F. and Knos, D. S., "The Use of Shading Patterns in Graded Series," *Annals of the Association of American Geographers,* Sept. 1961, pp. 316–34.

Lobeck, A. K., *Things Maps Don't Tell Us,* An Adventure in Map Interpretation, The Macmillan Co., 1956.

Macomber, Lenore, "Suggestions on Preparing a Movable Date Line Chart," *Journal of Geography,* May 1964, pp. 222–23.

McKinney, William M., "Experimental Proofs of the Earth's Rotation," *Journal of Geography,* April 1962, pp. 171–74.

McKinney, William M., *Geography Via Use of the Globe,* National Council for Geographic Education Center of Publications, Illinois State Normal University, Normal, Illinois.

Raisz, Erwin, *Principles of Cartography,* McGraw-Hill, 1964.

Thralls, Zoe A., "Maps and Globes are our Business," *The Teaching of Geography,* Ch. 2, pp. 19–75, Appleton-Century-Crofts, 1958.

Tobler, Waldo R., "Geographic Area and Map Projections," *Geographical Review,* Jan. 1963, pp. 59–78.

Chapter Three

Climatic Influences Upon Man

Climate may be defined as the total of meteorological phenomena that characterize the average condition of the atmosphere at any one place on the earth's surface. That which is called weather is only one phase in the succession of phenomena whose complete cycle, recurring with greater or less uniformity every year, constitutes the climate of any locality. To illustrate, one may say, "the weather in New England was very cold and snowy in December 1962," or "the weather in Massachusetts was pleasant in July 1963." It is also correct to say that the climate of England is mild and damp in December, although December of the year 1964 was colder than usual. However, the word *climate* is used incorrectly in the statement, "the climate of Denmark was rainy in the summer of 1964." As soon as one speaks of the atmospheric conditions of a specific short period of time, he should use the word *weather*.

Climate, which includes weather, may be the most important influence of the entire physical environment upon man's activities on land, on sea, and in the air. The type of clothing he wears, the kind and amount of food he eats, the character of the houses he lives in, his means of transport, the games he plays or watches—all these and many other features of everyday life are vitally affected by climate.

In a broad sense, climate acts upon man in three chief ways: (1) it sets up barriers which limit his movements; (2) it is the main physical factor influencing the nature and amount of most materials needed for food, clothing, and shelter; and (3) it has a direct and important influence upon health and energy.

Climatic Barriers

On the Ocean. Climate limits man's movements directly when a gale prevents ships from going out to sea. Its chief effects, however, may be indirect or in combination with other factors. For example, a large part of the difficulty in crossing oceans and mountains is climatic. America did not remain undiscovered so long merely because of the broad ocean but because people feared that conditions in the form of storms and winds would wreck them or prevent them from coming home again. Today, travelers do not fear the ocean when it is calm but only when it is disturbed by influences such as winds, waves, fogs, and icebergs; these sank the "unsinkable" Danish ship Hedtoft with 95 passengers and crew in January 1959. The effectiveness of the ocean as a barrier would be greatly reduced if climatic dangers could be eliminated.

Among Mountains. In the same way the barrier of mountains is largely climatic. In crossing the Himalayas from India to western China, steep slopes are indeed a great hindrance. Yet these direct effects of relief may be dreaded less than fierce snowstorms, followed by the blinding glare of the sun. Worst of all is the scarcity or absence of vegetation, which may lead to a corresponding scarcity or absence of people. Temperatures are so low that no one can dwell on vast stretches of high barren highlands, and not even grass can grow.

In the mountains of western United States, steep slopes and high altitudes provide a barrier for man's movements just as they do in the higher Himalayas. Again climate combines with altitude to slow down or bar transportation. In the Colorado Rockies there are 34 high passes between 10,000 and more than 13,000 feet high. During the summer, thousands of motorists use these routes to enjoy mountain scenery of surprising beauty and grandeur. But the winter climate closes these high passes by blocking them with deep snow. Farther west the Donner

Fig. 3–1   Train Stalled in the Deep Snow in the High Sierras. In the winter of 1952, the Southern Pacific train City of San Francisco was stuck in the snow near Emigrant Gap for three days. Annual snowfalls of many hundred inches have been recorded in the California Sierras; and in the mountains of Washington state, at Paradise Ranger Station, 1,000.3 inches fell in the winter of 1955–1956. (*Courtesy San Francisco Chronicle*)

Pass is the only major all year highway across the Sierras, and even it is kept open with difficulty at the height of the winter season. During early settlement days Donner's winter weather caused the death of scores of California-bound travelers, who were using what today would be called primitive means of transport; and the saga of this disastrous expedition is one of the most gruesome in mountain travel.

Even with modern surface transport, winter snows in the high Sierras can interrupt traffic completely for several hours and even for days. For example, in January, 1952 Southern Pacific's crack train, the City of San Francisco (Fig. 3–1), with more than 200 people on board, was stalled for more than three days at a point about fifteen miles east of Donner Summit. During this same period of heavy Sierra snowfall, motor travel on United States roads 40 and 50 in the

vicinity of Donner and Echo Summit passes was also halted for days.

Mountainous relief even exerts a barrier influence on air transport. The trouble is not so much with the mountain wall itself as it is with treacherous air currents that result from the rugged terrain. Aviators have known for a long while that air flow over mountainous country may be very erratic, especially when wind velocity is 30 miles an hour or more. Recently large amounts of money and time have been spent on mountain wave research; and from this research it has been learned that when a wave passes the crest of a mountain, the air breaks into a complicated pattern with downdrafts predominating. An indication of possible intensities can be gained from verified records of sustained downdrafts, and also updrafts, of at least 3000 feet per minute; other reports are well in excess of this figure. Thus, it behooves the airmen to know how to identify a wave situation and, having identified it, to plan flights so as to avoid the wave hazards. Even with these precautions, too many horrible air tragedies occur because of weather perils over mountainous terrain.

Within the High Latitudes. The climates of polar regions may be as much of a barrier as those of mountains and oceans. Surface transportation is so difficult over great fields of ice and snow that the North and South Poles were not discovered until the present century. Peary reached the North Pole and Amundsen the earth's southern extremity only after long experience had taught explorers (1) how best to use dogs and other means of transportation, (2) how to carry and store great supplies of food and fuel,

and (3) how to provide the warmest clothing and shelter.

In recent years man has improved air and sea transport so that enough supplies can be safely carried to polar regions to maintain a small number of carefully selected scientists. But transport and living costs are enormous, and only governments interested in polar research would make such an investment; and only men deeply interested in polar study are willing to endure the difficult human adjustments to be met in a short stay of a few months or a year. As yet few are interested in staking out claims for a permanent residence at the poles.

Deserts. Certain hot deserts of the world are almost as much of a climatic problem for man as the polar regions. In southern Arabia it was

Fig. 3–2   Pipe Lines Cross the Sahara Desert. Oil resources have increased the value of several deserts. These pipelines extend from distant desert wells to the gathering center at Zelten, Libya. The rich Libyan oil deposits have been developed only recently. (*Courtesy Standard Oil, New Jersey*)

Fig. 3–3   Jute Culture in the Amazon Basin, Brazil. Jute is growing in shallow water back of the stalks already cut in preparation for retting, (in the foreground). A few decades ago, Sakae Oti and other Japanese agronomists experimented with Indian jute and developed a commercial variety well adapted to the Amazon environment. As a result of these experiments, Amazonia farmers produced nearly three million kilograms of jute as early as the 1940's. Thus Asians proved to Brazilians that the Amazon Basin can produce other commercial crops besides rubber; and in the future the area may support a greater population than at present. (*Courtesy United Nations and the Pan American Union*)

not until 1932 that any explorer penetrated a forbidding desert region thousands of miles in extent. Men fear the region partly because of the difficulty of securing water and partly because of hardships encountered in climbing dunes of dry, sliding sand piled up for hundreds of feet by violent winds. As no rain may fall for years, dust becomes so deep that one sinks into it above the ankles, and every bodily movement raises fine dust into stifling clouds. Few people dare travel on foot for fear of being smothered. In some ways, however, the worst places of all are the vast smooth expanses of monotonous gravel stretching sometimes for 150 miles.

It is true that, with all the improvements in transport, in air conditioning, in clothing, and in shelter, man can penetrate the most difficult hot deserts. But the economic and health price may be extremely high, just as it is in the polar regions. The rewards of scientific research or of precious minerals and power resources (Fig. 3–2) may justify the expenditure of money and health; but there is little doubt that the hot climate may keep deserts like those of southern Arabia sparsely populated for years.

Tropical Rainforests. The damp heat of the tropical rainforest in such continental interior locations as the upper Amazon Basin creates a problem for human activities almost as serious as that of cold and hot deserts. Not only do high temperatures and excessive moisture assist the growth of dense forests through which surface travel is difficult, but the combination of these climatic elements is exhausting to human energy; and Amazonia's climate fosters some of the world's most deadly fevers. Thus, it may be a long while before much of the Amazon Basin reaches a population density of even five people per square mile. Of course the story may be different if Brazil encourages Japanese and Chinese settlers in rapid expansion of their already successful small scale tropical agricultural developments (Fig. 3–3).

CLIMATE AND FOOD SUPPLY

The effect of climate on man's material needs may be illustrated best by considering his food supply. Materials for clothing and shelter vary from place to place in the same way as food.

Climate more than anything else determines the nature and abundance of vegetation and hence of food. People who live in middle latitude humid continental climates, like that of the Corn Belt of the United States, find conditions favorable for producing a wide variety of feeds to fatten cattle and hogs as well as for growing cereals, fruits, and vegetables for direct human consumption. Inhabitants of the west coast marine climate of Northwest Europe live in a cool moist climate encouraging luxuriant growth of (1) grasses and hay—fine feed crops for dairy cattle—and (2) root crops like potatoes, turnips, and sugar beets. Farmers in Europe's Mediterranean region find that the climate is suitable for grapes, olives, and citrus fruit. Of course in an exchange economy characteristic of much of today's world, people in Iowa, Great Britain, and Greece can purchase from other countries commodities that they cannot produce themselves. Nevertheless, crop failures in any of the above mentioned places will reduce drastically the purchasing power and emphasize the importance of climate in determining the country's food supply; and in countries like India and China, which operate upon a subsistence economy, crop failure will bring malnutrition, disease, and death to thousands of people.

CLIMATE IN RELATION TO HEALTH AND ENERGY

Man's health and energy are influenced by climate both directly and indirectly. In the middle latitudes everyone knows that on some days the air is invigorating, and on others it is depressing. Most people work slowly on hot, muggy days; if they work rapidly, the result is considerable weariness. On a clear, bracing day in autumn, on the contrary, one may feel as if he could do anything, no matter how difficult the accomplishment. Still later, on an extremely cold winter day people sometimes run to keep warm, but in the house they feel much less desire for physical or mental effort. Thus in many ways man's activity in mind and body is influenced by the various elements of climate.

Temperature and Sunlight (Dr. Paul Siple). The following observations about Antarctic climates and man's activities are based upon comments made by Dr. Paul Siple after the first two Byrd expeditions to the polar continent.

The sub-freezing temperatures on Antarctica temporarily stimulate man's energy. The most strenuous work required of the men on each of the first two Byrd expeditions was during the period of unloading the ships. For weeks at a time, the men worked on an average of 15 hours a day doing heavy hard labor. Incentive may have encouraged, but it was not enough to fully explain this unusual display of energy. The contrast between middle latitude and high latitude temperatures seems more important. Of course twenty-four hours of sunlight during the summer period may have added a psychological influence.

Nevertheless, long continued work at low temperatures may prove detrimental to one's health. On several occasions, in the early spring, men labored when the thermometer registered more than 60° below zero. The heavy exercise of shoveling snow increased respiration enough to frost the men's lungs and slight hemorrhages resulted. As a precaution against serious damage, work was made optional when temperatures dropped to 50° below zero.

Man eats more food and different kinds of food in high latitudes. The actual food intake may be twice as much as the amount eaten in the tropics. This is really to be expected, for it has been estimated that heat energy consumed in warming the cold air breathed into the lungs at 14°F would take 270 kilogram calories per day in contrast to only 45 kilogram calories which would be required with a 77° temperature in the tropics. This is a difference of 225 kilogram calories that would be required as an output of heat energy in the polar regions over that of the tropics. There is in addition a great loss of body heat; and the lungs are further required to supply moisture to saturate the dry incoming polar air at the rate of nearly five times that required by warm tropical air. This is normal because of the physical fact that cold air can hold less moisture in suspension than warm air and consequently requires much more additional moisture to saturate it to the same extent.

In the polar regions the coarser vegetables and fat meats are relished or tolerated more than they would be in warmer climates. On this subject Dr. Siple made the following statement. "I have never found greasy bacon or fatty meats appetizing, but I recall how on my first sledging journey I drank with pleasure a half inch of liquid bacon fat from the top of my bowl of pemmican "hoosh" which itself was made up of one-third animal fats. When I returned to a warmer climate I once more reverted to my dislike for fats."[1]

Continuous summer sunshine and brilliant reflection from the snow are other important climatic influences upon man's polar activities. Continuous sunlight may be as disagreeable as the complete loss of sun during the winter night. Even with dark glasses one may develop snow blindness, a veritable sunburn of the delicate retina of the eye. With this affliction, one's eyes may become so sensitive that they may not heal for several days and opening them during this period may bring severe pain.

Temperature and Sunlight (Dr. Ellsworth Huntington). Another student of weather and climate had a good deal to say about the climatic elements and their influence upon man's health and energy. Dr. Huntington believed that the climates of the polar regions gave one of the most severe handicaps to man's progress, and he also looked with great disfavor upon the climates of the tropical rainforests. His favorite region for the encouragement of man's progress in civilization was the area of the west coast marine climate. There, temperature and other climatic elements closely conform to his ideas of the best conditions for high mental and physical activity.

These conditions may be summarized as follows: (1) average temperatures range from somewhat below 40° in the coldest month to nearly 70° in the warmest month; (2) frequent storms or winds from oceans or lakes that keep the relative humidity quite high except in hot weather and provide rain at all seasons; and (3) a constant succession of cyclonic storms that bring frequent moderate changes of temperature, but changes not severe enough to be harmful.[2]

Temperature and Sunshine (Dr. A. Grenfell Price). It seems pertinent here to call attention to major conclusions reached by another scientist interested in the effects of climate upon man. Dr. Price stated: "It appears from history, observation, and laboratory experiments that very high temperatures may damage the intellect and memory of adults. . . . It is fairly certain that tropical climates produce some decline in energy. . . . Apart from all questions of disease, the evidence from history, observation, statistics, and laboratory indicates that the majority of white and some of the colored peoples have an aversion for hot, humid climates, and that many Whites dislike all types of tropical climate. . . . Certain colored peoples such as Negroes and Chinese are more cheerful and docile than the white peoples in tropical environments, and are prepared to accept lower living standards. Similarly certain white groups of Mediterranean origin fare better in the tropics than the northern Whites. It is, however, impossible to say whether this superiority is due to ethnic characteristics, to differences in cultural development, or to variations in the tropical environments occupied by the invading groups."[3]

After citing the findings of Price, Huntington, and Siple, who stress the influence of temperature upon man's health and energy, a few other temperature relationships may be added. It is general knowledge that (1) basal metabolism is reduced in hot climates; (2) high temperatures of low latitudes encourage heat stroke; (3) long exposure to too much sunshine may bring painful sunburn, although exposure properly timed can make white skin tan. (4) The slower movements of many tropical people are related to the high temperatures of low latitudes. Heat also encourages the siesta, the closing of stores during

---

[1] "Recent evidence of polar activity indicates that men do not actually eat a great deal more in the cold, and that a conventionally balanced diet is better than the one higher in fat that we used to have. Actually, I think part of this new evidence is based upon better clothing and shelter and upon somewhat less heavy activity under full polar exposure as compared with the days when we drove dogs." (Quotation from Dr. Siple's correspondence, Dec. 1, 1964).

[2] For a more comprehensive description of the Huntington climatic theory see Dr. Huntington's several books on climate and civilization.

[3] For more complete information see A. Grenfell Price, *White Settlers in the Tropics,* American Geographical Society Publication 23, American Geographical Society, 1939.

the hotter parts of the day, and night travel through low latitude desert regions. The heat of desert countries may have influenced the belief that the area of eternal punishment after death is a region of extreme heat. In Norse mythology heaven was a place of warmth and hell a place of cold and mist. (5) Summer heat waves in middle latitudes cause man to lose weight, and they also increase death rates.[4]

(6) One of the most important items to add concerning the influences of cold temperatures is the fact that in Norway the winter period cuts down the hemoglobin in the blood about 25 per cent. (7) In middle latitudes severe variations between temperatures in and out-of-doors and heightened and fatiguing social activities team up to tear down man's body defense mechanisms and make him more susceptible to viral and bacterial invasion. Americans come down with a half billion colds a year; most of them, and especially the most severe ones, occur in the winter season. Thousands of sick and elderly people of middle latitudes seek warm temperatures and bright sunshine during the winter to improve their health and to lengthen their lives.

Precipitation and Humidity. In 1931, the author was doing geographic field work on St. Croix, the largest of the United States Virgin Islands. During that year St. Croix's rainfall was the heaviest in 80 years of record, and the island suffered one of the worst outbreaks of malaria in its history. These two phenomena are closely related.

An abundance of moisture producing ideal breeding grounds for millions of mosquitoes is one of three most basic factors involved in mala-

rial areas of the tropics. The other two are the presence of the anopheles mosquito and persons suffering from malarial fever (see Fig. 1–6).

The first factor is vital, for all anopheles are harmless during the greater period of their lives. For instance, out of each 100 anopheles mosquitoes, only a few will have a chance to bite a human being during the period in which his blood contains malarial parasites in the infective stage. Of those which do bite such a person, only a limited number will live the twelve days necessary for the plasmodium to attain its full development in the insect, and of those in which the twelve-day cycle is completed, some may die before they have an opportunity to attack a susceptible person. Thus, many interrelated factors must combine to produce an epidemic spread of the disease: the amount of rainfall necessary to provide favorable breeding places for the mosquitoes, the number of mosquitoes which are produced, the number of these insects susceptible to infection with the parasite, and the number of human carriers of that parasite. All factors must rise above those critical points if there is to be an epidemic.

From 1918 to 1930 only fifteen cases of malaria were reported in St. Croix, and with one exception all were confined to persons who had acquired the infection in Puerto Rico. Yet during this thirteen year period it was known by actual tests that anopheles mosquitoes were in the island. The rainfall was not sufficient, however, to furnish them breeding places for rapid multiplication.

The year 1931 gave the proper weather conditions. The malaria epidemic started in July in the most swampy part of Christiansted, St. Croix, the district of Gallows Bay. Before the malaria was checked, it spread throughout the island. Out of a total of a little over 12,000, St. Croix's population, over 900 cases received medical aid, and 22 deaths resulted from the disease. Probably many additional fatalities were induced by its weakening influence, the victims being left more susceptible to some other serious disease. Moreover, losses from sickness and death were not the only unfavorable results. There was an economic loss to laborer and employer in the number of days the workers were absent and in the lowering of the efficiency after their return. Again, St. Croix was attempting to build up a much-needed tourist industry to sup-

---

[4]The *New York Times* of July 27th, 1952, in an article entitled "Heat Wave Leaves Citizens Thinner" states that New Yorkers lost at least 3,200,000 pounds during the recent two-week heat wave. . . . If during a hot spell each New Yorker eats only 100 calories less a day, which is the equivalent of one large slice of bread, each person will lose two-fifths of a pound in two weeks. Another *New York Times* article during the same month, entitled "Heat Waves Make Death Rates Soar," includes the following information: For the first 24 days of June, when the temperature was seasonal, the average number of deaths reported daily was 213. For June 25 through June 27, however, when the mercury zoomed upward, the daily fatality average was 376. This was an increase of 77 per cent in those 3 sweltering days. . . . Most persons who succumb during protracted heat waves are the very young, the very old, and the chronically ill.

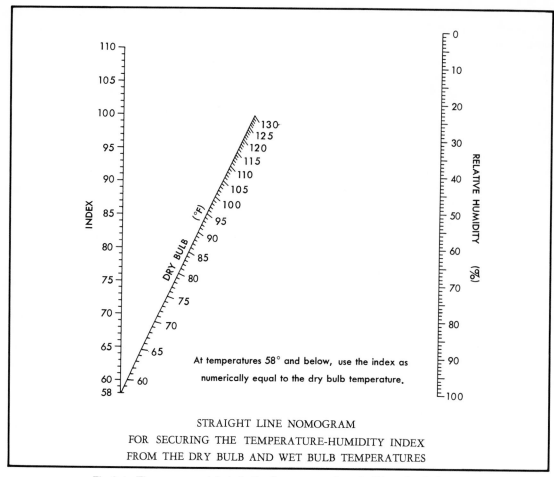

STRAIGHT LINE NOMOGRAM
FOR SECURING THE TEMPERATURE-HUMIDITY INDEX
FROM THE DRY BULB AND WET BULB TEMPERATURES

Fig. 3–4   There was a good deal of talk a few years ago about the Discomfort-Index, now called the Temperature-Humidity-Index. At least one national magazine published a United States map showing THI statistics. Average figures over a five-year period were based on relative humidity and temperature taken at noon; and these figures were plotted on the map for more than 20 major United States cities. July and August THI averages ranged from 64 in San Francisco to 85 in Yuma. The practice of publishing these figures was discontinued shortly after it started. (*Courtesy United States Weather Bureau*)

plement its declining sugar production. Word of the epidemic reached national dailies in the eastern United States, and passengers from more than one ship refused to stop at the island for fear of incurring infection.

Medical science has made definite advances in the control of malaria since 1931, but the American Medical Association stated in March 1961 that a million deaths from malaria occurred in India alone in 1960.

The Temperature-Humidity Index. The amount of moisture in the air (Fig. 3–4), or the

humidity, has a great deal to do with man's feelings, especially in the wet lowland tropics, and in the middle latitudes during hot summer days. In 1955 the first numerical measure of the effects of summertime conditions upon humans was developed by an engineer. The term Discomfort Index was coined; however, the Weather Bureau, in order to make the Discomfort Index agree more closely with the effective temperature reading at extremes of temperature and humidity conditions, extended and improved the method of securing the Index (now called the Temperature-Humidity Index or THI) by the development of three equations. One of these equations follows:

$$THI = 0.4 (T_{dry} + T_{wet}) + 15$$

With the dry bulb temperature 89° and the wet bulb instrument at 71°, the two temperatures[5] are added making a sum of 160. This figure is then multiplied by 0.4 and 15 is added. The resulting figure is the Discomfort Index or THI of 79. A reading this high makes nearly every one uncomfortable; a reading of 75 will make about half of the people uncomfortable; and very few people will suffer with a reading of 70. Of course, greater human comfort than is indicated by the Index results with a good breeze or other rapid air circulation. For a more complete description of the Index with numerous illustrations and many detailed explanations, see the United States Weather Bureau Washington D.C. map for August 21, 1959.

The Discomfort Index or THI is associated with both high temperatures and high moisture percentages in the air; but too much moisture alone in the atmosphere can create fogs that may be injurious to man. For example, the first great London fog of the 1952–1953 winter increased deaths during the seven days of its occurrence by approximately 4000 above average. Fogs also create transport hazards that bring numerous fatalities on the ground and in the air.

Death losses from floods, encouraged by heavy precipitation, are probably not as heavy as those resulting from fog. United States deaths brought on by floods reached 2764 between the years 1925 and 1956; and the property damage during the same period was 5½ billion dollars.

Winds and Pressure. Winds or the lack of them, may create havoc with man's health and energy. The lack of strong winds is one of several factors involved in smog, a health menace to many of the world's cities.

In appearance smog is a grey-brown haze, thin or thick. It can hang low, impairing visibility as close as a block away; or it can rise and become overcast. It may cling for days, especially in still, hot, weather, reducing sunlight to a brassy glare, irritating eyes, nose, and lungs; endangering ground and air traffic; damaging crops; and annoying and depressing people.

This haze occurs only when certain factors, many of them associated with the weather are present. These include (1) an inversion layer—a flat pancake of warm air above a cooler ground layer; (2) either no wind or a rim of surrounding hills to shut out a breeze capable of carrying away the smoke fumes, dust, etc; (3) hot sunlight; (4) a large concentration of people, almost all of whom own one or two automobiles and whose economy requires a steady stream of cars,[6] buses, and trucks day and night.

Probably the most famous smog city, but not the only one by any means, is Los Angeles. The city lies in the Los Angeles Basin, a valley about 60 miles long by 25 miles wide hemmed in on three sides by mountains; the steady pressure of cool air from the Pacific boxes in the fourth side. Hot air from the Mojave Desert, flowing westward over the mountains, overrides the cool Pacific air, creating higher temperatures above than below, or a temperature inversion. The hot air being light stays up, and the heavier cool air stays down, thus eliminating a vertical circulation.

When the lid caused by the inversion drops below 1500 feet preventing the incoming air from escaping over the mountains, the Los Angeles Basin becomes a gigantic stagnant receptacle into which are poured the discharges from millions of chimneys, thousands of industrial smoke stacks, more than a million home incinerators, and about three million auto and truck exhausts. Recently progress has been made in the control, limit, or elimination of some of these air contaminants.

Night may give little relief. Gentle off-shore breezes may waft the polluted air out to sea, but it may drift back in the morning. Each new day may add more airborne waste, so that the longer the inversion lasts, the worse the pollution becomes. Inversion conditions may prevail as many as 250 days a year.

Smog is not new to Los Angeles; for the early Spanish explorers, noticing how the smoke from Indian fires filled the Basin, named it the Bay of Smokes. But the Indian smog was not as serious

---

[5] Dry bulb readings are always the same for the same air temperature; wet bulb readings vary with the amount of moisture in the air. An instrument which includes both dry bulb and wet bulb thermometers is known as a psychrometer.

[6] California state laws now require use on motor vehicles of devices that will limit or eliminate harmful gas discharge from the exhaust.

Fig. 3–5   Funnel-shaped Tornado Cloud. At Grand Rapids, Michigan, a black funnel-shaped cloud spread death and destruction as it swept with savage fury over the area west of the city. This tornado of April 3, 1956, caused 16 deaths, approximately 200 injuries, and significant economic losses. (*Courtesy Stewart, Smith & Co., Inc.*)

Table 3–1.   Weather Bureau Warning Service Reduces Hurricane Death Loss

Comparison of Death Loss Trend with that of Property Loss. In the following Table a Unit of $10,000,000 is Used in Making the Comparison.*

PERIOD	PROPERTY DAMAGE	LOSS OF LIFE	FATALITIES PER UNIT OF DAMAGE
1926–1930	131,153,000	2108	161
1931–1935	60,910,000	494	81
1936–1940	257,333,050	663	26
1941–1945	296,924,100	107	4
1946–1950	253,700,000	69	2.74
1951–1955	1,733,385,000	416	2.4
1956–1960	610,863,000	507	8.3
1961–1963	446,060,000	61	1.4

* Most death loss is preventable, but this is not true of property loss. All statistics, Courtesy United States Weather Bureau.

as the eye smarting, lung irritating, and plant damaging plague of today.

While smog is encouraged by the absence of wind, a long list of winds may be damaging to man's health and energy. Tropical hurricanes endanger human life and property in many regions of the world: (1) the China Seas, especially in the Philippines, Southeast China, and southern Japan; (2) the Arabian Sea and the Bay of Bengal, located on either side of the Indian subcontinent; (3) the Caribbean Sea, with the West Indies, Yucatan, and east and southeastern United States all feeling the effects of hurricanes; (4) the eastern North Pacific in the region of western Mexico; (5) the south Indian Ocean east of Madagascar; and (6) the tropical waters of northeast and northwest Australia. An im-

provement in weather prediction is constantly lowering death and property losses, but these storms still pose a terrific threat.

Tornadoes (Figs. 3–5 and 3–6) are not distributed as widely throughout the earth as the tropical hurricanes; but they carry greater wind velocities over narrower paths. These violent winds take hundreds of lives annually and are an especial hazard to man in southern and central United States.

Besides the widely distributed disastrous winds associated with tropical hurricanes and tornadoes, there are many local winds which are injurious to man. For example the Italian sirocco is so depressing that judges may be more lenient with criminals when that wind is blowing; in France, some believe that the mistral is

Fig. 3–6 Destruction by Tornado. One of the most destructive tornadoes in the history of the United States struck Worcester, Massachusetts, and the surrounding area on June 9, 1953. This storm killed 94 people; injured 1310, some for life; left thousands homeless; destroyed 634 houses and damaged 2791; and caused a total property loss of more than sixty million dollars. (*Courtesy Worcester Telegram and Evening Gazette*)

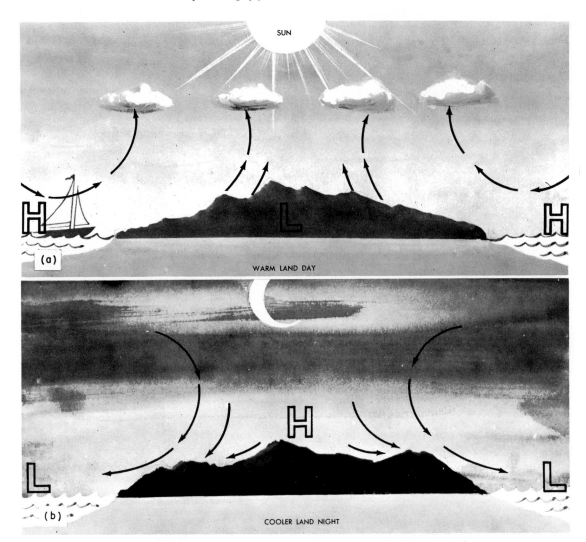

Fig. 3–7 Sea Breeze and Land Breeze. A sea breeze may develop on clear days because of more rapid heating of land than sea; this difference in temperature results in lower pressures for a few hundred feet above the land than at similar elevations above the nearby sea. Thus the sea breeze moves from sea to land. The land breeze may develop on a clear night when land cools more rapidly than the nearby sea and pressure conditions for a few hundred feet above land are higher than for similar altitudes above sea. Thus the land breeze moves from land to sea. (*Courtesy of United States Air Force, from AFM 105–5,* Weather for Aircrews, *Sept. 1, 1962*)

injurious to one's health; in Switzerland, before the advent of air conditioning, the extremely dry air of the foehn brought on extreme nervousness among invalids; this became so serious that surgical operations have been postponed until weather conditions improved.

T. E. Lawrence in his *Revolt in the Desert* vividly describes suffering from winds in the Arabian desert. "It was a breathless wind, with the furnace taste; and as the day went on and the sun rose in the sky, it grew stronger, more filled with the dust of the great sand desert of northern Arabia. . . . By noon it blew half a gale, so dry that our shrivelled lips cracked open and the skin of our faces chapped; while our eyelids, gone granular, seemed to creep back and bare our shrinking eyes. The Arabs drew their head-cloths tightly across their noses, and pulled the brow-folds forward like viziers with only a narrow loose-flapping slit of vision."

If some winds affect man adversely, there are others which bring him health and energy. A

Fig. 3–8   Mexico City's 7474 Feet Altitude Bothers Athletes. A *Life* article, March 28, 1955 was entitled "Pan-American Meet Proves a Lung Buster." The comment beneath the picture was "Alexis Bloem near suffocation fights painfully for air." Two other picture comments were (1) "Grim stretcher-bearers parade off the field with first altitude victim, Jamaica's Cynthia Mills who passed out during 60-meter dash"; and (2) "In need of oxygen after run, three athletes wear masks plugged into the same bottle, a common sight during the games." (*Mark Kauffman for* Sports Illustrated © *1955 Time Inc.*)

classic example is that of the sea breeze along hot tropical coasts. A few years ago in African Senegambia, measurements showed a drop in temperature from 102°F to 79°F in one-half hour; and during the same short period the relative humidity increased from 3 per cent to 61 per cent. Is it any wonder that the natives call such a cooling wind the doctor? (Fig. 3–7).

One of the most important contributors to man's health and energy through wind action comes from the summer monsoons of southeast Asia. More than a billion people, nearly half of the world's population, live in this part of the largest continent. And their very lives depend upon the moisture brought to their agricultural lands by this seasonal wind. When monsoon winds fail to bring sufficient precipitation, famines occur and millions of people may die. When monsoon winds produce normal or above normal rainfall, danger of famine is minimized or entirely eliminated.

When they move from low to high altitudes for short periods, people living near sea level are likely to suffer shortness of breath, headache, lassitude, and faintness. Pressure differences have been cited as responsible for high altitude mountain sickness. But in 1590, a Jesuit priest by the name of Acosta proved that the illness is due to oxygen deficiency. Because life expectancy is decreased at very high altitudes, it is fortunate that the higher regions such as those of Tibet and Bolivia are not densely populated.

In the 1940's, the Rockefeller Foundation made a study of the influence of Bolivian altitudes upon the length of human life. Researchers found that the life span of people living over 3000 meters is 31 years; from 1000 to 3000 meters, longevity increased to 34 years; and Bolivians living at altitudes of less than 1000 meters were living to an average of 37 years.

During the Pan American games of 1955, held in Mexico City, 7400 feet above sea level, athletes from low altitudes suffered severely from mountain sickness (Fig. 3–8). A girl sprinter from Trinidad fell unconscious to the track in the first event, and for the next six days contestants wobbled about the field with limp arms and agonized expression. As they dropped, stretcher-bearers rushed over to them, closely followed by men with oxygen bottles. Of course if man so desired, he could build a large building for the Pan American games, and with proper air conditioning he could do away with any danger of mountain sickness over the small enclosed area in the Mexican capital.

However, the Mexicans were ready for the outdoor rarified air, having trained in high altitudes. Moreover, while there is less air to breathe at the Mexico City elevation, there is also less atmosphere to resist moving objects, and some athletes gained from this advantage.

So far we have emphasized the influence of climate upon man and his activities, with particular stress on the dominance of nature over man. It must be noted, however, that as civilization advances, man has shown inventiveness in such areas as building better shelter, providing heating and cooling facilities for dwellings, developing better and faster transport equipment and making marked advances in medical science, in food preservation, and in clothing best adapted for each of the world's climatic regions. All these advances and many others designed to promote man's comfort and efficiency have enabled him to move into and work in areas where he could not become adjusted physiologically without them.

Although I believe that major emphasis in the study of geography should be placed upon relationships between earth and man and between man and the earth, students should also become familiar with each of the major features of the physical environment. Since Chapter Three has given an important stress to climatic relationships, the following chapter will include a brief general approach to the mechanics of the earth's climates.

QUESTIONS, EXERCISES, AND PROBLEMS

1. How does climate serve as a barrier on the ocean, among the mountains, on the desert, in the tropical rainforest, and within high latitudes?
2. Give examples to show how climate and weather effect man's food supply. Comment on the effects of climate on man's health and energy as described by Paul Siple, Ellsworth Huntington, A. Grenfell Price, and the author.
3. Tell of the causes for the malaria epidemic in St. Croix.
4. Why do certain cities resent Weather Bureau reports on the Discomfort Index?
5. What are the causes of smog, and what is being done about it in California?

6. Describe the differences between tropical hurricanes and tornadoes; between the sirocco and the foehn; between the sea breeze and the land breeze; between the mountain breeze and the valley breeze; and between India's summer monsoon and that of the winter period.

7. Give several illustrations which concern the influence of altitude upon man's activities.

8. What has man done to ease the hardships of life in areas of unpleasant weather and climate?

SELECTED REFERENCES

Curry, Leslie, "Regional Variation in the Seasonal Programming of Livestock Farms in New Zealand," *Economic Geography,* April 1963, pp. 95–118.

Curry, Leslie, "The Climatic Resources of Intensive Grassland Farming: The Waikato, New Zealand," *Geographical Review,* April 1962, pp. 174–94.

De Long, George C., "Temperature Trends in Southeastern United States, 1906–1960," *Journal of Geography,* Dec. 1962, pp. 387–93.

Dohrs, Fred E., Sommers, L. M., and Petterson, D. R., *Outside Readings in Geography,* pp. 58–156, "Climate and Man," Thomas Y. Crowell Co., 1955.

Gilliland, Minnio, "Bioclimatology: Weather and People," *Landscape,* Spring, 1964, pp. 11–12.

Headquarters, Quartermaster and Engineering Command, U.S. Army, *World Guide to Field Clothing Requirements,* Technical Report, EP–115, July 1959, Natick, Mass.

Humphreys, W. J., *Weather Proverbs and Paradoxes,* The Williams & Wilkins Co., Baltimore.

Kimble, G.H.T., "Handicap for New Nations: Climate," *New York Times Magazine,* Sept. 29, 1963.

Kolars, John F., *Tradition, Season, and Change in a Turkish Village,* University of Chicago Press, 1963.

Lebon, J.H.G., *An Introduction to Human Geography,* Ch. 2 and 3, "Climate and Man" and "Human Migrations and Climate," Longmans Green & Co., 1959.

Nuttonson, M.Y., "Crops and the Weather, the Role of Bioclimatology in Agriculture," *Landscape,* Autumn 1962, pp. 9–11.

Sopher, David, "Man and Nature in India: Landscapes and Seasons," *Landscape,* Spring, 1964, pp. 14–19.

Steen, Mary, "The Weather in the City," *Landscape,* Autumn 1961, pp.4–5.

Taylor, Griffith, editor, *Geography in the Twentieth Century,* Chapter IX, "Climatic Influences" by S. S. Visher, pp. 196–220, Philosophical Library, Inc.

Thralls, Zoe A., "The Teaching of Weather and Climate," Ch. 11, pp. 305–30, *The Teaching of Geography,* Appleton Century Crofts, 1958.

UNESCO, *Changes of Climate,* Proceedings of the Rome Symposium, Paris, 1963.

U.S. Dept. of Agriculture, *Climate and Man,* Yearbook of Agriculture, 1941.

Victor, Paul-Emile, Scott Sullivan, translator, *Man and the Conquest of the Poles,* Simon and Schuster, 1963.

Warntz, William, "Transatlantic Flights and Pressure Patterns," *Geographical Review,* April 1961, pp. 187–212.

Washington Weather Map—Index of special articles published on the back of the map, issue of Jan. 23, 1964. This index, usually published each January, includes titles and dates of articles published over the past few years that stress relationships between weather and climate and man's activities. In the 1964 issue, 18 articles were listed under Agriculture; 23 were devoted to Aviation; 4 to Cooperation; 5 to Forecasting; 7 to Hurricanes; 8 to Hydrology; 3 to Industrial Meteorology; 7 to Weather Instruments; 13 to Operations of the Weather Bureau; 2 to Recreation; 3 to Tornadoes; and 3 to Transportation. A sampling of these references is recommended for student study; and they are available at a low cost from the Weather Bureau, United States Department of Commerce, Washington, D.C.

Chapter Four

The Controls of Climate

Several approaches to the study of world climates may be utilized. For example, one may examine the major climatic elements—temperature, precipitation, humidity, winds, and air pressure; or he may look at the world climates on a regional basis, describing the climates of the continents and those of the various countries making up each of the large land masses; or he may study world climates by an examination of the major climatic controls. These include (1) latitude, (2) distribution of land and water, (3) prevailing winds, (4) cyclonic storms, (5) mountains as barriers, (6) altitude, (7) ocean currents, and (8) permanent and semi-permanent pressure cells. It may be best to use the controls approach.

Latitude. Latitude controls two of the most significant climatic conditions, (1) the amount of darkness and daylight a place receives during a 24 hour period; and (2) the position of the sun in the sky during the hours of daylight. In low latitudes the noonday sun is always close to the zenith or directly overhead; and on the equator, daylight and darkness are each approximately twelve hours long throughout the year. In fact throughout the tropics there is only a slight departure from the 12 hours of darkness and 12 hours of daylight.

In the high latitudes, length of day and night and altitude of the noonday sun contrast sharply with conditions on or near the equator. At the poles, the noonday sun is never higher than 67½° from the zenith or 23½° above the horizon, even in summer. In winter, darkness prevails throughout the entire period just as continuous daylight is characteristic of the summer. Between the Arctic and Antarctic Circles and the poles, (1) all continuous periods of daylight and darkness are shorter than those at the poles; and (2) the summer noonday sun is higher than at the top and the bottom points of the world.

In the middle latitudes, sun conditions depart from those of both equatorial and polar regions. In summer the noonday sun is relatively high, hours of daylight are long, and hours of darkness short; in winter the noonday sun is low, hours of darkness are long, and hours of daylight are short.

Daylight periods of approximately 12 hours every day of the year and a consistently high noonday sun combine to give the tropical lowland regions high yearly temperatures with very slight annual range. In equatorial lowlands, diurnal ranges are greater than annual ones.

In the middle latitudes, long summer days and high noonday sun produce relatively high temperatures; however, low temperatures result from the low winter sun and long periods of darkness on winter days. As a consequence, mean annual temperature range is significant, being considerably greater in the higher middle latitudes than in the lower ones.

In the high latitudes, especially near the poles, average annual temperatures are low. The persistence of snow and ice throughout the year minimizes the warming influence of the long daylight hours of summer. Although high-latitude-mean-annual range is greater than in the tropics, average temperature contrasts between summer and winter are not as great as those occurring in the higher middle latitudes.

The control of latitude upon pressure, another climatic element, in both high and low latitudes is significant. Speaking very generally, the low pressure belt of the equatorial region is closely related to the constancy of high temperatures—already described as controlled by latitudinal location. In the polar regions, however, the constancy of low temperatures exerts a different thermal control and brings about the more or less permanent high pressures at or near sea level.

Pressures in the middle latitudes result more from dynamic controls than from thermal ones; and while pressure distribution does show relation to latitude, the discussion of (1) sub-polar lows and (2) the gradual middle latitude pressure rise toward horse latitude highs will be delayed until an examination of the controls of pressure cells and prevailing winds.

Distribution of Land and Water. For a good understanding of this climatic control, it is necessary for one to compare the reactions of land and water to solar energy. He needs to understand what happens to land and water when each absorbs, transmits, and reflects the sun's heat.

Continental and ocean surfaces receiving the same amounts of incoming solar radiation during the day do not show the same increases in temperature; and during the night they do not show the same temperature decline. The main cause of this difference in heating and cooling is the fluidity of the water. The ocean is constantly on the move with (1) convectional currents moving up and down, (2) high and low tides occurring at fairly regular intervals, (3) waves varying from imperceptible ripples during periods of calm to heights of more than a score of feet during violent storms, (4) and numerous currents and drifts moving in a horizontal direction for thousands and thousands of miles. All these water movements distribute the sun's energy absorbed by the ocean throughout an extremely large mass of water; and as a result temperatures do not rise and fall rapidly on the ocean surface.

Land reacts to the receipt of solar energy in an entirely different way. Distribution of the heat absorbed at the surface does not affect nearly as large a volume of land as of water. One of the clearest proofs of this may be seen by noting the small distance beneath the surface that burrowing animals descend to escape the summer heat of middle latitude desert and steppe surfaces and the constant heat of the low latitude steppe and desert. On the average, diurnal temperature changes do not occur deeper than approximately three feet in the soil; while changes during the entire year normally extend no lower than about 47 feet. In contrast diurnal temperature changes in quiet water may extend down to 20 feet or more; and be-

cause of the turbulence usually present in deep sea and lake waters, it is probable that annual temperature changes in such areas may reach to depths between 500 and 2000 feet.

Fluidity contributes most to the conservative regime of heating and cooling in water, but there is also the lesser contributing factor of water's transparency. Light may penetrate sea water to depths of over a thousand feet, and water transparency also permits the transmission of solar energy for a score of feet at least. Since land is opaque, the element of transparency is of no significance in the heating of land masses.

Finally, the specific heat of water is greater than that of land. In other words, it takes twice to three times as much energy to heat a unit of water one degree C as the energy necessary to warm the same volume of soil.

For land masses as a whole, the loss of the sun's heat by reflection over the great diversity of surfaces is not greatly different from losses over the more uniform surface of the ocean. On the other hand, evaporation, which is a cooling process, is greater over the oceans than over most of the land; this is not true over the wet lowland tropics where evaporation exceeds that over the adjoining ocean.

From this comparison of land and water heating and cooling, it is evident that marine climates are conservative in daily and seasonal temperature changes in contrast to the more radical characteristics of continental climates (Fig. 4–1).

The control exerted by distribution of land and water over precipitation should be easily understood. Obviously, the ocean is the greatest source of moisture in the world, and locations close to the ocean, other things being equal, will receive more precipitation than continental interiors. Proximity to source of moisture also increases the humidity of the atmosphere.

For the earth as a whole, the average annual precipitation over land masses is approximately 26 inches, in contrast to an average of about 44 inches over all water surfaces. Since water covers about 72 per cent of the earth in contrast to the 28 per cent comprising the earth's land masses, a much greater total weight of moisture falls on the ocean, about 81 per cent, than that falling on land, about 19 per cent.

The time of occurrence of most precipitation

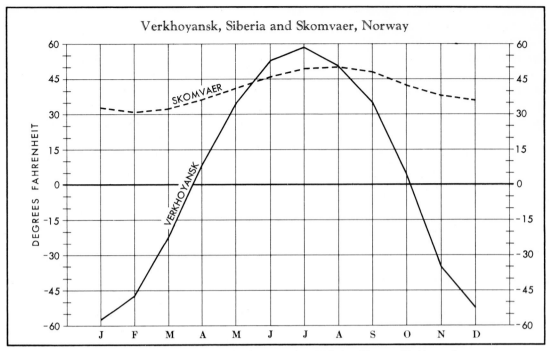

Fig. 4–1 Temperature Profiles for Continental and Marine Climates. Verkhoyansk, located at 67° 43′ N and 133° 33′ E, has a temperature profile showing its extreme continentality, with a mean annual range of 117.4° F. In contrast, Skomvaer 68° 26′ N and 13° 42′ E, located on Norway's Lofoten Islands at about the same latitude, possesses a truly marine profile with a mean annual range of only 19.6° F. The altitude for Verkhoyansk is 330 feet above sea level, and that for Skomvaer is 66 feet.

differs over land and sea. Over the former, the greater amount is likely to occur by day when thermal convection is at the maximum. However, night is likely to be the time of heaviest rainfall over the ocean. The reason is as follows: there is very little variation in temperature of the sea surface between day and night. Consequently, the air immediately above is likely to show little diurnal change. But this uniformity of temperature is not characteristic of the air at greater heights over the ocean. Here temperature is largely controlled by radiation and the upper atmosphere is warmer by day than by night. During the latter period, the lapse rate steepens between the cool upper air and the warmer air immediately over the sea surface. The steepening lapse rate encourages convective activity and night time showers. During the day, however, with the upper air warmer than ocean surface air, there is little to encourage convection.

Winds are also controlled in several ways by the earth's distribution of land and water. Over wide stretches of ocean with comparative surface uniformity, wind velocities are likely to exceed those of air moving over land. On the latter area, air encounters a diversity of topographic features.

Furthermore, the heating and cooling differences between land and water are likely to bring thermal control over pressures which may encourage differences in air movement. Diurnal temperature differences between land and the adjoining sea in middle and low latitudes may be sufficient to develop a sea breeze by day and a land breeze by night (see Fig. 3–7). Differences in temperature cause differences in pressure that in turn cause air movement from high to low pressures. On a clear day there is greater heating and lower pressure over land than over the nearby sea, and the breeze moves from sea to land—the sea breeze. On a clear night, temperatures cool more, and pressures are higher over land than over the adjoining sea and breezes move from land to sea—the land breeze.

Monsoon winds of southeast Asia are a much

larger example of air movements caused by the differential heating and cooling of land and sea. As previously indicated, land heats faster and more intensely at the surface than water. On June 21st, when the vertical ray of the noonday sun falls on the Tropic of Cancer, part of which passes through southeast Asia and (1) there is intense heating of the large land mass; (2) air is forced upward as a result of this heating, and at higher levels, several thousand feet, (3) this rising air spills over the less heated more compact air above the adjoining ocean. With the loss of some of this rising air to the ocean area, (4) pressure becomes lower over the land; and since the lost land air moves at higher levels over the sea, (5) pressure becomes higher over the adjoining ocean. Because surface air always moves from high pressure to low pressure, (6) the lower air of the Asian summer monsoon blows from sea to land (Fig. 4–2).

Asia's winter monsoon moves from land to sea in contrast to the direction of the summer monsoon. This reversal of wind direction is caused by the more rapid and more intense cooling of land surfaces than those of the sea.

As the vertical ray of the noonday sun moves towards the Tropic of Capricorn, far to the south of southeast Asia, (1) intense cooling commences over the huge land mass. (2) Air over the land contracts with cooling and gives opportunity for some of the less contracted air over the adjoining warmer seas to (3) spill over the contracted land air and move towards the land at high levels. With this movement (4) the sea loses air from above it at high altitudes and lower pressure results, whereas (5) the land gains air above it at higher levels and high pressure results. High pressure over land and low pressure over sea encourage (6) the lower winter air of southeast Asia to move from land to sea (Fig. 4–3).

The description above was the standard textbook explanation of the Asian monsoons for years, and there are still certain elements of truth left in this highly generalized simple story. However, modern meteorological research now shows that the causal explanation is much more complex than formerly believed. For example, (1) the monsoon of East Asia is now known to be different from that of South Asia. The outblowing winter winds of China are stronger than those that blow in from the ocean during the summer; in India conditions are exactly the reverse, with the summer monsoon winds stronger than those of winter. Again, (2) in East Asia the prevailing wind directions are interrupted in both winter and summer by locally developed cyclones and anticyclones. Finally, (3) it has been suggested that the Indian summer monsoon is merely a far northward advance of the Intertropical Convergence caused by the

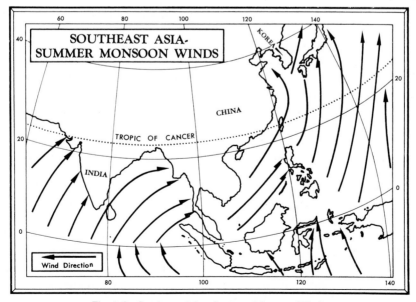

Fig. 4–2   Southeast Asia—Summer Monsoon Winds.

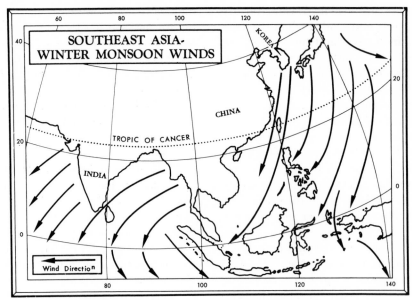

Fig. 4–3   Southeast Asia—Winter Monsoon Winds.

high summer temperatures of northern Pakistan and India. These are only a few of the complexities that are constantly being exposed by continued meteorological research. In short, there is no doubt that the Asian monsoons exist, but the causes are neither simple nor fully known. (A further discussion of the subject may be found in Colin S. Ramage, "The International Indian Ocean Expedition," *Washington Weather Map,* March 28, 1963.)

Pressure Cells and Winds. Pressure and prevailing winds are so closely related in their controls of weather and climate that they may be examined together. But before examining how they control climate, it may be well to study a few other facts about them.

A fundamental truth about the atmosphere is that it has weight, with air over each square inch of the earth's surface weighing approximately 15 pounds. Thus, since there are more than four billion square inches in one square mile and nearly two hundred million square miles on the world's surface, the total tonnage of earth air runs into nearly sixteen figures.

On weather maps pressure records usually appear in terms of inches of mercury or in millibars. A column of air having a cross section of one square inch, or any other area, and extending to the limits of the atmosphere will weigh the same as a column of mercury having the same cross-section area and extending vertically only about 30 inches. A bar is equal to 29.53 inches of mercury and a millibar is one thousandth of a bar. Lines on maps connecting places of equal pressures are called isobars.

Another useful fact about atmospheric pressure is that it declines with elevation; at ordinary, but uniform, temperatures the decrease is at the geometric rate of about $\frac{1}{30}$ of the pressure reading for a 900-foot increase in elevation. Thus, if the pressure at sea level is an even 30 inches, at 900 feet, it would be one inch less, or 29.0 inches; at 1800 feet it would be less by $\frac{1}{30}$ of 29 inches, or 28.03 inches, etc. At approximately 3.5 miles of altitude one half of the air in weight lies below and one half above.

As previously indicated the lowered pressure at high altitudes affects man physically. At about 18,500 feet, the oxygen content is only about half that at sea level. Furthermore, man's body is adjusted to the normal sea level pressure; and when he climbs a mile or more, his internal pressure is so much greater than that of the outside that he may suffer from headache, nausea, nose bleed, pain in the ears, and other troubles.

The temperature of air, as well as its moisture content, has a great influence upon its weight or pressure. Since most substances expand when warmed and contract when cooled, it becomes evident that warm air is usually lighter than cold air. Again, a cubic foot of water vapor weighs less than a cubic foot of dry air. Thus, moist air is lighter than dry air. And since the moisture of the air may change from hour to hour and from season to season, it follows that pressures may change in the same sequence.

Wind is always a result of difference in pressure between two areas, the movement of air being from the area of high pressure to the area of low pressure. Wind may be defined as air that moves essentially parallel to any part of the earth's surface; but the term air current should be applied to upward and downward moving air.

A wind is named for the direction from which it blows; for example a wind coming from the west is called a west wind, one from the east, an east wind etc. Two important terms associated with winds are windward and leeward. The former may be defined as the direction from which a wind blows, and the latter indicates the direction toward which it blows.

While winds and pressures everywhere show both daily and seasonal variations, there are a few major pressure belts or cells that remain in a more or less constant latitudinal location. In the equatorial latitudes, where temperatures are constantly high, a thermally controlled low pressure belt remains throughout the year. Between the equatorial low and latitudes of 30° to 40° North and South, pressures rise gradually to where the subtropical highs occur, a little poleward from the Tropic of Cancer and the Tropic of Capricorn. These horse-latitude highs probably have a dynamic rather than a thermal origin, but all the true causes are not definitely known.

Pressures decline gradually from the latitudes of 30° to 40° North and South to the Arctic and Antarctic Circles, where other low pressure belts occur. Like the subtropical highs, these subpolar lows are probably of dynamic rather than of thermal origin. Poleward from the Arctic and Antarctic Circles, pressures rise gradually to 90° North and South, where thermally induced high pressure belts occur.

In summary one may say that two thermally induced high pressure belts occur at the poles; one thermally controlled low pressure area is located in the equatorial latitudes; two dynamically caused highs lie in the horse latitudes; and

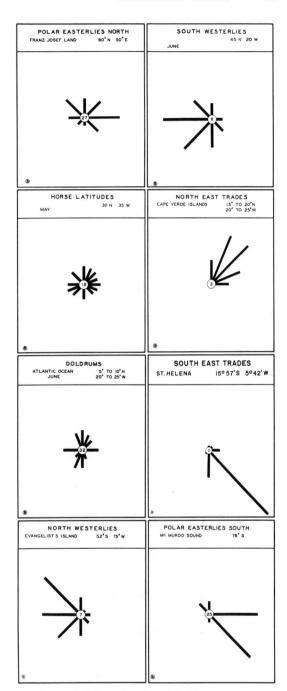

Fig. 4–4 Wind Roses for Major Wind Belts. This illustration shows winds as they actually occur at specific locations. However, three stations have wind roses based on but one month of the year.

two dynamically caused subpolar lows appear in the regions contiguous to the Arctic and Antarctic Circles (Figs. 4–4 and 4–5).

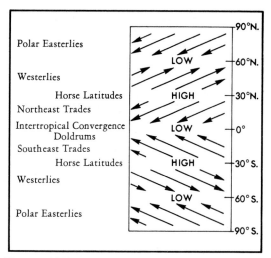

Fig. 4–5 Highly Generalized Arrangement of Zonal Wind and Pressure Belts at the Surface. Surface pressures at the poles are not shown, but they average higher than those of the subpolar lows.

The pressure distribution above shows considerable control over major world wind systems. From the polar highs air moves down and out towards the subpolar lows; and winds between the polar highs and subpolar lows generally receive the name of the polar easterlies. Although these winds start out as north winds in the northern hemisphere and south winds in the southern hemisphere, the deflection due to the earth's rotation gives them an easterly component, northeast in the northern hemisphere and southeast in the southern hemisphere.

Since both northeast and southeast polar winds are moving equatorward, they become warmer and increase their capacity to hold moisture. Consequently the polar easterly wind belt has little precipitation, partly because of the direction of air movement from the polar highs.

Descending air moves both equatorward and poleward from the horse latitude divergent wind system. The poleward moving air receives the name of the westerly winds. The starting air movement in the northern hemisphere is from the south and from the north in the southern hemisphere. Deflection gives a westerly component and the winds become the southwesterlies of the northern hemisphere, and the north-westerlies of the southern hemisphere.

Since the westerly winds have a generally poleward movement, they become cooler and

lose their capacity to hold moisture. This is one reason for the generally adequate amount of precipitation supporting humid agriculture throughout most of the westerly wind belt. The other major reason for significant rainfall is associated with the cyclonic storm climatic control, which is still to be discussed.

Air moving equatorward from the subtropical highs forms the trade winds, the northeast trades in the northern hemisphere and the southeast trades in the southern hemisphere. Equatorward air movement from the horse latitude highs is from the north, to start with, in the northern hemisphere and from the south in the southern hemisphere; but deflection caused by the earth's rotation brings the easterly component.

Trade wind air becomes warmer as it blows toward lower latitudes, and it increases its capacity to hold moisture. Like the horse latitude belt the trade wind region is one of the world's driest sections. In the former zone descending air encourages aridity; in the latter wind belt, precipitation is discouraged by warming equatorward moving air. Only when mountains force trade wind air to rise, cool, and condense is there any appreciable precipitation.

In the zone of equatorial low pressures, winds are light and variable with generally ascending air currents over wide areas. This ascending air is partly a result of high temperatures caused by the consistently high noonday sun and daylight periods of 12 hours or approximately 12 hours in length. Another cause for the rising air is the convergence of the northeast and southeast trade winds at or near the equator. The upward movement of equatorial air is one of the causes for condensation and generally heavy rainfall in such places as the Amazon and Congo basins.

Heretofore, consideration has been given to pressure belts as if they were zones extending completely around the world at certain latitudes. However, it would be more nearly accurate to describe them as cells of high or low pressure with their long axes extending in an east-west direction. For only in the southern hemisphere with its greater uniformity of water surface, do true zonal pressure belts exist. In contrast, north of the equator the northern hemisphere is an area of large continental masses with great seasonal contrasts in temperature, with great frictional effects, and with mountains as barriers. Here in this land hemisphere, pressure areas should be considered as pressure cells rather than east-west pressure zones.

There are also many departures from the diagrammatic representation of major world wind belts. For example, calms, variable winds, and generally rising air are not clearly marked throughout the equatorial zone; nor do these conditions exist at all times of the year. Again, air masses and air movements in the trade wind zone are not the same throughout the entire region. Dry trades occur more consistently toward the eastern ends of the subtropical high cells and at the poleward boundaries of the trade wind zone. Conversely more precipitation occurs at the western termini of subtropical highs and near the trade wind convergence zones. Departures can also be found from the general descriptions of westerly winds, polar easterlies, and air currents of the horse latitudes.

Thus the story of the earth's major wind belts, like that of the Asian monsoons is not as simple as formerly believed. There is still no doubt that the general atmospheric circulation is caused by the earth's rotation and by the differential heating of the lower and higher latitudes. Furthermore, there is a zone of equatorial calms in certain areas near the equator, a belt of trade winds poleward from the calms, high pressure cells between the westerly winds and the trade wind zones, and finally poleward from the westerlies are the subpolar belts of low pressures and outblowing winds from the polar areas.

However, explanations of the major wind belts and their exact locations are complex and becoming still more so with the constantly increasing information made available by the widespread meteorological research.

Cyclonic Storms. One of the most important climatic controls is that of cyclonic storms, especially those of the middle latitudes. In fact, middle latitude weather is largely controlled by a sequence of low pressure and high pressure systems—cyclones and anticyclones—moving around the world from west to east in the main stream of the prevailing westerlies. Lows have cloud, precipitation, temperature, and wind characteristics contrasting sharply with those of highs; the two pressure areas bring great variability to middle latitude weather; and they make the job of weather forecasting extremely difficult (Fig. 4–6).

The cyclone member of the team may be credited with an important assist in producing middle latitude precipitation. In short, this low pressure element contributes one of two major conditions necessary for rainfall. Given (1) adequate atmospheric moisture, the cyclonic storm provides (2) the lift to carry this moisture bearing air to higher altitudes where cooling and condensation bring precipitation in its various forms.

There is no general agreement upon the genesis of these air eddies, whirls, and cross currents that move from west to east in the great atmospheric river of the prevailing westerly winds. But it is safe to assume that the cyclonic storm may be formed where two contrasting air masses meet.

An air mass is an extensive portion of the atmosphere whose temperature and humidity properties are relatively homogeneous in a horizontal direction. Such a mass develops when the atmosphere remains at rest over an extensive area of uniform surface for a sufficiently long time so that the temperature and moisture characteristics of the air are brought into an adjustment with the underlying surface. These homogeneous portions of the earth's surface where air masses develop are designated as source regions. Examples of such source regions are the snow-covered plains of Canada in winter and the tropical waters of the Gulf of Mexico and the Caribbean Sea (Fig. 4–7).

Tropical air masses like those from the American Mediterranean (the Gulf of Mexico and the Caribbean Sea) are warm, moist, and unstable; and in the United States they are likely to move in from the south or southeast before a storm.

Polar air masses from Canada are usually cold, dry, and stable in winter. They generally move equatorward into the United States, but they also may have an easterly motion. When the Canadian air mass meets the one from the Gulf of Mexico, the contact zone is not along a sharp dividing line; on the contrary a great bulge of cold air may push in under the warm air like a wedge, and a great bulge of warm air may ride the cold air. These atmospheric conflicts of various kinds and degrees of intensity provide the conditions for the development of a mature cyclonic storm.

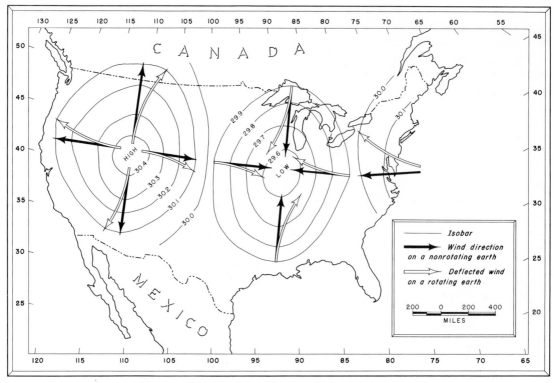

Fig. 4–6 Diagram of Cyclone and Anticyclone. Surface wind systems in cyclones (lows) and anticyclones (highs) are represented diagrammatically. The wind movement in the low is toward the center, counterclockwise, and upward in the northern hemisphere; toward the center, clockwise, and upward in the southern hemisphere. Air movement in the high is out-blowing from the center, clockwise, and downward in the northern hemisphere; out-blowing from the center, counterclockwise, and downward in the southern hemisphere. The general movement of the storm in either hemisphere is from west to east. A cyclone or anticyclone may cover an area of a million square miles or more.

In such a storm, the place where a warm air mass over-rides a cold one along the gently sloping atmospheric boundary surfaces is called a warm front. Air masses battling along this front may cause a rainy period ranging from a few hours to a few days in length. In time, the polar air, being heavier than the tropical air, will push under the warmer air and bring what is called a cold front (Fig. 4–8).

When this happens, the wind shifts to a west, northwest, and finally to a northerly direction. As a result, the temperature falls, and the drop may be quite significant during the winter season. Precipitation is likely to continue while the moist tropical air is being lifted, but cold front rain is usually of shorter duration than that from a warm front. The series of changes from south to north winds, from warm temperature

to cooler air, from fair weather to rain, and from rain to fair weather again is the result of the passing of a cyclone or low pressure system.

At the end of such a cyclone, descending, dry, cool, stable polar air brings the fair weather pattern usually associated with an oncoming anticyclone. In general a high follows a low or vice versa.

With the passage of a warm front in a cyclone or low pressure area, the cloud pattern generally changes from high altitude to middle and finally to low altitude clouds. Cirrus, at elevations of five miles or more, are likely to appear first, followed rapidly by cirro-stratus and cirro-cumulus only a little lower. These are usually followed by alto-cumulus and alto-stratus at medium elevations of from one to four miles; and finally the cloud series reaches closest to the ground—from a few hundred feet to a mile—in the low clouds which include strato-cumulus, stratus, nimbo-stratus, and nimbus. As the warm front passes and a cold front appears, the cloud pattern normally changes to numerous cumulus clouds that may soon disappear and leave the sky almost or entirely clear (Fig. 4–9).

Mention should be made of the almost certain, but little understood connection between the recently discovered jet stream and middle latitude cyclonic storms. The high altitude rapidly moving jet stream of air, discovered by the B-29 air squadron bombing Japan in World War II, probably has the effect of steering middle latitude cyclones and anticyclones around the world in the general path of the westerly winds. Furthermore, it is believed that

those cyclones moving immediately beneath the west-east jet path tend to intensify and produce heavier precipitation than would occur without the influence of the jet stream.

Cyclones of middle latitudes are not destructive storms themselves. But some of the most disastrous storms in the world, tornadoes, may form along sharply contrasting atmospheric conditions of a spring or summer cyclonic wind shift line; and the resulting funnel-shaped storm may leave significant death and property losses along a path less than a mile wide and only a few miles long (see Figs. 3–5 and 3–6).

Tropical cyclones, which may invade middle latitudes from the tropics, differ from the extratropical cyclones in many ways. They are usually destructive (Fig. 4–10), possess no wind

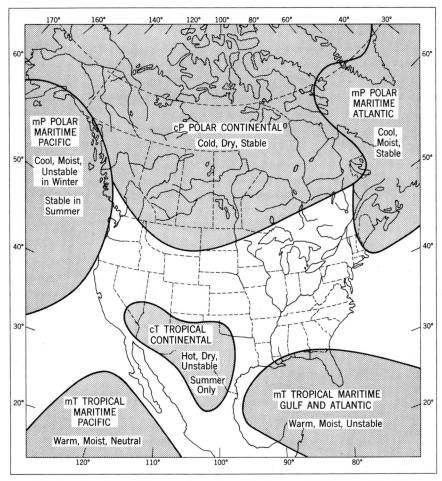

Fig. 4–7   North American Air Masses: Source Regions and Trajectories. (*From* An Introduction to Weather and Climate, *2nd ed., by G. T. Trewartha, Courtesy McGraw-Hill Book Co.*)

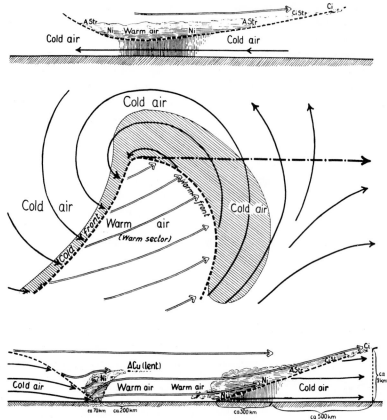

Fig. 4–8   Idealized Cyclone. A group of three diagrams shows the structure of an idealized polar-front cyclone by Bjerknes. The central diagram is a horizontal view of the distribution of air masses at the ground. For an orientation of directions for the central diagram the top is north, to the right is east, the bottom is south, and the left is west. The upper diagram represents a vertical west-east section, north of the center of the cyclone; the lower diagram shows a similar section south of the center of the storm area. *A str* means altostratus clouds; *Ni*, nimbus; *Ci Str*, cirrostratus; *Ci*, cirrus; *A Cu(lent)*, altocumulus lenticular. Distances in the lower diagram are approximate. (*Courtesy U.S. Weather Bureau*)

shift lines, move from east to west in the western hemisphere tropics, are somewhat smaller in size, have more circular isobars, and show a steeper pressure gradient with higher wind velocities.

Certain other low pressure areas in the tropics are called weak tropical lows. These cyclones are nondestructive storm systems with very slight pressure gradients and variable winds. They may be an important cause of precipitation in the wet lowland tropics.

Altitude. Altitude shows its climatic control well in the mountainous parts of the world. Here it affects all the climatic elements, humidity, precipitation, pressure, temperature, and winds.

In low latitudes of the Western Hemisphere, Spanish-speaking peoples refer to the *tierra caliente,* the *tierra templada,* and the *tierra fria* (Fig. 4–11). W. G. Kendrew, in his *Climates of the Continents,* describes these temperature zones in western South America north of the equator:

In the Andes the usual classification by altitude is: tierra caliente, from sea-level to 3000 feet, with a mean annual temperature from 83° to 75°, and luxuriant tropical vegetation, banana, sugar, and cacao plantations, and coconut groves; tierra templada, from 3000 to 6000 feet, temperature 75° to 65°, suitable for maize and especially coffee of which valuable crops are produced; tierra fria, 6000 to 10,000 feet, temperature 65° to 54°, where wheat, potatoes, and temperate fruits grow, but pasture predominates; paramos from 10,000

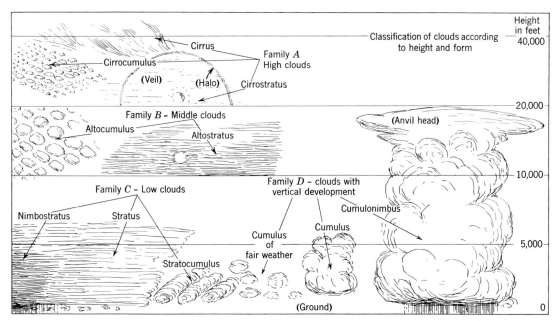

Fig. 4–9   Cloud Types. Cloud types are grouped into families according to height range and form. (*A. N. Strahler*, Physical Geography, *2d ed., John Wiley & Sons*)

Fig. 4–10   Destruction Caused by the New England Hurricane of September 21, 1938. Extremely high winds caused this damage to the First Unitarian Church, Worcester, Mass. Note the clock face formerly on the church spire. Wind gusts reached 186 miles an hour at Blue Hill Observatory, Milton, Mass. Storm statisticians placed the death loss at more than 600; injuries more than 2,000; and some 90,000 families suffered property loss. In fact, property loss of nearly one-third of a billion dollars was the greatest ever wrought by any storm in the world up to that time. For a good account of the meteorology of the hurricane, see C. F. Brooks, "Hurricanes into New England," *Geographical Review,* Jan. 1939. (*Courtesy* Worcester Telegram and Evening Gazette)

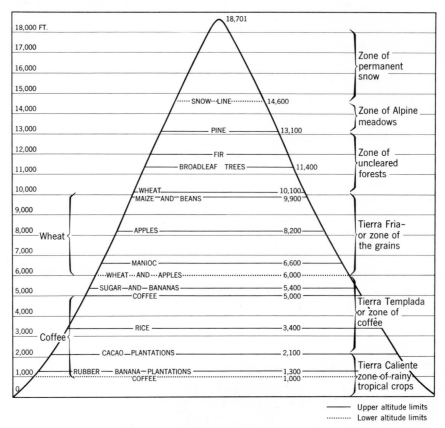

Fig. 4–11 Temperature Zones on Mount Orizaba. Mount Orizaba is located at
19° 0′ N and 97° 15′ W. The upper limits of each zone shown on this Mexican mountain extend higher on mountains located at or closer to the equator. (*after Karl Sapper
and Preston James,* A Geography of Man, *Ginn and Co.*)

to 13,000 feet, too cold for trees and cultivation, temperature 54° to 43°; above 14,000 feet there is per-
petual snow. Bogotá, 8700 feet above the sea, is in the
tierra fria, with a mean annual temperature of 58° and
an annual range less than 2°. (All temperatures are
given in °F.)

English names for altitude zones in the middle latitudes of Anglo-America are probably not
as picturesque as the Spanish zonal terms for
low latitude Latin America; but temperate
zones of Anglo-America exist just the same. Evidence of these zones may be seen in the broad
leafs at lower elevations in the Appalachians
and the conifers at higher altitudes. The conifer
is a more tolerant tree and can stand the lower
temperatures near the mountain tops. The same
vegetational response to temperature differences occurs in the mountains of western United
States and Canada.

It may be well to add that the average decline in temperature with each 1000 foot-in-
crease in altitude is approximately 3.3° F, varying with the location, season, and time of day;
and this decline in temperature with altitude
suggests that atmospheric heat is received directly from the earth's surface and only indirectly from the sun. The dry adiabatic rate of
cooling for rising air is 5.5° F per 1000-foot increase in altitude.

Altitude exerts a control over atmospheric
pressure as well as over the other climatic elements. It has been indicated previously that almost half the weight of the atmosphere lies below 18,500 feet, approximately three and one
half miles; and at the top of Mt. Everest, nearly
30,000 feet, the pressure is only between one-
third and one-fourth that at sea level. This lower
pressure and lower oxygen content of the air at
such high altitudes explains why Everest moun-

tain climbers carried oxygen tanks to make the successful ascent a few years ago.

High altitude pressures affect but a small portion of the world's population because the extent of land above 10,000 feet is quite limited; but small groups of people live permanently on the high Andes of Peru and in Tibet at altitudes of more than 15,000 feet. They probably go through some passes three and one half miles high in tending their flocks and herds.

Several years ago the United States Weather Bureau began carrying maps of North America showing upper air pressures; for it is known that conditions in the higher atmosphere have much to do with surface weather activities. Too, upper air pressure cells show marked contrast to surface pressure systems. As has been pointed out previously, at the earth's surface, pressures are low at the equator and high at the poles. However, at about 10,000 feet altitude, pressure maps show a pressure reversal with pressures low at the poles and high at or near the equator.

Winds at high altitudes also show differences from those at the surface. One of the main differences comes in the greater speed of air movement above and through the mountain peaks. At these elevations, friction hinders wind much less than it does a moving body of air at or near sea level.

Mountains as Barriers. Mountains as barriers exert a clearly marked control on all the elements of climate in any part of the world where highland regions occur.

Consider the barrier influences upon precipitation. Two of the rainiest stations in the world, Cherrapunji in Assam, India and Waialeali in the state of Hawaii have made their record because mountains lie at right angles to the prevailing winds (Fig. 4–12). In Hawaii, northeast trades sweeping over long stretches of the Pacific ocean strike the mountains of Kauai island and give up an average annual rainfall of over 400 inches. In Cherrapunji, the Khasi Hills squeeze about the same annual amount of moisture from the summer monsoons moving landward from the Bay of Bengal.

Again, rainfall in west coast marine climates is generally divided into two major types—that caused by prevailing winds striking mountain barriers closely bordering the coast and that resulting from cyclonic storms moving over lands of slight relief. The Andes mountains of southern Chile; the north-south trending highlands of New Zealand; the coastal ranges of Oregon, Washington, British Columbia and the Panhandle of Alaska; and the mountains of southwestern Norway all cause rainfall of the first type; this is called orographic rainfall.

Other places with mountain-caused rainfall include the trade wind Atlantic coast of Central America, the West Indies islands with east-west mountain backbones facing the northeast trades, the coast of east-central Brazil and the east coast of the Malagasy Republic both lying at right angles to the southeast trades, and the Western Ghats facing winds of the Indian summer monsoon. The Tibesti and Ahaggar mountains of the central Sahara rise high enough to block the northeast trades and thus encourage oases on windward sides of the mountains. Many other locations with orographic precipitation can be named.

If mountains as barriers can cause precipitation in the areas mentioned above, they can also cut off rainfall from other lands (see Fig. 4–12). One of the main reasons for the broad stretch of arid and semi-arid country in western United States is the group of highlands including the Cascade, Klamath, Sierra Nevada, and the Pacific Coastal ranges. These mountains receive significant amounts of precipitation on their windward slopes, but states lying to the leeward are blocked off from Pacific moisture by the mountains themselves.

It is fortunate that the Appalachians trend north-south in eastern United States rather than east-west across the southern states. If the latter situation existed, lands like Iowa and Illinois, two of our greatest food producers, might be as dry as Nevada and Arizona—all because mountains as barriers could shut off rain-bearing winds from the Gulf of Mexico.

In South Africa, the Drakensberg mountains block the southeast trades moving in from the Indian ocean, and descending air on the leeward side of the mountains brings aridity to the Kalahari desert. The Australian Alps block southeast trades from the Pacific ocean, and cause them to warm and withhold moisture as they descend into the Great Dead Heart of Australia. The Himalayas stop the summer monsoon winds from carrying moisture to central Asia. These and many other examples show

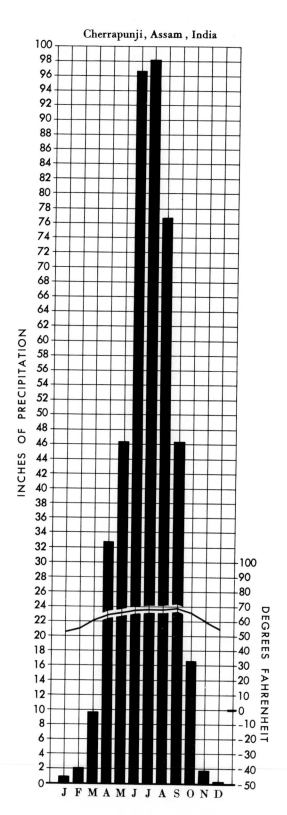

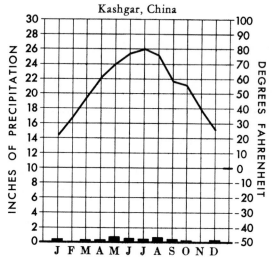

Fig. 4–12   Climatic Charts, Cherrapunji, India and Kash-gar, China. At Cherrapunji, rain-bearing winds not only are forced to rise by the steep mountain wall facing them, but air also piles up as it enters a wedge-shaped valley leading to the escarpment. Cherrapunji is located at 25° 16′ N and 91° 46′ E with an elevation of 4,309 feet. Mean annual precipita-tion is 427.8 inches. In contrast, Kashgar lies on the leeward side of the great Himalayan mountain barrier and near the interior of the continent, 39° N and 76° E. This location accounts for the low precipitation of 3.5 inches.

how mountains can cause aridity as well as heavy precipitation.

Mountains as barriers can control temperature as well as rainfall. The Riviera is the narrow and rugged strip of coast on which are located Nice in southern France and Genoa in Italy. The Maritime Alps and the northern Appenines, by blocking off cold winds from the north, contribute significantly to the mildness of the winter climate along this section of the Mediterranean shores.

In a like manner, the northern part of the Indian sub-continent has milder winters because the high Himalayas block cold outblowing air from the center of the great Asian continent. In North America the high Sierras guard the central valley of California against winds blowing out from the cold interior of the Intermontane Plateau and thus permit the growth of citrus fruit in relatively high latitudes.

The lack of an east-west mountain barrier across the great Central Lowland of the United States permits polar continental air to move equatorward without any obstruction. This cold air corridor between the Rockies on the west and the Appalachians on the east poses a frost hazard to all the southern states.

Mention has been made already of how mountain barriers exert control over temperature and precipitation by blocking winds. Mountains also develop local winds that may obscure the general weather conditions. Best known among these local air movements are the Mountain and the Valley winds. Both of these are a result of differential heating and cooling in a region of great diversity of land forms. For example, during a sunny morning the floor of the mountain valley becomes heated more than the valley slopes; at the same elevations in the upper air, pressure becomes greater directly over the valley floor than on the mountain sides leading up from the valley. With this development air moves from the higher pressures above the valley floor to the lower pressures along the valley walls and a daytime valley breeze begins moving up the mountain slope.

At night with a clear sky, the conditions are reversed. The air in the valley, cooling first, contracts and air from the nearby mountains moves in above the contracted valley air. Furthermore, after the surface air on the valley wall cools, it slides down slope into the valley. These downslope air movements form what is called the mountain breeze.

Besides the mountain and valley winds, there are mountain-caused air movements such as the bora, a wind characteristic of the northeast coast along the Adriatic sea. The origin of the bora is associated with a significant accumulation of cold air at the higher elevations of the bordering coastal mountains. This dense cold air from the high plateau and mountains is able to drain off to lower elevations because the air at lower altitudes has a lesser density. Bora air movements are likely to occur in winter when cold air has a tendency to accumulate under anticyclonic conditions.

Bora, mountain, and valley winds, all result from what may be called mountain climatic control although the barrier nature of the highlands has little to do with their origin. But there is one wind, the tropical hurricane, which is definitely controlled when it strikes a mountain barrier. For example some tropical hurricanes traveling from east to west across the Caribbean sea fail to turn north along the Florida coast and head straight towards Central America; here they soon lose their intensity when they strike the Central American mountain backbone.

Ocean Currents. Before pointing out climatic controls associated with ocean currents, it may be well to (1) examine the major and minor causes for movements of ocean water; to (2) explain differences between ocean currents (Fig. 4–13) and drifts (Fig. 4–14); and to (3) generalize upon the origin of warm and cold currents.

Major movements in the waters of the ocean result from two important causes, (1) surface friction brought about by the prevailing winds, and (2) differing densities influenced by differences in salinity and by differences in temperature. Sharp temperature contrasts exist between Arctic and Antarctic waters on the one hand and the warm waters found in equatorial locations. Again, waters in the dry horse latitude and trade wind zones have much greater salinity than ocean waters of the rainy westerly and doldrum wind belts.

Possibly a lesser influence upon ocean water movements is the deflective force of the earth's rotation; this force turns ocean currents and

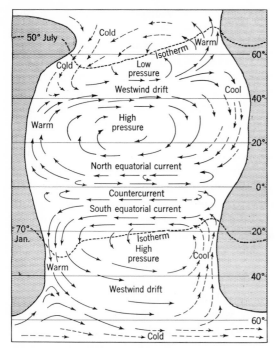

Fig. 4–13 Ocean Currents and Isotherms. This schematic map of an ocean shows the general system of ocean currents and their influence on isotherms. (*A. N. Strahler*, Physical Geography, *John Wiley & Sons*)

other moving bodies to the right in the northern hemisphere and to the left in the southern hemisphere.

To note this deflection, look at the course of the Gulf Stream on a map. When this great ocean river leaves the Straits of Florida, its general direction is from south to north; but deflection soon turns it northeast and then east-north-east as the Stream changes to the North Atlantic Drift and moves into higher latitudes. In the southern hemisphere, the Humboldt, Brazilian, and Benguela currents are all good examples of left-hand deflection.

Another influence upon movements of ocean waters is the configuration of coast lines. This situation is well exemplified by the splitting of the east-west moving South Equatorial Current when it meets Brazil's Cape São Roque head on.

One more cause for movements of ocean waters is the depth and degree of enclosure of the ocean basin. The Arctic ocean is sometimes called the Arctic Mediterranean because of its relatively enclosed location, somewhat similar to that of the Mediterranean Sea. But the Arctic has wide deep openings to the North Atlantic on

either side of Greenland in contrast to the shallow narrow opening to the Pacific by way of Bering Sea. As a result of this contrast, there is a much greater exchange of waters between the Arctic and the North Atlantic than between the Arctic and the North Pacific.

The term current or stream is applied to a horizontal movement of ocean water that is relatively narrow in width; and the term drift applies to a much wider horizontal movement of ocean water. The stream or current also is deeper, moves faster, and has better defined boundaries than the drift.

When these ocean rivers are moving from cold to warmer regions, they are usually designated as cold currents; when they are moving from warm to colder regions they may be called warm currents.

Warm currents have a tendency to parallel east coasts of continents equatorward from about 40°, whereas cold currents tend to parallel west sides of continents in the same latitudes. For example the Caribbean Current and Gulf Stream parallel the east coast of North America in the tropical and subtropical latitudes, and the Brazilian Current parallels the eastern shores of South America in similar latitudes. On the west coast of South America in the same latitudes the cold Humboldt or Peruvian Current bathes the coast, and in analogous latitudes on west coast North America, the California Current is active.

Poleward from 40° the reverse situation is generally true. Cool currents parallel the east coasts of continents, and warm ones parallel the continental west coasts. In North America, the Alaska Current, an offshoot of the North Pacific Drift, flows north along the coast of Alaska, and the Labrador Current flows south parallel to the eastern Canadian coast.

Climatic controls associated with these and other currents affect temperature, precipitation, and pressure. Examples of temperature control may be seen in Callao, Peru and Bahia, Brazil, west and east coast cities located in similar latitudes. Callao, on the coast of Peru, is bathed by the cold Humboldt Current and has an annual temperature of 67° F. Bahia, on the east coast of Brazil is influenced by the warm Brazilian current and has an annual temperature of 77° F. Durban and Port Nolloth are also in similar latitudes on the east and west coasts of South

Africa. Port Nolloth has a temperature of only 59° F for the warmest month largely because of the proximity of the cold Benguela Current. On the other hand, Durban has a warm month temperature of 76° F and gains warmth from the Mozambique warm current paralleling the coast.

Another good example of ocean current temperature control may be seen in the relatively high winter temperatures of northwest Europe when compared with those of the eastern shores of North America in the same latitudes. However, the influence of the North Atlantic Drift should not be given all the credit for the warm winter temperature anomaly of Europe's northwest coast. Westerly winds blowing for thousands of miles over an ocean warmer than the cold North American continent to the west contribute fully as much to mild west European winters as do the same winds blowing over the North Atlantic Drift—a drift warmer than the ocean through which it flows.

Ocean current control over temperature is again shown by converging and diverging ocean currents. The temperature gradient near the convergence of warm and cold ocean currents is much steeper than that occurring where ocean currents diverge. Not only do convergences tend to squeeze isotherms closer together, but they also are likely to cause advection fogs. Such temperature gradient and fog conditions may be seen in the vicinity of the Grand Banks off the coast of Newfoundland, where the cold Labrador Current and the warm North Atlantic Drift converge.

Where ocean currents diverge, as they do in the eastern North Atlantic, divergence tends to spread the isotherms and create a more gently sloping temperature gradient; the divergence also lessens the frequency of fog.

El Niño, a warm ocean current off the northern coast of Peru, provides one of the best examples of ocean current control over precipitation. El Niño is normally weak, but on infrequent occasions shows considerable strength. The name El Niño comes from the fact that the current normally appears about Christmas time.

Most every year north winds sweeping south across the equator bring with them a thin layer of warm ocean water that moves over the normally cold waters of the Humboldt Current paralleling the Peruvian coast. These cold ocean waters are usually augmented by upwelling of coastal waters brought about by offshore winds.

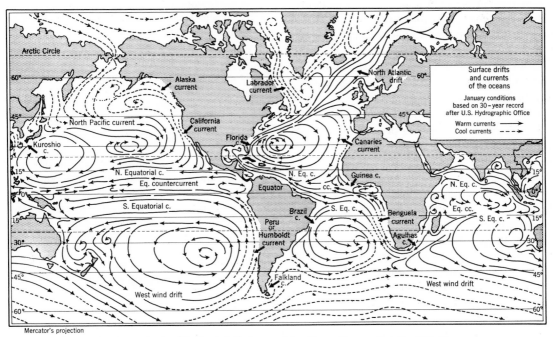

Fig. 4–14   Surface Drifts and Currents of the Ocean (January). (after U.S. Navy Hydrographic Office; From *A. N. Strahler*, Physical Geography, *John Wiley & Sons*)

Normally the warm El Niño surface current is so shallow that it has no effect upon the aridity characteristic of coastal Peru. But once in a long period of years, for reasons not fully understood, El Niño becomes a deep current of warm ocean water, and the normally arid Peruvian coast receives heavy precipitation. In 1925 at Trujillo, a place where only 1.4 inches of rain fell during the 7 years preceding 1925, 15.5 inches fell in one month; and 8.9 inches of this came in four days.

At this time a warm powerful El Niño greatly increased atmospheric humidity; warm moist air bounced upward when it struck the shores instead of rising sluggishly like the cold air normally does when it moves ashore from the cold Humboldt current; bouncing warm air produced towering cumulus clouds; and the towering clouds brought a deluge of rainfall.

Such heavy precipitation in a normally desert climate brought calamity; floods of water destroyed irrigation systems and covered fields with coarse gravel; houses built for dry weather crumbled and collapsed; roads and bridges were washed out; fever bearing insects increased; and inhabitants suffered from a variety of diseases. All this trouble came as a result of an unusual resurgence of El Niño into a deep, powerful, coastal paralleling ocean current—a warm current which replaced the cold Humboldt ocean river. Year after year the cold Humboldt lends encouragement to an arid climate; but 1925 brought a drastic climatic change. Historic records indicate that similar disastrous floods happened once in a long while even during the Inca period.

Ocean currents contribute at least some control upon the strengthening of pressure systems and upon the paths which they may follow. The winter strength of the Icelandic Low is influenced by the steep temperature gradient that occurs between the cold eastern side of North America and the warm waters of the North Atlantic Drift not far away. Winter also brings a much deeper Aleutian Low influenced by a similar steep temperature gradient between the cold eastern part of Asia and the warm ocean waters of the North Pacific Drift.

Ocean current control over paths of low pressure areas may be illustrated by citing two paths generally followed by Caribbean tropical hurricanes. One storm path follows the inside route of the warm Gulf Stream through the Caribbean Sea; and the second storm path generally coincides with the route of the warm current flowing north along the outer islands of the West Indies and the coast of Florida.

In studying the preceding pages describing climatic controls, the student should obtain a better understanding of causal factors accounting for various earth climates. Moreover, if he gains a general knowledge of the location and workings of these climatic controls, he may be able to work out for himself the climatic base for many countries and regions. And finally, with information about this base, he is better equipped to examine relationships between climates and peoples all over the earth.

QUESTIONS, EXERCISES, AND PROBLEMS

1. Name the controls of climate. What two significant climatic conditions result from latitude control?

2. Compare the reactions of land and water to seasonal heating and cooling. Be specific. How do oceans and lands compare in their reception of precipitation, both in amount and in time of occurrence? Explain causal factors involved in Southeast Asia's monsoon development.

3. List world wind belts from the North Pole to the South Pole. Comment upon (1) their tendencies to grow warmer or cooler and (2) upon the consequent changes in their capacity to hold moisture. What departures occur in the generalized system of world wind belts?

4. What is the origin of cyclonic storms in the belt of westerly winds? Give a detailed comparison of cyclones and anticyclones. What is an air mass? Name and locate several. Give a generalized description of weather sequences in a cyclone and in an anticyclone. Describe the jet stream, and tell of its discovery. Compare tropical and extratropical cyclones. Comment upon weak tropical lows.

5. Describe the "tierra" altitude zones of tropical Latin America. What is the difference between normal and adiabatic lapse rates? How does altitude affect humidity? Give the classification of clouds by altitude. What differences occur between winds at high and low altitudes?

6. What is meant by atmospheric pressure? Compare the pressure scales in inches and millibars. Comment upon the decline in pressure with an increase in elevation. Does air temperature influence pressure? Comment. What is the relation between (1) wind directions and wind speed and (2) atmospheric pressure? Give a generalized description of pressure belts between the equator and the poles.

7. Describe the influences of mountains as barriers upon precipitation, temperature and winds.

8. What are the differences between ocean drifts and currents? What generalizations can be made about warm and cold currents? What are the causes for movements of ocean waters in the form of drifts and currents? Comment upon location tendencies of ocean currents in the different latitudes. What influences do ocean currents exert upon temperature, precipitation, and pressure? Comment upon convergence and divergence of ocean currents.

9. Turn to the color plates at the end of the book and carefully study the Köppen-Geiger System of Climate Classification shown on Plate 2, "Climates of the World," and learn (1) the various climatic regions and (2) the bases for separating different areas into different climatic regions.

10. Examine Plate 1, "Mean Annual Precipitation of the World," and correlate major rainfall regions with the various climatic controls described in this chapter. How many centimeters are there in one inch? Learn other metric system measurements used in climatic control.

SELECTED REFERENCES

Bulletin of the American Meteorological Society, (monthly except July and August,) American Meteorological Society, Boston, Mass.

Clayton, H. H., *World Weather Records,* Smithsonian Institution, issued annually since 1927.

Dunn, G. E. and Miller, B. I., *Atlantic Hurricanes,* Louisiana State University Press, 1960.

Hare, F. Kenneth, "The Stratosphere," *Geographical Review,* Oct., 1962, pp. 525–47.

Haurwitz, B., "Atmospheric Tides," *Science,* June, 19, 1964, pp. 1415–22.

Kendrew, W. G., *Climates of the Continents,* Oxford University Press, latest revision.

Koeppe, C. E. and De Long, G. C., *Weather and Climate,* McGraw-Hill Book Co., 1958.

Larsson, Peter, "The Distribution of Albedo Over Arctic Surfaces," *Geographical Review,* Oct. 1963, pp. 572–79.

Logan, Richard F., "Winter Temperatures of a Mid-Latitude Desert Mountain Range," *Geographical Review,* April 1961, pp. 236–52.

Lokke, Donald H., *Teaching Weather and Climate,* Annotated Bibliography of Articles Published in *Journal of Geography,* National Council for Geographic Education, Publications Center, Illinois State Normal University, Normal, Illinois.

Morley, Thomas, *Climatological Atlas of Canada,* National Research Council and Meteorological Division, Dept. of Transport, Canada, 1953.

Schloss, Milton, "Cloud Cover of the Soviet Union," *Geographical Review,* July 1962, pp. 389–99.

Tanner, Gilbert, *Selected Climographs (640),* Eau Claire Wisconsin State Cartographic Institute, 1964.

Thiessen, A. H., *Weather Glossary,* U. S. Dept. of Commerce, Weather Bureau latest revised edition.

Trewartha, Glenn T., *An Introduction to Climate,* McGraw-Hill, 1954, especially part I, "The Elements of Climate," pp. 1–178.

Visher, S. S., *Climatic Atlas of the United States,* Harvard University Press, 1954.

Weather Bureau, U. S. Department of Commerce, *Climatography of the United States;* included under this heading are separates of climates of the various states with different dates of publication, different authors, different numbers of pages, and priced at approximately twenty-five cents for each state. The entire group is sometimes called *Bulletin W.* They are for sale by the Supt. of Documents, Washington, D. C.

Weather Bureau, U. S. Department of Commerce, *List of Selected Publications on General Weather Science Study,* Supt. of Documents, Washington, D. C.

Weather Bureau, U. S. Department of Commerce, *Meteorology and Atomic Energy,* Supt. of Documents, Washington, D. C.

Weather Bureau, U. S. Department of Commerce, *Monthly Weather Review With Supplements,* Supt. of Documents, Washington, D. C.

Weather Bureau, U. S. Department of Commerce, *Tornado Deaths in the United States,* Technical Paper No. 30, by Urban J. Linehan, 1957.

Chapter Five

The Earth's Major Surface Regions

The surface features of the earth are important influences upon climate, upon other features of the physical environment, and upon man and his activities. One way to become more familiar with the world's topography is to divide the earth into its oceans and continents and then subdivide these, especially the continents where man spends most of his time, into the most important physical regions. Thus, by examining major parts of the earth's physical landscape, one may become better acquainted with the physical world as a whole.

CONTINENTS AND OCEANS

The surface of the earth can be divided into major and minor physical features. Starting with major divisions, one can emphasize that nearly three fourths of the world, more than 140,000,000 square miles, is covered by water averaging approximately 2.5 miles in depth; and more than one fourth of the earth's surface, about 57,000,000 square miles, is land, rising to an average height of approximately one half mile above the sea.

This land mass is broken up into seven continents and adjoining islands: Africa, 11,635,000 square miles; Antarctica, 5,100,000; Asia 17,035,000; Australia, 2,975,000; Europe, 3,850,000; North America, 9,435,000, and South America, 6,860,000.

The 63,985,000 square miles of the Pacific Ocean account for nearly half the earth's water surface. This figure is larger than the total for the Atlantic, 31,529,000 square miles, combined with the Indian, 28,357,000 square miles. The Arctic ocean, almost completely surrounded by land, measures only 5,541,000 square miles. In addition to the four oceans, there are numerous seas, the largest of which are the Mediterranean,

the Bering, and the Caribbean, each covering about a million square miles.

The largest portion of the earth's water surface lies in the Southern Hemisphere; and so much of the land lies in the Northern Hemisphere that it is frequently called the land hemisphere. As previously suggested, land almost entirely encircles the Arctic Ocean.

The Continents

Three continental masses branch southward from the border of the Arctic ocean: (1) North and South America; (2) Europe and Africa; and (3) Asia and Australia. The Atlantic, Indian, and Pacific oceans fill in the hollows among the south-pointing land masses; finally, Antarctica rises where the southern continents would meet if prolonged toward the South Pole.

Four of the seven continents are triangular in shape. This is evident from a glance at North America, South America, and Africa, which taper notably toward the south. Europe's outline also resembles a triangle if we consider the Ural mountains as the base and the southwest tip of the Iberian peninsula as the apex. The other three continents, Asia, Australia, and Antarctica, show little resemblance to a triangle. In fact, if the ice were to melt from Antarctica, the continent would be seen as two separate bodies of land. Only the deep glacial cover gives it the appearance of a unified continent.

The Oceans

The Arctic Ocean is somewhat circular in form and the Atlantic's major curves resemble those of the letter "S." Africa, Asia, and Australia border the Indian Ocean on three sides; and the Americas, Asia, and Australia form all but the southern boundary for the Pacific. The name

Antarctic Ocean was once applied to the southern portion of the Atlantic, Indian, and Pacific oceans, which border the southernmost continent; but this term is seldom used in any description of the earth's major water bodies.

The Oceans, Submarine Topography. Water and land form the first major division of the earth's surface; continents and oceans comprise the second; and the third division should include the main topographic features of the continents and those of the ocean bottoms.

Man has merely started oceanographic research that will lead to a comprehensive picture of the earth's submarine geology. Some progress came during the IGY, and the scientists are now certain of a few important ocean-bottom features. One of the best known is the Mid-Atlantic Ridge (Fig. 5–1), which occupies at least one third of the Atlantic floor. Among the peaks which rise from the Ridge, two reach above the water surface and appear as land. These are Iceland and the islands of the Azores. The hot springs which appear on the island peaks give evidence of vulcanism, one of several geologic agencies responsible for the Atlantic's extensive submarine mountain feature.

The Ridge extends the entire length of the ocean and ranges in width from 300 to 1200 miles. Fracturing the submarine highland's surface is a huge graben,[1] thirty miles wide in places, and similar in origin to the rift valley of Africa. Near Antarctica, the Ridge swings east around South Africa into the Indian ocean.

The underwater topography of the Pacific is quite different from that of the Atlantic. The former ocean lacks the great north-south submarine ridge with its rift valley; on the other hand, there are fewer large stretches of Pacific underwater plains. The largest ocean possesses the greatest height measured from the ocean floor, that of Hawaii, 32,024 feet, and the greatest known depth, between 35 and 40 thousand feet, in the Mariana Trench. Other Pacific trenches extend for great distances in an east-west direction; one of these measures 3300 miles long, is about 30 miles wide, and 10,500 feet deep.

Although there is no great midocean ridge

like that of the Atlantic, there is an Eastern Pacific Rise along the west coast of the Americas. This rise reaches the surface in places such as the Galapagos and the Easter Islands; and the great submarine highland extends around southern South America where it joins the Mid-Atlantic Ridge. The Pacific contains many more sea mounts—flat-topped submarine peaks—than the Atlantic, many more deep trenches, and many more island chains.

Research undertaken largely by scientists of the 1962–1965 International Indian Ocean Expedition provides the first picture of the Indian Ocean's floor. Among the important topographic features are (1) a wall-like ridge 8000 feet high, which extends for 3600 miles in a north-south direction along the Eastern 90th meridian. Tentatively it has been called the 90-Degree Ridge. (2) Ridges from the Atlantic and Pacific Oceans enter the Indian Ocean from the south and form an inverted "Υ." (3) Deep faults split these ridges forming the inverted "Υ" near their central portions. (4) Although much of the Indian Ocean floor is mountainous, huge abyssal plains do occur, several of which lie near the mouths of continental rivers. For example, the Indian subcontinent is flanked by two such plains at depths of 10,000 to 15,000 feet, near the mouths of the Indus and Ganges rivers. A sketch map, showing important topographic features of the Indian Ocean floor, appeared in the Science Section of the New York Times, April 26, 1964. It is based upon the findings of the International Indian Ocean Expedition of 1962–1965.

Several features of the Arctic submarine topography were discovered during the scientific occupance of floating polar ice islands. Ridges and basins extend from the continental shelf of Eurasia to that of North America. The highest underwater ridge reaches more than 10,000 feet in height; and the deepest area is the Eurasian Abyssal Plain which lies nearly 15,000 feet beneath the sea.

The Continents, Physical Regions

For obvious reasons much more is known about topographical features of the continents than about those of the ocean floors. Thus it may be useful to divide each of the large land masses into a few major physical regions.

---

[1] A graben is a down-faulted portion of the earth's crust lying between two more or less parallel faults.

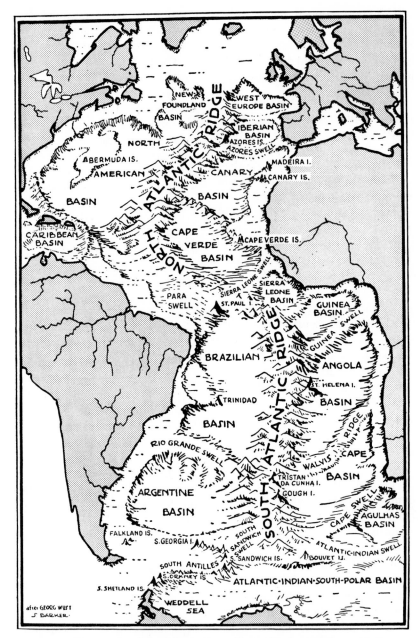

Fig. 5–1 Topography of the Atlantic Ocean Floor. Oceans comprise vast hollows lying among the continents, but the surface of ocean floors lacks uniformity just as that of the land surface. Great basin and ridge areas are dominant ocean-floor features that appear at some distance beyond continental shelves rimming many land masses. (*O. D. von Engeln,* Geomorphology *and Macmillan Company*)

North America. The land forms of North America (Fig. 5–2) fall into three major subdivisions, all showing a general north-south trend. On the west a great cordillera of mountains and plateaus extends from Alaska to Panama. On the east the Appalachian system reaches its southern limit in Georgia and Alabama and its northern in Labrador. Between the two highland units plains stretch from the Arctic and Hudson Bay to the Gulf of Mexico.

In the United States the western cordillera may be divided into the Pacific mountain sys-

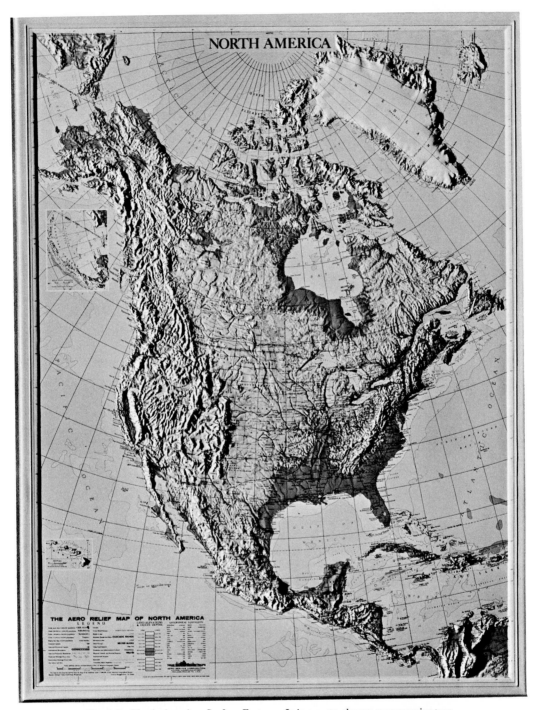

Fig. 5-2 North America, Surface Features. It is easy to observe many major topographic features, especially (1) the north-south trend of the Western Cordillera, the Interior Lowland, and the Appalachian Mountain System; (2) the broad Atlantic coastal plain and the narrow or absent Pacific coastal plain; (3) the Hudson Bay Lowland; (4) the Great Valley of California, the Willamette Valley, and the Puget Sound Trough; and (5) the Intermontane Plateaus of Canada, the United States, and Mexico. (*Courtesy Aero Service Corporation, a Division of A. J. Nystrom & Co.*)

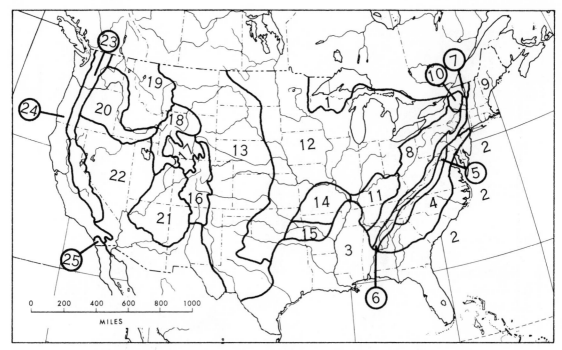

Fig. 5–3   Major Physical Regions of the United States. Nevin M. Fenneman divided
the United States into 25 major physical provinces, which are further subdivided into
a total of 86 land form regions. The 25 include (1) Superior Upland; (2) Continental
Shelf; (3) Coastal Plain; (4) Piedmont; (5) Blue Ridge; (6) Valley and Ridge; (7) St.
Lawrence Valley (including Lake Champlain); (8) Appalachian Plateaus; (9) New
England; (10) Adirondacks; (11) Interior Low Plateaus; (12) Central Lowland;
(13) Great Plains; (14) Ozark Plateaus; (15) Ouachitas; (16) Southern Rockies; (17)
Wyoming Basin; (18) Middle Rockies; (19) Northern Rockies; (20) Columbia
Plateaus; (21) Colorado Plateaus; (22) Basin and Range; (23) Sierra-Cascade;
(24) Pacific Border; (25) Lower California. (*Nevin M. Fenneman,* Physical Divisions
of the United States)

tem, the Intermontane Plateaus, and the Rocky
Mountains. The Pacific system slightly resem-
bles a capital letter "H." The Coast Ranges
form the left upright, the Sierra Nevada and
Cascades the right upright, and the Klamath
Mountains the cross bar which ties the two to-
gether. The Great Valley of California lies south
of the cross bar and the Willamette Valley to
the north. Intermontane Plateaus include the
Columbia, the Colorado, and the Basin and
Range physiographic provinces; and for con-
venience in study the United States Rocky
Mountains may be divided into the Northern,
Middle, and Southern Rockies (Fig. 5–3).

In Canada and Alaska the western cordillera
is narrower than in continental United States,
although all major subdivisions, Pacific mountain system, Intermontane Plateaus, and Rocky
Mountains are represented. Many of the coastal
ranges have been affected by subsidence and

form mountainous islands almost enclosing the
famous water route to Alaska, the Inside Passage. The Fraser and the Yukon are important
among the plateaus that separate coastal mountains from the Rockies to the east. (See Fig. 5–2
and A. K. Lobeck, *Physiographic Diagram of
North America.*)

In Mexico, mountain ranges continue in Baja
California, which is separated from the mainland by a graben, the Gulf of California. On the
mainland, other elements of the western cordillera include the Sierra Madre Occidental and
the Sierra Madre Oriental, which are separated
from one another by Mexico's Northern Basins
and Ranges, an equatorward extension of North
America's Intermontane Plateaus. The Western
and Eastern Sierra Madre come together in a
complex highland mass in the vicinity of Mexico City. To the south and east are the Sierra del
Sur and the Chiapas Highlands. The western

cordillera, much narrower, continues through Central America to join the Andes of South America. (See Fig. 5–2 and A. K. Lobeck, *Physiographic Diagram of North America*.)

Several of the mountains of southern Mexico and Central America have a structural trend in an east-west direction; and these east-west trending continental ranges are connected by submarine ridges, showing the same trend, with the east-west mountain backbones of the Greater Antilles. Most of the West Indies are mountainous. In general, the islands may be divided into two great arcs, an inner arc of volcanic islands with medium to high altitudes, and an outer arc of low-lying limestone islands. (See A. K. Lobeck, *Physiographic Diagram of North America*.)

North America's Appalachian system is shorter in a north-south direction, narrower in an east-west extent, and its highest elevations, approximately 6700 feet, are far lower than those of the western cordillera, more than 20,000 feet. The system may be divided into the Southwestern Appalachians and the New England-Acadian ranges. In the United States, an Atlantic Coastal Plain borders the Southwestern Appalachians on the east and south; in Mexico and Central America, a continuation of this plain is much wider than the narrow plain along the Pacific. An outlier of the Southwest Appalachians, the Ozark-Ouachita province, forms a separate physiographic unit within the Interior Plains. (See Fig. 5–2 and 5–3.)

The Interior Plains comprise the Laurentian peneplain, a horseshoe-shaped remnant of erosion almost encircling Hudson Bay; the Great Plains, lying just east of the Rockies and extending from the Arctic to Texas; and the Central Lowland, which borders the Appalachians to the east, the Great Plains to the west, and the Laurentian Shield to the north.

Many Canadian and United States surface features were greatly affected by Pleistocene glaciation (see Fig. 4–1). The equatorward boundary is approximately as follows: it extends from Long Island to Pittsburgh, where it follows the Ohio south to its confluence with the Mississippi. From there the edge of the glacial ice turned north along the Mississippi to the mouth of the Missouri. The latter stream forms the approximate equatorward boundary of the ice sheet west of the Mississippi. Within the general area of continental glaciation are at least two sections unaffected by ice action. One is located in southwest Wisconsin, northeast Iowa, southeast Minnesota, and northwestern Illinois; it is called the Driftless Area. The other includes a broad expanse in central Alaska. High mountains south of the glacier's general equatorward boundary were covered with an extensive ice blanket in Pleistocene time.

A significant service of glacial action for North America was the formation of the greatest inland waterway system in the world, the American Great Lakes. Moreover, the great ice rasp dug thousands of smaller lakes, and with its diggings it blocked drainage patterns so as to form thousands more. Numerous waterfalls developed when the continental ice sheet interrupted stream courses. Canadian and northern United States surface features afford many striking evidences of Pleistocene ice.

South America. South America's surface features (See Fig. 5–4 and G. H. Smith, *Physiographic Diagram of South America*) show several contrasts and similarities to those of North America. The southern continent (1) is slightly smaller in total area; (2) has a more regular shore line; (3) has fewer offshore islands; (4) possesses the highest mountain in the Americas, Mt. Aconcagua, 23,081 feet; (5) has fewer coastal indentations and peninsulas; (6) narrows into the middle latitudes, whereas North America narrows into the tropics; (7) has no great inland lake system like North America's Great Lakes; (8) and has a smaller area of continental shelf. (9) In North America the greatest river, the Mississippi flows from north to south and has built a great delta where it empties into the Gulf of Mexico; but in South America the great Amazon flows from west to east and has constructed no delta at its mouth.

However, there are a number of similarities in the surface features of the two continents. Both (1) are triangular in shape; (2) each has a great cordillera extending the entire length of the continent; (3) each has a mountain system in the east of greater age than the cordillera of the west; (4) each has an almost continuous lowland extending from north to south between mountains on the east and west; (5) both continents have a glacial history, present day glaciers,

Fig. 5–4 South America, Surface Features. Every one of the four major highlands—Andes, Guiana, Brazilian, and Patagonian—and the three major plains—Orinoco, Amazon, and Parana-Paraguay—can be recognized easily. (*Courtesy Aero Service Corporation, a Division of A. J. Nystrom & Co.*)

and fiorded coast lines at their poleward extremities; (6) each has a general slope from west to east; (7) both have large volcanic plateaus, the Columbia Plateau in North America and the Paraná Plateau in South America; (8) in both continents earth blocks are more stable on the eastern side than on the western side, and as a consequence earthquakes in both are more frequent along the Pacific coast; (9) each continent has active volcanoes; and (10) both have but small areas of interior drainage.

Regionally, South America can be divided into four highlands and three lowlands, making a total of seven major physical regions. The uplands include the *Andean Cordillera,* the *Brazilian Plateau,* the *Guiana Plateau,* and the *Patagonian Plateau.* The *Amazon Basin,* the *Paraná-Paraguay Plain* (including the Pampa) and the *Orinoco Plain* make up the lowlands.

The *Andean Cordillera,* extending over 4000 miles along the western part of South America, rises from the Caribbean Sea in three distinct ranges that continue into Venezuela and Colombia; remnants of the North American Cordillera also extend into Colombia from Panama. The three Andean ranges join together near the boundary of Colombia with Ecuador in a complex mountain group to which the name mountain knot has been applied by some geographers.

In the latter country, the Cordillera consists of two great ranges topped by volcanoes and separated by several high intermontane basins. The Andes of Peru are made up of three major elements: (1) high level surfaces with gentle slopes; (2) towering groups of peaks and high ranges; and (3) deep canyons cut by such rivers as the Ucayali, the Huallaga, and the Marañón. In Bolivia the Andes reach their greatest width in South America; this occurs at latitude 18° S between Arica on the Pacific coast and Santa Cruz on Bolivia's eastern plains, where the mountain complex stretches for 400 miles in an east-west direction.

The Bolivian Andes can be divided into 3 regions: (1) the Western Cordillera; (2) a north-south group of high intermontane basins known collectively as the Altiplano; and (3) the Eastern Cordillera.

South of Bolivia the Andes continue into northern Chile and northern Argentina, where a group of Alpine ranges enclose several relatively flat, dry intermontane plateaus. Poleward from about 27° S the Andes narrow to form one major range. Here are the highest elevations in the Americas, with Mt. Aconcagua rising to 23,081 feet above sea level. South of these high altitudes, elevations gradually decline until the Cordillera dips beneath the sea at the southern tip of the continent.

The *Brazilian Highland* as a whole possesses three major physical characteristics. There are (1) hilly uplands resting on a base of crystalline rocks; (2) in several places old worn down mountains display rounded forms similar to some of those in the Southern Appalachians of the United States; (3) in other areas, especially toward the interior, a mantle of sedimentary rocks lying upon an igneous and metamorphic base forms tabular plateaus with rather steep escarpments.

The eastern border of the Brazilian upland forms a steep escarpment which rises abruptly from the coast to over nine thousand feet (Pico da Bandeira 9462 feet, a little northeast of Rio de Janeiro). On most of the Atlantic border, the highland is broken into a series of steps forming parallel escarpments. From the coastal border, the highland slopes gently toward the interior; and rivers rising in the higher elevations flow a round-about way before they finally reach the sea.

The Brazilian uplands may be divided into several subregions: the Brazilian Oldland, the Paraná Plateau, the Goyaz Massif, the Mato Grosso Plateau, and the Chiquitos Plateau. Each of the first four divisions covers a large area; but the last named highland, lying far in the interior, is relatively small.

The *Guiana Highland,* which rises in the Guiana colonies, Venezuela, Colombia, and Brazil, is quite similar in surface features and geology to the Brazilian upland to the south. The highest elevations appear along the border between British Guiana and Venezuela on the north and Brazil on the south. Mt. Roraima, the highest point, 9219 feet is almost as high as Brazil's Pico da Bandeira. The Amazon lowland lies between Brazil's portion of the Guiana Highlands and the Brazilian upland.

The *Patagonian Plateau* borders the Pampa on the south and the Southern Andes on the west. The Plateau is really a series of plateaus ranging from a few hundred feet in altitude along the main streams and the Atlantic coast to over 5000 feet near the base of the Andes. The upland is covered by a series of sedimentary rocks resting upon a granitic base; and the surface is covered, in places, by recent lava flows. Patagonia is separated from the Andes by a fault zone called the precordilleran trough. The eastern plateau margin conforms essentially with the Atlantic coast line, for there is no true coastal plain in Patagonia.

The *Amazon Plain* is one of the largest and most homogeneous physical regions in South America. The greater portion of the lowland lies in Brazil, but bordering sections are included in Bolivia, Peru, Ecuador, Colombia, and Venezuela.

The plain has an east-west extent of more than 2000 miles; varies in width from 800 miles in western Brazil to 200 miles east of Manaus; and includes about two million square miles. About 10 per cent of the lowland is subject to flooding. Within this flood district are broad disconnected swamps and old channels or sloughs. Only a small portion of the remaining 90 per cent of the Amazon Basin is covered with water or imperfectly drained.

The *Plain of the Orinoco* lies between the eastern ranges of the northern Andes and the Guiana Highlands. The Caribbean Sea lies to the north; and a small low plateau separates the Orinoco from the Amazon to the south. The Plain is underlain by sedimentary rocks which are covered with savanna vegetation. In fact, the lowland is sometimes called the Llanos; but the Llanos grassland actually covers a greater extent than that of the Orinoco Plain.

The *Plain of the Paraguay-Paraná* lying between the front ranges of the Andes and the southern extension of the Brazilian Plateau may be divided into three subregions, the Gran Chaco, the Pantanal, and the Pampa.

The Chaco has been formed by streams such as the Pilcomaya and Bermeja carrying enormous quantities of unconsolidated sands and clays eastward from the Andes mountains. These and other rivers follow winding, shifting courses over the Chaco; and as their braided channels change in pattern after each flood season, they leave a new series of crescent shaped swamps and abandoned levees. Bolivia, Paraguay, Brazil, and Argentina all share parts of the nearly flat featureless plain, site of the Chaco

War between Bolivia and Paraguay in the 1930's.

The Pantanal is a basinlike area drained by headwaters of the Upper Paraguay. This lowland is almost enclosed by the Mato Grosso on the east and north, the Chiquitos Plateau on the northwest, and an extension of the Brazilian Highland on the south. In recent geologic time the plain was probably an inland sea; at present it is a great alluvial morass with difficult drainage problems, especially during the rainy season.

The Argentine Pampa, one of the world's great agricultural regions, lies south of the Chaco and west of the Rio de la Plata. Its relatively flat surface is made up of alluvial and aeolian deposits overlying a series of horizontal sedimentary strata resting on a granitic base. Only two interruptions occur in the nearly flat topography, the Sierra de Ventana and the Sierra Tandil, both of which may be called inselbergs.

Europe. Europe's arrangement of surface features (See Fig. 5–5 and A. K. Lobeck, *Physiographic Diagram of Europe*) is far different from that in the United States. In the midsection of North America, from east to west, the Atlantic Coastal Plain, the Appalachian Mountains, the Central Lowland, the Great Plains, the Rocky Mountains, the Intermontane Plateaus, and the Pacific Highlands all lie more or less parallel to each other with the greatest length in a north-south direction.

In Europe, the distribution of mountains, plateaus, and lowlands shows more resemblance to a checkerboard than to a series of parallel lines. Here, irregularly shaped highlands and lowlands alternate with each other over most of the map, and only in a few places do the mountains and plains show a definite regional continuity. The bordering waterways are partly responsible for the topographic confusion.

In no other continent do bays, gulfs, and seas penetrate so deeply. For example look at the Baltic Sea, the Gulf of Bothnia, the Gulf of Finland, the North Sea, the English Channel, the Bay of Biscay, and the Mediterranean Sea and all of its tributaries; and note how these water bodies separate the continent into numerous and, in places, somewhat isolated pieces. Europe has been called a peninsula of Eurasia, but

Europe is also possessed of more peninsulas than any other continent.

Not long ago, geologically speaking, water areas such as the North Sea, the Bay of Biscay, the Tyrrhenian Sea, and the Adriatic Sea, now contributing to these many peninsulas, stood above sea level. Thus, before subsidence took place, there was much more continuity to the land. Again, in recent geologic time, mountain groups have been separated from one another by the formation of trough-like depressions such as the Rhône Valley, the Rhine Graben, and the Scottish Lowland. Downward earth movements have produced isolated uplands of Central France, the separation of the Vosges Mountains from the Black Forest, and the isolation of the Southern Uplands of Scotland from the Scottish Grampians. Other examples of an interrupted continuity of highlands and lowlands may be cited.

A careful examination of a physical map of Europe will show that the continent cannot be divided as easily into a small number of major topographic regions with definite regional unity

Fig. 5–5 Europe, Surface Features. On this heterogeneous mixture of mountains, plateaus, and plains, we can see with a little careful study main parts of the four major regions described in the text. The Northwest Highlands show up clearly, located northwest of the Great Central Plain; the Alpine Mountain System beginning with the Pyrenees on the west does extend in a general west-east direction; and finally notice the Spanish Meseta, the Central Plateau of France, the Rhône Valley and the Rhine Graben as parts of the fourth region of Central Massives with Associated Lowlands. (*Courtesy Aero Service Corporation, a Division of A. J. Nystrom & Co.*)

as is possible for North America. But a general division of Europe into major physical regions can be accomplished. This can be done by considering areas as related units when they are similar in topographic pattern and in physiographic history although detached from one another.

For example Norway, Sweden, Finland, all of Great Britain except the extreme southeast, Ireland, and Brittany can be grouped together into one region called the *Northwest Highlands*. This is possible because these lands possess the same general types of ancient disordered rocks and because all show more rugged topography than the region to the south.

In a similar way the basins of Aquitaine and Paris in France, the plain of southeast England, the plains of Denmark, Holland and Belgium, the north German Plain, and the extensive plains of Russia and Poland all can be grouped together into one major topographic region, Europe's *Great Central Plain*.

Another region may include the great massives and bordering lowlands of Central Europe such as the Spanish Meseta, the Central Plateau of France, the plateaus of southern Germany, and the Bohemian plateau of Czechoslovakia, together with the Rhône valley, the Rhine graben, the Andalusian lowland, the Portuguese lowland, and other plains contiguous to the ancient massives. This major topographic region may be named the *Central Massives with Associated Lowlands*.

Finally the name *Alpine System with Associated Massives and Lowlands* may be applied to the fourth region. Mountain ranges of this area extend from the Pyrenees to the Caucasus; and folded mountains arranged in arcs border old massives like the Balkan and Rhodope Plateaus and productive plains like the Po and the Danube Valleys.

Although several of the subregions have been mentioned in delimiting the major regions, it may be useful to mention all of them. The *Northwest Highlands* may be subdivided into the Scottish Highlands, the Southern Uplands of Scotland, the Central Lowland of Scotland, the Pennine Range, the Lake District, Wales, Cornwall, Ireland, Brittany, the Norwegian Highlands, the Swedish Highlands, the Smaland Highland, the Central Swedish Lowland, the Lapland Plateau, and the Finnish Lowland.

The *Great Central Plain* includes the Aquitanian Basin, the Paris Basin, the English Lowlands, the Baltic Plain, the Central Russian Tableland, the Black Earth Belt, the Arctic Tundra Belt, and the Caspian Depression.

Subregions of the *Central Massives with Associated Lowlands* number more than a dozen. They are the Spanish Meseta, the Andalusian Lowland, the Aragon Lowland, the Portuguese Lowland, the Central Massive of France, the Rhône Lowland, the Vosges, the Black Forest, the Rhine Graben, the Slate Mountains, the Highlands of Central Germany, the Bohemian Massive, and the Bavarian Plateau.

The *Alpine System with Associated Massives and Lowlands* numbers among its subdivisions, the Alps, the Carpathians, the Balkan Range, the Caucasus, the Dinaric Alps, the Pindus Range, the Rhodope Massive, the Apennines, the Sierra Nevada, the Pyrenees, the Tyrrhenian Massive, the Jura, the Swiss Plateau, the Po Basin, the Hungarian Plain, and the Rumanian Plain.

Asia. (See Fig. 5–6 and A. K. Lobeck, *Physiographic Diagram of Asia.*) Surface features on the continent of Asia, with nearly one third of the earth's land surface, make almost as much of a checkerboard as those of Europe. However, six major regions with a considerable degree of physical unity can be noted. They are the great *Central Triangle of Plateaus*, the *Plateaus of Western Asia*, the *South Pointing Plateau Peninsulas*, the *Northwest Triangle of Plains, Plateaus, and Mountains*, the *Great River Valleys of South and Eastern Asia*, and the *Island Arcs of the East and South*.

The *Central Triangle of Plateaus*, located in the heart of the continent, is the largest of the six and is buttressed by high mountains on every side. The most extensive of these plateaus are (1) the Highlands of Tibet between the Himalayas to the south and the Kun Lun to the north; (2) the Tsaidam Basin between the Kun Lun on the south and the Altyn Tagh on the north; (3) the Tarim Basin bounded by the Kun Lun and Altyn Tagh ranges on the south and the Tien Shan range to the north; (4) the Gobi and Ordos deserts lying northeast of the Tsaidam Basin; and (5) the Vitim and Aldan Plateaus situated somewhat northeast of the Gobi desert.

The western apex of the triangle of plateaus is formed by the Pamir mountain knot; mountains of northeast Asia form another corner of the triangle; and mountains of southeast China lie at the third angle.

The lofty Himalaya Mountains form a continuous chain along the plateau triangle's southern border. On the northwest side of the triangle several ranges form the boundary, including the Tien Shan, the Altai, the Sayan, the Baikal, and the Cherskiy. But this northwestern boundary is not nearly as definite and consistent as the Himalayas to the south; for among the various northwestern ranges surrounding or extending out from the plateau complex are great trenches like that of Dzungaria with a general east-west direction—trenches that have formed routes of travel for migratory groups going from Asia to Europe for untold centuries. The mountains along the eastern border of the plateau triangle include the Khingan, the Stanavoi, and the ranges of southeastern China.

The plateaus included in the triangle are of unequal altitude, ranging from 2000 to 16,000 feet in height. Several of the tablelands have mountain ridges rising above the general level, and as previously indicated, many have high

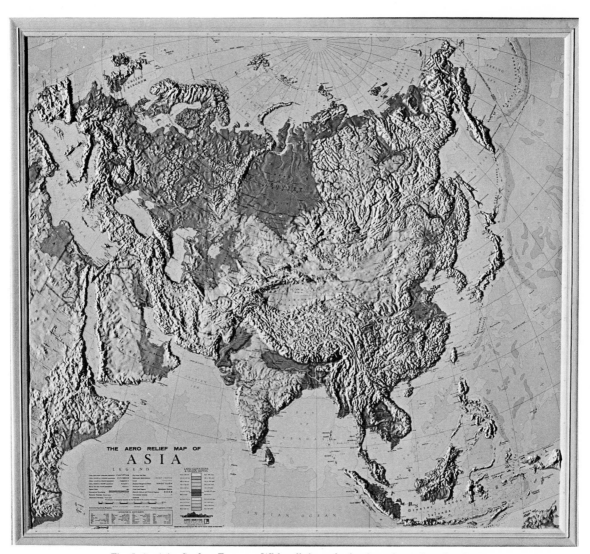

Fig. 5–6   Asia, Surface Features. With a little study the six major regions described in the text can be observed. Notice also that there is no physical separation between Europe and Asia; and that Eurasia joins Africa by the isthmus of Suez. (*Courtesy Aero Service Corporation, a Division of A. J. Nystrom & Co.*)

bordering ranges. Over all of this mountain and plateau region, there is great similarity in surface features and in the harsh climate and sparse vegetation that are a response to the topography. Here in the same latitudes that provide abundant commercial agriculture in both Europe and North America, farming is extremely difficult because of the unfavorable environment.

The *Plateaus of Western Asia* extend from the Pamir Knot on the east through Afghanistan, western Pakistan, Iran, and Turkey. Mountain ranges rimming the plateaus of Baluchistan, Afghanistan, and Iran join in western Iran and eastern Turkey to form the Armenian Knot, a mountain complex of western Asia somewhat similar to the Pamir Knot near the center of the continent. Branching west from the Armenian Knot, the Taurus range on the south and the Pontic range on the north rim the dry barren Anatolian Plateau of Turkey. The plateaus of western Asia possess the same monotony in rugged topography, in xerophytic vegetation, and in desert or steppe climate as those encountered in Asia's central plateaus; and man's response to these harsh physical conditions shows very little difference in the two regions.

The third major topographic region, the *South Pointing Plateau Peninsulas*, shows certain characteristics similar to those of the two regions previously described. But it differs in two important ways: (1) the three parts of the region are not contiguous; and (2) all three sections are peninsulas which point towards the south—the Arabian Peninsula; the peninsula of India, sometimes called a subcontinent; and the peninsula of Indochina.

In the Arabian peninsula, the general slope is from southwest to northeast—from the high mountain fringe of Yemen to the Tigris and Euphrates lowland. On the Indian plateau, slopes descend in the same general direction from the Western Ghats to the plain of the Ganges.

The third south pointing peninsular plateau is more complex than the other two. Mountains rim it on the west, the Naga and Arakan Hills, and on the east, the mountains of coastal Vietnam; and within the major region mountains and valleys alternate with plateaus (the Shan Plateau in Burma and Thailand and the Yunnan in southern China). Moreover, mountains

extend almost the entire length of the Malay Peninsula, which forms an extreme southern extension of the eastern subregion.

The *Northwest Triangle of Plains, Plateaus, and Mountains* differs from the three major physical regions already mentioned in that lowlands dominate the topographic pattern. Here, plains occur (1) in the southwest around the Aral Sea and in the Amu Darya and Syr Darya river valleys, (2) in western Siberia where the Ob and Irtysh rivers and their tributaries drain a huge subarctic lowland, and (3) in northern Siberia where a tundra plain fringes the Arctic coast. The region's plateaus are sometimes called the Central Siberian Highlands and are drained by the Yenisey and Lena rivers; its mountains occupy the extreme northeast part of the regional triangle. It should be emphasized that Siberia has three well-defined topographic regions— plains in the west, plateaus in the center, and mountains in the east.

The fifth region, the *Great River Valleys of South and Eastern Asia,* differs from the fourth in that (1) it is made up entirely of plains; and (2) these plains are widely separated from one another. Plains include those of the Tigris and Euphrates, Indus, Ganges, Brahmaputra, Irrawaddy, Salween, Menam, Mekong, Si, Yangtze, Hwang, Liao, Sungari and Amur rivers. This group of river valleys supports by far the largest per cent of Asia's more than a billion people.

The sixth and final region, the *Island Arcs of the East and South* include Sakhalin, the Kuriles, and Japan with its four major islands and many minor ones; Formosa or Taiwan, Hainan, and the Philippine archipelago; and the islands of the East Indies—Sumatra, Java, Borneo, Celebes, New Guinea, and scores of smaller islands.

On all of these islands, mountainous topography exceeds lowland by a large margin. And these mountains, together with those on Asia's eastern coast, form about one quarter of the highland rim that borders almost the entire Pacific ocean—the mountains of eastern Asia on the northwest; the Australian Alps on the southwest; the Andean cordillera of South America on the southeast; and the Western cordillera of North America on the northeast.

Africa. In contrast to the checkerboard pattern of surface features found over Asia and

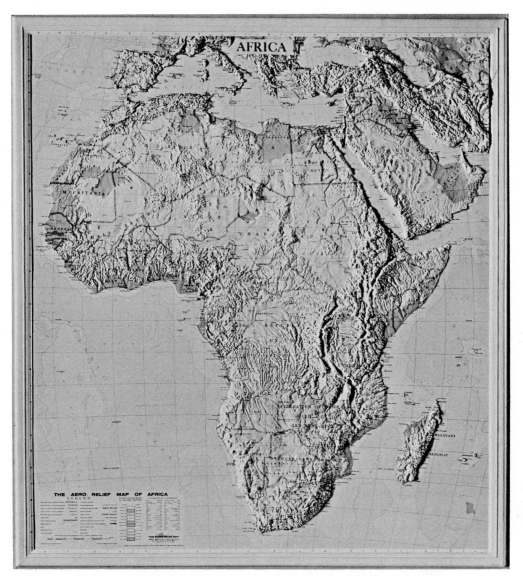

Fig. 5–7   Africa, Surface Features. Notice the dominance of highland, the small amount of lowland, the narrow or absent coastal plain, and the Great Rift Valley— all these topographic features stand out clearly. (*Courtesy Aero Service Corporation, a Division of A. J. Nystrom & Co.*)

Europe, those of Africa are relatively simple (See Fig. 5–7 and A. K. Lobeck, *Physiographic Diagram of Africa*). In general the continent may be described as a huge plateau with a narrow coastal plain; and the broadest division into physical areas would number but two regions, one extremely large and the other extremely small.

The large one, the plateau, extends in an east-west direction from Somaliland to the Gulf of Guinea coast; and in a north-south trend from the northern Sahara to the central part of the Cape provinces. Two small regions of fold mountains are crumpled against the continental plateau, the Atlas mountains in the north, and ranges including the Langebergen and Zwarte-bergen in the south.

On the African plateau, greatest elevations occur in the south and east, where average altitudes rise to five thousand feet or more. But the striking feature of both high and low tablelands is the vast extent of level or gently undulating surfaces; in fact at high levels, plateau topography appears monotonously flat.

Several of the major rivers on the plateau flow through somewhat circular basins throughout most of their courses. Basins of the Congo, the Upper Zambezi, and the Orange rivers are around 1000 feet above sea level; and they are rimmed by edges of higher parts of the plateau rising to altitudes of 3000 to 4000 feet. Near the coast they break through the rim of these saucer-like topographic features and reach the sea through a narrow defile over falls and rapids. The location of these falls and rapids at a place where the river has its greatest volume helps to explain the great hydroelectric potentiality of the African continent.

The broad, approximately circular, and relatively shallow river basins may have been formed during the general uplift of the African plateau; and they may have been occupied by inland seas during past geologic time.

Another unique feature of Africa's tableland is the great rift valley which extends, with several branches, from Mozambique to the Red Sea. Beyond the Red Sea the rift is occupied by the Jordan river in western Asia. Several fresh water lakes cover parts of the African depression—Nyasa, Tanganyika, Kivu, Edward, Albert, and Rudolf, but not the largest central African lake, Lake Victoria.

Along the course of this downfaulted section of Africa's crust, outpourings of volcanic material have produced the continent's highest mountains—Kilimanjaro, Kenya, Elgon and Ras Dashan; but not Ruwenzori, which is probably an uplifted fault block. Vulcanism is also responsible for the huge lava tableland of Ethiopia, a highland similar in origin to the Deccan of India, the Paraná Plateau of Brazil, and the Columbia Plateau of northwestern United States. Volcanic action also produced the 13,000 feet high mountains of the Cameroons near the Gulf of Guinea coast and far to the west of the rift valley.

Other mountains rising above the plateau are the Futa Jallon-Liberian massive, the Tibesti and Ahaggar mountains of the Sahara, and the Drakensberg mountains of South Africa. The latter are merely the steep sea-facing escarpment of the South African plateau.

In no other continent does the amount of plain below 600 feet represent such a small portion of total area. Great flood plains such as are common in the Americas—the Mississippi and the Paraná—and in southeast Asia—the Ganges, Yangtze, and Hwang—do not appear in Africa. Usually Africa's narrow coastal plain extends only a few miles inland before it reaches the edge of the continental plateau; a distance of 20 miles is not too conservative for an average figure. In fact the term coastal plain when applied to Africa should be used almost in a relative way because plateau cliffs form a significant portion of the coast line. Exceptions to the narrow or absent coastal plain are found in Mozambique, and in the Gulf of Guinea coast of Nigeria.

Africa resembles South America in its regular coast line, its small number of coastal indentations, its scarcity of peninsulas, and the absence of numerous off shore islands. Moreover, there are few good natural harbors except at the estuary of the Congo and along the irregular mountainous northwest coast. In several places currents paralleling the coast discourage good harbors. For example, the good port of Alexandria, Egypt, is possible largely because it lies west of the Nile delta rather than east of it. If the city were situated east of the delta, shore currents flowing from west to east would carry delta silt into the harbor and make constant dredging necessary.

Australia. Australia, (See Fig. 5–8 and A. K. Lobeck, *Physiographic Diagram of Australia*) with less than three million square miles, is the smallest of the continents, and smaller than the United States minus Alaska and Hawaii. With the exception of Antarctica, it is the only continent completely separated from other land masses. Its shape is roughly rectangular, extending 2600 miles from east to west and 2000 miles from north to south. Relatively few indentations penetrate the generally regular coastline, and offshore islands are as limited as they are around Africa and South America. Altitudes are lower than those on any other great land mass with the highest mountain, Mt. Kosciusko, reaching only 7328 feet.

Major physical divisions number but three, the *Western Shield,* the *Eastern Basins,* and the *Eastern Cordillera.* Although each major region shows considerable unity, a detailed study permits further subdivision. For example, Gentilli[2] and Fairbridge divide the Western Shield into 20 subregions and these into 40 parts; the Eastern Basins into 3 subregions with 5 parts; and the Eastern Cordillera into 18 subregions with 24 parts.

The *Western Shield*, sometimes called the Great Australian Peneplain, comprises more than half of the continent and consists essentially of a rather low plateau, averaging about 1200 feet above sea level. The rocks of the southern part are extremely old, of Archean age, those of the north are somewhat younger, Proterozoic in age; and both are overlapped by more recent sediments. A folded belt comprising

[2]Joseph Gentilli and Rhodes W. Fairbridge, *Physiographic Diagram of Australia,* The Geographical Press, 1951, C. S. Hammond and Company, Maplewood, New Jersey.

the Macdonnell Range, which may be connected with the Flinders Range beneath the surface, separates the northern and southern portions of the Shield.

In the south, the more or less monotonous peneplaned surface is interrupted here and there by rounded granite outcrops rising only a few feet above the surrounding country. Farther north, differential erosion has interrupted the topographic monotony with the rather widespread occurrence of flat-topped sedimentary hills, buttes, and mesas. A climate with limited rainfall occurring in heavy downpours greatly influences the erosional features.

The *Eastern Basins* bordering the Western Shield on the east may be subdivided into three major sections, the Carpentaria on the north, the Great Artesian Basin in the center, and the

Fig. 5–8 Australia, Surface Features. Notice how clearly the Western Shield, the Eastern Basins, and the Eastern Cordillera stand out as major physiographic regions. (*Courtesy Aero Service Corporation, a Division of A. J. Nystrom & Co.*)

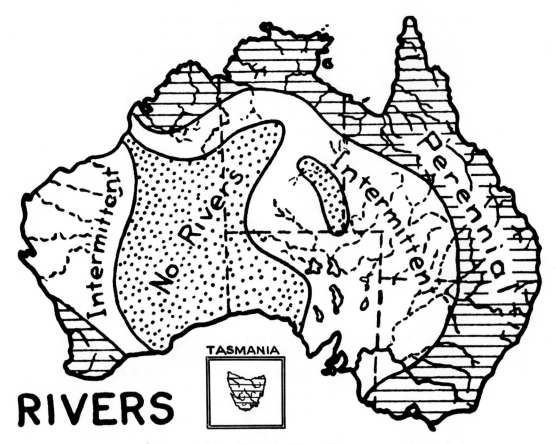

Fig. 5-9 Diagrammatic Map of Australian Rivers. The map suggests that much of the continent receives little precipitation. Note the influence of the Great Dividing Range. (*The Australian News and Information Bureau*)

Murray Basin at the south. A rough analogy to the topography of the three basins may be made by placing on a table a soup dish to represent the Carpentaria, a plate to represent the Great Artesian, and a saucer to represent the Murray. The soup plate shows the Carpentaria of medium size but deeper than the others; the plate shows the dominance of the Artesian in size; and the saucer shows the Murray to be the smallest and the shallowest of the three. If the plate is tilted slightly to the south, one may visualize how some drainage disappears by way of the Darling river; but no stream carries drainage of the Carpentaria Basin into the Great Artesian depression. On the contrary, the Carpentaria drains to the Arafura Sea (Fig. 5-9).

All three basins were once arms of the sea into which porous sands were deposited; but uplift brought about the ocean's departure. Since

uplift there has been down warping of the underlying Paleozoic rocks to give the region its present topographic outline. Average basin elevations are about 500 feet above sea level apart from the bordering rims.

Artesian water is derived principally from rain falling on the exposed portions of the underlying porous sandstones and massive limestones. These sedimentary rock strata are tilted and reach the surface on the western flanks of the bordering Eastern Cordillera.

Groups of mound springs occur in various parts of the basins where water bearing strata reach or closely approach the surface. Mounds range from 15 to 30 feet in height and may be 100 feet in diameter. Lake Eyre, one outlet of the Great Artesian Basin, is in reality a large area of salt marsh and crusted salt flats lying below sea level. Since the lake was an arm of the sea in recent geologic time, the salinity of the water is not entirely due to the evaporation of ground water.

The *Eastern Cordillera*, bordering the Artesian Basins on the east, extends for 2400 miles from Torres Straits in the north to Tasmania on the south. This mountain complex has an average width of 200 miles, although its east-west extent broadens to twice that figure in a few places. On the northern portion, the Cordillera is paralleled by the Great Barrier Reef; but this unique feature ends at about 25° S with a change in the shape of the continental shelf.

Widespread folding featured the early geologic history of ranges making up the Cordillera. Later, in Tertiary time, extensive faulting took place and gave rise to tilted fault blocks, block mountains, and some very steep escarpments facing east towards the Pacific. These steep slopes contrast sharply with the gently sloping mountainous terrain on the west. Lava flows have added further complexity to the Cordillera geologic history that has given the region mineral and power resources of considerable economic significance.

Agencies Shaping Surface Features

It is well to know the major physical regions of the world, but it is also well to learn of the controls that have shaped their surface features. These controls are of two major types: those which originate within the earth and those which have their origin on or above the earth's surface. The former include diastrophism and vulcanism, two agencies which encourage irregular land forms. The latter include erosion (degradation) and deposition (aggradation). These agencies tend to regularize topographic features and include the work of rivers, oceans, lakes, ice, ground water, wind, plants, and animals. A brief examination of each agency, with examples of specific surface features resulting from its activities, may be useful for the student.

Diastrophism. Diastrophism can be defined as any movement of the earth's crust, vertical, horizontal, or angular (Fig. 5–10). These movements may uplift, depress, bend, tilt, warp, or break the earth's crust. Where breaks occur and there is an appreciable displacement, either vertical or horizontal, these breaks are called faults. Earth blocks may move up, down, or

horizontally along such faults. Displacements are not likely to be more than a few feet at any one movement. But over long periods of geologic time, millions of years—the earth is believed to be about three billion years old—some earth blocks may move up until they become block mountains thousands of feet high, such as the Wasatch and Sierra Nevada ranges of western United States.

If downward movement of an earth block occurs between two more or less parallel faults, a graben develops. Numerous well known examples may be cited: the Rhine valley between the Black Forest and the Vosges mountains; the Scottish Lowland between the Grampians and the Southern Uplands; the Jordan Valley; the Great Rift Valley of Africa; the Gulf of Lower California and many others.

Diastrophism may bend the earth's crust into folds called anticlines and synclines. The anticline is an upfold in the rock strata, and the syncline is a downfold. It is well to remember that such folds refer to a bending in the rock strata which may conform to the surface features or may not, depending largely on the recentness of folding or the amount of erosion, or both. Good examples of fold mountains may be seen in the Appalachians of Maryland, Pennsylvania, and West Virginia, and in the Jura mountains on the border between France and Switzerland.

Diastrophic movements may also raise former sea bottoms into plains like that of Florida; or lift former sea floors still higher into plateaus like the Appalachian Plateau of eastern Ohio and Kentucky and the loftier Colorado Plateau occupying parts of Colorado, Arizona, New Mexico, and Utah.

Vulcanism. Like diastrophism, vulcanism (Fig. 5–11) has formed mountains and plateaus throughout the world. The Hawaiian Islands have been built by outpourings of volcanic materials from the sea bottom—Mauna Kea and Mauna Loa reach nearly 14,000 feet above sea level. Mount Whitney, of volcanic origin, the highest mountain in the contiguous 48 United States rises 14,495 feet. There are numerous high volcanic peaks in the Andean Cordillera of South America, with Chimborazo of Ecuador touching 20,577 feet.

Mountains also may be formed by arching

Fig. 5–10   Earth Movement Wrecks School. A slippage of earth blocks along California's San Andreas fault zone caused the wreckage of this Long Beach school building in 1933. Fortunately school was not in session when the earthquake occurred. (*C. R. Longwell and R. F. Flint,* Introduction to Physical Geology, *2d ed., John Wiley & Sons*)

the earth's surface above a lens-shaped intrusion of molten material forced into the outer part of the earth's crust. Doming of this type may increase erosion to such an extent that rocks overlying the volcanic intrusion may be worn away and the underlying volcanic rocks become exposed. Good examples of such domed mountains are the Henry Mountains of Utah and the Black Hills of South Dakota.

A plateau differs from a mountain in possessing a greater amount of summit level. Both are significant elevations, but the plateau has a greater area of relatively flat surface. Well known lava plateaus include the Paraná Plateau of Brazil, the Deccan of India, the Ethiopian Plateau, and the Columbia Plateau of northwest United States. Quiescent outpourings of lava creating land forms with a minimum of slope may be seen in many other parts of the world.

Work of Streams. Once forces from the interior of the earth have built mountains, plateaus, and less elevated topographic features, the controls on or above the surface of the earth start tearing down the work of vulcanism and diastrophism. One of the most active degrading agents is running water. This agency may wear down mountains and plateaus completely if given sufficient time. One may see convincing evidence of such erosion if he stands on the rim of the Grand Canyon and looks at the enormous gash made in the Plateau by the mighty Colorado River.

The geologist calls the Colorado a youthful stream, and the Colorado Plateau a region in youth. He is not speaking of the number of years since the stream started canyon cutting. On the contrary he is thinking of the amount of erosion the stream has accomplished in comparison to what remains to be done before the high plateau is eroded to a relatively low featureless plain called a peneplain.

When the peneplanation has been accomplished by stream action and by other erosive agencies, the former plateau will be in old age. Long before this takes place, erosion may change the present relatively flat surface to one of gently rolling hills and indefinite divides, a stage in the cycle of erosion known as topographic maturity. It is well to remember that the three different stages, youth, maturity, and old age refer to the amount of wearing down done in relation to the amount of erosion to be done; and these terms and proportions refer to streams as well as to land forms.

The same Colorado River is a depositing stream as well as an erosive one. Much of the sediment taken from the Plateau is carried to the Gulf of Lower California, where the Colorado delta is being extended slowly into the Gulf —a long narrow arm of the sea.

Many other surface features besides deltas and canyons result from the work of streams. These topographic types include gorges, rapids, waterfalls, pirated streams, wind gaps, water gaps, monadnocks, natural levees, oxbow lakes, alluvial fans, alluvial cones, flood plains, meandering streams, stream terraces, braided streams, streams in youth, streams in maturity, and streams in old age.[3]

Ice Action. Glacial action, or the work of ice, has been and still is important in shaping surface features of the earth. The northern parts of

[3] An explanation of all these and other features together with the geologic processes responsible for them may be found in any good textbook on physical geology. Student assignment to examine illustrations of the geological features mentioned in this chapter is suggested.

Fig. 5-11   Paricutin and its Work. In February 1943, San Juan Parangaricutiro, the largest town near Mexico's Paricutin volcano, was overridden completely by lava except for the towers of this church. (*C. R. Longwell and R. F. Flint,* Introduction to Physical Geology, *2d ed., John Wiley & Sons*)

North America and Europe retain even today many of the physical characteristics forced upon them by Pleistocene ice—ice which largely disappeared on these continents about twenty-five thousand years ago. One great example of ice work occurred on the Canadian Shield, a great horseshoe-shaped physiographic region surrounding Hudson Bay on three sides. Here, in many places, rocks were scraped bare by the huge ice rasp; and Canadian soil was carried as far south as what is now the Corn Belt of the United States.

Stream drainage also was interrupted by the ice flow and thousands of glacial lakes were formed, some by glacial gouging and some by glacial damming. Pleistocene ice created North America's Great Lakes and played an important part in the formation of Niagara Falls. For climatic reasons, not entirely understood, the Pleistocene ice covered but little of Asia. Southern South America was affected by the ice over a considerable area, especially in Argentina and Chile, but Africa and Australia were disturbed but little. Today, glaciation is active in shaping surface features of Antarctica, Greenland, mountains of polar and subpolar latitudes, and high mountains of middle and low latitudes.

Other physical features formed by ice action besides interrupted stream drainage, lakes, and rocks scraped bare of soil are ground, lateral, terminal, and recessional moraines, glacial striae, cirques, hanging valleys, U-shaped valleys, fiords, drumlins, eskers, kames, kettle holes, erratics, and outwash plains.

Work of the Sea. A third agency of erosion, as well as of deposition, is the sea. Today's action is largely confined to present shore lines; but evidence of ocean activities in past geologic time may be observed in various parts of all the continents. For example, ancient seas extended from what is now the Gulf of Mexico northward to the present Arctic Ocean. North America's Rocky Mountains have been created from folded and faulted floors of former seas; and so have mountains in other parts of the world. The Colorado Plateau, previously described in connection with the work of the Colorado River, is a former sea bottom uplifted by diastrophism to many thousands of feet above present sea level. Numerous other examples could be cited.

Seas are active forces of both erosion and deposition just as glaciers and streams are. A few examples of significant erosion may be mentioned. The seaward shores of Cape Cod and the islands near it yield to the sea from 1 to 6 feet each year, and at the present rate, these lands will disappear entirely at the end of about 4,000 years, leaving only submarine banks to mark their former positions. Certain stretches of the Yorkshire coast of England have been worn back a mile since the Norman conquest, and two miles since the time of the Romans. In the space of 200 years the town of Egmont on the Dutch coast, was undermined and entirely destroyed by the persistent work of the waves. Cliffs near Dover on the English Channel are receding at the rate of 15 feet each year, and east of them the Goodwin Sands, now a shallow submarine bank, were formerly an island. The island of Helgoland off the mouth of the Elbe, once very large, was being eaten away so rapidly that it would by this time have disappeared entirely had erosion not been checked, near the end of the nineteenth century, by the construction of a strong sea wall.

Examples of deposition by the sea can be seen along the Gulf and Atlantic coasts of the United States, where nearly continuous bars, with bays and lagoons, are developed on a large scale. At Cape Hatteras the bar is about 20 miles from the mainland, but along the east coast of Florida, as at Palm Beach and Miami Beach, it is near shore, and the lagoon in consequence is very narrow. Both Atlantic City, New Jersey, and Galveston, Texas, are built on sand bars made by the sea.

Other physical features on which the sea shows some element of control in their formation include beaches, spits, hooks, wave built terraces, wave cut terraces, sea caves, spouting horns, stacks, barrier reefs, fringing reefs, and atolls. Shorelines, as classed by geologists, may be youthful or mature; and they may be submerging, emerging, compound, or neutral.

Wind Action. Wind is a powerful agent aiding the sea in shaping shorelines; it drives waves and currents against the bordering land, eroding in some places and depositing in others. Winds also carry moisture from the oceans to the land, where precipitation is used by streams, ground water, and ice in the processes of erosion and deposition. And wind may act alone, as an agent of tearing down and building up the surface of the earth.

Wind may erode in two ways. First, loose particles such as grains of sand are picked up by air in motion and carried from one place to another. This process is called *deflation*, from the Latin *de-flare*, to blow away. Second, in their movement, the wind driven particles strike against each other and against pebbles, boulders, and exposed bed rock on the ground; as a result, additional particles are removed from the bed rock and from the loose rock materials. This process is called *wind abrasion*.

The work of the wind is (1) especially conspicuous along shore lines, where materials brought in by waves and dried out by the sun may be piled into dunes by wind action; (2) in arid lands where mechanical weathering and the absence of vegetation facilitates work of the wind; (3) in humid lands during periods of drought, particularly when soil particles have been broken up by cultivation; and along river flood plains when droughts follow flooding and dried-out-river deposits are easily picked up by winds.

Surface features fashioned by winds may include dunes of various types—transverse, longitudinal, and crescentic (barchans), some reaching hundreds of feet in altitude as in the Sahara; loess deposits found over large areas of the Missouri-Mississippi Valley, the Rhine Valley, the Paraná-La Plata Valley, and the Hwang Ho Valley; numerous shallow undrained depressions in arid lands, sometimes called *blowouts;* and the widespread occurrence of *ventifacts,* polished and peculiarly shaped pebbles that have laid for a long time in wind-swept areas.

Solution Processes. The earth's superficial rocks constitute a vast reservoir of *subsurface water,* which not only is of prime human importance, but also plays an important part in the endless process of geologic change. Ground water dissolves some substances of which rocks are composed, and thus prepares them for attack by other erosive agencies. Conversely it acts as a transporting medium for substances that cement loose sediments to form new rocks. Again, the quantity and distribution of water beneath the land surface influence the flow of rivers, the levels of lakes, and the location of swamps.

Subsurface water, like surface water, effects hydraulic action, abrasion, solution, transport, and deposition. However, its hydraulic action and abrasion are effective only in restricted localities where there are underground streams. As the chief factor in adding to the weight and mobility of rock or soil mantle on slopes, it is important as a mechanical agent in processes which geologists call mass wasting. But the greatest geologic work of ground water lies (1) in its chemical reactions upon rocks—reactions called solution processes; (2) in its transport of substances dissolved by solution processes; and (3) by the deposition of these materials through precipitation. So widespread are such activities that the soluble mineral matter in the rocks of continents is being slowly eaten away and delivered to streams by subsurface water.

Ground water features include the *water table,* or the surface below which rocks are saturated; springs of various types; natural artesian wells; underground rivers such as those found in Puerto Rico; caves[4] and caverns, some very large like the one at Carlsbad, New Mexico that extends to a depth of 1300 feet, with one chamber 4000 feet long, 625 feet wide, and 325 feet high; cave deposits that include stalactites and stalagmites; geodes; replacement deposits, especially the ones that form economically valuable ores; concretions; siliceous sinter and travertine found around springs; and sink holes. Where the latter are numerous, the resulting combination of surface features may be called *karst* topography, a name which was originally applied to land forms resulting from the work of ground water in Yugoslavia. Karst regions are also widespread in Missouri, Florida, Indiana, Kentucky, Puerto Rico, and other regions of the United States where limestone formations are widespread.

Work of Plants and Animals. Plants and animals influence the character of the earth's surface features as well as other agencies previously mentioned. Erosion on slope lands may be

---

[4] In 1962, at the time of the Cuban missile crisis, there was a good deal of talk about Cuba's limestone caves in which Russian missiles were stored or could be stored. One of the most likely areas for such storage is the karst region of Pinar del Rio province in the western part of the island. It is known locally as the Guaniguanicos region. Beneath the hills are many intricate passage ways of channels, galleries, caverns, and caves—all the result of active solution processes.

prevented by a covering of forest or grass. Sand dunes can be stabilized and migration stopped by the planting and growth of grasses, shrubs, and trees. Cultivation of various agricultural crops may make possible serious erosion by wind and water. And finally, vegetation is the mortal enemy of lakes, which are ephemeral features from the standpoint of geologic time.

Animals, by overgrazing pasture plants contribute conditions that make wind and water erosion easier. In the tropics, ants may build hills many feet high and add a unique diversity to the physical landscape. Thousands of such topographic features may be seen on the route between São Paulo and Rio de Janeiro, Brazil. Again, burrowing animals aid both geologic processes of weathering and erosion. Before the European settlement of North America, grazing animals, seeking easiest passage through rugged lands, developed trails that were later followed by explorers and still later covered by modern roads. But animal power followed man power in pulling plows and other machines for cultivating land; and machines, together with man, have hastened erosion in many parts of the world.

QUESTIONS, EXERCISES, AND PROBLEMS

1. Name, locate, and describe the major physical regions of Canada, the United States, Mexico, Central America, and the West Indies. How do the Pacific land forms of the United States resemble the letter "H"?
2. What is the highest mountain of the Appalachians; of the United States; of North America; of South America; of Europe; of Asia; of Africa; of Australia; and of Antarctica? What are the equatorward limits of Pleistocene glaciation in the United States?
3. Point out ten contrasts and ten similarities between the physical geography of South America and that of North America. Name, locate, and describe four major highlands and three major plains in South America.
4. Name, locate, and describe the four major European physical regions. Compare the alignment of European and North American physical features. Identify the following: Rhine Graben, Scottish Graben, the defenses of Paris, the Iron Gate, the Rhône-Saone Gate, the Moravian Gate, the Brenner Pass, the Morava-Vardar Depression, the Lorraine Gate, the Belfort Gate.
5. Name, locate, and describe the six major physical regions of Asia. Identify and locate the Pamir Knot, the Armenian Knot, the Dzungarian Trench, Khyber Pass, Shipki Pass, Karakoram Pass, Jade Gate, Deccan, Western Ghats, Tsinling Mountains, Bolan Pass, and three major physical regions of Siberia.
6. Name, locate, and describe the major physical features of Africa. Describe the basins of the major rivers. What is meant by stream piracy? Where is the Rift Valley? Give one explanation for its formation. Does it extend into Asia? Explain. What is the average inland extent of Africa's coastal plain? Where is it the widest? How does Africa resemble South America?
7. Name, locate, and describe the major physical features of Australia and New Zealand. Make a comparison between the three subregions of the Eastern Basins of Australia and some china ware. What is the geologic history of each of the three major physical regions of Australia?
8. What major physical agencies shape the surface features of the earth? Give examples of the work of each one of these agencies.

SELECTED REFERENCES

Atwood, Wallace W., *The Physiographic Provinces of North America,* latest edition, Ginn and Company.

Barton, T. F., "The Earth's Surface: Three Substances and Nine Major Physical Divisions," *Journal of Geography,* Oct. 1962, pp. 321–25.

Dohrs, F. E., Sommers, L. M., Petterson, D. R., *Outside Readings in Geography*, Thomas Y. Crowell and Co., 1955, especially Section 3, "Landforms: Processes and Types," pp. 157–232.

Hammond, E. H., "Analysis of Properties in Land Form Geography: An Application to Broad-Scale Land Form Mapping in the United States," *Annals of the Association of American Geographers,* March 1964, pp. 11–19.

James, Preston, *Latin America,* latest revision, Odyssey Press, especially sections on Surface Features in General and Surface Features for each political unit.

Kikolski, Bohdan, "Contemporary Research in Physical Geography of the Chinese Peoples Republic," *Annals of the A.A.G.,* July 1964, pp. 181–89.

Lobeck, A. K. and others, *Physiographic Diagrams of Africa, Asia, Australia, Europe, North America, South America, and the United States* together with pamphlet texts of various dates, C. S. Hammond, Maplewood, New Jersey. Large or small scale copies of these maps should be made available for student assignment during the study of Chapter V.

Longwell, C. R. and Flint, R. F., *Introduction to Physical Geology,* 2d edition, John Wiley and Sons, 1962.

Pratt, R. M. "The Ocean Bottom," *Science,* Oct. 26, 1962, pp. 492–95.

Stamp, L. D., *Africa,* 2d edition, John Wiley and Sons, 1964, especially Ch. 3, "The Physical Background."

Stamp, L. D., *Asia,* 15th edition, John Wiley and Sons, 1961, especially the section on "The Physical Background."

Taylor, Griffith, *Australia,* 6th edition or later revision, E. P. Dutton, especially Part II, "The Natural Regions and Their Varied Environments," pp. 129–234.

United States Geological Survey, *Amazon River Investigation: Measuring a Mighty River,* Feature Material, 1964.

Van Cleef, Eugene, "A Letter to the Editor: Continents," *Journal of Geography,* December 1962, pp. 424–25.

Van Valkenburg, S. and Held, C. C., *Europe,* 2d edition, John Wiley and Sons, 1952, especially Chs. 3, 4, and 5, "The Northwestern Uplands," "The Central Lowland and Uplands," and "The Alpine Division."

Washburn, Bradford, "A New Map of Mount McKinley, Alaska: The Life Story of a Cartographic Project," *Geographical Review,* April 1961, pp. 159–86.

Chapter Six

Man's Use of Plains, Mountains, and Plateaus

In the preceding chapter, emphasis was placed upon the distribution of major surface features of the world, significant topographic elements of the ocean floors, important physical divisions of the continents, and finally the agencies both within and without the earth which shape world topography. Now it may be useful to examine another approach to the earth's surface features, namely how the differences in man's utilization of plains (Fig. 6–1), mountains, and plateaus may be affected by their differences in geologic age, slope, dissection, drainage, altitude, and other physical characteristics.

Plains

Youthful Plains. (See A. K. Lobeck, *Panorama of Physiographic Types.*[1]) The question may be asked, does the fact that a plain is in geologic youth, maturity, or old age have any influence upon man's use of the topographic feature. A few examples will suggest an affirmative answer.

A youthful dissected plain may be defined as one with broad nearly level interstream areas, widely spaced major river valleys, and few tributary valleys. Good examples include recently dissected glacial plains of Illinois and Iowa and the High Plains east of the Rockies in Colorado, Kansas, New Mexico, Oklahoma, and Texas.

Man uses the broad interfluves in humid regions for row-crop farming, for easy transport routes of various types, and for urban centers. Major stream valleys may possess flood plains also useful for agriculture, transport, towns, and cities. Such valleys in dry lands are better suited for irrigation agriculture than inter-

[1] The full reference is given in the Selected References at the end of this chapter.

stream sections, for obvious reasons. Tributary stream valleys may be too steep either for farming or for transport.

Recently upraised sea bottoms too youthful to show significant dissection are likely to contain large areas of swampy ground of little agricultural use to man. The Florida Everglades are a good example of such recent uplift, and they have been set aside as a National Park. Parts of the entire Atlantic-Gulf Coastal Plain are of similar geologic age and have witnessed little economic development by man.

Mature Plains. (See A. K. Lobeck, *op. cit.*) Plains dissected enough to be classified in the geologic age of maturity may contain too much slope land for the best row-crop agriculture and for easy transport routes. The formerly level plains of southeast Iowa and northern Missouri illustrate this situation; since the time of Pleistocene glaciation that smoothed out the rolling preglacial topography, stream action has made the land forms rolling once more.

Plains in Old Age. (See A. K. Lobeck, *op. cit.*) Few old age plains approaching base level exist in today's world; but one such erosional surface occurs in British Guiana. Here several remnant hills stand above the relatively flat topography of crystalline rocks that millions of years ago stood at a much higher level. These hills would suffer serious erosion with row-crop agriculture, but level portions of the region offer little topographic handicap for such farming.

Glacial Plains. Many other factors influence the use of surface features besides the factor of geologic age. One, glacial action, has given the earth many plains (see Fig. 6–1), some formed largely by glacial erosion and some dominated by glacial deposition. The Laurentian Shield of

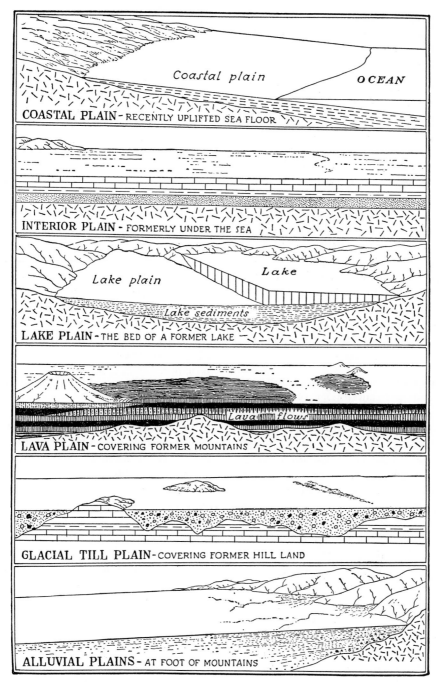

COASTAL PLAIN – RECENTLY UPLIFTED SEA FLOOR

INTERIOR PLAIN – FORMERLY UNDER THE SEA

LAKE PLAIN – THE BED OF A FORMER LAKE

LAVA PLAIN – COVERING FORMER MOUNTAINS

GLACIAL TILL PLAIN – COVERING FORMER HILL LAND

ALLUVIAL PLAINS – AT FOOT OF MOUNTAINS

Fig. 6–1   Types of Plains. The plains regions of the world are of many different kinds. (*Courtesy McGraw-Hill Book Co. and A. K. Lobeck*, Geomorphology)

Canada is a good example of the former. Here rocks have been scraped bare[2] of soil over a wide expanse, thus limiting agriculture even if climate

[2] Bare rock surfaces may offer little encouragement for farming, but they make the discovery of minerals much easier.

were favorable. Several hundred miles to the south, glacial deposition became more important than glacial erosion; and the deep soils of the relatively flat surface encourage wide spread commercial agriculture. The significance of glacial topography and soil upon successful farming has been proven statistically by a comparison of the Driftless Area[3] with that of the glaciated lands nearby.

Piedmont Plains. Piedmont plains (see Fig. 6–1), especially ones in dry regions offer better than average conditions for crop agriculture; and the outermost sections of such plains are likely to be more productive than portions closest to the base of the mountains. This condition results because the outliers are more nearly flat and are made up of better soils. If the mountains rising above the piedmont plain lie at right angles to prevailing winds, crop agriculture gains a precipitation advantage. The Sierra Nevada range rises above the piedmont plains of California's Great Valley and faces the prevailing westerlies; and the Ahaggar mountains, which face the northeast trades crossing the Sahara desert, cool the rising air until it precipitates moisture for alluvial piedmont plains contiguous to the northern slopes.

River Flood Plains. (See A. K. Lobeck, *op. cit.*) The many different topographic features occurring upon river flood plains show a variety of human uses. With a youthful stream, there may be no flood plains or very small ones for man to utilize. As the river reaches a mature stage and starts to meander, sufficient overflow may take place to provide level areas for cultivated crops. And finally near the mouth, the stream may exhibit abandoned stream channels, natural levees, and wide stretches of flat land behind the levees—all characteristic features of an old age stream. While all of these old age areas may be risky for farming because of flood danger, their relative smooth topography and alluvial soils favor row-crop agriculture. A second problem besides flooding may be good drainage, especially on abandoned channels and upon the lowlying plains behind natural levees.

Bridging the wide, swampy, old age portion of the stream may be a serious, expensive problem. If there is a delta at the river mouth, man may also find it necessary to straighten, confine, and deepen one of the distributaries. To provide easier access to the sea, this has been done on

the Mississippi near New Orleans and on the La Plata near Buenos Aires. On the other hand, the delta may provide mankind with some of the best agricultural land in the world and enough to support millions of farmers. During recent geologic time, China's Hwang Ho has extended its delta seaward far enough to tie the Shantung Peninsula, a former island, to the mainland, and to add thousands of square miles to China's limited amount of tillable land.

Lake Plains. Lake plains (see Fig. 6–1) in most humid areas provide easy means of transport, level land for expanding urban centers, and above all favorable sites for subsistence and commercial agriculture. The lake plains surrounding the North American Great Lakes provide a good example for each of the above-mentioned types of land use. Note the dense rail and road patterns on both Canadian and United States sides; notice also the large cities of both countries, which are numerous around these inland waterways; and finally observe the rich agricultural lands of the United States that lie to the south and west and those of Canada to the northeast.

Strategic Plains. Just as isolated desert plains may encourage utilization for military purposes, so may plains among or near mountains along international boundaries facilitate invasions during war time. At the start of the first World War Germany chose to violate Belgian neutrality to take advantage of plains[4] topography rather than to move into France through the mountainous French-German border.

Man has taken advantage of many long narrow stretches of plains lying between mountains on both sides for transport purposes. An easy, nearly level access to the West through the Appalachian mountains by way of the Mohawk-

---

[3] The Driftless Area was unaffected by ice action and is located in southwest Wisconsin, northeast Iowa, southeast Minnesota, and northwest Illinois.

[4] A more recent example of military rivalry for a strategic plain involves the many battles which occurred on the Loatian Plaine des Jarres (English equivalent, Plain of Jars) during the early 1960's. Communists, non-Communists, and neutrals were active in these engagements. Military strategists have called the plain the key to the control of Laos. It has an east-west extent of approximately 20 miles and a north-south measurement of about 15 miles. Its altitude averages about 3,000 feet above sea level; and low mountains ring it on all sides with elevations ranging from 1500 to 3500 feet above those of the plain. Not far from the airport, large jars, with an origin dating back about 2000 years, are scattered through the natural grass cover. The use and origin of these man-made features from which the plain takes its name, are unknown.

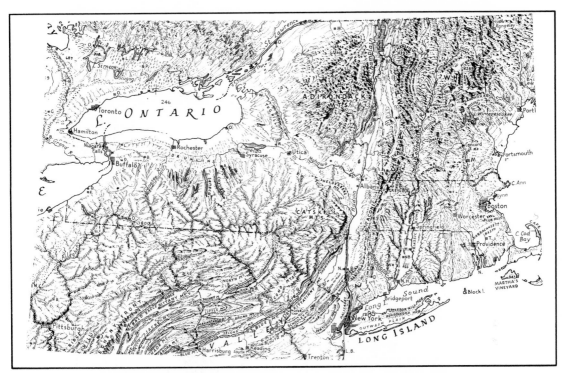

Fig. 6–2   The Hudson-Mohawk Gateway to the West. The trade of New York City was greatly encouraged by its splendid natural harbor and by its easy accessibility to the productive central plains of the United States. Easy access could be attained by tht Hudson-Mohawk Valley and Great Lakes route. Note the absence of shading, showing plains topography, in the Hudson Valley and on west from Albany by way of the Mohawk Valley to Buffalo and the Great Lakes. (*W. W. Atwood,* Physiographic Provinces of North America, *Ginn and Co.*)

Hudson Gateway gave early opportunity for canal building; and as a result, New York City grew much faster than many other competing cities without such a water level access (Fig. 6–2).

Plains and Major World Cities. Before leaving the subject of human adjustment to plains topography, it may be well to enumerate some of the world's great urban centers which are located on plains. Tokyo, the earth's largest city lies on the Kwanto Plain, Japan's most extensive nearly level area; London extends along the lower valley of the Thames; New York spreads out across lowland contiguous to the mouth of the Hudson and over Manhattan, Long, and several other relatively flat islands. Los Angeles occupies a large section of the coast facing Los Angeles Basin. Buenos Aires lies on the coastal section of the Argentine Pampa; Moscow is situated near the center of the huge Russian Platform, a great division of the European Plain; Cairo is located near the mouth of the Nile where the river starts building its delta; Shanghai's millions live on the wide plain near the mouth of the Yangtze; and Peiping is built on the Hwang Ho lowland. Further study will show that plains topography has been a significant factor in the location of most of the world's cities, great and small.

Mountains, Major Utilization. Man's ability to adjust to and better utilize mountains (Fig. 6–3) has progressed considerably during the last century. Nevertheless, many highland regions are still undeveloped and characterized by sparse population. Some uplands will remain that way indefinitely.

In general the words "mountaineer," "high-

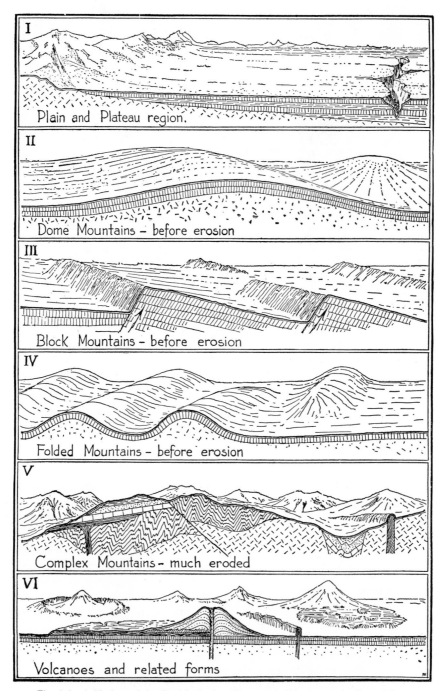

Fig. 6–3 A Variety of the Earth's Surface Features in Diagrammatic Form. Most upland regions of the world include mountains of many types such as domed mountains, fault blocks, folded structures, volcanic cones, and erosional forms. (*Courtesy McGraw-Hill Book Co. and A. K. Lobeck,* Geomorphology)

lander," and "hillman" suggest people who differ from plainsmen in modes of life, habits, and physique. They may be sturdier and more daring than people of the lowlands. On the other hand, a mountaineer may mean a man who goes to the Alps, Rockies, Himalayas or other high mountains for the pleasure of climbing; or the mention of mountains often brings to mind vacations and beautiful scenery. It may also call up the idea of mines, lumber camps, water power, or water supplies for great cities of the plains. Certain tropical plantations, such as those producing coffee, are more successful on highlands than upon lowlands. Many of these benefits of mountains are comparatively new. For example mountain mines, water power, and recreation were not one-tenth as important a hundred years ago as they are now. Hence, the value of mountains today is far more appreciated than formerly.

High Mountains. Life in mountains differs from that in plains for three chief reasons, namely altitude, climate and slope. Altitude alone is relatively unimportant. Some people with heart trouble, to be sure, cannot live even at an altitude of 5000 feet, and many find difficulty in breathing at altitudes of 10,000 feet or more. Nevertheless, when people stay at high altitudes, their bodies soon become adapted to the new conditions. An increase in the number of red corpuscles enables the blood to absorb oxygen more rapidly, and thus the rarity of the air, which is the great difficulty at high altitudes, is robbed of much of its effect. When people come down from the mountains this excess of red corpuscles makes them feel strong, but the extra strength quickly passes away. The prompt change in the blood enables people to adapt themselves to any altitude where the climate and relief make it possible to earn a living. Denver, for example, has become a great city a mile above sea level; Mexico City is a half mile higher; Quito prospers at an altitude of nearly two miles. And certain villages in the Andes and Tibet raise barley and sheep nearly three miles above the sea. In each case a comparatively level upland makes it possible for the city or village to grow up in spite of the altitude.

It should be remembered that only a small percentage of the population suffers until an altitude of 6000 feet or more is reached. Such altitudes are scarce in the eastern two-thirds of the United States, and form scarcely a quarter of the western two-thirds. In Europe they are rare, in Australia at a minimum, and in Africa limited to Abyssinia and a few other minor areas. Only in the Tibetan region of Asia and in the Andean region of South America are there large areas where altitude alone makes it difficult for people to live.

How Mountains Influence Climate. The contrasted climates which arise from differences of altitude influence man more than the direct effects of altitudes. In the loftiest villages of the Andes and Tibet, the villagers think less about altitude than about climate. But altitude influences climate in at least four ways: (1) Temperature decreases with altitude. In the free air the decrease is about 1° F for 330 feet of altitude in summer and for 400 feet in winter. The decrease is more marked where mountains rise steeply above a lowland, as in the Alps, than in regions like the Great Plains where one can rise from near sea level to Denver almost without noticing any grade. Nevertheless the average yearly temperature at Denver is about 3° lower than at Indianapolis, which lies in the same latitude but 4500 feet lower. (2) The greater the altitude the more variable is the temperature. Rarity of the air allows the sun's heat to pass through it readily. Thus the earth's surface is quickly warmed, but the same condition also allows the earth's heat to pass away rapidly at night, so that there are great diurnal extremes. Relief also causes variability, for cool air may flow down a valley at night and warm air rises by day. (3) Mountains also are more cloudy and rainy than plains, for the currents of air that approach them must rise. Hence the air is cooled and its water vapor condenses into clouds and rain. On a perfectly clear day on the plains of California, one can often see great banks of clouds enshrouding the crests of the Sierras only 40 miles to the east. While the dry brown grass of the Great Valley shows that no rain has fallen for months, the dense pine forests of the mountains and the little brooks flowing amid rich green grass or thick brakes of flourishing bushes give evidence of plentiful rainfall. (4) High altitudes bring lower pressures. In fact, atmospheric pressure is halved at approximately 18,000 feet above sea level.

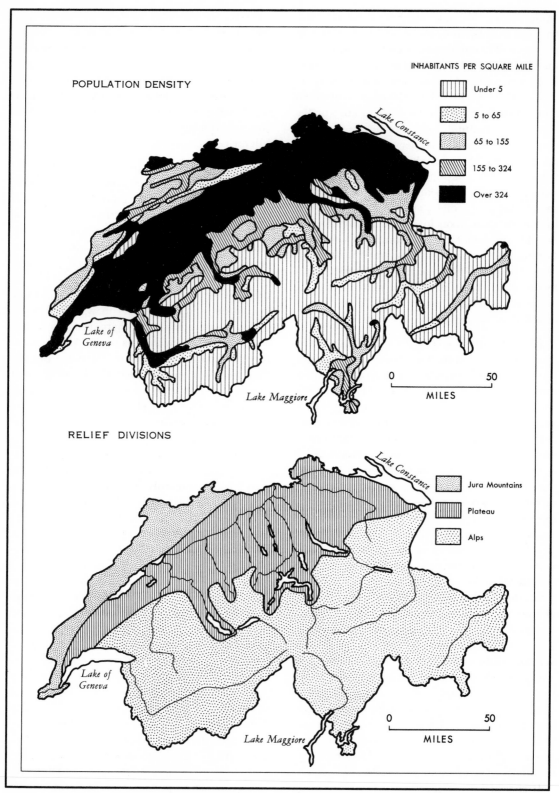

Fig. 6–4 Topography Influences Swiss Population Density. Land forms are a major influence in Switzerland's population distribution. The greatest concentration occurs in the northern plateau with its relatively low relief. On the other hand, the Alpine region and that of the Jura are sparsely settled. Both relief and population distribution are highly generalized.

Although climatic differences between highlands and lowlands are everywhere important, they influence man most in regions close to the colder margins of human occupation and within the tropics. England lies so far north that in the lowlands the summers are not warm enough for corn and barely warm enough for wheat oats and potatoes. Accordingly a rise of 1500 feet may be enough to make row-crop agriculture impossible and to prevent the growth of the best forests. Near the coast and in the valleys, luxuriant trees, fine gardens, and rich hayfields surround comfortable villages and picturesque farmhouses. Mild winters actually permit the growth of semi-tropical plants such as the fuchsia. Only a few miles away the cool summers of the rolling uplands, 1500 feet higher permit little except grass, heather, drifting mist, and shepherds.

Mountains in the Tropics. In tropical countries, high altitudes are beneficial because of the cool air. Near sea level the temperature much of the year may average close to 80°. This temperature is too warm for the greatest comfort, the best health, or the highest efficiency. Up to an average of 72°, however, high temperature is not particularly uncomfortable or unhealthful and does not greatly diminish efficiency except as it remains monotonously at the same level. Accordingly, an altitude sufficient to lower the temperature of the warmer months by eight to ten degrees is a great advantage to health in the tropics. Hence the coffee-growing plateau of southern Brazil, 2000 to 3000 feet high, has a climate better for man's activity than that of the Amazon lowlands. High Kenya and Uganda in Africa also provide far more pleasant climatic conditions than the equatorial coasts of the continent. Bogotá, at an elevation of 8000 feet is more healthful than the hot steaming jungles of Colombia, Ecuador, Peru, and Bolivia at the eastern base of the Andes.

Population on Mountain Slopes. The influence of steep mountain slopes on population distribution may be seen more easily by citing two specific examples. In Switzerland, population reaches the greatest density on the Swiss Plateau, a gently rolling upland situated between the higher and steeper Jura on the north and the Alpine heights of the south, both sparsely populated; and even in the Jura and Alps, most of the small number of people live along the main river valleys (Fig. 6-4). Again, Bhutan, on the rugged southern slope of the Himalayas, contains only about thirty-five people per square mile, whereas in the Indian province of Bengal, a short distance to the south, the flat Ganges plain supports more than five hundred persons per square mile.

Mountain Slopes, Transportation. Slopes of mountains (Figs. 6-5 and 6-6) also present many handicaps to surface transport. (1) In going up slope a load must not only be carried forward but also must be lifted against the pull of gravity; (2) attempts to minimize this difficulty are likely to involve greater distances and larger expenses than in crossing plains; (3) travel will be slower on slope land than on level terrain; (4) the wear and tear on transport equipment will be greater on sloping than upon level topography; (5) and the cost of power for trains and motor cars will be greater in going through mountains than over plains.

A short description of transportation in the mountains of western United States and Canada will illustrate the transport handicaps listed above. The Denver and Rio Grande has spent enormous sums to provide a faster schedule and a less difficult route. In 1902, Daniel H. Moffat envisioned a route between Denver and Salt Lake City which would save 175 miles of difficult mountain travel, eight hours for trains moving freight, and six hours for passenger trains; the prospective route would permit transport during winter when travel over the high passes is blocked by snow.

Moffat's vision involved the 6-mile-long Moffat tunnel and the Dotsero cutoff of 38 miles. Thirty-two years elapsed before the Moffat-Dotsero route was officially opened, June 15, 1934; for the project which involved the expenditure of millions of dollars faced financial problems as well as the mountain barrier. Today, the tunnel provides a short passage for trains, telegraph, telephone, and electric power lines, and also carries a pipe-line to bring water to the city of Denver, Colorado.

Two other transcontinental railroads, the Santa Fe and the Southern Pacific really do not cross the Rockies, but avoid them completely by taking the southern route. Routes of the Northern Pacific, the Great Northern, and the

Fig. 6–5   Winding Road from India to Nepal. Notice the trucks moving up and down the difficult "Nine Turns" or switchbacks of the mountain road. (*Standard Oil Company, New Jersey*)

Chicago, Milwaukee, and St. Paul go through the mountains in Montana, thus taking advantage of the narrower Northern Rockies. The first railroad to cross the continent, the Union Pacific, follows a route over the relatively favorable terrain of the Wyoming Basin, which separates the Central Rockies from the Northern Rockies. Only two Canadian railroads cross the Rockies, the Canadian Pacific with its western terminus at Vancouver, and the Canadian National, which reaches the Pacific at Prince Rupert. These two railroads take advantage of breaks through the Rockies. Only the nine railroads named above cross the continent to the Pacific in Canada and the United States (Fig. 6–7).

Motor transport has found the mountains as much of a barrier as the railroads, and most through traffic uses the Wyoming Basin and routes south of the Rockies to reach the Pacific.

In spite of modern travel over and through mountains by motor car, train, and airplane, the old primitive transport still persists. Pack trains still carry loads even in the more progressive mountain countries. A unique use of pack animals has existed for a long time in the Southern Appalachians of the United States. In the more inaccessible parts moonshiners still distill whiskey illegally. Corn, one of the main bulky crops, cannot be transported cheaply to lowland markets for the lack of good roads. Whiskey is only a small fraction as heavy as the corn from which it is made. By loading a few containers of liquor on a pack animal, transport of a crop, processed from much heavier grain, to the lowland market is relatively easy whether there are good roads or not. All this is a good illustration of a basic principle in economic geography. In isolated regions the best money crop is one which has high value per unit of weight and one which will not deteriorate in quality over long periods of time.

Mountains and Agriculture. Row-crop farm-ing is also difficult in rugged regions. Every rain carries away some soil, especially when the fields have been freshly plowed. In the Carolinas, Georgia, and other southern states, the Appa-

Fig. 6–6 Mountain Bridges over the Rimac River in Peru. A train of the Central Railroad of Peru is crossing over the middle bridge, while the other two bridges form part of the Lima-Cerro de Pasco Highway. The railroad was surveyed by Henry Meiggs, a North American engineer. As the main line follows the Rimac valley towards Cerro de Pasco, it passes over numerous bridges, through many tunnels and around many switchbacks. At one place the rails follow the bed of the stream, which is diverted through a boring on one side. The highest point on the Ferrocarril Central reaches over 15,000 feet. (*Courtesy Standard Oil, New Jersey*)

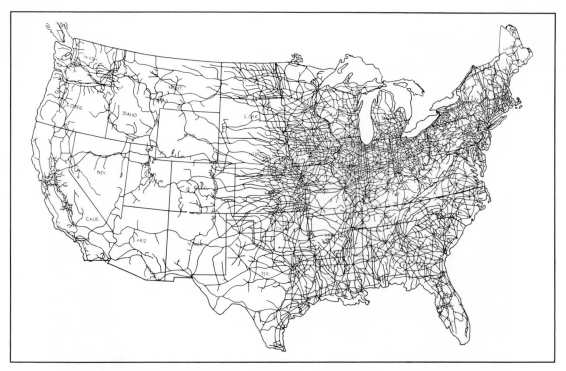

Fig. 6–7   Railroads of the United States. The student may point out areas in which relief is an important influence discouraging railroad construction. (*Courtesy Association of American Railroads*)

lachian foothills have suffered almost irreparable harm in this way. Under the influence of unwise cultivation, the soil of hundreds of farms has been gullied so that fields are ruined. Where the slopes are fairly gentle, this difficulty can be overcome by plowing so that all the furrows are horizontal and the rainwater stands in them instead of running down the slope. This is called contour plowing because the furrows run horizontally like the contour lines on a map. In other places, the gullies can be checked from spreading further by building little dams at their heads. The planting of grass or small grains such as wheat and oats instead of hoed crops such as corn and potatoes often helps to stop erosion. The washing away of soil is doubly harmful, for the material carried from the fields is often spread out on valley floors, where for a time it may ruin other fields.

In mountain regions the farmer finds an ex-

treme scarcity of level places for planting crops. He uses the valley bottoms, but to get more level land, he may construct terraces on the hillside. In China, Japan, and Lebanon this has been done on an enormous scale. Whole mountain sides are often covered with terraces, where walls 5 or 10 feet high have been built in order to form terraces 20 or 30 feet wide. The labor of making such terraces and of keeping them in repair is very great. Moreover, machinery cannot be used in such places.

Since row-crop farming is so difficult, mountaineers may try to make a living in other ways, for instance by keeping cattle and sheep. These animals can easily graze on slopes too steep for cultivation. Throughout the Rocky Mountains, the Sierra Nevada, the European Alps and other rugged sections of the world, sheep and cattle are driven to highland pastures to graze during the summer. In Switzerland, the high meadows or "Alps" have given their name to one of the world's most famous mountain groups. Every year when warm weather comes and mountain snows disappear, some Swiss farmers move with their flocks and herds to chalets or huts among the pastures near the snow line. There they spend the summer caring for the cows and making butter and cheese. In the western United States improved roads have made it possible to truck sheep to the high pastures during the summer grazing season (Fig. 6–8).

Tree Crops. In many respects tree crops are to mountains what grain crops are to plains. Probably the world's most important food products are the cereals, including rice, corn, wheat, rye, barley and oats. In order to make a good living, especially if he raises wheat, barley, rye, or oats, the farmer must cultivate a relatively large acreage. He can do this only if he uses machinery. On slopes such machines as gang plows, seeders, mowing machines, and harvesters are not adapted to the terrain.

With trees the situation is different. Many kinds of trees grow as well on hillsides as on plains, and the land doesn't have to be plowed. Moreover, since there is no cultivation, the soil is not washed away as easily as where the crops are planted anew each year. Roots of trees hold the soil in place, and their leaves increase its depth.

Because of these conditions tree crops are highly profitable in regions of rugged relief. For example in France and Italy rough rocky hillsides may be planted with chestnut trees, and these hillside crops may be as profitable as yields of wheat grown on plains. Walnuts, chestnuts, beechnuts, pecans, filberts, and butternuts all furnish good food for man and can be raised on slope land. So, too, can the olive, which provides one of the best vegetable oils.

Acorns also grow well on slopes. They furnish good swine feed in rugged lands of Yugoslavia, Spain, Portugal, and even in the southern Appalachians of the United States. In medieval time, European forests were valued as much for the feed they provided for swine as for their supply of wood products.

Slopes have a real advantage for orchard fruits, not only because the land may be cheap, but also because hills diminish the danger of frost in the spring when trees are flowering. Hillsides also lengthen the season that is warm enough for ripening in the fall, a fact which is especially critical for apples, an important tree crop in the United States. This is because the earth cools faster at night than does the air. It thereby cools the air that touches it. Since cool

Fig. 6–8   Cattle Grazing in the Swiss Alps. Transhumance, the seasonal movement of animals with the necessary herders from lowland to highland pastures is practiced in many mountainous lands.

air contracts, it becomes relatively heavy and begins to flow down the slope. Its place is taken by warmer air which has not yet touched the earth. Most people have noticed how this process of air drainage causes the hollows to be cooler than the land a little farther up slope on a still summer night.

In tropical countries where there is no frost, the slopes often have another great advantage, both for trees and all kinds of crops. Gentle slope soils may be better than those found anywhere else. This is because soil on level tropical lands is often so badly leached that it becomes infertile. Moreover, in the valley bottoms it may be waterlogged. Some tropical farmers may not understand why slopes are better, but long experience has taught them that it pays to use slopes and to depend on trees as much as possible.

Lumbering as a Mountain Industry. Trees for lumber as well as for food probably always will be more abundant in rugged regions than in plains. Many plains that are now densely populated were once covered with trees; today, however, in middle latitudes, forests are largely restricted to rugged areas that cannot be used for row-crop farming. In the United States, such forest lands are found in northern New England, the Adirondacks, the Appalachians, and the northern parts of Michigan, Wisconsin, and Minnesota. The Ozark region of Arkansas, parts of the Rocky Mountains, and much of the Sierra Nevada, Cascade, and Coast ranges are likewise forested. In Europe, the words *forest* and *mountain* are almost synonymous. The terms *Black Forest* and *Black Mountains* are both used for the same part of Germany. Similarly in most of France, the forests have been cut away so completely, except on the rugged uplands, that a term such as *Argonne* means both forest and highland.

Until the latter part of the last century, lumber and firewood were abundant in both United States plains and mountains. Now, however, except for the sandy pine lands of the South, the main reliance of the country is almost entirely upon the forests of rugged areas.

Winter Occupations in Isolated European Mountains. European mountaineers may use the winter period to engage in occupations such as the woodworking of Switzerland and the German Black Forest. Since there is plenty of wood around them, people have taken to carving it into all sorts of toys for children and also into elaborate patterns such as clock cases and paneling for churches. Women often make lace or embroidery. Carved wood and embroidery, like moonshine whiskey, previously described, represent a high value per unit of weight, and hence can be transported easily out of the mountains. The mountaineers really export their skill, their raw material being of little value.

Mountains May Attract Plains People. Just as the wealth of the plains has long attracted people of mountains, so the scenery and pure air of the mountains now attract the people of the plains. A century or two ago civilized people such as those of the English and German lowlands regarded mountains as places to be shunned. In old books mountains are often referred to as terrifying, gloomy, and frightful. Now the vast majority of civilized people regard mountains as a pleasure ground. With improvement of mountain transport, thousands of families escape from the city each summer in order to gain strength and happiness among mountains. They want to enjoy the wild forests, climb rugged peaks, and feel the exhilaration of the view from a mountain top.

The Alps, White Mountains, Adirondacks, Rockies, and Sierras are full of people who make a large part of their living by taking boarders, running hotels and motels, supplying milk and vegetables, selling small articles made during the winter, acting as guides, and in other ways caring for the tourists. In such communities disadvantages of mountain life are diminished. Since people no longer depend wholly upon local products, their prosperity increases. They can have better schools, better roads, more books, better professional men and artisans, and more advantages in many ways. Contact with people from many lowland regions brings new ideas, and mountain life is broadened and deepened.

Mountain life and mountain utilization may be influenced by the geologic age and the geologic genesis of the mountain group. Obviously there are differences in the ruggedness of mountains in youth and in old age. As a result of such differences, transport facilities are more easily developed through the old worn down mountains of New England, for example, than through the youthful Himalayas and Andes.

Again, mountains resulting from vulcanism still may be active and threaten the life of a farming community built along the flanks to take advantage of the rich volcanic soil. This has happened in the new state of Hawaii. Or communities like those in the Southern Appalachians may develop a transportation pattern according to the direction of mountain folding. In the Appalachians transport facilities follow the general northeast-southwest trending synclines found among the anticlines with the same general trend. Many other relationships to differences in mountain age and type of origin could

be cited, but the few described above should be enough to emphasize the point.

Plateaus

Man's utilization of plateaus (Figs. 6–9 and 6–10) will depend upon such factors as location, height, amount of dissection, origin, mineralization or the lack of it, and other factors. Greenland is sometimes described as an ice covered plateau, and glaciers also cover plateau terrain in parts of Antarctica. Polar location makes these areas of little use to man whether land forms beneath the ice are mountain, plain, or plateau.

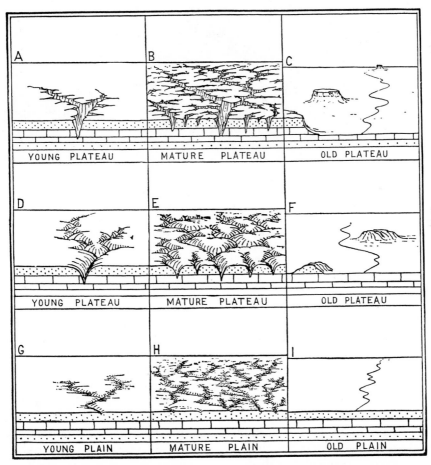

Fig. 6–9 Erosional Cycle in Plains and Plateaus. The sketches above show plains and plateaus in youth, maturity, and old age. Notice (1) the horizontal structure characteristic of many plains and plateaus; (2) the poorly developed drainage patterns of youth and old age; (3) the well developed mature drainage pattern; and (4) the greater amount of relief in plateaus than in plains. (*Courtesy McGraw-Hill Book Co. and A. K. Lobeck*, Geomorphology)

Fig. 6–10 Llama Pack Train Near Cuzco, Peru. A considerable area of plateau topography occurs in central Peru between the Pacific—facing ranges and those fringing the Amazon Basin to the east. Elevations reach 15,000 feet or more and make many types of land utilization difficult. Precipitation is low; diurnal ranges of temperature are great; natural vegetation supports only limited grazing; and agriculture is not a dependable occupation. The llama, still an important burden bearer, is especially tolerant of low atmospheric pressure so characteristic of the region. (*Courtesy Standard Oil, New Jersey*)

The middle latitude Tibetan Plateau is the highest in the world and shows a marked contrast in economic development to that of the lower Piedmont Plateau in eastern United States. Agriculture is extremely difficult on the former, but much less hazardous and much more profitable on the latter. In South America, differences in height make life considerably easier on the Brazilian Plateau than on the Bolivian Plateau several thousand feet higher. Moreover, the Paraná portion of the Brazilian Plateau originated in the form of quiescent lava flows. These have added fertility to the soil and have made the lands more attractive for agri-cultural utilization. The Deccan Plateau of India, the Ethiopian Plateau, and the Columbia Plateau of northwestern United States are of the same volcanic origin and possess similar advantages for farming.

Little dissection has occurred on the Columbia Plateau in contrast to that which is evident on the Catskill portion of the Appalachian tableland. As a result the Catskills are of little use for agriculture, whereas grain farming on an extensive scale has been dominant in eastern Washington and Oregon for many decades.

In many parts of the Appalachian Plateau other than the Catskills, rocks contain millions of tons of high grade coal. Thus the geologic history has made possible the extraction of fuel, an important phase of Appalachian Plateau land use.

Forestry, tourism, and other types of land use besides mining and farming may be found on most middle and low latitude plateaus. In fact most industries characteristic of mountain lands may be found on plateaus, especially those showing considerable dissection.

Hills. Hilly terrain may be better suited for agriculture than that of dissected plateaus and mountains but less adaptable for row crops than plains topography. However, gently rolling hill land may be farmed with a minimum of danger of erosion if man employs contour farming, strip cropping, and other modern methods of preventing rapid runoff. Nevertheless, most hill land should be left in grass or planted with tree crops rather than subjected to the plow.

Hilly terrain shows striking relationships to man's activities in urban geography. Different parts of cities can often be classified according to both altitude and slope. As a rule, the better houses are located on higher land. In some cities the steepness of certain slopes makes them undesirable so that they may be left unused, or occupied by people with low incomes. The character of lawns and gardens is much influenced by slope of the land. Terraces, rock gardens, and in some cases miniature brooks and pools are characteristic of sloping houselots far more than of flat ones. Artistic people sometimes build their houses on pieces of land so high, rough, or steep that other people do not want them. Hilltop sites are often chosen because of their view. In winter the view may be paid for in fuel because of the wind, but compensation may be found in coolness and freedom from mosquitoes in summer.

Another effect of hill lands in cities is often seen in the extent to which streets depart from straight lines and a rectangular pattern. For example, in Worcester, Massachusetts, a city with more than seven hills, roads occupying the few locations possessing long cross-town valleys carry the bulk of the traffic. As a consequence traffic snarls are much more frequent than in towns and cities with no hill problems. Traffic snarls also occur on Worcester's hilly roads during the winter period when snow and ice bring an added handicap to hill travel over that on plains. Another urban headache of many hill towns like Worcester is the distribution of water to people living on the higher elevations. Numerous other contrasts between man's adjustments to hills and those to plains could be cited for both urban and rural areas.

QUESTIONS, EXERCISES, AND PROBLEMS

1. Explain the cycle of erosion as it refers to land forms in youth, maturity, and old age. Give examples of youthful, mature, and old age plains; tell how the geologic age of a plain may influence its utilization by man.

2. How does man's life in the mountains differ from that on plains? Show mountain influences upon temperature, precipitation, pressure, and winds. Be specific. What differences in population density occur in mountains? Why? Describe the effects of mountains upon transport by air, motor, and train. What adjustments can be made to make agriculture profitable in mountainous lands?

3. Give examples of tree crops best adapted to mountains in the tropics and in the middle latitudes; explain these adaptations in some detail. How do isolated mountain locations in the middle latitudes affect man's winter occupations?

4. What differences occur between man's use of plateaus and that of mountains? Explain man's adjustments to life on hilly terrain.

5. Identify the following: Laurentian Shield, Driftless Area, piedmont plain, peneplane, La Plata estuary, strategic plain, lacustrine plain, the world's ten largest cities and their topographic situation, Mohawk-Hudson Gateway, Moffat Tunnel, transcontinental railroads crossing the United States, row crop, four well-known lava plateaus, contour farming, strip cropping.

SELECTED REFERENCES

Bishop, Barry C., "How We Climbed Everest," *National Geographic*, Oct. 1963, pp. 474–507.

Bishop, Barry C., "Wintering in the High Himalayas," *National Geographic*, Oct. 1962, pp. 503–47.

Burton, Ian, "Education in the Human Use of Flood Plains," *Journal of Geography*, Nov. 1961, pp. 362–71.

Burton, Ian, *Types of Agricultural Occupance of Flood Plains, in the United States,* University of Chicago Press, 1962.

Carley, A. J., "Mountain Train, Peru," *Canadian Geographical Journal*, Feb. 1963, pp. 60–63.

Douglas, William O., "The People of Cades Cove," *National Geographic*, July 1962, pp. 60–95.

Dyrhrenfurth, N. G. and Bishop, Barry C., "Six to the Summit of Mt. Everest," *National Geographic,* October 1963, pp. 460–73.

Eyre, John D., "Mountain Land Use in Northern Japan," *Geographical Review,* April 1962, pp. 236–52.

Graves, W. P. E., Miller, M. M., Thomas, T. P., "Alaska Earthquake of 1964," *National Geographic,* July 1964; photographs especially useful.

Hidore, J. J., "The Relationship Between Cash-Grain Farming and Landforms," *Economic Geography,* Jan. 1963, pp. 84–89.

High, James, "A Reappraisal of Terrain Appreciation," *Professional Geographer,* Jan. 1963, pp. 11–16.

Hornbein, Thomas F., and Unsoeld, W. F., "The First Traverse," *National Geographic,* Oct. 1963, pp. 508–13.

Karan, Pradyumna P. "Bhutan and Sikkim," *Canadian Geographical Journal,* December 1962, pp. 200–09.

Kates, Robert W., *Hazard and Choice Perception in Flood Plain Management,* University of Chicago Press, 1962.

Lobeck, A. K., *Panorama of Physiographic Types,* C. S. Hammond, Maplewood, New Jersey; students should be required to study these illustrations on the map and read about them in the pamphlet.

Marten, E. J., "The Trans-Canada Highway," 1963, *Canadian Geographical Journal,* Sept. 1963, pp. 74–91.

Murphy, Francis C., *Regulating Flood Plan Development,* University of Chicago Press, 1958.

Plafker, G., Kachadoorian, R., Grantz, A., *Alaska's Good Friday Earthquake, 1964,* Geological Survey Circular 491, U.S.G.S., 1964.

Robinson, K. W. and Burley, T. M., "Flood Plain Farming on the Maitland Flats, Hunter Valley, N.S.W., Australia," *Economic Geography,* July 1962, pp. 234–50.

Shaw, Earl B., *Anglo-America,* John Wiley and Sons, 1959, refer to "The Middle Atlantic Coastal Plain, pp. 92–113; "The Southwest Appalachians" pp. 146–80; "The Rocky Mountains," pp. 315–41; "The Intermontane Plateaus," pp. 342–81; and "The Pacific Borderlands," pp. 382–448.

Sheaffer, J. R., *Flood Proofing: An Element in Flood Damage Reduction Program,* University of Chicago Press, 1960.

Smith, Marinobel, "Roads to Reform," *Landscape,* Spring, 1962, pp. 9–14.

Stanislawski, Dan, "The Monchique of Southern Portugal," *Geographical Review,* Jan. 1962, pp. 37–55.

Thorne, Wynne, *Land and Water Use: With Special Reference to Mountain and Plains Regions,* American Association for the Advancement of Science, 1963.

Vance, James E. Jr., "The Oregon Trail and Union Pacific Railroad: A Contrast in Purpose," *Annals of the Association of American Geographers,* Dec. 1961, pp. 357–80.

Wagner, Philip L., "The Path, the Road, the Highway," *Landscape,* Fall 1960, pp. 36–40.

White, G. F., *Papers on Flood Problems,* University of Chicago Press, 1961.

Chapter Seven

Influences of Oceans Upon Man

Why Oceans are Important

Few features of man's geographical surroundings are more important than the division of the earth's surface into continents and oceans. At first thought one might say that only the lands are really necessary. We live on them; their soil yields food for man and beast; they contain most of the mines from which we extract minerals. We travel chiefly upon the lands. It might seem that the ocean merely covers about three-fourths of the earth's surface in place of fertile plains supporting millions of people. Such a view is wrong, for the oceans are as necessary to man's well being as the lands. They are probably of greatest service climatically as a source of rain and as regulators of temperature. They serve as an aid to health and as a source of minerals and food. Oceans also profoundly influence man's life through transport, for they act as barriers to and carriers of commerce.

The Climatic Effect of Oceans

As a Source of Water for Clouds and Precipitation. Even in the heart of a continent, much rain is derived from the ocean. If crops depended only on moisture evaporated from the lands, including lakes and rivers, most of them would wilt and die. Nebraska and the Dakotas, although in the middle of a continent, raise millions of bushels of grain by means of water from the Gulf of Mexico and the Atlantic more than 1000 miles away. A large per cent of the world's corn crop depends upon summer rains from oceans hundreds of miles away. This is not surprising. Evaporation from land is usually less than from the same area of water, as is evident from the dampness of a sea breeze compared

with the dryness of the land breeze. Then, too, the area of the oceans is about 2½ times that of the lands, and 200 times that of all the lakes, rivers, swamps, and other bodies of inland water. If all the lakes in the world should dry up within a single year, they would supply only about one-fifteenth of the rain that falls annually on the lands.

Oceans as Regulators of Temperature. In addition to supplying moisture, the oceans reduce the extremes of heat and cold upon the land. Water requires much more heat to warm it than does land, and is correspondingly slow to cool. Moreover, since water is easily movable, the winds give rise to currents which carry warm water from the tropics toward the poles and cold water from polar regions toward the equator. Because water heats and cools more slowly than land and because the warm and cool parts are mixed by currents, the ocean is warmer than the land in winter and cooler in summer. Hence winds that blow across the oceans are warmed by the water in winter, and cooled in summer. On reaching land they make the summers cooler and the winters warmer than they would otherwise be. How great this effect is may be seen by comparing Seattle, Washington, where west winds from the Pacific Ocean greatly influence temperature, with Bismarck, North Dakota, which is far from either ocean. In January, while the farmers around Seattle are plowing in an average temperature of about 40°, those around Bismarck, where the average is only about 7°, can do little except feed their livestock and protect them from blizzards. In July, the average of Seattle is about 64° and at Bismarck about 70°. If there were no oceans, all parts of the United States would have extremes much greater than those of Bismarck; summers

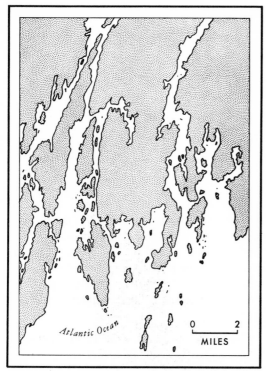

Fig. 7-1   Generalized Diagram of a Shoreline of Submergence. Shorelines of submergence are likely to possess offshore islands, peninsulas, and deep indentations making the coast very irregular.

would be unbearably hot and winters unbearably cold. Climatically it is well that the continents are surrounded by great oceans.

The Oceans as an Aid to Health

The Seacoast Climate. The coast is the place where the ocean exerts its influence upon the greatest number of persons. There, oceans may be a wonderful aid to health because, in general, extremes of temperature and dryness are rare. These favorable conditions of temperature and humidity are brought by winds from the sea. When land winds cause extreme heat in summer or extreme cold in winter, a sea breeze may arise to moderate the temperature.

The healthfulness of the coast is one of the main reasons why so many people throng to the seashore in summer. Health joins with opportunities for recreation in causing much of our coast to be lined with summer cottages. Because of west winds from the sea, Los Angeles, for example, averages only 70° during July and August, while Yuma, Arizona, 150 miles from the coast, averages 90°. In tropical countries the cooling effect of the sea is less conspicuous. Tropical oceans within 10° of the equator usually have a temperature well toward 80° at all seasons. The main exceptions are northern Peru, where the Humboldt Current from the south cools the water, and the mouth of the Congo in Africa, where the Benguela current performs the same function. Nevertheless, tropical seacoasts have a great advantage because the wind is stronger and more steady than inland. Such winds from the sea temper the constant heat and make people feel more like work. Such air movements also drive away mosquitoes and other insects that are a great menace to health and comfort. Hence the people of equatorial Africa, for example, build their houses along the shore in far larger numbers than elsewhere.

Seacoasts and Recreation, Submerged Coasts. The variety and beauty of seacoasts (Fig. 7-1), and the opportunities for sports such as swimming, sailing, and fishing, join with the climate in attracting visitors and improving health. In Maine, the summer visitor delights in the beauty of a submerged coast. Innumerable deep bays dotted with picturesque rocky islands have come into existence because of the subsidence of the land and the consequent flooding of coastal valleys by the sea. Such conditions tempt one to sail and enjoy their beauty even if he does not care to catch fish which abound in the cold water at these high latitudes. Intervening peninsulas with their coniferous forests and their rugged cliffs worn by the waves tempt the visitor to go on long walks or to sit at the top of a bluff and watch the waves. Materials worn from rocky cliffs on the outer parts of the peninsulas and capes are carried by currents to the heads of innumerable bays and there form little beaches where boats can be drawn up safely.

Emergent Coasts. Farther south in Florida the land has risen and given an emerging coast with its broad sandy beaches. Surf rolls in magnificently to the pleasure of spectators and bathers. Between the levels of high and low tide, the damp beach is so hard and smooth that it offers a good place for automobile races. Many of the world's speed records have been made here. Good harbors are not as numerous as on the submerged coasts of Maine, for emergence has shallowed the water level in Florida's coastal valleys in contrast to the deepening of waters in Maine's subsiding shores. Land has also been rising along the Ohio shores of Lake Erie, since the enormous load of Pleistocene ice has melted because of increasingly warmer climates (Fig. 7–2).

The Ocean as a Purifier. Another important function of oceans is their help in the expensive work of getting rid of sewage in such a way that it will do no harm. In general, sewage is conducted into some neighboring coastal water. If the water is in motion, the sewage is carried away and greatly diluted. In a short time the water purifies itself so that even the most careful analysis fails to show pollution. On seacoasts, especially where there are strong tides, difficulties of disposing of sewage are reduced to a minimum.

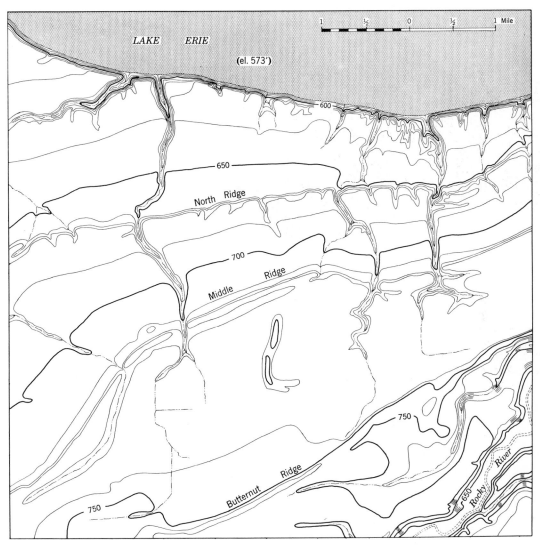

Fig. 7–2   Emerging Shoreline of Lake Erie. Lake Erie, whose present shoreline is located in the northern part of this map, formerly stood higher than at present. Three ridges mark previous higher stands of the water level; Butternut Ridge, the highest, is also the oldest; Middle Ridge and North Ridge mark progressively lower stages of the water mark. The regular outline of the emerging Lake Erie shoreline is in marked contrast to the submerging coast of Figure 7–1. (*Courtesy A. N. Strahler,* Physical Geography, *2d edition, John Wiley & Sons*)

The Ocean as a Storehouse for Minerals

Since about 3½ per cent of the weight of sea water consists of solid mineral matter in solution, the ocean serves as a storehouse of minerals. Every stream and river carries a small amount of dissolved material. Water which reaches the sea is eventually evaporated and goes back to the land, but the mineral matter remains. An average cubic mile of sea water contains 117 million tons of various types of salt, 6 million tons of magnesium, 300,000 tons of bromine, 15 tons of silver, 70 tons of uranium, 450 tons of copper, 900 tons of iron, and 2000 tons of iodine.

Salt. The dissolved material that man takes from the water in largest quantities is salt. On warm, sunny coasts where the water is shallow, large ponds are often banked off by dikes. Here the water evaporates until the salt crystallizes; on the shores of the Mediterranean Sea and on the coasts of Central America and Java, great piles of white salt crystals often form gleaming cones. Most of the world's salt, however, comes from ancient deposits like those of Syracuse, New York, and Stassfurt, Germany, and was laid down long ago in salt lakes whose waters very slowly dried up in the same way that the water of enclosed ponds on the seashore now does. In addition to common salt, or sodium chloride, many other salts can be recovered from sea water.

Limestone. Aside from salts one of the most valuable minerals in sea water is lime. Shellfish constantly use this for their shells. Some shells are thick and heavy like those of clams, oysters, and the great edible abalone of the Pacific Coast of the United States. Others are beautifully branched like many corals. Still others are so small and thin that they cannot be seen by the naked eye. Globigerina ooze, a soft mud which covers large areas of the sea floor, consists of such shells. It would form chalk if converted to stone. Shells have given rise to large deposits of limestone. Long ago the sea once encroached far into what is now the continental interior. Hence, large deposits of limestone are found in most parts of the country. Without them we should be at a loss for lime to make cement and concrete, to make mortar and plaster, to give

the flux so essential in the smelting of iron, and to provide fertilizer needed on many soils.

Potash and Phosphate. Certain other valuable materials, although present in quantities too small to be profitably extracted by man, are taken from the sea water by plants and animals. One of these is potash. A large seaweed called kelp contains so much potash that it is gathered by seacoast farmers as a fertilizer. According to the U.S. Dept. of Commerce, the kelp crop on our Pacific Coast would be worth millions of dollars annually if it could be economically harvested. Another valuable fertilizer, phosphate, is taken from sea water by fish. It is found in their bones and scales and in the guano deposited by birds that live on fish. Millions of tons of guano have been taken from islands off the coast of Peru as fertilizer. It is still accumulating there, for millions of seabirds roost on the islands at night and fly over the sea searching for fish by day.[1]

Fisheries

The presence of plankton and hence of fish in the waters above the Continental Shelf permits coastal people to carry on fisheries as well as occupations of the land. The word "fisheries" has a broad connotation including catching fish like menhaden, salmon, and tuna, the leading commercial fish in the United States during a recent year, as well as gathering shell fish like the oyster and clam, crustaceans like the lobster and crab, and even mammals like the whale and seal. Norway and Japan are examples of countries in which fish form a most important source of food. This is partly because the deeply indented coasts are favorable for navigation. Even more important is the fact that cool parts of the nearby continental shelf, where fish are abundant, offer a better chance to get a living than do the rugged slopes which form a large share of these countries.

Shallow-Water Fisheries. Fisheries may be divided into two classes according to whether

---

[1] In Chapter 17 of *Sail Ho,* Sir James Bisset, the author of this Criterion Books, 1958 publication, gives a good description of Peru's Chincha Islands and their guano deposits. Trade in guano was important in the time of sailing ship dominance of ocean commerce. Student assignment is suggested.

they are carried on in shallow waters near the coast, or in deeper waters out in the open sea or on ocean banks. Many shallow-water fisheries are devoted to exploiting shell fish. Clams, for example, are dug in large numbers at low tide on the New England and Middle Atlantic Coasts. The oyster crop of the Gulf Coast may be dredged from the bottom in water not over 100 feet deep. The lobster, which lives in shallow waters, especially on the Atlantic Coast from Delaware Bay to the St. Lawrence, is so highly prized that the United States has been compelled to pass stringent laws to conserve the supply.

Salmon Fisheries. Shallow water fisheries are concerned not only with organisms such as oysters and lobsters that spend their lives in one locality at the bottom of the sea, but with fish

such as shad, sardine, herring, and salmon. These fish travel long distances in great shoals to reach their feeding grounds, or to find safe places where they may lay their eggs and the little fish may be hatched. By some strange instinct the adult salmon go back to the stream where they were born. If they are prevented from going back they may kill themselves in the attempt, and no more salmon will be found unless the stream is restocked. During the spawning season the lower parts of the rivers that empty into the Pacific from California to Alaska and on to Japan are crowded with salmon. In order that the salmon and sea trout may still reach upper waters and thus keep streams well stocked, large sums have been spent upon fishways. At each great dam on the Columbia River, for instance, fishways (Fig. 7–3) have been built which are somewhat like stairways

Fig. 7–3 Fishway at Bonneville Dam. A fishway may consist of a water-filled lock, channel, or a series of connected pools by means of which fish may swim past a dam or a natural barrier. The photograph gives an upstream view of a fish ladder that aids salmon in reaching their spawning grounds. (*Courtesy Fish and Wildlife Service*)

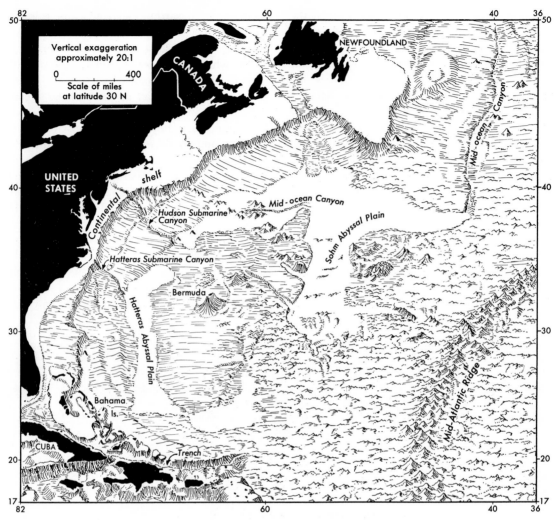

Fig. 7–4   Generalized Sketch of the Western Portion of the North Atlantic Ocean Basin Topography. Notice the broad area of continental shelf, one of the world's great fishing grounds, adjoining Cape Cod, Maine, Nova Scotia, Prince Edward Island, New Brunswick, and Newfoundland. (*Courtesy C. R. Longwell and Richard F. Flint,* Introduction to Physical Geology, *John Wiley & Sons, 1962*)

with sloping steps many feet wide between little waterfalls two or three feet high up which fish can jump easily. Besides migrations by fish because of spawning, they may migrate because of changes in water temperature, salinity differences, pollution of the water, and on account of the movement of their food supply which comes primarily in the form of plankton. Those fish which obtain food along the surface of the water are called pelagic fish, those which feed on or near the bottom of the sea are known as demersal types.

Deep Sea Fisheries. Most deep sea fisheries are centered in banks. These are almost synonymous with continental shelves, portions of the continental masses now submerged to a depth of not more than 200 meters, or 6562 feet; during past geologic time these shallow sea bottoms formed part of the land itself and may do so again (Fig. 7–4).

Continental shelves are of great importance to the fishing industry on account of the shallow depths of water lying above. Because of this shallowness, the sun's rays may penetrate far enough to encourage a plant growth which provides an abundant source of fish food. Furthermore, plant nutrients such as nitrates and phosphorus are more easily available in sea water of slight depth because of the greater possibility of their being carried upward by vertical currents from the floor of the sea. Some of these nutrients may be returned to the surface after organisms which contain them have disintegrated on the bottom or in the deeper water. This factor is of great significance in the production of diatoms, foremost among the primary fish foods of the sea. Rivers issuing from shores contiguous to continental shelf areas also contribute soluble salts that favor the rich plankton life of the shallow sea waters. As a consequence of all these and other influences, the continental shelf, so far as is known, has been more productive of fish food per unit area than the economic province of greater depths. Some of the greatest of world fisheries are found on the continental shelves, not only because they are a natural fish habitat, but also because the mechanics of fishing can be carried on more easily in these shallow seas.

The most productive continental shelves, or banks fishing areas, of the world include those near Newfoundland, those of the North Sea, those near Japan, and those along the North Pacific Coast of the United States and Canada. The European banks lie near countries whose religion encourages large fish consumption, near many lands of dense population, near areas several of which have a submerged shoreline favoring sea activities, near many rugged sections unfavorable to agriculture, and near lands whose forests aided ship building in the earlier days of the fishing industry. Most of these conditions, except that related to religion are found near Japan. The limited domestic animal supply in the Japanese islands impels the Japanese to look to the sea for protein foods. North Pacific and Newfoundland banks fishing is exploited by people from lands characterized by most of the above conditions.

Methods of Banks Fishing. Methods of fishing are influenced by the habits of the fish and the environment in which the fish are found. An example of the ways and means used to catch mackerel—a pelagic fish, one feeding near or at the surface—will serve as an illustration. Mackerel travel in large schools of hundreds of thousands, and as they swim very close to the surface they can be seen from great distances. When a

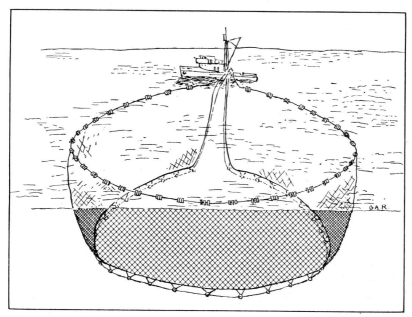

Fig. 7–5 Purse Seine. The purse seine accounts for the major catch of the pelagic schooling species of fish. Seines vary in size according to the size of the vessel, the size of the mesh, the species of fish sought, and the depth to be fished. (*Courtesy John Wiley & Sons, George A. Rounsefell and W. Henry Everhart,* Fishery Science, *1953*)

school is sighted from the masthead or located by the use of sounding devices, crew men of the mackerel ship put off in a boat with a purse seine (Fig. 7–5). As they reach the school, one end of the seine is thrown over. This end is picked up by one man in a dory from the mackerel ship, who keeps the end where it was placed. The purse seine boat moves at full speed, letting out the seine until it has completely surrounded the school with the net, and returns to the dory where both ends of the purse lines, as they are called, are brought into the seine boat and attached to a purser, which is a drum winding the purse line from both directions at once to close the bottom of the seine. The mackerel ship is then brought alongside the two smaller boats, and the catch is taken aboard. Herring, menhaden, and other pelagic fish may be caught in a somewhat similar manner.

Demersal fish, in contrast to the pelagic or surface feeding types, obtain their food on or near the bottom of water bodies; these include cod, haddock, and halibut as well as such shell fish as oysters, lobsters, shrimp, and crab.

The cod has been very important in the economy of New England, adjoining eastern Canada, and now in the waters south of Greenland. Modern codfishing calls for a trawl (Fig. 7–6), or a large, flattened, conical-shaped bag about 150 feet long, made of strong manila twine with a mesh of about 3 inches square in the forward third of the bag, one of 1½ inches square in the central mesh, and one slightly smaller and doubled in what may be called the cod end of the trawl. Steamers tow the bag along the bottom at a rate of about 2 or 3 miles an hour. It literally scoops up everything in its path; later it is drawn to the surface of the water and hoisted to the deck of the trawler. Much of the hazard of the sea is thus eliminated, for all the men remain aboard the powerful trawler, which operates the fishing gear. Operations of trawlers are facilitated by shallow water lying over relatively smooth banks. Obviously to drag such a meshed bag over extremely rugged sea bottom would ruin the equipment.

Oceans as Barriers

From earliest times the ocean has been a barrier, but its importance in this respect is decreasing steadily. For thousands of years the Atlantic, Pacific, and other oceans were such barriers that people never crossed them. This is one chief reason why the native race of men and the species of animals and plants in Australia are so different from those of other continents. This is also the reason why the great land mass on one

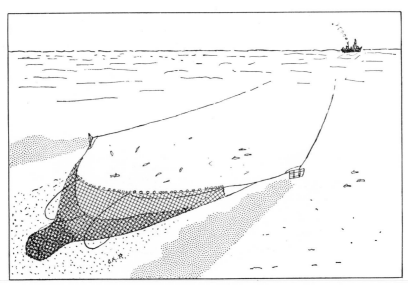

Fig. 7–6 Otter Trawl. The otter trawl is one of several types of trawls in which the water is strained through the meshes of a moving net, leaving the fish in the bag. It is especially useful for demersal fishing. (*Courtesy John Wiley & Sons, George A. Rounsefell and W. Harry Everhart,* Fishery Science, *1953*)

side of the world is called the *Old World,* while the two continents on the other side are the *New World.* Not until 1492, save for sporadic visits, did men of the Old World succeed in crossing the Atlantic barrier to America. They marveled at the Red Men; they found a new grain known as maize, a new vegetable called the potato, a weed which people smoked in pipes, and many other things unknown to them because they had not been able to cross the water.

How effective the ocean barrier may be is illustrated by the life of Napoleon. After he had been conquered by the English, Spanish, and Germans he was sent to the island of Elba as an exile. There, however, the water that separated him from France was so narrow that he escaped from exile and returned to lead his armies once more. Then when he was again conquered, at Waterloo in 1815, he was sent to the little island of St. Helena, separated even from Africa by a barrier of 1200 miles of water and from France by 5000. He could not escape, and so spent the rest of his life there. Like the lighthouse keeper on a rocky island during a storm, he was held in one small place because he had no means of crossing the ocean barrier.

Water as a Defense Against Enemies. Water barriers were as effective in keeping people out as in keeping them in. In prehistoric times some of our ancestors protected themselves by building huts of poles and bark on piles in shallow water near the shores of lakes. The same method may still be seen in New Guinea and in other East Indian Islands. A narrow walk leads from the shore across the water to the huts. Part of the walk consists of a plank that can be lifted from the village side. Thus when a community is gathered in its huts with canoes tied under them and the plank raised, primitive enemies have hard work to approach because of the barrier of water.

The British Isles illustrate the way in which the influence of the geographic environment changes when new inventions are made. Until the airplane was invented, Great Britain was almost like a home on piles with the plank drawn up. It lay close to the coast of the most progressive part of Europe and could communicate freely with the rest of the world when it so desired. Yet it was separated by a narrow body of water which checked invaders who approached uninvited, and obliged them to come in ships and first win mastery of the sea. In primitive times, to be sure, the twenty miles of water between Dover and Calais made England isolated and backward, but later for many centuries the water barrier was of incalculable value. In the later decades of the last century and the first of the present one, when the other great powers of Europe were spending untold millions in preparing vast armies, England was content with only a small army, and saved her money either to develop industries of peace or to build warships. She knew that because of the water no large army of invaders could quickly be landed on her coasts, and even if it were landed, it could not easily be kept supplied with provisions, ammunition, and reinforcements. So much did she value her island position that, after a tunnel under the English Channel was actually begun, the project was abandoned. England did not wish to build an easy entrance to her front door and thus perhaps give an enemy the opportunity to bring in an army. For the sake of safety she proposed to compel those who came to her to come in boats.

When the First World War came in 1914, Germany could do little harm to the island empire, try as she might. Even dirigibles and airplanes wrought only intermittent and local destruction on the English coast and in London. The island as a whole was unaffected. In the end, because England's water boundaries had led her to develop a great navy, she maintained control of the sea, and cut off a large share of Germany's foreign commerce, while she herself was being greatly helped by supplies and ammunition from America and elsewhere. When America was ready to enter the war, British ships carried more than a million of our men overseas.

When the next war began in 1939, however, airplanes had improved so much that Britain's water barriers had lost much of their value. Nothing gave the British such anxiety as fear that German fliers would bomb cities and destroy not only ships but also railroad bridges, factories, and the docks which hold ships at the level of high tide. By that time, safety against air raids demanded a far greater barrier of water such as the whole Atlantic, and now this water barrier has lost much of its historic value for defense.

Aside from Great Britain, other large islands have had the advantage of protection by water. For example, Japan also is located so close to a continent that it has profited by an advantage similar to that of Britain. Japan, to be sure, has the disadvantage of being far from the center of the land hemisphere. On the other hand, her island position has allowed her to develop her civilization without being swamped by barbarous invaders who have again and again entered China from the bleak deserts of Central Asia.

Oceans as Carriers of Commerce

Low Cost of Ocean Transport. Although oceans have served as barriers, they have helped world trade. To carry a ton a mile in the air is expensive, although the rate is decreasing. Cost by rail is far lower, and on oceans this low rate falls still lower. Sea transport costs are far less than on land for several reasons. First, since the ocean is a ready-made highway free to all, ocean transport is not burdened with three classes of expenses that are borne by railroads, buses, and trucks. (a) Tracks must be built for trains and hard surfaced roads for motor vehicles. Costs of these road beds are high and are increasing all the time. (b) Large sums are paid by railroads to maintain the roadbed in good condition. Since tracks wear out, they must constantly be watched by track walkers and repaired by section men. Motor roads, too, need constant supervision and repair. (c) Taxes are another item. Even in good years a railroad pays taxes amounting to a large fraction of its net operating revenue. Trucks and buses do not pay such heavy taxes as railroads, but other taxpayers have to stand the cost of the roads.

Another important advantage of sea transport is that less power is needed by ships than by trains to do the same work. In proportion to the work they do, trucks and buses use more power than trains. Airplanes, of course, use vastly more.

Again, a given load requires fewer men on ship than on a train; and the cost of building a ship is less than that necessary for the construction of trains or trucks capable of carrying an amount of tonnage equal to that of the ship. Moreover, from the point of view of safety, water transport has an advantage. The proportion of passengers lost at sea is less than that on land, and in the number of accidental injuries to employees, the conditions at sea are still more favorable. Every accident does some damage which somebody has to pay for, so that even in this respect transport by water costs less than by land. In the same way trucks and buses have relatively more accidents than trains.

The Tides

The tides not only influence ocean transport by their variability in height, time of occurrence, and other characteristics but also as a result of this variability they bring contrasts in coastal landscapes.

Along the shore at low tide, great stretches of oozy mud flats may invite barefoot clam diggers to wander over them with short handled pitchforks. Elsewhere, acres upon acres of sea grass growing in salt marshes lie flat on the ground; broad sandy beaches are strewn with stranded bits of seaweed, broken shells, and translucent daintily tinted jellyfish; on more rugged coasts, rocks are carpeted with brown seaweed. In coves many small boats lie keeled over where they have been left by the retreating tide. A smell of decay burdens the air. Then the tide turns, and the water rises slowly. After three or four hours, mud flats and weed-strewn rocks are covered, marsh-grass begins to stand erect in the water, fishermen with their nets embark in the boats which are now afloat, bathers appear on sandy beaches, strong currents flow up inlets where previously the water was flowing outward. The whole appearance of the shore suggests life and activity, which reaches a maximum at high tide. Then the sea seems to be brimming full, all signs of death and decay are hidden, and a strong, life-giving odor pervades the air.

The Nature of Tides. The tides are great waves with a length from crest to crest equal to half the earth's circumference. As the wave approaches the shore and reaches shallow water, it behaves like the ordinary small waves seen in any body of water. Its speed decreases; the crest rises and the trough sinks, making the height greater. Height of the earth's tidal wave varies from about 2 feet in the open ocean to 5 or 10 feet on the average shores. Where tides enter narrow bays the increase in height is sometimes impressive, reaching approximately 50 feet at the head of the Bay of Fundy between Nova Scotia and New Brunswick (Fig. 7–7). Very high tides present a serious problem in some of the world's greatest harbors, such as Liverpool, Bristol, and London. At the mouth of the Thames below London the range between high and low tides is 20 feet. At such places basins with great gates have been built so that water can be held uniformly at a high level and the ships will not move up and down against the wharves with every change in the tide. Gates are opened for ships to go out only near the time of high water.

Curiously enough, although the range of the tide is 20 feet at the mouth of the Thames, it is only about 5 feet on the Dutch coast less than 100 miles away. This is because waves of the tide enter the North Sea from two directions— through the English Channel on the south and around Scotland on the north. Tides coming in the two directions move at such rates that in some places they reinforce one another, but elsewhere neutralize one another.

Sometimes a tidal wave forms breakers in the same way as an ordinary wave. This occurs where the tidal wave forces its way into a narrow opening such as the mouth of a river. In the northern mouth of the Amazon River such a tidal bore, as it is called, rushes up the river at the rate of 10 or 15 miles an hour in the form of a breaking, foaming, splashing wall of water 5 to 12 feet high. No small boat is safe in it, and a steamship may be endangered.

Kinds of Tides. Habits of tides in different parts of the world are far from uniform. The largest ocean, the Pacific, has two unequal tides. A narrower ocean, the Atlantic, has two nearly equal tides each day at an average interval of about 12 hours and 25 minutes. Partially enclosed seas, such as those hemmed in by the East and West Indies, together with the Gulf of Mexico and the east side of the Sea of Japan, have only one tide a day. Seas such as the Mediterranean, Baltic, and parts of the Caribbean, as well as the enclosed Arctic Ocean, are practically tideless, or at least have tides that rise and fall less than 2 feet.

Causes of the Tides. Tides are caused by the attraction of the moon, sun, and earth (Fig. 7–8). They occur at regular intervals because of

Fig. 7–7 Ship at Low Tide in Bay of Fundy Harbor. One can see from this photograph the seriousness of shipping problems brought about by great tidal range. While such a tidal range may be a problem for shipping, it can be the basis for significant power production. Recent development of such power near the ancient French town of St. Malo is a good example. Furthermore, Robert Gibrat, active in the St. Malo project, lists about 90 world coastal sites with tidal range high enough to deserve tidal power study. Near the head of this list is the Bay of Fundy. For further information see "Moon Power over St. Malo," *Popular Mechanics,* June 1964.

the rotation of the earth, and the revolution of the moon around the earth. A water surface always places itself at right angles to the pull of gravitation. Since the moon as well as the earth exerts a gravitational pull, the surface of the ocean or any other body of water must place itself at right angles to the combined strong pull of the earth and weak pull of the moon. But the strength and direction of the moon's gravitational pull keep changing, because the earth's rotation, as well as the moon's own revolution around the earth, introduce constant and regular variations. The result is an extremely complicated series of tidal waves moving in all directions according to the part of the ocean that one

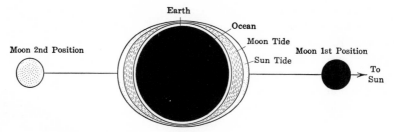

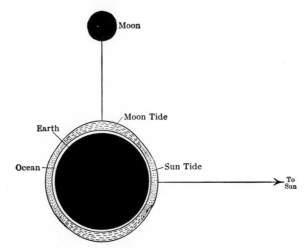

A—The Cause of Spring Tides. Moon and sun act together.

B—The Cause of Neap Tides. Moon and sun act at right angles.

Fig. 7–8   Tides and Their Causes.

happens to observe. Often a tide lags many hours behind the condition of the moon which causes it. In deep bays there may even be two tides at the same time. For example, as a tidal wave progresses up Chesapeake Bay from Old Point Comfort, the shallowness of the bay hinders it so much that, by the time it reaches the head of the bay north of Baltimore, a second tide has entered the lower part of the bay.

The sun causes tides like those of the moon, but in most places not so high. The usual way in which sun tides become apparent is by increasing or decreasing the lunar tides. When moon, earth, and sun are in a straight line at full moon or new moon, the two tides combine so that the high tides are higher than usual and the low tides lower. These are *spring* tides. When the sun and moon are at right angles to one another, they partially counteract one another so that *neap* tides neither rise so high nor fall so low as ordinary tides. The exact time of occurrence of either spring or neap tides varies from place to place, and in some regions may be sev-

eral days before or after the combination of lunar and solar activity which causes them.

The chief practical application of our knowledge of how moon, sun, and earth influence tides lies in the construction of tide and current tables. These calculations depend not only on the relative position of the sun and moon, but also on variations in the height of these bodies above the horizon at noon in different seasons. The tables record such complex relations that they require laborious calculations which are now performed by machines. The information on the tables sums up all the different effects and determines for years in advance how high the normal tide will be in any given place at any given time. Tides have to be separately computed for each port. Those at nearby places can be roughly deduced from those at the principal ports. Alterations in the usual course of tides because of storms and winds, however, cannot readily be predicted. At London, for example, a storm with east winds has been known to make the tide several feet higher than was predicted.

How Tides Improve Harbors. Tides have an important effect upon harbors. Many ship channels such as those of New York, Boston, and Liverpool are kept from silting up by tidal currents that scour them out daily. In many cases where it has not been worth while to dredge channels, tides enable ships to enter harbors which would otherwise be inaccessible; and harbors which would not be deep enough if there were no tides, may admit ocean liners because of depths at high tide.

The Role of Harbors in Water Transport

Transportation on the ocean would be as difficult without harbors (Figs. 7–9 and 7–10) as railway traffic would be without stations and freight yards. A good harbor must furnish (1) *protection* from winds and waves; (2) good *depth* of water in channels and close to shore; (3) abundant *anchorage* room; and (4) plenty of *space for wharves or docks.* A harbor may possess all these qualities, however, and yet not lead to the growth of a great city, as may be seen at Mount Desert in Maine and in the many deep bays that border the coast of Labrador. It needs also (5) abundant *level land* for city building; (6) *easy lines of communications* with the interior, and far above all else (7) *a rich hinterland or back country* in which to sell imported products in exchange for abundant exports.

Fig. 7–9 The Port of San Francisco. The bridge in the distance, upper left, spans the Golden Gate entrance, the best-known and most-significant break in the California coast line. The Golden Gate and the adjoining bays, San Francisco and San Pablo, make up one of the world's best natural harbors. (*Courtesy San Francisco Chamber of Commerce*)

Fig. 7–10   Lightering in the Caribbean. Workers are wading ashore from the lighter and carrying bags of wheat flour, one of the main import food items of the Caribbean region. At many small ports, harbors are so shallow that lightering is necessary. The steamers must anchor far from shore, and the cargo is then transferred to shallow-draft boats.

Why Harbors Need Protection. No matter whether people use primitive canoes or huge modern steamships, navigation is hampered unless harbors are well protected. Islands and headlands break the force of the waves and winds and thus, by preventing boats from being tossed about and perhaps dashed against the shore or against one another, make it easy to load them at all times.

The Constant Demand for Deeper Harbors. For small sailing ships, harbors 10 to 20 feet deep may be suitable. So long as such ships were the largest that sailed the ocean it was possible for a port such as Salem, Massachusetts, with only a shallow harbor, to do more business than Boston, and almost as much as New York. Now large ships are more economical than small ones; some are over 1000 feet long, 100 feet broad, 60 feet from keel to upper deck, and draw as much as 40 feet of water. For such steamers a shallow harbor is useless, no matter how well protected. With the growing tendency to build large ships, ports with deeper channels and better harbors are likely to grow more and more at the expense of those with shallower channels.

The Need for Roomy Harbors. Deep water is needed not only in the channel but also in places not far from shore where vessels can find room to anchor and to turn around. A 1000-foot vessel needs nearly half a mile of free space in which to turn around, even though it has the

help of tugs. Because of the large area required to maneuver modern steamships, a river such as the one which forms the harbor at Savannah is rarely as valuable as a bay along a submerged coast like that of the Atlantic from Norfolk northward, or the Pacific from San Francisco northward.

Dockage Space as a Necessity of a Good Harbor. In bays formed by submergence the long shoreline and deep water close to shore enable wharves to be built, so that steamers can be loaded directly from land. It is expensive when a ship costing millions of dollars has to spend two-thirds of its time in port lying idle while waiting to come up to the wharves; charges for interest, for depreciation, and for obsolescence count up while the wages of the crew also continue. Hence shipowners prefer to send their ships to places where abundant docks and wharves make it possible to receive cargoes directly from warehouses or from trains and trucks which come alongside, so that their loads may be hoisted from the cars to the ship's hold. New York probably has the most extensive docking facilities in the world.

How Land for City Building Affects the Value of a Harbor. If a harbor does much business, it should have a large city beside it. Such a city needs level land, especially for its business sections. Some cities, such as San Francisco have grown great in spite of hills, but those like Philadelphia which have plenty of level land are more fortunate. So necessary is this that in many places shallow bays have been filled to make artificial land. One of the residential sections of Boston is the Back Bay, where once the tide ebbed and flowed. It paid Seattle to spend millions of dollars to cut down a steep hill of gravel in the heart of the city. By means of great streams of water squirted against the hill it was washed into the shallow part of the bay. Thus level land was obtained both by cutting down the hill and by filling the bay. In San Juan, Puerto Rico, marshy land along the shore was filled in with dredged materials from the floor of the harbor; by one action an air field was built and San Juan harbor dredged.

How Lines of Inland Communication Make or Mar a Harbor. A modern seaport can become of much importance when it is served by numerous lines of inland transportation. Along the Pacific Coast for example, the twin ports of San Francisco and Oakland are helped because the combined Sacramento and San Joaquin Valleys enable railways to reach the interior of California easily. Northward to the mouth of the Columbia River, on the other hand, no great city is likely to grow even if there were a good harbor, because high mountains everywhere hinder communication with the interior.

How the Hinterland Determines the Trade of a Harbor. The region tributary to a harbor is called its *hinterland.* The importance of a hinterland depends not only on its size, but much more upon the number of inhabitants and their power to produce goods and to buy them. Pará is a seaport of minor rank, largely because its hinterland, the enormous basin of the Amazon, is sparsely populated and undeveloped. Providence, on the other hand, is also a minor port mostly because the more accessible harbors of New York and Boston limit its hinterland to a small area, mainly in Rhode Island. Even such important places as Boston and Philadelphia have much smaller hinterlands and much less trade than they would have if the many advantages of New York did not draw trade away from them. New York's great advantage lies in the fact that it has not only a magnificent harbor, but in addition a nearly level route inland up the Hudson and Mohawk Valleys (see Fig. 6–2). Moreover, it lies in the very heart of the region where climate, other natural resources, and accidents of historical development bring the activity of America to its highest level.

Concentration of Population in Seaports. The remarkable way in which transportation by water influences the size of cities is shown by an analysis of the site location for the 50 largest cities of the United States. Of the first twenty cities in the United States with a population over one-half million, ten are on the ocean, five on the Great Lakes, three on navigable rivers, and two without water transportation. Of the next twenty between 300,000 and 500,000, four are on the ocean, one on the Great Lakes, four on navigable rivers, and eleven are without water transport. Of the next ten, between 250,-000 and 300,000, five are on the ocean, one on the Great Lakes, and four are without water transport. Not only in the United States, but in all parts of the world, the demands of commerce usually cause the largest cities to be located on navigable water bodies.

QUESTIONS, EXERCISES, AND PROBLEMS

1. Comment upon the influences of oceans upon temperature, precipitation, health, and recreation. What minerals are contained in sea water? Tell of the progress in the desalting of ocean water.
2. How do the habits of the fish and the ocean environment influence methods of fishing? Give illustrations of several types of fishing.
3. Illustrate the barrier nature of oceans. Explain in detail why costs of ocean transport are low.
4. What are the causes of tides? What conditions cause an extremely high tidal range? What are the ideal characteristics of a harbor for successful port development? Apply these criteria to several of the world's great ports. Do water transport facilities influence the size of the world's largest cities? Comment.
5. Identify coastal submergence and emergence, various types of fish migrations, fish ladders, continental shelf, demersal fish, pelagic fish, four of the world's major fishing banks, trawl, spring tide, neap tide.

SELECTED REFERENCES

Abelson, P. H., editorial, "Economic Benefits from Oceanographic Research," *Science,* p. 461, Jan. 29, 1965.

Alexander, Lewis M., *Offshore Geography of Northwestern Europe,* Rand McNally, 1963.

Boehm, G. A. W., "Inexhaustible Riches from the Sea," *Fortune,* Dec. 1963.

Boehm, G. A. W., "The Economic Realities of Water Desalting," *Fortune,* Jan. 1962.

Boxer, Baruch, *Ocean Shipping in the Evolution of Hong Kong,* University of Chicago Press, 1961.

Britton, J. N. H., "The Transport Functions of the Port of Port Kembla," *Economic Geography,* Oct. 1962, pp. 347–58.

Carson, Rachael L., *The Sea Around Us,* Oxford University Press, 1951.

Carter, R. E., "A Comparative Analysis of United States Ports and Their Traffic Characteristics," *Economic Geography,* April 1962, pp. 162–75.

Cousteau, Jacques-Yves, "At Home in the Sea," *National Geographic,* April 1964, pp. 465–507.

Dietrich, Gunther, *General Oceanography,* John Wiley and Sons, 1963.

Helin, R. A., "Soviet Fishing in the Barents Sea and the North Atlantic," *Geographical Review,* July, 1964, pp. 386–408.

Hill, M. N., editor, *The Sea: Ideas and Observations on Progress in the Study of the Seas,* (3 volumes), John Wiley and Sons, 1962 and 1963.

Huxley, Anthony, *Encyclopedia of the World's Oceans and Islands,* G. P. Putnam's Sons, 1964.

Ough, J. P., "The Polar Continental Shelf Project," *Canadian Geographical Journal,* July 1962, pp. 2–13.

Padgett, H. R., "Sea Industries: A Neglected Field of Geography," *Professional Geographer,* Nov. 1961, pp. 26–28.

Rogers, A. L., *The Industrial Geography of the Port of Genova,* University of Chicago Press, 1960.

Sears, Mary, *Oceanography,* 2d printing, 1962, American Association for the Advancement of Science.

Spiegler, K. S., *Salt Water Purification,* John Wiley and Sons, 1962.

Sullivan, Walter, "Charting the Seas: Study of Indian Ocean Aids Understanding of the Earth's Crust," *New York Times,* Science Section, Sunday, April 26, 1964.

Thoman, R. S. and Patton, D. J., *Focus on Geographic Activity,* Chs. 12 and 13, "Long-Distance Trawling out of Hull, England" and "Mother-Ship Whaling Operations," McGraw-Hill, 1964.

Chapter Eight

Inland Waters and Their Human Relationships

The most important inland waters comprise lakes, both salt and fresh, rivers, and canals. Like oceans, these serve as (1) regulators of temperature, (2) sources of moisture, (3) an aid to health, (4) a source of minerals, (5) a source of food, (6) barriers, and (7) carriers of commerce. They also serve as (8) sources of water supply, (9) a source of power, and (10) a means of irrigation and drainage.

Inland Waters as Regulators of Temperature

As regulators of temperature even the largest lakes are of little importance compared with oceans. Yet the southeastern shores of Lakes Michigan and Erie are great regions for grapes and other fruit (Fig. 8–1) because water, which retains the heat of summer in the fall, warms northwest winds and prevents early frosts. Also in spring, lakes retain the low temperature of winter. Thus they keep winds cool and prevent fruit trees from flowering too early and being nipped by frost. Summer heat may also be relieved by cool lake breezes which blow like the sea breezes in the afternoon.

Inland Waters as Sources of Atmospheric Moisture

Although the effect of lakes upon cloudiness and rainfall is small, it may be important in large lakes. At the southern end of the Caspian Sea, the northern slopes of the Elburz Mountains, well watered by rain from this great salt lake, form a striking contrast to the barren deserts on either side. Again, an inland body of water as large as Lake Michigan receives a little more precipitation on its eastern or leeward side (in the belt of the westerlies) than on its western, windward side. It is well to note the difference in lakes and mountains with reference to winds and rainfall. The windward side of a mountain is normally the rainy side, whereas the leeward side of a large lake is likely to be more rainy.

Inland Waters as Aids to Health

When it comes to health and recreation, inland waters take high rank, although they are probably not as important as the ocean. How high they stand is evident from the way in which summer cottages and camps skirt the shores of lakes, ponds, and rivers all over the United States. Few summer resorts are more famous than those around the Rangeley Lakes, in Maine; at Lakes Champlain, George, and Placid, in New York; and along the shores of the Upper Peninsula in Michigan. The Thousand Islands in the picturesque St. Lawrence River are equally noteworthy, as are Lakes Louise (Fig. 8–2) and Tahoe in the western mountains of Alberta and California.

Inland Waters as a Source of Minerals

Inland bodies of water are a source of medicinal salts, iron ore, peat, salt, and potash. Many springs such as those of Saratoga, New York, and Warm Springs, Georgia, are full of dissolved minerals which may have healing quality. Bog iron ore is often deposited at the bottom of swamps. For example, such swamps of glacial origin abound in the sandy region of southeastern Massachusetts. Because of them, that region was the main source of iron ore for the early New England settlers. The first iron foundry in America was established at Saugus, Massachusetts in the 1640's to smelt ore from neighboring bogs. Today bog iron ore is of little importance because the deposits are so small. Swamps also furnish peat, which may be called a half-mineralized vegetable product. Most of the world's coal appears to have been formed in ancient swamps that were part of the earth's inland waters.

Salt lakes also furnish rock salt such as is obtained by leading the water of the Dead Sea into little ponds along the shore and there letting the hot sun evaporate it. Such water also yields rare minerals like potash, which is also found in many little lakes in western Nebraska, and at Searles Lake in southern California.

Inland Waters as Sources of Food

Some larger lakes such as the American Great Lakes and the Great Slave Lake of Canada have important fishing industries; and rivers like the Penobscot and Columbia, where salmon, shad, and sea trout come in from the ocean, support far more fishermen in proportion to their size than do the seas. In Russia, also, the Volga, Don, and other rivers support extensive fisheries. The most famous of these are the sturgeon fisheries, which produce caviar, as the roe, or eggs, of this fish are called. Inland waters of the world's underdeveloped lands are extremely important as sources of food for the native population.

Inland Waters as Barriers[1]

The Mississippi River illustrates many ways in which inland waters serve as barriers. On the map notice how largely this great river forms the boundary between states. This is natural, for the stream is so wide, so deep, and so subject to great floods that it is difficult to cross it in boats, and very difficult to bridge it. Not till 1930 was there any bridge over the main river below Memphis, 500 miles from the mouth; and until 1939 people and trains had to cross by ferry at New Orleans. Even now the lower 1400 miles of the river is crossed by bridges at only a few places. To sum it all up, the chief reason why the Mississippi and other bodies of water are barriers is that they require a change in method

---

[1]The author is not in any way denying the unifying influences of rivers and river valleys upon man and his culture by suggesting that many rivers do form a barrier to surface transport. In fact the need to eliminate such physical transport barriers may be one of many factors encouraging unity between people living on different sides of a river.

or equipment of traveling. A train must run on to a ferryboat, or must make use of an expensive bridge or tunnel; the pedestrian must swim or get a canoe or other boat. Change is what makes the trouble.

How Water Barriers Encourage the Location of Cities. London. Since bodies of water act as barriers, the places where it is easy to cross them are likely to develop into urban centers (Fig. 8–3). This is because roads converge at such places, and people are often obliged to stop there. London is a good example. Ten or more centuries ago, the two most important parts of England were the southeastern corner (Kent, Surrey, and Sussex) and the region between the lower Thames and the curious square-cornered indentation called "The Wash" (Essex, Suffolk, Cambridge, and Norfolk). They were important partly because they were near the European mainland. Still more important was the fact that with favorable topography, soils, and climate, they were the best places for farming, which was then the most important occupation.

Inasmuch as these two best sections were separated by the Thames, the silk merchant, for example, who went from Cambridge to Paris, or the pilgrim who was returning from Rome to Norfolk, was obliged to cross the Thames, or else go around its head. The lower reaches of the river were not easy to cross because the stream widens toward the sea and is bordered by marshes. Hence traffic converged at the lowest point where the stream is narrow and the banks are firm, and there London grew up. The site was where the water barrier could be crossed easily.

Other Cities. Paris with its center on the little islands of St. Louis and Le Cite, where the Seine is easily crossed, is another city whose location was originally influenced by a river acting as a barrier. These islands also served as a stronghold protected by water. In the same way Cairo is located at a point where the Nile begins to divide into the many branches, or distributaries of its delta. Even in ancient times an important ferry was maintained there, since it was easier to maintain one large ferry than several small ones. Chicago's growth in the first favorable location west of the southern end of Lake Michigan is due to the fact that the lake is a barrier as well as a waterway. All road and rail traffic from the North Atlantic States to Wisconsin, Minnesota, and the Dakotas must converge at the lake's southern end. Hence a great railroad center had to grow up there.

The Expense of New York City's Water Barriers. The city of New York, unlike London and Paris, owes its location not so much to water barriers as to excellent water communication with which it is provided. The very water which affords such good means of communication, however, is a hindrance to local communication. This is because New York, with 22 islands within her harbor limits, is a city of islands. Largely because of the island status, vertical travel in the metropolis probably exceeds horizontal. In other words elevators prob-

ably carry more passengers than do all the cars, trains, taxis, buses, and subways combined.

While the city was small, the so-called "rivers" that separate the islands and the mainland caused little trouble. In time, however, the lower end of Manhattan island became thickly covered with buildings. As this went on, the price of land kept rising. When land became extremely valuable people began to try to overcome the difficulty by erecting higher and higher buildings. New York's tallest skyscraper, the Empire State Building with 86 stories towers a quarter of a mile. Some skyscrapers accommodate 15,000 workers. Streets between such huge buildings are like deep canyons (Fig. 8–4).

When the skyscraper type of architecture was being developed as one response to water bar-

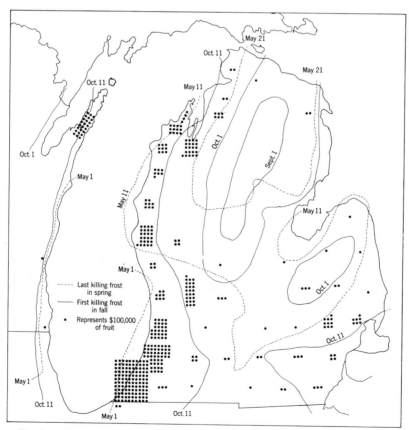

Fig. 8–1   Fruit Production in Western Michigan. Lake Michigan and the westerly winds are significant factors in modifying the climate of western Michigan and in influencing the kinds of crops produced. In a narrow belt along the leeward shore of Lake Michigan, nearly seven-tenths of the total value of all fruit grown in Michigan is raised; and nearly four times that for the entire state of Wisconsin situated on the windward side of the lake. (*Courtesy John Wiley & Sons and G. J. Miller, A. E. Parkins, and Bert Hudgins,* Geography of North America, *1954*)

Fig. 8–2 Lake Louise. This water body lying within the forested snow-capped Canadian Rockies of western Alberta is one of the most beautiful lakes in the world. Lake and mountains attract thousands of tourists each year. Flowers in the foreground grow on the grounds of a large hotel. (*Courtesy Canadian Pacific Railroad*)

riers, ferries were coming into existence as another response. In addition, New Yorkers in their desire to overcome water barriers of their island home have built bridges and tunnels. If the ferries, bridges, and tunnels by which New York overcomes water barriers had to be built anew, they would cost billions of dollars. Although New York harbor is one of the chief causes of the city's progress, the water separating different parts of the city is a most expensive hindrance. San Francisco and the combined city of Norfolk, Portsmouth, and Newport News in Virginia are other cities where water barriers involve great cost and inconvenience.

Inland Waterways as Carriers of Commerce

Inland waterways, including rivers, canals, and lakes are especially important as carriers of commerce, but no single waterway is satisfactory in each of the commercial qualities desired.

Depth and Breadth. If a river comes from a region of heavy rainfall, it is likely to have a great volume and hence be deep enough and broad enough for important traffic. The Amazon is such a river. For a distance of over 2000 miles, its vast volume gives it an average depth of 120 feet and a width of one to six miles. So huge is the river that while still beyond sight of land sailors, not knowing the facts, have actually died of thirst when adrift on the fresh water of the enormously wide mouth of the Amazon.

The Rio Grande illustrates the opposite condition. Although half as long as the Amazon, it is practically unused for navigation. The rainfall of its basin is so sparse that the river has little volume and only slight depth and breadth. Even at its mouth it is shallow, and in its middle portion it sometimes runs dry.

Navigable Length. The length of navigable stretches on a river is of first importance. The Yangtze, for example, is navigable for 1000 miles in one continuous stretch from its mouth far into the heart of China. The Orange River, on the contrary, although about 1300 miles long, is not nearly as valuable for navigation because the stretches where boats can ply extend only for a few score miles. Thus, a waterway is valuable for commerce only if its navigable portions are long and uninterrupted.

Character of Course. Straight rivers like the Amazon, Hudson, and St. Lawrence are far the best for navigation. On winding rivers not only are distances increased, but also the channel is so crooked that little speed can be made and there is danger of running aground. The extremely winding Mississippi meanders so much that after flowing ten or fifteen miles around a horseshoe curve, the stream in some places comes back to within a few hundred yards of its earlier position.

Current. The gentler the current of a river the better it is for navigation. The great Volga River, even at its source, is only 665 feet above sea level, while 1500 miles from its mouth it is

Fig. 8–3 Stratford Upon Avon, Royal Shakespeare Theatre. Stratford Upon Avon is a very famous river town developed originally because of location near a good fording place. Levi Fox, in his book, *The Borough Town of Stratford Upon Avon,* comments as follows: "The name *Stratford,* that is a road or *streat* across a *ford* aptly reminds of the town's origin as a river crossing settlement." In fact there is no historical record of a bridge until 1235; although archeological discoveries indicate that the earliest human occupation belongs to the late Bronze Age. Human activities of this earliest settlement, of people in the early Romano-British village, and of the early Saxon invaders—all these were influenced primarily by the physical environment. But within the last century Stratford economy has been influenced largely by the works of man, one man, William Shakespeare. Today Shakespeare theaters, Shakespeare's birthplace, and all the elements associated with Shakespeare's life and works bring thousands of tourists to the town originally built to take advantage of a useful fording place across the Avon River. (*Courtesy British Travel Association*)

Fig. 8–4 New York's Skyscrapers. Land is so valuable on Manhattan Island that buildings are likely to expand vertically rather than horizontally. (*Courtesy Skidmore, Owings & Merrill*)

only 190 feet above ocean level and 280 feet above the Caspian Sea. Hence throughout most of its course it flows so gently that ships are little impeded and locks and dams are unnecessary. Contrast the Volga with the Brahmaputra, which rises 15,000 feet above the sea and flows so swiftly over rapids and falls that along much of its course no one ever uses a boat.

Seasonal Changes. Practically every river is subject to strong seasonal changes. Floods and droughts are more or less universal, and freezing is common in middle and high latitudes. The rivers most free from floods come from great lakes, as does the St. Lawrence, or receive an abundant supply of rain at all seasons, like the two greatest equatorial rivers, the Amazon and the Congo. However, in contrast to the constant ice-free flow of the latter two rivers, ice in both the St. Lawrence, and in the Great Lakes which feed it, blocks navigation for about five months of the year (Fig. 8–5).

Hinterland. No matter how good an inland waterway may be in other respects, it does not carry much commerce unless a well-populated hinterland supplies raw materials, food, or manufactured goods in exchange for goods brought from afar. Compare the Rhine and the Yukon. The Rhine flows through some of the most densely populated and progressive parts of the world. Hence it carries thousands of boats of all sizes from small ocean steamers and large canal barges down to rowboats. In contrast, the Yukon hinterland is sparsely populated with people who neither consume much nor furnish articles of export in quantities large enough to supply significant cargo.

Direction. The direction in which a large inland waterway extends is an important feature which man cannot control. He can deepen and broaden a river, increase navigable length, and overcome falls and rapids by building canals and locks. He can straighten windings, control the current, overcome effects of seasonal changes, and populate the hinterland; but he cannot change the general direction in which a long river flows. Yet this condition is vital in determining the value of an inland waterway. The Rhine is a relatively small river. Nevertheless, from parts of Switzerland, Germany, and France which are rich in lumber, coal, iron ore, and manufactures, it flows toward the great market represented by the German manufacturing center around Essen and the great cities of Rotterdam, Amsterdam, Brussels, and London. Therefore it supports an incredibly active commerce. The Mackenzie and the Ob are far larger than the Rhine, but in a year they carry about as much commerce as the Rhine does in a day, for they flow toward the frozen Arctic Ocean.

Examples of Great Inland Waterways

The St. Lawrence and the Great Lakes. How do some of the great inland waterways meet the seven requirements mentioned above? The St. Lawrence River and the Great Lakes furnish a broad, deep, and relatively straight waterway penetrating as far as the western tip of Lake Superior, about 1700 miles away from the

Fig. 8–5   Winter Ice on the Great Lakes. One of the main arguments used by opponents of development on the Great Lakes–St. Lawrence Seaway is the fact that ice makes shipping difficult for four or five months of the year. (*Courtesy U.S. Department of Commerce, Weather Bureau*)

Fig. 8–6   The Rhine is a Busy River. The Rhine is probably the world's busiest river and is of great economic significance to nations along its course. This photograph was taken at Duisburg, Germany, and shows barges loading coal from the Ruhr; they are coming from Belgium, France, Germany, the Netherlands, and Switzerland. Duisburg is the largest inland harbor in Europe. (*Courtesy United Nations*)

Pacific Coast. The Lachine Rapids above Montreal, the falls of Niagara, and the Sault Sainte Marie at the lower end of Lake Superior, to be sure, present difficulties. Nevertheless, these have been partly overcome by canals and locks so that ships of 27 foot draft can go from the Atlantic to Chicago or Duluth. Another and a more serious difficulty is that, although seasonal changes have no great effect upon depth of the water, as previously indicated, ice closes the St. Lawrence River and the Great Lakes for several months. Such difficulties, however, are much more than outweighed by the wonderful hinterland, which includes the rich farmlands of the Corn Belt, large iron deposits near Lake Superior, immense coal mines of Pennsylvania, and the busy manufacturing region from Buffalo to Milwaukee. Thus the waterway extends in the right direction to connect regions producing food, raw materials, fuels, and manufactured goods (see Fig. 1–8).

Excellent Waterway of the Rhine and German Canals. The system of inland waterways,

of which the Rhine (Fig. 8–6) is the main artery, owes its importance to its hinterland and its direction. Because the Rhine flows through an extremely populous and progressive region and toward the center of the world's activities, Germans and Dutch have found it worth while to deepen and broaden it; to increase its navigable length by canalizing certain parts; to straighten out windings; to provide cables to pull ships up through strongest currents; and to make provision for the regulation of floods. To take further advantage of this good waterway, Germans have built many canals to connect the Rhine with the Weser, the Elbe, and other rivers farther east. Canals greatly enlarge the hinterland and enable traffic to move east and west as well as more nearly north and south along the line of main rivers. Canal building was made easy by old east-west trending glacial stream courses, remnants of a time when major north-flowing streams were forced to parallel the front of the glacier for long distances before emptying into the sea. The Rhine and the German canals illustrate the tendency of commerce to aim straight at the most thickly settled industrial regions.

The Superior Inland Waterway of the Yangtze. The Yangtze fulfills conditions of a good waterway to a remarkable degree. It is so broad and deep that even with little artificial improvement ocean steamers of several thousand tons can usually reach Hankow about 700 miles from the coast. In this stretch, windings are not particularly troublesome, and the current is negligible, for the river falls only about an inch per mile. Although floods raise the river forty or fifty feet at Hankow, they do not seriously hinder traffic. In fact, for these 700 miles, advantages for navigation are little inferior to those of the Amazon, while the hinterland is far superior. Above Hankow, small steamers can go another 300 miles to Ichang, where the river is still only 130 feet above sea level. There the rapids intervene for 350 miles. In spite of rapids, so large is the river, so excellent its direction, and so rich and populous the Szechuan hinterland that for hundreds of years Chinese workers on the river bank laboriously dragged junks over the rapids. The stream is again navigable beyond them.

For nearly 2000 miles the Yangtze flows through a region with a dense population about as large as that of the Western Hemisphere. If ever these people should become as productive and prosperous as those in the Rhine and St. Lawrence hinterlands, ships might pass as frequently as at the Straits of Dover. The direction of the Yangtze is ideal, for the river runs through the heart of the most fertile part of China directly toward the part of the coast where the greatest cities are located and where trade is most active. The importance of the stream is increased by large navigable tributaries, the chief of which joins the main stream near Hankow, and by the Grand Canal, which connects the mouth of the river with Tientsin and the great cities of the Hwang Valley. Contrast this with the slight navigation of the Indus because of its shallow channel and swift course and because it flows out of huge mountains into a desert.

An Appraisal of the Mississippi Waterway. In proportion to its size and length, the Mississippi River is used less than the St. Lawrence, Rhine, or Yangtze. This may seem surprising in view of certain advantages of the river. The channel has a depth of 9 feet to St. Louis, 1270 miles from the mouth, whereas the Rhine has an equal depth only a quarter as far, to Mainz. Length of the Mississippi is an advantage; with the Missouri it is one of the longest rivers in the world. The river's current, though rapid in places, is also comparatively favorable; for south of St. Louis the river falls only 4 inches a mile and the heavier traffic is downstream. Finally, the hinterland includes the most fertile parts of the United States.

Against these advantages stand several disadvantages. Two of these are a very winding lower course and seasonal floods. A more important disadvantage, however, still remains in the insurmountable drawback that the river lies at right angles to main lines of traffic and does not flow toward eastern manufacturing districts and Europe, which are the great markets for food and raw materials of its rich hinterland.

The Value of a Large Water Supply

One of the most valuable functions of inland waters is the use for domestic, municipal, and industrial purposes. In fact the water required for daily living in the United States weighs more than 100 times as much as all other materials consumed including food, fuel, gravel, lumber, metals, plastics, sand, and stone. In the United States, water is usually obtained so easily, by simply turning a faucet, that people do not realize its importance unless there is a drought such as occurred in the early 1930's, in 1939, and in the early 1950's. In the early 1930's Dust Bowl conditions occurred on the Great Plains and the region suffered a major disaster. In 1950 and in 1963, restrictions on the use of water in New York City brought home the importance of an adequate water supply to every New Yorker as well as to people visiting the city. During this shortage no water was served with meals in restaurants and hotels unless it was requested by the customer. In 1953 nearly one third of United States 200 cities with a population above 50,000 experienced water shortages.

In spite of these periodic regional droughts, there is now no general national water shortage, and the 30 inch average annual precipitation for the country as a whole is adequate. But many authorities worry about the future and emphasize the need for conservation; among other things, they point to the fact that while our population has doubled since 1900, the use of water has quadrupled.

Most of the water for domestic, municipal, and industrial purposes comes from surface waters. In 1955, 91 per cent of the industrial water supply procured by industries themselves came from streams and lakes. In contrast, ground water furnished three times as much domestic supply as surface water in the rural areas; however, ground water contributes only about 20 per cent of the water withdrawn for public supply, rural, self-supplied industrial, and irrigation.

What Kind of Water Supply Is Needed

Quality of a water supply is as important as its quantity. Every up-to-date city employs skilled engineers not only to determine the best sources of water and the best means of protection against contamination but also to construct purifying works if necessary and to test water continually for harmful impurities. Major requisites of a good water supply include several freedoms: freedom from mud, freedom from taste and smell, freedom from chemical impurities, and freedom from bacteria.

A little mud is harmful chiefly because it does not look attractive. This is a major reason why cities build settling basins where water stands for hours and drops its load of silt. Sometimes, however, even a prolonged period of quiet will not cause the finest clay to settle, and some of the wholesome water supplies are a little cloudy.

Neither unpleasant taste nor smell necessarily indicates that the water is unwholesome. Nevertheless, since both are disagreeable, and since either may indicate that the water is bad, cities go to great expense to get rid of them, either by filtration or by chemical treatment.

Some chemical impurities reveal themselves by their taste or smell. A large number, however, such as the lime that causes hardness, do not make the water disagreeable, while some—such as iron—that produce both taste and smell may be beneficial. Lime is the most common chemical impurity of water and the hardest to eliminate. When hard water is used in boilers, it causes the deposition of a limy cake on the inside of the boiler and soon ruins it. In man's body, it

may increase the susceptibility to certain diseases. When hard water is used for washing, it does not form a good lather easily, and special kinds of soap are needed. Yet such water may be sparkling and clear, without odor, and with an excellent taste. In general, the central part of the United States has the surface water areas with the greatest amount of dissolved calcium, and the East coast and Pacific Northwest are notable as areas with unusually soft surface water.

Freedom from bacteria is the most important quality of a water supply. Water that is ideal in other respects may contain germs of typhoid fever, dysentery, and other diseases. Even though water seems to have become perfectly clear and has no mud, taste, odor, or chemical impurities, disease germs may still live and do vast harm. In Europe, for a long while, the prevalence of disease germs in the water supply of many places was one reason why wine and beer were used so extensively. In practically all American cities, however, and in most of those of Europe, the water supply can now be drunk with safety. On the contrary, in several countries, especially in the rural parts of Africa, South America, and Asia disease germs still may be abundant in the water. There people have found by long experience that the best way to get rid of bacteria is to boil the water, a lesson which people should remember when obliged to use doubtful supplies of water where such diseases as typhoid and dysentery are common.

How a Water Supply Is Procured and Distributed

Primitive Methods. The simplest way of getting a water supply is to dip it from a stream, spring, or lake by hand. In countries such as Jordan, Iran, and Egypt one can see scores of women walking gracefully to the stream or the fountain with earthenware jars poised on their heads or shoulders. In the same areas and in other underdeveloped lands, men with plump goatskin bags on their backs or driving barrel-shaped little donkey carts bring water from the river and fill big earthenware pots that stand in a shady corner of the courtyard.

Ordinary Wells. Among rural people wells are the most common source of water. This is because the soil and solid rock everywhere are saturated with water below a certain depth. The varying level at which permanent water is found is called the *water table*. This table may be only a few inches below the surface in swamps, but generally a few hundred feet below in deserts. To make water available at all times, a well must penetrate below the lowest level to which the water table falls in dry seasons. The chief difficulty with most wells is to raise water to the surface. Now primitive methods using hand and animal power are fast being replaced by machinery. The simplest machine for drawing water is the hand pump, but pumps run by animal power, wind, or gasoline are used in many places. Use of such pumps may lead to building tanks or reservoirs, and this makes it easy to have running water in the house at all times.

Artesian and Driven Wells. Use of machinery has made it possible to drill wells to great depths. Artesian wells (Fig. 8–7) are those in which the well penetrates to porous layers of rock lying between impervious ones. Layers must be tilted sufficiently so that considerable areas of the porous layer are exposed at the surface at a level above that of the bottom of the well. These areas receive rain that seeps slowly along in the porous layer and fills it completely not only at the surface, but also in its deeper portions far away. When a well penetrates into this deeper portion, the pressure of the water all through the porous layer causes the water to rise in the well.

Artesian wells are especially important in dry regions such as the Sahara, where they support many small oases. There, deep sources are tapped for water derived from rain that falls upon mountains many hundreds of miles away. Kharga and other oases in the Libyan portion of the Sahara, west of the lower Nile, are supported by springs that are natural artesian wells. There the wind may have scoured deep depressions in the solid rock, and water flows out where they reach an artesian layer. In America, water for livestock and human use may be obtained from deep wells, many of them reaching the Dakota sandstone, a water-bearing stratum outcropping over thousands and thousands of square miles on the Rocky Mountains and the Black Hills. This stratum underlies large parts of Saskatchewan, the Dakotas, Wyoming, Montana, Kansas,

and Nebraska. The first well was drilled into the aquifer in 1882; since that time more than 15,000 have been drilled.

City Water Systems. Sources of city water are various. Some cities like Pittsburgh pump water from rivers and must spend much money in purifying water and in lifting it high enough to supply the hilly parts of the town. Others such as Chicago, get water from lakes close at hand and have the same problem of purification and pumping, although the cost of pumping is slight because the city lies so close to lake level. Chicago's main problem is not the physical process in getting and distributing lake water, but it is in court fights with other lake districts over the enormous amount of water taken by Chicago. The case has even become an international problem with Canada objecting to Chicago's so-called water steal. New York's Ashokan Reservoir lies among the Catskill Mountains 85 miles from the city, and its water is brought to New York by a great aqueduct that goes under the Hudson River in a deep tunnel. Now New York is reaching still further to obtain water from the Delaware River.

Boston, in the same way has constructed the largest lake in Massachusetts in order to use the water of the Quabin branch of the Con-

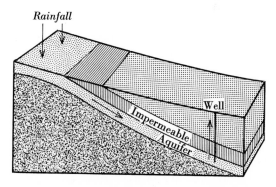

Fig. 8–7   A Simple Artesian System. A permeable sandstone layer (aquifer) outcrops on the left and absorbs precipitation, which descends along the sandstone sealed in beneath a capping layer of impermeable rock. A hole bored down into the aquifer, farther down its slope, becomes an artesian well. For an orientation to an actual situation, consider the area where rain is falling as Dakota sandstone outcropping on the Rocky Mountains and the well located in the North Dakota section of the Great Plains region to the east. (*After C. R. Longwell, A. Knopf and R. F. Flint, Physical Geology, 3d ed., John Wiley & Sons, 1948*)

necticut River. Water goes under the hills north of Worcester in one of the world's great tunnels, 26 miles long. San Francisco has also driven a huge tunnel under the neighboring Coastal Ranges to bring water from high mountain reservoirs along the Hetch Hetchy River. Los Angeles, located in a region where there is a long dry season, has to bring its water much farther than New York does. Among other sources, it taps the Owens River on the east side of the Sierras at the foot of Mt. Whitney, and brings water under the Sierra Nevada Mountains in a tunnel. This aqueduct, about 250 miles long, is one of the largest in the world, but Los Angeles wants still more water; and is now bringing it from the more distant Colorado River.

Cities also get water from artesian and driven wells. Although London gets its supply chiefly from the rivers Thames and Lea, it likewise has a huge system of artesian wells driven into the underlying chalk. So numerous are these wells, and so great the demand of London for water, that the water table has been lowered over a large area. Many similar examples could be cited.

One of the most unusual methods of getting a water supply is that of Aden. The city is located in a region so dry that fresh water is very scarce. Hence the best method has been to piece out the meager supply with distilled sea water. Fuel for distillation must be brought in from a distance, and the treatment of sea water in the early 1960's is a costly process. Still more unusual is the method long employed at some of the nitrate ports on the desert coast of northern Chile and even on the island of St. Thomas, one of the United States Virgin Islands. There water has been brought in by steamer on many occasions.

Water for Industry. Industry in general is urban in its location, and in the United States it is common practice to use city water; for example, in 1955 industrial concerns used over thirty per cent of the public water supply. However, 95 per cent of industrial water is self-supplied.

Industrial water may be used for many purposes; these include thermal generation of electric power, cooling, as a solvent, a raw material, a diluent, a waste carrier, a carrier of powdered coal, and for flotation and energy transfer. The amount of water used for some factory products is enormous: 65,000 gallons are necessary for the production of each ton of steel; 365,000 gallons are consumed in producing a ton of rayon yarn; and a million gallons are used to produce 1000 gallons of aviation gasoline. Nevertheless, much of the water used by industry is reused. While the average reuse may be no more than 25 per cent, most paper plants reuse over 50 per cent, and many petroleum products plants reuse as high as 98 per cent.

Irrigation

Irrigation (Fig. 8–8) is needed in many climatic regions—the Wet and Dry Low Latitudes, Low and Middle Latitude Deserts, Mediterranean Lands, and the Monsoon Countries all need it. In fact, wherever there is a dry season, especially if the weather is warm at that time, irrigation is an enormous advantage. In the Indian subcontinent except in the south, all the millions of people who depend directly upon agriculture would practice irrigation if they could, because they have a long and warm dry season. Even though the supplies of water are limited, about a fifth of the cultivated land is irrigated. In China a similar condition prevails. In the south, although some rain falls in winter, irrigation is a great help and is practiced wherever possible. In the north, where rains do not begin until May or even June, the farmer who can lead water to his fields is fortunate. The same can be said of Korea, where droughts may do much damage.

In the Mediterranean type of climate characteristic of southern California, Chile, parts of Australia, southwest Africa, and especially around the Mediterranean Sea, irrigation is widespread; and in deserts and dry continental interiors, there is a similar need for irrigation of agriculture. How often geographers have stated that Egypt is the Nile! Probably more than half of all the world's farmers need irrigation and practice it where possible.

In continental United States, the 17 western states have 94 per cent of the nation's irrigated land but only 25 per cent of the annual national precipitation. Leaders in irrigation among the 17 are California, Texas, Idaho, and Wyoming.

About three-fourths of the irrigation water comes from streams and lakes, with wells and springs accounting for most of the remainder.

Of the total water taken for irrigation in a recent year, approximately one-fourth was lost by evaporation and seepage on the way to the farm. But irrigation water lost by seepage is not entirely useless, because after sinking into the ground it may return to wells and once more enter irrigation ditches.

The Origin of Crop Agriculture. Looking back into very ancient history one origin-theory credits irrigation along the Nile, Euphrates, Indus, and Hwang rivers for the beginnings of crop agriculture. At this time, primitive man had no metal tools; and his stone implements were arrowheads, scrapers, grinders, and other tools for hunting, preparing skins, or grinding

wild seeds. Suppose he observed that certain seeds such as wheat and barley are good to eat and can keep a long time. The idea of saving seed and planting it may have come into his mind as the result, perhaps, of some accident. Under what kind of environment would this idea prove fruitful? Not in the shade of a forest; not in a prairie where every square inch is crowded with plants already; and not on a sea beach where the salt will kill the wheat. A flood plain is the place which may have encouraged such an idea. Each flood leaves tracts of bare mud in some places. Seeds need merely be scattered there, and they will grow. The ground remains moist a long time, for the level of the river and of ground water falls slowly. Other

Fig. 8–8 Irrigation Farming. The farmer uses small siphons to irrigate individual rows on his farm near Grand Junction, Colorado. (*Courtesy United States Department of Agriculture*)

plants may not choke the seed, for they may not start soon enough. So according to the flood plain theory, the primitive farmer could sow his seed, go off to hunt or gather wild seeds, and at length come back to find his wheat ripe and ready for harvest.

But the flood plain story, long accepted by many, now is receiving competition from another theory which may be generalized as follows. Somewhere in the Middle East ten to fifteen thousand years ago, primitive man observed that a common plant which he had collected for eating was growing where he had previously spilled some seeds—maybe on the upland, the hill slope, or the lowland. After he had thought about this incident and talked it over with his family and friends, they may have decided that this spot where wheat or barley was growing profusely had some magic about it. After a few years more of planned crop planting on the magic acres, he and his family may have decided to become primitive sedentary farmers instead of nomadic hunters of game and collectors of plants; and thus sedentary agriculture may have come into being in any one of several places of the Middle East.

Irrigation May Encourage Civilization. Just as irrigation may have been significant in the early stages of crop agriculture, this type of farming may have contributed to man's advances toward higher civilization in several ways: (1) only sedentary peoples are successful in irrigation agriculture. Thus, every improvement that such people make in their fields and homes is a more or less permanent value and stimulates them to do more; (2) such people have to learn forethought, for otherwise their ditches and dams will not be ready, and their crops will not grow. They also learn industry, for they cannot put off their work. If water is led on to fields too late or allowed to remain too long, there will be a poor harvest. Forethought and industry are at the base of all advances in civilization. (3) Irrigation also promotes civilization by teaching people to live in peace. They soon realize that if anyone begins to tamper with the water, all the rest may suffer serious loss because their own crops may be left dry. Hence strict laws are passed, and public opinion usually enforces them sternly. (4) Irrigation also helps to teach self-government. For example,

in parts of northern Italy, the users of water from a given ditch meet and elect representatives to represent all who are supplied by one large canal. Each village plans what crops it will raise; then the water is divided according to the needs of each.

Irrigation Gives Special Advantages to Agriculture. The farmer in irrigated regions enjoys certain distinct advantages: (1) Although the soil of dry regions may be deficient in humus, it is rich in other plant foods. The low precipitation carries away few of the soluble ingredients. (2) In addition to plant food in the original soil, new food may be provided from muds in the irrigation water. This serves as fertilizer. (3) Since the sun shines much of the time, growth is rarely hindered by cool cloudy weather. (4) Plants do not suffer from drought or from too much rain, for they can be given as much or as little water as is needed. (5) Fruits grown on irrigated lands can be dried easily. (6) Hay and grain ripen perfectly and can be harvested without getting wet. In rainy lands vast quantities may be spoiled by rain at harvest time.

Water Power

Bases for Power. The two basic conditions for potential water power are rugged relief to provide sufficient head or slope and ample well distributed precipitation to furnish water. If the rainfall is seasonal, lakes or reservoirs will give more consistent stream flow. However, the presence of these conditions may not assure actual development because (1) A cheap competing source of power such as coal, oil, or natural gas may discourage new power development; (2) The location of the potential water power site may be too far from market; but improvements constantly are being made in long distance power transmission over wires without serious loss of original voltage. Such losses plagued earlier hydroelectric developments. (3) The availability of sufficient local raw materials that can be processed profitably into the finished product may influence the change from potential to actual water power; (4) Hydroelectric installations have been most numerous in countries showing greatest industrial progress; or in underdeveloped areas assisted by technicians and capital from such progressive states.

World Distribution of Water Power.
Among the continents, Africa has the greatest
hydroelectric potential (Fig. 8–9). Broadly
speaking, continental surface features are dominated by a huge plateau complex bordered by
a narrow coastal plain. Abundant rainfall in
equatorial sections encourages large rivers, and
these streams have their greatest volume where
they drop from the edge of the African Plateau
to the bordering coastal plain. Thus land forms
and surface water combine to give Africa more
than one third of the world water power potential. In the decades of the 1950's and 1960's,
there has been a faster tempo of changing potential into actual with the help of European and
American capital and technology. These
changes are occurring on the Nile, the Volta, the
Congo, the Zambezi, the Orange, and on other
African streams.

South America and Latin North America also

have great potential. For example, most of the
huge Amazon Basin lies in the climatic belt of
the doldrums and receives heavy rainfall; but
the land forms of the Basin are not as favorable
as those of Africa. Both surface features and
precipitation are more favorable along Brazil's
coastal escarpment; and most of the country's
hydroelectric installations are there. Also terrain
and rainfall give significant potential in southern Mexico, along Central America's Atlantic
coast, in southern Chile, and on South America's northwest coast. But little of the potential
has been changed to actual. Moreover, two of
the world's greatest water falls, British Guiana's
Kaieteur and the Iguazu, along the borders of
Brazil, Argentina, and Paraguay, both await
hydroelectric development.

Precipitation in Europe and Anglo-America
is not generally as heavy as in equatorial Africa
and South America, but many surface features

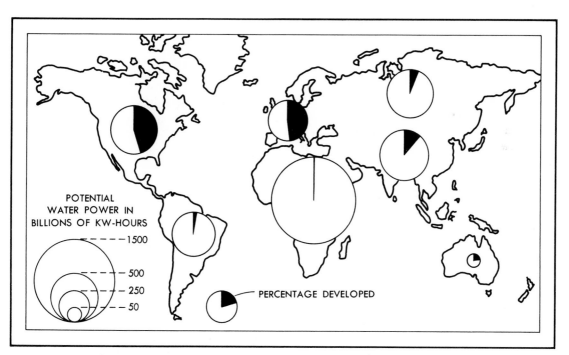

Fig. 8–9 The Continents and Their Water Power: Potential and Developed. As you
look at this map, recall the land forms, rivers, lakes, climatic controls, and climatic
elements of Africa, all of which are largely responsible for the continent's enormous
water power potential. Consider also the history, material progress, and other characteristics of the population, a combination which may aid in understanding the
extremely small amount of Africa's developed water power. Then follow the same
procedure in studying the background for potential and developed water power in
each of the other continents. (*Courtesy E. Willard Miller and* The Journal of Geography,
Sept. 1959)

are ideal. Europe's Alps and North America's Appalachians and Western Cordillera all give proper terrain. Moreover the original rugged surfaces have been made more useful by Pleistocene glaciation. This great ice flow contributed thousands of lakes that make stream flow more consistent; and the ice rasp gave many hanging valleys among the European Alps and America's Western Cordillera.

After the United States and Canada, which lead the world in installed hydroelectric plants, Europe has several countries which stand high among world producers. These include Austria, France, Germany, Italy, Norway, Sweden, Switzerland, and the U.S.S.R. Note that all of these nations except Germany and Russia have limited coal resources—and England, with ample reserves, is not included among the group.

More than half of the United States potential water power lies in the five states of California, Idaho, Montana, Oregon, and Washington. Great federal power developments of the West include the Bonneville, Chief Joseph, Grand Coulee, Hoover, McNary, and Shasta dams; but in spite of larger potential of the West, the great power market of the East has encouraged greater actual hydroelectric development there than in the West.

Asia has suitable land forms for water power development over wide areas; but the continent's precipitation is far from ideal. Deserts and steppes cover enormous sections, and this continent with the largest area of monsoon climate possesses marked contrasts in seasonal precipitation. These and other conditions hold back actual hydroelectric development.

Japan leads in Asian water power development. Over 80 per cent of the land is mountainous, with more than adequate precipitation and with less than national requirements in coal reserves. In the Bratsk manufacturing area of Asiatic Russia's Baikal Region, the Angara River offers huge resources of hydroelectric power; and since 1963, Bratsk has been the largest single hydroelectric producer in the world according to the Russians.

Australia, like Asia, has land forms suitable for hydroelectric development, but distribution and amount of precipitation lack much to be desired. New Zealand, more than a thousand miles to the south, has surface features just as favorable as those of the island continent, and

the rainfall is far heavier and more evenly distributed throughout the year. Little of the potential has been changed to actual in either country.

Floods

Sizable floods (Fig. 8–10) have swept down the streams of all the continents for thousands of years, but flood damage has plagued modern man more and more as the centuries pass by. In the United States, for example, rivers out of their banks caused little or no loss to the Indian civilization because most villages were located above the lowlands. In contrast, man in modern cities builds industrial districts, railroad yards, highways, warehouses, and mills near the stream. When floods come, the river climbs into buildings, houses, and mills, many of which are ruined.

Man has done other things to increase flood damage. He has cut forests, and in many instances failed to replant them; his paved city streets and roads afford quick runoff for rain; he has plowed hillsides carelessly; smoke and fumes from home and factory have denuded hillsides; and large areas have been covered with buildings whose roofs are no check to runoff of rainfall. In 1955, drenching rains from Hurricane Diane caused over a billion dollars damage to urban districts in New England, most of which lay too close to river banks. Local and national action for flood control is needed throughout the world.

INLAND WATERS AND THEIR ASSOCIATION WITH RELIGION

The association of rivers with man's religion is one of the best known of human relationships. The Jordan (Fig. 8–11) provides a good example, for the name appears scores of times in the Bible. Jordan is mentioned early in the Old Testament with the selection of the river valley by Lot as a grazing place for his flocks; and it is mentioned numerous times in the new testament throughout the history of Christ's ministry.

In many of the hymns and spirituals of the Christian Church, the Jordan River has a special place and a definite significance. Millions of people are familiar with the song that goes, "Deep River, My Home is Over Jordan"; and the crossing of the Jordan is a Christian symbol for finding peace and a spiritual home.

Another river closely associated with man's religion is India's Ganges. According to the Hindu religion it was at the junction of the Jumna with the Ganges that the god Brahma made preparation to create the world. Allahabad, located at this junction, and Benares, another city along the Ganges have hundreds of temples overlooking the river. Bathers constantly crowd the banks at these sacred cities and funeral parties spread ashes over the hallowed waters. It may be recalled that in 1964 the ashes of Jawaharlal Nehru were scattered over the Ganges at its junction with the Jumna. This act was carried out in conformance with a last request of India's famous prime minister.

Finally, mention may be made of the Nile, for ages one of the most sacred of rivers. I recall with interest, the veneration which even modern Egypt holds for the well known stream. During the early 1950's, when I accompanied a group of college students on a field trip from Cairo to Helwan, I warned my class to take along canteens of pure city water and not to drink from the waters of the Nile. Several took the canteens, but several also drank directly from the river; for natives still believe that water from the Nile will give strength and vigor to man and will help him spiritually as well as physically.

Fig. 8–10   Serious Flood Damage of Rampaging River. Hazard, Kentucky, lies in the narrow valley of the North Fork of the Kentucky River and was inundated by floodwaters during March, 1963. Other cities such as Louisville, Kentucky, and Cincinnati, Ohio, have suffered millions of dollars damage from Ohio River floods on many occasions. (*Courtesy* Louisville Courier-Journal, *photograph by Billy Davis* ©)

Fig. 8–11 The Jordan River. One of the most sacred spots for the Christian World is Makhadet al Hajla, or the Ford of the Partridge, where St. John baptized Jesus. This peaceful shaded bend of the river has been a goal of thousands of pilgrims. They come here to get a bottle of the precious water or to bathe in the famous stream. Some bathe in the river fully clothed and take home these garments to be worn when they are buried. (*Courtesy Arab Information Center and Jordan Tourist Authority*)

QUESTIONS, EXERCISES, AND PROBLEMS

1. How do inland waters influence temperature, precipitation, atmospheric pressure, winds, health, and food supply? Describe the barrier nature of inland waters and give many illustrations to stress the points you make.

2. List the characteristics of a river that will make it most useful as a carrier of commerce; apply these ideal characteristics to several of the world's major inland water ways. Comment upon the historical changes in the levels of the Caspian Sea.

3. Point out the most desirable qualities of an urban water supply. Describe several methods of obtaining municipal and industrial water requirements.

4. In what climatic regions is irrigation needed to improve agriculture? Comment on the amount and distribution of developments in each region. Did irrigation promote civilization? If so, How?

5. What are the bases for water power, both potential and developed? Where are the greatest installations? Where is the greatest potential? What are the causes of floods? How can man eliminate some of their disastrous effects?

SELECTED REFERENCES

Abelson, P. H., editorial, "Water for North America," *Science,* p. 113, Jan. 8, 1965.

Arab Information Center, "The Jordan River," *The Arab World,* March-April 1964, p. 15.

Bardach, John, *Down Stream: A Natural History of the River,* Harper and Row, 1964.

Behre, Charles H. Jr., "Our Most Important Mineral—Water," *Focus,* Jan. 1957.

Bradley, Charles C., "Human Water Needs and Water Use in America," *Science,* Oct. 26, 1962, pp. 489-91.

Burton, Ian and Kates, R. W., "The Floodplain and the Seashore: A Comparative Analysis of Hazard-Zone Occupance," *Geographical Review,* July 1964, pp. 366-85.

Dahlberg, R. E., "The Concord Grape Industry of the Chautauqua-Erie Area," *Economic Geography,* April 1961, pp. 150-70.

Fox, Levi, *The Borough Town of Stratford Upon Avon,* Corporation of Stratford-Upon-Avon, 1953.

Hendricks, E. L., "Hydrology," *Science,* March 1962.

Laidly, W. T., "Submarine Valleys in Lake Superior," *Geographical Review,* April 1961, pp. 277-83.

Lewis, Robert A., "The Irrigation Potential of Soviet Central Asia," *Annals of the Association of American Geographers,* March 1962, pp. 99-114.

Michel, Aloys A., "The Canalization of the Moselle and West European Integration," *Geographical Review,* Oct. 1962, pp. 475-91.

Revelle, Roger, "Water-Resources Research in the Federal Government," *Science,* November 22, 1963, pp. 1027-33.

Thoman, R. S. and Patton, D. J., *Focus on Geographic Activity,* McGraw-Hill, 1964, Chs. 18, 29, and 30, "A Hydroelectric Plant on the Susquehanna River"; "Volga River Transportation: Problems and Prospects"; "Recreational Resources of Ontario's St. Lawrence Frontier."

U. S. Department of Agriculture, *Water, The Yearbook of Agriculture,* 1955.

Weather Bureau, U. S. Dept. of Commerce, "Ice Reporting on the Great Lakes," *Washington Weather Map,* March 25, 1964.

Wolman, M. G. and Leopold, L. B., "River Channel Patterns: Braided, Meandering, and Straight," *Geological Survey Professional Paper, 282-B,* U. S. Geological Survey, 1957.

Wood, Donald S., "The New Volga: A Soviet Transformation of Nature," *Journal of Geography,* Feb. 1963, pp. 49-56.

Chapter Nine

World Distribution of Natural Vegetation

The reader may remember that in the beginning chapter attention was called to the way man has changed the face of the earth greatly by changing its natural vegetation. Such alterations, both destructive and constructive, cover millions of square miles. The constructive activities include planted forests, grasses, and agricultural crops, all a part of what geographers call the cultural landscape.

An analysis of this landscape will be made in the section on economic geography, and in the following paragraphs emphasis will be placed primarily upon (1) major vegetation types and (2) the great world regions of natural vegetation (Fig. 9–1).

The Three Great Types of Vegetation

The earth's garment of vegetation may be divided into three great groups: (1) trees; (2) bushes, scrub, and woody perennials; and (3) grasses and other herbaceous forms. While soil and relief have much to do with the local distribution of these three groups, their general distribution over the world as a whole depends chiefly upon two climatic factors: (a) length of season warm enough for growth; and (b) proportion of that season during which there is moisture enough to promote growth.

Trees. Although trees are the largest form of vegetable life, they are in many ways more sensitive than bushy or grassy vegetation. As a rule they are sensitive to drought, especially when young. In traveling from a well-watered region to one that is dry, one sees that the trees diminish in size and become scrubby, or else they become few in number and are limited to areas that are usually damp. Most trees need a fairly long growing season. That is why the tree line on mountains is lower than the upper limit of grasses. On the higher slopes of mountains, although there is plenty of moisture, the warm period when growth is possible is so short that quickly growing grasses have a great advantage over slow-growing trees and can drive them out. Accordingly regions in which trees attain a fine growth and form great forests generally have a moderately long warm season with fairly abundant moisture. Such regions may be as varied as the Amazon Basin, Siberia, eastern United States, and the Andes of southern Chile.

Bushes and Scrub. Plants classified under this heading range all the way from scrubby trees to perennials with more or less woody stems that die in part after each growing season. Such plants are mixed with trees in most forested regions. Where the conditions of climate or soil become unfavorable to trees, however, bushes crowd them out and become the chief growth. This can be seen near the tree line on the sides of mountains where low temperature hampers trees more than bushes. It is also seen on the edges of swamps, where too much moisture in the soil prevents many kinds of trees from growing, but does not drive out the bushes. Again where the soil becomes thin, and hence dry, trees give place to bushes. The most noteworthy habitats of bushes are subtropical and desert regions, or parts of the tropics where the dry season is particularly long. The mountains of Sicily with their scrubby "dry forests," the sagebrush desert of Utah, and the bushy desert of Arizona are all examples of this type.

Bushes, shrubs, and trees of dry regions are well fitted to maintain themselves through protracted droughts provided they have water at occasional intervals. Many of them have drought-resistant leaves. In some, like the laurel and live-oak, the leaves are hard and shiny; in others such as the sage, they are soft and furry.

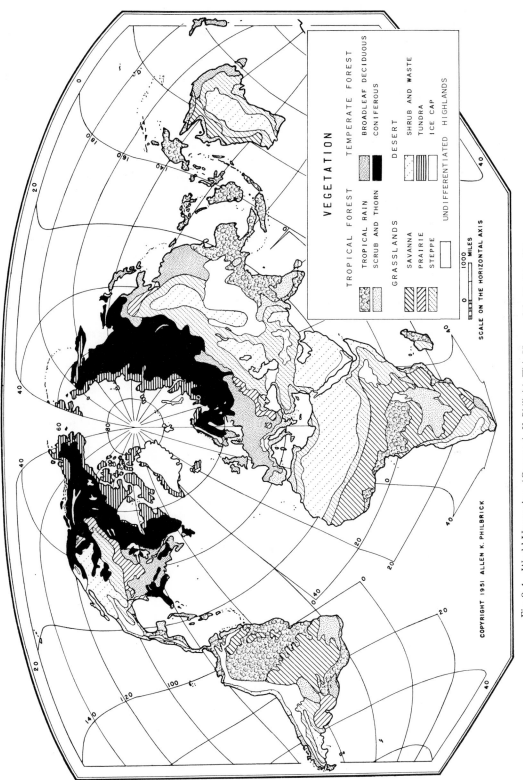

Fig. 9–1 World Vegetation. (*Courtesy A. K. Philbrick, This Human World, John Wiley & Sons, 1963*)

Both types have coverings that hinder evaporation and thus protect the plants during the long dry season. Many such plants also bear prickly leaves or spines. These incidentally protect the plants against the ravages of animals, but in most cases they originate through a progressive reduction in the plant's evaporating surface. The plants in which evaporation is restricted have the best chance of survival in the desert.

Grasses. Grass grows under a greater variety of conditions than trees or bushes. Many grasses can complete their growth and mature their seeds in a few weeks, so that a single shower in the desert may be enough for them; others can thrive on high mountains where the warm season is too short for trees or bushes. Hence, above the tree line lofty green pastures or "alps" furnish food for sheep and cattle in Switzerland. Grasses can also endure excessive moisture that would be fatal to trees and bushes, as on the dripping hills of Ireland, Scotland, and Wales, and the soggy marshes of Holland. Wherever other forms of vegetation are at a disadvantage, as in deserts, steppes, and regions with short

seasons or much cool moisture, grasses are likely to oust them.

A Mountain Showing the Three Main Types of Vegetation. An illustration of the relation of climate to trees, bushes, and grasses is found on the western slope of the Sierra Nevada in California (Fig. 9–2). At the base, the climate is so dry that the plain and the lower foothills are clothed with grass which is green only a few weeks of the year. A little higher up, where rainfall increases, one finds bushy vegetation of many sorts including the wild lilac, the yucca, and the manzanita. The live oak with its hard, prickly leaves also appears, and before one has climbed far he is in the midst of a dry forest, that is, one composed of drought-resistant trees many of which are scrubby. At higher altitudes, where there is abundant rain, the dry forest is replaced by a wet forest of broad-leaved trees like the oak and sycamore. Then, where the air is colder, the type changes to coniferous forests of pines, giant sequoias, spruces, and firs. Next, where the growing season becomes too short for trees, one struggles through a dense thicket of

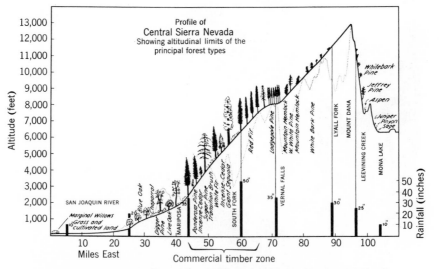

Fig. 9–2 Vegetation on the Sierra Nevada Mountains. Notice that the 10-inch rainfall (annual) at the western base of the mountain discourages tree growth but permits a natural grass vegetation. Higher up, with a 20-inch rainfall, chaparral and other drought-resistant trees crowd out grasses. Still higher, the 35-inch rainfall encourages commercial forests, which reach optiumum development at the 50-inch isohyet near 3500 feet altitude. Thereafter precipitation gradually declines to about 25 inches near the summit, where cold temperatures rather than lack of precipitation discourage tree growth. Notice the 10-inch rainfall near Mono Lake on the eastern (leeward) mountain side, where vegetation is restricted to drought-resistant varieties of piñon and sage. (*U.S. Department of Agriculture, Yearbook of Agriculture, Trees*)

bushes bent down by many months of snow each year. Finally, the open grassy slopes appear where the temperature is too low for other plants; here grasses thrive far better than they do in the dry hot desert climate of the lowlands. Thus within a day's climb one may find most of the world's main types of vegetation.

World Distribution of Natural Vegetation

The distribution of trees, bushes, and grasses over the earth's surface follows fairly definite laws. Distribution is affected not only by the zonal arrangement of temperature (Fig. 9–3), but also by the relief and especially by the presence of moisture. Far larger areas bear sparse vegetation because of aridity than because of low temperature.

The Tropical Rainforest. The tropical rainforest (Fig. 9–4) occupies much of the land surface close to the equator; and includes among its trees a significant number rising to heights of a hundred feet or more. The broad branching of these trees at the top and the sparsity or absence of branches from the lower fifty feet or

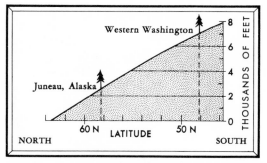

Fig. 9–3   Altitude, Latitude, and the Upper Tree Line. In a distance of 11° of latitude from western Washington to Cross Sound near Juneau, Alaska, the upper tree line drops from 7000 feet to 2500 feet. A little farther north it drops to sea level. South of western Washington the upper tree line rises.

more of the trunk has encouraged the term *umbrella-shaped* to describe tall trees of the tropical rainforest. Although the broad expanse of upper leaf-covered branches causes considerable shade, it is the density and complexity of vegetation beneath the uppermost canopy that most limits the amount of light that penetrates to the forest floor.

S. R. Eyre in his book *Vegetation and Soils,* (Al-

Fig. 9–4   Tropical Rainforest in Coastal British Guiana. Notice the umbrella-shaped tree in the distance, which gives proof of at least two distinct tree layers in the forest.

Fig. 9–5   Parklike Savanna in Africa. Acacia-tall-grass tropical savanna here shown is an even cover of grasses with flat-topped acacia trees quite evenly spaced. In some places trees form clumps, and there are also many open grassland areas. This photograph was taken between Meru and the Uaso Nyiro River, Kenya. (*Courtesy H. L. Shantz and* Economic Geography)

dine Publishing Co., 1963) stresses this variety of tree heights in the tropical rainforest; and divides trees according to heights into three different groups. For example, in one tropical rainforest region he tells of the upper tree layer averaging about 110 feet in height; a second layer rising to about 65 feet; and a third layer reaching an average elevation between 45 and 50 feet. It is this combination of tall, medium, and low growing trees rather than the tall umbrella-shaped ones alone which account for the deep shade of the forest floor and the consequent sparsity of plant life there.

However, on the poleward borders of the forest, where rainfall is still abundant but where the dry season is longer, more light can penetrate the lesser density of leafy branches. As a result there is less shade on the forest floor and a much heavier vegetation floor cover than in areas with an extremely short or no dry season. One of the best known groups of plants adding complexity to the dryer parts of the tropical rainforest are the lianes. These climbing plants which may achieve a length of more than a hundred feet may entwine themselves around several trees and even penetrate the crowns of some of the taller ones. Besides the liane, the tropical rainforest includes other vegetation forms such as epiphytes, parasites, stranglers, and saprophytes.

It is well to remember that the tropical rain-

forest does not form a continuous equatorial belt around the world, because it is interrupted not only by oceans but also by mountains and plateaus. Nevertheless it covers vast areas in the Amazon and Congo Basins, the East Indies, and other portions of southeast Asia. Smaller sections are found on the rainy Atlantic coasts of Central America and Brazil; on the windward coasts of Puerto Rico, Hispaniola, Jamaica, and Madagascar; on the west coast of India; and in a few other places. In many of these locations the forest is almost uninhabited; and certain groups among the rainforest population still remain at a very low stage of civilization.

Tropical Scrub. Although tropical rainforests are often considered the most typical vegetation in the warmest parts of the earth, tropical scrub and grassland occupy larger areas. Both of these are more or less mixed with each other by reason of variations in soil, altitude, and relief. Moreover, rivers may be bordered by what is called a gallery forest composed of trees resembling those in the lower layers of the tropical rainforest. In the scrub regions, the bushes are green during the wet half of the year but may lose their leaves during the dry season; at this time they may look like a second growth in an American woodlot in late autumn. Occasionally, however, a bare bush covered with great red, yellow, or purple flowers makes one realize that he is within the tropics, and only ten to twenty-five degrees from the equator. Areas of tropical scrub occur in north, central, and southern Africa; in northern Australia; in northwest Venezuela; in the Ceará region of Brazil; in the Yucatan Peninsula; in the dryer portions of the India Plateau; and in other places of the tropics.

Savanna. As one proceeds farther from the equator, tropical scrubby trees and bushes gradually give way to broad grassy areas. Sometimes these grasslands are dotted with clumps of trees or bushes, the outposts of the tropical rainforest and the scrub. In other places they are almost treeless except along the rivers. The Chaco of Argentina, the Campos of Brazil and the Llanos of Venezuela are three of the best-known tropical savannas. In central Africa among the highlands and farther north in the great plains of the Sudan, similar grasslands are developed on a vast scale; and in northern India and northern Burma they occur in large patches. Parts of such savannas, where trees alternate with grass are almost ideal for big game (Fig. 9–5). Trees furnish shelter, while the grass furnishes food for innumerable animals such as buffaloes, antelopes, giraffes, zebras, elephants, and many smaller herbivorous species, which in turn supply food for lions, tigers, leopards, and other carnivores. For man, however, savannas are not always ideal. Grass, to be sure, furnishes food for cattle, although it is likely to be much tougher and less nutritious than grass of middle latitude regions. In the long dry season, in many places, water can be procured by digging wells. Sod is so tough that it is difficult to plow. Consequently many natives of tropical grasslands wander with their cattle. A good example may be seen in the Dinkas of the African Sudan, among whom prices are reckoned largely in terms of cattle. Many tropical highlands also have large areas of grasslands, and these are among the best parts of the tropics for comfortable living (see Fig. 9–1).

Steppe. In the low latitudes, steppe may form a transition zone between tropical savanna and the desert. In the middle latitudes, steppe generally occurs between prairie and desert. The term steppe refers to vegetation made up largely of grasses shorter than those of the savanna or prairie; and steppe vegetation usually makes a less consistent ground cover than either of the above (Fig. 9–6).

In Africa, steppe lies both north and south of the Sahara and Kalahari deserts. In fact Africa is a good continental example of a similar sequence of tropical rainforest, savanna, steppe, desert, steppe, and scrub forest both north and south of the equator. In Australia steppe surrounds what is often called the Great Dead Heart of that continent on all sides except that of the west. In Eurasia, North America and in South America's Argentina, steppe usually borders desert in both low and middle latitudes. Steppe lands are more densely populated than deserts, except in desert oases, but the steppe is always a risky place for humid agriculture. No one learned this better than Russia's Khrushchev after his disastrous grain farming experi-

Fig. 9–6   Roundup of Hereford Cattle in Idaho's Copper Basin. The grazing of cattle and sheep is a characteristic industry of the steppe lands of western United States. Notice the small bushes and widely separated grass clumps in the foreground, both typical of steppe vegetation. However, trees may be seen on the distant mountains, where higher elevations better exposed to the prevailing westerly winds bring heavier precipitation. (*Courtesy Standard Oil, New Jersey*)

Fig. 9–7   Desert Vegetation in Southern Arizona. Saguaro, or giant cactus, with smaller cacti and greasewood bushes below them. Notice the beautiful white flowers of the saguaro in the upper corner.

ment on the Eurasian steppe lands during the early 1960's.

Deserts. Poleward from the tropical savanna and steppe, large deserts may occur between about 25 and 40 degrees from the equator. Here the subtropical high pressure cells and the trade winds prevail alternately according to the season. As previously indicated, both of these climatic controls contribute very little precipitation. However, deserts usually occupy these latitudes only on the western sides of continents; while, in general, rainy areas lie on the east coasts.

Both grasses and bushes are found in deserts. Plants that support wandering people, such as some of the Arabs, consist of grasses and other small herbaceous forms which sprout quickly after the infrequent rains, remain green only a few weeks, and then quickly wither and disappear so that one hardly knows they existed. In most deserts, however, there is also a more permanent type of vegetation, consisting of bushes spaced far enough apart so that each has a large area where it can spread its roots horizontally and thus get as much water as possible from each infrequent shower. Some types, which grow on hollows, form what may be called an inverted forest, for the roots reach far down to groundwater, and are so large that they form as it were an underground forest, far bigger than

the small plants that rise above the surface. Throughout much of the desert, however, the water table, or level of permanent groundwater, lies so far below the surface that plants are unable to reach it.

Although the total number of plants in a desert is small compared with moister regions, the number of species is large. Not only are there the relatively long-lived bushy types, the temporary grasses, and the other herbaceous forms that grow quickly after rains, but moist spots support the kinds of vegetation that grow in regions of abundant rain, and the salt lakes are surrounded by species similar to those that grow on the seashore. In addition to this the desert is full of highly specialized plants, like the cactus, adapted for storing large quantities of water (Fig. 9–7). Because of the necessity of adapting themselves to extreme aridity, many of the genuine desert plants are peculiarly awkward in appearance. Their fat, hairy stems, their spines, and their fuzzy or leathery leaves seem uncouth compared with the graceful vegetation of moister regions.

Subtropical Dry Forest. On the cooler borders of the desert, especially on the western sides of the continents, the vegetation in latitudes of approximately 30° to 40° consists of subtropical dry forest, the Mediterranean type. This is also found on many mountains which rise above the desert itself. It is composed of small gnarled, hard-leaved trees or bushes which often form open parklike expanses through which it is easy to travel. In some places, however, they change into a tangle of bushes above which rise frequent trees. For example, along the southern coast of Asia Minor the lower mountains are clothed with scattered trees and occasional bushes that give an open, friendly aspect like a park. Higher up, however, toward the level where the coolness and moisture of the mountains cause them to be clothed with coniferous forests, there is a bushy belt almost impossible to cross. This belt may include the laurel, olive, holly, and live oak. Winter temperatures in these latitudes are often quite high and as the rain comes chiefly in the winter, the trees can grow even at that season. This makes up in part for the dry summer when growth is sharply limited.

Prairie. Subtropical dry forest, desert, steppe, prairie (Fig. 9–8), and deciduous forest all occur in the same latitudes in both North America and in Eurasia. Forests usually occur near the coasts; and the deserts, steppes, and prairies may be found in the interior. Distribution of prairies depends on the season of rainfall. Grasses are such assertive, tenacious plants that they can drive out the trees in places where trees could grow if nothing else interfered with them. Thus large parts of the American prairies and the steppes of Russia and Hungary are located in regions where certain kinds of trees can flourish if they are protected when young. Grasses, however, because of their more rapid growth and greater hardiness, have driven out the trees. Over most of the prairie region, the rainfall is likely to be deficient not only in winter, so that the ground is dry when the temperature becomes warm enough for growth, but also in the spring when the trees need it especially. Hence when seedling trees begin to grow, they are at a disadvantage and are strangled by the more rapidly growing grasses. If such a region is swept by fires, or is grazed by herds of animals like the buffalo, grass and seedlings both suffer, but the grass springs up again in a few weeks, while the

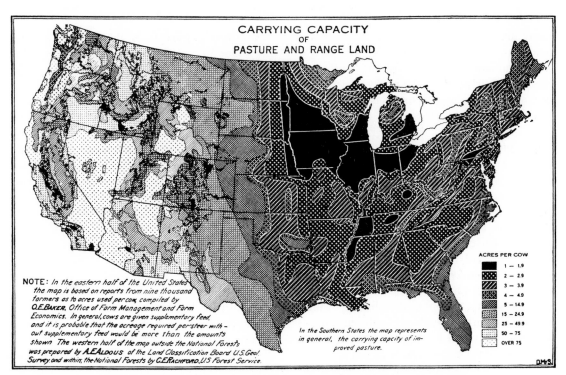

Fig. 9–8   The Prairie Has the Grazing Potential in the United States. The blackened sections of Iowa, northern Illinois, northern Indiana, southwestern Minnesota, and the extreme eastern parts of Nebraska and the Dakotas all belong to the region of natural prairie. However, most of this prairie grass land is producing cultivated crops now. *(Courtesy U.S. Department of Agriculture)*

Fig. 9–9   Merchantable Tulip Poplar. This Poplar is a deciduous tree, which drops its broad leaves in the autumn. (*U.S. Forest Service*)

young trees must start from new seeds and hence are ousted in the long run. Because of their stimulating climate, rich soil, and gently rolling to nearly level topography, the prairies hold high rank in agriculture as is shown by the United States Middle West.

Deciduous Forests. In eastern United States and western Europe, prairies give way to deciduous forests. These are composed of trees like maple, beech, oak, and poplar that drop their leaves in autumn (Fig. 9–9). In many places these trees are mixed with conifers, like pine. The mixed forest grows in places where winters are cold but not extremely long, and where the summers are warm, or even hot for a while, but with plenty of moisture at all times. Cyclonic storms dominate the climate of these regions, a climate which not only encourages deciduous or mixed forest growth, but also favors man and a great variety of his activities. Because of such favorable conditions most of the forest area has been cleared, and the regions now support a dense population engaged in profitable agriculture, manufacturing, and com-.merce.

Coniferous Forests. In the latitudes averaging about 50 degrees, various types of vegetation merge irregularly into vast forests of spruce, fir, pine, hemlock, and other coniferous trees (Fig. 9–10); these forests grow in a climate with winters that are long and cold and summers fairly warm and rainy, although relatively short. This evergreen forest forms a great belt across Canada and another belt extending from the Scandinavian peninsula through European and Asiatic Russia. On the whole the coniferous forest region is too cold for profitable agriculture. Hence it is well settled only in the southern portions. The rest still stands as the world's greatest forest reserve outside the tropics. (See Fig. 9–1.)

At this point it may be well to include a few statistics about tropical, middle latitude, and high latitude forests. A recent United Nations report on world forest resources states that about 64 per cent of the total productive forest area of the world consists of broadleaf species. Of this proportion, so-called temperate hardwoods account for 14 per cent, and tropical hardwoods make up the remaining 50 per cent. About 36 per cent of the world's productive forests are coniferous, but more than 70 per cent of the demand for wood for use in construction and for industrial purposes is for coniferous species. It is estimated that slightly less than 50 per cent of the world wood consumption is used for construction and for industrial purposes and slightly more for fuel. Also, total consumption is almost equally divided between coniferous and broadleaf species. Of the coniferous forest wood, a little over 70 per cent goes to building and industry and nearly 30 per cent is burned. For the broadleaf species these proportions are almost exactly reversed.

Besides the areas classified as productive forests, other forests comprise areas which bear a greater or lesser degree of tree cover, but where site conditions are so unfavorable that the trees are of very slow growth and of dwarfed and stunted form. Forests of this kind occupy vast areas near the southern margins of the treeless tundras of the far north and in the arid savanna formations fringing the deserts of Africa. Others are found at high altitudes near the upper limits of tree growth and on poorly drained sites of high acidity. Some of the last-mentioned group may eventually be transformed into productive forests by drainage, but it is highly improbable

that the other groups will ever be able to provide forest products other than small and irregular supplies of fuel wood. In some continents the total forested area, meaning the whole area bearing tree cover, is useless as an indication of potential forest productivity because of the preponderance of areas which properly fall into the nonproductive category just described.

Considering the productive and other forested areas of the continents as a whole, 38 per cent of Europe and the U.S.S.R.; 31 per cent of North America; 43 per cent of South America; 28 per cent of Africa; 20 per cent of Asia exclusive of Russia; and 9 per cent of Oceania are forested; and the percentage for the 6 continents is 30 per cent.

Russia has more forests than any other country in the world, about 2½ times the acreage of the United States. In both countries, however, the balance between annual use and natural growth of accessible forests is now favorable, that for Russia being 700 annual growth and 600 used; for the United States 345 annual growth and 283 used. (The unit of measurement is in millions of cubic meters of roundwood, solid content without bark.) Corresponding fig-

Fig. 9–10   Seed for a Crop of Coniferous Forest. Pine cones are collected from selected trees in seed orchards to provide healthy stock for future planting. (*Courtesy West Virginia Pulp and Paper Company*)

Fig. 9–11   Tundra Landscape Near the Town of Umiat. Umiat is located on the Colville River north of the Brooks Range in Alaska. While mosses and lichens are significant elements of tundra vegetation, bushes and even dwarf trees occur in many places. The man in the photograph is the late Dr. Richard Lougee of Clark University, who in 1956 visited the region to study its glacial history. (*Courtesy Dr. Robert Anstey, U.S. Army Natick Laboratories*)

ures for other countries show the United Kingdom, 2.75 and 3.37; France, 25.30 and 25.47; Germany, 22.10 and 39; Italy, 14.30 and 14.68; Sweden, 53 and 36.60; Canada, 80 and 94.66; China, 44 and 10; Japan, 40 and 66; Australia, 8 and 8; and New Zealand, 1.5 and 2.5.

Tundra. On its poleward side the coniferous forest gradually breaks down into a belt of bleak tundra (see Figs. 9–1 and 9–11). Plant life resembles that of the dry deserts in several respects. Leaves are small; root systems may expand in a horizontal direction like those of the desert; the plant makes this adjustment to take advantage of thawing, which reaches only a few inches below the surface during the summer. Plants are compact, stunted, and make haste to complete their life cycle as quickly as possible during the short growing season.

As an adaptation to the short Arctic summer,

almost all truly Arctic plants are perennial and develop the next year's flowering buds before the onset of winter. Summer is too short for annual species to complete a life cycle in one season. The failure of a single seed crop might exterminate the species in a local population. Most Arctic plants require many years from germination to the first flowering. Many do not depend entirely on seed production for their propagation, but are protected against unfavorable seasons by various means of vegetative reproduction.

In the Arctic, there are few climbing plants, few plants that sting or poison, and few that are protected by spines or thorns. The implication, of course, is that such protection is not needed. Many are xerophytes, that is plants adapted to withstand prolonged drought by having rather small, leathery leaves, often covered by densely matted hairs that provide a felt-like covering for the stomata. These xerophytic adjustments are necessary, for it should be remembered that precipitation is low in the cold deserts just as it is in the hot ones.

Arctic plants numbering more than a thousand species were identified at the beginning of the 20th century—250 species of mosses, 330 of lichens, and 760 flowering plants. Flowering plants outnumber the nonflowering, and in tonnage the preponderance of flowering is still greater. Plants in the Arctic do not grow haphazardly along side one another. Those having similar requirements as to soil, moisture, and wind or snow protection generally grow together in more or less well-defined communities.

Only a few native plants show a direct relationship to man's economy. In North America, none of the woody species is large enough for constructional purposes by the Eskimo, who formerly at least, obtained what little wood he needed chiefly from driftwood. However, heather and berry bushes, stunted willows, alder, and ground birch are used for cooking; and nearly all the larger lichens are highly inflammable when dry and may be used to cook food. Raw peat, particularly heath turf but also partly decomposed sphagnum moss, is available nearly everywhere.

Indirectly vegetation is of great importance to man because it furnishes feed for grazing animals—reindeer, caribou, and muskox. Seeds, buds and roots, and stems or leaves of many species are eaten by birds and small rodents that, in turn, constitute the feed of some of the fur-bearing animals sought by trappers. Likewise, the comparatively rich marine plant life furnishes feed for the sea mammals, long so important in the economy of the tundra dweller. Some Arctic Eskimos obtain needed "greens" from the stomachs of sea mammals and caribou that have fed on plants.

Polar Deserts. Near the poles in latitudes above 75°, the temperature almost everywhere is so low that the snow does not disappear in time to permit much vegetation other than minute bacteria of various forms or lichens that cling to rocks (see Fig. 9–1). Yet the prolonged summer sunlight provides such steady warmth that beautiful flowery vegetation can be found in small isolated patches with sunny exposures. Nevertheless, this region, as a whole consists of polar deserts like Greenland and Antarctica, which are sparsely settled.

It is worth noting that in polar deserts, the long period when the ground is frozen prevents the plants from getting enough water even though it is available in icy form. There is no way in which loss of water by transpiration can be balanced by absorption of water through the roots.

QUESTIONS, EXERCISES, AND PROBLEMS

1. Comment upon tolerance characteristics of grasses, bushes, and trees. Describe the vegetation sequence occurring upon the western slope of California's Sierra Nevada Range. How is this sequence related to altitude and climate?
2. Describe major botanical characteristics and the relationships to climate in the tropical rainforest. Tell of its latitudinal location and of the nations which include large portions of the forest within their borders.
3. Comment upon botanical features, climatic relationships, and latitudinal and national locations of the tropical jungle, the tropical scrub, the tropical savanna, the deserts, the subtropical dry forest, the prairies, the deciduous forests, the coniferous forests, the tundra, and the polar desert.
4. List pertinent statistics about low, middle, and high latitude forests. Compare the tropical savannas with the middle latitude prairies.
5. Starting at the generally east-west flowing Congo river, name in sequence the vegetation regions north to the Mediterranean Sea; south to the Cape of Good Hope.
6. Study Fig. 9–1, "World Vegetation;" turn to the color plates at the end of the book and study Plate 4, "Natural Vegetation Regions of the World." List the ways in which the two maps are similar and the ways in which they are different. Notice that Plate 4 shows considerably more detailed information.

SELECTED REFERENCES

American Geographical Society, *A World Geography of Forest Resources,* The Ronald Press, 1956.

American Forest Products Industries, Inc., *American Tree Farmer and Forestry Digest,* 1964 (Official yearly magazine of the voluntary American Tree Farm system).

Dansereau, Pierre, *Biogeography: An Ecological Perspective,* The Ronald Press, 1960.

Doerr, A. H., "A Preliminary Survey of Plant Succession on Coal Mine Spoil in Oklahoma," *Journal of Geography,* Oct. 1962, pp. 301–10.

Eyre, S. R. *Vegetation and Soils,* Aldine Publishing Co., 1962.

Fuson, R. H., *The Origin and Nature of American Savannas,* Geographic Education Series No. 2, National Council for Geographic Education, 1963.

Geographical Record, "An International Vegetation Map on the Millionth Scale" *Geographical Review,* July 1964, pp. 434–37.

Polunin, Nicholas, *Introduction to Plant Geography,* McGraw-Hill, 1960.

Thoman, R. S. and Patton, D. J., *Focus on Geographic Activity,* McGraw-Hill, 1964, Chapter 11, "An Integrated Forest Industry in the Pacific Northwest."

U.S. Department of Agriculture, *Grass, Yearbook of Agriculture,* 1948; *Trees, Yearbook of Agriculture,* 1949; *Managing the Family Forest,* Farmers Bulletin No. 2187, 1962.

Wagner, Philip L., "Natural and Artificial Zonation on a Vegetation Cover: Chiapas, Mexico," *Geographical Review,* April 1962, pp. 253–74.

Weaver, J. E. and Clements, F. E., *Plant Ecology,* McGraw-Hill, latest revised edition.

Chapter Ten

Soil Formation and Distribution

Soil has often been defined as a mixture of weathered particles of rock, of decaying organic matter, of moisture, and of air—a mixture that covers the earth in a thin layer, from a few inches to several feet thick. Generally about half of the volume of soil is made up of solids and the other half consists of open spaces which contain air and water. Genetic factors in soil formation include parent rock material, relief of the land, flora, fauna, time, and probably the most important of all, climate.

How Soil is Formed

Mechanical Agents. A major part of the soil is derived from rocks by means of mechanical, chemical, and organic processes. The mechanical processes consist of breaking rock into small fragments in the following ways: (1) When rocks are heated by the sun and cooled by the wind and precipitation, they alternately expand and contract, a process that causes them to crack. The Egyptian Sphinx has been cracked and chipped in this way. (2) Rocks are also broken by movements of the earth's crust. Large movements may result in earthquakes. (3) Into cracks formed in these and other ways, water percolates sooner or later. If it freezes, it expands and thus widens the cracks and forms new ones. When it melts the former ice, now water, settles into the enlarged openings; then if it freezes again the cracks are enlarged still more. (4) Where small particles of rock lie on the surface, running water, waves, and winds move them and grind them still finer. At the same time, the removal of the soil by these agencies exposes new rock susceptible to soil formation.

Chemical Agents. Cracks formed by mechanical agents make it easy for chemical agencies to convert the rock into soil. Water that percolates into the ground is sure to contain impurities. From air it gathers some of the carbon dioxide given off by volcanoes, by animals when they breathe, and by decaying vegetation. On the surface of the ground, water seeps among rotting leaves, roots, and other organic matter, and dissolves humic acid, ammonia, and other chemicals. Thus the water becomes a weak chemical solution, usually acid, and is able to dissolve some minerals and weaken others.

Air itself, especially when moist, produces similar results. Water, oxygen, carbon dioxide, ammonia, and other substances which air contains in minute quantities cause decay. The process is like rusting or oxidizing of iron, which sometimes goes on so rapidly that a bright blade may become red when left out of doors overnight. Oxidation is one of the commonest methods by which rocks are converted into soil. The red, yellow, or brown coating on the outside of rocks is the result of oxidation.

Organic Agents. Anything which exposes bits of rock to the attack of air or water aids in soil formation. (1) A lichen helps when it attaches itself to the side of a bare, solid rock. Higher plants help when they send rootlets into cracks. As the roots grow the cracks are forced open. (2) Animals such as woodchucks, prairie dogs, earthworms, ants, termites, and crustaceans expose bits of rock to the air. Earthworms get their food by eating the fine soil. In the process of digestion they take out the decaying organic matter as the soil passes through them and is subjected to chemical action.

If all the soil of a given region were swept into the ocean, the mechanical, chemical, and organic processes described above would in time break up the exposed rocks and form a new cover of soil, but it might take thousands of years.

Texture of Soils

Gravel Soils. The value of soils varies greatly according to their texture. Gravelly soils, such as are formed by swiftly running water, are too coarse for most plants. They allow air and water to penetrate freely to the roots, but do not retain the water; and in regions of marginal precipitation, crops are likely to dry up. Moreover, although the roots can find their way easily among the particles, the soil does not furnish soluble chemicals in sufficient quantities. Gravelly soil is also hard to plow and cultivate because of the stones.

Sandy Soils. Although sandy soils may need heavy fertilization, they are easy to cultivate; they also allow root expansion of crops like potatoes and sugar beets better than tight clay soils; and on farms like those of the North Atlantic Coastal Plain, they warm up more quickly in the early spring than the heavy textured inland soils. This warming quality encourages the growing of early vegetables. Thus it is untrue to say that sandy soils are poor soils. For whether a soil is good or poor depends largely upon the purpose for which it may be used.

Clay Soils. Clay has many qualities which differ from those of sand. Clay soil grains may be so small and stick together so closely that they are difficult to cultivate. Furthermore, because of their water retentiveness, they dry slowly, and fields may be covered with clods if plowing takes place too soon after rains. Yet clay soils have good qualities as well as bad ones. For example, they have a capacity to retain water for a long time in the subsoil, a feature ideal for rice production; and most of Cuba's large sugar cane crop thrives on clay soils.

Loam Soils. Probably the best textured soil, loam, is a mixture of sand, silt (very fine sand), and clay. Some sand is desirable to make a soil friable so that it is easily broken up by the plow or hoe and easily penetrated by roots. Silt is desirable for the same reason, and because its particles are so small that they can readily be weathered into clay, thus providing fresh chemicals in soluble form. Both sand and silt, be it noted, are genuine rocks in spite of their size, and are of no immediate use as plant food. The food comes from clay, which is rock that has been oxidized and otherwise altered so that parts of it are soluble. Only these soluble parts ever get into plants. Thus some clay is useful.

Soil Structure

Kinds and Importance of Structure. Soil structure (Fig. 10–1) refers to the manner in which the individual grains are arranged. Arrangement may be influenced by the texture of the soil, chemical nature of the fine clay portion, aeration, kinds of plants and other organisms growing in the soil, and similar factors. Soil grains may be grouped into plates, crumbs, granules, prisms, nutlike units, or one of many other types. These forms may vary considerably themselves as to hardness and plasticity under different degrees of moisture.

Not only is structure highly significant in scientific studies of the soil itself, but it is of great direct importance in determining the soil's reception of plant roots, its amenability to cultivation, and its susceptibility to blowing by the wind or erosion by water. For example during dry periods, some soils, even those containing large amounts of clay, may blow badly if the grains are grouped into fine crumbs or granules. On sloping land more care is required to prevent erosion by water if the subsoil has a massive structure, relatively impermeable to water, as compared to subsoil having a crumb or nut structure permeable to water.

Transported Soils

Transportation and Soil Fertility. The character of a soil depends partly on the degree to which soils from various sources have been mixed, so that all the necessary chemical elements are present. Soils that have not been moved from their place of origin are sometimes called residual, because they reside, as it were, where they were first formed. Residual soils derived from quartz rocks, such as quartzite or sandstone, are likely to be sandy and infertile. Residual soil derived from dark heavy lavas, or from limestone, on the other hand, may be rich in essential chemicals, but often has the disadvantage of being sticky. If fine sand is mixed with such soils they form loams which are soft, pliable, easily worked, and highly fertile.

Fortunately a large portion of the earth's soil

does not remain where it was formed. It is carried by running water, glaciers, or wind and may be mingled with other soils. Thus sand and clay are brought together to form loams. A soil that is poor in one essential ingredient is mixed with a soil that is rich in that respect. Hence transported soils are on the whole better than residual soils. They are found as a rule in plains and lowlands, whereas residual soils may predominate in highlands. That is one reason why plains may be more prosperous than mountains.

Alluvial Soils. The most valuable transported soils may be found in alluvial deposits laid down by streams. At their best such soils are derived from so many sources that all necessary chemical elements are well represented. They may also consist of a well-proportioned mixture of sand, silt, and clay. In addition to this they are likely to have sufficient humus and sufficient maturity but not old age. Therefore it is not surprising that the world's densest population is found on great alluvial plains such as those of China, India, Egypt, the Rhine Valley, and the Mississippi Valley. Regions that were recently parts of the sea floor or of lake bottoms share these good qualities, as in Denmark, the Netherlands, and the old lake bed of the Red River region in Minnesota and North Dakota.

Glacial Soils. Glaciers, as well as rivers, may deposit good soil. One of the most characteristic actions of ice sheets is that they scour off hilltops and deposit materials thus obtained at other points that may be far away. This "drift" material, as it is called, consists of fine soil mingled with boulders. It often is deposited in low places and tends to fill hollows. The transported soil thus formed is improved by mixture of materials from one region with those from another. This is especially true in the Corn Belt of the United States. In regions such as eastern Canada and Finland, however, the glaciers in many sections scraped away the good soil leaving only bare rock.

SEVERAL IMPORTANT TYPES OF SOIL STRUCTURE

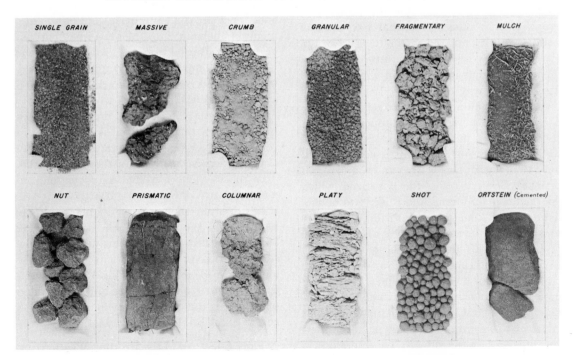

Fig. 10–1   Structure of soils is of great importance in studying their genesis or ecological relationships; and it is harder to change than their fertility. (*C. E. Kellogg, "Development and Significance of the Great Soil Groups of the United States,"* Miscellaneous Publication 229, *U.S. Department of Agriculture*)

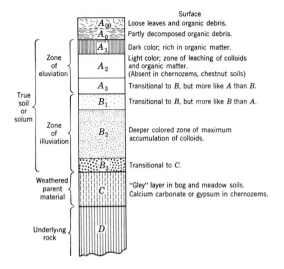

Fig. 10–2   The Idealized Soil Profile. (*Courtesy A. N. Strahler, Physical Geography, 2d edition, John Wiley & Sons, 1960—after* U.S. Department of Agriculture Yearbook, 1938)

Movement of Materials Within the Soil

Soil Profiles. While a soil is decaying on top of the original rock, or is being built up by water, ice, or wind, it by no means remains the same for century after century. On the contrary, it grows older in stages somewhat like those of youth, maturity, and old age in living creatures. Part of the process of aging consists of the movement of materials up and down within the soil itself. In this way a typical soil in regions of moderate rainfall acquires three parts (Fig. 10–2). One, the A horizon, is the upper layer that contains humus and is the most essential part so far as the growth of plants is concerned. It may be of any thickness from an inch to a foot or more. Below it comes the B horizon, which does not contain humus and is likely to be of a lighter color than the A horizon. Rainwater soaking down through this layer dissolves some of the chemicals that have been set free by weathering and carries them downward. It also often carries down some of the finest clay. These materials ordinarily do not go very far. At a depth of a foot or two deposition may start. This gives rise to a third or C horizon of still a different color, called the subsoil. The materials in this horizon have not been sufficiently oxidized to be good for the immediate use of plants.

Not all soils show the three major zones, A, B,

and C, characteristic of the mature soil. For example youthful soils on steep slopes are carried down slope long before they have an opportunity to start the process of aging in place; and water logged soils develop no normal profile because the stagnant water doesn't permit leaching and weathering.

Climate and Soil

Soils of Different Ages. In the long run, the quality of a soil depends on its age and the climate under which it has developed more than upon the rocks from which it is derived. All very old soils in any given climate are much alike, no matter what their origin. They have decayed so much that almost everything which can become soluble, even though very slowly, has been carried away. Thus old soils may become so completely leached that they are mere skeletons. They often take the form of extremely fine, deep, and sticky clay, which becomes very hard and stiff when dry, but sometimes they are almost granular like sugar. Such old soils are exceedingly poor for crops, although even the oldest support some sort of vegetation, especially grass. Very young soils are not much better than old ones. They are shallow, coarse, and full of fragments of unchanged rock. Only a small part has yet been converted into real clay and thus has become fine enough to yield up chemical elements needed by plants. Moreover, such soils are usually deficient in humus.

Between the young and old soils there is a mature stage. In this the soil is fairly deep; it contains at least a moderate amount of clay, but also some coarse material in the form of sand. This makes it more friable than old soil, but more retentive of water than coarse young soil. It has decayed enough to allow plant foods to be available, but not so much that they have been thoroughly leached. Thus maturity is the stage of a soil best fitted to agriculture. Of course any soil can be improved by being plowed and fertilized, but in a well-drained and well-aerated mature soil, this is far easier than in either a coarse young soil or a clayey old soil.

The Effect of Climate on Weathering. Weathering, like practically all chemical processes, is greatly accelerated by heat as well as by moisture. When soil is frozen, chemical changes almost cease. At temperatures near 90°, on the other hand, weathering processes are greatly accelerated, especially if moisture is abundant. Moreover, at low temperatures plants are scarce, so that the water in the soil is comparatively free from acids and other chemicals. With high temperatures and rainfall, on the contrary, there is invariably much vegetation which decays quickly so that the water is strongly charged with chemicals. Such conditions speed weathering, so that in warm moist regions the soil may grow old a hundred times as fast as in very cold regions, where frost prevails a large part of the year. Hence if all soils were of the same age in years, in going from polar to equatorial regions, one would see a gradual change from young types in high latitudes to old types in low latitudes.

A Soil Section from North to South. The geographical distribution of soils (Fig. 10–3) agrees largely with what one should expect from the preceding paragraphs. In general, they are young, shallow, coarse, and of poor quality in the far north of the Northern Hemisphere. The worst of such soils are found in the tundra, where the only vegetation is lichens with some grass and flowering plants. Soils become better in the podzols or light-colored soils of the northern forests, but are still lacking in fertility and structure. Farther south, on the east side of North America, for example, mixed forests of conifers and broad-leaved deciduous mingle. There the higher temperature and the more varied vegetation tend to produce browner soils that are fairly mature and reasonably fertile. Of course soils here, as everywhere, vary greatly according to a great variety of nonclimatic conditions, including the nature of the underlying rock, glaciation, volcanic activity, uplift from under the sea, and deposition in floodplains. Nevertheless, on the average, the humid brown earths, as these soils may be called, are mature, moderately fertile, and better than those in either cooler or warmer regions. They provide one of the many advantages of the middle latitudes.

Farther toward the equator, the soils on average become older and more leached. They tend to assume yellow and red colors. Warm climates cause these red earths and yellow earths to decay so rapidly that in many places they have passed the most favorable conditions of maturity and are declining in quality. This means that they are too clayey, and are so leached that they have lost much of their plant food. Finally, soils of equatorial regions are largely lateritic. True laterites are very old soils from which practically all the soluble material has been leached. They are red, very deep, and practically useless for agriculture. These very old soils in low latitudes have the same practical effect as very young soils in high latitudes.

The Importance of Soils in Low Latitudes. The character of the soil in low latitudes is extremely important. In high latitudes the poor quality of young soils makes little difference because the climate is too cold for agriculture. In middle latitudes, even though there are many poor soils, the tendency is toward maturity and fertility. In the humid low latitudes, however, climatic conditions which foster a luxuriant growth of vegetation also foster poor, leached soils. For this reason any condition that leads to younger soils is advantageous. The best of such soils are derived from recent volcanic eruptions. Java is the prime example of this. That island, only about the size of Iowa, is able to support more than fifty million people partly because it possesses much recent volcanic material, which under the influence of the tropical climate soon forms mature and rich soil. A major reason why neighboring islands, such as Borneo and New Guinea cannot support as many people is partly because their soil is older and partly because their lava flows have not yielded as good a soil. Many of the West Indies also have areas of volcanic soil, as do the Hawaiian Islands. This helps to make them among the best of the tropical countries.

Residual soils on gentle slopes furnish another tropical type that is likely to be mature in spite of the warm moist tropical climate. On such slopes the topsoil is gradually washed away, and thus the underlying soil is exposed before it is too old. If the slope is very steep, as in mountains, the soil may be washed away before it is mature, but in any given region some slopes are likely to be just steep enough so that their soil has the right degree of maturity. For this and other reasons, coffee and various other tropical plantation products may be found on gentle slope land.

The alluvial deposits of valley bottoms and the coastal plains along coasts that have been recently uplifted also provide good mature soils in tropical regions. The valley deposits are usually derived from mountains where the slopes are so steep that the soil is washed away while still young. If it has a chance to weather properly, with periods of moisture alternating with those of dryness, which allow entrance of air into pores of the soil, it soon forms rich soil. A great many tropical valley bottoms, however, suffer because they are water-logged much of the time or else flooded by heavy seasonal rains. This is true of large areas along the Amazon and on the coasts of New Guinea and Borneo. There the land is so nearly flat that it is difficult to drain it in such a way as to bring about proper aeration. This has much to do with the backwardness of such regions. Sediments at the bottom of the sea also have no chance to be oxidized and turn into mature soil. When they are uplifted, however, they soon become mature under the influence of tropical climate. Hence within the tropics the coastal soils are often quite fertile. This condition, together with ease of transport by water, helps explain why most of the world's sugar cane is raised on plantations near the seacoast. From the comments above it appears that, although enormous areas within the humid tropics are hampered by poor soil, certain sections such as volcanic regions, slopes that are neither too steep nor too flat, and well-drained young plains in valley bottoms or along the seacoast may have good soil. Hence the great majority of tropical people are found in such places, while vast areas, like the Amazon Basin are sparsely populated.

Wet Soils versus Dry Soils. Soils may be divided into two great classes, pedalfers and pedocals. *Pedalfers* are soils that have been formed under conditions so humid that the calcium (lime) in the upper parts has been carried away, although the aluminum and iron are left. The syllable "al" in the word pedalfer indicates aluminum; "fer" indicates the Latin word for iron which occurs in such words as *fer*ric iron ore and *fer*romanganese. Pedocals get the last syllable of their name from the word calcium. The syllable "ped" comes from the Greek word meaning ground, which occurs in such words as *ped*iment. These are soils that have been formed

in climates so dry that the calcium is not removed from the upper soil layer. This may be advantageous up to a certain degree, but it may be accompanied by two disadvantages. One is that in dry regions vegetation is not abundant, and hence the chances to accumulate humus are few. The other is that, where the soil is too dry, the water does not flow away underground but comes up again to the surface and there evaporates into the air. The result is that lime and other materials which water dissolves are not carried away, but are left near the surface in a cake known as hardpan, which makes it difficult to cultivate the soil.

Grassland Soils and a Cross Section from East to West. In middle latitude United States (Fig. 10–4) a cross section from east to west shows that the soil improves as one goes from the seacoast inland. Then some deterioration ensues in the arid regions of the interior and on the humid west coast. The best soils of the East are found in the mature humid brown earths of places such as Pennsylvania. Farther west, however, in the prairies of Illinois and Iowa, soils change into darker and better ones known as prairie earths. These are almost black, and the black part is often a foot deep. In colonial days the settlers first made their farms close to the rivers. There they had the advantage of being among trees and near running water, but the soil was of the brown forest type like that farther east. The settlers soon discovered that the darker soil back from the rivers on the open grasslands was much more desirable. It was harder to get water and wood there, but the soil gave much larger yields. One of the main differences between the soils of forests and grasslands lies in the fact that grass has a far larger proportion of roots than trees have and grass roots are short-lived. Dig into a piece of turf, and see how closely the upper soil is packed with roots. Then dig a bit in the woods, and see how much more scarce the roots are. Bear in mind, too, that many grasses are annuals, and even the perennials are by no means as long-lived as trees. The result is that innumerable grass roots die each year in the grassland, but not in the forest. The coolness of the climate and the moderate rainfall allow the grass roots to remain in the soil and form humus. Moreover, since the grasslands are drier than the forests, more lime remains in the soil.

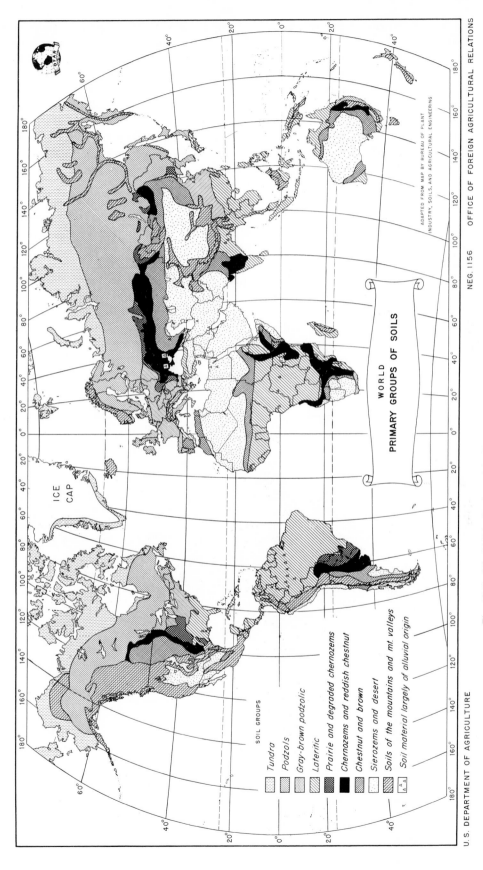

NEG. 1156   OFFICE OF FOREIGN AGRICULTURAL RELATIONS

ADAPTED FROM MAP BY BUREAU OF PLANT
INDUSTRY, SOILS, AND AGRICULTURAL ENGINEERING

Fig. 10-3 World Distribution of the Principal Zonal Soil Groups. (*Courtesy U.S. Department of Agriculture*)

Thus one sees factors contributing to the richness of the prairie soils.

In the western parts of the American prairies and in the southeastern parts of the corresponding grasslands in European Russia, the climate becomes quite dry. Grasses still grow, but there is not rain enough to wash the lime out of the soil. Nevertheless, there is rain enough so that little hardpan accumulates. Hence in a belt from Saskatchewan through Nebraska to Texas and again in the Black Earth Region of Russia, one finds the best soils of the entire earth. Unfortunately the largest crops per acre are not also found there because the dryness of many years keeps average yields per acre low except in a few favored places.

West of the United States black earths the soil begins to assume a redder shade, and one sees a belt of chestnut-colored soils. These arid brown earths are fertile although not quite equal to the black earths. Their great defect is that the climate is so dry that the crops often suffer or fail completely. They occupy the climatic area where dry farming is especially important. Still farther west, where aridity is greater, occur the gray earths, typical soils of dry regions. Where there is no hardpan, they contain a great amount of all sorts of plant food aside from humus, for they suffer very little from leaching. The lack of humus is a serious defect, but if a crop like alfalfa is planted, which is able to take nitrogen from the air, the presence of other plant foods insures fine crops, provided of course there is irrigation.

In the discussion of soil above it was necessary to speak in very general terms. The very nature of soil as largely decayed rock causes an infinite degree of local variety, so that some good soils and some bad ones and soils of almost every quality and color may be found close together. Nevertheless, as a general rule, soils improve as one goes from high latitudes to middle latitudes, and then deteriorate again toward the equator. They also improve as one goes inland in middle latitudes and from the humid coast through forests to grass lands. Then they deteriorate

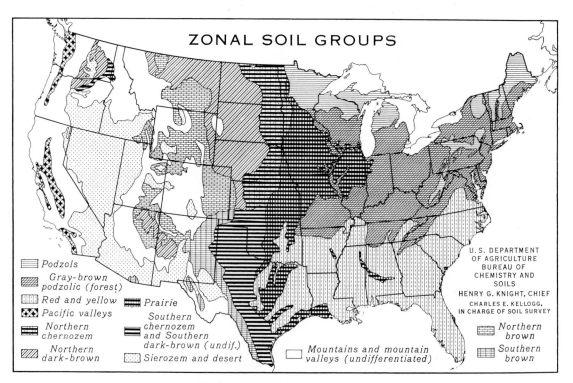

Fig. 10–4   Zonal Soil Groups, United States. Note that in eastern United States the long extension of the soil groups is in a general east-west direction; in the central and western parts of the country, the belts extend in a general direction of north-south; causes for this alignment are largely climatic. (*Bureau of Agricultural Economics, U.S. Department of Agriculture*)

Fig. 10–5   Abandoned Farm in South Carolina. Uncontrolled soil erosion leads not only to the decline of the land but also to social decay and abandonment of farmsteads. This South Carolina Piedmont plantation was ruined by erosion that could easily have been prevented. (*Courtesy H. H. Bennett, U.S. Soil Conservation Service*)

again as climate becomes drier and drier. Where the soil reaches the highest quality along both of the cross sections, described above, the finest soils of the world are found in places such as in western Iowa and in the Russian Ukraine.

It is also well to remember that all sorts of soils, varying widely in productivity, color, and chemical composition, may be derived originally from the same rock type. Climate and vegetation may influence soils more than parent rock material. Whereas rocks are distributed more or less promiscuously over the earth, as far as present environment is concerned, areas of individual kinds of soil occur in an orderly, discoverable geographic pattern. Each distinct combination of climate, flora and fauna, parent rock, relief, and time—sometimes called the five

genetic soil factors—give soil a unique set of characteristics.

No better analogy concerning different types of soils coming from the same parent rock material can be given than the following: "Give a log apiece to a Swiss wood carver, to a Polynesian boatman, and to a Canadian frontiersman, and behold how different their final products. So given loess, the humid subtropical climate of Mississippi makes weak-structured, impoverished yellow soils; the cool rainy climate of Illinois makes fair-structured, moderately leached brownish soils; and the subhumid climate of Nebraska makes strong structured, rich black earths therefrom." (Louis A. Wolfanger, "A Simple Key to Soil Geography", *Journal of Geography*, Vol. XXX, No. 8)

Fig. 10–6   A Farm Completely Treated for Conservation. Terracing, strip cropping, crop rotations on the contour basis, cover crops, gully control, retirement of steeper land from cultivation to trees and kudzu (a hay crop) are all practiced on this South Carolina Piedmont farm to fit the needs and adaptabilities of the different kinds of land. (*H. H. Bennett, U.S. Soil Conservation Service*)

Soil Conservation

Living beings depend upon the soil for existence: plants directly and animals and man indirectly. The functions of the soil may be summed up as follows: (1) to act as a physical support of vegetation; (2) to serve as a medium for storing water and bringing it in contact with the roots; and (3) to supply a small but essential percentage of materials (3 to 7 per cent of the dry weight of plants) that are converted into plant food by means of light. This small percentage is absolutely necessary. In a certain way, it bears to the main elements a relation analogous to that of salts, acids, and vitamins to the carbohydrates, fats, and proteins that form most of the food of man. Various chemical elements derived from soil, air, and water are not exactly plant foods

when first absorbed by the plants. Before they can nourish the plant they must pass through the chlorophyll cells and be changed into starch, sugar, proteins, fats, and other substances like those which nourish animals. They cannot do this unless chemicals of the soil as well as those of the air are present.

Because the soil is essential for the formation of chlorophyll, and thus for all growth, the soil becomes a great human problem (Figs. 10–5, 10–6, and 10–7). Although water and carbon dioxide supply most of the bulk of plants, they create no such problem because there is less danger of exhausting the supply. The necessary chemicals of the soil, on the other hand can be rapidly exhausted. In a state of nature most plants die where they grow. Materials that they contain are thus returned to soil through decay.

Moreover, there are usually many varieties of plants on the same area, so that the same kind of food is not demanded by all. On farms, on the contrary, it is usually necessary to devote the whole of a given area to a single crop at any given time. When the crop is reaped, it is carried away and consumed somewhere else. Thus there is a great drain on the soil.

Wise Use of the Soil: Rotation of Crops. A farmer may lessen this drain on soil in two important ways: (1) by rotation of crops and (2) by using commercial fertilizers. Rotation of crops means that the farmer plants different crops from year to year, so that on a given area the same elements are not constantly required in large amounts. It is called rotation because after a few years the same series of crops is planted over again (Fig. 10–8). In planning a rotation, the object is not only to use crops that do not

require the same food, but to include some, such as clover, that can be plowed under to serve as fertilizer. For instance, beets need a great deal of potash, while wheat in proportion to its bulk requires only half as much, but needs nearly twice as much nitrogen. Clover and peas on the other hand, do not require much nitrogen from the soil. Indeed their bacteria actually take nitrogen from the air and give it to the soil. Hence beets, wheat, and peas might make a good rotation from the standpoint of soil conservation.

The rotation of crops has still another value, as it provides a degree of insurance against unfavorable weather and low prices. For example, in the American Corn Belt, where crop rotation with a diversified field pattern is widely practiced, seldom if ever is there a year with complete failure of crops; a cool moist spring gives little encouragement for the early planting of

Fig. 10–7   Conservation of rainfall in the furrows between ridges plowed on the contour is practiced on this Oklahoma farm. (*H. H. Bennett, U.S. Soil Conservation Service*)

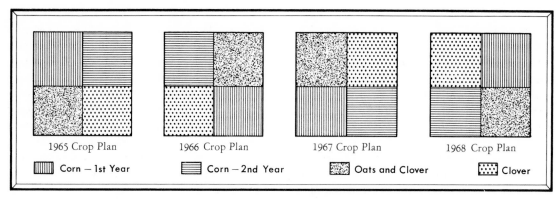

Fig. 10–8 Crop Rotation. Corn, oats, and clover may be used to illustrate a 4-year rotation cycle. Other crops may be added to or substituted for oats and clover; for example sweet clover planted in place of oats and clover can shorten the crop cycle to 3 years. Choice of crops depends upon soil conditions, disease hazards, relative prices for crops, major farming aims, and many other factors.

corn, but it is ideal for oats and hay; a rainy autumn, delays corn harvest but favors fall pastures; and greater-than-average rain through July and August is not good for drying hay, but it assures a large corn crop. Thus a farmer seldom misses ideal weather for one crop at least.

Again, price fluctuations are less serious in areas with crop rotation. On declining markets all prices may be depressed; but some crop will bring relatively higher prices than the others. Therefore, the farmer gains a stability of profits with an emphasis upon crop rotation and the normal resulting diversity of crops. The rotation of crops also helps in checking the ravages of insects and of bacterial plant diseases.

Commercial Fertilizers

What Chemicals Plants Need from the Soil. In order to provide the right kinds of commercial fertilizers, it is necessary to know (1) what chemical compounds plants need, and (2) how much of these the soil contains. Plants take at least fifteen chemical elements from the soil. Silicon, chlorine, sodium, and manganese are of slight importance and seem almost always to be present in sufficient quantity. Magnesium, iron, sulphur, copper, cobalt, nickel, zinc, and boron must be present in soluble form that can readily be absorbed by plants. The farmer rarely needs to worry about these, however, for they are practically always present in sufficient abundance

for any kind of a crop. Calcium, phosphorus, potassium, and nitrogen, on the contrary, often cause much trouble because they are not available in sufficient quantities.

Lime. Almost all the main agricultural parts of the world contain limestone, and it is merely a question of finding the cheapest means of grinding the rock and making it easily accessible to the plants.

Phosphates. Phosphates are not as widely distributed as lime. The main resources of the United States lie far apart. In four western states —Idaho, Montana, Utah, and Wyoming—billions of tons of the fertilizer are available; and in six states of the Southeast, Arkansas, Florida, Kentucky, the Carolinas, and Tennessee, phosphate is present in much lesser quantity. However, because the Southeast deposits lie closer to the nation's greatest farming country, they account for over three fourths of our annual production.

Russia has large reserves of phosphate in the Kola Peninsula, far from the best agricultural area; and other European countries may obtain supplies from Tunisia and Morocco, lands with much rugged topography and low rainfall.

Historically, phosphates from the South Pacific in the form of bird excreta and bones, called guano, became so important to the United States in the 1850's that Congress on August 18, 1856, passed an act which permitted Americans to claim unoccupied islands in the name of the United States government for the purpose of obtaining shipments of this fertilizer. Claims to approximately fifty islands were made under this act and now form one of the best bases for United States ownership of certain islands.

Again, history records that from 1830 to 1880, guano worth nearly a billion dollars was taken from the Chincha Islands off the coast of Peru and carried around Cape Horn to be sold to Europe and America. The Peruvian government was largely supported by taxes on guano until the deposits were seriously depleted. Only a limited amount is now available.

Potash. For many years the United States had much more difficulty in obtaining potash than phosphates. In fact, before World War I, the main world resources were located around Stassfurt, Germany, and Alsace, France; and U. S. imports were necessary from the German-French cartel. With this foreign source cut off by World War I, a careful search took place in

the United States to add to limited local reserves—salt lakes of western Nebraska, the well brines in Michigan, kelp along the Pacific Coast, and potash extracted from cement mills and blast furnaces. As a result of war-time prospecting, large deposits of sylvite and langbeinite were discovered in the Carlsbad region of southeastern New Mexico. Now New Mexico supplies are large enough to provide for United States needs; but like the largest phosphate reserves, they lie far away from our major farm lands. Recently more potash was discovered in the Four Corners mineral complex, where Colorado, Utah, Arizona, and New Mexico join one another. And in neighboring Canada, source of the world's largest potash beds, active exploitation began in the early 1960's in Esterhazy, Saskatchewan (Fig. 10–9).

The Search for Nitrogen. Among the essential ingredients of the soil, nitrogen is unique in that much of it comes from the air, where re-

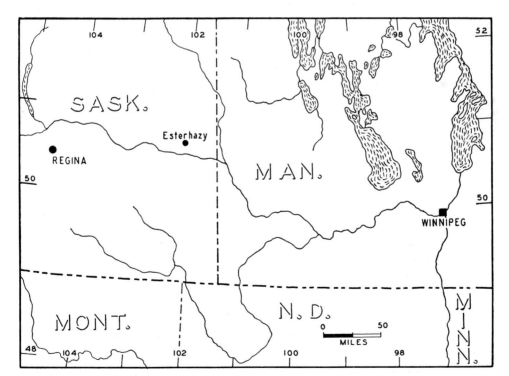

Fig. 10–9 Vicinal Location of Esterhazy. Not far from Esterhazy in Canada's Saskatchewan Province, there is enough potash to supply the entire earth, at the present rate of consumption, for several centuries. Here man accepted the challenge of a great mining problem, conquered it, and by so doing enlarged world capacity for food production. (*Courtesy Earl B. Shaw and* The Journal of Geography, *Jan. 1962*)

serves are inexhaustible. Until the 20th century, however, this reserve was almost useless to the farmer, for no one knew how to convert it into a soluble compound that could be carried into the roots of plants by water. This is because nitrogen is one of the most inactive chemical elements. Quite unlike such an active substance as oxygen, it will not readily unite with other elements.

Because of this the Atacama Desert in northern Chile long had a great importance. It contains the only well known large deposits of compounds of nitrogen. Before their value was known, the Atacama Desert was such a barren waste that almost no one lived there, although Chile, Peru, and Bolivia all laid claim to parts of it. When the value began to be appreciated, however, about 1879, all three countries wanted it. This led to a long war in which Chile was the victor.[1] Then followed a period when the nitrate fields were exploited to the value of millions of dollars each year. Taxes paid by companies working the nitrate fields were long one of the chief sources of revenue for the Chilean government. Today these natural supplies of nitrates are no longer so important to the nitrate trade nor to the tax structure of Chile.

One result of the prolonged search for sources of nitrogen has been the discovery that bacteria that cause "nitrification" can be raised artificially and shipped anywhere. When clover seed is inoculated with them, the roots become covered with unusually large tubercles that contain nitrogen, and thus the fields are fertilized.

Another result of the demand for nitrogen was first seen in Norway. After the value of nitrates was realized, people began to search for means of utilizing the unlimited supply of nitrates from the air. Success was at last obtained by means of strong electric currents that cause the atmospheric nitrogen to unite with lime or other substances. Much power is required for electric discharges, so that the process is commercially profitable only where power is cheap. Power from waterfalls is especially abundant in Norway. Since raw materials of most kinds are not abundant there and nitrogen in the canopy of air is present everywhere, the manufacture of nitrogenous fertilizers has be-

come an important industry. Nevertheless, this is not now the only source of nitrogen fertilizer. New processes using cyanamide, ammonia, and distillates from coal have been devised, so that a great source of nitrate comes from the manufacturing regions.

Cheaply available, naturally occurring nitrate reserves are almost nil in the United States, but as previously indicated, nitrogen-fixation plants offer adequate substitute where low-cost power is available.

Work in obtaining fertilizers from various sources may seem remote from the lives of many people. Yet it concerns everyone. Farmers supply man with most of the materials for food and clothing that play so large a part in life. If agricultural workers do not have rich soil and cannot raise their crops abundantly and cheaply, the price of food and clothing goes up and many people suffer. It is of great importance that an abundant supply of good fertilizers be available for farmers throughout the world.

QUESTIONS, EXERCISES, AND PROBLEMS

1. Give a definition for soil, and list major factors which influence its formation and significant features. What mechanical, chemical, and organic agencies encourage soil genesis? Classify soil as to texture, and tell of the agricultural advantages of sand, clay, and loam. Define soil structure and list several structural types.
2. Comment upon the advantages of transported, alluvial, and glacial soils for farming. Describe the A, B, and C soil horizons.
3. Illustrate the effects of climate upon soil. Tell of major changes in soil groups from Arctic North America to the Amazon in South America. Name the exceptions to the general rule that rainy low latitude lowland soils are infertile.
4. Give the names and locations of the major soil groups east of the Mississippi river in the United States. What soil groups occur west of the Mississippi river? Which contribute more to soil fertility, trees or grass? Explain.
5. What are the major functions of soils? What is meant by crop rotation? What major minerals are essential for best fertility in soils? What is the position of the United States with reference to resources of lime, potash, phosphates, and other mineral fertilizers often needed to replenish soils? Give the location of these resources.
6. Identify the following: pedalfer, pedocal, cher-

[1] See James, Preston, *Latin America*, Odyssey Press, 1959, pp. 258–61.

nozem, podzol, gray-brown podzolic, red and yellow earth, laterite, guano, Kola Peninsula, Atacama, leaching, chlorophyll, prairie earth.

7. Study Fig. 10–3, "World Distribution of the Principal Zonal Soil Groups"; then turn to the color plates at the end of the book and study Plate 3, "Great Soil Groups of the World." List the ways in which the two maps are similar and the ways in which they are different.

SELECTED REFERENCES

Eyre, S. R., *Vegetation and Soils,* Aldine Publishing Co., 1962.

Higbee, Edward, *American Agriculture,* John Wiley and Sons, 1958.

Higbee, Edward, *The American Oasis,* Alfred A. Knopf, 1957.

Highsmith, R. M., Jr., Jensen, J. G., Rudd, R. D., *Conservation in the United States,* Rand McNally, 1962, especially section on soils.

Jacobsen, T. and Adams, R. M., "Salt and Silt in Ancient Mesopotamian Agriculture," *Science,* Nov. 21, 1958, pp. 1251–58.

Marbut, C. F., *Soils of the United States,* U. S. Dept. of Agriculture, Latest revision.

McNeil, Mary, "Lateritic Soils", *Scientific American,* Nov. 1964, pp. 96–102.

Megill, W. J., "Potash in Canada's Past and Saskatchewan's Present," *Canadian Geographical Journal,* June 1964, pp. 178–87.

Parson, Ruben L., *Conserving American Resources,* Prentice-Hall, 1964, especially section on soils.

Parsons, James J., "Potentialities of Tropical Soils," *Geographical Review,* July 1951, pp. 503–05.

Simonson, Roy W., "Soil Classification in the United States," *Science,* Sept. 28, 1962, pp. 1027–34.

Smith, G.-H., editor, *Conservation of Natural Resources,* John Wiley and Sons, 1958 or later revision, especially chapters "The Great Soil Groups and their Utilization"; "Soil Conservation"; and other sections related to soils.

U. S. Dept. of Agriculture, *Soil, Yearbook of Agriculture,* 1957.

Vann, J. H., "Developmental Processes in Laterite Terrain in Amapa, Brazil," *Geographical Review,* July 1963, pp. 406–17.

Chapter Eleven

Minerals

At the outset it may be well to define a few terms. A mineral is a naturally occurring inorganic substance with definite physical characteristics capable of expression by a chemical formula. Under a strict interpretation of this definition, coal, petroleum, and natural gas cannot be included with minerals because they are organic in origin. Probably they should be classified as power resources, but they will be studied with minerals in the following paragraphs.

An ore is a mineral whose extraction from an ore body, including the ore and other materials called gangue, can be made at a profit. Profit is a key word in this definition. Rocks are made up of one or more minerals, and most of the hard, naturally formed substance of the earth's crust may be classified as belonging to one of three major types of rocks: the igneous, the sedimentary, or the metamorphic group. Rocks may contain organic as well as inorganic material.

Where Minerals are Found

Minerals and Mountain Building. Metallic minerals are likely to be found in mountains or in regions where mountains formerly existed. Several reasons account for this situation: (1) Mountains result from earth movements, folding and faulting, which make it easier for molten magma, the mineral bearer, to rise in folds and along faults from the interior of the earth. As the magma rises, it cools, and like mineral elements contained in the magma tend to come together. Thus, a mineral deposit may be concentrated and brought near the surface by the upward flow of molten material resulting from the processes of mountain building. (2) Erosion, encouraged by high mountains, also aids in bringing minerals nearer the surface. Without erosion most of the metallic deposits, even though up-

lifted, would be buried under an enormously thick layer of dense rock. During the lapse of millions of years, the work of running water and other geologic erosive agents has carried away thousands of feet of rock and exposed many deep-seated deposits. An immeasurable quantity of valuable minerals has thus been carried to sea and lost, but, in this process, erosion has exposed the underlying rocks so that at least a part of the earth's metallic wealth is accessible.

Coal. Coal beds (Fig. 11–1) owe none of their original formation to mountains, although the quality of coal may be improved by pressure exerted through certain folding and pressure processes characteristic of mountain regions. The formation of coal began in swamps (Fig. 11–2) under climatic controls that encouraged luxuriant plant growth during geologic eras of long ago. The continents, which at that time possessed large areas of ill-drained lands and humid tropical or semitropical climates, are the continents leading in today's coal resources. Most of these resources lie in the Northern Hemisphere, with Asia leading all the continents in total proven reserves. The Southern Hemisphere, however, possesses less than 5 per cent of it, with South America accounting for the least of all the inhabited continents.

Oil and Gas. Mountain building that gives aid to the formation of metallic minerals may destroy deposits of oil and gas (Fig. 11–3, 11–4, 11–5, and 11–6). It is generally believed that oil forms from the remains of marine life entombed in the muds of shallow seas; now oil may be found in the sedimentary beds of ancient seas, which at some periods of past geologic time covered a total of 22 million square miles of the almost 60 million square miles included in the continents today. The geologist's knowledge of where the former seas were situated has established four great basins—North Polar, Mediterranean, Indonesian, and American Mediterranean (Caribbean and Gulf of Mexico)—as major world centers of oil and gas accumulations. Such resources may also be discovered on the earth's 10 million square miles of continental shelf.

Most of the sedimentary beds in the four great basins are geologically young rocks. Old rocks retain their heritage of petroleum only where they have been spared the contortion and the induration periodically visited over most of the earth's crust by its rhythmic pulsations; such areas are the midcontinental regions, particularly the Mississippi valley of the United States and the plains on either side of the Ural Mountains in Russia and Siberia. Even geologically young rocks may lose their content of petroleum and natural gas if they are subjected to extreme earth movements.

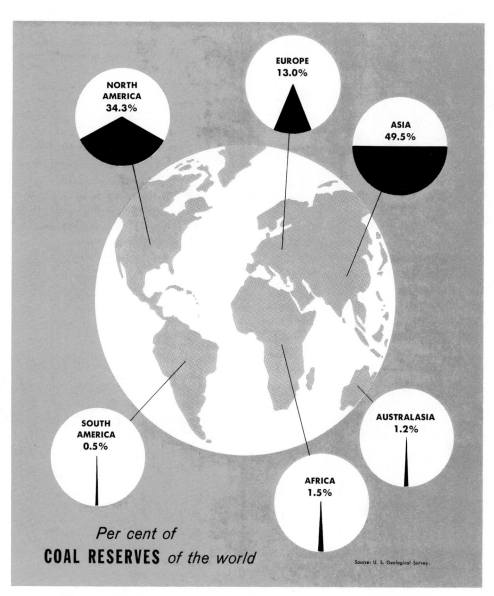

Fig. 11–1   Coal Reserves of the World. Notice the dominance of the Northern Hemisphere in reserves of coal. (*Courtesy U.S. Geological Survey and National Coal Association*)

Fig. 11-2   Prehistoric Swamps. The formation of bituminous coal began millions of years ago in great swamps presumed to have looked like this. As the vegetation died and fell into the water, it decomposed only partially, forming layers of peat. Sediment later covered these deposits, and as the land rose and fell in vast geological upheavals, increasing pressure for eons transformed the peat into lignite and then into bituminous coal. In a few areas, still more pressure turned the bituminous coal into anthracite. (© *Chicago Natural History Museum*)

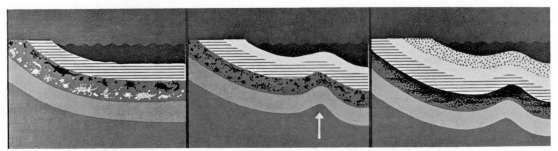

Fig. 11-3   Formation of Oil. Although scientists do not know exactly how oil was formed in the earth, many believe that the formation proceeded in steps like these. Plant and animal matter from land and ocean were deposited on the sea bottom in layers of ooze (*left*); accumulation of sediment created pressure that compacted the organic matter and generated heat (*center*); over eons of time, bacteria or other agents transformed the decaying matter into tiny drops of oil (*right*). (*Standard Oil Company, New Jersey*)

Methods of Mining

Open-Pit and Strip Mining. (Figs. 11–7 and 11–8). The type of mineral occurrence will influence the manner of exploitation and the cultural or man-made landscape associated with the mine. Where metallic deposits or coals of economic importance are present near the earth's surface with very little overburden, or overburden of such a nature that it can be removed easily by mechanical processes, open-pit or strip mining will be used in exploiting the deposit. Such surface mining is employed in the Mesabi region of the United States (Fig. 11–9), at Kiruna, Sweden, beyond the Arctic Circle; in Itibira, Brazil, said to be the largest deposit of rich iron ore in the world; at Schefferville, Labrador, from where iron moves by rail to Seven Islands for shipment by water on the adjoining St. Lawrence river; and at Krivoy Rog, Russia, whose iron becomes a partner with Donetz coal in the Donbas industrial region.

Open-pit mining techniques are also used in exploiting copper at Bingham, Utah; Chuquicamata, Chile; Katanga, in the former Belgian Congo; and in Kounradskiy and Djezkazga, U.S.S.R., south of Lake Balkash; in mining tin in Malaya; bauxite in Dutch and British Guiana; phosphates in Florida; nitrates in the Atacama desert of northern Chile; and in mining limestone, granite, marble, sandstone, clay, shale, gypsum, sand, gravel, and other building materials in various parts of the world.

The term "strip mining" is applied to surface exploitation of coal more frequently than "open-pit mining." In Illinois it is considered practical to strip off as much as 50 feet of overburden to reach a 5-foot coal seam. In Pennsylvania, stripping operations have been used to reach anthracite that is more than 175 feet below the surface of the ground.

Shaft Mining. This method is employed to

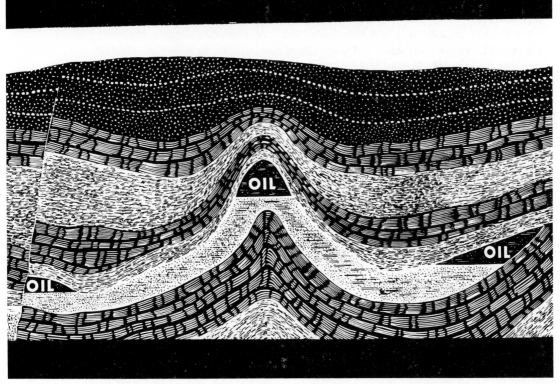

Fig. 11–4   Traps for Oil. Oil deposits are usually found in traps of the types illustrated above; (*left*) a fault; (*center*) an anticline; (*right*) a stratigraphic trap. (*Standard Oil Company, New Jersey*)

Fig. 11-5   Off-shore Oil Drilling. This off-shore oil-drilling rig in the Gulf of Mexico is capable of drilling for petroleum in water depths exceeding one hundred feet. (*Courtesy Allied Chemical Corporation*)

exploit minerals lying at great depths beneath the surface or resting at shallower depths beneath overburden too difficult to blast or remove (see Fig. 11-7). Some of the deepest shaft mines of the world, almost two miles down, are the Rand gold mines of South Africa. As a consequence of the great depths, these mines require artificial cooling. Another deep gold mine is near Mysore, India, where the shaft reaches a depth of 9200 feet.

Obviously shaft mining usually is more expensive than open-pit or strip mining. But in all latitudes it may be carried on throughout the year; climatic conditions in middle- and high-latitude countries generally make winter mining impossible for open-pit or strip mines.

Drift and Slope Mining. Both drift and slope mining employ methods of reaching the underground deposit that differ from the technique necessary for the vertical shaft mine (see Fig. 11-7). Slope mines are opened by driving an inclined entry through overlying strata to the mineral; and a drift mine leads to the mineral through a horizontal shaft. Many Appalachian Plateau mines use drift mining to extract the coal, and a description of the process may provide a useful illustration.

Appalachian coal formation took place on lowland swamp topography millions of years ago. After the coal beds were formed, uplift of many hundreds of feet took place with a minimum of folding and faulting. Following uplift, stream erosion cut deep valleys, making it easy for man to extract thick horizontal beds of coal from the valley by drift mining. Thus coal can be brought to the edge of the valley by underground transport moving horizontally or nearly horizontally, and from there the fuel moves down grade to the bottom of the stream valley, where it may be moved by barge or rail through an easy valley route to market. Of course, stream erosion, which made mining and transport of the product easy, removed some coal during the dissection of the plateau.

Placer Mining. (Fig. 11–10) A placer is a deposit of sand or gravel that contains particles of a valuable mineral in sufficient quantity to be workable at a profit. In the most primitive methods, the gravel may be placed in a large pan with water and swirled about so that the water and gravel gradually spill out. The mineral, being heavy, stays at the bottom of the pan. Gold, tin, platinum, and diamonds are substances commonly taken from placers. Most placers are

stream gravels, but a few are marine beach gravels.

Placers are so easily found and so readily worked, without special equipment or capital, that they have been sought from the beginning of history by the prospector and explorer. Gold placers have been the strongest incentives in this search, and most of our gold mining districts have been located by the placer miner.

Extraordinary ingenuity has been applied to the problem of working the leaner placers. So brilliant are the results in the more advanced methods of placer mining—hydraulicking and dredging—that they are some of the most efficient forms of mining, in the sense that a lower grade of material can be worked by them than by any other method. In hydraulic mining a jet of water under heavy pressure is directed against a bank of gravel. The gravel thus loosened is swept by a current of water into a long sluice, where the mineral, because of its high specific gravity, settles rapidly to the bottom and is caught by an appropriate device at the head of

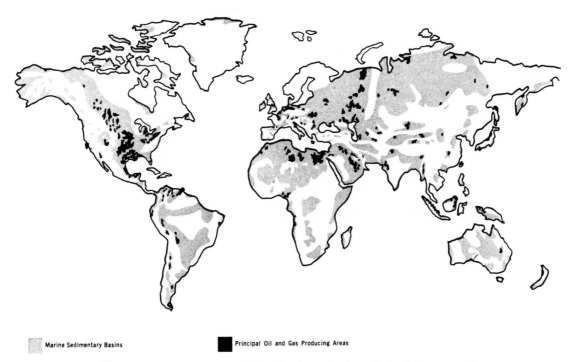

Marine Sedimentary Basins   ■ Principal Oil and Gas Producing Areas

Fig. 11–6   Actual and Potential Oil and Gas Producing Areas. Notice the large areas of marine sedimentary basins, the most likely places for future oil discovery and production. (*Courtesy American Petroleum Institute*)

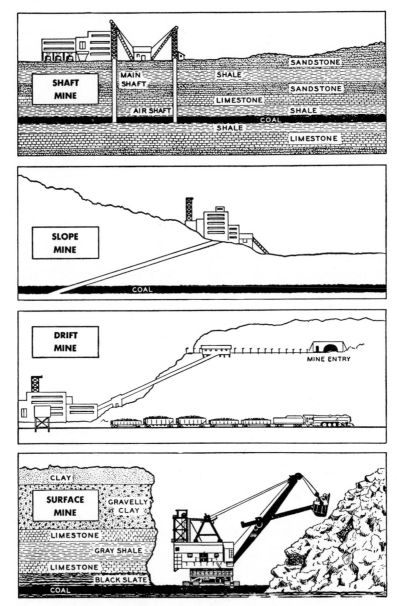

Fig. 11–7   Diagram of Mining Methods. The drawing above illustrates several ways in which coal and other minerals may be removed from the earth. In underground bituminous coal mining, there are three modes of ingress: shaft mines are opened by sinking a perpendicular shaft through the overlying strata to the coal seam; slope mines, by driving an inclined entrance through the overlying strata to the coal seam; and drift mines, by driving horizontally into the coal seam. In surface mining the overlying material is removed, usually with steam shovels, and the coal is mined at the surface. Surface mining also has been called strip or open pit mining. (*Courtesy Bituminous Coal Institute*)

Fig. 11–8   Strip-Mining Machinery. This giant stripping shovel towers about 170 feet into the air; and mining with machines of this kind accounts for about one fourth of the United States production of coal. A major problem is the restoration of strip-mine spoil banks to farm crops, grass, or trees; for if left untouched, the spoil banks become a hideous scar on the landscape. Restoration laws should be enforced strictly. (*Courtesy National Coal Association*)

Fig. 11–9   Hibbing, Minnesota, on the Edge of an Open Pit Mine. The present city of Hibbing borders the edge of a huge open-pit iron mine. In the 1920's part of old Hibbing was moved. The underlying iron was so valuable that mineral exploitation became more important than the permanence of that part of the town site.

Fig. 11-10   Primitive Placer Mining in Malaya. A small amount of tin is still washed from the gravel by panning— an oriental version of the technique practiced by the forty-niners in the California gold rush. (*Courtesy American Iron and Steel Institute*)

the sluice; and the lighter material, the gravel and sand, is carried through the sluice.

In dredging, the digging apparatus and the entire concentrating plant are contained on a boat, the dredge. The dredge floats on a pond; it digs and takes in the gravel at its forward end and discharges at its stern the tailings—the gravel from which the mineral has been separated. Thus the pond and the dredge on it gradually move up the valley.

Other Types of Mining—Salt, Sulphur, and Magnesium. Besides open-pit, strip, drift, shaft, slope, and placer mining, there are other kinds in which the manner of mineral exploitation fits an unusual type of occurrence in a somewhat unique way. Sulphur, salt, and magnesium mining may illustrate this mineral group.

Important sulphur deposits in the United States are located in Texas and Louisiana, where the mineral occurs in the cap rock overlying salt domes at depths varying from 300 to 2000 feet. Sulphur is brought to the surface by the Frasch process, named for the man who invented it in 1891. The method (Fig. 11–11) consists of melting the sulphur *while it is underground* by pumping heated water to it and then raising the melted sulphur to the surface, where it may solidify in vats or be shipped in liquid form. This takes advantage of the fairly low melting point of sulphur (about 240° F).

The occurrence of a high percentage of so-dium chloride in desert lakes, and of lower percentages in ordinary sea water, has encouraged man to build settling basins for obtaining common table salt in commercial quantities. The high rate of evaporation in dry climates soon removes all water from the shallow basins, and only the salt is left. Man-made basins may be located near the sea or lake and arranged so that water from the sea may move in at high tide and then be cut off entirely from its source; or in the case of the lake, water may be pumped into the settling basin for separation of the sodium chloride from lake water by evaporation.

A successful plant for processing sea water to extract minerals is at Freeport, Texas. Here the Dow Chemical Company separates the four parts of magnesium chloride contained in each one thousand parts of sea water; this process is accomplished by letting the sea water stand in huge settling tanks containing crushed calcined oyster shells and other materials useful in the process of chemical separation. Later the magnesium chloride is changed to metallic magnesium by treatment in electrolytic cells. Thus does the type of occurrence of the mineral—magnesium chloride in sea water—influence the manner of exploitation—huge settling tanks and electrolytic cells located close to the raw materials available in the Gulf of Mexico.

The Use and Exhaustion of Minerals

The use of a mineral body and the time of its exhaustion will depend upon several conditions, among the most important of which are the following: location; amount; metallic content of the ore; stage of technical advance employed by the group exploiting the ore; the ease of exploitation; the demand; and transportation. Comment on a few of these factors may be useful.

Location. Two iron deposits of world significance will illustrate the significance of location in mineral use and exhaustion: those near Mayurbhanj, India, and those near Lake Superior. Shipments of Lake Superior ore have moved out to markets over the easy Great Lakes routes at the rate of approximately 100 million tons annually for several decades. These markets are encouraged by people laying greater and greater stress upon the machine age. Partly as a result of location on easy transport lines to a big American market, the richest ores, those of the Mesabi, are nearing exhaustion.

On the other hand, India's iron deposit of nearly ten billion tons lying about one hundred miles west of Calcutta, has experienced little exploitation, only about one to two million tons annually. Thus, this resource will last for many generations at the present rate of utilization. Indian markets offer little encouragement to expanded production of ore, largely because Indians have been interested but little in big-scale manufacture of iron and steel. Furthermore, shipments of Indian ore to American markets involve a long haul even in peace time, and during war periods delivery would be almost impossible.

Metallic Content of the Ore. The approaching exhaustion of high-grade hematite ores in the Mesabi district has forced steel men to spend millions of dollars in research for practical processes permitting use of billions of tons of low-grade Lake Superior ore still remaining. Not far from the Mesabi, ore containing approximately 51 per cent metal, lie enormous supplies of 20 to 30 per cent ore called taconite.

This ore bed, about 100 miles long, several thousand feet wide, and up to 200 feet thick, has been known to steel men for years; but because of low metallic content and the difficulty of beneficiating the ore—changing it to a higher percentage of metal—the use of the mineral has been delayed. With depletion of high-grade Mesabi ore, only a few years away and with unit production slower and unit costs mounting as better deposits near exhaustion, steel producers are turning to taconite.

Magnetic taconite scattered through the mining region's ore-bearing hard rock is crushed with the rock and ground to fine pieces; iron particles are separated magnetically from the gangue; and powdered metal is concentrated into small pellets (Fig. 11–12) or balls that are usable in blast furnaces. In the early 1960's Canadian mills could produce 20.7 million tons of the pellets annually compared with a capacity of 17.4 million tons in the Lake Superior iron district of the United States. Continued expansion is raising these capacities significantly, especially in the United States. The 1964 election in Minnesota helped the growth of this taconite processing expansion. For many

years steel companies have paid higher-than-average taxes on their operations associated with handling high grade Mesabi iron ore. They resented this method of taxation and threatened no more investments in taconite refinement unless the special tax was removed. In short, they insisted that their operations should receive the same tax as that for other industries. The threat became serious enough to endanger Minnesota's taconite industry. As a result, the so-called Minnesota taconite amendment passed by a 7 to 1 margin.

Within 36 hours after passage of the amendment, United States Steel announced plans for a taconite project costing between 120 and 150 million dollars; and Jones and Laughlin, Hanna

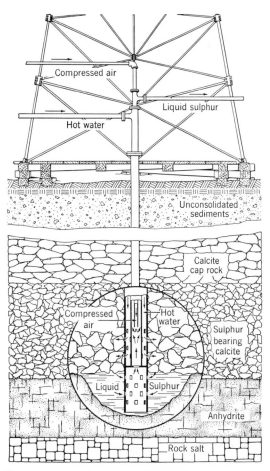

Fig. 11–11 Sketch Showing Sulphur-Well Piping. This method of mining melts the sulphur while it is underground by pumping heated water to it and then raising the melted sulphur to the surface. The process takes advantage of the fairly low melting point of sulphur. (*Courtesy Texas Gulf Sulphur Company*)

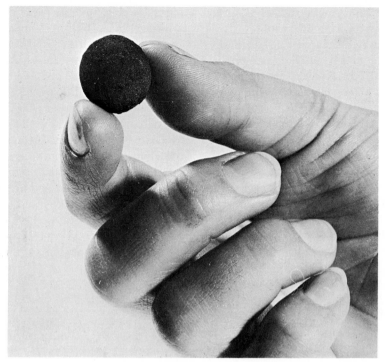

Fig. 11–12   A Finished Pellet. (*Courtesy Reserve Mining Company*)

Mining, and other steel companies also made significant expansion announcements. Minnesota expects, as a result of this change in taxing policy, an increase of a direct half-billion investment in taconite plants with 5,000 direct and 10,000 indirect jobs. The taconite amendment, to the Minnesota constitution, guarantees that for the next 25 years at least, taconite output will not be taxed at a rate higher than that of the general corporate tax level.

Stage of Technical Advance. Several conditions may delay use of an ore body until the stage of technical advance overcomes such difficulties. In the war of 1870 between France and Germany, the defeated French lost the now valuable Lorraine iron ores to the Germans. At that time no economical process was available to remove excess phosphorus contained in the ores. Exploitation had to await discovery of a practical formula by Thomas and Gilchrist in 1878.

Another example of use of a known ore body awaiting technical progress in mining technique is the Witwatersrand gold deposit in South Africa. Rand ores were known for years before the development of the cyanide process made the utilization of these low-grade ores profitable.

Finally it may be mentioned that the large taconite deposits of the Lake Superior region are of two kinds—magnetic and nonmagnetic. Processes for beneficiating the magnetic taconite became economical in the early 1950's after years of research; but so far a practical means for extracting metal from the much larger amount of nonmagnetic ore awaits further study to achieve success.

Mining Is a Robber Industry. Something should be said about the fact that minerals once removed from the earth are irreplaceable within human time. It is true that active volcanoes, at times of increased activity, may give off heated gases including such minerals as lead and iron. But the amounts are too small to be of economic significance. It is also a fact that minerals like iron can be used over and over again. Mineral technology has made it possible for blast-furnace use of as much as 50 per cent scrap iron mixed with ore fresh from the mine. Building stone can be taken from one building and used to construct another. But coal and petroleum, so-called minerals, serve for fuel but once. And, in general, the statement is true that *mining is a robber industry*.

The Western United States has more than one ghost town to remind us of the statement above. If, however, the mining property is located in a rich agricultural region, the adverse economic effects of mineral exhaustion will not be as serious to the community. Farming will cushion the shock of depleted mineral supplies. In short, what happens to the economy of a mining region, a mining state, or a mineral country after these resources are gone depends largely upon the remaining elements of the physical environment.

National Ownership of Minerals

Many illustrations can be given of how the rise[1] and fall of nations are influenced by the control or lack of control of adequate mineral resources. It was a common saying after World War I that the Allies floated to victory on a sea of oil; and in both World War I and World War II the Lake Superior iron resources contributed significantly to Allied success. One may ask now, what are the mineral resources of today's two great powers, the United States and Russia, and of other important nations in the world.

[1]"Human activity has been determined by the accident of mineral occurrence far more than most historians recognize. Flint was sought for the hunter, clay for the potter, metal for the wealthy, even at history's dawn. Later, as tribes merged and nations evolved, liquidation of those quick assets of a country, its mineral wealth, yielded revenue that many times led to power. But commonly we fix our attention on the power, not on the ores in which it had its roots. The success of Alexander the Great came not alone from his genius, but from the well-equipped army with which he started his campaigns—equipment and men available because of the many thousands of talents of gold accruing to him and to his father from the Macedonian gold bonanzas. Some thirteen centuries later, the long-lived Rammelsberg silver mines, discovered about A.D. 920, were a vital factor in the birth of the Holy Roman Empire; bullion from these mines provided both Henry the Fowler and Otto the Great with much of the capital used in their successful campaigns. Mineral deposits also contributed immeasurably to the expansion and power of ancient Egypt, the success of the exploring Phoenicians, the civic and military vigor of ancient Athens, the rise and fall of Venice, and the brief hegemony of Spain." T. S. Lovering, "The Exploitation of Mineral Resources," *Scientific Monthly,* Feb. 1949.

Mineral Resources in the United States. No nation is self-sufficient in mineral and power resources, but the United States probably approaches that status as closely as any country in the world. National supplies of coal will last for centuries at the present rate of consumption. In 1961, United States miners produced about four hundred million tons of coal, a figure lower than that for peak years, not because of declining resources, but because of strong competition from petroleum and natural gas. Most coal fields produce a high-quality product; many are adaptable to strip, slope, or drift mining, the easiest methods of exploitation; and the average thickness of seams makes the use of machines practical so that almost all United States coal is machine-mined; various favorable factors combine to make the daily and yearly tonnage per miner the highest in the world.

Many oil fields contribute to United States needs for petroleum; the Appalachian, Ohio-Indiana, Illinois-Indiana, Midcontinent, Gulf Coast, Rocky Mountain, and California fields yield the greatest annual totals reached by any nation; and new proven resources are maintaining reserves about as fast as annual consumption depletes them. Furthermore, transport of oil and gas is easy by pipe line and tank car as well as by tank ships on both inland and ocean waterways.

Uranium discoveries have increased so rapidly in the United States, especially in the Colorado Plateau, that the nation is self sufficient in the relatively new power resource. In the early 1960's, with local supplies more than adequate the United States failed to renew contracts for Canadian uranium.

Mention has been made already of the successful technical processes now being used to extract magnetic iron from low-grade Lake Superior taconite ore. Billions of tons of taconite will insure local supplies when high-grade Mesabi ore is depleted by, perhaps, the early 1970's. Steel producers also can turn to the less-well-located but rich Birmingham, Alabama, ores little used yet; and to the well-located Labrador ores of Canada, which are being produced by both Canadian and United States capital. All in all, the United States is well supplied with easily accessible iron resources; and not only leads the world in national production, approximately one hundred million tons annually in the early 1960's, but also has the capacity and resources to raise that figure significantly.

The situation is not as bright for the nonferrous minerals. Although the country is a production leader in copper, stock piling from foreign sources took place for some time; and supplementary shipments from Chile, Africa's Katanga, and other regions will probably continue in demand. Production of zinc and lead is also high, but local supplies, largely from the Midwest and Tristate district, are not sufficient, and imports for current consumption and stock piling have been necessary. Local supplies of tin are nil; deficiencies are also evident in bauxite and mica as well as in many metals such as vanadium, nickel, tungsten, antimony, chromium, and manganese. No imports of molybdenum are necessary.

Resources of mineral fertilizers are adequate, in the main, but not always well located. Supplies of phosphates are ample both in the Southeast and in the West. Unfortunately the Southeast supplies in Florida, Tennessee, Arkansas, South Carolina, and Kentucky are smaller than those of the West in Idaho, Montana, Utah, and Wyoming; and the Southeast probably needs commercial fertilizers more than any other agricultural section of the United States. On the other hand, the large supplies of the West are situated where lack of rainfall and rugged land forms discourage agricultural production, and long distances separate these phosphates from the major United States agricultural regions.

Sulphur is available in large quantities along the Gulf Coast. The Carlsbad, New Mexico, region and nearby areas have huge potash deposits, but like the western phosphates, they are not well located with reference to most of the nation's best agricultural regions. No natural nitrates are found in the country, but synthetic manufacture to supply national needs in their entirety only awaits the building of sufficient power resources.

In summary, the United States has large supplies of power minerals and iron ore, formerly important criteria of a great power. Mineral fertilizers abound in sufficient quantity to keep the country's soils in good agricultural condition. Copper, lead, zinc, and molybdenum are in fair supply. But tin, bauxite, mica, and many alloys used in the manufacture of iron and steel must be imported.

The U.S.S.R. Mineral Resources. Russian coal resources are large and widely distributed throughout the great empire that stretches between the Atlantic and Pacific for more than 5000 miles. Heavy production comes from the Donets field lying close to the Black Sea and a few hundred miles to the east of the rich Krivoy Rog iron fields; and from the Kuznetsk area located southeast of the Urals and not far from Karaganda iron ore. Besides these important resources, Russian coal deposits include the Caucasus, South Moscow, Pechora, Minusinsk, Yenisey, Kansk, Irkutsk, Tunguska, and Lena fields as well as several others. Russia's total tonnage in 1961 was well over 500 million tons, a figure more than a hundred million tons greater than that of the United States.

Known deposits of petroleum and natural gas are not as widely distributed as coal. The bulk of the country's proven reserves are located within the borders of an irregular rectangle bounded on the south by a line extending near the Black Sea through Maikop, Grozny, Baku, and across the Caspian Sea to Emba; the eastern boundary extends from Emba in a northerly direction along the slopes of the Western Urals to a little north of Moscow's latitude; the northern boundary extends west from the western slopes of the Middle Urals to a point north of Moscow; the western boundary turns south from this point towards the Sea of Azov. However, in 1962 *Tass* reported the finding of oil in Eastern Siberia, where none had been discovered before. This will supplement the long exploited resources on Sakhalin Island to the north of Japan. Geologists believe that there is one and a half to two times as much oil in Russia as in the United States; and compared to the United States, Russia has scarcely begun to exploit the nation's petroleum resources. Russian production in 1962 reached 1,457,000,000 barrels, a little over half that of the United States.

Knowledge of uranium resources beyond the Iron Curtain is limited; but it is known that deposits in Czechoslovakia have been worked for years, and that Siberia has large resources (1) to the east of Lake Balkash and (2) north of the Mongolian border.

Russia probably has iron reserves as large or larger than those of the United States; and they are widely distributed throughout the empire.

The Krivoy Rog deposits form the partner of Donets coal in the well-known Donbas industrial region. Proven reserves are also located at Kerch, Kursk, Magnitigorsk, Nizhni Tagil, and elsewhere in the Urals, Karaganda, Angara, and other fields. Although United States steel capacity is much greater than that of the Soviet, growth in steel production is much faster in Russia. Steel ingots produced in the U.S.S.R. in 1950 totaled 25,500,000 tons—in 1960 72,-090,000 tons; figures for the United States show 96,836,075 tons for 1950 and 99,281,601 tons for 1960.

Russian supplies of copper, lead, and zinc probably give the country an approach to self-sufficiency; and manganese is mined not only for local needs but also for export. As for tin, nickel, vanadium, tungsten, chrome, bauxite, and a few other minerals, it is likely that proven reserves are insufficient. Gold and platinum resources place Russia among the world's great producers.

Russian soils needing phosphate may be supplied from the deposits of the Kola Peninsula; and adequate potash comes from Solikamsk in the western Urals. As in the United States, no natural nitrates of significance are available; but demand may be met by the use of synthetics when or if sufficient power facilities are built.

In conclusion, it may be said that Russia compares with the United States in the possession of large coal, iron, petroleum, and natural gas resources. Fertilizers are available, with the addition of sufficient power, for all the country's needs. Possession of a wide variety of other minerals is equal to and possibly more than any other nation.

Minerals in Other Countries, Britain. Not one of the five former great powers, Britain, France, Germany, Italy, and Japan, has mineral resources comparable to those of the United States or Russia. Mineral supplies of the British Commonwealth, of which England is but one member, may equal or exceed those of Russia or the United States; but the parts of the British Commonwealth are widely separated, and transport is an important element in the way countries make a living and retain world position in both peace and war.

Britain's coal resources, in spite of high-cost production due partly to deep mines, thin, contorted seams, and other unfavorable physical factors, may supply the island for many years at the present rate of consumption. Much coal remains in Wales, along the flanks of the Pennines, and in the Scottish graben. But iron is another story. Britain has been dependent upon foreign sources for years; and India's rich Mayurbhanj deposit, Labrador's several fields, and Australia's iron in every province are a long distance away from the English heart of the Commonwealth.

The same situation exists in oil and gas. Geologists long guessed that the rocks of Britain contained no oil. Technically they guessed wrong because a little local oil has been produced, but the total is so small that it scarcely deserves mention. Canada's oil boom can provide excess for shipment to Britain; Borneo's oil resources may be underestimated; or the Middle East, where Britain has long been active, can contribute to British needs. It may be that recent large discoveries of oil and gas in the Netherlands will be only the first of many more to come in coastal areas bordering the North Sea as well as beneath its waters. If this sea yields as well as some optimists suggest, Britain's future petroleum supply will lie very near her borders; furthermore, the success of North Sea oil wells will help power needs of other West European countries. Another modern power resource, uranium, is available in Australia, Canada, South Africa, and other parts of the Commonwealth, but little has been found in the home island.

Cornwall's tin declined long ago. Copper, lead, zinc, bauxite, and most of the alloys are available in British dominions, but no adequate supply exists at home. The same can be said for mineral fertilizers, although, with ample supplies of coal and physical conditions favoring more water power installation, Britain could become locally self-sufficient in nitrates.

France. Across the channel, French coal supplies cannot compare with those of Britain and are far from adequate for home needs. Furthermore, much of the French coal is located along the country's borders, a bad situation for national economy in time of war. French coal deficiency is being overcome by expanding hydroelectric power; but oil and natural gas are insufficient. Limited production of petroleum takes place at Pechelbronn, too near the country's eastern boundary, and also in southwest France.

Iron in Lorraine, bauxite in Provence, and potash in Alsace, all occur in large amounts, more than adequate for the country's needs. Outside of these minerals, however, local supplies of other types are seriously lacking, and the country must look beyond her borders for many of her mineral supplies.

Germany. The Ruhr or Westphalian coal field has been the economic bulwark of Western Germany, just as it was for prewar Germany. Ruhr coal resembles that of the Appalachian field in several ways: in thick, but not quite as thick, seams, in good quality bituminous, in large resources, in mechanization but not as much as in the United States, and in relatively easy mining. Located near the Rhine, it surpasses the Appalachian coal in accessibility for export. But Western Germany lacks petroleum just as the entire country has always felt an oil shortage. Germany's oil needs were so serious that German scientists, many years ago, made great progress in extracting gasoline from lignite, of which the country has enormous amounts.

Both West and East Germany have limited iron resources, forcing the West to look to Lorraine in France and to Kiruna in Sweden for the best means of utilizing Ruhr coal, namely, in the manufacture of iron and steel. Leadership in chemicals has long been evident, based largely upon availability of great potash deposits, near Stassfurt, a mineral resource now located largely in East Germany. Outside of plentiful supplies of potash and coal, Germany has limited mineral resources.

Italy. Italy is short of all major power resources except hydroelectric facilities. The nation leads the continent in developed water power. Coal and petroleum are in limited supply, but oil has been discovered in the Po Valley and in Sicily, and increased production will help the national power situation. Small quantities of iron in Elba, bauxite in the heel of the Italian peninsula, lead and zinc in Sardinia and Tuscany, and sulphur in Sicily supplement large amounts of mercury in Tuscany. But even with

these the country has a weak background in minerals.

Japan. Japan must turn to other nations for most of her mineral requirements. A wide variety of minerals is present, but only in copper, silver, gold, and sulphur do local supplies meet national demands. The country has some petroleum, zinc, tin, lead, and iron, and almost a self-sufficiency in coal. Had Japan retained the far-flung Asian empire of the 1940's, the nation would have been much better supplied with the minerals so badly needed by an industrial power. In fact, a basic cause stressed by Japan for entrance into World War II was the need for minerals and other raw materials.

China. Part of Japan's ephemeral expansion took place in territory belonging to China, the neighbor to the west. Postwar changes in this large country suggest to some that it must be considered a great world power. How is China supplied with coal, petroleum, and iron, formerly important indices of powerhood?

China has coal in every province, but more than three-fourths of the resources are in two provinces, Shensi and Shansi. Petroleum reserves appear to be inadequate, but more detailed exploration may reveal greater proven supplies. Significant quantities of low-grade iron occur in Manchuria, and better ores along the Middle Yangtze and in the province of Szechwan. Copper, lead, zinc, tin, tungsten, antimony, manganese, sulphur, bauxite, mercury, and uranium are present, some in significant amounts. It must be remembered, however, that China has an enormous population, over six hundred million, and per capita amounts of mineral resources fall far short of those in the United States and in Russia.

Years ago, appraisals of China's mineral supplies were very optimistic; estimates of a later date were slightly pessimistic for such a large country; the actual truth probably lies somewhere in between.

QUESTIONS, EXERCISES, AND PROBLEMS

1. Be able to locate the mining centers mentioned in the text on a world map.
2. What is the relation between the occurrence of coal and geologic history? Explain the same relationship

for petroleum and natural gas. Show the relation between the occurrence of metals and mountain building.

3. Explain the following mining principle by aid of examples in open-pit mining, shaft mining, drift mining, and placer mining. The type of mineral occurrence will influence the manner of exploitation and the cultural or man-made landscape.

4. Show how the following conditions will influence the use of a mineral body and the time of its exhaustion: location, amount, metallic content of the ore, stage of technical advance, the ease of exploitation, the demand, transport facilities, etc. Explain how the statement "mining is a robber industry" may be true.

5. Compare the mineral resources of the United States and the Soviet Union.

6. Describe the mineral position of the British Commonwealth, of France, of West Germany, of Italy, of Japan, and of China.

7. Identify the following: strip mining; gangue; ore; overburden; folding; faulting; dissected plateau; dredge mining; hydraulic mining; sulphur mining; magnesium mining; beneficiate; taconite, cyanide process; alloy; marginal producing mine; continental shelf; Thomas and Gilchrist.

SELECTED REFERENCES

American Iron and Steel Institute, *Steel Facts,* published monthly, 150 E. 42nd St., New York 17, New York.

American Iron and Steel Institute, *Steelmaking: Flow Charts.*

American Petroleum Institute, *Petroleum Facts and Figures,* 1964 or later edition, 1271 Avenue of the Americas, New York 20, New York.

Boericke, William, "Quest for Iron Ore," *Barron's,* July 24, 1961.

Bureau of Mines, *Mineral Facts and Problems, Bulletin 556,* Govt. Printing Office, 1956 or later edition.

Cannon, R. L. "Botanical Prospecting for Ore Deposits," *Science,* Sept. 1960, pp. 591–598.

Garnett, W. A., "The Australian Breakthrough," *Fortune,* Sept. 1962.

Goodwin, William, "Outlook for Aluminum," *Focus,* Jan. 1961.

Hess, W. N., "New Horizons in Resource Development," *Geographical Review,* Jan. 1962, pp. 1–24.

Hoy, D. R. and Taube, S. A., "Power Resources of Peru," *Geographical Review,* Oct. 1963, pp. 580–94.

Leasing, Lawrence, "The Mighty Mix of New Materials," *Fortune,* May 1962.

Meyerhoff, H. A., "Mineral Raw Materials in the National Economy," *Science,* Feb. 1962, pp. 510–16.

Miller, E. Willard, "World Patterns and Trends in Energy Consumption," *Journal of Geography,* Sept. 1959, pp. 269–79.

Miller, Elbert E., "Outlook for Uranium," *Focus,* March 1960.

National Coal Association, *Bituminous Coal Facts,* 1964 or later edition, Coal Bldg., Washington, D.C.

Odell, P. R., *An Economic Geography of Oil,* G. Bell and Sons, Ltd., London, 1963.

Riley, Charles M., *Our Mineral Resources,* John Wiley and Sons, 1959.

Rodgers, Allan, "Coking Coal Supply: Its Role in the Expansion of the Soviet Steel Industry," *Economic Geography,* April 1964, pp. 113–50.

Shaw, Earl B., "Esterhazy and its Potash," *Journal of Geography,* Jan. 1962, pp. 31–35.

Sherman, J. V., "Iron Ore Expansion: Industry is Investing Heavily in High-Grade Pellet Capacity," *Barron's,* Feb. 3, 1964.

Thoman, R. S. and Patton, D. J., *Focus on Geographic Activity,* McGraw-Hill, 1964, Chs. 14, 15, 16, and 17, "A Bituminous Coal Mine in the Appalachian Highlands,"; "Iron Ore Production in Quebec-Labrador"; "A Diamond Mine in South Africa"; and "Geography of an International Petroleum Firm."

Part Two

Introduction to Regional and Economic Geography

Chapter Twelve

The Humid Tropics:
Tropical Rainforest and Tropical Grasslands

One of the significant contributions of geography is the recognition that in spite of numerous variations in the earth's landscape the world can be divided into major more or less similar areas which may be called geographic regions.

There are several views of what constitutes a geographic region. George Renner says that a region is an area homogeneous enough in its physical environment to possess either actual or potential unity in its cultural aspects. *American Geography: Inventory and Prospects* states that a region is an area of any size that is homogeneous in terms of specific criteria and that is distinguished from bordering areas by a particular kind of association of areally related features. Other geographers may word the definition slightly differently, but all of them show general agreement.

One important advantage of the regional approach is that it gives a better knowledge of the different parts of a unit, their relationships to each other and to the unit as a whole. This is true whether the unit is a country, a continent, or the world.

In the following five chapters the student may look at major world regions divided from one another on the basis of climate. Climate is chosen as the divisor because the larger fraction of mankind is still making a living on farms; and climate is extremely significant in defining limits for natural vegetation, for planted crops, and for domestic animals. A brief geographic analysis is made of each region—an examination based on the region's geographic environment and its land utilization.

The Physical Environment: Tropical Rainforest

Location. Latitudinally most of the tropical rainforest lies only a few degrees from the equator, with outlying portions extending farther poleward along the windward sides of continents (Fig. 12–1). The largest and most typical sections are found in the Amazon Basin and the coastal lowlands of Brazil, the Guinea Coast and Congo Basin of Africa, and the plains and lower windward slopes of monsoonal lands of southeast Asia. Smaller portions occur where trade winds are forced to rise over uplands or where a combination of convectional and orographic influences may provide heavy rainfall. Examples of the orographic influence may be noted in the eastern part of the Malagasy Republic, at the eastern base of the Central Andes and in parts of Central America and the West Indies.

Climate. Major climatic features include high temperature, averaging not far from 80°F at sea level; very slight seasonal temperature changes; and heavy rainfall, usually 80 inches or above, with either no dry season or a very short one. The most critical requirement is enough precipitation to support rainforest vegetation (Fig. 12–2).

Vegetation. Tropical lowlands, where there is no distinct dry season, or where the dry season is not long and severe, produce very luxuriant forests; for moisture, temperature, and light are continuously favorable. In keeping with the luxuriance of the vegetation, the number of

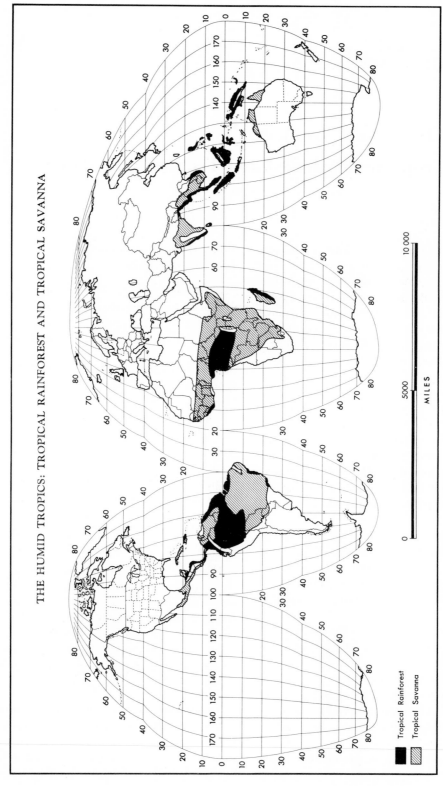

THE HUMID TROPICS: TROPICAL RAINFOREST AND TROPICAL SAVANNA

Tropical Rainforest

Tropical Savanna

Fig. 12-1   The Humid Tropics: Tropical Rainforest and Tropical Savanna. The bulk of the tropical rainforest is found in three major areas, the Amazon Valley, the Congo Basin, and the East Indies. Smaller sections appear in Latin America, Africa, and southeast Asia. Notice the large areas of tropical savanna in Latin America, Africa, southeast Asia, and in northern Australia. (*Projection based on the homolosine projection copyright by the University of Chicago. Map by permission McGraw-Hill Book Co. and G. T. Trewartha,* An Introduction to Climate)

species of trees, vines, epiphytes, and parasites is greater than in either the middle latitude hardwood or the subarctic coniferous forests. More than a hundred species of trees have been counted in an area of little more than a half acre.

Trees in the true tropical rainforest are often described as umbrella-shaped, with thick trunks branchless until near the wide-spreading tree-top. This top may shield the ground so closely that little understory vegetation occurs. Such conditions are found in the wet tropics, but they are not general. In fact, in many sections two- and three-story vegetation is characteristic, with undergrowth such as tree-connecting vines so thick that travel through the forest is difficult. In the Amazon and Congo Basin, trees ten or more feet in diameter, at the base, may reach a height of 100 to 200 feet. One of these trees contains many times as much lumber as the average tree of the middle latitude hardwood or subarctic conifer forests. Nevertheless, the rainforest and the subarctic are alike in being little disturbed by human invasion. Only where the forest borders the ocean or some great river, has exploitation even started.

Soil. Lateritic soils are typical in the nearly level areas such as large sections of the Amazon Basin and the coastal plain of New Guinea. The ground is waterlogged much of the time. Milpa agriculture, characteristic of widespread areas, necessitates a change of land every two or three years because of soil depletion and the rank growth of weeds.

Land Forms. Ill-drained plains, such as those of the Congo and Amazon rivers, dominate surface features. Slopes, like those leading from the eastern Brazilian coastal plain to the interior plateau, may be included, but they comprise a minor fraction of the total region.

Land Utilization

Man has not conquered this region. In many cases he is dominated by the physical environment. In the most isolated sections, small groups, often but a few families, roam the forests gathering fruits and vegetables and killing animals and fish. Their dwellings, many of them built on posts or on platforms in the trees, are little more than roofs of palm leaves that serve merely

as a refuge from animals and a shelter from storms. No matter whether natives of the rainforest are Pygmies of the Congo Basin or Indian head hunters of the Upper Amazon, they all live a similar type of life, one of the least developed forms of human existence found anywhere on earth.

The tropical rainforest region could be divided into two sections on the basis of location: the more accessible continental coasts and islands and the less accessible continental interiors. In better-located parts, life rises above the level of food gatherers and hunters. Houses are of fair quality—rude, palm-thatched huts with walls of rough sticks. They may be surrounded by small patches of rice, corn, yams, manioc, taro, and other crops. Swine and poultry may add to the food supply. Although still almost seminomadic, moving on after the soil is exhausted, these people have a higher culture than those with little or no agriculture (Fig. 12–3).

Probably nowhere else are certain diseases more virulent (Figs. 12–4 and 12–5). Man must contend with fevers, dysentery, and other dangerous ailments. He must combat stinging insects that make sores which fester a long time. Disease, enervating climate, poor soil in most areas, excessive vegetation, difficulty in keeping domestic animals, human inertia, all unite in

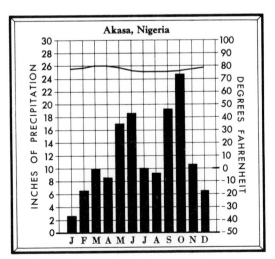

Fig. 12–2   Climatic Chart, Akasa, Nigeria. Akasa shows a double maximum in its precipitation, which may be influenced somewhat by the twice-yearly passage of the vertical ray of the noonday sun. Only one month shows an average below 3 inches of rainfall; and the average monthly precipitation is 12 inches.

Fig. 12–3   Corn Growing in the Congo Basin. Oil palms have been left standing purposely for food supply. A few other trees have survived the brush fires characteristic of milpa agriculture; these trees possess the bare straight appearance of most tropical rainforest growth. Note the trunks and branches of trees still lying on the ground. (*Pierre Gourou,* The Tropical World, *Longmans, Green & Co. Ltd. and John Wiley & Sons, Mr. Goldstein, photographer*)

preventing significant economic progress in much of the tropical rainforest. Industries contributing most to regional economy include (1) tropical plantations, developed in the more accessible, better soil areas, (2) forest products, and (3) mineral and power materials.

Tropical Plantations. Tropical plantations, like livestock ranches, are a relatively recent agricultural development (Figs. 12–6, 12–7, and 12–8). These large farms became productive in response to the demands of middle-latitude peoples, Europeans first, for various commodities—products which can not be grown outside the tropics or subtropics. Cane sugar was the first plantation crop to achieve commercial significance, but now at least a dozen more appear on world markets. Many are grown in regions far removed from their native habitat.

Rainy low-latitude plantations are characterized by the following practices: emphasis is placed upon commercial rather than subsistence production; commodities are usually forwarded to middle-latitude markets; a plantation once established may remain in existence for many years; and in this respect differs markedly from

milpa agriculture, which is subsistence and migratory in nature. Monoculture, or crop specialization, is the rule; in many cases but one crop is produced on the plantation. Laborers may not raise enough fruits and vegetables for their own use.

Extreme care is taken with seed selection, methods of cultivation, and other production practices. Disease prevention and control receive careful attention for both crops and workers. Management usually comes from the middle latitudes.

Most tropical plantations are found near ocean transport either on islands or along the mainland coast. Such a location provides advantageous shipping facilities and insures health-giving ocean breezes so favorable for the best working conditions in the wet lowland tropics. Not only do sea winds lower the daily maximum temperature, but also the salt air discourages disease-bearing insects that often menace health of the workers. Better-than-average soils on recently upraised sea bottoms or on well-drained coastal alluvium may also encourage the coastal location.

The land to be planted must be cleared of its

rainforest cover. This is a difficult job, for the forest is made up of a dense stand of large trees. For sugar cane and similar commodities, roots, stumps, and boulders must be removed so that the ground can be plowed. For other crops such as tea, cacao, rubber, abaca, or bananas, much less preliminary preparation for planting is necessary, since the land does not have to be plowed. A few crops, such as bananas, are shipped almost as they are harvested, but many others are processed in varying amounts with equipment located on or near the plantation.

Although laborers may be indigenous to the country where the plantation is located, very often workers are imported from other low-latitude or subtropical regions. A good example of this occurred in the Caribbean area on some of the earliest of tropical plantations. Negro slaves were shipped from similar low latitudes in Africa to work on Caribbean sugar plantations; and the importations are largely responsible for the many colored peoples who occupy this area at present.

Forest Industries. Forest industries are little developed commercially, for several reasons. (1) Laborers are limited in numbers, and those available are less efficient than workers in middle latitude forests. (2) The scattered occurrence of trees of the same species makes cutting and assembling the finished product more difficult than exploiting the more consistent tree stands in areas outside the tropics. (3) Transportation is a problem, especially in forests far from navigable waterways. There are few roads; and road and rail building is more expensive in time and materials than in the middle latitudes. Even in the use of available streams, transport faces a problem in the high specific gravity of many hardwoods. Some are so heavy they do not float; and rafts of light wood, such as balsa, must be built to move the weighty logs downstream. (4) Not the least of hardships is finding a market for tropical hardwoods. They are little known in the nontropical industrial world; and their uses are far more limited than those for middle latitude hard and soft woods. (5) In spite of difficulties, some companies have found the exploitation of tropical hardwoods profitable.

Fig. 12–4   Severe Case of Elephantiasis. Elephantiasis, which causes enormous swelling of the legs and sometimes other parts of the body, is caused by a minute worm transmitted by mosquitoes. (*Paul Popper Ltd., Photographic Agency*)

Fig. 12–5   Tsetse Fly (*Glossina palpalis*). This fly transmits *trypanosoma gambiense* causing sleeping sickness in man. (*Paul Popper Ltd., Photographic Agency*)

©

Fig. 12–6   Rubber Plantation in Southeast Asia. These 8-year-old Sumatra rubber trees are planted in rows 20 feet apart; 10 feet separate one tree from the next in each row. The ground is planted with a cover crop to add soil fertility and to prevent soil erosion and noxious weeds. The southeast Asian tropics accounted for more than 90 per cent of the 1962 world production of natural rubber, totaling 2,145,000 long tons. Indonesia and Malaysia each produced approximately one third of the world total.

This is no place for the individual lumberman. This is the environment for big corporations willing to risk and to plan every operation carefully from the task of obtaining logs in the forest to the delivery of the finished product to the ultimate consumer.

Besides offering limited opportunities for exploiting mahogany (Fig. 12–9), ebony, teak and other tropical hardwoods, the rainforest supports an industry which may be called forest gathering. It is one of the oldest ways of making a living known to man, probably comparing with fishing and hunting as to age. Today certain primitive peoples still gather products of the forest for subsistence purposes, just as their ancestors did thousands of years ago. People collect nuts for their food, leaves, bark, and roots for beverages and medicinal purposes, fiber for cloth, thatch for houses, and many other items for food, shelter, and clothing.

Forest gathering has also entered the stage of exchange economy. Natives in the Amazon Basin gather latex for rubber (Fig. 12–10); in the forests of Guatemala, chicleros tap the trees for chicle, the base for chewing gum; on the eastern slopes of the Peruvian Andes, Indians collect cinchona bark for quinine and coca leaves for cocaine; in Colombia, Venezuela, and Ecuador, workers gather tagua nuts for making vegetable ivory buttons; along Africa's Guinea Coast, Negroes collect palm nuts for palm oil; in the Pacific Coast forests of northern Ecuador and Southern Colombia, the toquilla palm provides fiber for so-called Panama hats; and several other forest products from these and other rainforest lands move into commercial trade.

Minerals and Power. Minerals are exploited in several areas. One which attracts world attention is the Katanga region of the former Belgian Congo. That area contains large deposits of copper, tin, zinc, cobalt, diamonds, uranium, and other mineral and power resources. Richest of the Congo's provinces, Katanga sought independence from the rest of the country; and kept political conditions unsettled for a long time in the early 1960's.

Another important mineral development is in Malaya and the Indonesian Republic, especially in two small islands, Bangka and Billiton, where large tin deposits occur. These resources lie near the surface, are rich in metallic content, and are easily accessible to coastal shipment.

Petroleum exploration is also active in Brazil and Peru along the flanks of the Andes bordering the Amazon Basin; some day population clusters will occur wherever profitable exploitation takes place.

One of the most important exports from the colonies of Dutch and British Guiana comes from their bauxite deposits in the heart of the

Fig. 12–7   Harvesting Cacao in Tafo, Ghana. The West African Cacao Research Institute (WACRI) has its headquarters at Tafo. Cacao grows well in Ghana's warm, wet, low-latitude tropics with their high frequency of calms. Windy weather is a hazard to the heavy pods, about the size of a large cucumber, which hang from the trunk and branches of the tree on weak stems. Africa's tropical rainforest region produced two thirds of the 1963 total world crop of 1,191,700 metric tons. Ghana accounted for one third, Nigeria one sixth, and Brazil one tenth of the world total. (*Courtesy United Nations*)

Fig. 12–8   Mature Bunch (stem) of Bananas Hanging from a Full-Grown Plant. The Latin American tropics accounted for about five sixths of the 1961 world trade in bananas, amounting to 183,289,000 stems. Ecuador, the leading exporter, shipped about one fourth of the total. The picture above shows the Gros Michel banana, long dominant in Latin American production. However, the United Fruit Company is replacing "Fat Mike" with the valery banana on its plantations; this fruit is immune to Panamá disease and is more resistant to wind damage because of its lower height. *(Courtesy United Fruit Company)*

rainforest. Large quantities of this profitable base for aluminum are shipped by cheap ocean transport to Canada where they are processed in the huge hydroelectric power development at Arvida along the Saguenay River.

Recently Bethlehem Steel Corporation is shipping significant quantities of rich iron ore to its Sparrows Point steel mill in Maryland from African Liberia. And in nearby Sierra Leone, diamonds form the most important export in that little country.

The mining developments mentioned above do not make up the entire list of mineral activi-

ties now taking place in the rainforest lands; in fact minerals and power probably hold as much promise for future development as any of the resources of the region.

Summary and Conclusions. In summarizing rainforest economy, it may be well to look at the population map. It shows only a small number of people in the region. Over half the area supports less than 2 persons per square mile; on the bulk of the remainder the density is between 2 and 25 per square mile. Only along the coast bordering India's Western Ghats, in western Java, southern Ceylon, the tip of the Malay Peninsula, small areas along Brazil's east coast, Africa's Gulf of Guinea Coast, and in a few small coastal and island areas elsewhere are population densities significant.

Natural rubber, cacao, bananas, and several other tropical plantation products; small amounts of forest-gathered commodities; shipments of tropical hardwoods valued less than forest-collected articles; and minerals, especially from the African rainforest and the southeast Asia peninsular and island region—these make up major items contributed by the tropical rainforest to world trade. On the whole this contribution represents but a small fraction of total world commerce.

Most of the region belongs to the world's underdeveloped lands. These are poor, non-industrialized areas, where most people live under conditions approaching misery; and there is mass poverty that is not the result of a temporary calamity. Well over half the population is engaged in farming, hunting, and forest gathering. The inhabitants—with the exception of those on tropical plantations, mining enterprises, and a few other developments, all largely managed and financed by persons from the middle latitudes—employ antiquated methods of production and little inanimate power. The birthrate is high but mortality is declining, the diet on all counts is inadequate, life expectancy is low, and illiteracy is the rule. Expressed in one word, most of the rainforest people belong to the "havenots" of the earth.

Physical Environment: Tropical Savanna

Location and Climate. The tropical savanna includes more land than the tropical rainforest, which lies on its equatorward margin. Major portions of the savanna extend from about 5° to 15° on both sides of the equator. Seasonal rainfall is influenced by relatively stable dry descending air of the horse latitudes on the poleward margins, and by unstable wet ascending equatorial air near the savanna's opposite

Fig. 12–10   A Seringueiro in the Amazon Basin. These forest gatherers search for wild rubber trees of the tropical rainforest and tap them for latex. The white ball at his feet is the rubber he has collected. The black ball is the vessel for holding the latex. An open fire is used for coagulating the latex. (*Pierre Gourou,* The Tropical World, *Longmans, Green & Co., Ltd. and John Wiley & Sons*)

Fig. 12–9   Tropical Hardwood for Export. The men at the left give an idea of the enormous size of tropical rainforest timbers. These mahogany logs have been sorted, graded, and made ready for shipment from Kumasi to Takoradi. At this Ghana port they will be loaded on shipboard for sale in Europe or the United States. (*Courtesy United Nations*)

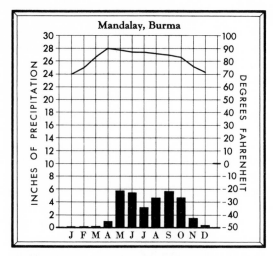

Fig. 12–11   Climatic Chart, Mandalay, Burma. The Irra-waddy Valley, in which Mandalay is located, is cut off from rain-bearing monsoon winds by mountains; thus the annual rainfall limits natural vegetation growth to tropical grasses.

boundaries. In southeast Asia air masses are not distributed as described above; there, monsoon conditions dominate, with winds blowing towards land in summer and towards sea in the cool season. Seasonality of rainfall, so character-istic of tropical savanna climates, is the same.

Rainfall follows the sun (Fig. 12–11). During the season of high sun and long days, precipita-tion is heaviest. When the sun is lower and day-light shorter, a dry period prevails. Rainfall is usually less, more seasonal, and more variable than in the rainforest. On the equatorial mar-gins, precipitation differs little from that of the rainforest. However, on the savanna's poleward margin, rainfall becomes more like that of the steppe or desert. Boundaries among these re-gions are transitional.

Maximum temperatures are higher and the minimums lower than those of the rainforest. Averages are similar, but ranges, both diurnal and annual, are greater. Reasons for these dif-ferences are not hard to understand. Length of daylight and altitude of the noonday sun show greater seasonal variation in the savanna; there is also greater seasonality of precipitation, drier air, and less cloud. All these factors affect annual range.

Vegetation. Vegetation is influenced by cli-mate. In the more rainy savanna, open forest may be found in the midst of heavy grass. In less

rainy sections forest gives way to genuine park-like savanna with only scattered trees. This gradually merges into immense treeless grass-lands broken only by narrow strips of dense forest along rivers where abundant moisture supports tree growth. Finally, where climate becomes semiarid, grass becomes short, or the ground may be covered with scrubby bushes.

Tall and abundant grasses, in many places from three to fifteen feet high, form the habitat for millions of wild animals. Many of them feed on the savanna grasses, but others are flesh-eaters; the latter include the tigers of Asia, the lions of Africa, and the jaguars of South Amer-ica. Along various rivers in the African savanna, one may see huge hippopotamuses and savage looking crocodiles. Jackals and vultures are the scavengers of dead and dying animals left by the carnivorous beasts.

Fever-bearing mosquitoes are numerous just as they are in the rainforest, especially in the rainy season and in all seasons on flat lands like the Sudd of the African Sudan, where drainage is poor. In many sections of the African savanna, the tsetse fly menaces the health of man as well as that of his domestic animals; and ticks bring great irritation to cattle as well as to human beings.

Soils. Savanna soils have more humus, more mineral plant foods, and better structure than those of the rainforest; but they belong to a relatively infertile soil group. Nevertheless, un-certainty of rainfall, both in amount and dis-tribution, is probably a greater agricultural handicap than tropical grassland soils.

Surface Features. Land forms may be di-vided into tropical lowlands and uplands. Be-cause of elevation, the uplands are cooler and more habitable than the lowland savannas de-scribed in the preceding paragraphs. An in-crease in altitude of 3000 feet may lower tem-perature approximately 10° F, a decrease of great importance to human settlement in the tropics. Large plateaus appear in Brazil and in East Africa. Upland surface features may be eroded by stream action, which is accelerated by the heavy seasonal rainfall. In fact, tropical downpours may cause severe dissection on up-land slopes, and the eroded material may be spread out at lower elevations on flood plains and deltas. Steep slope farming necessitates careful conservation practices to be successful; and these are advisable even on the gently rolling surfaces. Soils are likely to be better on gentle slopes than upon the level plains.

Land Utilization

In general, the responses of man to the savanna environment follow the same pattern in every continental region, but they differ considerably in stage of development. An extremely primitive economy may be seen among the few "black fellows" of northern Australia. In the South American savanna, the economy is higher. Before the coming of the European, Indians followed an occupation with hunting the dominant element. Europeans introduced cattle, and grazing has now become a main source of income. Although land is cheap, cattle raising has many handicaps on Latin American savannas as well as upon those of other continents. The coarse grass does not provide good pasture except when it first sprouts; the dry season may bring suffering or even death from lack of water; ticks and other insects not only impair the health of animals but aslo injure their hides by making sores which leave holes or weak spots in their skins. Transport is difficult because of the mud in the wet season, the scarcity of water in the dry season, and the absence of good roads at all seasons. The Llanos of the Orinoco, the Gran Chaco in Paraguay and Bolivia, the uplands on the gentle western slope of the plateau of eastern Brazil, and the great central Brazilian Campos and Mato Grosso are still sparsely populated, wide open spaces awaiting modern economic development.

In the African savanna on the low plateau extending from Senegal to Upper Nigeria crops are raised as far north as the rainfall is adequate. In spring, the air is full of smoke, where dry grass is being burned to clear the fields. Millet, cotton, and peanuts are important crops. Large villages of conical grass huts protected by mud walls show a relatively high level of native culture. Farther north, where the climate becomes drier, stock raising takes the place of crops, houses made of mud replace the grass huts, and finally nomadic life of the desert becomes dominant.

In East Africa, distinct local differences are common. Uganda, on the Lake Plateau, with a comparatively dense population and, with money crops of coffee, bananas, millet, and cotton contrasts sharply with the less favorable environment in much of the lowland of southern Sudan. Cattle raising persists within a few degrees of the equator in the southern Sudan. Tall, slender Shilluk, Nuer, and Dinka tribes wander almost naked with their cattle. In the dry season South Sudanese build huts of grass beside perennial streams or in low places, where water can be procured by digging wells. Just before the rains, dry grass is burned, and crops are planted on higher ground.

In the grasslands of Rhodesia and contiguous areas, similar conditions prevail. An unhealthful physical environment joined with local wars and raids of slave dealers to keep population sparse. Now, on Rhodesian uplands, farmers raise cattle, sheep, corn, wheat, and cotton. Here, as in all parts of the savanna region, the summer rain may be late or scarce, thus bringing disaster. It is well to remember that the lower the average rainfall, the greater the variability from year to year.

In Asia, savanna climate is found on most of the Deccan Plateau and in small sections of Burma, Thailand, and former French Indochina. In the Deccan, climatic conditions are slightly different from those of South America and Africa. Here, a monsoon rainfall occurs, precipitation brought mainly by southwest winds. The mountain wall of the Western Ghats diminishes rainfall for the leeward Deccan.

Farmers of India's Deccan combine cattle growing with crop raising. Where water is available, rice is raised, but jowar, a kind of millet, covers a far greater acreage and forms a main item in the diet. Not much is heard about millet in the western world, probably because so little enters world commerce; but the crop is important to millions of people in the dry lands of the eastern hemisphere. Indian corn; pulses, which are legumes resembling peas; and, in the north, wheat are the other main food crops. A rainfall of approximately 40 inches is ample for crop maturity if it comes at the right times; but failure of rains is common. Terrible famines are the result, unless food can be brought from sections with a more favorable geographic environment. Only a few fruits and vegetables are raised. Livestock plays an important part in land use, yet most animals are of poor quality.

Fig. 12–12 Native Cattle in Burundi. These long-horned animals, on an experiment station near Kitega, are typical of those grazing on tropical savannas of Burundi, Rwanda, Sudan and neighboring states. Here, cattle ownership carries considerable prestige, and cattle raising is a dominant feature of the economy. (*Courtesy United Nations*)

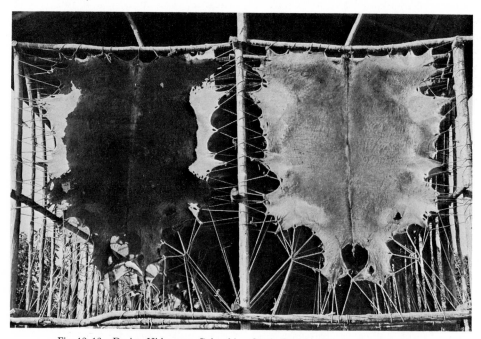

Fig. 12–13 Drying Hides on a Colombian Cattle Ranch. Hides are a good money crop from far inland portions of tropical savannas. These lands have poor transport facilities and need a market commodity with high value per unit of weight, together with an ability to retain quality over long hauls and for long periods of time. Hides, properly dried or salted, will retain their original qualities a long time. (*Courtesy Standard Oil, New Jersey*)

Cows give little milk, and the ox is used mainly for draft purposes. Probably the animal's usefulness in plowing is an important reason why the Hindu religion prohibits meat eating. In the fertile soils of the northwestern and western Deccan, cotton is the main crop.

On the Burmese savanna, millet, sesamum, cotton, and peanuts exceed the acreage in rice. Cattle raising is dominant in the Korat Plateau of Thailand, where the permeability of the soil makes it too dry for crop agriculture, even though rainfall is normally sufficient.

Although cattle raising is important in most of the tropical savannas, tropical cattle cannot compare in quality of meat or perfection of hide with those of the middle latitudes (Fig. 12–12 and 12–13). The high sun, coarse grasses, insect

pests, floods, droughts, and other unfavorable factors are too much of a handicap. European breeds suffer much more severely from the handicaps named above than native animals when grown in the same environment.

Within the last few years, large numbers of breeding animals, such as the Santa Gertrudis, are being forwarded from the middle latitudes to the tropical savanna cattle country. The Santa Gertrudis combines the best qualities of the Shorthorn and the Brahman, or Zebu—two types used in developing the breed. The Brahman's high tolerance of heat, humidity, poor pastures, and resistance to insects and disease is combined with the Shorthorn's fine beef-producing quality and quiet temperament. This combination may give an economic boost to

Fig. 12–14 Puerto Rican Bookmobile Travels Roads Lined with Sugar Cane. Note the height of this cane in relation to the children and the motor car. Most of the world's sugar cane grows in the humid tropics where a twelve-month growing season is assured. Total world cane sugar, centrifugally produced, for the 1962–1963 season reached 31,111,000 tons; noncentrifugally produced 6,845,000 tons. Cuba, Brazil, and India lead in centrifugal in the order given; but India, with about two thirds of the noncentrifugal, is the world's greatest producer of cane sugar. For more detailed statistics see Foreign Agricultural Service, U.S. Dept. of Agriculture. (*Courtesy Commonwealth of Puerto Rico*)

Fig. 12–15   Coffee Plantation, State of Caldas, Colombia. On Colombia coffee plantations, located within a few degrees of the equator, shade trees are needed to protect coffee plants from the high sun. Care also may be used to select trees that will contribute to soil enrichment. (*Courtesy Standard Oil, New Jersey*)

cattlemen in the tropical savanna and steppe lands.

Sugar and Coffee. Besides grazing and subsistence agriculture, the tropical savanna supports other industries which contribute significantly to world trade. Two of these are agricultural crops that rank high among United States imports—cane sugar and coffee (Figs. 12–14, 12–15, and 12–16). True, not all of the world's commercial cane sugar grows in savanna climates, but all of it is produced in the tropics or subtropics (see Figs. A-5, and A-6, pp. 385 and 386).

Because the natural vegetation consists largely of grassland rather than forests, the problem of preparing the ground for plowing is much easier than in the dense tree vegetation of the tropical rainforest.

Sugar cane is a member of the grass family that grows best in frost-free climates which average from 70° to 80° F throughout the year. Thus the best growth of sugar cane is confined to the tropics. Certain short-maturing varieties can be grown in the subtropics, but yields are lower, and expenses of production are likely to be higher.

Well distributed annual rainfall of at least 45 inches is needed for a good cane crop. Heavy rainfall is not necessary in every month, for before harvest relatively dry weather is good for storing up sucrose in the stalk. The tropical savanna, with a long wet season and a short dry period, possesses approximately the climatic optimum. Another advantage of the short dry season is the opportunity it gives for cutting the cane and transporting it easily to the central sugar-manufacturing plant. Wagons and trucks loaded with cane can quickly bog down in moving over fields of sticky mud.

Gently rolling topography which offers little difficulty for mechanized agriculture is highly desirable, especially with the prospects of more and more machine culture in cane growing.

Moreover, the slight departure from levelness encourages good drainage and better tropical soils.

Cuba possesses all of the environmental factors listed above together with good harbors and a location close to the greatest of the world's sugar markets. For more than a half century most of the island's main commercial crop reached the United States with a considerable Cuban price advantage. Only in the early 1960's, after Communist Castro's takeover, did the isle lose this economic concession in price. Probably in time old commercial relations will be restored, and a high tonnage of cane sugar will again move from the tropical savanna island to its large middle latitude neighbor.

Although much of the world's cane sugar grows on the lowland savannas, most of the world's coffee thrives on the upland savannas, especially on the East Central Plateau of Brazil and on the plateaus of tropical Africa. As in the case of sugar cane, not all of the coffee crop comes from savanna lands; but such a large percentage is produced there that it may be called an upland savanna crop.

Like sugar cane, coffee is extremely susceptible to frost, and that fact limits its production to the tropics. Not until Hawaii became a part of the United States was any coffee grown in that country. The 55° F isotherm for the coldest month is the poleward limit of coffee growth; and the annual isotherm of 77° F is the equatorward boundary. High temperature alone will not exclude coffee from any region, but high temperature plus high moisture may be detrimental. It is necessary to protect coffee trees from long periods of the high sun found in latitudes on or near the equator; but Brazilian

Fig. 12–16 Picking Coffee on a Colombian Plantation. The coffee plant is really a large shrub. Its ripe fruit has a red skin, pulp like that of a cherry, size about the same as a cherry, and a parchment within the pulp that covers a silver skin containing two oval coffee beans. These green beans, when roasted, form the base for the drink called coffee. World production of green coffee 1963–1964 reached 65,912,000 bags of 132 pounds. Latin America still produces nearly three fourths of the total with Brazil accounting for about one half; but Africa's share is increasing rapidly and amounts to almost one fourth. (*Courtesy Standard Oil, New Jersey*)

coffee savannas lie near the Tropic of Capricon, and consequently few areas have shade trees (see Fig. A–6, p. 386).

The precipitation needed for best coffee growing depends upon rainfall efficiency. The amount generally given for ideal growth ranges from 50 to 70 inches of well-distributed annual rainfall. Ribeirao Preto, in the heart of the Brazilian coffee-producing area has an average of about 55 inches annually with a definite summer maximum and no month without rain. An annual rainfall distribution with some rain each month is good for coffee trees, which need no real rest period. Moreover, the drier season, which correlates with the cool season in Brazil, makes better conditions for picking coffee and trimming the trees.

Soils with adequate amounts of iron, potash, and nitrates are favorable. Brazil's volcanic terra rossa soils rank well in these qualities and extend over a wide area. On the savanna upland, much of the Brazilian coffee land has gentle slopes which encourage soil drainage, air drainage, and water drainage, all a help for successful coffee culture. Furthermore, slope land is not a handicap to tree-crop agriculture, since frequent cultivation is not essential.

Most savanna land coffee as well as the savanna cane sugar is grown on tropical plantations described earlier in this chapter. On the Brazilian plateau, these plantations are called *fazendas,* but they are known as *fincas* on the Central American plateaus.

Other Savanna Resources. Besides commercial and subsistence agriculture, occupations of the savanna people include mining, manufacturing, and even forest industries in a few places. Obviously forestry occurs only in the park-like savannas or in the gallery forests, along the streams such as those in Paraguay. Here in the Chaco, among the species of scrubby trees is the quebracho (*Quebrachia lorentzii*), a tree valuable as a source of tannin. Logs of the quebracho tree are brought from the woodlands along the river to tannin factories for processing at such towns as Puerto Cooper, Puerto Pinasco, and Puerto Casado.

Manufacturing is more important in the savanna lands than in the tropical rainforest; but the greater portion occurs in the uplands. For example Brazil's east central plateau is one of the most highly industrialized sections of all Latin America. Both heavy and light manufacturing are present. The Brazilians are proud of progress made in cloth manufacture, and they have almost eliminated imports of textiles. They also point with pride to the growing iron and steel plant at Volta Redonda.

Just as in the tropical rainforest, many sections of the savanna country possess rich deposits of minerals and power resources. Two of the world's greatest iron fields occur at Itabira, Brazil, and at Singhbum, India, both in the savanna; and from the Venezuelan llanos both United States Steel and Bethlehem Steel import iron ore for their tidewater steel plants along the eastern coast of the United States.

Venezuela also can be cited as a country rich with petroleum resources; so can Mexico, Boliva, and certain other Latin American countries. Within the last decade oil corporations have become increasingly active with exploration in the savanna country of Africa and Australia.

While world savannas contain large areas almost as sparsely populated as the rainforest, there are highland, island, and coastal regions that support significant numbers of people. These latter areas show far more potential for economic progress than either the tropical rainforest or the lowland savanna country.

QUESTIONS, EXERCISES, AND PROBLEMS

1. Outline the general features of humid tropical climates, vegetation, and soils.
2. In what countries does the tropical rainforest climate occur? What ones have a tropical savanna type?
3. Where are the major world producers of commercial bananas, cacao, rubber, cane sugar, and coffee? Give details on how each crop is produced; prepared for export; the exporting cities; the means of transport; and the major market areas. This information may be obtained from various regional geographies on the several continents. Describe the general characteristics of tropical plantations. Where are the best locations for tropical agriculture in the humid tropics? What are the advantages and disadvantages of the lowland tropical savanna for cattle raising?
4. Comment upon the major tropical diseases of man. Describe diseases and pests afflicting commercial crops of the tropics.

5. Describe major characteristics, distribution, and numbers of population in the humid tropics.

6. How attractive are the humid tropics to the world's great powers?

7. Summarize major uses of the land in the humid tropics.

8. Compare the areal distribution of the tropical rainforest climate shown in Fig. 12–1 with that of the *Af* and *Am* climates shown on Plate 2 at the end of the book; point out similarities and differences in locations. Compare the areal distribution of the tropical savanna climate shown in Fig. 12–1 with that of the *Aw* climate shown on Plate 2; point out similarities and differences in locations.

SELECTED REFERENCES

American Geographical Society, "Resources of the Tropics: Africa," *Focus*, December 1952; "South America," *Focus*, April 1953; "World's Underdeveloped Lands," *Focus*, Sept. 1959; "Human Starvation," *Focus*, June 1961.

Augelli, John P., "The Controversial Image of Latin America: A Geographer's View," *Journal of Geography*, March 1963, pp. 103–12.

Barton, Thomas F., "Rainfall and Rice in Thailand," *Journal of Geography*, December 1963, pp. 414–18.

Brazilian Trade Bulletin, "Immense Amazon Basin has Great Mineral Potentials," Feb. 1, 1963.

De Blij, H. J., *A Geography of Subsaharan Africa*, Rand McNally, 1964.

Deshler, Walter, "Cattle in Africa: Distribution, Types, and Problems with Map," *Geographical Review*, Jan. 1963, pp. 52–58.

Eidt, Robert C., "Pioneer Settlement in Eastern Peru," *Annals of the Association of American Geographers*, March 1964, pp. 107–26.

Fosberg, F. R., Garnier, B. J., and Kuchler, A. W., "Delimitation of the Humid Tropics," *Geographical Review*, July 1961, pp. 333–47.

Fuson, R. H., "House Types of Central Panama," *Annals of the Association of American Geographers*, July 1964, pp. 190–208.

Gourou, Pierre, *The Tropical World*, translated by E. D. Laborde, 3d ed., Longmans, Green & Co. Ltd., and John Wiley and Sons, 1961.

James, Preston E., *Latin America*, Ch. 17, "Brazil: The North," pp. 539–54 and sections on the humid tropics of other Latin American countries, 1959 or later edition.

Linke, Lilo, "Down the Changing Amazon," *The Americas*, Feb. 1961, pp. 7–12.

Morello, T., "Jungle Cutlas: the Machete," *The Americas*, Feb. 1958, pp. 26–29.

Parsons, James J., "Potentialities of Tropical Soils," *Geographical Review*, July 1951, pp. 503–05.

Shaw, Earl B., "A Reconnaissance Journey in the South Sudan," *Journal of Geography*, March 1955, pp. 111–21.

Sopher, David E., "The Swidden Wet-Rice Transition Zone in the Chittagong Hills of East Pakistan," *Annals of the Association of American Geographers*, March 1964, pp. 107–26.

Stevens, R. L. and Brandao, P. R., "Diversification of the Economy of the Cacao Coast of Bahia, Brazil," *Economic Geography*, July 1961, pp. 231–53.

Stuchen, Philip, "Malaysia: Implications and Potentialities," *Canadian Geographical Journal*, August 1963, pp. 62–73.

Thoman, R. S. and Patton, D. J., *Focus on Geographic Activity*, McGraw-Hill, 1964, Chs. 1, 2, 6, and 7, "Shifting Cultivation in the Humid Tropics," "A Cattle-Keeping Tribe in East Africa," "Bananera: A Tropical Plantation," and "Cane Sugar Production on the Queensland Coast."

Tosi, Joseph A. Jr., and Voertman, Robert F., "Some Environmental Factors in the Economic Development of the Tropics," *Economic Geography*, July 1964, pp. 189–205.

Townsend, Derek, "Green Gold, West Indian Bananas for British Tables," *Canadian Geographical Journal*, Nov. 1963, pp. 172–77.

Trewartha, Glenn T., *An Introduction to Climate*, McGraw-Hill, 1954, Ch. 7, "The Tropical Rainy Climates," pp. 239–66.

Wood, Donald S., "The Pattern of Settlement and Development in Liberia," *Journal of Geography*, Dec. 1963, pp. 406–13.

Zahl, Paul A., "Malaysia's Giant Flowers and Insect-Trapping Plants," *National Geographic*, May 1964, pp. 680–701.

Chapter Thirteen

The World's Dry Lands: Steppe and Desert

THE STEPPE

Steppe climates are named for their characteristic vegetation. When steppe is used in a climatic sense, it implies low precipitation, a little more than the desert on the dry side, a little less than the humid lands on the moist boundary. Variability in precipitation is an important feature, more variability than in the humid lands and less than in deserts. In an economic sense, the word steppe implies risk—more risky for crop growing than for grazing, but some risk is implied for either economic activity. Steppe climate covers about 14 per cent of the earth's land surface, an area more than twice the size of the United States and almost the size of North America.

The Physical Environment

Location. (Fig. 13–1) Steppes appear in every continent except Antarctica; they total a much smaller area in the southern hemisphere than in the northern one. Difference in areal extent results primarily from much greater continentality in the northern half of the world. In North America, steppe lies in a long north-south band from southern Canada to northern Mexico, in general west of the hundredth meridian. Shape is influenced by the source of the summer maximum in precipitation—rainfall from American Mediterranean (Gulf of Mexico and Caribbean) air masses. The farther the steppe is from this moist air, the lower the precipitation. Steppe merges into desert as it extends westward—desert brought about partly because of greater distance from the eastern sources of moisture and partly because of the mountain barrier extending north and south near the western coast from Canada to Mexico.

In European and Asiatic Russia, the steppe also extends in a long, relatively narrow zone; but in contrast to the north-south-trending North American steppe, the Russian short grassland stretches in a general east-west direction. This is related to summer air masses moving in from both Atlantic and Pacific oceans. Moisture from the Indian ocean is cut off from the deep interior by high mountains; and air coming from the Arctic moves from high to low latitudes, a direction which increases its capacity to hold moisture.

In southwest Asia, a large section of tropical and subtropical steppe occurs in Turkey, the Arabian Peninsula, Iraq, Iran, Afghanistan, northwest Pakistan, and in a few other areas. Various factors may account for low precipitation, but a central location in the World Island (Africa, Europe, and Asia) provides continentality, an important influence. India's steppe land, lying directly east of the Western Ghats, is influenced by the mountain barrier stretching at right angles to the southwest summer monsoon.

In South America there are three strips of steppe, one in northeast Brazil, and the other two in Argentina. Trade winds and local relief may encourage aridity in the Ceará, sometimes called the famine region of Brazil. The Andes barrier against westerly winds is an important drying influence upon Argentine steppe land.

The equator divides Africa in such a way that it has steppe climates near both extremities. To the north of the equator, two narrow bands lie north and south of the Sahara. South of the equator, steppe land rings the Kalahari on all but the seaward side, where contact with the cold Benguele current is a strong desert influence.

Australia's steppe resembles that of southern Africa in almost completely surrounding the desert. Only on the Indian-Ocean side does it

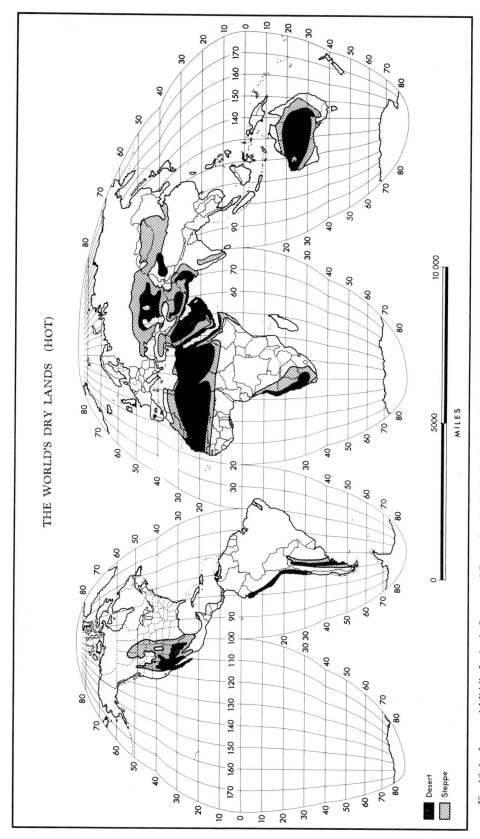

THE WORLD'S DRY LANDS   (HOT)

Desert
Steppe

Fig. 13–1   Low and Middle Latitude Steppe and Desert Lands. (*Projection based on the homolosine projection copyright by the University of Chicago. Map by permission McGraw-Hill Book Co. and G. T. Trewartha, An Introduction to Climate.*)

fail to encircle the great dead heart of the continent. Arid portions of Australia and Africa result largely from descending air of the horse latitudes, equatorward-moving trades, proximity to cold currents, and continentality. Not all these causes may be involved in each case.

Climate. Middle-latitude steppe lies poleward of the 32° F isotherm for the coldest month; low-latitude steppe lies on the equatorward side of the line (Fig. 13–2).

No general precipitation figures can be given for the boundary between dry lands and humid areas, because precipitation, temperature, and wind all influence the aridity of a location. For example, a rainfall of 20 inches may give a humid climate when coupled with relatively cool temperatures and infrequent periods of windy weather; but if temperatures are constantly high, and if they are accompanied by consistent windiness, 20 inches of precipitation may result in a dry climate rather than a humid one. The main point to remember about dry climates is that evaporation, influenced sharply by temperature and windiness, exceeds precipitation.

Rainfall is likely to show considerable variation from year to year, or from one series of years to another series. A classic example of variability occurs in the United States along the hundredth meridian, which marks the approximate boundary of the 20-inch-rainfall line. Rainfall comes in cycles. Wet cycles of varying length follow dry ones, and the 20-inch-rainfall line may change several hundred miles in an east-west direction over a period of years. Economic consequences of wet and dry cycles are significant, both in the United States and elsewhere. A well known historical result of rainfall variability is the migration of people from Central Asia during dry cycles. The great Asian Volkerwanderung of centuries ago was made up of vast folk migrations of peoples seeking more humid conditions, migrations which brought them from Asia to Europe.

Low-latitude steppes may have as high a mean annual temperature as that found in the tropical savanna and tropical rainforest; but there is greater diurnal and annual range. Temperatures in the middle-latitude steppe are high in summer, but because of latitude, winter temperatures may fall considerably below freezing (see Fig. 13–2).

Like all dry climates steppes are characterized by considerable wind. With a limited vegetation cover, friction is low and air movement re-

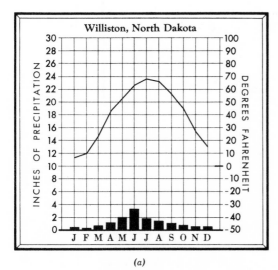

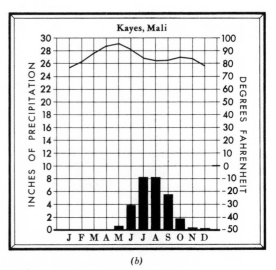

(a)   (b)

Fig 13–2   Kayes represents low latitude steppe climate and Williston that of middle latitudes. The boundary between low and middle latitude steppe is the 32° F isotherm for the coldest month. Williston is located in the Spring Wheat agricultural region of the United States, with winter monthly temperatures far below 32° F, too cold for planting winter wheat. Notice that both stations have low rainfall with a definite summer maximum.

ceives little obstruction. A well-known wind, not confined to the steppes but well developed there, is the American blizzard. Extreme cold, high wind velocity, and blinding wind-driven snow make this storm unfavorable to man and livestock. The Russian buran is similar in its effects to those of the American blizzard. A favorable steppe wind of economic significance is the chinook. The warm air from this winter wind descending the eastern slopes of the Rocky Mountains removes snow quickly and makes grass available for much-needed cattle feed.

Vegetation. Middle-latitude steppe vegetation is made up of short grasses with trees only along stream courses. Grass may cover the ground completely, or stretches of comparatively bare surface may lie between grass clumps. Surface cover may appear almost lush during a long rainy period. Low-latitude steppe has shorter grasses than the tropical savanna; but the long season without rain makes grasses as coarse and unpalatable for livestock as those in the dry-season savanna. At that time animals may pasture along perennial streams if any are available.

Soils. The limited rainfall of the low-latitude steppe brings little soil leaching, and soils limit agriculture less than risky precipitation. Middle-latitude soils are of better quality and include the richest of the pedocals, the chernozems. Fertility is high; grass cover, although not as luxuriant as that of the prairie, encourages humus development; low rainfall and moderate temperatures discourage leaching. However, the meager precipitation which aids soil fertility brings risk to agriculture.

Land Forms. Surface features vary from high plains to plateaus. Although total rainfall is low, heavy downpours may bring widespread erosion to sections lacking consistent grass cover. Wind is also important in shaping surface features.

Land Utilization, Low Latitude Grazing. Grazing of domestic animals, sheep, goats, and cattle, is the most widespread occupation of the steppe lands. Like low-latitude desert grazing, much of the pasturing on low-latitude steppes is nomadic. In the Middle East, for example, sheep are more numerous than goats or cattle (Fig. 13–3). They are smaller than most animals in the United States middle-latitude

steppe lands. Sometimes ewes are milked; but a sheep gives less milk than a goat, which in turn gives less than a cow. Much Middle East wool is of poor quality and is used for rugs and carpets. For centuries many of these floor coverings, with their beautiful designs, were made by hand; now most of them are machine made.

The small sheep of the Middle East is well adapted to the environment. The animal can get along with less water than a cow; it can survive on poorer pastures; it travels long distances between good pastures with a minimum of discomfort; and the fat-tail sheep stores fat in periods of plenty for times of adversity. Moreover, the Arab considers the fat tail a delicacy; these dressed tails are sold on meat markets of Jerusalem, Damascus, and in other Middle East cities. Away from large markets the size of a sheep fits the family meal better than that of a cow, for in the hot climate a family group can eat a sheep with much less danger of part of the carcass spoiling than if a cow were slaughtered.

The goat will thrive on poorer pastures than the sheep; he is more nimble than the wooled animal and can get grass from more difficult terrain. More goats may be seen along the desert fringe of the steppe than on the humid boundary. Goat hair is also useful in making tents for the nomad, fitting the purpose better than wool. Middle East cattle are small and poor milkers, and the carcass and hide possess the inferior quality characteristic of animals in the tropical savanna.

Steppe Grazing in Middle Latitudes. Grazing is an important economic activity of middle-latitude steppe country such as that of the United States Great Plains. Here man's adjustments to the environment follow a pattern somewhat different from that of the Middle East. Part of the difference may be ascribed to a slightly higher latitude. But contrasts in people, history, and living standards are more significant. It is well to remember that similar physical environments may not receive similar utilization by different peoples. Man is a very important element in geography.

Cattle, sheep (see Figs. A-8 and A-10, pp. 388 and 390), and Angora goats are pastured on the Great Plains steppe lands. Cattle and sheep may be found throughout the region, but

Fig. 13–3   A Kuwaiti Shepherd and His Sheep. Notice that the sheep are of various colors. Many are fat-tailed sheep, a type common in the Middle East. (*Courtesy Gulf Oil Corporation*)

Angora goats are most numerous in the Edwards Plateau of Texas (Fig. 13–4).

One of the most important requisites of raising beef cattle on the Great Plains, as on every other steppe land of either low or middle latitude, is an adequate water supply. This may be a river, a spring, a reservoir, or even a deep well. Deep wells are much more numerous now than in the early days of ranching, a situation made possible by the invention of well-drilling machinery. Many wells are pumped by windmills. Winds on the plains are active almost constantly over the wide expanses of flat lands supporting low types of vegetation that provide very little wind friction.

The rancher in the southern Great Plains needs little shedding for his animals; although without protection they may suffer damage from an occasional winter norther. Northern ranchers must protect their animals from winter cold and snow, and must purchase or raise supplemental winter feed for those cattle not marketed before the cold season. Supplemental feed may be lessened by a more frequent occurrence of the chinook, already mentioned, which may keep pastures open on many winter days.

Ranches range in size from a few thousand to a half-million acres or more. Usually the smaller ranches are found near the humid border of the Great Plains steppe and the larger ones near the desert fringe. Carrying capacity may vary from 10 to 30 acres a cow. On the desert fringe the number of acres needed for an animal may rise to 50, and on the desert itself as many as 75 may be necessary. For comparison, 1 to 2 acres of grass in the Corn Belt will support a cow (see Fig. 9–8).

Sheep ranches on the Great Plains are operated in about the same way as cattle ranches; in fact, sheep and cattle may be pastured on the same ranch. In the north, sheep and cattle may be driven to the mountains for summer pasture, where they eat grass that is unavailable during winter because of snow. Snows probably menace sheep more than cattle, and much care is necessary to keep the animals from drifting with cold winter winds and becoming lost in snow drifts. Furthermore, sheep need more protection from wild animals than cattle. Shearing time shows seasonal adjustments. Animals are shorn in the spring after cold and snow have passed and warm days show summer is on the way. Wool is a primary product of Great Plains sheep; but more and more emphasis is placed upon the sale of lambs for feeding in more humid areas.

Angora goats are handled on ranches like sheep. As previously mentioned, the Edwards Plateau is the goat center of the United States. Its pasture land, too poor for good sheep and cattle ranching, will support Angora goats, which are browsing animals. They thrive on good grass but do well on bush pasture where sheep and cattle would starve to death. Goats are raised primarily for mohair, just as they are in the steppe lands of Turkey and South Africa, the two other important Angora goat regions of the world. In the United States the market for goat meat is limited because of a well-established popular prejudice. No such prejudice is present in countries of the Middle East, where living standards are much lower.

Contrasts in Low- and Middle-Latitude Grazing. Contrasts in low-latitude grazing of the Middle East with middle-latitude ranching in the Great Plains include the following:

Fig. 13–4 Angora Goats on the Edwards Plateau. Texas' Edwards Plateau provides grazing for many of the Angora goats raised in the United States. Most of the world's goats graze steppe and desert lands of low and middle latitudes. (*Courtesy Fort Worth Clearing House Association*)

1. Middle East grazing is largely for subsistence—for local use, with low-grade wool and hides providing money crops. Both money crops have high value per unit of weight and keep well for a long time. These factors are important in this isolated area with limited transport to market.

2. Great Plains grazing is for commercial purposes. Cattle go to feeding markets or to beef markets. Hides form an unimportant money crop for the rancher; these commodities are sold to the tanner by the meat packer. Cattle are shipped to market by train or truck in a country with well-developed transport facilities.

3. Great Plains wool is of better quality than that of the Middle East. Many sheep and lambs are sold to midwest markets for fattening or to eastern markets for meat. Again, transport facilities and market demand make this practice possible. Animals of the Great Plains are generally larger and of better quality and receive more scientific care.

4. Labor is hired to look after Great Plains animals, whereas family groups may travel as nomads in the Middle East.

5. Much more capital and equipment is used in Great Plains grazing.

6. People of the Great Plains are of different historical background and have far higher standards of living than those found in the Middle East.

7. In general, Great Plains ranching, although it involves large areas, is made up of fenced lands belonging to some individual or corporation. Middle East nomadism may involve larger areas and more distant movements, but upon unfenced lands and lands under far less personal control.

Major similarities between Middle East Grazing and that of the Great Plains include:

1. Both involve extensive use of the land.

2. Both involve sparsely populated areas.

3. Both show far greater areas devoted to grazing than to crop raising.

4. In both, animals receive most of their feed from native pastures.

5. In both, animals move to fresh pastures from time to time.

Dry Farming. Although great emphasis is placed upon grazing by people of the world's steppe lands, they may also undertake crop raising either by irrigation or dry-farming methods. In Anglo-America, dry farming is one of three major types of land use that extend in a belt-like pattern across the Great Plains steppe: (1) near the streams, water is available for irrigation; (2) on the land which borders these irrigated lands, man resorts to dry farming practices for cultivating crops; and (3) still farther away from the streams, grazing is the dominant type of farming. This arrangement of belted activities is highly generalized, and the plan may not be followed throughout the steppe. Nevertheless, the pattern persists enough to be noticeable to the careful observer.

Since steppe rainfall is marginal for the production of many crops and is also cyclic (Fig. 13–5), man has developed techniques of dry farming that are designed to get the most efficiency from a rainfall regime of this kind. These practices involve fallow farming. In following this procedure, (1) the farmer will let the land lie idle for a while, for example one year out of three, or every other year, in order that sufficient moisture for a successful crop may accumulate in the soil. Even if he lets the land lie fallow, he is likely (2) to plow the ground when necessary to keep down weeds, which take moisture from the soil; to make the land more receptive to water storage; and to interrupt evaporation channels which may develop in the soil during periods of dry weather. In plowing the land the farmer may plow (3) in such a way as to create deep furrows along the contours; these will not only store the water for a maximum period but will also prevent runoff at the time the rains come. Trenchlike furrows at right angles to the prevailing winds may also counteract soil blowing. If dust starts to blow badly, the farmer may resort to chiseling the land with a plow that strikes deep enough to turn up clods that will stabilize the loose soil. (4) He will also select drought-resistant crops such as wheat, barley, millet, and grain-sorghum. (5) A new development among Great Plains farmers has been called trash farming. All accumulation of refuse after harvest may be left on the field until the ground is cropped again. This technique not only protects the ground from excessive moisture loss by evaporation, but the trash will also serve as a gigantic sponge to soak up more moisture from each rain. (6) Another moisture preserver is the planting of trees, sometimes called a shelter belt, to the windward of the crop land. Such trees create a barrier to the prevailing winds, thus slowing up velocity and causing air to rise over the barrier, and to descend beyond the crop zone. In addition the shelter belt may trap winter snow, which will encourage better tree growth as well as that of the crops. Farmers also plant trees around building plots and feed lots. Plantings like this will save fuel and feed bills. (7) Farmers in the United States and Canadian steppe study the long range weather forecasts for the coming crop season. These predictions are becoming dependable enough for man to decide whether to fallow the land another year, to select extremely drought-resistant seeds, or to take advantage of a growing season with above average precipitation by planting crops demanding more than normal seasonal moisture. All these dry farming practices have proved helpful to steppe farmers, especially in Anglo-America.

Wheat (Figs. 13–6, 13–7, and 13–8) is an important dry farming crop in all the steppe lands with high production in Argentina, Australia, Canada, China, Russia, and the United States (see Fig. A–1, p. 381). Barley is also widely grown especially in the drier sections of these lands. Millet has achieved great popularity on the steppes of Asia and Africa. In the United States production of grain sorghum has expanded significantly in the southern Great Plains steppe since 1950 and now is actively competing with wheat for crop land.

Other Steppe Resources. Besides dry farming, irrigated agriculture, and grazing, the steppe lands possess other valuable activities. In Anglo-America, the Great Plains are rich in power resources, including low-grade coal, petroleum, and natural gas. Oil and gas fields include the Leduc area, the Williston Basin straddling the international boundary, the United States Mid-continent, and other fields.

Fig. 13–5   The Dust Bowl of the United States During the 1930's. The photograph shows a dust cloud approaching Springfield, Colorado, at 4. 47 PM on May 21, 1937. Total darkness lasted for thirty minutes. (*U.S. Soil Conservation Service*)

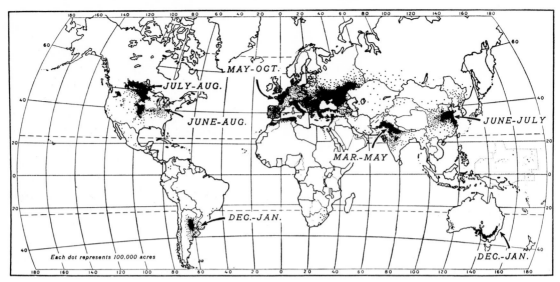

Fig. 13–6 World Wheat Growing Lands. Notice the influence of location upon the time of harvest. Total world production reached 8 billion 240 million bushels in 1963–1964. Normally the Soviet leads with about 1½ billion bushels, followed by the United States with over a billion and Canada with ½ to ¾ of a billion bushels. China may produce nearly a billion bushels, but no reliable figures are available. Most Russian, United States, Canadian, and Chinese wheat grows in steppe country; but part of the 22 per cent of the world's harvested crop land occupied by wheat may be found in other climates. (*Courtesy U.S. Department of Agriculture*)

Fig. 13–7 Grain Elevators and Drilling Rig. The drilling rig of an Imperial Oil well at Smiley, Saskatchewan, Canada, dwarfs prairie wheat elevators. In both Canadian and United States sections of the North American Spring Wheat Region, recent oil discoveries and expansions have added new wealth to a land long dependent upon one-crop farming. Imperial Oil brought in the discovery well in Saskatchewan in September 1953. (*Courtesy Saskatoon Board of Trade and Imperial Oil Limited*)

More petroleum and natural gas are constantly being discovered, and new discoveries will continue because the geologic environment is favorable.

Potash and phosphate occur in large deposits. In fact, the world's largest potash resource is now receiving its initial development near Esterhazy in Saskatchewan, Canada. A smaller potash deposit occurs near Carlsbad, New Mexico. The largest United States phosphate occurrence lies to the north in Wyoming and Montana. Although these United States fertilizers are valuable, they are far removed from the large farm section of eastern United States, which could use them to the best advantage. Metallic minerals, especially gold, occur in the Black Hills, where the well-known Homestake Mining Corporation leads in production.

It is doubtful that the Anglo-American steppe lands will ever become a great manufacturing region. To prosper, manufacturing needs a big market; the local one is too small, and distant markets are too far away. Emphasis is placed upon processing local raw materials and the utilization of cheap power. Meat packing plants and flour mills are widespread throughout the region. Petrochemical industries are based upon the presence of large supplies of petroleum and natural gas. Some ores move east from the Rocky Mountains to the steppe to take advantage of low processing costs which are influenced by cheap fuel. However, big cities are not

Fig. 13–8 Chinese Man in Field of Growing Millet. Millet and grain sorghum, both crops resistant to drought, occupy 10.1 per cent of the world's harvested area of principal crops; about half as much as that of wheat, 22.1 per cent. (*Courtesy U.S. Department of Agriculture*)

numerous, and manufacturing is far from the dominant industry.

Russian steppe lands form an area extending east from the Black Sea to the Altai Mountains, and they form a part of the so-called fertile triangle. Boundaries of this triangle run south from Leningrad to Odessa, east from Odessa to Omsk, and northwest from Omsk to Leningrad. The triangle contains the economic heart of Russia, the best climate, land forms, soils and minerals, and the most people. The steppe portion of the triangle has the best soil in Russia, the famous chernozem. The absence of tree cover, except along the streams, makes cultivation easy. Here is grown a significant portion of the Russian grain crop; here are found many domestic animals; and here is the famous Donbas region—Donets Basin coal and Krivoy Rog iron—well located for mining, for market, and for Black Sea transport; and the equally well known Kuznetsk region with coal and iron lies nearby. Here too are several of Russia's great cities, Kiev, Odessa, Rostov, Omsk, Tomsk, and Volgagrad. Not far from Volgagrad is oil; and other mineral resources are easily available. In spite of its risky climate for farming, the Russian steppe contributes significantly to national economy in food supply, in power and mineral resources, and in industrial development.

China's steppe country includes Inner Mongolia, a portion of the Loess Plateau, and the drier northern section of the North China Plain. Much of China's wheat, millet, and kaoliang comes from the eastern more humid parts of the steppe, whereas the dryer western area is devoted mainly to pastoral pursuits. Population pressure has been heavy on the land to the east; and in the wet phase of the steppe's cyclic rainfall, farmers have been pushing deeper into the area of the pastoralists. Possibly in the future, the mineral and power resources of the region may become almost as significant as the food supply. Enormous reserves of coal, the largest in China, occur in Shensi and Shansi provinces of the Loess Plateau. Oil and gas have been discovered, and iron is available not far away. With the coming of modern transport, modern equipment, and much better management, the minerals and power may contribute far more to the economy than at present.

From the brief description above it may be noted that minerals and power of the steppe contribute, or may contribute, significantly to national economy in China, Russia, and Anglo-America; and these resources are also important in the steppe country of the Middle East, Africa, and Australia, where they add diversity to a risk farming economy.

THE WORLD'S DESERTS

Deserts are found in low, middle, and high latitudes (see Figs. 13–1 and 13–14). Popular concept seldom envisions Arctic and Antarctic lands as deserts; but they conform to the botanical desert definition, a region of sparse and highly specialized plant life. Since this is true, it seems proper that cold deserts may be studied with the less icy deserts of middle and low latitudes. The latter will be described in the first part of the chapter and the former in the final section.

Low and Middle Latitude Deserts

Location. (Fig. 13–9, see also Fig. 13–1) Low- and middle-latitude deserts occupy a large portion, nearly one eighth of the earth's land surface. Translated into continental terms these deserts would approximate the size of South America; low and middle latitude steppe and desert together give a dry-land total the size of both the Americas. Dry deserts lie within 5° of the equator in South America. They extend to 50° N in Asia and to 50° S in South America. From the Atlantic coast of Africa near the Tropic of Cancer, they reach across the continent into Asia's Arabia, Iran, Afghanistan, and Pakistan. Farther north another desert band runs from the Caspian Sea through Turkmenistan, Uzbekistan, and other parts of Asiatic Russia to China's Sinkiang. Smaller deserts lie in southwestern United States and northern Mexico; and the narrow desert strip along the Pacific coast from Ecuador through Peru into Chile is one of the world's driest places. Its southward counterpart east of the Andes in Argentina extends in slightly mitigated form into Patagonia. Southwest Africa displays similar features in its Kalahari desert, and a large part of Australia in these same latitudes is also desert.

Causes of Deserts. Most low- and middle-latitude deserts result from one or more of the following causes: location (1) on leeward sides of mountains such as the desert east of the Sierra Nevada Range in the United States; (2) in the trade-wind zone where air is moving equatorward, warming, and consequently increasing its capacity to hold moisture, as in the Sahara; (3) in the belt of subtropical calms or horse latitudes, as in Arabia, where air movement is largely downward; (4) on a coast bathed by cold ocean currents like the Humboldt Current along the western shore of South America and the Benguela Current along the western border of Africa; or on these and similar coasts where the upwelling of cold waters encourages aridity just as cold ocean currents do; (5) where prevailing winds parallel the coast as along the Atacama desert in Chile; (6) in the continental interior, such as the Takla Makan of Central Asia, cut off from the sea by mountains, by great distances, or by both.

Precipitation. Amount of rainfall is extremely low. In fact there are stations with relatively short records showing no precipitation at all, as at Calama, Chile; and at nearby Iquique no rainfall came for four years, and only slightly more than one inch fell in five years. Rainfall is variable in occurrence. Its variability recalls the principle that, the lower the total, the greater the variability. When rain does come, it is likely to be torrential and to cause disastrous flash floods on land with so little vegetation. French army orders long prohibited making camp in desert wadis (dry stream beds).

Temperature. Desert temperatures are the highest in the world. At Azizia, in Libya, not far from Tripoli, a shade temperature of 136.4° F has been recorded. Of course low-latitude mean-annual temperatures reach higher levels than those of middle latitude, but summers are likely to provide many readings of 100° F in both. Winters may show low readings in middle latitudes, and diurnal range is likely to be extreme regardless of distance from the equator. A range of nearly 70° F has been recorded in the mid-Sahara. Desert air is so clear, and so little heat is lost by evaporation, that the unbroken sunshine warms the earth very rapidly by day. Cooling takes place just as rapidly by night because of the swiftness of outgoing earth radiation through the same clear air. In low-latitude deserts, diurnal range is likely to be greater than seasonal range. In middle latitudes, the significant seasonal change in length of day and altitude of the noonday sun makes seasonal range higher than diurnal.

Vegetation. General features of desert vegetation vary little, regardless of latitude. The most typical plants are small bushes with various de-

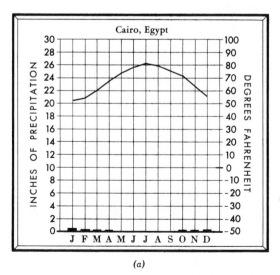

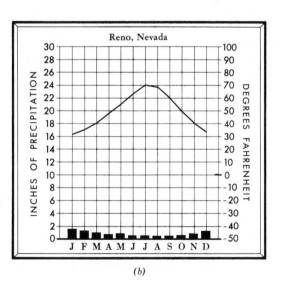

(a)   (b)

Fig. 13–9   Climatic charts, Cairo, Egypt and Reno, Nevada. Cairo temperatures and precipitation illustrate low latitude desert climates; those for Reno, with the coldest month below 32° F, represent middle latitude desert climates.

vices to limit evaporation. The leaves may be small, thick, and hairy, or perhaps plump and watery with skins that prevent evaporation. Sometimes leaves are reduced to sharp spines or little bracts. Other plants may be leafless, but have chlorophyll, or green matter, in their stems. Another plant device to save moisture is a fat stem full of water. The object of all these features is to reduce evaporation to the lowest limits, and to store up water which cannot easily escape. In many deserts no vegetation at all may be visible for long distances; often an occasional little bush is seen at intervals of scores of feet. Such bushes can live without rain for years. In other deserts bushes are fairly numerous, and there is also an annual cover of sparse short grass that becomes dry and brittle soon after the end of the rainy season so that much of it is blown away by the wind. In southern Arizona, creosote, mesquite, many kinds of cacti with brilliant flowers, and feathery grasses in isolated clumps make the desert most attractive. Even in the driest deserts a single shower may cover the land with a superbly flowered carpet of grass. Plants are likely to extend their roots deep into the ground in search of ground water, or they may expand their root system widely in a horizontal direction so as to take every advantage of the limited rain which falls. These tendencies give rise to a desert term "up-side-down vegetation."

Desert Land Forms. Topography of many kinds may be found in the world's deserts, but many dry lands are featured by basins enclosed by mountains and with no outlet to the sea. L. Dudley Stamp classifies what he calls the true deserts of Arabia as follows: (1) Dahanah is a comparatively hard gravel plain, covered at intervals with sand belts of varying width. Ground water may be present at depth, but dahanah may elsewhere form a complete barrier. (2) Nefud is a continuous area of deep gravel or sand, formed by wind action into high dunes. (3) Ahqaf is very soft dune country and cannot be crossed except in narrow belts, owing to the extreme physical labor involved. It is rare in Arabia. (4) Harrah is the name given to tracts of rough lava surface that cuts the feet of man and animals.

In the Takla Makan Desert of western China, millions of sand dunes of many tones of yellow, brown, and pink look like the waves of a huge dry sea several hundreds of miles long. Wind piles the dunes up to a height of five hundred feet or more and thus causes them to be an almost impassable barrier. Although sandy deserts do not occupy any larger area than those of bare rock, gravel, and clay, they present the most unusual appearance, largely because of the presence of dunes of every size and description. That is why the most familiar pictures of deserts show sand dunes. Both wind and water are active in shaping desert land forms.

Soils. Desert soils lack humus, but show little loss of mineral constituents through leaching. Some are saline; in fact, the many ephemeral lakes found in deserts may dry up and leave salt-encrusted surfaces in their former bottoms. Deposits like this may bar agriculture but may be of such a character as to provide mineral fertilizers like the potash of Searles Lake, California. Other desert areas may be made up of alternate beds of sand and mud with salts at lower levels. Such soils pose a problem for irrigation. When man turns water on to this land, the moisture seeps down and dissolves the salts. Saline material may rise to the surface by capillary attraction, and when evaporation takes place, the salt remains. About the only thing the farmer can do then is to wash the salts from the soils; and this may be an expensive process.

Land Utilization

Grazing. Land use in deserts presents two major agricultural patterns, nomadic herding and irrigation farming. The former, one of several phases of pastoral life, occurs over huge areas. One may note the limited economic importance of this activity by looking at a population map and observing the few people on the earth's deserts and desert-margin steppes.

In early times, before the advent of modern weapons and transport, ancestors of these few people achieved an importance far out of proportion to their number. With well-planned military movements, they conquered large groups of sedentary populations who possessed a much higher degree of civilization. Modern transport and weapons have removed most of the former military advantage held by desert nomads.

Desert herders may pasture cattle, sheep, goats, or camels, depending largely upon carrying capacity of the range and somewhat upon the choice of nomadic groups. Animals graze over wide expanses with daily movements from place to place in the vicinity of the camp site and movements for longer distances seasonally or during shorter periods. Availability of drinking water as well as of pasture may govern the time of stay in any location and the direction of travel when leaving a certain grazing area.

Grazing areas are not fenced, and little land is privately owned. But many tribal groups have what might be called a gentleman's agreement over grazing limits for each tribe. Acreage per animal is high everywhere.

Equipment of the nomads is necessarily limited, light, and unbreakable, showing adjust-ment to constant movement from place to place. The black tents of the Bedouins can be taken down easily, folded into small compact bundles, and carried on the backs of camels. Cooking utensils are few. Many eat with their fingers, dispensing with knives and forks. Rugs and blankets may take the place of furniture. Living equipment must conform to occupational movements (Fig. 13–10).

Nomad activities generally emphasize a production for subsistence rather than for commerce. Animals provide food, shelter, and clothing. Yet nomads do furnish a few articles for world trade such as hides, wool, and rugs. All these commercial products have high value per unit of weight and possess qualities that will survive long-distance transport and long periods of time.

Fig. 13–10   Bedouins of the Hasa District Serving Coffee. Bedouin hospitality has long been well known, for the nomad knows the hardships of desert travel. Although the characteristic black tent is small, there is usually a curtain separating the men's section from that of the women. (*Courtesy Standard Oil, New Jersey*)

Irrigation Agriculture Oases. Irrigation agriculture is practiced on oases, which make up a very small percentage of the desert total and which may result from several physical conditions, some of which are mentioned below. (1) Irrigation water may be available from exotic streams, rivers such as the Nile and the Colorado which receive their water, flowing through the deserts, from far-away sources. For example, the Blue Nile rises on the Ethiopian plateau, where a strong seasonal monsoon inflow of air, striking against mountains that act as barriers, gives up rainfall—water which provides 70 per cent of the agricultural life blood of Lower Egypt. As much as 20 per cent of Egypt's much-needed moisture comes from the White Nile, rising in Lake Victoria, where the heavy tropical precipitation occurs for many months. The other 10 per cent comes from the Atbara, which like the Blue Nile, rises in the Ethiopian highlands and reaches the main Nile north of the Blue and White Nile junction.

(2) Within the desert itself, or located close by, mountains may rise sufficiently to wring moisture from prevailing winds—moisture enough to carry mountain streams to mountain bases, where successful agriculture may develop on alluvial fans. Utah is sometimes called an oasis at the foot of the Wasatch Mountains. The Wasatch rise over 10,000 feet, high enough to force moisture from prevailing westerly winds. This moisture feeds streams that have contributed water for irrigation agriculture since the times of the early Mormon settlement near the present Salt Lake City.

(3) Artesian wells are especially important in dry regions such as the Sahara, where they support many small oases. In this huge desert man has tapped deep sources of water derived from rain that falls many hundreds of miles away. At places like the Atlas Mountains precipitation may fall on permeable sandstone exposed at the surface for hundreds or thousands of square miles. Water may be absorbed by this porous rock and move through the gently dipping sandstone (see Fig. 8–7) at considerable depths for long distances. Ideal conditions for continuous flow occur where the buried sandstone is sealed from above by a capping layer of impervious rock. Five hundred miles distant in the desert, a hole bored through the impervious cap becomes an artesian well. The Kharga oasis in

Egypt and several oases in the Libyan portion of the Sahara, west of the lower Nile, are supported by springs which are natural artesian wells. There the wind appears to have scoured deep depressions in the solid rock, and water flows out where these depressions reach an artesian layer.

Oases Crops. Desert crops show as much variety as the physical conditions that encourage the water supply. On the desert coastal plain of Peru, about fifty streams flow down the western slopes of the Andes and provide water for large land holdings producing Peru's two main export crops, cotton and cane sugar. In Argentine Patagonia, streams from the eastern slopes of the Andes, the Chubut, Negro, and Colorado, give moisture to the country's pear crop, for large vineyards, and for broad valley plains planted to alfalfa.

Several crops such as cotton, citrus fruits, grain, hay, and vegetables depend upon waters of the Colorado, the Rio Grande, the Gila, and other streams flowing through lands of desert climates in North America. Near the eastern edges of the desert covering most of central Australia, waters of the Murray-Darling system are tapped to produce vineyards, citrus groves, orchards of peaches, apricots, and pears, grain, and other crops. Water is also being drawn from the Murray through a 240-mile pipe line leading to the Whyalla steel production district on Spencer Gulf. This pipe is only 110 miles shorter than the one extending from near Perth in western Australia to the Kalgoorlie gold fields, 350 miles away and at a level 1290 feet above the Mundaring reservoir. In the Australian desert physical conditions do not stop man completely from mining gold, manufacturing steel, and producing crops. In Pakistan, the Indus and its tributaries supply water in the Punjab and lower Indus valley, where irrigation crops include rice, wheat, and cotton.

Nearly all Russian cotton is produced in the desert region east of the Caspian. Irrigation agriculture is important around the urban centers of Tashkent, Merv, Bukhara, and Samarkand. During World War II, when the Germans took over much of the great food-producing Ukraine, it was necessary to turn this cotton land to wheat culture in order to feed military and civilian population. Now, irrigation cotton, growing again, is a leading crop in desert agricultural economy.

The date palm dominates agriculture on the Shatt al Arab irrigation district, southern Iraq, which annually produces about three-fourths of the world's commercial dates. The palm also provides a very important food crop for other arid lands of southwest Asia and for arid parts of northern Africa as well (Fig. 13–11). Date palms on irrigation districts of desert lands in the United States contribute to the American market, but fall far short of supplying total needs. Supplementary shipments must be imported from the Old World.

Methods of Irrigation, Egypt. Probably in no other country of the world, is the entire farming population so dependent upon irrigation as in Egypt. Because of this a description of its irrigation facilities may serve as an example for irrigation in desert lands.

Egypt has two major types of irrigation, basin and perennial. The former is older and less complicated than the latter; it simply involves building earth embankments, a few feet high, along the flood plain of the river. At the time of flood, waters spread over the earthen barriers; when flood crest is past and recession of flood water starts toward the main channel, trapped water remains on the bank-enclosed sections. During flood, rivers carry much silt; swirling flood waters become quiet as they are ponded in the shallow basins and deposit their fertile load on the soil. Thus basin irrigation permits an annual soil rejuvenation—a rejuvenation with rich volcanic materials carried by the Blue Nile from the Ethiopian Highlands.

Whereas annual natural fertilization gives definite advantage, basin irrigation permits but one yearly crop in Egypt. The Nile reaches a crest in September, and planting takes place when the waters recede in the autumn. More-

Fig. 13–11 Al Hasa, Saudi Arabia, an Oasis in the Desert. An Arab farmer washes in a little canal running through date groves surrounding Qatif. These small areas of date palms provide a sharp contrast to the broad, brown, sandy expanses encompassing such green islands in the desert. (*Courtesy Standard Oil, New Jersey*)

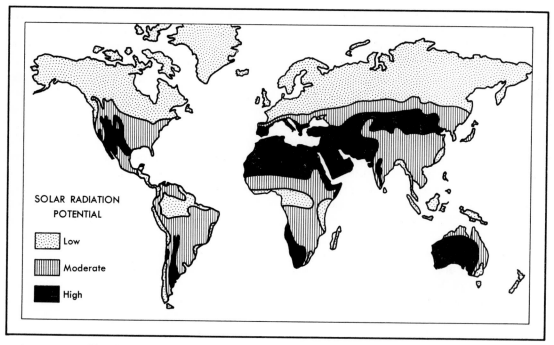

Fig. 13–12   The Continents and Their Sun-Power Potential. The areas of high sun-power potential correspond quite closely to the world's deserts and steppe lands. Sun power may become a major source of energy at some future date, when man perfects cheap, efficient, large-scale methods of reception and of long-distance transmission. (*Courtesy E. Willard Miller and* The Journal of Geography, *Sept. 1959*)

over, the one annual planting is limited to certain crops that can withstand Egypt's cool season. Wheat, barley, and berseem (a hay crop) are well adjusted to fall seeding; but cotton, millet, rice, and maize do not thrive so well. Very little of Egypt's irrigation is of the basin type, and most of this is in the south, Upper Egypt.

Perennial irrigation involves a series of barrages for control and distribution of the water at all times during the year. During time of flood, excess water is stored for the dry season. Thus, year-round water supply makes possible three crops a year on the same land. Summer crops of maize, rice, and cotton can be raised, and these are of extreme importance to Egyptian economy; maize and rice supply food for many people; cotton is the important money crop. Perennial irrigation may increase food supply and furnish a much-needed money crop, but it raises a problem of soil depletion. The deposition of silt, so advantageous in basin irrigation, now takes place in the bed of the Nile, not on its

crop lands. Moreover, three crops a year draw much fertility from the soil in spite of generally close attention to proper rotation plans. Egypt buys more fertilizer per acre than the Netherlands and Belgium; and during World War II, when sources of fertilizer were cut off, Egyptian crop yields declined significantly.

Irrigation has permitted a doubling of Egyptian population since the start of the century. But present population increases cannot be supported by the irrigable land now available. Egypt is seriously worried about this problem and is making plans to extend the cultivable area mainly by increased water supply. Plans for extension of cultivable land include (1) the building of the new Aswan Dam, already well started; (2) Century Storage, which envisions the use of Lakes Victoria and Albert for storage of rain waters in years of heavy rainfall; (3) building of a Sudd canal that will allow the Nile (Bahr el Jebel) to run between the seventh and tenth parallels, north latitude, without excessive losses from evaporation; and (4) drainage of salty coastal lagoons and proper soil treatment that will add thousands of acres for crop production (see Fig. 20–10).

One more point should be mentioned in connection with expanding desert irrigation in low latitudes like those of Egypt. Irrigation extension may increase disease hazards from malaria and bilharzia; increase of water will enlarge the breeding places for organisms carrying these and other diseases and thus increase the health problems.

Other Desert Resources, Minerals and Power. (Fig. 13–12) Minerals and power make

significant additions to irrigation agriculture and grazing, previously described. Southwest Asia's dry lands contain at least half of the world's proven oil reserves; and the petroleum reserves of the Sahara are becoming increasingly important. No doubt Algerian petroleum discoveries were one of the causes for a delay in the French-Algerian peace settlement. Other useful desert oil fields are Russia's Emba deposits east of the Caspian Sea and Argentina's resources in the Patagonian dry lands. The recent finding of large uranium resources in the Intermontane Plateau has made the United States self sufficient in the bases for atomic power. Finally,

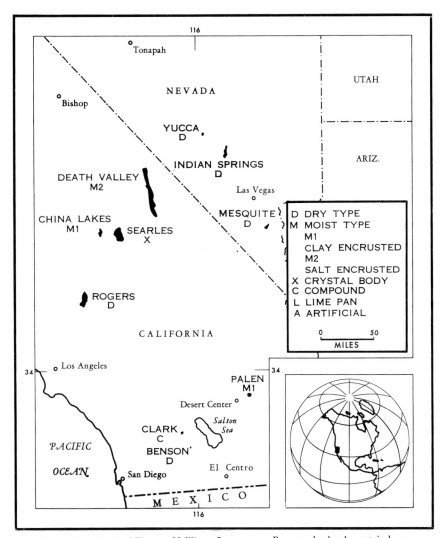

Fig. 13–13 Dryland Playas of Military Importance. Because dry lands contain huge areas with low economic value and sparse population, some of them are useful for military maneuvers. (*Drawn after map of Quartermaster Research and Development Center, Environmental Protection Research Division, U.S. Army, Natick, Mass.*)

abundant sunlight is another important desert resource. Sometime in the not-far-distant future, we may be able to trap power from sunlight cheaply and transmit it economically.

Significant desert minerals already discovered include the world's largest supply of natural nitrates in the Atacama Desert of Chile; a big deposit of potash near Carlsbad, New Mexico; one of the earth's great copper areas in the Atacama Desert, especially near Chuquicamata, Chile; and gold in the western part of Australia's Dead Heart, around Kalgoorlie, previously mentioned. All these and others suggest that minerals and power are of economic importance in the world's deserts.

Military Use. The United States dry lands provide an example of how deserts are being utilized for military purposes (Fig. 13–13). Such use results from the low economic value and sparse population in large areas. During and since World War II, the dry lakes of California and Nevada have been of great use to the armed services. The flat, hard-packed, vegetation-free areas in sparsely populated regions have proven ideal for aircraft landing fields, gunnery ranges, bombing ranges, and for testing such new weapons as guided missiles and atomic bombs.

The most noted of the dry lakes used by the military is Rogers Lake (Muroc), where Edwards Air Base is located. The lake, which is roughly thirteen miles long and five miles wide, provides a landing field more than sufficient for all types of aircraft. The bearing strength of the massive clay body (measured as three fourths of an inch depression for a single wheel loading 150,000 pounds) can easily support the heaviest aircraft. Its isolated location is ideal for the testing of secret and experimental equipment. At nearby China Lake, the Navy has a similar installation, where guided missiles and experimental aircraft are tested. Yucca Flat in southwestern Nevada has been the site of experimental tests of atomic bombs and atomic[1] weapons.

Other dry lakes that are being used by the military are Benson Dry Lake, where the Navy maintains a gunnery and bombing range, and Indian Springs Dry Lake, Nevada, where the Air Force has a gunnery and bombing range. During World War II a primary flying school and glider school was in operation at Mesquite (Twenty-nine Palms) Lake and a gunnery range at Clark Dry Lake. The Palen Playa near Desert Center was extensively used by General Patton in the training of armored divisions in desert warfare.

High Latitude Deserts

High Latitude Deserts (Fig. 13–14) resemble low and middle latitude deserts in several ways. These regions are similar in (a) low precipitation; (b) scanty vegetation; (c) limited agriculture, manufacturing, and commerce; (d) considerable dependence of man upon animals; (e) sparse population, in some places nomadic, in other places centered around mines or military installations; and (f) a relatively primitive stage of civilization especially in the more isolated sections.

Ownership. Polar regions include about 16 per cent of the world's land surface but only about 0.01 per cent of the world's people. Such a contrast in percentages shows the remarkable effect of high latitude and resulting cold and ice upon man's choice of a habitat. Six per cent of the world's land area is in the Arctic, 10 per cent in the Antarctic. In the Arctic, 40 per cent of the land surface belongs to Russia, 28 per cent to Canada, 26 per cent to Denmark, 5 per cent to the United States, and 1 per cent to Norway and Iceland. In the Antarctic, claims have been staked by some nations, but it is to be hoped that all claims remain as spheres of influence.

Climate. Polar climates, by definition, lie on the poleward side of the tree line, the 50° F isotherm for the warmest month (Fig. 13–15). The tundra climate includes the area between the warm-month isotherm of 50° F and that for 32° F. The icecap region extends poleward beyond the 32° F warm-month isotherm.

High latitude is probably the most important control on polar climates. It is responsible for the striking seasonal differences in length of daylight and darkness. Poleward beyond the Arctic and Antarctic circles, at least one day of the year will have 24 hours of darkness. The noonday

---

[1] France and Communist China also used a desert environment for testing atomic bombs. The former nation tested in the Sahara desert; and the latter country entered the atomic power club in the Lop Nor section of the Takla Makan desert in Sinkiang Province during October 1964.

THE WORLD'S DRY LANDS (COLD)

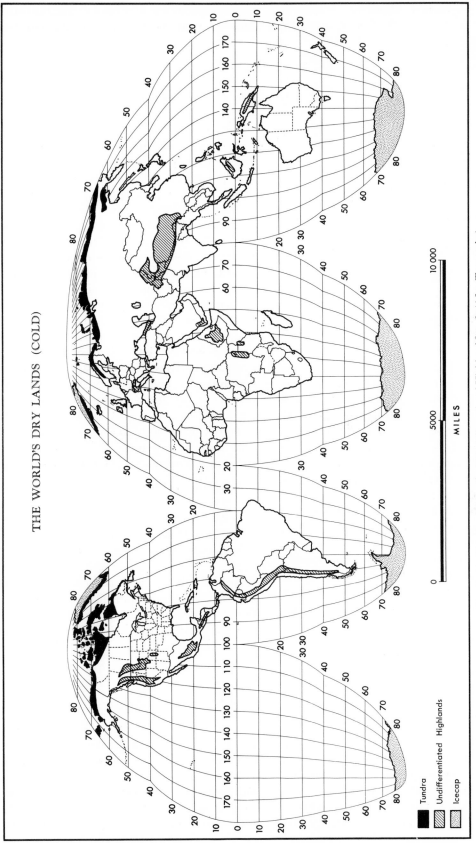

Tundra

Undifferentiated Highlands

Icecap

MILES

0   5000   10 000

Fig. 13-14 Tundra, Icecap, and Undifferentiated Highland Lands (After Trewartha). Icecap lands are less productive than deserts of low and middle latitudes; and so is much of the tundra and undifferentiated highlands. (Projection based on the homolosine projection copyright by the University of Chicago. Map by permission McGraw-Hill Book Co. and G. T. Trewartha, An Introduction to Climate)

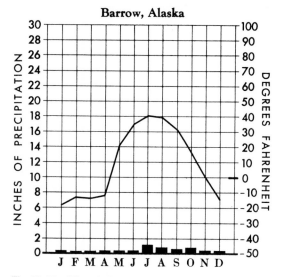

Fig. 13–15   Climatic Chart, Barrow, Alaska. Barrow, Alaska (71° 15′ N, 156° 12′ W; altitude 10 feet; mean annual precipitation 5.6 inches; mean annual temperature 10° F). Barrow temperatures and precipitation illustrate high-latitude desert climates. Note that no month averages as high as 50° F.

sun is never closer than within 43° of the zenith even at the Arctic and Antarctic circles; and it will be 90° from the zenith on one day of the year at these circles. Low altitude of the sun at all times and the short period of daylight for half the year provide a combination accounting for the lowest mean annual temperature and the coolest summers of any world climate.

Precipitation is low both in the tundra and on the icecaps, because (1) cold air can hold but little moisture; (2) descending air of the semipermanent high-pressure systems discourages precipitation; and (3) there are few cyclonic storms and little development of convection. Most of the precipitation comes during the warmer season.

Polar climates are characterized by high winds in winter. These blizzards are worse than those in the subarctic, for there is little vegetation to slow down the gale. In the tundra, high winds and low precipitation are responsible for large areas entirely free from winter snow.

Soils. Soils are of no importance in ice cap climates, for ground is constantly covered with ice. Moreover, the temperatures would not permit plant growth. In the tundra, the unfavorable characteristics of the soils themselves would do little to encourage agriculture even if temper-

atures were favorable. They are leached of their mineral constituents and contain but little humus.

Surface Features. In general, surface features of the tundra show little relief. The greater part of mainland Arctic Canada, outside Yukon Territory, is a lowland plain. Most portions of the Alaskan-Canadian tundra have so little relief that it is difficult or impossible for the unaided eye to judge which way it slopes. The drainage system gives the best clue. Hummocky surfaces may result here, as well as in other parts of the tundra, from winter freezing of surface soils, many of which are semifluid in consistency during the warm season. Generally speaking, the coast of Arctic Siberia resembles that of Alaska, although at places the mountains come nearer the less regular coast line.

Coastal areas of Greenland and Svalbard (Spitzbergen) possess deep fiords eroded by tongues of ice moving out to sea from the ice-covered interior. Lakes and swamps abound everywhere on the Alaskan, Canadian, and Siberian tundra, and during the summer months they encourage the large number of insects for which the tundra is so well known (Fig. 13–16).

Terrain featured by plateau or mountainous land forms is characteristic of the icecap areas of Antarctica, Greenland, Svalbard, and Iceland.

Vegetation. Mosses and lichens dominate vegetation on the tundra. Along equatorward boundaries many shrubs and trees, such as dwarf willow, are found. At this transition zone between tundra and subarctic, trees are especially numerous along streams and in areas protected from high winds. Tundra vegetation will pasture reindeer on something like the acreage basis for cattle grazing in the arid intermountain plateaus of western United States. In each case approximately 40 acres is needed for each animal.

Land Utilization

The story of the sparse population in the millions of square miles of the Arctic lands cannot be written as it was a few decades ago. Then, many of these people had little or no contact with modern civilization. Many depended entirely upon the local physical environment for food, shelter, clothing, and tools. It took considerable natural ingenuity for survival under such circumstances. Now contact with middle-latitude people has changed them; it has helped them in several ways, although it may have harmed them in such features as disease and depleted game supply.

Greenland may serve as an example of recent change in Arctic economy. This Danish colony of more than 25,000 Greenlanders, mixed European and Eskimo, has doubled in population since the start of the century. At that time people lived largely by subsistence hunting. Owing to a slight warming of the North Atlantic, cod have migrated poleward toward Greenland and have given the island's people commercial fishing as a major occupation. A progressive Danish government is aiding the economy with a good colonial administration.

Canada, like Denmark, is seeking to improve conditions for those inhabiting the north coast mainland and adjoining island sections. At least once a year government patrol ships call at lonely outposts of northeastern Canada, where a few thousand Eskimo and a few hundred

Whites maintain permanent residence. These ships bring supplementary food, clothing, medical supplies, and other essentials to Canada's isolated people. A little more than a decade ago, August 1953, nearly half of Canada's Eskimos voted in the nation's general election. Voting equipment was taken to isolated settlements by plane, helicopter, and icebreaker. Thus the life of the Eskimo takes on modern characteristics. The old isolation is disappearing.

One of the most serious problems of the North American and Eurasian Arctic is the adjustment of modern settlements to a widespread occurrence of permafrost (perennially frozen ground). In fact it generally occurs anywhere in the world where the average annual temperature is below 32° F and underlies large parts of Greenland, Canada, Alaska, and the U.S.S.R. Scientists estimate that it may underlie one fifth of the earth's land surface.

Lying above the permafrost, is a thin layer of earth that thaws during the long period of sunlight of summer and freezes again during the short days and long nights of the winter season.

Fig. 13–16   Mosquitoes on Army Caps, Churchill, Canada. Churchill is located in a transition zone between the subarctic or taiga climate and that of the tundra. Permafrost lies a short distance below the surface of the earth; during the summer period large areas of undrained land produce conditions ideal for the breeding of millions of mosquitoes. There are probably 10 times as many mosquitoes per square mile over at least two thirds of the land north of the tree line as the highest average over an equivalent area in the tropics. (*Courtesy C. R. Twinn, Arctic Institute of North America Collection*)

This layer, which usually consists of soil, is deeper near the southern limits of permafrost than it is near the poles.

It is this soil lying above the permafrost that causes trouble for settlers of the tundra and northern taiga regions. One of the major difficulties concerns the proper method of constructing a firm foundation in the permafrost so that pilings and footings will not shift and crack the building they support. Another problem is how to lay a paved road or airstrip over permafrost with any certainty that it will remain relatively flat a year later. At Inuvik, Canada, near the mouth of the Mackenzie river, many buildings are constructed of wood—for lightness—and they rest upon wooden piles driven into steam thawed permafrost. There, they are enclosed in pilings that prevent weight or heat from causing the structure to buckle or heave. The Inuvik air strip, costing more than 6 million dollars, is insulated with about eight feet of crushed rock, a scarce commodity near the Mackenzie delta.

As early as the close of the 19th century, the United States attempted to improve living conditions for Alaskan Eskimos by importing reindeer. This venture achieved some success but also encountered many difficulties. Some of the problems include the following. Most Eskimos are natural hunters, and they do not easily become interested in the exacting occupation of reindeer herding. Herds need to be guided to the better grazing areas, to be protected from wild animals, and to be carefully watched to keep them from being assimilated by wild herds of North American caribou. Even if Eskimo interest were adequately developed, shipping and marketing problems are legion. They include lack of suitable docking facilities, the expense of refrigeration shipping space, a short ice-free shipping season, the expense of shipment by aircraft, competition with beef in the American markets, lack of cooperation from American packers, the average American's preference for beef, and several other problems.

In the Eurasian tundra, reindeer have been domesticated for centuries; and through domestication of animals, groups of Eurasian Arctic people reached a higher stage of civilization than that achieved by the North American Eskimo. In northern Norway, Sweden, and Finland many Lapps still live with their reindeer herds and supplement products of their domestic animals by exploiting life of the sea. But homes, food, and clothing show many changes from those utilized several decades ago. Moreover, several Lapps have given up herding reindeer and have taken up work in the forests to the south, in mining, or in other occupations. The three countries of Sweden, Norway, and Finland have made it possible for Lapp migrations to cross country boundaries without any government interference.

Changes are also taking place in the Russian Arctic. Like the reindeer people of the Scandinavian peninsula, native tribes have lived largely on reindeer products and fishing for a long while. Homes have been primitive; meat, fish, and summer berries have dominated food menus; and furs and skins of animals have provided clothing. Remnants of old food, shelter, and clothing practices persist. But the Russian government has started reindeer farms, provided better fishing nets, and in some places substituted motor boats for the less dependable canoes. Natives are taught to grow cold-resistant vegetables, build better houses, attend school, and all in all gain a better standard of living. Life is changing for most people of the sparsely populated Arctic, for the Eskimo, the Greenlander, the Lapp, and the many tribes of the Russian Arctic.

Power and Mineral Resources. In any appraisal of power resources in the Polar regions, one would call attention to the large areas of continental shelf found in Hudson Bay, the Bering Sea, and the Arctic Ocean. The Arctic Basin shelf is always mentioned as one of the great petroleum reserves of the world. Little exploitation has taken place, but exploration has started in several places. For example, the United States Navy has important leases known to contain oil, in the vicinity of Point Barrow, along the northern shores of Alaska.

Coal is found near the shores of the Arctic both in North America and in Eurasia. Low-grade coal serves a useful purpose after it is mined from Disko Island along the west coast of Greenland. Significant tonnage is mined annually on Svalbard (Spitzbergen). In the southern hemisphere, Antarctica is known to have coal deposits. This suggests that icecap climate did not always dominate atmospheric conditions on the glacier-covered continent. It seems evident also that man will need power resources far more than at present before Antarctic coal exploitation will become important.

Many minerals are available in the Arctic lands that include parts of the Laurentian and Scandinavian Shields and other geologically old physiographic regions with highly mineralized igneous and metamorphic rocks. Iron is being exploited on both sides of the Norwegian-Russian border at Norway's Kirkenes and Russia's Kirovsk. The Kolyma river area in Northeast Siberia contributes to the high rank of Russian gold production. Lead and zinc mining is in the development stage at Mesters Vig in northeast Greenland. Large nickel, copper, iron, and other mineral deposits are known resources on the Ungava Peninsula of northern Labrador. A variety of minerals have been discovered around both east and west shores of Hudson Bay and along the Arctic coast.

Although many mineral resources have been and will be discovered in the Polar deserts, only those that are particularly valuable, easy to extract and refine, and close to economical transport will be developed in the near future; it is a well-known fact that the expenses incurred in bringing in labor, supplies, and equipment; in shipping out products; in heating; and in providing amenities for workers and their families are all factors that weigh heavily against profitable mineral production in the Polar Deserts.

Military Activities. Military activities are increasing in the Arctic. In North America a radar line of bases extends across Canada's Arctic islands between Greenland and Alaska; this line is called the DEW LINE (Distant Early Warning), and lies farther north than the Mid-Canada and Pine Tree radar barriers. Eskimos already are being trained to operate radar and weather stations; many have mechanical ability, and they are better adjusted than the white man to live and work in the low temperatures (see Fig. 1–11).

Military air transport is making rapid strides, even on floating islands, because of the strategic location of the Arctic basin. Routes over the Arctic shorten distances between North America and Eurasia. Over-the-pole air flights have also been inaugurated for commercial purposes.

In 1961 Russia held the atomic tests in the Polar Desert region. This emphasizes the utility of an area of low economic value and sparse population for conducting military maneuvers involving guided missiles and atomic bombs.

In summary it may be said that the Polar Desert environment includes a climate too cold for commercial agriculture; grazing land with low carrying capacity; few trees and none of large size; inadequate development of transport facilities; no manufacturing except of local raw materials; much wild life upon land and in the adjoining seas; a location exposed to over-the-pole attack; and resources of petroleum, natural gas, and metallic minerals, many of them located in isolated areas.

Human use of the geographical environment by a sparse population has resulted in emphasis on hunting, trapping, fishing, grazing, mining, and military activities. Further changes in regional economy may be slight, but they will include greater emphasis upon the extraction of power and mineral resources and further improvements in transportation.

QUESTIONS, EXERCISES, AND PROBLEMS

1. Outline the general features of steppe and desert climates, vegetation, soils, and land forms. What are the causes of deserts?

2. In what countries do steppe lands and deserts occur? What is the geographic significance of the 100th meridian in the United States?

3. Point out relationships between nomadic herding, a feature industry of deserts, and the geographic environment. What are the causes for water supply in desert oases? What conditions make the sheep better adapted to Middle East grazing economy than the cow? Compare Great Plains and Middle East grazing industries. Describe the practices of dry farming, stressing relationships to the geographic environment.

4. What are the advantages of irrigation farming? How may an increase in irrigation be related to an increase in disease hazards? Give arguments against increased irrigation in the United States. Describe irrigation potential and practices in Egypt.

5. Wheat can be grown in many climates. Name them. What advantages and disadvantages does the middle latitude steppe have for growing wheat? Describe man-made limits to wheat production. What is the difference between spring wheat and winter wheat?

6. Describe major characteristics, distribution, and numbers of population in the world's steppe and desert lands.

7. Summarize major uses of the land in the world's dry lands. How attractive are the world's deserts and steppes to the great powers?
8. Compare the areal distribution of low and middle latitude steppe climates shown on Fig. 13–1 with those of the *Bsh* and *Bsk* climates shown on Plate 2 at the back of the book. Point out similarities and differences in locations and boundaries.
9. Compare the areal distribution of the low and middle latitude desert climates shown on Fig. 13–1 with those of the *Bwh* and *Bwk* climates shown on Plate 2. Point out similarities and differences in locations and boundaries.
10. Compare the areal distribution of high latitude tundra and ice cap climates shown on Fig. 13–14 with those of the *E* climates shown on Plate 2. Point out similarities and differences in locations and boundaries.

SELECTED REFERENCES

Abrahamson, Gunther, "Canada's Reindeer," *Canadian Geographical Journal,* June 1963, pp. 188–93.

Barbour, K. M., "North and South in Sudan: A Study in Human Contrasts," *Annals of the Association of American Geographers,* July 1964, pp. 209–26.

Bone, Robert M., "The Fertile Triangle of Soviet Russia," *Canadian Geographical Journal,* Nov. 1963, pp. 166–71.

Clarke, J. I., "Oil in Libya: Some Implications," *Economic Geography,* Jan. 1963, pp. 40–59.

Clarke, J. I., "Studies in Semi-Nomadism in North Africa," *Economic Geography,* April 1959, pp. 95–108.

Clawson, Marion, *The Western Range Livestock Industry,* McGraw-Hill, 1950.

Cressey, G. B., *Crossroads: Land and Life in Southwest Asia,* J. B. Lippincott, 1960.

Dozier, C. L., "Mexico's Transformed Northwest," *Geographical Review,* Oct. 1963, pp. 548–71.

Dunbar, Moira and Greenaway, Keith R., *Arctic Canada From the Air,* Canada Defence Research Board, Ottawa, 1956.

Dutcher, Flora, "A Sod House," *Journal of Geography,* December 1949, pp. 353–62.

Fonaroff, L. S., "Conservation and Stock Reduction on the Navajo Tribal Range," *Geographical Review,* April 1963, pp. 200–23.

Geographical Record, "Problems and Prospects of Pastoral Nomadism," *Geographical Review,* April 1961, pp. 310–11.

Geographical Record, "The Coast Lapps of Norway," *Geographical Review,* October 1959, pp. 570–72.

Gerster, Georg, *Sahara: Desert of Destiny,* Stewart Thomson, translator, Coward-McCann, 1960.

Gulick, Luther H., Jr., "Irrigation Systems of the Former Sind Province, West Pakistan," *Geographical Review,* Jan. 1963, pp. 79–99.

Hodge, C. and Duisberg, P. C., *Aridity and Man: The Challenge of the Arid Lands in the U.S.,* American Association for the Advancement of Science, 1963.

Hudson, James, *Irrigation Water Use in the Utah Valley, Utah,* University of Chicago Press, 1964.

Ives, J. D. and Sagar, R. B. "Return to the Ice Age: Geographical Branch Research in Baffin Island," *Canadian Geographical Journal,* Aug. 1963, pp. 38–47.

Lewis, Norman U. "Malaria, Irrigation and Soil Erosion in Central Syria," *Geographical Review,* April 1949, pp. 278–90.

Macinko, George, "The Columbia Basin Project: Expectations, Realizations, and Implications," *Geographical Review,* April 1963, pp. 185–99.

Quartermaster Research and Engineering Command, U. S. Army, *Southwest Asia: Environment and its Relationship to Military Activities,* Technical Report EP-118, Natick, Mass., July 1959.

Robertson, O. C. S., "Geographers, the Arctic, and the Canadian World Exposition," *Canadian Geographical Journal,* May 1964, pp. 144–55.

Rudolph, William E., *Vanishing Trails of Atacama,* American Geographical Society, 1963.

Rue, Aubert de la, "Caatinga, The Dry Country of Northeast Brazil," *Landscape,* Autumn, 1962, pp. 18–24.

Rutherford, John, "Interplay of American and Australian Ideas for the Development of Water Projects in Northern Victoria," *Annals of the Association of American Geographers,* March 1964, pp. 88–106.

Shaw, Earl B., *Anglo-America,* John Wiley and Sons, 1959, Chs.—2—3—11—13.

Stead, G. W., "Arctic Probes by the Canadian Coast Guard," *Canadian Geographical Journal,* June 1963, pp. 176–87.

Thoman, R. S. and Patton, D. J., *Focus on Geographic Activity,* McGraw-Hill, 1964, Ch. 9, "Commercial Crop Operation in the Northern Great Plains."

Trewartha, Glenn T., *An Introduction to Climate,* McGraw-Hill, 1954, pp. 267–88; and 358–77.

Twitchell, K. S., "Water Resources of Saudi Arabia," *Geographical Review,* April 1944, pp. 365–86.

U. S. Department of Agriculture, *Grass, Agricultural Yearbook,* 1948, pp. 203–60.

U. S. Department of Agriculture, *Shelter Belts for the Northern Great Plains* Farmers' Bulletin, No. 2109, 1961.

Vanderhill, B. G., "The Farming Frontier of Western Canada," *Journal of Geography,* Jan. 1962, pp. 13–20.

Weaver, J. E. and Albertson, F. W., *Grasslands of the Great Plains: Their Nature and Use,* Johnson Publishing Co., Lincoln, Nebraska, 1956.

Chapter Fourteen

The Mediterranean and Humid Subtropical Lands

The subtropical regions described in this chapter are only two in number, the Mediterranean and Humid Subtropics, because deserts and steppes located along the poleward boundary of the tropics have received consideration in previous chapters.

The Mediterranean Region, Physical Environment

Location. (Fig. 14–1) Mediterranean regions may be found in six of the seven continents; but the climatic type includes only 2 per cent of the earth's land. Most of this small fraction lies along or near the Mediterranean Sea, which gives its name to the climate. The European section includes the bulk of three south-pointing peninsulas, the Iberian, the Italian, and the Balkan with parts of Portugal, Spain, France, Italy, Yugoslavia, Albania, Greece, Bulgaria, and Russia's Crimea. In northern Africa only the coasts of Morocco, Algeria, and Tunisia have Mediterranean climates; and in southern Africa this climate occurs only in a small area around the city of Capetown. Asia's Mediterranean climate lies in the southwest, and includes (1) Turkey's Black Sea coast; (2) the Mediterranean coast of Turkey, Syria, Lebanon, and Israel; and (3) *a* a considerable portion of western Iran, including the well-watered section at the base of the Elburz Mountains lying just south of the Caspian Sea; *b* part of Iraq where it joins Iran to the east; and *c* a portion of Russia immediately south of the Caucasus Mountains. Mediterranean climates also appear in South America's Middle Chile; in North America's Southern California; and in west-facing portions of southern Australia, especially around the city of Perth and Spencer Gulf.

Climate and Land Forms. The Mediterranean climate might be called a transition one,

for it lies equatorward from the middle latitude humid lands and poleward from the low latitude deserts and steppes. It is found on the west sides of continental masses and occupies a latitudinal position approximately between 30° and 40° North or South.

Air masses from three wind belts may affect these northern and southern hemisphere latitudes. In summer, descending air of the horse latitudes and equatorward-moving air of the trade winds are likely to be in control—thus summer months are dry (Fig. 14–2). High temperatures are likely to be common in this period of low precipitation; but in every case except along shores of the Mediterranean, Caspian, and Black Seas, cold currents lower summer temperatures. In winter, low-pressure cyclonic storms of the westerlies contribute the bulk of the precipitation. Cool temperatures prevail in this season.

In all areas of Mediterranean climate, mountains or plateaus lie near the coast and prevent the extension of the climatic type far inland. But the highland background, so near the sea, encourages heavy precipitation for both coast and mountain and plateau backdrop. In California, the lofty Sierras receive heavy winter precipitation, and the melting snows add significantly to water needed for irrigation in the long dry summers. The Andes perform the same function for Middle Chile. California's Sierra Nevada and Klamath Mountains and the European Alps protect coastal areas from cold air moving equatorward out of the interior. Uplands also encourage local winds such as the mistral and bora of the European Mediterranean.

Vegetation. The natural response of vegetation to relatively hot, dry summers and mild, moist winters (Los Angeles has about 78 per cent of its precipitation from December to March in-

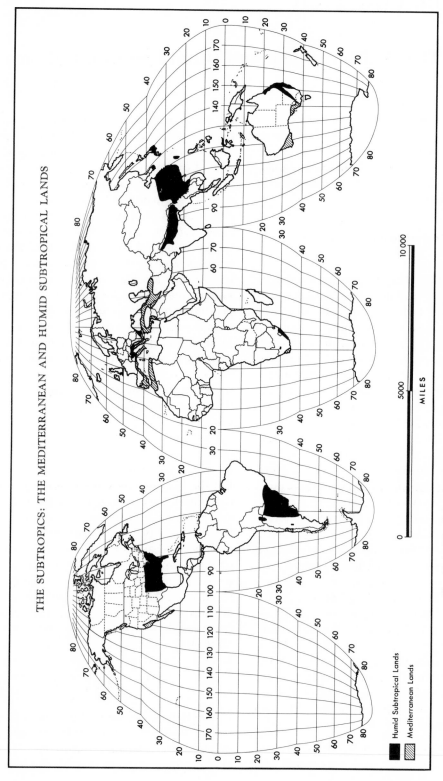

THE SUBTROPICS: THE MEDITERRANEAN AND HUMID SUBTROPICAL LANDS

Humid Subtropical Lands

Mediterranean Lands

MILES

Fig. 14-1   The Subtropics: Mediterranean and Humid Subtropical Lands. (*Projection based on the homolosine projection copyright by the University of Chicago. Map by permission McGraw-Hill Book Co. and G. T. Trewartha, An Introduction to Climate*)

clusive and less than 2 per cent from June to September inclusive) is largely bush or scrub forest such as the chaparral of southern California and the maquis of the Mediterranean Sea countries. The annual precipitation (usually 10 to 25 inches) is too light to encourage luxuriant forest growth. In no place is there a heavy stand of commercial timber. A further retarding influence for forest growth, especially in the Mediterranean Sea lands, is the work of sheep and goats, which discourages heavy tree cover. Vegetation is likely to possess many of the characteristics of desert plants, thick bark, small leaves, thorns, leaf hairs, thick cuticle and small stomata on leaves, deep roots or ones covering a large area in a horizontal direction, and many other features, all of which are designed to prevent the loss of moisture.

Soils. Soils are of various types. Many lack humus, although low rainfall discourages leaching. Since most Mediterranean lands have rolling terrain, soils are likely to be thin on the more rugged areas; valley alluvium presents the best opportunities for agriculture. Soils are not generally as great an agricultural handicap as the low uncertain precipitation.

Land Utilization

Agriculture. Agriculture, much of it irrigation farming, is a dominant occupation, if not the most important, in every one of the lands with Mediterranean climate. The warm temperatures give opportunity for year-round growth; but there is always danger of frost in at least one month. Locations closest to the sea and those protected by mountains from cold winds moving out of the continental interior have the best chance for a twelve-month growing season.

Mediterranean Sea Lands. The area in the vicinity of the Mediterranean Sea is the largest region. Here a wide variety of both commercial and subsistence crops feature farming activities. One of the most typical products is the olive, which will grow without irrigation upon hill slopes and plains and on clay, sandy, gravel, or limestone soils. Its leaves are small; its bark is thick; and its roots spread out a considerable distance in order to take advantage of all available water supply. Furthermore, the crop gets help from man who makes the limited moisture more efficient with dry farming practices.

Lands around the Mediterranean Sea lead in

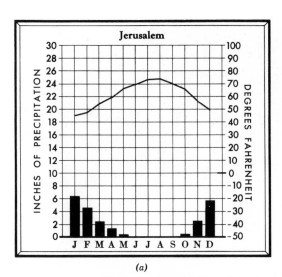

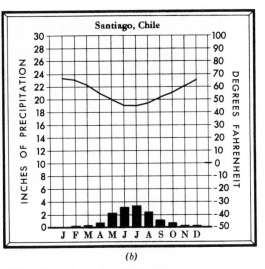

(a)   (b)

Fig. 14–2 Climatic Charts, Jerusalem and Santiago, Chile. Notice the definite winter maximum in precipitation and the extremely dry summer; both conditions are characteristic of the typical Mediterranean climate. Remember that the cool rainy season occurs in northern hemisphere Jerusalem at the time of southern hemisphere Santiago's dry period.

Fig. 14–3   Harvesting Olives in an Italian Olive Grove. One of the typical tree crops of the region around the Mediterranean Sea is the olive. In fact it is thought by some people to have originated in Syria, and from there its culture was carried around the shores of the Mediterranean. Joseph E. Williams in his *World Atlas* 1963, credits Spain with 29 per cent of world production, Italy 22 per cent, Tunisia 11 per cent, Greece 9 per cent, and Turkey and Portugal 7 per cent each. Thus these Mediterranean countries account for about 85 per cent of the world total. (*Courtesy Standard Oil, New Jersey*)

the production of olives (Fig. 14–3) and commodities processed from them. Olive oil contributes an important vegetable fat, a substitute for animal fat, in the diet of rich and poor. This

is a significant contribution to the economy because the climate is far from the best for dairy breeds of cattle. They suffer from summer heat and especially from the absence of nutritious grasses, curtailed by the dry summers.

Citrus fruits, extremely important in production and export, are not indigenous to the Mediterranean. Man has brought them into an environment that is relatively favorable, and by care and forethought he has achieved for the region a high place in world citrus production. Most countries lack enough natural precipitation for profitable citrus farming; so man takes water from streams, rising in nearby mountains, where precipitation is heavier, and irrigates his citrus groves. He plants these orchards on gentle slopes to take advantage of air drainage and thus minimize frost hazard. Frost temperatures, if they come, never last long, and many fruit growers use smudge pots (Fig. 14–4) to heat the air and also to prevent out-going radiation. Some farmers have huge revolving fans to keep the air in motion.

The hot, dry Mediterranean summers favor natural drying (Fig. 14–5) of figs and other fruit; but in some Mediterranean lands, and in all humid areas where figs, prunes, and raisin grapes are grown, artificial drying has become important. This eliminates any possible damage

Fig. 14–4   Heating Fruit Orchards. Freezing temperatures may occur for a day or two in both Mediterranean and humid subtropical climates; thus it may be necessary to start fires in orchard heaters and to use other frost prevention devices. (*Courtesy U.S. Deptrtment of Commerce, Weather Bureau*)

Fig. 14–5 Drying Fruit in Mediterranean Lands. The dry summers of Mediterranean climates provide much sun for drying raisin grapes and assure relative safety from rain damage. (*Courtesy U.S. Department of Commerce, Weather Bureau*)

from a passing shower, something that can occur in almost any climate.

Wine grapes are much more important in lands bordering the Mediterranean Sea than raisin grapes; and wine drinking is widespread. In caring for his vineyards, man makes careful adjustments to limited moisture supply. Vines may be pruned carefully; kept close to the ground to lessen evaporation from winds; protected against excessive loss of moisture by wind breaks; and planted at wide intervals to assure sufficient root expansion for tapping sources of ground water.

Lands along the western shores of the Mediterranean Sea have an almost complete monopoly on natural cork production (Fig. 14–6). The cork oak is native to the region and forms a part of the climax vegetation of southern Spain and Portugal and the adjoining shores of North Africa. The thick bark is well adjusted to hot, dry summers and winters with limited rainfall. Bark protection also helps the tree survive possible damaging effects of the leveche, a hot wind, which sweeps in from the dry Sahara in front of a passing low-pressure area.

In any discussion of lands bordering the Mediterranean, mention should be made of

cereal growing, especially of wheat. Winter rains and summer droughts provide a cool, moist period for growth and a dry sunny spell for ripening the grain; both these conditions are vital for successful production. Italy is one of the world's leading wheat producers, and normally is not far below Canada. The main difference is that Canada has 18 million consumers and Italy 50 million. As a consequence, Canada is one of the leading wheat exporters, while Italy consumes the entire locally produced crop. In the drier Mediterranean areas barley may supplant wheat because the former is more drought resistant. Rice growing reaches its poleward limits in northern Italy, where streams fed by mountain rainfall provide irrigation and mountain barriers give protection from cold winter air masses.

Animal industries show striking adjustments to the environment. Goats are found in large numbers; and in some places they are driven from customer to customer and milked at the place of sale. The animal's ability to exist on bush, coarse grasses, and tree sprouts makes him adaptable to the natural vegetation. His appetite has been blamed for the depletion of Mediterranean forests, consequent greater stream erosion, and the destruction of marginal farm lands.

The Merino sheep (see Fig. A–10, p. 390), one of the world's best breeds for dry lands, is believed to have originated in Spain or North Africa. Like the goat, it is well adjusted to the

Fig. 14–6 Transporting Cork Oak Bark in Spain. Donkeys almost completely covered with light-weight bark from the cork oak, indigenous to Mediterranean lands, provide the best means of transport over mountain trails. (*Courtesy Armstrong Cork Company*)

environment, but it will not thrive on as poor pastures. Transhumance is still practiced, but not as extensively as it was some centuries ago when sheep men dominated the economy and politics of Spain.

More donkeys are raised than horses. They can adapt themselves better than the horse to poor grazing conditions; and they work better over rugged mountain trails. Poultry raising is important with Mediterranean breeds such as the Leghorn and Minorca quite disease resistant and willing to rustle for the limited grain supplies. They also have better egg-laying records than many of the larger types.

Southern California. Probably the most progressive agricultural area is Southern California, where farming by European settlers began at the Spanish missions in the 16th century. About 300 years later the gold rush stimulated food production when population in the 1848 to 1857 period increased from 15,000 Whites to over a half million. The modern agricultural period began about 1900. Since then southern California, as well as the state as a whole, has changed huge grain fields and pastures into thousands of acres of citrus groves, orchards, and vineyards. Now the state has become the largest producer, fresh shipper, processor, and exporter of commercial fruit in the world.

Most of the four major areas accounting for the large share of California's fruit and nut production lie in the region of Mediterranean climate. (1) The San Joaquin Valley accounts for over three fourths of California's grapes, two thirds of the peaches, one half of the plums, 15 per cent of the citrus crop, 90 per cent of the figs and nectarines, and 40 per cent of the olives. (2) The Sacramento Valley with 10 per cent of the fruit and nut acreage and production has more precipitation and lower temperatures than the San Joaquin area; as a response there are more deciduous fruit trees than those of the citrus variety. (3) The Central Coastal area north of Santa Barbara County has no commercial citrus fruit, but accounts for 80 per cent of the apples, 75 per cent of the prunes, 65 per cent of the apricots, nearly half of the pear acreage and almost half of the cherry acreage. (4) The eight counties south of the Tehachapi mountains produce nearly all the commercial avocados and lemons, 60 per cent of the state's navel oranges and 90

per cent of the valencias; the latter are highly concentrated in the coastal areas, where the moderate and equable marine climate favors production of the best quality of fruit with the least risk of frost damage to the winter blossoms.[1]

More than thirty varieties of commercial vegetables are grown, and national leadership is definite in lettuce, cauliflower, carrots, cantaloupes, and honey dew melons. Most of the vegetables are produced in the four major fruit and nut growing regions. Field crops include hay, barley, wheat, cotton, beans, rice, and sugar beets. Practically all the hay, most of it alfalfa, is grown by irrigation; but barley and wheat are planted at the start of the cool period to take advantage of the winter rains for growth and the dry summer following for ripening. Southern California cotton gives the state second place in the nation. Rice may be planted on some alkali soils; the large amount of water needed for rice growth will wash salts from the soil. Another crop showing tolerance to certain alkali soils is the sugar beet, always grown by irrigation in California. California's field crops make up one of several factors responsible for the state's growing livestock industry. Many cattle and lambs fattened in the Great Valley on beet pulp and molasses, cottonseed concentrates, fibrous barley, and the all-important alfalfa hay. The foothills surrounding the valley have annual and perennial grasses on which the livestock are dependent.

In summary, California shows great diversity in its modern commercial farming with fruits and nuts, vegetables, field crops and livestock. A large share of the crops is grown by irrigation (Fig. 14–7) in a state that has spent millions on the conservation and distribution of water. Rainfall increases from south to north, but level land increases from north to south. Thus a major problem has been to move water of the north to the dry lands of the south, and from well-watered mountains, almost surrounding the Great Valley, to the drier plains.

Middle Chile. All Chile, like all Gaul of old,

---

[1] The percentages quoted for fruits grown in southern California represent production in a recent year. Obviously such statistics change; but whatever changes have taken place do not alter the fact that this Mediterranean climatic region is one of the greatest producers of fruits and vegetables in the world.

is divided into three parts. At the north is the Atacama with its low-latitude desert climate; at the south is southern Chile with its west-coast marine climate; and in between north and south is middle Chile with its Mediterranean climate.

Middle Chile is also divided into three sections. Near the coast are low mountain ranges set apart from the Andes region to the east by a down-faulted Central Valley, the economic heart and life of Chile. Here are the most of the wealth, the industry, the farming, and the people.

Middle Chile's physical environment is largely similar to that of Southern California, but economic development has moved at a much slower pace. Much of the land is still in large farms; and too much of it remains in pasture for cattle, instead of being utilized for crop

agriculture. No fruit and vegetable culture has reached the importance or intensity of that of the great state in the Southwest. One important retarding factor is the great distance to a tariff-free profitable market for fruits and vegetables. No tourist industry like that of California is present. In spite of magnificent scenery, distance from a dense population with high living standards will discourage tourist development until the length of time to make the journey and costs can be lowered satisfactorily. Local manufacturing and commerce are progressing, but they need more capital from local and foreign sources in order to reach the desired economic goals.

Africa's Southwest Tip. Southwest Africa's share of Mediterranean climate occupies the

Fig. 14–7   An Irrigated Mountain Valley of Southern California. Mountain barriers against prevailing westerly winds, active in the winter season, encourage precipitation for irrigating valley lowlands. Note the snow-clad mountains in the background; farmers are vitally interested in this source for irrigation. (*Courtesy Keystone View Company*)

smallest area of any of the world regions. It includes the southwest tip of the continent, where one of the few folded mountain sections of Africa may be found. Elevation of the Cape Range is not as high as that of the Sierras which form the backdrop for Mediterranean California, or the Andes to the east of middle Chile, or the Maritime Alps which protect Nice from cold winter air masses from the north; but the Cape Range reaches 7000 feet and makes striking temperature contrasts between highlands and coastal lowlands.

Some of the lowlands around the westernmost ranges have been farmed for more than three centuries by Dutch and French colonists and their descendants. Wheat, which probably occupies most of the farm lands, has always been an important crop, but it is so only because man protects local production by import tariffs. Grapes, like wheat, are grown in areas with a minimum of 15 inches of rainfall; and the manufacture of good-quality wine is based upon local viticulture. Many sheep feed on areas of low rainfall. Soils and climate are not unfavorable to the growing of Turkish types of tobacco, but the environment does not seem to favor one of the most typical Mediterranean crops, the olive.

South Africa's Mediterranean region is favored with beautiful scenery, mountains, seacoast, deep gorges, spectacular waterfalls, and many other features. But like Middle Chile and Mediterranean Australia, South Africa is far distant from dense populations with high living standards, a very important necessity for developing a large tourist industry. At present, race problems may also minimize tourist attraction.

Mediterranean Australia. Australia's Mediterranean climate includes (1) the southwest coast of the province of West Australia. Here the Swan River cuts through the Darling escarpment, lying to the east to reach the sea near Perth. Its waters are used for irrigation. (2) In South Australia Province, the Gawler Ranges lie back of the Eyre Peninsula portion; and both sides of Spencer Gulf, St. Vincent Bay, and east and west foothills of the southern part of the Flinders Range are included. The mouth of the Murray River, Kangaroo Island, and Adelaide belong in the region. (3) The Victoria section comprises the southwest part of the province, where waters of the Murray encourage irriga-

tion agriculture just as they do in the province of South Australia.

Australia is a leading world exporter of wheat, wool, and mutton (see Fig. A–1, p. 381); and a significant portion comes from the Mediterranean section. Irrigation for citrus crops and fruits for drying is increasing. Southern-hemisphere fruit has a market advantage in a ripening season occurring during the winter of the northern hemisphere. This factor was of little importance until progress was made in transport both from the standpoint of speed and refrigeration facilities. These man-made advantages encourage fruit orchard expansion not only in Australia but also in the Mediterranean climate of southwest Africa. Australia, a member of the British Commonwealth, has a tariff advantage over southern-hemisphere Chile.

Other Resources. Proven oil reserves are significant only in California and in the Mediterranean areas of the Middle East. Coal supplies are at a minimum in Mediterranean climates. Water-power resources are much larger than those of coal, but most of the water comes from adjoining high mountain regions. Forest resources are meager, and Mediterranean fisheries make no great world contribution. Heavy manufacturing is of little importance because basic raw materials of coal and iron are limited in supply. Resources of metallic minerals are not large. Only in California and to a lesser extent in Australia is manufacturing expanding rapidly. In Australia it is encouraged by widespread occurrence of iron and adequate supplies of coal together with a small market. In California encouragement comes from a rapidly expanding population in Pacific coast states, and from high living standards. All in all the Mediterranean regions do not stand out as areas of great economic strength; and one of the main reasons is small size, a fact emphasized at the beginning of the chapter.

The Humid Subtropical Region, Physical Environment

Location. The humid subtropical climates (see Fig. 14–1) include lands in six continents. A large section lies in southeast Asia—in China, India, and Japan; in southern Korea, all of Formosa (Taiwan), the extreme northern parts of Siam (Thailand) and former French Indochina, and a portion of Pakistan. Africa has only a little coastal stretch east of the Drakensberg escarpment and the small Australian region along the Pacific coast is interrupted slightly by the Australian Alps. Very little appears in Europe—much of the Po valley plus a small part of Yugoslavia east of the coastal ranges, and a small area west and east of the Black Sea belonging to Bulgaria and Russia. Brazil, Argentina, Uruguay, and Paraguay are represented in South America; and the North American section lies in southeastern United States.

Climate, Humid Subtropical, and Mediterranean Contrasts. (1) Humid subtropical climates have an east coast position; the Mediterranean climates have a west coast location (Fig. 14–8). (2) The former have either a summer maximum in rainfall or well-distributed precipitation throughout the year in contrast to the winter maximum of the latter. (3) On an average the humid subtropical climates have a higher total annual precipitation than that of the Mediterranean. (4) East-coast locations, between 30° and 40° north or south latitude, are paralleled by warm ocean currents in contrast to the cold ones usually found along similar west-coast latitudes. This condition alone encourages heavier summer precipitation in the humid subtropical regions. (5) Mediterranean climates, as a rule, have cooler night temperatures. Those of the humid subtropical climates may be extremely unpleasant in summer and may exceed summer readings for the tropical rainforest region. (6) Humid subtropical regions, especially in the United States, have many summer thunderstorms. This is not the case on west coasts in the same latitudes. (7) Mediterranean locations are more marine in their climatic characteristics than locations in the humid subtropics. In fact, the great continentality of the latter climates, especially in Asia, encourages monsoon conditions. (8) It is true that both climates may appear transitional in type, but the Mediterranean lies between steppe or desert on its equatorward side and the west-coast marine on its poleward boundary. The humid subtropical, on the other hand, merges with the tropical savanna or rainforest on the equatorward boundary and with the humid continental, especially in Asia and North America, on the poleward side. (9) The humid subtropical climate receives part of its precipitation from tropical hurricanes, but there is little danger of these violent windstorms in Mediterranean climates.

Climate, Humid Subtropical and Mediterranean Similarities. Similarities between the

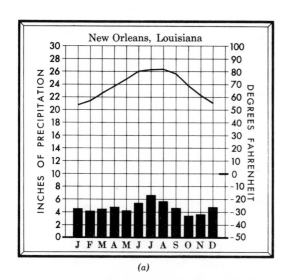 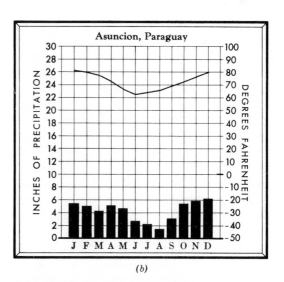

Fig. 14–8   Climatic Charts, New Orleans and Asuncion. Both northern and southern hemisphere stations show a definite summer maximum in rainfall. Note the contrast with stations in the Mediterranean climate.

two climates include the following: (1) Both lie in similar latitudes 30° to 40° north or south, although in some cases the humid subtropical may extend a few degrees closer to the equator. (2) Both are transitional climates. (3) The annual temperature range is relatively small in both. Absolute range (difference between highest and lowest temperatures ever recorded) is likely to be greater in the humid subtropical, a situation especially characteristic in the Gulf Coastal Region of the United States. (4) Equatorward portions of both climates suffer frost hazards over such short periods that commodities sensitive to cold may be grown with relative security in many sections of both regions, provided, of course, that the farmer takes special precautions against frost damage. (5) Cool-season rainfall in both is likely to result from the passage of cyclonic storms in the belt of westerly winds. (6) Snow may fall in both regions, but that occurring on equatorward margins probably will last approximately a day or less.

Surface Features. Whereas the land forms of the Mediterranean region are dominated by hills and mountains, those of the humid subtropical lands are made up largely of plains. These include the Atlantic and Gulf Coastal Plains of the United States; the Pampa in eastern South America; the Ganges, the Yangtze, and the Si river plains in Asia; the Po valley in Europe; and the narrow coastal plains of South Africa and eastern Australia.

Vegetation and Soils. In contrast to the drought resistant characteristics of tree, bush, and grass vegetation in the Mediterranean climates, that of the humid subtropical areas has far less need of such adjustments in the moister atmosphere. Here natural vegetation is largely forest, which, on the whole, is dominated by the broad leaf deciduous; but in some cases there is a large acreage of conifers. As an example of the latter situation, the conifer forests of southern United States have crowded out the broadleaf because of greater conifer tolerance to sandy soils and fires. Moreover, in that same region small areas of natural grass lands, now mostly in crop, were discovered by early explorers. Such pastures as the Alabama Black Belt and the Black Waxy Prairies of Texas are thought to be a response to edaphic conditions.

One may also find grasslands in the South American Humid Subtropics. Some believe that the Argentine Pampa was formerly forested but has lost its tree cover because of fires set by the Indians; whatever the cause, the Pampa, which early Latin American explorers saw, was one of the finest prairie grasslands in the world.

The remaining South American portion of the subtropical region is a mixture of trees and grasses. In Uruguay, tall grass prairie makes up a larger total than forest, which is found mainly along stream courses. Both semi-deciduous and grass vegetation occur in southern Brazil; and the distribution may be related to the underlying rock formations. Eastern Paraguay supports a semi-deciduous forest.

Monsoon forests originally covered most of the Asian humid subtropics. Now, however, in India's Ganges valley population pressure is so great that practically the entire area is under cultivation. This is not true in China, where some of the best forests of the nation still remain —ranking next in value to the tree cover of eastern Manchuria. On the subtropical coastal section of Africa, much of the forest, mainly deciduous, has been reduced by clearing for sugar plantations. The eastern Australian subtropics support both deciduous and conifer trees with most of the latter lying to the west of the Great Dividing Range.

Humid subtropical soils belong to the pedalfer group, with those in the United States classified largely as red and yellow earths. The grasslands are more fertile than forested sections because the grasses provide more humus than trees. Where rainfall is heaviest, soils may be leached seriously.

Land Utilization

Southern United States. Slight differences in climate and other features of the physical environment as well as contrasts in race, population density and, historical factors bring about economic differences among the several humid subtropical regions.

In southern United States cotton (Fig. 14–9) continues to be a very important agricultural crop, but diversification of crops and livestock is gaining rapidly. In fact, *change* is a good theme to describe the economy of the United States subtropics. Crop rotation, soil conservation, dairying, beef cattle, poultry, the use of legumes, hybrid corn, citrus fruit, cane sugar, rice, truck crops, and deciduous fruit, together with other competitors, are threatening cotton's former dominance. Furthermore, textile manufacturing, forest industries, mining, petroleum and natural gas production, and other industries are now actively competing with agriculture.

The United States subtropics may be divided into two major subregions, the Cotton Belt and the Humid Subtropical Coast. Again, the former is not a continuous area of cotton growing but may be divided into several areas that now produce about two-thirds of the crop (see Fig. A–7, p. 387). In each of these subdivisions, cotton occupies less than half the farm land; in fact, more land may be devoted to each of two or more other crops. The choice of crops, other than cotton is not the same among the several regions. In the west Texas High Plains, a three-crop pattern includes cotton, grain sorghum, and hay forage for beef cattle. Beef cattle, and the growing of hay to feed them, are important in every one of the regions; but the third item of the crop pattern may be different. In the Mississippi alluvial valley it is soybeans, except in

central Arkansas where it is rice; in northern Alabama it is corn or soybeans; the Piedmont produces winter small grains; the Georgia and South Carolina Inner Coastal Plain produce corn and peanuts; but North Carolina produces tobacco on the same plain; and on the Black Waxy Prairies of Texas, corn, legume seed, and peanuts along with cattle and cotton are raised. Thus, instead of a similar crop pattern all over the Cotton Belt, different sections specialize in diversified crops best suited to their needs. Diversification is the rule, but field plans vary from place to place.

On the Humid Subtropical Coast farming shows similarities to and differences from that of the so-called Cotton Belt. A major difference is the small amount of land devoted to cotton; another appears in the large production of rice; still another is the greater emphasis upon truck crops; and finally, a decided contrast occurs in the stress upon cane sugar and citrus fruits, which are entirely absent from the Cotton Belt. Probably the greatest similarity appears in the growth of beef cattle and in the trend toward agricultural diversification in both subregions.

Fig. 14–9   The Cotton Picking Machine. At harvest time, in the Cotton Belt of the United States, machines move down the rows methodically plucking cotton from bolls and blowing it into cage-like hoppers behind drivers. In 1963, the United States accounted for less than one third of world production, 49,573,000 bales. Russia produces nearly 8 million bales—mostly by irrigation; China and India about 5 million each; and Brazil, Egypt, Mexico, and Pakistan each raise about 2 million bales. Although much of the world's cotton grows on humid subtropical lands, especially in the United States, other subtropical and tropical climates account for a large share. (*Courtesy Standard Oil Company, New Jersey*)

South America. In South America, the Humid Subtropics include four major areas, Southeast Brazil, eastern Paraguay, Uruguay, and the Argentine Pampa.

In Southeast Brazil, natural vegetation changes from a mixture of grass and trees on the equatorward section to a more or less continuous grass cover in the south. In the north, during the latter part of the 19th century, Germans, Italians, Polish, and other nationalities migrated from Europe and developed small farms. Here among the hills and valleys one may see crops of corn, beans, potatoes, rye, wheat, grapes, and even more diverse produce, rather than coffee, cacao, sugar, and bananas that dominate the plantation agriculture of tropical Brazil.

The Argentine Pampa has South America's largest expanse of nearly level land, with fertile soils, and a mild, moist climate. Most of it lies relatively near the coast, where crops of corn, flax, wheat, and livestock products are forwarded for export from several great ports. Corn and flax are grown in the more humid sections; alfalfa and wheat in the drier areas; and high grade livestock are pastured and fattened throughout the entire Pampa. During the past few decades, the region has suffered from government attempts to subsidize industry at the expense of agriculture. Now there has been at least a temporary halt to this trend.

The economy of Uruguay is closely geared to the raising of livestock, sheep, and cattle. These animals graze almost entirely upon natural pastures, for the acid soils are not as adaptable for growing alfalfa as in the Argentine Pampa to the south. Some crops, especially corn, wheat, and flax are grown in the south; but diversified agriculture has made slight progress in competition with the dominance of livestock-raising estancias, which are spread out all over the country.

The eastern portion of Paraguay may be divided into the quebracho section of the west, the farming and grazing area of the south, and the lumbering and yerba mate gathering lands of the east. Most of the people live in the south, where they raise cotton, sugar, rice, tobacco, subtropical fruits, and other crops for subsistence and for the local markets. Low grade cattle provide a small export of hides and canned meat, but many factors keep the national economy at a stage far below its potential.

Asia. Asia's share of the humid subtropical lands is large with big areas in China, India, and Japan. Much of China's portion occupies the drainage basins of two great rivers, the Yangtze and the Si; and the terrain is more rugged than that of the western hemisphere's humid subtropics. Most of the people live on the relatively flat valley lands and coastal plains, where a pattern of intensive agriculture dominates the landscape. Some terracing occurs on the hillsides, but most highland areas are left in forest; however, many slopes have been stripped of their tree cover.

Crops such as rice (see Fig. A–2, p. 382), sugar cane, tea, and sweet potatoes make an attractive rural scene throughout the long growing season—long enough in much of the area for two crops a year. Along the northern fringe wheat, barley, and soy beans occupy small portions of the crop land. Throughout the region agriculture dominates the economy, and over half of China's millions of people gain their livelihood on humid subtropical intensive farms.

At present only a small percent of the region's population is engaged in other occupations. But expansion is possible in mining, especially in Szechwan and the Yunnan Plateau; in fishing, already well established along the coast; in manufacture, the Communists having had only limited success in making the change from handicraft to modern industry; in forestry; and in commerce.

India's subregion of Asia's humid subtropics lies largely in the Ganges valley, with the exception of the delta. Terrain is almost flat, monsoon seasons are well developed, forests are limited to small groves and narrow strips along river banks, and the alluvial soils are deep and fertile. As in China, intensive agriculture dominates the economy with sugar cane, corn, cotton, rice, and millet important among the warm-season crops; and wheat and barley featured in cool-season plantings.

Rice occupies a smaller acreage than in the Ganges delta because of the grain's excessive demands for moisture; and monsoon rainfall shows a definite decline from the mouth of the Ganges toward its source (Fig. 14–10). With a more definite dry season than in any of the world's humid subtropics and great variability in the summer monsoon rainfall, farmers have many wells and canals to provide a supplementary supply of water for the crops.

In no other place in the world are people more dependent upon agriculture. There is little manufacturing, except handicraft, almost no minerals, no forestry, and very limited activity in other occupations.

As in China, most of Japan's people live in the subtropical climate of Kyushu, Shikoku, and southern Honshu; and as in the larger country, the greater part of the terrain is rugged with less than twenty per cent of plains topography. Average population density on each square mile of agricultural land exceeds 3000 persons. Two-crop intensive agriculture includes rice (Fig. 14–11), tea, fruits, vegetables, and mulberries; wheat and barley may be raised only in the cool season as summers are too hot and humid for these grains. Rainfall is generally heavier than in either the Chinese or Indian subtropics, and there is no sharply-marked dry season.

Besides supporting a dense farming population, southern Japan includes important de-velopments in manufacturing, mining, fishing, forestry, and commerce. Here, too, are many of the nation's largest cities, and possibly the world's largest city, Tokyo, with over eight million people, 1960 census.

Africa. Africa's humid subtropical land is limited to a narrow strip of coastal plain extending a short distance north and south of Durban. Everywhere rainfall is adequate for both subsistence and commercial farming, with sugar cane, citrus fruits, and vegetables featuring the crop pattern. In some years, enough sugar is produced for export; and the southern hemisphere location gives seasonal advantages for shipments of fruits and vegetables to the European market.

While climate is not the best for dairy cattle, settlers from Britain, where many dairy breeds originated, have achieved some success with the dairy industry. Here is an example of man being more important than environment in the development of an economic activity.

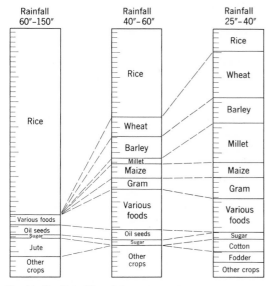

Fig. 14–10   Rainfall and Crops in the Ganges Valley. In the Lower Ganges region rice dominates; in the Middle Ganges, it leads among the various crops; in the Upper Ganges, it ranks below millet and wheat. Southeast Asia normally produces about 90 per cent of the world's rice. The 1963–1964 production, excluding China, amounted to 154,304,600 metric tons. China, India, Indonesia, and Japan are usually the largest producers; but Burma, Thailand, and the countries of former French Indochina—all with low population density—are the major exporters. (*Courtesy E. P. Dutton and Company and L. Dudley Stamp,* Asia)

Fig. 14–11   Transplanting Rice Near Fujiyama. Transplanting requires more time and labor than broadcasting; but it saves seed and produces higher yields, which are of great importance in densely populated southeast Asia. When seedlings are taken from nursery beds to fields, they are placed in 2 to 4 inches of water. Growing rice shows some resemblance to oats, although leaves are narrower and stalks are more slender. A single rice seed sends up a large number of shoots, forming a thick clump of slender stems crowned with heads of grain. Grains are enclosed in tight husks that may prevent spoiling in regions of wet climates. In many areas farmers will not remove the husk until the grain is used for food. (*Courtesy Robert O'Connor*)

A dense population of Europeans, Africans, and Indians occupies the humid subtropical coastal plain. Many live in or near Durban, a great African port, which numbers among its exports coal from the nearby Newcastle field.

Australia. Like Africa, Australia's humid subtropical area is small. This narrow north-south strip extends along the coast from 20° S to 30° S, where it splits and continues on both sides of the Great Dividing Range to approximately 35° S. Natural vegetation varies from grassland to forest, mainly eucalyptus. In the north, sugar is produced at considerable expense by white labor. Farther south agriculture becomes more varied with dairying important near the many population centers and beef cattle grazed and fattened in the more rural sections. Cultivated crops include a diversity of fruits and vegetables.

Location near the coast and close to mineral and power resources gives impetus to commerce, mining, and manufacturing enterprises.

Europe. The small European area falls into the humid subtropical climate statistically, but lacks the typical east coast location characteristic of the other five continents.

Italy's plain of the Po, the largest European humid subtropical section is an Alpine piedmont plain with gently sloping terrain and fertile alluvial soils; it makes up about 15 per cent of the country and is one of the richest agricultural lands on the continent. Moreover, besides providing the country's largest, most modern, and most intensive farming region, the area supports Italy's major industrial developments and the nation's greatest density of population.

Summary. Humid subtropical farming occupies some of the world's most valuable lands. If one were to choose a half dozen of the world's richest agricultural regions, he could hardly omit the Yangtze basin, the Ganges valley, the Lower Mississippi valley, the Argentine Pampa and the Po valley. Other good, but less valuable farming sections would include southern Japan, the Brazilian Panhandle, and Uruguay. These farmlands already support about one-fourth of the world's population, mostly in southeast Asia. Such lands as the Mississippi valley, but not the lands of the Amazon and Congo valleys, are probably the best potential areas for future

dense populations with relatively high standards of living.

Not only do humid subtropical lands stand high in agriculture, both actual and potential, but they also contain valuable forests, minerals, and power resources; good forests occur in southern United States and Japan; coal and iron in the Yangtze Basin and southern United States; petroleum in southern United States; water power in Japan, the Yangtze Basin and southern United States. These are other resources that make the humid subtropics so valuable to nations fortunate enough to own or control them.

QUESTIONS, EXERCISES, AND PROBLEMS

1. Outline the general features of the Mediterranean climates, vegetation, soils, and land forms. Locate the Mediterranean regions as to country and as to world wind belts. What percentage of the earth's land surface is affected by Mediterranean climates?

2. Compare and contrast the humid subtropical climates with those of the Mediterranean type. What differences in vegetation and soils occur among the several humid subtropical regions? What nations possess humid subtropical climates?

3. Tell of geographical relationships in the production of cotton and rice. What man-made limits affect commercial rice and cotton production? Describe world trade in rice and cotton. Describe major agricultural uses of humid subtropical lands in Asia, southern United States, South America, southeast Africa, and along the east-central borderlands of Australia.

4. What adjustments do the following crops show to the Mediterranean environment: olives, citrus fruits, figs, grapes, cork oak, wheat? What type of sheep probably originated in Mediterranean lands? How do these sheep show adjustments to the environment?

5. Summarize land utilization, other than that of agriculture, in both the Mediterranean and humid subtropical lands. Describe major characteristics, distribution, and numbers of population in these two regions. How attractive are they to the world's great powers?

6. Identify the following: summer monsoon, boll weevil, Eli Whitney, paddy rice, Klamath, climax vegetation, merino, minorca, California's four fruit regions, Chile's three regions, Middle Chile's three regions, Black Waxy Prairies, Alabama Black Belt, Cotton Belt subregions, quebracho, yerba mate, Szechwan, Yunnan.

7. Compare the areal distribution of the Mediterranean climates shown on Fig. 14–1 with those of the *Cs, Csa,* and *Csb* climates shown on Plate 2 at the back of the book. Point out similarities and differences in locations and boundaries. Note the significant difference in North America.

8. Compare the areal distribution of the humid subtropical climates shown in Fig. 14–1 with those of the *Cfa* climates shown on Plate 2. Point out similarities and differences in locations and boundaries.

SELECTED REFERENCES

American Geographical Society, *Focus,* various dates, "Australia," "California," "Chile," "Los Angeles," "Union of South Africa," and other issues.

Amiran, D. H. K. and Shahar, A., "The Towns of Israel," *Geographical Review,* July 1961, pp. 348–69.

Baggett, R. T., "Cotton: A Decade of Change," *Foreign Agriculture,* Feb. 4, 1963.

Church, R. J. Harrison and others, *Africa and the Islands,* John Wiley and Sons, 1964, Ch. 24, "The Republic of South Africa and Southwest Africa."

Cressey, George B., *Asia's Lands and Peoples,* McGraw-Hill, 1963, Chapter 8, "Regions of China"; Chapter 16, "Regions of Japan"; Chapter 29, "Regions of North India."

Efrat, Elisha, "The Hinterland of the New City of Jerusalem and its Economic Significance," *Economic Geography,* July, 1964, pp. 254–60.

Fall, Bernard B., "A Grain of Rice is Worth a Drop of Blood," *New York Times Magazine,* July 12, 1964, pp. 10–16.

Gregor, Howard F., "Industrialized Drylot Dairying: An Overview," *Economic Geography,* 1963, pp. 299–318.

James, Preston, *Latin America,* Odyssey Press, 1959 or later edition, "Middle Chile," pp. 241–254; "Argentina: The Humid Pampa," pp. 324–55; "Brazil: The South," pp. 503–27; "Paraguay," pp. 281–93; and "Uruguay," pp. 366–83.

Jensen, R. G., "The Soviet Subtropical Argiculture: A Microcosm," *Geographical Review,* April 1964, pp. 185–202.

Kakiuchi, G. H. and Setsutaro Murakami, "Satsuma Oranges in Ocho-Mura, Japan," *Geographical Review,* Oct. 1961, pp. 500–518.

Padgett, Herbert R., "The Sea Fisheries of the Southern United States," *Geographical Review,* Jan. 1963, pp. 22–39.

Parsons, James J., "The Acorn-Hog Economy of the Oak Woodlands of Southwestern Spain," *Geographical Review,* April 1962, pp. 211–36.

Parsons, James J., "The Cork Oak Forests and the Evolution of the Cork Industry of Southern Spain and Portugal," *Economic Geography,* July 1962, pp. 195–214.

Prunty, Merle, Jr., "The Woodland Plantation as a Contemporary Occupance Type in the South," *Geographical Review,* Jan. 1963, pp. 1–21.

Shaw, D. J., "The Problem of Land Fragmentation in the Mediterranean Area: A Case Study," *Geographical Review,* Jan. 1963, pp. 40–51.

Shaw, Earl B., *Anglo-America,* John Wiley and Sons, 1959, pp. 250–86 and 382–449.

Taylor, Griffith, *Australia,* E. P. Dutton, 1951 or later edition, Ch. 4, "The Climates of Australia."

Thoman, R. S. and Patton, D. J., *Focus on Geographic Activity,* McGraw-Hill, 1964, "An Estancia in Argentina: Commercial Livestock Raising," Ch. 10.

Thompson, Kenneth, "Location and Relocation of a Tree Crop—English Walnuts in California," *Economic Geography,* April 1961, pp. 133–49.

Trewartha, Glenn T., *An Introduction to Climate,* McGraw-Hill, 1954, pp. 290–312.

Walker, D. S., *The Mediterranean Lands,* John Wiley and Sons, 1960.

Williams, Owen, "Sugar Growing and Processing in the Union of South Africa," *Economic Geography,* Oct. 1959, pp. 356–66.

Chapter Fifteen

Middle Latitude Lands:
West Coast Marine and Humid Continental

Middle Latitude deserts and steppes have been described in Chapter 14, and this chapter will be devoted to humid middle latitude areas—the West Coast Marine and Humid Continental regions.

West Coast Marine Lands

Location. (Fig. 15–1) Regions of west-coast marine climates are found in four continents.[1] In North America, the area extends from approximately 40° N to almost 60° N and includes the coasts of California north of San Francisco, Oregon, Washington, British Columbia, and the Panhandle of Alaska. Most of southern Chile and a little of southern Argentina form the South American section. Australia's portion includes the southeast coastal area, Tasmania, and the Eastern Highlands about as far north as the Queensland-New South Wales border, approximately 27° S. All of New Zealand has a west-coast marine climate. Europe has the largest area, which includes northern Spain; all of France except the Alpine section and the Mediterranean lands of the southeast; Belgium, the Netherlands; and Denmark; western Germany's Rhine country and most of the north German plain; the southwest coast of Norway; and the British Isles.

Climate. (Fig. 15–2) West-coast marine climates lies along west coasts of continents and receive their greatest climatic influence from adjoining seas. Extension into the interior depends upon surface configuration; mountains may limit the climate to a coastal fringe. Mediterranean climates form the equatorward boundary, and tundra or subarctic lands the poleward one.

Summers are cooler than average for the latitude, and winters are warmer. This is a natural result of the sea as a dominant control. In winter, frost conditions may last several days, and greatest cold comes from air moving out of the continental interior.

The distribution of precipitation resembles that of the Mediterranean climate except that summers have low rainfall rather than drought conditions. Both climates show maximum precipitation in the cool season; the maximum is more pronounced, in west coast marine climates, at locations possessing strong marine influences or at places where mountains lie near the coast. Winter snow may fall on the coastal lowlands, but it never lasts long. Heavy snow may accumulate on adjoining highlands.

Precipitation comes largely from cyclonic storms. With more storms and better-developed ones in winter than in summer, it is easy to account for the winter maximum. Very little convectional rain falls because summer air masses are relatively stable and temperatures are seldom high. Where mountains border coasts, orographic (mountain influenced) precipitation is important. An abundance of cloud is characteristic, and northwestern United States has the questionable honor of the lowest annual percentage of sunny hours.

Vegetation and Soils. There is enough winter cold to keep most vegetation relatively dormant, a contrast to Mediterranean conditions where

---

[1]A small section in South Africa that could be included is omitted from description because it departs somewhat from the typical rainfall regime and lacks a location on a continental west coast. The extreme tip of South America and part of Iceland are not described because their summers have less than 4 months of temperatures above 50° F, conditions hardly typical of the average west-coast marine climates.

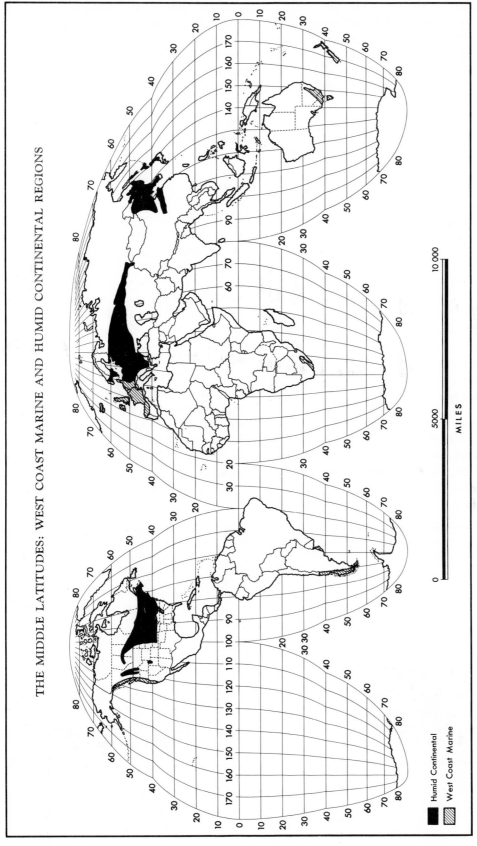

THE MIDDLE LATITUDES: WEST COAST MARINE AND HUMID CONTINENTAL REGIONS

Humid Continental

West Coast Marine

MILES

Fig. 15–1   The Middle Latitudes: West Coast Marine and Humid Continental Lands. *(Projection based on the homolosine projection copyright by the University of Chicago. Map by permission McGraw–Hill Book Co., and G. T. Trewartha, An Introduction to Climate)*

growth continues throughout the year. Forests, many of them coniferous, originally covered the lands; but in several places reckless exploitation has occurred, especially in western Europe and in New Zealand. Now, a change to widespread scientific forestry is well started. Where removal of the original forest has taken place, planted grasses flourish and provide feed for some of the world's best dairy cattle. Soils belong to the pedalfer group and with proper care will yield good crops.

Surface Features. Most land forms are characterized by large percentages of rugged terrain especially those of northwest Anglo-America, southern Chile, southern Africa, southeast Australia, and New Zealand. Even western Europe, with a significant portion of the North European Plain, has mountains or plateaus in almost every country; for example the English Pennines, the Scottish Highlands, the Central Plateau of France, the Ardennes of Belgium, and the uplands of western Germany.

Land Utilization

Europe and North America. The west coast marine region of Europe is larger than that of Anglo-America largely because of the position and direction of major mountain systems. In Anglo-America, high mountains trending gen-

erally north and south effectively block marine influences before they move far toward the interior. In western Europe, on the contrary, east-west trending Alpine ranges permit deep penetration of sea air; and only in Norway do mountains hold the marine climate to a coastal fringe.

Differences in population totals and density are quite marked between European and Anglo-American regions. Although population in northern Spain and Ireland is relatively sparse, the number per square mile is not nearly as low as in the Alaskan Panhandle. And the continental United States and Canadian sections cannot compare in density with England, Holland, Belgium, and Denmark.

A dense population is one good reason for the low percentage of forest on most of the European section in comparison to heavier stands, largely conifer, found along the less densely populated coasts of northern California, Oregon, Washington, British Columbia, and the Alaskan Panhandle. In all west coast marine regions, forests have been cleared to provide farmland where agriculture has developed. Dairying is an important industry in the European area, especially in the countries of Denmark and the Netherlands. Root crops grow nearly as well as grasses and may supplement them in the dairy cow's ration.

Dairying is less intensively developed in the

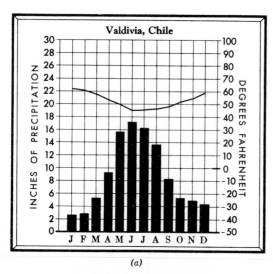

(a)

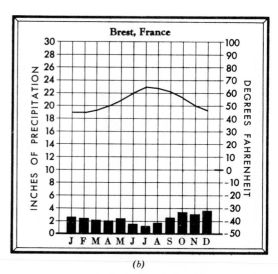

(b)

Fig. 15–2   Climatic Charts, Valdivia and Brest. Notice the contrast in total precipitation between Brest with no mountain background and Valdivia, which lies to the windward of the high Andes.

Fig. 15–3 Dairy Farm in Netherlands' Friesland Province. Friesland is well known for its dairying and for its Holstein-Frisian cows. Note the modern methods of milking which are increasing rapidly throughout the west-coast-marine dairy belt. The gabled roof in the background suggests that the farm is typically Frisian. (*Courtesy Netherlands Information Service*)

American section; especially is this true in the sparsely populated lands of the Alaskan Panhandle and British Columbia. Surplus dairy products from Washington and Oregon show adjustment to the great distances from the large eastern market of the United States. Much milk is processed in dried and powdered form. In western Europe surplus milk is processed not only into powdered and dried products, but also into butter and cheese (Fig. 15–3). Large quantities of these products move into exports. Skim milk and whey, left after processing dairy solids, may be fed to swine that provide pork for local and foreign markets.

It should be pointed out that livestock raising, in Denmark and the Netherlands especially, may be so intensive that it is sometimes called stall feeding. Animals are kept in barns or sheds and feed and drink are brought to them for the greater part of their lives.

In rugged sections of England, Scotland, Ireland, and northwestern United States, livestock raising loses this intensiveness. On these uplands cattle and sheep graze over natural pastures during the warmer months. Grass feeding receives a supplement of hay during the colder periods when the animals may be protected from inclement weather by proper shelter. Hay grows well in the west coast marine climate, but curing

may suffer from too much rainfall in the wetter sections.

Besides root crops grown for livestock, the sugar beet and potato are raised for human food. Potatoes (see Fig. A–4, p. 384) flourish so well in the European region that Ireland and Germany have higher yields than those of the United States. There is one serious handicap, however; too much cloud and precipitation in critical stages of plant growth may encourage crop diseases. For example, a costly Irish famine occurred in the 1840's largely as a result of potato-crop failure. Heavy rains fostered a blight so virulent that few potatoes were produced. As a consequence 200,000 to 300,000 people died of famine and from diseases associated with malnutrition.

The extraction of sugar from beets first made important progress in west-coast marine climates. When a British blockade cut off sugar from Napoleon's armies, the great general encouraged research to find a substitute for cane sugar. Following the Napoleonic wars, there were times when beet sugar production, much of it grown under government subsidy, exceeded cane production. More cane sugar is produced today than beet sugar, but the latter constitutes a significant portion of world totals.

Beets do well in the west-coast marine climate

Fig. 15–4 Sugar-Beet Farming near Mannheim Germany. The farmer is spreading chemicals on his beet field to control insect pests. World total beet sugar production in the 1962–1963 season reached 23,399,000 tons, a figure somewhat less than the world yield of cane sugar. Europe accounts for more than three fourths of the yield and the Soviet alone for nearly one third. The United States contributes about one tenth. Most sugar beets are raised in west-coast-marine and humid-continental climates. For more detailed statistics write Foreign Agricultural Service, United States Department of Agriculture. (*Courtesy German Information Center*)

(Figs. 15–4 and 15–5), which is cooler than the optimum for corn. Summers lack the hot days and nights ideal for maize, but this lack of heat is just what beets and potatoes need. Aside from a climatic advantage, many areas possess loose, sandy loam glacial soils which permit easy root expansion for the two tuber crops. Northwest Europe emphasizes beet and potato production far more than the North American region (see Fig. A–5, p. 385).

Besides grasses and root crops, certain cereals such as oats and the soft wheats yield well. Belgium and the Netherlands show the highest national wheat averages in the world. Choice of best land, intensive agriculture, and dependable and adequate rainfall all contribute to these high yields.

Environment favors many kinds of fruits. Apples, pears, plums, and loganberries feature farming in northwestern United States and adjoining British Columbia. Here some fruits are sun dried, as they are in the Mediterranean cli-

mate of southern California; but the low percentage of sunshine necessitates artificial drying for most processing. In Europe grapes are grown for table use and for wine. The French wines and those of the Rhine valley are known all over the world. A highly specialized example of intensive agriculture is the bulb industry, well developed in the Netherlands and becoming important in northwestern United States and in British Columbia. In 1962, the Netherlands exported nearly 70,000 metric tons of bulbs, valued at more than $46 million.

Dense population provides a valuable market for farm products in western Europe, but relatively low population density gives less market encouragement in northwest Anglo-America. The large cities in the latter area can be counted on the fingers of one hand. Portland, Oregon, Seattle, Washington, and Vancouver, British Columbia, are good-sized cities; each has more than 100,000 people, and each performs an important market function to a wide hinterland.

Western Europe has literally scores of urban centers, each as large as the few Anglo-American cities, and each contributing a good market for west coast marine farm products. Little danger exists here of producing a farm-products surplus whose transport to market will eliminate the farmers' profit. Although France is more than self-sufficient in farm products, surplus movement is easy to nearby Britain and Germany, only about one-half and three-fourths self sufficient respectively.

It is in manufacturing more than in farming, however, that western Europe excels. Although supplies of petroleum are limited, Britain and Germany have large quantities of coal, and France is more than self-sufficient in iron. Britain's coal lies in three major districts, on the flanks of the Pennines, in Wales, and in the Scottish Lowlands. In the Ruhr or Westphalian district of western Germany, there is one of the world's largest coal fields; and a westward extension of the field continues through southern Netherlands, Belgium, the Saar, Luxembourg, and northern France. The Ruhr coal-and-

Fig. 15–5 Sugar Beets, Together with Tops and Root Systems. This illustration shows sugar beets nearly ready for harvest. Note that the plant extends several feet into the earth—see spade at the left—and that the main beet root sends out smaller side roots. When the beet is pulled from the ground, many of the small roots remain and add fertility to the soil. After the sugar has been extracted, the entire vegetable portions of the beet are available for livestock feeding purposes. An average acre of beets produces about 3500 pounds of pure sugar and 300 pounds of meat. (*Courtesy Great Western Sugar Company*)

Fig. 15–6 Steel Plant in West Germany. This photograph, taken at the Thyssen steel works in Duisburg, shows two of the rollers of a hot-steel rolling mill for the continuous lamination of steel into reels, thin sheets, or heavy plates. The mill is only one of thousands of factories manufacturing iron, steel, chemicals, textiles, and machinery —factories that make up the great Ruhr industrial complex. Plenty of coal is available locally, but most iron ore is imported from Sweden, France, Spain, North Africa, and elsewhere. (*Courtesy United Nations*)

manufacturing district is the area that, more than any other, kept Germany in World War I for 4 years and in World War II for 6 more. It is no wonder that all world powers are deeply interested in who controls the Ruhr and what use is made of Ruhr resources (Fig. 15–6).

French iron occurs in the Lorraine. In the past, this peripheral location of an important asset near a strong aggressive neighbor has been costly to the French; for Germany has taken over these deposits three times—in the war of 1870, in World War I, and in World War II. Besides possessing iron and many other raw materials for bases of manufacturing, west European nations have been dominant in world trade for centuries, a factor which gave export markets for an expanding industry.

Northwest Anglo-America lacks both petroleum and coal in significant amounts; but hydroelectric power, an abundance of raw materials, a coastal location encouraging world trade, and a rapidly increasing population all combine to

stimulate a growing emphasis upon manufacture and other industries besides agriculture.

South America, Southern Chile. The region of west-coast marine climate in Chile is quite similar to that of British Columbia and the Alaskan Panhandle. There is the same heavy orographic rainfall in both, brought about by prevailing westerlies rising over the Coastal Ranges in the North American section and over the southern Andes in Chile. The poleward parts of both are made up of a maze of islands, suggesting geologic subsidence in each case. Vegetation consists of heavy forest cover in southern Chile as it does in the Alaskan Panhandle. Heavy rain throughout the year, cool temperatures, and forests encourage the formation of gray-brown podzolic and podzol soils. Above the forested zone are snow-capped mountains; and live glaciers move down toward the fiord-bordered seacoast just as they do in southern Alaska.

The first men found by early Spanish explorers were Indians; but the Spanish never did conquer the natives, because the forests aided the energetic defence by the Indians just as forests have aided defending forces throughout history. Spanish settlement in southern Chile was never large, and the largest present-day settlements are German. Several thousand left the rolling plateau country of south Germany during the mid-nineteenth century, and their descendants now live on farms in the equatorward part of south Chile. Carefully tended fields of root crops and planted grasses furnish feed for livestock, many of them dairy cattle. Population centers are few, but those that are there have an air of permanence and prosperity.

Crop agriculture is almost absent in the island-studded poleward part of Chile south of the German settlements. Two provinces, Aysen and Magallanes, make up the major portion of this section and total an area about the size of Great Britain. Leeward portions of the provinces get less rainfall than the more rugged windward areas. As a result natural grasses of the east contrast with the forests on the west. More than two million sheep, held on large ranches, graze these Chilean pastures.

Heavy precipitation, mountains, and many islands interfere with road building in west-coast-marine Chile. Mediterranean Chile, the economic heart of the country affords markets for farm produce, but transport costs lessen profits. A little petroleum has been discovered, and mining may expand and provide more markets. More tourists would increase demand for agricultural commodities; they would find the southern region's scenic qualities ranking with the world's best; but few tourists are likely to come, for the area lies far away from dense populations having relatively high living standards. Today, southern Chile is a sparsely populated land contributing but a few farm, ranch, and forest products to the nation's economy.

Australia, the Southeast. Eastern Australia extends into a higher latitude than western Australia. In fact parts of New South Wales, Victoria and Tasmania bulge south far enough to receive a west coast marine climate; and a northern strip of the first two provinces is included because of altitude.

Most Australians live in urban centers where manufacturing is developing rapidly. Industrialization was literally forced upon the continent by two world wars. The Dominion lies thousands of miles distant from Britain which long traded manufactures for agricultural raw materials such as wool, mutton, wheat, and dairy products. Australia still exports these farming commodities in large quantities, but the nation is becoming less and less dependent upon outside markets for processed goods. Iron occurs in every province, and coal sufficient for the country's steel production is found in several coastal sections. Recently, promising discoveries of petroleum have been made.

As in other west-coast marine regions, dairying is important; and milk is processed into solids to cheapen transport to foreign markets. Dual-purpose sheep share pasture and hay crops with dairy cattle.

Forests are no longer considered objectionable vegetation to be cleared from the land in order to use it for farming purposes. Of the country's remaining native forests 90 per cent belong to the eucalyptus family. Local pulp mills manufacture paper from these trees, but some of the best timber comes from western Tasmania, where beech and pine are grown. Tasmania also raises a large percentage of the country's apples. This island markets about one half of Australia's crop from approximately one fourth of the nation's apple trees. In this respect, Tasmania resembles the rich apple-producing valleys of northwestern United States and British Columbia. Other middle-latitude fruits are also important in Australia's marine climate.

New Zealand. This British dominion is made up of two main islands comprising about 100,-000 square miles or approximately the size of Colorado. When such a small area lies far out at sea, more than 1000 miles from any continental mass, the ocean will exert a dominant control on its climate. Mountains exceed plains and these highlands extend practically the entire length of the north-south trending islands. Moreover, they are high mountains in many places; Mount Cook rises to over 12,000 feet, and far exceeds Australia's highest, Mount Kosciusko, approximately 7000 feet.

Like Australia, New Zealand is a long distance from a major export market for dairy products, and milk is processed into solids for foreign shipment. All-year grazing favors sheep just as it does dairy cattle; and sheep provide the country with exports of wool and mutton. In fact, New Zealand leads the world in export of mutton. On moist lowlands, sheep farms of a few hundred acres specialize in dual-purpose animals well adapted to a cool marine climate. The Romney Marsh and similar breeds, developed long ago in European marine climates are raised in large numbers. On the colder uplands, ranches of thousands of acres specialize in raising the hardier Merino, which are better suited to the more difficult environment.

A small industrial activity is based upon local supplies of coal and iron. No large tourist trade is likely to develop because of the economic principle that hampers isolated locations. It seems unfortunate that scenic beauty, including mountains, sea, glaciers, fiords, and even geysers lies so far away from densely populated lands with high standards of living.

Summary and Conclusions. Several decades ago, especially in the 1930's, Ellsworth Huntington of Yale University provoked considerable discussion with his climatic theories on the progress of civilization. Among other things he stated that the west coast marine climate closely approaches his ideal for the greatest stimulus to progress. The ideal included:

(1) average temperature ranges from somewhat below 40° F in the coldest month to nearly 70° F in the warmest month; (2) frequent storms, or winds from oceans or lakes, should keep the relative humidity quite high except in hot weather, and provide rain at all seasons; (3) there should be a constant succession of cyclonic storms to bring frequent moderate changes of temperature, but not severe enough to do damage.[1]

Whether there is anything to his theory is debatable, but there is no question that the west coast marine climate does conform closely to the above guide lines. Again no one doubts that northwestern Europe has a progressive population with three of the great powers, or at least former great powers. In these and other west European countries, economic progress has been brought about through advances in farming, manufacture, trade, and other industries, all of which support one of the world's most dense populations enjoying high standards of living. Density of population is much less in other west coast marine regions, but living standards are just as high.

Humid Continental Lands

Location and Climate. Continentality, the result of location within large land masses, is the

[1] Ellsworth Huntington and Earl B. Shaw, *Principles of Human Geography*, 6th ed., John Wiley & Sons, 1951, p. 408.

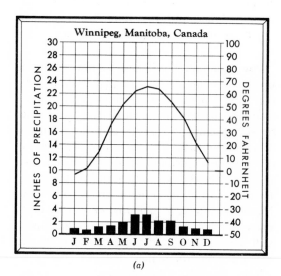

(a)

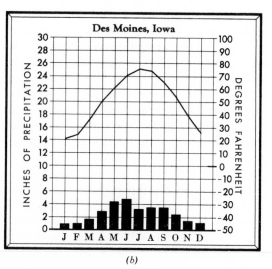

(b)

Fig. 15–7 Climatic Charts, Winnipeg and Des Moines. Winnipeg is a good example of spring-wheat climate, and Des Moines a representative station for corn belt climate.

Fig. 15–8 Harvesting Corn in the Corn Belt. The corn harvester is cutting and husking the grain in one operation. In 1963 the United States raised slightly over half of the 8 billion 20 million-bushel world crop of corn. Most of United States corn grows in the Humid Continental climate. Brazil and Russia with 400 million and 385 million bushels each rank next to the United States. Other countries producing approximately 200 million bushels are in sequence Union of South Africa, Mexico, Yugoslavia, Rumania, and Argentina. (*Courtesy International Harvester Company*)

important climatic key to humid continental climates (Fig. 15–7, see also Fig. 15–1). Note that they do not occur in the southern or water hemisphere.

The great heating of continental interiors during the summer months, especially in North America, gives the humid continental long summer subdivision its popular name, the corn belt climate. Corn (Figs. 15–8 and 15–9) does well where high temperatures continue through the night as well as through the daylight period; and it also flourishes because of the rainfall encouraged by the indraft of moist air from the oceans during the summer season.

In latitudes poleward from the Corn Belt, summer is shorter, winter is longer, and temperatures are lower in both seasons. The climate is known popularly as the spring-wheat type (Fig. 15–10). Here, with temperatures too cool for corn, spring wheat rather than autumn-planted grain, for which winters are too cold, is grown. Although there is less rainfall in the

Spring Wheat Region of United States and Canada than in the Winter Wheat Belt of the United States, precipitation is sufficient to mature a crop in the higher latitudes. Cooler temperatures bring lower rates of evaporation, and rainfall efficiency is increased.

Middle-latitude location places both corn belt and spring-wheat climates within the belt of the prevailing westerly winds. However, these winds are interrupted by monsoons in the Asian sector. The lack of mountains as barriers permits marine influences, carried by the westerlies, to penetrate interior Europe, Consequently, European west coast marine climates border Europe's humid continental climates on the west. The situation is different in North America, where mountains parallel the west coast and cut off oceanic influences not far from shore. This accounts for steppe climates bordering the North American humid continental area on the west. Steppe lands also form the western boundary of humid continental areas in Asia.

Fig. 15–9   Iowa Farms. Nearly 500 square miles of Iowa farms are shown on this photograph. Light patches show harvested small grain such as oats and wheat; dark-colored areas include corn, pasture, and forage. Note the rectangular fields so characteristic of the nearly level Corn Belt topography. (*Courtesy of the* Des Moines Register)

Humid subtropical climates border east Asia's long summer humid continental climate on the south as they do in North America. But in Europe, Mediterranean climates lie south of the mountain barrier. This barrier cuts off ocean influences from Europe's humid continental long summer climate so well that more rainfall variability occurs than in the same type of climate in North America without such mountain barriers. Rainfall variability in the Balkans is reflected in frequent fluctuations in annual yields of the corn crop.

Land Forms. In describing topographic features, it is possible to generalize and say that the area shows but slight relief. In detail, however, there are several contrasts: the worn-down mountains of New England with many fertile valleys; the fertile St. Lawrence Valley with the old Laurentian Highlands on the north and the Adirondacks and associated mountain groups across the border in the United States; and the Annapolis valley bounded by old worn-down mountains in Nova Scotia. To the west of these coastal mountains and valleys lie the glacially formed Great Lakes. These water bodies are of

some importance as a climatic influence upon crop production, but of far greater importance in another economic capacity: they provide the greatest inland water transport in the world. West and south of the lakes lie productive plains, largely of glacial formation. These include the great American Corn Belt and the Spring-Wheat Region of the United States and Canada.

In Europe, the Plains of Skane, the most productive part of Sweden; Poland, whose plains topography has always tempted invaders; the Bohemian Basin of Czechoslovakia; most of the Rumanian and Hungarian plains; these and the more productive plains of European Russia show the dominance of plains topography. A few low mountains, such as the Urals, cover minor areas just as they do in North America's humid continental climates.

Beyond the Urals, a wedge-shaped plains section narrows to nothing about the ninetieth meridian east. Here plateau elevations and continentality encourage subarctic climate. In east Asia the Hwang Ho plain and that of central Manchuria lie among low mountains of Manchuria, China, Korea, and Japan.

Vegetation. Originally, natural vegetation on interior locations consisted of subhumid grasslands, and near the coast, forested areas. The former include the prairies of central United States, sometimes called the tall grasslands; and the plains of Hungary, Rumania, the Ukraine, western Siberia, and Manchuria. Original forests, consisting of broadleaf deciduous on equatorward margins, conifers at the north, and mixed forests in the center, were some of the best in the world. But in climates such as these, so favorable to crop production, man considered forests a barrier to food supply and carelessly exploited them. Now forest concepts have changed, and land may be set aside for a tree crop on almost every woodland farm in the more humid sections. Natural grasslands are practically all under cultivation. These areas support some of the world's most productive agriculture.

Soils. (See Figs. 10–3 and 10–4) Soils of humid continental climates cover a wide range. The podzols of the conifer forests are leached, have poor structure, and contain little humus. Fortunately most of these are located where growing seasons are short, and other climatic hazards discourage farming. Where crop periods are longer, and natural vegetation that of broadleaf deciduous trees, gray-brown podzolics occur. These soils have a fair structure, are not badly leached, and accumulate more humus than those developing under conifers. The grasslands show the best soils, however, for lower precipitation and winter freezing lessen leaching, grass cover contributes humus both above and below ground, and structure is excellent. The prairie earths are characteristic of the humid grasslands, and the finest soils in the world, and chernozems, develop on the drier sections.

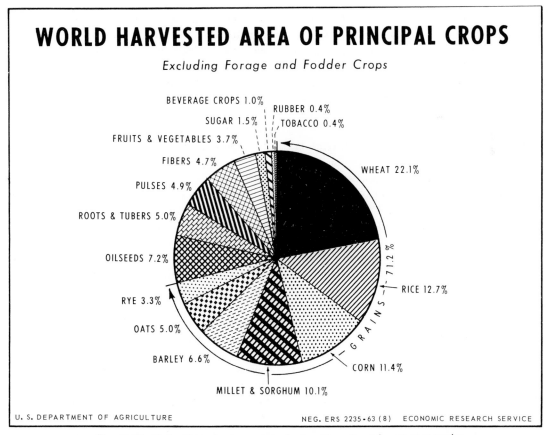

WORLD HARVESTED AREA OF PRINCIPAL CROPS
Excluding Forage and Fodder Crops

BEVERAGE CROPS 1.0%   RUBBER 0.4%
SUGAR 1.5%   TOBACCO 0.4%
FRUITS & VEGETABLES 3.7%
FIBERS 4.7%
PULSES 4.9%
ROOTS & TUBERS 5.0%
OILSEEDS 7.2%
RYE 3.3%
OATS 5.0%
BARLEY 6.6%
MILLET & SORGHUM 10.1%
CORN 11.4%
RICE 12.7%
WHEAT 22.1%
GRAINS — 71.2%

U. S. DEPARTMENT OF AGRICULTURE   NEG. ERS 2235-63 (8)   ECONOMIC RESEARCH SERVICE

Fig. 15–10 Notice that wheat, grown in the humid-continental, west-coast-marine, and many other climatic regions, occupies a larger harvested area than any other of the world crops—almost one fourth of the world's harvested crop lands.

Agriculture

North America. In the Corn Belt portion of North America's humid continental region, corn, oats, soybeans, clover, and alfalfa are featured crops; and hogs and beef cattle dominate livestock production. Diversified farming, with its many economic advantages, is practiced almost everywhere (see Figs. A–3, A–8, and A–9, pp. 383, 388, and 389).

The Spring Wheat Region shows certain resemblances to the Steppe Region, which is a little more arid, in its emphasis upon one-crop farming, in its cyclic rainfall, and in its variability in harvests. Of course diversified farming isn't as easy to practice as it is in the Corn Belt; for the ease of successfully producing a multiplicity of crops is lessened as one goes into poleward sections or into deep continental interior areas of the humid continental climates. But a greater crop diversity can be achieved; and more agricultural variety can bring increased economic stability.

Dairying is practiced in both the Corn Belt and the Spring Wheat Region, but it becomes a dominant type of farming as one goes east of these two areas. Dairy products are not the same throughout this dairy belt. Near large cities, and there are many of them, fluid products are sold widely; but in more isolated sections, butter and cheese dominate sales.

Environment favors dairying throughout much of the humid continental region, especially in the areas bordering the Great Lakes, in the St. Lawrence Valley, and in New England. Land forms are not so favorable to mechanized agriculture as in the Corn Belt and Spring Wheat Regions. But in the cool moist climate, this country produces rich grasses and fodder crops ideal for dairy cattle, and the region possesses an all important market made up of millions and millions of people with relatively high living standards. Silos and dairy barns dominate the cultural landscape. Barns and silos are needed for winters are cold; and ground that is covered with snow for weeks at a time provides little opportunity for winter grazing.

Fruit raising competes with dairying in many sections. (1) Apples are raised on gentle slope lands in New England; in the Annapolis Valley of Nova Scotia; and in New York state, one of the leading apple producers in the United States. (2) Cherries are important in Michigan and surrounding states, where a cherry festival may be held each year. (3) Cranberry bogs are found in Massachusetts, New Jersey, and Wisconsin. (4) Peaches take more careful attention in humid continental long-summer climates than in lower latitudes; but they are grown and marketed in many sections. (5) Grapes and other fruits are found on the leeward sides of the Great Lakes. Orchards on the east and south sides of water bodies, such as the Great Lakes (see Fig. 8–1), in middle latitudes have advantages in frost protection.

The European Wedge of Humid Continental Climates. The east European and adjoining Asian section includes the following areas: eastern Germany, Poland, Czechoslovakia; Yugoslavia and Albania except the Adriatic coast; Greece and Bulgaria beyond the lands bordering the Black and Mediterranean Seas; and Hungary and Rumania. A southern strip of Sweden, the extreme south coast of Finland, and the southeastern part of Norway extend the climate almost to the Atlantic. Russia's portion west of the Urals and east of these mountains to the 90th meridian East forms a large part of the wedge-shaped climatic area, over a thousand miles wide in the west and only about two hundred miles across in the east. As previously indicated, the narrowing of the eastern part comes through greater continentality and through the presence of higher elevations to the north, east, and south.

Agriculture is more successful in the humid continental climate than in the subarctic or taiga to the north, where poorer soils and danger of frost every month of the year make farming hazardous; and it is likely to be more consistently profitable than steppe land areas to the south, where rainfall is less and its occurrence more variable.

Various crops are produced. Food crops include rye, barley, wheat, corn, oats, millet, sugar beets and potatoes. Flax and hemp are important among the fibers grown for textile production. Swine are raised on corn, mast, and potatoes. Cattle are grown for milk and beef; and sheep raising gives wool and meat, with greater emphasis on wool in the Balkans.

The wide spread planting of sugar beets is influenced by the following factors: (1) climate and soil either permit or favor crop growth; (2) war may cut off shipments of cane sugar; (3) cheap labor assures low cost of production (women and children take care of thinning and weeding and other tasks); (4) livestock may be fattened on by-products of the sugar beet; and (5) livestock manures replenish fertility taken from the soil by beet plants. As a result of the above and other conditions European humid continental and west coast marine regions account for over three-fourths of the world's sugar beet production (see Fig. A–5, p. 385).

These same European regions produce nearly 90 per cent of the world's potatoes (Fig. 15–11). Environment is favorable; women and children do most of the light work; potatoes provide a good food crop; and Europeans use the tuber in more ways than Americans do. For example more are utilized for swine feed, for flour, for starch, and for alcohol (see Fig. A–4, p. 384).

Wheat is grown in humid continental climates with planting of winter varieties in the Balkan long-summer climatic areas; much larger wheat lands are found in Russia, where spring wheat dominates farming practices over wide sections. The Russian wheat belt extends along the wetter northern part of the steppe climate and the drier southern portion of the humid continental short-summer type (see Fig. A–1, p. 381). Fluctuation in yield is significant because of great continentality, which is responsible for variable precipitation. Added to this, problems of collective state-owned production are many. Incentive is often lacking; bureaucratic control sometimes takes too many workers from actual production; and delays of various kinds may be costly.

Most of the world rye crop, like that of potatoes and sugar beets, is European grown; and most of it comes from lands with humid continental climate. It is fairly well adjusted to the moister phase of the spring-wheat climate and makes better adjustment than wheat to the podzol soils. In fact, it has been called the grain of poverty, a name largely due to its usefulness on moderately poor soils. Barley is much less important than rye because it requires better soils for a good crop. Its ability to mature in a short season encourages high latitude production where soil is adaptable. In the European spring-wheat climates barley is grown on the few good soil sections at relatively high latitudes.

The largest flax-production area in the world lies in the spring-wheat climate of Poland and Russia. Here, approximately three fourths of the world's flax grown for fiber is produced. Climatic conditions of sufficient summer rainfall, high relative humidity, and mild but not hot summer temperatures all conform to requirements. An adequate labor supply is needed for several weedings of the crop; to attend to dew wetting; and to separate fibers from the stalks. Labor willing to do this and many other tasks associated with flax fiber culture is found, not in America, but in Europe. In Russia and Poland the farmer and his family look after these processes and take care of other farming tasks as well.

An area of hemp production lies just south of the major flax fiber region of Russia. Here farm labor is found that is willing to apply work processes to hemp raising similar to those described for growing flax. In fact the hemp plant is related to that of flax and produces fiber of coarser quality.

Dairying and raising livestock for meat supplement or dominate farm practices in the European humid continental climates. Laws and attitudes of the government regarding ownership, growth, and sale of livestock have kept

Fig. 15–11   Harvesting Potatoes in West Germany. Most of the world's potatoes are grown in the humid-continental and west-coast-marine lands of Europe. United States potato production lags behind that of each of the countries of Russia, Poland, West Germany, France, and East Germany. In 1963 the world total reached more than 5 billion hundredweight. (For more statistical information write Foreign Agricultural Service, U.S. Department of Agriculture. *Courtesy German Information Center*)

Russian production below or near that of the pre-revolution period.

The East Asian Region. The East Asian portion of the humid continental climates includes Korea, all but the southeast tip, northern Honshu, Hokkaido, Manchuria, southern Sakhalin, the Shantung Peninsula, and the southern Hwang Ho plain.

These areas are affected by the Asian monsoon, a prevailing wind which exerts a climatic control by blowing from one direction part of the year and from a direction almost directly opposite during the rest of the time. The wind is related to the enormous size of the continent with its great contrasts in summer and winter temperatures.

Although extreme southern Korea belongs to the humid subtropical climate, the bulk of the country may be included in the humid continental region, and the following comments refer to the country as a whole. Far northern Korea has a long cold winter with 5 months of below-freezing temperatures. In the south, winter temperatures are less severe although low for the latitude. Summer temperatures show more uniformity throughout the country, but the warm period is shorter in the north. Similarly the rain-bearing summer monsoon lasts several weeks longer in the south than in the north.

Besides these differences between north and south, there are marked contrasts between east and west. In summer, the east coast is usually sheltered from the prevailing southerly winds and is therefore relatively fog-free; the more exposed south and west coasts, on the other hand, may be hidden from view days at a time during the height of the monsoon.

Local climatic diversity is paralleled by local diversity in surface features. The western part has much less rough land than the eastern portion; the latter has several high mountain ranges, many deeply entrenched valleys, few large areas of lowland, and practically no coastal plain. The western part has most of the large rivers and a virtual monopoly on the richer alluvial lands.

These differences in terrain and climate are reflected in the land-use and population patterns. Rice and barley are the dominant grains in the south and west, and, with the help of the long summers and heavy rain, two crops may be

obtained. In the north, the farmers harvest one crop; because of the shorter growing season and lower rainfall, this is likely to be wheat, millet, corn, soybeans or some other dry-field crop, though rice is grown in the better-favored places.

The population also reveals great regional differences. About twice as many people live south and west of a line from Pyongyang to Pusan as live northeast of the line.

To a remarkable degree, the products of north and south complement each other. The north needs rice and barley from the south for its factory workers. The south is in constant need of fertilizers for its paddy fields, fertilizers that could be supplied by chemical plants of the north when they are in full operation. The north needs textiles, manganese, tungsten and copper produced in the south; the south needs wood, coal, iron, machinery, and power from the north. Here is a case where physical conditions encourage commerce, but political conditions interfere with trade.

Diversity of land forms is as widespread in northern Honshu as it is in Korea. Three mountain ranges trend in a north-south direction and leave very little level land for agriculture. Farming takes place in the valleys and along the narrow coastal plains where mountains fail to reach the sea. Farms of 3 to 5 acres average larger than in the humid subtropical climates of southern Japan, where two harvests a year are possible in the longer growing season. Crops include barley, potatoes, millet, and buckwheat as well as a small acreage of rice. A cool ocean current moving equatorward along the east coast, plus the inblowing summer monsoon, increases fog frequencies and cool summer temperatures. Along the western side, the outblowing winter monsoon from the continent passes over the Japan Sea, where it picks up moisture to leave in heavy winter snows along western slopes. Population is sparser than in southern Japan because of several conditions, among which are (1) a shorter growing season; (2) less level land; and (3) the general Japanese desire to remain in milder climates.

Hokkaido, the northern island of Japan may be compared with Canada's Nova Scotia, for they have several similar features. Both short-summer climatic sections have a strong marine influence, much rugged land, heavy forests over large areas, podzolic soils, a cold current paral-

Fig. 15–12　Kaoliang and Soy Beans in Manchuria. Kaoliang and soy beans are important food crops in Northern China. Kaoliang is a grain sorghum which looks something like broomcorn when matured. It grows eight to ten feet tall and has a cluster of kernels the size of a small pea. It may be eaten as a cheap grain, fed to livestock, or made into wine. Stalks may be used for fuel or building material.

leling the eastern coast, much fog, crops such as potatoes, apples, oats, hay, together with dairy products, all produced on scattered farmsteads; and industries such as lumbering and fishing. Much of the land discourages agriculture, and the sea beckons with richer harvests. Population, like that of Nova Scotia, is sparse.

The richest Manchurian agricultural land lies in the plain, carved and partly occupied by the Liao and Sungari rivers, the former in the south and the latter in the north. Little agricultural land is found in the mountains that lie both to the east and west of the central plain. The Manchurian lowland is much more densely peopled than the surrounding highlands. Soybeans, corn, kaoliang (Fig. 15–12), wheat, and millet are important farm crops. Farmers live on scattered farmsteads just as they do in Japanese Hokkaido.

Southern Sakhalin, like Manchuria, owes several changes of ownership to its location near China, Japan, and Russia. Karafuto, as the Japanese called southern Sakhalin, became Nipponese as a result of the Russo-Japanese war of 1904–1905; it changed back to Russia with the disastrous Allied concession to the U.S.S.R.

near the close of World War II. Its main economic value is in its oil resources, although nearby fishing grounds encourage some villages along the coast. Agriculture is discouraged by mountainous terrain and long cold winters.

Unlike the Manchurian plain, which is a plain of erosion, the southern Hwang Ho Plain is one of deposition. It is made up of sediments laid down by the Hwang Ho, which has worked so long and well that it not only has fashioned a great productive plain but also has changed a former island into the present Shantung Peninsula (Fig. 15–13).

Relief is so slight throughout the area that the river has changed its course on several occasions during historic time. Sometimes it is south of the former island, and other times it lies to the north of the Shantung Peninsula, as it does now. Monsoon rains, level land, and built-up dikes all conspire to cause disastrous floods causing loss of property and life.

The Hwang Ho plain is a wheat country rather than rice land like south China. It is a well-known fact that many northern Chinese eat rice only on special occasions; probably some have never eaten it. Besides wheat, other crops

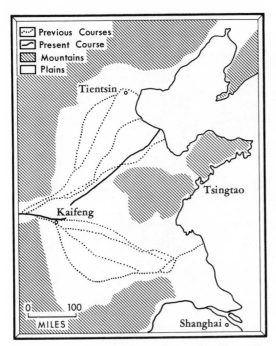

Fig. 15–13 The Changing Lower Course of the Hwang Ho. The Hwang Ho has changed its course over the relatively level North China Plain many times in the past few thousand years. (*Drawing based upon map in* China's Geographic Foundations, *G. B. Cressey, McGraw-Hill, p. 160*)

include cotton, corn, kaoliang, and millet. Farms are larger than in south China, where a longer growing season permits greater unit production.

On the Shantung Peninsula, crops are similar to those of the adjoining Hwang Ho plain, but the rugged terrain gives a small proportion of arable land. Coal of good quality is available, a contrast to the situation on the Hwang Ho plain, where rich soils are practically the only mineral resource. Another contrast between peninsula and plain occurs in Shantung's coastal indentations, which have encouraged the development of a few good ports such as Tsingtao and Chefoo.

Summary and Conclusions. On the basis of size alone, the humid continental region holds an important rating because it is one of the world's largest. Moreover, the region includes all or major parts of such agriculturally productive plains as the Corn Belt of the United States; the Spring Wheat Region, the Lake Plain, and the St. Lawrence Valley of Canada; the best part of Russia's Fertile Triangle; the Polish

plain; Sweden's Plain of Skane and the southern parts of Finland and Norway; the Hungarian and Rumanian plains in the Balkans; and the Manchurian plain and best part of the Hwang Ho plain of China. These farm lands make a major contribution in food supply to the United States, Russia, China, Canada, Poland, the Scandinavian countries and the Balkan nations.

Humid continental areas also have important lumber resources in the mixed forests of northern United States, southeastern Canada, Russia, Manchuria, Japan, and other parts of the region.

Power resources include fields of petroleum and natural gas in the United States and Canada; important Russian fields between Moscow and the Urals; and other proven oil and gas reserves. Coal deposits are large. Among them are the northern Appalachian field in the United States; the reserves of Poland and larger ones in Russia; the thick coal seams of Manchuria and Japan's best in Hokkaido. Developed water power includes that on Niagara Falls; installations on several of Russia's streams; hydroelectric power plants in northern Japan; and many other developments actual and potential.

Minerals include the iron mines that have contributed the greatest annual tonnage in the world, those of the Lake Superior region of the United States; production from these mines travels on the best inland water transport on earth, the Great Lakes system, almost entirely within the humid continental climates. Besides the Lake Superior mines, there are the Silesian mining region of Poland; the rich mining area of the Middle Urals; and diverse if not rich metallic minerals in the East Asian region.

To resources of size, agriculture, forests, power, and minerals should be added an energizing climate. The humid continental climate, next to the west-coast marine, probably has given man the greatest stimulation towards progress in a materialistic civilization.

QUESTIONS, EXERCISES, AND PROBLEMS

1. Outline the general features of the West Coast Marine and Humid Continental climates, vegetation, soils, and land forms. Locate these areas as to country and as to world wind belts. Why doesn't Asia have any west coast marine climates? Why are there no humid continental climates in the southern

hemisphere? Point out major differences between West Coast Marine and Humid Continental climates.

2. Compare land utilization in the North American West Coast Marine lands with that in the European section. Why does the European section extend much farther into the interior of the continent? Why is there a difference in the boundary climates of the West Coast Marine lands in Europe and those in North America? List the factors that favor great manufacturing development in western Europe. Describe land utilization in southern Chile, extreme southeastern Australia, and New Zealand.

3. What conditions favor corn production in the humid continental climates of North America? Describe the raising of root crops, especially sugar beets and potatoes, in the European Wedge of humid continental climates. What other crops are raised here? Describe the agricultural land use of the East Asian humid continental lands. Why are certain parts of the humid continental region called risk climates for agriculture? Outline land use, other than utilization for agriculture, for the humid continental lands. Name well known plains regions within the humid continental climates.

4. Identify the following:

orographic	Mt. Kosciusko
root crop	dual purpose sheep
stall feeding	Ellsworth Huntington
Irish famine of the 1840's	Annapolis Valley
bulb industry	Mukden
Pennines	spring wheat
Saar	Grampian
Ruhr	Wicklow
Lorraine	Cantabrian
Alaskan Panhandle	Willamette
Vladivostok	Ketchikan
geologic subsidence	Puerto Montt
fiord	Valdivia
pedalfer	Pyongyang
eucalyptus	Pusan
Tasmania	Harbin
Mt. Cook	

5. Compare the areal distribution of the west coast marine climates shown on Fig. 15–1 with those of the *Cfb* climates shown on Plate 2 at the back of the book. Point out similarities and differences in locations and boundaries. Note the significant difference in North America.

6. Compare the areal distribution of the humid continental climates shown on Fig. 15–1 with those of the *Dfa, Dfb, Dwa,* and *Dwb* climates shown on Plate 2. Point out similarities and differences in locations and boundaries.

SELECTED REFERENCES

American Geographical Society, *Focus,* various dates, "Alaska"; "Australia"; "California"; "Canada"; "Chile"; "Czechoslovakia"; "Denmark"; "European Economic Community"; "Hungary"; "New Zealand"; "Soviet Union, Agriculture"; "Soviet Union, Resources and Heavy Industry"; "Romania"; and others. The student should select portions of these issues emphasizing west coast marine and humid continental regions.

Coppock, J. T., "Postwar Studies in the Geography of British Agriculture," *Geographical Review,* July 1964, pp. 409–26.

Curry, Leslie, "The Climatic Resources of Intensive Grassland Farming: The Waikato, New Zealand," *Geographical Review,* April 1962, pp. 174–94.

Cressey, George B., *Asia's Lands and Peoples,* McGraw-Hill, 1963, pp. 122–30, "The Yellow Plain"; pp. 134–38, "Manchuria and the Shantung Hills"; pp. 588–652, "The Soviet Realm"; especially portions emphasizing the humid continental region.

Cumberland, K. B., *Southwest Pacific,* McGraw-Hill, 1956, pp. 50–126.

Durand, Loyal Jr., "Major Milksheds of the Northeastern Quarter of the United States," *Economic Geography,* Jan. 1964, pp. 9–33.

Freeman, Otis W. and Martin, Howard H., editors, *The Pacific Northwest,* John Wiley and Sons, 1954, or later edition.

Garland, John H., *The North American Midwest: A Regional Geography,* John Wiley and Sons, 1955, or later editon.

Hoffman, George W., editor, *A Geography of Europe,* The Ronald Press, 1961, The student should select countries and portions of countries within the west coast marine and humid continental regions for emphasis.

James, Preston, *Latin America,* Odyssey Press, 1959 or later edition, "Chile: The South," pp. 262–71.

Koeppe, C. and De Long, G. C., *Weather and Climate,* McGraw-Hill, 1958, especially parts of Chs. 20 and 21.

Lewthwaite, G. R., "Wisconsin and the Waikato: A Comparison of Dairy Farming in the United States and New Zealand," *Annals of the Association of American Geographers,* March 1964, pp. 59–87.

Lowenthal, David and Prince, H. C., "The English Landscape," *Geographical Review,* July 1964, pp. 309–46.

Norton, Harold L., "The Netherlands' $46-Million-A-Year Bulb Trade," *Foreign Agriculture,* pp. 4–6, May 4, 1964.

Shaw, Earl B., *Anglo-America,* John Wiley and Sons, 1959, pp. 92–146; 180–250; and 382–449.

Taskin, George A., "The Soviet Northwest: Economic Regionalization," *Geographical Review,* April 1961, pp. 213–35.

Thoman, R. S. and Patton, D. J., *Focus on Geographic Activity,* McGraw-Hill, 1964, Ch. 8, "Vestergaard: A Farm in Denmark."

Trewartha, Glenn T., *An Introduction to Climate,* McGraw-Hill, 1954, pp. 312–48.

Chapter Sixteen

The Subarctic or Taiga Region

The Physical Environment

Location and Climate. The subarctic covers one of the largest land areas of any world climatic region, extending from the Pacific to the Atlantic in North America and from the Atlantic to the Pacific in Eurasia (Figs. 16–1 and 16–2). Two great countries, Canada and Russia, include most of the taiga; well over half the lands of each possess this climate. The subarctic also spreads over Alaska, except the southern Panhandle and the northern coasts. The mountain boundary between Norway and Sweden and the extreme south are the only two parts of these countries without a taiga climate; and Finland's subarctic gives way to humid continental only along the southern coast and changes to tundra along the northern fringe. No taiga climate occurs in the southern hemisphere because the continents either do not extend far enough in to the higher latitudes, or they narrow so much there that oceans dominate atmospheric conditions.

The taiga climate has several outstanding characteristics: (a) long cold winters; these more than (b) the short summers account for (c) the greatest temperature range of any of the world's climates. The temperature rise above zero in summer may be greater than the temperature fall below zero in winter. (d) Some of the world's coldest temperatures occur in this climate. Summers have (e) long days and short nights and winters short days and long nights. (f) In subarctic latitudes, the summer noonday sun is never high. (g) Transition seasons of spring and autumn are short or almost nonexistent. (h) Frost is a hazard every month of the year—in great contrast to the situation in subtropical climates where the danger is confined to about one month of the year. (i) Wide areas are characterized by permafrost. (j) Anticy-

clonic conditions dominate winter months and block the consistent movement of cyclonic storms found at lower latitudes. (k) Precipitation, with a summer maximum, is relatively low; a few areas show an annual average of more than 20 inches. Winter precipitation in the form of snow remains a long time because of forest-cover protection from sun. (l) Polar continental air, widespread in the tundra, frequently covers the subarctic.

Surface Features, North America. The Canadian taiga includes all or parts of five major physiographic regions: the Laurentian Shield, the Interior Plains, the Hudson Bay Lowland, the Appalachian Highlands, and the Western Cordillera. The Laurentian Shield underlies more than half of Canada, and includes a 2-million square mile horseshoe of ancient Precambrian rock encircling Hudson Bay. From the air it resembles a plateau broken by rounded hills, numerous lakes, and areas of muskeg. It slopes towards Hudson Bay, and rises in the direction of Labrador.

Geologically the Shield is the peneplaned remnant of Precambrian mountains. Mountain building and later peneplanation have greatly influenced the economic life of Canada. Valuable mineral deposits were brought nearer the surface by the folding and faulting coincident with uplift, and the higher altitudes resulting from diastrophism accelerated erosion of rocks overlying the metallic formations. All of this made it possible for man to recover minerals at much shallower depths. Most of Canada's gold, silver, copper, nickel, platinum, cobalt, uranium, and iron comes from the Laurentian Shield.

Peneplanation that favored mineral exploitation was not so encouraging to agriculture. Pleistocene glaciation acted as a huge rasp, leav-

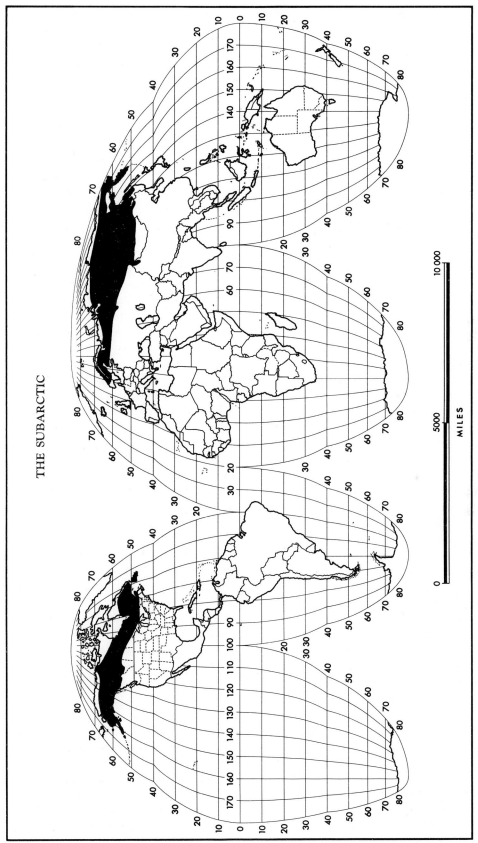

THE SUBARCTIC

Fig. 16–1 Subarctic Lands (*Projection based on the homolosine projection copyright by the University of Chicago. Map by permission McGraw-Hill Book Co., and G. T. Trewartha, An Introduction to Climate*)

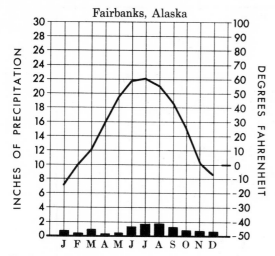

Fig. 16–2 Climatic Chart, Fairbanks, Alaska. Note the small amount of precipitation and the great mean annual temperature range.

ing widespread areas of bare rock completely stripped of soil. Some soils were carried as far south as the United States Corn Belt. This same glacial action was responsible for the many lakes, swamps, and disarranged stream drainage that are characteristic of the Laurentian Shield; such conditions, discouraging to farming, favor hydroelectric power so important in Canadian economy.

West of the Laurentian Shield, the Interior Plains, a poleward extension of the United States Great Plains, continue central Canada's low-lying topography to the Rocky Mountains. In contrast to the Laurentian Shield, the taiga portion of the Interior Plains is more nearly level, and is for the most part, underlain by sedimentary rocks little affected by folding and faulting. Here are most of the great Canadian oil fields. Land forms rise gradually from approximately 1000 feet above sea level to a few thousand feet near the base of the Rockies. Glaciation has been active over this section of the taiga just as over the shield section; lakes, moraines, and interrupted stream patterns, although somewhat less numerous, are similar to those of the peneplane to the east.

The portion of the taiga known physiographically as the Hudson Bay Lowland also differs from the Laurentian Shield. The nearly-flat lowland, underlain by youthful sedimentary rocks, has its greatest length, approximately 800 miles,

towards the southeast; the narrowest dimension, east-west, varies from 100 to 200 miles. Deposition of sediments, now forming rocks of the lowland, took place as the ice sheet receded poleward beyond the divide between the St. Lawrence and Hudson Bay drainage. Many of the sediments are lacustrine clays, laid down in waters ponded in front of the retreating continental glacier.

The Appalachian Highlands appear in Newfoundland, which is also a part of the Canadian taiga. The island is shaped like an equilateral triangle with each side of its 43,000-square-mile area approximately 320 miles in length. Inland from the 6000 mile subsiding shoreline, with its many coastal indentations and islands, is a rolling plateau dotted with numerous glacial lakes and hills. The surface slopes gently from about 2000 feet in Long Range on the west to about 700 feet near the eastern coast.

Pleistocene glaciation brought both erosion and deposition to Newfoundland, and drainage patterns were badly interrupted. Metallic deposits of iron, lead, zinc, and other minerals occur in the widespread crystalline rocks, and a little coal is present in the stratified sedimentaries of the southwest.

The Western Cordillera of Canada includes mountains and plateaus lying west of the Interior Plains. Some of these surfaces reach an altitude that gives them a tundra or ice cap climate, but they have all been included in the subarctic to simplify the regional approach.

The Yukon Plateau occupies the largest area of the Alaskan taiga with elevations ranging from 2000 to 4000 feet on its peneplaned surface. This plateau is cut off from the Pacific by the Alaskan and other ranges to the south, and from the Arctic by the Brooks Range to the north. Both mountain areas are included in the taiga region, but like Canada's Western Cordillera they possess climates other than the Subarctic.

Surface Features, Eurasia. In the huge Siberian section, west of the Yenisey, agents of both erosion and deposition have combined to produce a relatively flat terrain, where the Pleistocene ice sheet has left very few traces. To the east of the Yenisey, between that river and the Lena, plains topography changes to that of a dissected plateau. Here is the ancient Siberian Shield, which has resisted folding since Archean time; although there are no fold mountains, enough uplift has taken place to encourage accelerated erosion and consequent dissection. East of the Lena River, many mountain groups alternate with several plateaus. The mountain ranges include the Stanovoy, with closely packed folds; the rocky and irregular Dzhugdzhur, which form a serious obstacle to the Pacific; and the folded Verkhoyansk and Cherskiy, more or less Alpine in type.

Surface features of the subarctic in European Russia show considerable similarity to those of western Siberia. To be sure there are the uplands of the Kola Peninsula and Karelia and the low Timan highlands; but these are only a few hundred feet above the basins of Onega, Dvina, Mezan, and Pechora, all shallow depressions streaked with trails of glacial moraines.

The taiga of the Scandinavian countries is dominated by the Scandinavian Shield, a feature with surface characteristics and geologic history similar to that of Canada's Laurentian Shield.

Vegetation and Soils. Although the taiga is almost entirely forest (Fig. 16–3), the climate is not ideal for rapid tree growth. Many trees are small; stands are not close over wide expanses of territory; and it takes many years for a tree to reach maturity. Where trees are widely spaced and penetration of light is easy, an understory bush vegetation is characteristic; where trees are closer together and only a little light reaches the ground, mosses and lichens may occur; and where stands are dense and no light penetrates through the branches, nothing but a thick bed of leaves covers the ground.

Softwoods make up nearly three-fourths of the forest with spruce, balsam fir, pine, hemlock, cedar, larch, and cypress prominent among the conifers. Poplar, birch, and maple are important among the hardwoods.

Fig. 16–3 Coniferous Forest and Big Games. Subarctic lands are better adapted for forestry, hunting, trapping, and mineral exploitation than for farming. Here, in the western Canadian taiga, a moose looks up after drinking from one of the thousands of glacial lakes. (*Courtesy I. McT. Cowan*)

Fig. 16–4   Matanuska Valley, Palmer, Alaska. Spring wheat in the shocks near Pioneer Peak four and a half miles southeast of Palmer. (*Courtesy United States Department of Agriculture*)

The dominantly conifer vegetation of the subarctic contributes little in humus to the soils, much less than that contributed by deciduous forests and grasses in regions to the south. The podzol soils belong to the nonlime-accumulating pedalfer division; they are low in humus, leached, and possess unfavorable structure. Neither the thin podzol soil nor the widespread occurrence of bare rock scraped clean by Pleistocene ice handicaps agriculture as much as climate.

Land Utilization

Agriculture, North America. One may well start with Alaska (Fig. 16–4), the only state in the United States with taiga climate. In this area of 586,000 square miles only about 20 square miles have been cleared for farming. Most of this land lies between the Yukon Plateau city of Fairbanks and the coastal city of Anchorage.

For the period 1932–1947 inclusive, the highest temperature recorded at Fairbanks was 99° F and the lowest was −65° F. During the growing months, beginning with May, the normal temperature shows a steady rise, reaching its peak in July. The growing season for hardy plants such as grains and grasses averages 123 days on the south-facing slopes. For tender plants, such as potatoes, the growing season averages 105 days. On the valley floors, the growing period is several days less.

Total precipitation ranges from 8.5 inches to 16 inches, with approximately half coming during the growing season. This is enough for cereal crops in view of the relatively low temperatures and the favorable evaporation-precipitation ratio. During the growing season, the long daylight contributes to the rapid growth of plants. Earth in the Tanana Valley, near Fairbanks, is frozen to varying depths with some lenses or blocks of ice of various sizes. When the natural vegetation cover is disturbed by clearing the land, summer thawing may be deep enough to melt the ice blocks mentioned above; as a result the surface area may sink. Because of such sinkings, a number of fields in the vicinity of Fairbanks have become too hummocky and rough for cultivation. Soils developed from stream alluvium are low in organic matter and deficient in nitrogen and phosphate. A few dairy herds feed on oats and peas grown for hay; garbage from the nearby military base is fed to hogs and chickens; potatoes are the chief cash crop.

Economic handicaps for Yukon agriculture, and that for Alaska in general, are as serious as those of the physical environment. These handicaps include (a) expensive labor and equipment —clearing land costs from $100 to $200 per acre; (b) high cost of transporting crops to local markets; (c) inefficient marketing practices; (d) the lure of high industrial wages tempting farmers to leave the land; (e) high clearing and development costs preventing would-be farmers from agricultural investment; (f) and danger of overproduction for Alaska's market of only a few hundred thousand people. This last handicap throttles any significant expansion, for any surplus, with added transport costs to outside markets, could not hope to meet competition from better located producing areas.

Probably 85 per cent of Canada's nearly 4 million square miles is unfit for farming; more than half of this lies in the subarctic. Within the latter area, however, there are sections where opportunities for successful farming are better than those for the bulk of Canada's northern forest region. One of these is the section known as the Clay Belt, south of James Bay; another lies in the valley of the Mackenzie and in the valleys of some of its tributaries; and another stretches along the foothills of the Rocky Mountains, where air drainage is frequent and where winds occur that are similar to the chinook in Rocky Mountain lands of western United States.

Although farmers face danger of frost almost every month of the year, latitude is high enough to give long daylight periods in summer to encourage plant growth. With careful planting of cereal types maturing in a short season, and of root crops that complete their life cycle in similar short periods, the farmer may receive a crop in more than half the years of planting. Farmers should also include livestock raising, with cultivation of root crops and hardy cereals. Animals provide meat, milk, hides, and wool, and they furnish manures needed to add fertility to the soil and to improve soil structure. If the farm lies close to mining centers or paper towns, as some farms do, the farmer has a better market for animal products and cultivated crops.

Farms in the Canadian taiga need people who are willing to work hard and to suffer privation to achieve success. Not many people are willing to do this; not many are willing to engage in a variety of activities to make a living. Assurance of economic success is encouraged by supplementing farming with work in the forests, in the mines, or by hunting, fishing, and trapping. Settlement has been aided in some sections by the church acting as a semicolonizing and semi-cooperative agent. In the Clay Belt church organizations have been more successful in establishment of farm settlements among the French Catholics than among other groups. Even so, probably not more than 5 per cent of the best farm land available is devoted to crops. Pressure of population upon North American land must be much greater than at present before a poleward movement of farmers to the Canadian taiga takes place. If the present upward trend in world temperatures continues a few more centuries, and if the icecaps of Greenland, Antarctica, and the Arctic islands approach complete dissipation, taiga farmland may attract a rush of purchasers; but these occurrences are extremely unlikely within the next few hundred years.

Agriculture, Eurasia. In the European subarctic west of Russia, there is a larger percentage of approximately flat terrain in Finland than there is in Norway and Sweden; and there are more gentle slopes in Sweden than in Norway. In fact Norway has been described as all mountains and sea; a country almost without plains; only fjords and high fields. Along the fjords there are small areas of coastal flats where farmers raise some wheat, rye, hay, and potatoes. They also keep a few cows, which they drive to the highlands for pasturage during the summer season.

The Swedish taiga contrasts with that in Norway not only in terrain, but also in being located on the leeward side of the mountain backbone separating the two countries. This location gives more continentality to the climate, with less precipitation and colder winters. Most Swedish farming takes place on the plain of

Fig. 16–5 Newfoundland Paper for Export. Only Russia and Brazil have greater forested areas than Canada. Out of a total of 3,845,144 square miles, about 1,300,000 square miles are forested with 503,000 classified as accessible and productive. (*Courtesy Newfoundland Tourist Development Office*)

Skane, south of the mountain belt and in the humid continental climate. Here, as well as on the slope lands of the subarctic, root crops, hay, hardy cereals, and dairying dominate the agricultural pattern.

In Finland, the cultivated area covers about 8 per cent of the land, with hay and oats by far the main crops, although there is a considerable acreage devoted to rye, wheat, barley, and potatoes. Dairying has achieved significant importance, and enough butter and other dairy solids are produced to provide a considerable surplus for export.

Finland's economic potential is sometimes compared with that of the Alaskan Yukon; but the former has several advantages over the latter. In the first place Finland's climate is favored by slight marine influences in contrast to that of the Yukon, which is completely cut off from the oceans by mountains. Again, Finland has better forests than the Yukon, thus giving the Finns a winter occupation to supplement their summer farm activities; and probably most important among Finland and Yukon differences is Finland's proximity to a good European market for crop and animal products. As a result of these and other reasons, Finland has far more land in agriculture than the insignificant acreage of Alaska.

At least half of the Russian Empire's more

than 8 million square miles lies in the region of subarctic climates. This fact strengthens the economic principle that area alone does not insure great agricultural production, nor does it assure economic returns commensurate with size.

Taiga agriculture is mostly of a subsistence type except where farms lie near lumber mills, mines, or river-port cities. As in other taiga lands, the farmer may cultivate root crops, raise a few garden vegetables, grow hardy cereals, and gather wild fruits from bushes forming a second-story vegetation in the forest. Growing of fruit trees is almost impossible in the subarctic, except along equatorward edges or where local topography ameliorates temperatures. As a consequence of tree-fruit shortage, the gathering of blueberries, wild apples, raspberries, strawberries, and other vine and bush fruits becomes of more than average importance and adds dietary assistance to taiga farmers.

Cattle raised by subarctic peoples are likely to be small and resistant to low winter temperatures. In the European Russian taiga, animals descended from European wild cattle belong to the Veliko-Russian black and red breed. Their carcasses may weigh no more than 110 to 285 pounds, but they withstand cold well and survive on small amounts of feed. In Siberia, cattle are descended from small wild stock and are also able to get along with a minimum of feed; they have shaggy long hair that protects them from low temperatures in the cold season. In eastern Siberia the Yakuts raise horses for meat and milk, and they may keep cattle for the same purposes as well. Along the Yenisey, the Tungus are reindeer people, and in some places taiga farmers have started to domesticate the moose. Domestication is said to be easy, and the animal may be used for draft purposes as well as for meat. Captivity works no hardship on reproduction, and the female usually gives birth to two calves. These may reach maturity in about sixteen months.

In all the Russian subarctic, settlements are likely to show greater concentration along streams. Here, fishing may supplement farming; hunting and trapping will probably be better along water courses; and contacts with the outside world may be more frequent. Farming conditions are better in the taiga of western Siberia than in that of the east. The western part has plains topography, is less cold in winters, and precipitation is likely to be less variable.

Other Resources

Forest Industries, North America. The economic development of Canada has always been associated with forests. It was in the forest that the earliest settlers secured fur, the first commercial product of continental Canada. Forests also provided wood for fuel, timber for ships, lumber for homes, barns, and sheds, and a

combination of forests products for export. However, problems of clearing the forest delayed agricultural development, and forests gave shelter for Indian enemies. Today, Canada's annual output of pulp and paper totals over a billion dollars, and forest products normally provide about one fourth of Canadian exports (Fig. 16–5).

Although most Canadian subarctic trees are small in size, slow growing, and weak in structure, they are low in resin content and react well to chemical and mechanical processing. Other

Fig. 16–6   Hamilton Falls, Labrador. About 700 miles northeast of Montreal, the Hamilton River drops 245 feet—1½ times the drop of the Niagara—into Bowdoin Canyon. Estimates of power potential run as high as 6 million hp, which would place Hamilton Falls in the same category as the world's largest hydroelectric power project at Bratsk on the Soviet's Angara river. No definite plans for development have been made, but in 1964 New York's Consolidated Edison Company deferred construction plans in New York; and announced it was negotiating with Canadian interests for "a large block of firm hydroelectric power." (*Courtesy the British Newfoundland Corporation Ltd.*)

advantages for paper making include proximity to cheap hydroelectric power (Fig. 16–6) and to the greatest of the world's paper and pulp markets, that of the United States. In fact, several United States corporations have moved their factories to Canada. By such a change they save on labor costs and, what is more important, they cut down transport charges. This economy comes through shipping the lighter, more compact finished product rather than the bulky heavy logs.

Availability of facilities for transport is very significant in the location of paper pulp and paper mills. Most all are located where railroads cross large streams. Thus, certain supplies may be brought in by rail and the finished product moved by the same means of transport; and with the along-stream location, the bulky logs may be floated down river to the mill. A situation near a stream also gives opportunity for hydroelectric power development; and enormous amounts of power are needed for the manufacture of wood pulp. The town of Kapuskasing is a good example of such a location. It lies well within the taiga, near the southern edge of the Hudson Bay Clay Belt where the Canadian National Railroad crosses the north-flowing Kapuskasing River.

Little commercial exploitation of forests takes place in the Alaskan taiga, largely because of poor quality and limited quantity of suitable trees. The best Alaskan timber is in the region of west coast marine climate along the Pacific coast, especially in the Tongass and Chugach National Forests.

Forest Industries

Eurasia. Forest industries are commercially important in Norway, Sweden, and Finland. In Sweden sawmills and planing mills alone employ almost as many men as all the iron mines, machinery factories, and other metal work for which Sweden is famous. Most of the lumbering is done in winter, making it possible for the people to combine farming and lumbering. In many cases, however, the Swedish lumber crews are considered permanent labor, and some sawmill companies furnish houses and gardens for their workers. In the summer, trees to be cut the following winter are marked. Lumbering begins when the first snow falls. The marked

trees are felled, the branches cut, the bark peeled, and the trunks sawed into proper lengths. Branches and bark may be used for tar or for making charcoal to be used in the iron industry. Timber is transported to the nearest river and piled on the ice to await the spring thaw. Transport is important in lumbering, because the product is bulky and heavy in proportion to its value. Moreover, lumber comes largely from uplands or other regions where population is scanty and the roads poor. In Sweden, as in Norway, Finland, and Russia, snow greatly facilitates transport. Sledges pulled by horses or driven by motor power bring the timber over the smooth snow surface to the nearest river.

The fact that Sweden has many short parallel rivers is an advantage, for a haul of only 2 or 3 miles brings most of the lumber to a river. When logs are piled there on the ice, the main labor of transport is done, for the spring thaw carries the wood to the seashore (Fig. 16–7). Drivers, with long poles, prevent the floating timber from forming jams at rapids or bends of the river; or in calmer water they direct it to workers in tugboats who gather it into rafts. The chief remaining task is to tow the chained timber rafts across the glacial lakes which may interrupt the rivers. Finally, the timber reaches the mill or paper pulp factory, which usually is located near the mouth of the river. Sawmills and pulp mills are often combined. The northern part of the seacoast is lined with such mills from which the final product is shipped to market. The direction of the rivers and their rather steady water supply are of great importance. The fact that most of Sweden's rivers run from northwest to southeast gives them an advantage of thawing first at their mouths in spring and then having high water when the snow melts higher up.

Although Norway possesses but little arable land, most cultivated sections lie within or near forests so that many farmers are employed part time in cutting and transporting timber. Forest industries furnish the bases for paper, pulp, and electro-chemical plants and provide approximately one fourth of the country's exports.

No other country in the world, not even Sweden or Canada depends so heavily upon forest industries as Finland. Over half of the country is forested; rivers, lakes, and winter snow provide easy transport; water falls furnish good bases for hydroelectric power; and many good accessible harbors encourage shipments of wood products and their derivatives which dominate the country's exports.

Russia has more forest land than any other country, two and one half times as much as the United States and probably at least a quarter of the world forest acreage. Of the 628.3 million hectares covered with commercial timber, 23 per cent lies in European Russia and 77 per cent in Asiatic Russia. Pine and spruce are leading tree types in the north of European U.S.S.R.; larch predominates in Siberia, where there are also extensive birch and aspen forests.

Out of the estimated 58.7 billion cubic meters of standing timber, only about 30 billion are available for exploitation, either immediately or in the near future. At present only about 1 per cent of the total timber stand is being cut each year, a very low cut. This 1 per cent, however, is obtained, not from the entire timber-covered area, but from the most accessible forests, which therefore are being cut in excess, while at the same time, overmature timber on millions of hectares in inaccessible localities remains unused, deteriorates, and rots on the stump. Furthermore, forest fires, often set by natives to improve hunting or wild berry crops, rage unchecked in remote regions, and insects and diseases exact an enormous toll. Thus, it becomes evident that vastness of area alone is far from being a sufficient basis for appraising realistically the forest wealth and potentialities of the U.S.S.R.

Asiatic Russia, where 77 per cent of all the forests of the country are located, has only 19 per cent of the population. In European Russia, it is just the reverse. With 81 per cent of the population, European Russia has only 23 per cent of the forests. This necessitates bringing timber from constantly longer distances from the north and east to the densely populated industrial centers.

In 1959 a seven-man team of experts was assigned to study the Russian forest industries by the United States State Department. Among the findings of the group were the following:

1. Saw mills employed several times as much manpower per unit of production as that used in the United States.

2. Pulp and paper mills were much more efficient than the saw mills.

3. More than half of Russia's annual gross timber cut goes for fuel.

4. Paper consumption per capita was 32 pounds compared with 435 pounds in the United States.

5. There has been heavy overcutting of accessible timber in western Russia.

6. The ratio of forest research workers in Russia as against Canada is ten to one.

7. North America will receive tough competition in forest products from the Soviets in seven to ten years.

In any discussion of forest resources of the subarctic as a whole, something should be said about the fur industry, which is important throughout all the taiga. The fur industry has many advantages here: (a) the cold climate encourages good quality furs; (b) adequate feed is

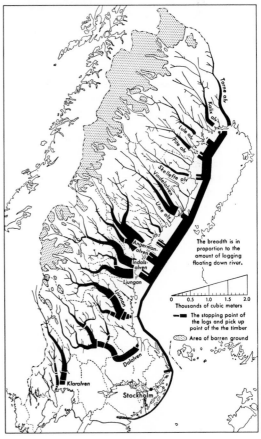

Fig. 16–7   Logging in the Norrland of Sweden. In the Norrland which covers about 100,000 square miles of Sweden, logs are floated down the rivers to the Gulf of Bothnia coast towns. (*Courtesy Holt, Rinehart, and Winston, Jean Gottman,* Geography of Europe)

Fig. 16–8   Headframe of a Mining Development Shaft at Thompson, Manitoba. Much of the North American and Eurasian Subarctic region is underlain by highly mineralized igneous and metamorphic rocks. At Thompson, International Nickel has invested more than a hundred million dollars for mining, power, and town building facilities; and has made the area the world's second largest producer of nickel. The ore body extends about 80 miles in length and nearly 10 miles in width. Transportation to market is available through a 30-mile spur line that links Thompson with the Canadian National's Hudson Bay Railroad. Notice the typical coniferous forest in the background. (*Courtesy International Nickel Company of Canada Ltd.*)

available for fur-bearing animals; for example beaver thrive on bark of local trees, and muskrats enjoy many aquatic plants growing in the numerous lakes and rivers; (c) these waterways provide trappers with a route to market; (d) snow aids in tracking animals; (e) although mining, forestry, agriculture, and other industries have invaded the quiet of Taiga forests, thousands of square miles remain to give the isolation sought by wild animals; (f) world standards of living are rising, a factor which encourages a broader market for furs.

Although furs taken from wild animals in the taiga have been important items in world commerce for centuries, fur farming is becoming constantly more significant. In the early 1960's

fur farms, many in the taiga, contributed about one half of Canadian production.

Mineral Industries, North America. Mention has been made of the old rock masses in the subarctic, the Laurentian Shield of Canada, the Scandinavian Shield of northwest Europe, and the Shield of Central Siberia. Many metallic minerals have been discovered in the igneous and metamorphic rocks of these shields and many more will be found when careful geologic mapping of the huge areas—now only started—is completed.

Besides old metallic bearing shield rocks, there are also younger sedimentaries such as those of the interior plains of the Canadian taiga. These youthful strata hold promise for the discovery of petroleum and natural gas.

It may be well to mention a few of the great mineral and power resources now being exploited in the subarctic. In Alaska, gold bearing intrusive rocks occur near Fairbanks; and the state possesses nearly all of the more than 30 minerals listed by the United States as strategic or critical. In 70 years—from 1870 to 1950—Alaskan mineral production, most of it in the Taiga, amounted to more than a billion dollars.

In Canada, the well known Sudbury nickel mine on the equatorward edge of the taiga has provided most of the world's supply of that mineral for decades. Now its production is supplemented from a new mine at Thompson (Fig. 16–8), not far from Hudson Bay. Another significant mining development, for copper, is located at Chibougamau, about 320 miles north of Montreal. This copper strike serves as a good example of how actual mining of nonprecious minerals awaits the arrival of adequate transport facilities. Copper ore outcrops at Chibougamau were discovered more than a half century ago, but no road gave easy accessibility to markets. In 1957, the Canadian National Railway completed a branch line to the copper region. With an outlet assured over both rail and road, by 1959 mining corporations had invested more than fifty million dollars in the mines. Taiga iron is available in large quantities in Ontario, north of the United States Mesabi region; in Labrador; and in the Bell Island Wabana mines of Newfoundland. The Labrador ore receives much publicity because of its location with reference to the St. Lawrence

River. A railroad (Fig. 16–9) built to move the iron to market connects Schefferville with Seven Islands on the St. Lawrence, and iron can move easily by deep water to the North American steel centers. In 1964 Texas Gulf Sulphur announced the discovery of a huge deposit of metallic ores—mainly copper, lead, and zinc—at Timmins, Ontario. Company stock more than doubled in value within a few weeks and Timmins took on all the aspects of a booming mining town.

In conclusion it should be emphasized that Canada is one of the world's leading mineral producers. In the late 1950's the country led in the production of nickel, platinum, and asbestos; ranked second in gold, zinc, cadmium, and selenium; third in silver, molybdenum, and barite; and fourth in copper and lead. It may be that the nation has the world's largest iron resources. For example in 1962, while a survey party was exploring the Yukon for oil, they found a huge iron ore body of high quality, possibly greater than any earlier Canadian discovery. But exploitation will wait a long while

in this isolated section of the taiga (Fig. 16–10).

Eurasia. In Sweden great deposits of rich iron ore occur at Kiruna and nearby areas. In fact Sweden's iron and forest products make up the bulk of the country's exports. Minerals also contribute to Finnish and Norwegian economy, but less significantly than to that of Sweden. However, one of the largest European copper deposits has been discovered at Outokumpu, Finland, where zinc ore is also present.

In Russia's Kola Peninsula, which lies in both the Arctic and subarctic climates, the U.S.S.R. has a mineral storehouse, producing copper, aluminum, phosphates, and many other minerals. The northern Urals are also highly mineralized as is the Russian Far East, where large quantities of gold have been, and continue to be, extracted from the Aldan and Kolyma river valleys. Other taiga mineral locations include the Pechora oil and coal district, the Lower Tunguska Valley with coal, graphite, mica, and magnetite, the Olekma Valley with salt and petroleum, and the Yakutsk

Fig. 16–9   Trains on the Labrador Mineral Railroad. The Labrador Peninsula is one of the most highly mineralized regions in the world. Loaded cars on the left are moving from the Schefferville iron mines, about 300 miles north of the St. Lawrence river, to the St. Lawrence port of Seven Islands. Empty cars on the right are returning to Schefferville. Notice the landscape of dominantly coniferous forest. (*Courtesy Iron Ore Company of Canada*)

Fig. 16–10 Transportation at Norman Wells, in the Canadian Subarctic. In a territory with winter snows, summer muskeg, and few roads and railroads, planes are important means of transport for passengers and freight both summer and winter. In the latter season, dogs may supplement air travel. (*Courtesy Standard Oil Co., New Jersey*)

district with high and low grade coal. In fact metallic minerals and the power resources of coal, petroleum, and natural gas are present in abundance throughout the Russian taiga.

As in other subarctic areas, the development of the Russian mineral and power deposits depends upon quality and quantity; for most of the distances to market are so great that only the best and largest resources will be extracted in the forseeable future.

These long distances also emphasize the problem of exploiting the dominantly coniferous forest cover of the huge world region. Like the minerals, only trees of the best quality and those most accessible are likely to be exploited within the next few years. Moreover, the present agricultural development is extremely limited, and growth will be slow unless maximum and minimum temperatures rise much more rapidly than they have in the last few centuries. In short, the taiga is doomed to remain a sparsely populated and little developed land for several decades to come.

QUESTIONS, EXERCISES, AND PROBLEMS

1. Outline the general features of the subarctic climates, vegetation, soils, and land forms. Locate these areas as to country and as to world wind belts. Why doesn't the southern hemisphere have any subarctic climates?

2. Describe subarctic land utilization in North America, the agriculture, forest industries, mineral resources and exploitation, etc.

3. Describe subarctic land utilization in Eurasia, the agriculture, forest industries, mineral resources and exploitation, etc.

4. Comment upon the character and distribution of population in the subarctic lands of both North America and Eurasia. Consider this problem in the countries of Alaska (state), Canada, Norway, Sweden, Finland, and Russia.

5. Identify the following:

Laurentian Shield	Veliko-Russian
peneplanation	Kiruna
Stanovoy	Olekma
Cherskiy	Kapuskasing
Pechora	Sudbury
Population of Alaska	Timmins
Mackenzie	lacustrine clays

Newfoundland's shape
Dzhugdzhur
Kola Peninsula
Scandinavian Shield
Tanana
Skane
Schefferville
Kolyma
Yakutsk
fur farming
Chibougamau
Yenisey

Siberian Shield
Verkhoyansk
Timan
Area of Alaska
permafrost
Alaska-Finland comparison
Bell Island
Tunguska
Lena
strategic minerals
forests and fur relationships

6. Compare the areal distribution of the subarctic climates shown on Fig. 16–1 with those of the *Dfc, Dfd, Dwc,* and *Dwd* climates shown on Plate 2 at the end of the book. Point out similarities and differences in locations and boundaries.

SELECTED REFERENCES

American Geographical Society, with various authors, *A World Geography of Forest Resources,* The Ronald Press, 1956, especially Ch. 18 by Raphael Zon, pp. 393–419.

American Geographical Society, *Focus,* "Canada"; "U.S.S.R.: Agriculture"; "U.S.S.R.: Heavy Industry"; various dates; especially portions emphasizing the subarctic region.

Cressey, George B., *Asia's Lands and Peoples,* McGraw-Hill, 1963, "The Soviet Realm," pp. 588–652, especially portions emphasizing the subarctic region.

Department of External Affairs, Information Division, Ottawa, *Fact Sheets: Canada,* 1957 or later edition; emphasize subarctic region.

Department of Mines and Technical Surveys, Ottawa, *Selected Bibliography of Canadian Geography,* 1956 or later revision; emphasize subarctic region.

Department of Resources and Development, Ottawa, *Forests and Forest Products Statistics,* Forest Research Bulletin, latest revision.

Geographical Record, "Burning in the Boreal Forest of North America," *Geographical Review,* January 1961, pp. 127–28.

Harrington, Lyn, "Yukon's Wilderness Roads," *Canadian Geographical Journal,* August 1962, pp. 127–28.

Hoffman, George W. editor, *A Geography of Europe,* the Ronald Press, 1961, The student should emphasize portions of countries within the subarctic climatic region.

Jackson, W. A., "The Virgin and Idle Lands of Western Siberia and Northern Kazakhstan: A Geographical Appraisal," *Geographical Review,* Jan. 1956, pp. 1–19.

Jackson, W. A., "The Virgin and Idle Lands of Western Siberia and Northern Kazakhstan Reappraised," *Annals of the Association of American Geographers,* March 1962, pp. 60–69.

Jorre, Georges, *The Soviet Union: The Land and its People,* translated and revised by E. D. Laborde, 2d ed., John Wiley and Sons, 1961; emphasize Ch. 17, pp. 226–67, "The Forest Belt."

Koeppe, C. E. and De Long, G. C., *Weather and Climate,* McGraw-Hill, 1958, stress parts of Ch. 21 describing the subarctic region.

Lydolph, Paul E., *Geography of the U.S.S.R.,* John Wiley and Sons, 1964, especially Ch. 7, "The European North"; Ch. 11, "Western Siberia and Northern Kazakhstan"; and Ch. 12, "Eastern Siberia and the Far East."

McDermott, George L. "Frontiers of Settlement in the Great Clay Belt, Ontario and Quebec," *Annals of the Association of American Geographers,* Sept. 1961, pp. 261–73.

Ross, W. Gillies, "Power on Hamilton River, Labrador," *Canadian Geographical Journal,* March 1963, pp. 74–87.

Shaw, Earl B., *Anglo-America,* John Wiley and Sons, 1959, Ch. 4, "The Taiga, or Subarctic Region of Canada," pp. 64–91.

The Queen's Printer, *The Canada Yearbook,* 1964 or later edition; stress portions describing the subarctic region.

Trewartha, Glenn, *An Introduction to Climate,* McGraw-Hill, 1954, "The Subarctic Climates," pp. 348–57.

Chapter Seventeen

Manufacturing

The concept of manufacturing involves man's work in changing materials, usually raw materials, into products (1) that possess a form and nature differing from the original and (2) that normally become more useful as a result of the change.

Primitive Manufacturing. (Fig. 17–1) Where manufacturing is carried on depends upon the kind of manufacturing one has in mind. Primitive manufacturing may occur wherever there are people and materials available for manufacture. Primitive subsistence manufacturing takes place in many different environments. Eskimo women, far away from modern civilization, not long ago ruined their teeth in chewing animal skins to get them into workable condition for making family clothing. They sewed these skins together with needles fashioned from the bones of animals and with thread made from animal hides. In Bedouin encampments of the Middle East, tents and robes are woven from the hair of goats and camels. These animals, together with sheep, provide shelter, clothing, food, and transport in a feature industry, nomadic herding, of Middle East desert and steppe land environment. In the near-rainforest environment of the southern Sudan, spear points and arrowheads may be made from iron; the iron ore is freed from most of its impurities in crude native furnaces.

A few examples of primitive manufacturing for commercial purposes may be cited. In the Cairo Mouska, and in a similar market in Damascus, there are streets where men do handwork only in gold; alleys where copper trays are decorated by hand with silver skillfully pounded into the cheaper metal; shops where leather is made into bags; and household factories where ornamental screens and boxes are carved from wood and decorated with various types of metals. In Ecuador, native workers skillfully weave palm fibers into hats and baskets. Many other examples of primitive commercial manufacturing could be given.

Modern Manufacturing. (Fig. 17–2) Modern manufacturing involves more than raw materials and people in answering the question "where can manufacturing be carried on." Besides (1) products from field, forest, mine, or ocean, modern industry needs (2) an active, energetic, inventive type of people stimulated by (3) an energizing climate; (4) fuels and other sources of power; (5) easily accessible and economically operated transport facilities; (6) skilled and unskilled labor; (7) capital; (8) markets; (9) favorable government attitude; and several other conditions.

It may be well at the outset to point out contrasts between modern manufacturing and other productive industries. (1) Most raw materials used in manufacturing are not produced in the place where they are manufactured but are transported from other localities. In contrast, local climate and soil produce crops which may be fed to animals raised on the farm; minerals are found in the mine; lumber industries are based upon local forests; hunted animals are found on hunting grounds; and fish are exploited in the waters of rivers, lakes, and oceans, where fishing takes place. (2) Manufacturing is more widespread than any other industry, for some kind of manufacturing is present wherever there are people. (3) The ground area covered by factories, a feature of modern manufacturing, is small in comparison to that covered by other productive industries. (4) In general, the value of production per unit of area in manufacturing is probably greater than that of any industry except mining. (5) One of the greatest differences between manufacturing and the other productive industries is the contrast in cultural landscapes. The factory landscape looks far different from that of the tropical plantation, the tree farm, the open-pit mine, or the steam trawler. (6) Most factories, but not all, are located in urban areas, whereas farms and forests, at least, are definitely rural. (7) Most factory areas are characterized by greater population density than the areas of other productive industries. (8) Usually, but not always, factory sites occupy surface area more valuable than that occupied by forests, farms, fisheries, and hunting grounds. Mines, however, may be situated in places where the unit area is much more valuable than that of the factory site.

World Distribution of Manufacturing. (Fig. 17–3) Two major regions and several smaller ones stand out in world manufacturing. A major one occurs in the United States east of the Mississippi River together with southern Canada; the second appears in northwestern Europe, in-

Fig. 17–1   Egyptian Pottery Worker. Water jars like these are used for carrying water and for cooling it in the summer. The potter's work illustrates primitive manufacturing. (*Courtesy Dawlat Sadek*)

cluding European Russia and an eastward extension to the Kuznetsk Basin of the Soviet Union. In these two areas 90 per cent of the world's industrial output is produced by 30 per

Fig. 17–2   Can Manufacturing Machine. The American Can Company is one of more than 500 manufacturing corporations from continental United States to establish plants in Puerto Rico. Important tax incentives and man-made factors influence this migration of industry. The Commonwealth of Puerto Rico offers qualified manufacturers ten to seventeen years tax exemption; and United States federal taxes do not apply in Puerto Rico. (*Courtesy Commonwealth of Puerto Rico*)

cent of the earth's population. Most of the remaining 10 per cent is processed in (1) Japan, sometimes called the Britain of the Orient, largely in southern Honshu and Kyushu; (2) the California, Washington, and Oregon portion of western United States; (3) India, especially the areas around Calcutta, Madras, Bombay, and the Central Ganges; and (4) eastern China, particularly around the Lower Yangtze, Peking-Tientsin, and southern Manchuria.

Within these world manufacturing regions, one or more of the factors which encourage major concentrations of manufacturing may be most important in the location and distribution of certain industries. Several of these factors will be examined individually, and examples will be given to stress the importance of each factor in the distribution of specific industries.

Raw Materials. Among the many factors that influence the location of an industry, the distribution of raw materials is one of the most obvious. Cane-sugar manufacturing is localized in the United States humid subtropics largely because this is the only part of the country where the combined conditions of temperature, rainfall, and relief make it worthwhile to raise sugar cane. However, cane would not be produced in this region, which lacks a 12-months growing season, were it not for a government favorable to tariff protection. Thus the presence of raw materials is not alone responsible for cane sugar manufacturing in extreme southern United States. Inasmuch as the raw material (the cane as it comes from the fields) weighs far more than the sugar made from it, and has only slight value after the sap has been squeezed out, sound business policy requires that it be transported as little as possible. Hence, mills for the manufacture of raw sugar are almost invariably located close to the cane fields. This kind of simple industry is by far the largest type of manufacturing in Cuba and many of the other West Indies, and occupies a high position along the northeast coast of Brazil, the middle and upper Ganges Basin of India and Pakistan, the Peruvian coastal plain, eastern Java, and in several other tropical and subtropical locations.

North of cane-sugar manufacturing, factories for converting cotton seed into oil, cake, and meal are located in a belt extending across the United States. This industry is developed only in cotton-raising states especially from Georgia to Texas. After an interruption in the western part of Texas, it revives in the irrigated West, especially on areas watered by the Rio Grande in New Mexico and Texas and by the Colorado in Arizona and the Imperial Valley of southern California. North of the western part of the belt where cottonseed industries prevail, lies a large area in which beet sugar is manufactured. The location depends on the presence of raw materials encouraged by a relatively cool but nevertheless fairly sunny climate where sugar beets grow well with the help of the natural rainfall or irrigation. Many other examples of the importance of raw materials upon industrial location could be described.

Markets. The importance of the market in determining where industries are located may be seen in the manufacture of bread. For bread, the raw materials play only a minor locational part; the main factor is the market. In the United States bread is one of the most common foods. A small fraction is made in homes, but today most bread is bought from bakeries.[1] The bread-making factories are no more abundant in wheat-raising states such as the Dakotas and Kansas, where the raw material is plentiful, than in states like Massachusetts and Florida, which raise little wheat. Transportation, too, seems to have only a slight effect upon the nationwide distribution of bakeries. One of the main reasons for this is that people want their bread fresh. Another is that bread making is a simple kind of manufacturing which does not require much capital or any kind of skill that is not easily acquired. Hence bread is baked close to where it is eaten.

Transportation. In the business of manufacturing automobiles, Detroit is well located for the transport both of the finished product and of raw materials and fuel. Detroit also lies near the center of the automobile market. A circle

---

[1] Bread, cakes, and pies belong to what might be classified as soft bakery products; crackers, biscuits, and similar commodities belong to hard bakery goods. The location of factories for hard bakery items, which will keep long periods of time without deterioration, is not so dependent upon market location. These goods may be marketed far from the place of manufacture; in fact, shipments of such hard bakery goods appear in overseas markets.

slightly more than 600 miles in diameter with its center at Detroit includes Boston, New York, Philadelphia, Baltimore, Washington, Atlanta, Memphis, Kansas City, Omaha, and Montreal as well as many less distant cities. This area now owns a large portion of United States motor vehicles and almost half of those of the entire world. Nowhere else does a similar circle include as many auto users. Cheap transport on the Great Lakes and to a much lesser extent on the St. Lawrence, makes the central location still more important. Cars can be carried by water to within 300 miles of practically the entire area. Thus from the standpoint of transport to the main market for motor vehicles Detroit's location is good. From the standpoint of raw materials and fuel the location is almost equally as good. Detroit can bring iron ore at a small expense by water from the Lake Superior region; coal can come cheaply from mines in Pennsylvania and Ohio. It is not strange that Michigan and other states bordering the Great Lakes produce such a large percentage of the world's cars.

The making of heavy agricultural machinery is another kind of manufacturing in which transport is especially important. The location of the market is even more significant than that of the raw materials, but both play a part. Many agricultural machines are bulkier than automobiles and more expensive to ship. Much of the market lies farther west than that for automobiles. This is not only because large sections of the Middle Atlantic and New England states are too rugged for farming but also because those states generally have small farms which require less bulky machinery. As yet, the South, with many small tobacco farms and much corn still harvested by hand, does not purchase as much bulky machinery as the Middle West. The large market lies mainly in the plains of the North Central states from Ohio to Kansas, Nebraska, and the Dakotas, with a southward extension to Oklahoma and Texas. Chicago's position at the southern end of Lake Michigan causes railroads from all directions except north and northeast to converge upon it. Thus it lies in an admirable position for shipping agricultural machinery to the entire prairie region from Ohio westward. It is also well located for bringing coal, iron, and

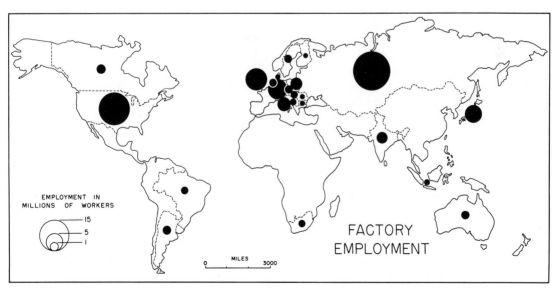

Fig. 17–3 World Factory Employment. In 1960 it was estimated that 185 million workers were engaged in manufacturing and handicraft industries of the world. Possibly not more than 95 million were employed in industrial establishments that could be called factories. Among the countries for which statistics are available, the Soviet Union ranked first in total number, followed by the United States, Germany, the United Kingdom, Japan, France, and Italy. In these seven countries, factory manufacturing employed about 70 million workers or over 70 per cent of the world total. (*Courtesy E. Willard Miller*, A Geography of Manufacturing, *1962, Prentice-Hall, Inc.*)

wood by water from Pennsylvania, the western end of Lake Superior, and the forests of northern Michigan. Southern Wisconsin shares these advantages and is especially well located in respect to the northern wheat region of Minnesota and the Dakotas where much large machinery is used. Hence, Milwaukee and Racine are centers of agricultural machinery. The part played by transportation is also illustrated by sugar refineries. Raw sugar from Puerto Rico and Hawaii is brought by cheap water transport to convenient seaports, where it is refined and either used locally or shipped by rail to the interior.

Fuel and Other Power Resources. The presence of some source of power is important for the majority of modern manufacturing industries. Certain factories that require much fuel show a general tendency to be located on or near coal fields. Iron and steel factories illustrate this situation. The separation of iron from its ore requires fuel and limestone as well as ore. The fuel, usually coal, supplies the heat; the limestone acts as a flux which, when melted, unites with the nonmetallic parts of the ore and separates them from the iron. Only in rare sites, such as the Birmingham district in Alabama, are all three—coal, iron, and limestone—found close together. If the three are located in separate places, the cost of transport may be lowest if iron furnaces are placed near coal rather than near ore or limestone. The amount of coal for making coke to smelt a ton of iron may be bulkier than the iron ore required in the same process. If this is so, transport costs for bringing coal to iron will be greater than those for bringing iron to coal. Another consideration is that coke, made from coal, is entirely lost in the smelting process, so that, if the steel plant is located near coal, no transport cost will be involved in assembling the coal and none will be involved in any added weight given to the finished product by coal, because it does not add any.

Probably more important than either of the conditions above in influencing location of steel plants near or on coal fields is the fact that most majo. coal fields lie near the major markets for iron and steel products. This is true of the Appalachian coal field, the Ruhr, the English coal fields, and many others.

In the United States the best deposits of iron

ore, now largely exploited, are located close to the western end of Lake Superior. Good Appalachian coking coal, on the other hand, together with abundant limestone, is located within easy access of the southern shore of Lake Michigan, and especially that of Lake Erie. This part of North America has a dense population with productive skill and great buying power. Thus the region along the southern lake shores is accessible to iron, fuel, and limestone and also supplies two other important factors influencing industrial location—labor and the market. Most of the iron and steel furnaces in the United States are located along the Great Lakes water transport route and close to the northern Appalachian coal fields.

Pittsburgh factories, large producers of United States iron and steel, are well located with reference to limestone and to the Connellsville seam of Appalachian coal, which lies within easy barge distance of the steel furnaces. Iron, however, must be transferred from lake steamers docking at Lake Erie ports and shipped by rail to Pittsburgh. Rail shipments are more expensive than lake shipments for the same distances; in view of this, plans for canal building from lake shore to Pittsburgh have been considered; and another transport plan envisages an endless-belt system to carry the iron ore from steamer to Pittsburgh furnaces.

At present some of Pittsburgh's mills, now a half-century old, face a prospect of replacement. This may occur, not in Pittsburgh, but in more recently developed steel-manufacturing areas along the southern shores of the Great Lakes, sometimes called the "Ruhr of North America," or along the lower Delaware River in the heart of the eastern coastal market. Thus, certain manufacturing areas may profit by an early start, but later they may receive strong competition from better-located plants with more modern machine processes.

The Chicago district's iron and steel manufacture lies some distance from Appalachian coal; but coal shipments are cheapened by the fact that there is more competition among lake boats seeking west-moving freight than among those moving east. Iron ore and grain account for heavier east-going tonnage than that created by coal and other commodities seeking shipment to the west. Chicago is really located at the market, with iron ore and coal moving to the sales area for iron and steel. The Chicago district's plants, on broad acreages of the Lake Michigan shore plain, show better site location than the Pittsburgh plants; those factories are confined to a narrow river valley of the lower Monongahela and Allegheny, which join at Pittsburgh to form the Ohio (Figs. 17–4 and 17–5).

Market is often fully as significant as fuel in determining factory location. Although Bethlehem Steel's Sparrows Point plant, near Baltimore, is not far from Appalachian coal, with iron ore coming by sea, the market is probably the most significant factor in choice of plant location. The decision of United States Steel to build a new plant along the banks of the lower Delaware is closely related to market accessibility.

Since large supplies of water are used in iron and steel manufacture, the availability of water may be as influential as the availability of fuel in determining location. Water became a key factor in the expansion of the Birmingham, Alabama, plant facilities. Another factor of constantly increasing importance in steel-plant location is the availability of scrap iron. As much as 50 per cent scrap is now used in many iron and steel factories.

Location of the aluminum and newsprint industries is greatly influenced by hydroelectric power, for both commodities take enormous amounts of power in their manufacture. Thanks to water power, Canada ranks high among the world's newsprint producers. Thanks to the power of the upper Saguenay with its access to tidewater, the Aluminium Company of Canada produces the world's lowest cost aluminum at Arvida, Quebec, and has duplicated its Arvida facilities in British Columbia.

Because it takes nearly 10 kilowatt-hours to make a pound of aluminum, a reduction plant can be located with profit in a remote part of the earth if only power is cheap enough. Cheap power is the reason the Aluminium Company of Canada has built one of the world's largest power-aluminum projects near Kitimat in northern British Columbia, a somewhat remote part of the world (Fig. 17–6). The water for Kitimat's power is dammed in a chain of lakes that make a reservoir 150 miles long. At the west end

Fig. 17–4   Valley Location of Pittsburgh Steel Mill. Note that the road and railroad occupy an area cut from the valley wall of the Allegheny Plateau and that easy plant expansion is limited by the narrow valley and by the steep bordering slopes shown at the left. (*Courtesy Pittsburgh Photographic Library*)

Fig. 17–5 Steel Plant, Indiana Harbor. Enormous amounts of flat land are available on the broad plain adjoining Lake Michigan. The location is also easily accessible to cheap water transport for raw materials as well as for the finished product. Moreover, there is an excellent market for iron and steel within the general region, including Chicago and its periphery. (*Courtesy the Youngstown Sheet and Tube Company*)

of the chain a ten-mile tunnel conducts water through a mountain and lets it fall 2600 feet, 15 times Niagara's drop, to the hydroelectric plant. Its power costs about a third as much as power generated in the southern part of the United States. In order to avoid landslides and to solve certain construction problems, the power plant was located at Kemano in a giant cavern hewn out of solid rock. Power is transmitted 50 miles to the smelter at the port of Kitimat. Hydroelectric power at low cost has contributed greatly to Canada's industrial growth.

Labor. Availability of the proper kind and amount of labor is an important influence upon the location of factories. Yet labor is one of the most mobile factors in the development of man-

ufacturing regions. Labor will move toward industry, even in Greenland, if wages are made sufficiently attractive. Publicity on wages paid laborers working on Arctic air bases suggests proof of this point.

Cheap immigrant labor, working in buildings apportioned with small amounts of floor space per worker, gave New York City an early start in the clothing business. In spite of a decline in immigration after the 1930's, a strengthening of labor unions among clothing workers, and higher wages, New York has been able to maintain clothing-manufacture leadership. It is well to remember that, although labor is important, it is not entirely responsible for the city's high clothing production. The region's dense population, and a location attracting buyers from all parts of the country provide a strong market factor. This may be augmented slightly by the fact that New York is the nation's foremost style center.

Although not as important as the clothing industry, the cigar and jewelry industries also require large numbers of laborers; and labor is an extremely important item in the final cost of the factory product. Again market may be as critical in the choice of factory location as in the availability of labor.

Skilled labor is a significant influence upon the location of certain industries, especially that of machine tools. New England still accounts for a sizable share of machine-tool manufacture partly through long years of training machine-tool labor skills. But the importance of market in factory location again comes to the forefront. With the enormous development of agricultural machinery and automobiles in the Middle West, demand came for regional machine-tool factories. Today, Cincinnati, Chicago, Detroit, Milwaukee, Indianapolis, and St. Louis, and other cities located in the Middle-West heart of the automobile and agricultural machinery manufacturing belt account for over half of national production. It is pertinent to note, however, that some of the present factories started as branches of New England firms; or they were staffed with skilled workers from New England when machine-tool production began. Skilled New England shoe workers also gave an impetus to the development of an important boot and shoe industry in St. Louis.

Labor laws or the absence of them, together with limited unionization of workers, have influenced factory location, especially in southern United States. The South was slow in taking legal steps to eliminate child labor, and some factories were started to take advantage of this situation. But cheap adult labor, cheap land, cheap power, low taxes, and even subsidies extended to manufacturing plants were of more significance in plant location than the absence of restrictive child labor laws. Cheaper labor in the South rests upon the South's geographic advantages of low costs for shelter, fuel, and clothing in a warm climate, and low prices for food in an area with a long growing season.

Not only has the southern section of the United States encouraged factory location through cheap labor, but also countries outside the United States gained leadership in manufacturing and in international trade through the payment of low factory wages. Before World War II, Japan spread shipments of cotton textiles and other factory products all over the world. Although, no doubt, other factors influenced the great rise of manufactures among the Japanese, the cheapness of Nipponese labor was an extremely strong encouragement.

Factory expansion may be discouraged by a long history of strike-bound plants. Strikes may be the fault of manufacturers, laborers, or both; but whatever the cause, they raise the cost of production, and, with constantly rising costs of labor, they encourage the invention and manufacture of labor-saving devices.

In plotting manufacturing areas on a map, in the United States and other parts of the world, questions sometimes arises concerning the criteria to be used. Some argue that maps showing industrial distribution should be based upon the number of workers employed; others believe that the amount of power, the value added to the original product by manufacture, the total value of the manufactured commodity, or some other factor or a combination of all factors should be employed as a base. There is no base generally acceptable to all.

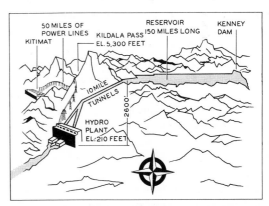

Fig. 17–6 Diagram of Kitimat-Kemano Aluminum Plant. Note the Kenney Dam, which reverses the direction of an east-flowing river and forces water over a long, steep drop from the Pacific mountain escarpment. The smelter at Kitimat now has an annual capacity of 232,000 tons based upon power supplied by the Kemano hydroelectric plant. Future plans call for doubling smelter capacity; however, when this takes place, a second 10-mile tunnel will be necessary to supply additional hydro-electric power. Kitimat is located at 54° 01′ N and 128° 11′ W. (*Courtesy Aluminum Secretariat Ltd., ALCAN*)

Capital. Capital, like labor, is one of the most mobile factors involved in influencing plant location. One illustration concerning the source and significance of labor and capital in the development of manufacture is associated with the textile industries of New England and the South.

From the standpoint of both labor and capital, New England had a greater advantage over the South in the past than at present. A combination of poor farms and energetic farmers was a factor in leading the early New Englanders to carry on hand industries. The same conditions encouraged their sons and daughters to work in factories. After the textile industry had become well established, cheap and relatively efficient immigrant labor was readily available in southern New England. The South, on the contrary relied on inefficient slave labor until after the Civil War. Now, however, a large, efficient labor supply actually gives the South an advantage because, as previously indicated, wages are lower than in the North. Financial resources were probably more important than labor in developing the textile industry in New England rather than in the South, where the raw material is grown. Personal wealth in early America was mainly held by two groups, the planters and the merchants. The southern planter held riches in the form of land and slaves, but rarely had ready money beyond the limits of what came each year from the crops. In other words he had little readily available capital. The northern merchant made his money by taking risks, putting a large sum of capital into a single venture, and waiting for profits. His capital was liquid at frequent intervals after a ship returned with a profitable cargo. Thus it was not at all revolutionary for the merchant to buy stock in a corporation, or even to start a factory, whereas it required a complete change of habits for the planter to do so. Moreover, the War of 1812 made foreign commerce unprofitable in New England at the very time when money was needed for textile factories, which were proving highly profitable. Hence, in the early nineteenth century, almost every merchant in Boston owned shares in cotton mills. This advantage, like various others, still persists, but has lost most of its importance. People are much more ready to invest capital in distant parts of the country than they were a century or more ago. Many large cotton mills in the South are owned by northern companies, which still have mills in the North.

Attitude of the Government. The influence of the government upon the building of manufacturing plants finds expression in several ways: (1) in absolute control of general manufacturing areas and factory site location, building, and operation as in Russia; (2) in choice of factory location, building, and operation as a wartime measure, such as occurred in the United States in World War I and in World War II; (3) in gifts to private enterprise for factory expansion, repair, and operation; again the United States may be used as an example; (4) in favorable taxes, laws, and interpretations of laws, a situation that occurs in many countries.

In Russia, many of the factors generally conceded as encouraging or discouraging manufacturing do not apply as they do in noncommunist countries. In the Soviet, the government may decide to build factories in locations which might never be chosen if left to private enterprise.

In World War I, the United States built huge shipyards near Hog Island, along the Delaware River; and in World War II, the government was forced to construct 28 synthetic-rubber and rubber-ingredients plants which were sold to private industry after the war. These plants were widely distributed throughout the United States; the wide distribution came partly from political pressure exerted by certain states and partly through a desire to scatter the risk of attack from the air. During the same war, the United States made gifts to private industry, or what was practically the same as gifts, for expansion of steel plants and other manufacturing facilities of military necessity.

Since World War II, America granted billions to Europe in the form of Marshall Plan aid, much of which was used for repairing and rebuilding old factories, and for constructing new ones; and in the past two decades, aid from the United States, Russia, and other powers has gone to India, Japan, China, Indonesia, the Middle East, Latin America, the new countries of Africa, and other nations. Large sums from these gifts have been allocated for building manufacturing plants. Many other examples of government aid to manufacturing can be cited.

Climate and People. The factors of energizing climate and an active, energetic, and inventive type of people may be considered together. The areas of greatest industrial development, east central North America and Europe, largely belong to humid continental and west-coast marine climatic types. In general, the west coast marine and those parts of the humid continental climate with the greatest oceanic influences have cold, but not extremely cold winters; warm but not hot summers; generally high relative humidity; ample, well-distributed precipitation; and frequent variability of weather brought about by a constant sequence of west-east moving cyclonic storms. Many believe that such atmospheric conditions are likely to encourage the greatest mental and physical activity, two very important factors in man's successful operation of the complexities of modern industry.

World Distribution of Manufacturing

The United States. (Figs. 17–7 and 17–8) One of the most striking facts about the distribution of manufacturing in the United States is the size of the nonindustrial sections. Even in the East the rugged terrain of the Appalachians discourages factory building except along mountain borders or along passes like that of the Mohawk gateway. Large regions of the West such as the Great Plains, the Rocky Mountains, the desert and semi-desert Intermontane Plateaus, the Cascades, the Klamath, and the Sierra Nevada Mountains show up as blank or nearly blank sections on any manufacturing map of

Fig. 17–7   United States: Major Manufacturing Regions. When a line is drawn (1) from Baltimore through central West Virginia, Louisville, St. Louis, to Kansas City; (2) northward to Minneapolis-St. Paul; and (3) east through central Wisconsin, Michigan, New York, and central New England; the area of northeastern United States included in the irregular quadrilateral encompasses nearly three fourths of the nation's manufacturing. The term "belt" is sometimes applied to this quadrilateral; but if "belt" is used it should connote a series of distinctly separate manufacturing regions. Other manufacturing regions of the United States are growing, but those of the Northeast keep growing at the same time. (*Courtesy E. Willard Miller,* A Geography of Manufacturing, *1962, Prentice-Hall, Inc.*)

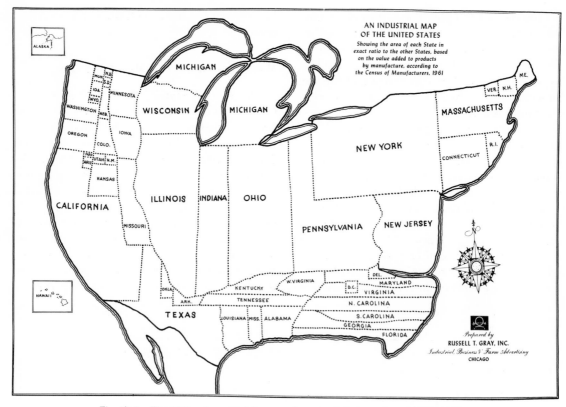

Fig. 17–8   The 1961 value added by manufacturing is 5 times that of 1929, $164,-292,449,000 to $30,591,435,000. The 9 leading states in order of importance, 1961, New York, California, Ohio, Illinois, Pennsylvania, Michigan, New Jersey, Indiana, and Wisconsin add more to the value by manufacturing than all the rest of the states put together. Production workers in 1961 numbered 11,790,056; in 1920 the figure was 8,369,705. The wage figure for 1961 was $54,792,236,000 as against $10,884,919,000 for 1929. (*Courtesy Russell T. Gray, Inc.*)

the United States. Along the west coast, however, industrial concentration appears, especially around Los Angeles, San Francisco, Portland, and Seattle. Comparisons of current manufacturing intensity with that of earlier years show a great proportionate increase in the West. A map of the South shows many blank places, but manufacturing there is increasing rapidly, and future maps may show less empty space.

The greatest United States industrial concentration lies in a quadrilateral extending from Baltimore northeast to Boston; north from Boston through the Connecticut and Mohawk valleys, the Lower Lakes area, and on to Minneapolis and St. Paul; from the twin cities south to Kansas City; and on east through St. Louis and the Ohio River region to Baltimore. Minor areas may be found beyond the border of the

quadrilateral, but industrial intensity is not nearly as great.

This great industrial region, one of the greatest in the world, is based upon all or nearly all the factors already listed and described as encouraging industrial development. These include a great variety of raw materials needed in industry, but not all; great quantities of high-grade easily mined Appalachian coal; hydroelectric power based upon dependable precipitation and suitable land forms; regional supplies of petroleum and natural gas or ample quantities available by pipe line, barge, or ocean-tanker transport; excellent roads for trucks; railroads for trains; and the Great Lakes inland waterway for ships; an energizing climate for a large labor supply with high living standards; this, together with the remaining population, densely concentrated and also with high living standards, provides a good market and ample capital for industrial development and expansion.

One dangerous disadvantage to such a huge concentration of industry is the excellent target it offers to enemy attack. The North American Ruhr has many advantages for peace-time production, but it must be strongly guarded to minimize damage in case of war.

Canada. The greatest manufacturing region of Canada lies in the country's south-pointing lake peninsula and in the St. Lawrence valley, both just to the north of the United States industrial quadrilateral. Power is available in the form of coal down the St. Lawrence from Nova Scotia or across the lake from Pennsylvania; much of the power used, however is hydroelectric, which is based upon ample precipitation and rolling terrain resulting from contact between weak rocks of the lowland and the bordering resistant rocks of the more rugged Canadian Shield. Oil and gas are now piped to the head of the Great Lakes from the petroleum fields of the prairie provinces. Labor and markets are important factors also because most of Canada's population with its high living standards lives in the manufacturing region. Iron for steel, forests for newsprint, and grain for flour are important raw materials that are not far away. The climate is energizing. Both American and Canadian capital are available for industrial investments. No wonder the United States quadrilateral could well be extended north with the total result listed under the name of the Anglo-American industrial quadrilateral.

Western Europe. (Fig. 17–9) Most of the great west European industrial region had its beginnings in highly developed home industries even before the Industrial Revolution; but, with the coming of factory methods, manufacturing expansion was aided by the presence of nearby coal fields. This power factor, so important in the location of many manufacturing regions, is found around the Pennines in England, as well as in Wales and Scotland; a westward extension of the Ruhr field lies in northern France and in Belgium; in Germany the Ruhr coal underlies the area between the Ruhr and Lippe rivers. In Saxony, lignite replaces bituminous coal, which is available again in the Bohemian basin of Czechoslovakia and in the Silesian fields of Poland.

Ample coal with Lorraine ores lying within western Europe is supplemented by foreign iron to supply heavy industries. Blast furnaces, steel rolling mills, and foundries are located on or close to the coal fields; and glass, pottery, textiles, chemical, and other industries are not far away.

Germany, Britain, and France are the three leading industrial countries of western Europe, and have been for many decades. The first two are self sufficient in coal, but France is not, and partly as a result has made more progress with hydroelectric power than her two neighbors. None of the three has an adequate local supply of oil and gas; in fact there is an insufficient quantity in all of western Europe. However, North African and Middle East fields are relatively near and the great industrial region receives most of its petroleum from these foreign sources.

West European industry was badly hurt by two world wars; and after World War II, it could be said truthfully that the region had too much old industrial equipment, too limited amounts of private risk capital, shortages in many raw materials, and a lack of political and economic unity.

In the early 1960's the above disadvantages are no longer active; and the change has come largely as a result of man-made factors. Important among these influences has been the Marshall Plan, which gave the war torn countries a big push on the road to economic and political recovery. This Plan, that gave western Europe 50 billion United States dollars between 1945 and 1957, contributed new industrial equipment, risk capital, many needed raw materials, and a lift to economic and political morale.

Trends toward economic unity advanced with the formation of the European Coal and Steel Community in 1951—a Community composed of Belgium, France, West Germany, Italy, Luxembourg, and the Netherlands. Its main purpose was to provide free trade in coal, iron ore, iron and steel, and steel scrap among the participating countries. In 1959, these same nations started Euratom to provide a common market for nuclear products; and in the same year they fashioned the Common Market to be completely implemented within a decade or

MANUFACTURING
REGIONS

CENTRAL
SWEDEN

SCOTTISH
LOWLANDS

NORTHEAST
ENGLAND

EASTERN PENNINES

LANCASHIRE

MIDLANDS

SOUTH WALES

LONDON   LOWER
RHINE   BERLIN

MIDDLE
ELBE

NORTHERN FRANCE   MIDDLE
BELGIUM-LIMBURG   RHINE   SILESIA

PARIS   WESTERN
CZECHOSLOVAKIA

LORRAINE   NECKAR
BASIN

ALSACE

SWISS
PLATEAU
CENTRAL   PO PLAINS
FRANCE

MILES
0   300

Fig. 17–9   European Manufacturing Regions. Europe has been a leader in manufacturing for more than two hundred years. In 1960, European factories (the Soviet
Union not included) employed about 40 million workers. The United Kingdom (8
million), West Germany (7½ million), and France (5 million) accounted for approximately half of the 1960 total. In eastern Europe (8 million), Czechoslovakia, East
Germany, and Poland are the major industrial countries. (*Courtesy E. Willard Miller,*
A Geography of Manufacturing, *1962, Prentice-Hall, Inc.*)

more. In 1961, the United Kingdom and several
additional European countries applied for
membership in the Common Market.

The lowering of trade barriers brought about
by the formation of these organizations has increased industrial progress significantly; for
trade moves among the Common Market countries somewhat as it does among the various
states of the United States. An increase in intercontinental trade has paralleled inter-European

commerce. One factor contributing to this advance has been the zeal of West European manufacturers to produce products that meet the
exact specifications of buyers in other continents.
West Germans have been particularly zealous in
this practice.

Besides encouraging trade agreements that
have stimulated manufacturing, west European
governments have actively assisted industry in
low interest government loans, tax inducements

to promote private investments, and preferential rates for electricity, gas, and water. Moreover, it is customary for several West European governments to invest more in both nationalized and private industry than they receive from industrial taxation.

Again, government industrial planning has helped. For example, the Monnet Plan of France, established in 1947 has specific aims to channel investments into six key industries—agricultural machinery, cement, coal, electrical power, iron and steel, and transportation—all of which are considered basic for industrial growth.

As a result of these and other man-made factors, manufacturing in western Europe has advanced steadily since World War II—much faster than in the United States. To cite one example, western Europe's output of steel rose from 57 million tons in 1950 to 118 million tons in 1960, a ten-year growth of over 100 per cent. During the same decade the United States had a growth in steel production from 97 million tons to 99 million tons, an advance of but 2 per cent.

Russia. (Fig. 17–10) With the implementation of the first five-year plan in 1928, efforts were made to develop new centers of industry. But great expansion meant a huge capital outlay for factories and also for rail facilities. Largely because of these obstacles, the initial

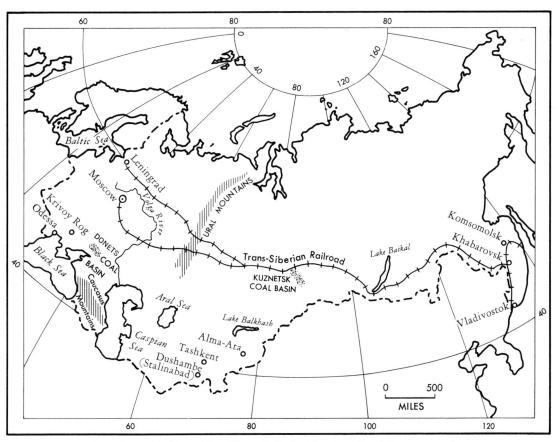

Fig. 17–10 Significant Place Names in Soviet Manufacturing. All place names included in the text description of Russian manufacturing appear on the map; these locations may assist students in learning the areas of Russia's major industrial regions. No attempt was made to show any Soviet railroads except the Trans-Siberian direct from Moscow and from Leningrad. Even the rail connection between Moscow and Leningrad is not shown.

industrial emphasis was placed upon the utilization of known mineral bases and the existing railway system.

Although the Soviet Empire now is known to be rich in coal, petroleum, and other power resources as well as in a great diversity of minerals, the minerals best known and most highly developed during the tsarist period were coal and iron ore. Of course these were essential to planned Soviet industrialization. Some of the already utilized coal and iron resources in the late 1920's were the Donets and Kuznetsk coal basins and the Krivoy Rog and Ural iron ores. Between 1928 and 1940 great concentration of heavy metallurgical industries near these resource bases took place. Iron and coal moved between Krivoy Rog and the Donets Basin, and the same bases of heavy industry moved between the Kuznetsk Basin and the Urals.

It is a good thing for Russia that Stalin developed the Ural metallurgical complex before World War II, because the Germans took over the Donbas Region completely during the early stages of the invasion; they also damaged the Central and Leningrad industrial areas with aerial attack about the same time. In all, the Germans occupied Russian territory where approximately 40 per cent of the population lived and where they produced about 60 per cent of the pre-war coal, iron ore, steel, and aluminum.

Russia is a good example of war influence upon the movement of factories and upon the changes in site location for the development of new manufacturing plants. In 1941 the Russians moved over 400 factories to the Urals, over 200 to western Siberia, and over 200 into Central Asia. Moreover during the war years of 1941 to 1945 over 2000 large factories were newly built in these regions.

After the war, industrial objectives stressed the reconstruction of war devastated areas as well as a continued growth of manufacturing in the East. In spite of the major emphasis upon expansion of eastern industry, the region west of the Urals possessed about two thirds of the nation's fixed assets in the late 1950's.

The main reason for Russia's enormous industrial growth since the Revolution has been the consistently followed goal to change a predominantly agricultural economy into an industrial one. This has been achieved by (1)

making enormous capital investment in industrial facilities; (2) by instituting allied technical programs for training engineers and skilled workers; and (3) by widespread exploration for industrial raw materials within the Soviet Union. Since the early 1950's, a full range of geological surveys has been in progress, and the discovery and development of natural resources, especially minerals has been phenomenal.

Another goal stressed in all the plans since 1928 was the growth of capital goods industries over the manufacturing of consumer goods. Examples to show that this goal has been achieved follow. Between 1928 and 1959, production of capital goods increased 90 fold while the increase for consumer goods was only fifteen times. The 1959 output of machine tools was about 90 times that of 1928, steel 14 times greater, coal 19 times more, and sulphuric acid 40 times more. In contrast the manufacture of cotton fabrics in 1959 was only a little over twice the rate of 1928.

Today the factories of European Russia lie largely in a triangular-shaped area outlined by Leningrad on the north, Odessa on the south, and the Urals to the east. Within this triangle are five major industrial regions that produce about 70 per cent of Russia's manufactures. The five may be called (1) the Leningrad District, which because of its outlet on the sea, was an important manufacturing center in tsarist days; (2) the Central Region, which focuses upon Moscow and leads all regions in industrial production; (3) the South, which includes the Donets coal and Krivoy Rog iron ore; (4) the Middle Volga with the richest oil fields of the Soviet Empire together with a great development of hydroelectric power; and (5) the Urals, which are highly mineralized and which provided a great industrial support to the Russian military effort in the Second World War.

Outside Russia's major industrial triangle, other prominent manufacturing sections include (1) the Kuznetsk Basin, which has one of the richest coal deposits in the world and which originally procured iron from the Urals to develop an important steel industry. Now enough iron has been discovered within the general region to make the area almost self-sufficient in iron ore. The growth of steel manufacturing together with a wide diversity of other factories has made the Kuznetsk Basin the greatest industrial region in Siberia; (2) the Caucasus with its rich metallic minerals, a long history of handicraft industry, and the first Russian oil development; (3) Central Asia from Dushambe (Stalinabad) through Tashkent to Alma-Ata, where isolation has forced (a) the development of as many industries as can be closely allied with the regional economy; and (b) has limited production for national consumption; (4) Lake Baikal, where a small industrial growth has occurred along the Trans-Siberian railroad largely to assist in agricultural and mineral development; (5) Far East, where again the industrial expansion lies close to the Trans-Siberian railroad and focuses upon the towns of Vladivostok, Khabarovsk, and Komsomolsk. Railroads and water routes are major influences in the choice of site locations for industrial expansion.

In conclusion it may be noted that Russian factory development is characterized by adequate power, a wide diversity and a large quantity of raw materials, not the best transport (with about 90 per cent of the traffic moving over long distances by rail), a climate less favorable to manufacturing than that of western Europe and eastern North America; generally adequate labor supply (especially with the use of enemy laborers in slave labor camps within comparatively recent time), good markets; government capital; and a large industrial population. Finally in evaluating the great progress of Russian manufacturing during the past few decades, it should be stressed that man-made factors have contributed fully as much as the physical environment, which in general has favored great industrial expansion.

Japan. (Fig. 17–11) Like Russia, the growth of large scale industrial activities in most Asian countries is comparatively recent. However, Japan is an exception, and long before World War II this Britain of the Orient had made considerable progress in modern manufacturing. In fact, well established handicraft industries provided bases for the evolution of a fast growing industrial development after 1870. By 1937, industrial production was probably twice that of the entire continent of Asia excluding Russian Siberia. And during the decade of the 1930's, when Japan was committed to a program of military conquest, growth of heavy industry and

domestic machinery manufacturing was impressive.

All types of Japanese industry were badly damaged in World War II. Moreover, after-war recovery was extremely slow. This was caused partly by repressive measures of the conquering powers who feared another surge of Nipponese industrial power. However, in the late 1940's and early 1950's the war victors, primarily the United States, started to encourage an expanded manufacturing growth, largely to counteract the growth of Chinese communism. The Korean War stimulated a further redevelopment of industry when the demands of the United States and its allies gave a ready market for manufactured goods from Japan. Progress has continued throughout the 1950's and early 1960's. In 1963 emphasis is placed upon heavy machinery, electrical equipment, and chemicals, with lesser stress given to the traditional industries such as textiles and nonendurable consumer goods. Nevertheless, textiles still employ more people than the manufacture of industrial machinery, but the latter contributes more to the national product.

Japan's leading advantage over most competitors selling manufactures in international trade has been cheap labor. Other than that, the country has a great variety of metals, but limited in amounts, with reserves of copper and silver leading. Hydroelectric power resources give more promise than coal or petroleum. Reserves of oil are insufficient for national needs; and those of coal are generally adequate in tonnage, but not all of them are of good coking quality. Japan needs many raw materials, a dependable foreign market, and more capital. On the constructive side, the country has an energizing climate with a strong marine influence; people are energetic and industrious; dense population, with low, but rising, living standards gives a fair local market; but Japan must export, or be subsidized, in order to survive. Transport is good by rail, by road, and by sea; and the size, narrowness, and good natural harbors of the islands all make cheap ocean shipping easily accessible to most sections.

Most Japanese manufacturing areas are located along the coast and upon relatively level terrain, a scarce topographic type in Japan. Major regions include (1) the Kwanto Plain,

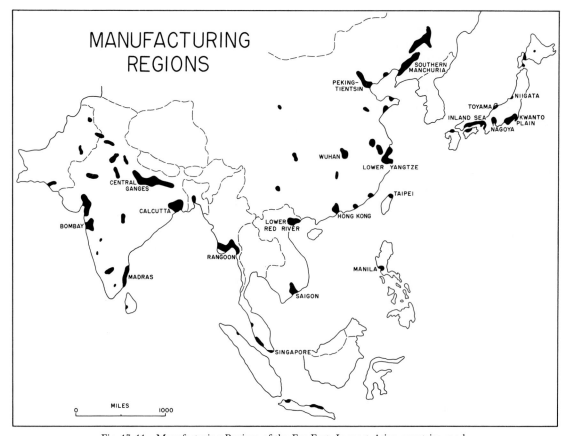

Fig. 17–11   Manufacturing Regions of the Far East. In most Asian countries, modern, large scale industry is of recent origin. Since 1945, the greatest expansion has occurred on mainland China, Taiwan, Hong Kong, India, Pakistan, South Korea, the Philippines, and Japan. Perhaps Japanese post-war industrial growth has been the most spectacular of all; and that island nation may well deserve the name "Britain of the Far East" as far as manufacturing is concerned. (*Courtesy E. Willard Miller,* A Geography of Manufacturing, *1962, Prentice-Hall, Inc.*)

(2) the Kinki Node, (3) the Nagoya Node, and (4) the Kita-Kyushu Node.

The Kwanto Plain centers on Tokyo and Yokohama. Factors favoring manufacturing include Tokyo's political and cultural leadership, good banking and commercial facilities, a large local market of about ten million people, a consistent supply of pure water, good harbors, skilled labor, and the country's largest area of level land. Industry is characterized by great diversity and accounts for Japan's greatest regional production.

The Kinki Node centers upon the cities of Osaka, Kobe, and Kyoto. Like the Kwanto Plain, industry here is also diversified. The district produces about one third of Japan's iron and steel, a little less than half of the country's rolling mill output, and significant quantities of aircraft, chemicals, processed food, foundry products, machinery, refined oil, shipbuilding, and textiles.

The Nagoya Node developed at the head of Ise Bay on the Mino-Owari Plain and is noted for its light manufacturing and small scale industry. It is the only Japanese manufacturing region in which textiles are most important; and its pottery industry, based upon local clays, is the largest in the islands.

The Kita-Kyushu Node occupies northern Kyushu and the extreme southwestern part of Honshu and is well known for its stress upon heavy metal industries. Nearness to Japan's most important coal fields gave early encouragement to the Yawata Iron and Steel Works, which might be called the United States Steel of Japan. This manufacturing region is the only Nipponese industrial section where textiles are of little significance.

China. Since World War II, several factors have encouraged industrial growth in Asian countries other than Japan. First, political changes have been numerous. Before the Second World War, Afghanistan, China, Iran, Japan, Nepal, and Thailand were the only independent nations of the Far East. After 1945, eleven more countries gained independence—Burma, Cambodia, Ceylon, the Federation of Malaysia, India, Indonesia, Korea, Laos, Pakistan, the Philippines, and Vietnam. In most of these newly independent countries economic planning became one of the first aims of the new governments; and industrialization, together with technical training for workers appeared conspicuously in almost every plan. It is the hope that an increase in manufacturing will raise living standards, and all countries are deeply interested in that. Some have given aid to private industrial enterprise, some have eliminated private industry with the government becoming the entrepreneur, and all have been receptive to foreign aid from one source or another.

The most industrial progress since 1945 has occurred in China, both the mainland and Taiwan; India; Hong Kong; Pakistan; the Philippines; and South Korea. It may be useful to look briefly at conditions in mainland China and India.

China has one of the world's largest resources of coal. It is found in every province, with especially large quantities in Shansi and Shensi. Known reserves of petroleum are small, and little hydroelectric power is developed; however bases for waterpower are good in several places, particularly at Ichang on the Middle Yangtze. Significant quantities of iron occur in Manchuria, along the Middle Yantgze, and in the province of Szechwan. Antimony, bauxite, copper, lead, manganese, mercury, sulphur, tin, tungsten, and zinc are present, and some in significant amounts. It must be remembered, however, that China has over a half billion people and that the per capita mineral resources fall short of those in Russia and the United States.

The greatest Chinese industrial development is located in North China, especially in Southern Manchuria and in the provinces of Hopei, Shantung, and Shansi. The main reasons for manufacturing in these locations are (1) the availability of coal and iron; (2) a good start upon heavy industry in Southern Manchuria had been made by the Japanese in the 1930's; (3) transportation is better developed than in most of China; and (4) the area lies close to Russia, which once gave assistance and protection. Other manufacturing centers appear in the Yangtze Lowlands and in the Canton region. Here again, raw materials, power, and useful transportation are easily available.

In the first government planning, emphasis was placed upon heavy industry in a few large centers; but the later planning includes stress upon a wide distribution of smaller manufacturing activities with more attention given to the processing of agricultural products.

India. Manufacturing in India resembles that in China with certain differences. Handicraft industries are widespread. The nation has far more iron, but probably less coal, than China. Neither country has much petroleum, but hydroelectric developments are promising in both nations. Since 1956 iron and steel, other metallurgical development, engineering, and chemical industries have increased significantly; but textile manufacturing, mainly cotton and jute, still accounts for about 40 per cent of the country's industrial output. Cheap labor, as in China and Japan, may be the country's greatest manufacturing asset, but cheap labor suggests a limited local market for manufactured goods among a dense population with low living standards. Tropical and subtropical climates are hardly stimulating factors for the hundreds of millions of people. Although long British occupation brought a fair railroad net, built largely for military control, neither rail nor road transport lends enough encouragement for rapid growth in large scale manufacturing. Few good harbors indent the regular shoreline for ships that should bring many raw materials that are lacking. In most industries skilled technicians, heavy machinery, progressive management, and private capital are in short supply.

Four manufacturing regions are important: (1) the Bengal-Bihar Triangle includes Cal-

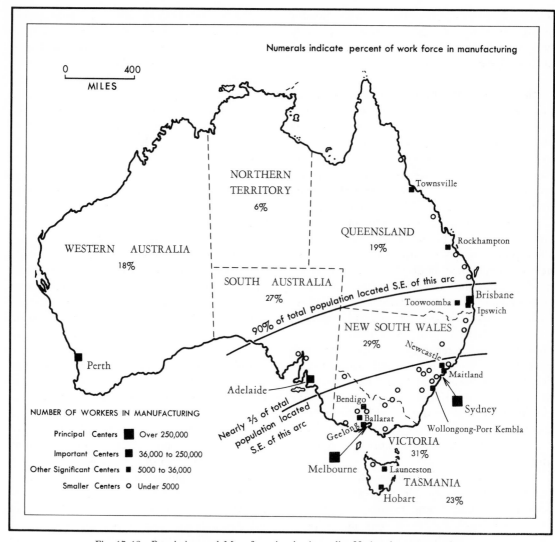

Fig. 17–12   Population and Manufacturing in Australia. Notice the concentration of population and manufacturing in southeast Australia. Melbourne and Sydney each have over 250,000 workers engaged in manufacturing. (*Drawn from Map issued by the Department of Trade and Industry, Australia*)

cutta, Jamshedpur, and Asansol; and is favored by land and sea transportation, Damodar Valley coal, Singhbhum iron ore, and nearby jute; (2) the Bombay-Sholapur Node is located near Dekkan cotton, which it uses in textile manufacturing; but other industries are slowly expanding; (3) the Ahmadabad-Surat region also produces large quantities of cotton goods together with pottery and chemicals; and (4) the Central Ganges region has the largest woolen and leather industries in India as well as flour mills, sugar refineries, cotton factories, chemical

works, and many plants producing small consumer goods.

Australia. (Figs. 17–12 and 17–13) Continents of the southern hemisphere generally lack one important asset, coal, so significant in world manufacturing for centuries. Hemisphere reserves are probably less than 5 per cent of the world total. Yet Australia has most of these southern hemisphere reserves, an adequate amount to power manufacturing for a population slightly over 10 million. Iron is available in every province, but most iron and steel is produced in southeast Australia with high grade coal from the local Newcastle field, and iron ore from the Eyre Peninsula. This heavy industry contributes an important portion of southeast Australia's 80 per cent of the continent's industrial output.

A major demand for iron and steel is for agricultural implements, railway equipment, autos, ships, and similar products. Besides these commodities, local manufacturing produces a large fraction of the country's requirements in a great diversity of products such as paper, rubber, chemicals, plastics, and drugs. Nevertheless, the nation still imports from one fifth to one fourth of its manufacturing needs.

One Australian worker out of three is busy in industry. The production of machines and the assembly of vehicles rank first in worker employment. Textiles and clothing industries rank second, with half as many employees. Food processing, brewing, and related industries are third in importance.

The growth of Australian manufacturing has

been aided by overseas industry. Foreign firms developed a strong demand for their products and then built factories inside the tariff wall rather than risk the loss of markets to local manufacturers. Another significant fact about Australian manufacturing, and that of all southern continents, is the part played by World Wars I and II. These conflicts literally forced Australia into greater industrial development.

Added power for future industry may come from recent discoveries of petroleum, long a dream of the Commonwealth. While present production in Queensland meets only a fraction of the demand, its discovery bears out the claim of geologists that the continent is worth probing. A pipeline now carries oil from the Moonie field to Brisbane 200 miles away.

Latin America. (Fig. 17–14) Latin American manufacturing has been slow in making progress for several reasons: among these are, (1) the prevailing poverty and illiteracy have limited both the local market and the availability of skilled labor; (2) for centuries land ownership

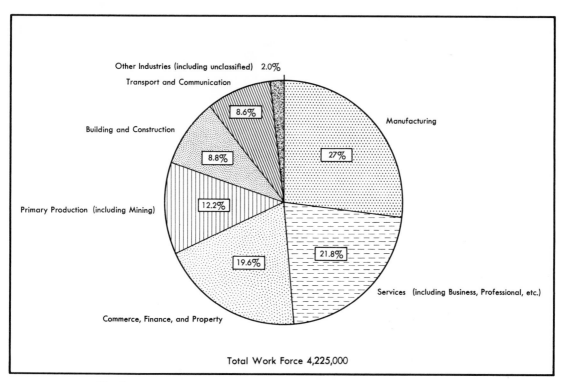

Fig. 17–13   Composition of Australian Work Force. (*Statistics from Department of Trade and Industry, Australia*)

Fig. 17–14   Latin American Manufacturing. Latin America's entrance into modern manufacturing is of recent origin; and until about 1945 most end products resulted from the processing of local raw materials. Now more complex industrial developments are beginning to emerge in the A-B-C countries of South America as well as in North America's Mexico. Puerto Rico, not shown on the map, has hundreds of branch factories belonging to parent concerns in the United States. (*Courtesy E. Willard Miller,* A Geography of Manufacturing, *1962, Prentice-Hall, Inc.*)

has given the individual more prestige than any commercial or industrial investment; (3) of all the continents, South America has the least coal, long the major base for industrial development; moreover, few if any countries approach the self-sufficiency needed as a base for modern manufacturing; and (4) transport within each country and among the various countries is inadequate.

The A-B-C Latin American countries (Argentina, Brazil, and Chile), Colombia, and Mexico show more industrial progress than the remaining nations. Brazil has a small but well developed iron and steel complex at Volta Redonda. Iron comes from the Itabira region, rich in quantity and quality. Some inferior coal moves from Santa Catarina and Rio Grande do Sul; much potential hydroelectric power is available nearby. Other manufactures include electrical goods, chemicals, textiles and many processed local raw materials. Three fourths of the huge country's manufacturing takes place on the East Central Plateau, in the Federal District and in the states of Espirito Santo, Minas Gerais Rio de Janeiro, and Sao Paulo.

Argentina's manufacturing district is located around the urban center of Buenos Aires. The nation lacks iron and coal as well as many raw materials for modern industry. Local petroleum may be sufficient, but Argentina long kept out foreign exploitation and so far has been unable to produce enough oil for national requirements. Although costs of production are high, the country has several well-developed consumer and capital goods industries. Leather and textile needs are well supplied, and advances have been made in repairing and building ships.

Almost all of Chile's modern manufacturing occurs within the middle portion of that elongated country—the portion with the Mediterranean climate. The processing of local raw materials is important, and a small but uptodate iron and steel plant is in operation. Local wool is available for textiles, but cotton is imported. The national market is small in a country with only about eight million people.

Most of Colombia's population lives in the highlands, and here one may see a start towards modern industry, especially in the region around Bogotá, Medellín, and Cali. Local raw materials provide bases for the manufacture of apparel, chemicals, food products, footwear, and textiles. The country has a fair supply of

petroleum, little coal, and considerable hydroelectric power potential. No great supply of iron, as in Brazil, is available.

Probably Mexico is making more manufacturing progress than any other Latin American country. It has a flourishing iron and steel plant in the Northeast—an industry based upon Durango iron and Sabinas coal. Another prosperous manufacturing area, much more diversified, occurs around Mexico City. Here, textile manufacturing, especially cotton based upon local production, is well advanced. Petroleum reserves are large, hydroelectric power potential is good, and there is a fair supply of coal. Silver, lead, zinc, iron, and other metallic minerals are present in adequate amounts; and huge quantities of sulphur are being exploited. Thus, with a growing local and export market, and a relatively favorable government attitude toward local and foreign investment, modern industry seems likely to continue to expand.

Africa. (Figs. 17–15 and 17–16) African manufacturing is largely in the beginning stage, but the industrial situation is spotty. For example good progress has been made in the Union of South Africa; fair advances have

Fig. 17–15 Making Cloth in Ghana. The center of the Kente cloth industry is at Bonwire, near Kumasi. This material has been used traditionally for making the robes of Ashanti Chiefs. The primitive handicraft industry shown here contrasts sharply with the modern cotton manufacturing at Mahalla, Egypt. (*Courtesy United Nations*)

Fig. 17–16   Steel-Making Materials at Helwan's Iron and Steel Plant near Cairo. While Egypt's major manufactures, textiles, leather goods, and food stuffs employ thousands of workers, great priority is now given to the development of heavy industry. Local limestone, manganese, feldspar, and iron, all important in steel making, are available; but there is no coal and only limited amounts of local oil. The new Aswan Dam will increase power facilities; and with a good iron supply only 30 miles to the east, more steel mills may be built. (*Courtesy United Arab Republic Tourist Office*)

occurred in North Africa, especially in Egypt; and little change appears in much of the Congo.

Modern industry faces several handicaps: (1) colonial powers long looked at Africa as a source of raw materials and as a market for manufactured goods; (2) in the majority of countries, industry started with non-African capital and entrepreneurship, and the local population supplied nothing but labor; (3) transportation is developed inadequately in most countries; (4) the market is small, for the natives have low buying power, and foreigners with high living standards are limited in number.

In South Africa two manufacturing districts stand out, (1) the Southern Transvaal and (2) the coastal cities of Capetown, Durban, and Port Elizabeth. The first district has well developed iron and steel plants at Vanderbjil Park and at Pretoria. These supply 90 per cent of national requirements. South African iron and steel provides 80 per cent of the country's needs in heavy machinery. Access to local or nearby coal, iron, and limestone is favored by a well developed rail net.

Manufacturing in the coastal cities is quite diversified with an emphasis upon apparel, auto assembly, footwear, metal fabrication, paper, and textiles. In both manufacturing areas a subtropical climate is generally favorable.

In Egypt, lack of coal and a limited supply of petroleum force the country to take advantage of hydroelectric possibilities of the Nile. These appear primarily at Aswan, where the contact zone between weak and resistant rocks produces natural water falls; and man accentuates the natural fall by building a huge dam. Aswan power is used for many industries; but one of the most important occurs in the manufacture of fertilizers needed to stimulate Egypt's annual two- and three-crop agriculture. A modern textile mill is located at Mahalla. Besides Egyptian manufactures of cotton, wool, rayon, and silk, factories supply glassware, soap, pottery, sugar, leather, and other items made from local and imported materials. Climate, low standards of living, with resultant limited market, poor transport, limited raw materials and capital, all handicap progress. However, industrialization is one way to relieve the great population pressure on the land and to take advantage of the major manufacturing asset, cheap labor.

QUESTIONS, EXERCISES, AND PROBLEMS

1. Give examples of primitive manufacturing for subsistence purposes; for commercial purposes.
2. Contrast modern manufacturing with other productive industries. Where is the greatest concentration of modern manufacturing? Explain the influence of raw materials on the location of manufacturing. Do the same for each of the following conditions: markets, transportation, fuel and power resources, labor, capital, attitude of the government, climate, and people.
3. Describe the location of the major manufacturing areas in the United States. Point out locations of lesser industrial development. Describe the location of Canada's leading industrial area. What causes this concentration of manufacturing?
4. Comment upon the location of western Europe's industrial region. Give major bases for manufacturing development here. Name and describe major manufacturing regions in the U.S.S.R. Do the same for Japan, India, South Africa, and China.
5. Indicate the causes for Russia's great industrial growth; causes for the slow growth of manufacturing in Latin America; the handicaps for African manufacturing; the bases for Australian industrial development; causes for greater industrial development in North China than in South China; direction of Russia's war time factory movement. Summarize major principles for industrial location.
6. Identify the following: hard bakery goods; flux; sources of scrap iron; Connellsville seam; Pittsburgh-Plus; Monongahela; Sparrows Point; Birmingham; Arvida; Kitimat; source of original capital for New England's cotton industry; American Ruhr; Port Kembla; Volta Redonda; Wankie; Pretoria; Bogotá; Medellín; Itabira; Sabinas; Durango; Mahalla; Aswan; Donbas; A-B-C countries; Monnet Plan; Common Market; European Coal and Steel Community; United States manufacturing Quadrilateral; Mouska.

SELECTED REFERENCES

Bank of Montreal, "Industrial Expansion in Canada," *Business Review,* Oct. 26, 1962.

Burck, Gilbert and Parker, Sanford, "The Prime Mover Begins to Move, Investment Made by Manufacturing Industries," *Fortune,* Feb. 1963.

Chang, Kuei-sheng, "Geographical Bases for Industrial Development in Northwestern China," *Economic Geography,* Oct. 1963, pp. 341–50.

Chilcote, R. H., "Spain's Iron and Steel: Renovation of an Old Industry," *Geographical Review,* April 1963, pp. 247–62.

Clark, Paul, "Kitimat—A Saga of Canada," *Canadian Geographical Journal Reprint,* Ottawa.

Drake, Francis and Katherine, "They're Thinking Big Down Under," *Reader's Digest,* Oct. 1964, pp. 106–11.

Duncan, Craig, "The Aluminum Industry in Australia," *Geographical Review,* Jan. 1961, pp. 21–46.

Estall, R. C., "The Electronic Products Industry of New England," *Economic Geography,* July 1963, pp. 189–216.

Eyre, John D., "Industrial Growth in the Suwa Basin, Japan," *Geographical Review,* Oct. 1963, pp. 487–502. "Tokyo Influences in the Manufacturing Geography of Saitama Prefecture," *Economic Geography,* Oct. 1963, pp. 283–98.

Federal Reserve Bank of Boston, "Wages Across the Country," *New England Business Review,* Feb. 1962. See other Federal Reserve Bank Reports throughout the United States related to manufacturing.

Gildea, Ray Y. Jr., "Geographic Aspects of Industrial Growth in the Monterrey Region of Mexico," *Journal of Geography,* Jan. 1960, pp. 34–41.

Hamilton, F. E. I., "Location Factors in the Yugoslav Iron and Steel Industry," *Economic Geography,* Jan. 1964, pp. 46–64.

Linge, G. J. R., "The Diffusion of Manufacturing in Auckland, New Zealand," *Economic Geography,* Jan. 1963, pp. 23–39.

Lubar, Robert, "Old Europe's Young Again-and Fretting," *Fortune,* Feb. 1963.

McGovern, "Industrial Development in the Vancouver Area," *Economic Geography,* July 1961, pp. 189–206.

Michel, A. A. and Klain, S. A., "Current Problems of the Soviet Electric Power Industry," *Economic Geography,* July 1964, pp. 206–20.

Miller, E. Willard, *A Geography of Manufacturing,* Prentice-Hall, 1962; student assignments are suggested for this basic text.

Pred, A. R., "The Intrametropolitan Location of American Manufacturing," Annals of the Association of American Geographers, July 1964, pp. 165–80.

Rodgers, H. B., "The Changing Geography of the Lancashire Cotton Industry," *Economic Geography,* Oct. 1962, pp. 299–314.

The Conference Board, 460 Park Avenue, New York 22, N. Y., *Value Added by Manufacture,* June 29, 1962; also see many other graphic reports from the Board related to manufacturing.

Thoman, R. S. and Patton, D. J., *Focus on Geographic Activity,* McGraw-Hill, 1964, Chs. 19, 20, 21, 22, 23, 24, 25, and 26; "Lock Making: A Handicraft Industry in India"; "A Company in Potteries of England"; "A Soviet Iron and Steel Plant"; "An Organized Industrial District"; "A Modern Producer of Cotton Fabrics in an Underdeveloped Economy"; "A Textile Plant in Poland"; "Industrial Structure of the New York Garment Center"; "A New Hampshire Plant of Semiconductor Products."

Thompson, J. H. and Miyazaki, M., "A Map of Japan's Manufacturing," *Geographical Review,* Jan. 1959, pp. 1–17.

Thompson, J. H. and Lonsdale, R. E., "A Map of U.S.S.R. Manufacturing," *Economic Geography,* Jan. 1960, pp. 36–52.

White, Langdon and Chilcote, R. H., "Chile's New Iron and Steel Industry," *Economic Geography,* July 1961, pp. 258–66.

White, C. L. and Forde, H. M., "The Unorthodox San Francisco Bay Electronics Industry," *Journal of Geography,* Sept. 1960, pp. 251–58.

Chapter Eighteen

The Geography of Trade

Trade is likely to develop among nations or among individuals when one has a surplus of some commodity in which the other has a shortage and the other has a surplus in a product in which the first is short (Fig. 18–1). Surplus creates a desire or a demand to trade; shortage creates a desire or a demand to trade. Surpluses and shortages may occur in goods and services or in money, which is only a medium of exchange representing goods and services. Surpluses and shortages stimulate market development, and market prices are greatly influenced by supply and demand, unless, of course, a government institutes price controls.

An important fraction of the earth's economic products enters domestic and foreign trade before it reaches the ultimate consumer. Almost the entire output of certain crops moves thousands of miles to market. For example most natural rubber travels from southeast Asia to the United States and Europe. On the other hand, some commodities go no farther than local manufacture, local trade, and local consumption. Bricks exemplify this type of commodity, for, in contrast to natural rubber, almost the entire output is utilized in the immediate vicinity of the kilns.

Differences in Natural Resources Encourage Trade. Surpluses and shortages in commodities differ from country to country and from individual to individual. These differences may result from various causes, such as contrasts in the physical environment. Because Florida's east coast subtropical climate has a long growing season—in some years all 12 months are without frost—the state can produce surpluses of cane sugar and citrus fruit. New England's humid continental climates are unfavorable for both crops. But New England's Cape Cod produces a large fraction of the nation's cranberries;

and in the cold waters off the Maine coast, lobsters of high quality are trapped in surplus, and they are in demand in many parts of the entire country. Thus climatic differences create bases for interstate trade.

The highlands of Colombia produce some of the world's best coffee in the tierra templada climate. In the nearby tierra caliente lowlands of the Cauca and Magdalena valleys, bananas, sugar cane, cacao, and other tropical lowland crops are grown. Thus through differences in altitude, based upon differences in land forms, there is a good basis for intracountry trade within a horizontal distance of a few miles.

Near the mouth of the Volga River, where it empties into the Caspian Sea, are large sturgeon fisheries, the source of well-known Russian caviar. This resource is found in but few of the world's water bodies and offers the Soviet a basis for trade with the United States. Such a basis does not encourage important exchanges between the two countries, however, because trade is discouraged by two sharply opposed government philosophies. Differences in surpluses, may bring little trade when contrasts in basic human philosophies, such as that between communism and democracy, create international friction.

On the volcanic soils of the Deccan Plateau, just east of Bombay, fertility and soil-water retentiveness of the earth create conditions favorable for the growth of cotton. Here soil cooperates with marginal monsoon rainfall in contributing a background for surplus Indian cotton, an important export item. India, near Singhbhum, also has one of the largest deposits of high-grade iron ore in the world. Although local iron and steel are being produced in increasing quantities, large amounts of ore are available for international trade. Japan needs raw cotton and iron ore for her expanding manufacturing industries. Nearby fishing banks and

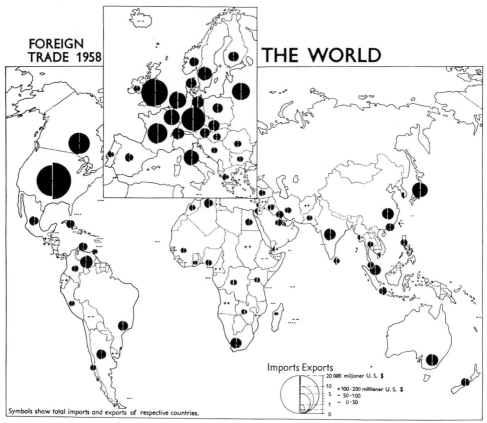

Fig. 18–1   World Foreign Trade 1958. Although the map is based upon 1958 statistics, the general pattern has not changed sharply. Note the large commerce of Anglo-American and Western Europe and the smaller amounts for Africa, Asia, Australia, and Latin America. The Japanese commerce looks large in comparison with that of India and China. Circles just north of South America are for the Dutch West Indies and for Trinidad. (*Courtesy G. Alexandersson and G. Norstrom,* World Shipping, *John Wiley & Sons, 1964*)

energetic Japanese fishermen provide millions of pounds of fish for local consumption and for export. Fish and cheap manufactured goods offer a good basis for exchange between iron-and-raw-cotton-poor Japan and dominantly agricultural India.

Trade based upon differences in plants, animals, minerals, soils, water bodies, land forms, and climate—the important features of the physical environment—may be termed an exchange of goods based upon contrasts in natural resources. This commerce is likely to show a greater degree of permanence than that based upon other conditions.

Differences in Stage of Industrial Development. For many years a large part of the United

States trade with Europe involved an exchange of American raw materials for European manufactured goods. It took America more than a century to catch up with the industrial nations of western Europe. Now the United States not only has become generally self-sufficient in manufacturing but a major exporter of industrial commodities as well. England exchanged manufactured goods for the raw materials produced in her colonies and dominions for centuries. India long complained about British discouragement of Indian industrial growth. This was an important cause for the achievement of Indian independence. Australia imported iron and steel manufactures from Britain for many years in spite of iron deposits in every province and coal resources in southeastern Australia.

Two World Wars cut off British industrial supplies and forced the continent down under into a path that is reaching closer and closer to industrial self-sufficiency. Canada has now awakened to her manufacturing opportunities and is depending less and less upon industrial shipments from Britain and other countries.

United States trade with Latin America is largely that of manufactured goods for raw materials. But Brazil, for example, is becoming aware of her own bases for manufacturing. She has one of the largest iron deposits in the world at Itabira in the province of Minas Geraes, and she is justly proud of her iron and steel plant at Volta Redonda, not far from Rio de Janeiro. Purchases of textile manufacturing machines from the United States have been significant. These purchases mean larger Brazilian manufacture of cotton cloth, so large that the largest Latin American country not only supplies her own needs for cotton cloth but also sells to other Latin American countries, a market formerly held more closely by the United States and other countries. Brazil lacks good coal, an important manufacturing base, but the nation may trade local iron for United States or European coal; and this Portuguese-speaking country can develop an important hydroelectric power potential to satisfy growing demands.

Highly industrialized Japan used a desire for raw materials as an important reason for entering World War II. The nation still needs trade based largely upon differences in the stage of industrial development. The country can well use natural resources from China, India, Burma, the various countries of former French Indochina, Thailand, Malaysia and Indonesia, and other countries of southeast Asia. Because of Japanese industrial advances such a trade could last several years. But the time will come when nations now supplying Nippon with raw materials will combine them with cheap labor, power, and metallic minerals to supply most of their own manufacturing needs. In each of the trading situations just described—Western Europe and the United States, England and her Dominions and colonies, United States and Latin America, Japan and southeast Asia—differences in stage of industrial development either have disappeared or are tending to disappear with the passage of time. This trade basis fails to show the permanence characteristic of commerce resulting from contrasting natural resources.

Trade Based on Differences in National, Tribal, or other Group Characteristics and Customs. A small part of world commerce is still based upon differences in national, tribal, or other group characteristics and customs (Fig. 18–2). Today, Iranian rugs, beautiful in design and with other unusual qualities of handwork are becoming rare. Such rugs are rapidly being superseded by machine made types. Thus, trade resulting from skills of Persian rug-makers' handwork is rapidly declining. For many years Navajo rugs, made in the United States, provided extra income for Indians of this tribe. Authentic Navajo rugs peculiar to the group are still produced, but quantities are limited.

In the Mouska of Cairo, Egypt, beautiful inlaid boxes are made by Egyptian hand labor with Egyptian designs; metal trays carry patterns and qualities peculiar to the Egyptian workers, who design and produce them, and to the country where they are made. Other com-

Fig. 18–2 Sunday Market in Cuzco. Not all of the interesting markets are in the Old World, for the New World has its share too. One unique trading area is that of the Sunday market in Cuzco, the capital of the old Inca Empire and now third largest city of Peru. (*Courtesy Standard Oil, New Jersey*)

Fig. 18–3 Swiss Wood Carver. The long cold season of a middle-latitude mountain location encourages an indoor industry taking time and skill to produce relatively valuable handicraft products from nearby forests. (*Courtesy Schweizer Heimatwerk and Consulate General, Switzerland*)

modities whose value depends upon qualities peculiar to a particular group custom, or national character include French perfumes, Madeira and Irish linens, Swedish and Czechoslovakian glassware, Swiss woodcarving (Fig. 18–3). British tweeds, Florentine leather goods, Indian brasswork, Italian statuary, and Guatemalan Indian blankets. This type of trade is small in comparison to that based upon differences in natural resources; and the amount is becoming smaller. True representatives of distinct tribal groups are gradually disappearing; national characteristics are becoming less noticeable; and old customs are slowly giving way to more uniformity.

Transportation. Easy routes of communication have an important bearing on the development and continuance of trade (Fig. 18–4). A useful example of this importance may be chosen from the early economic history of the United States; the opening of the Erie Canal route across the Mohawk gateway lowered freight rates materially. Carriage costs for goods dropped from $100 to $5 per ton because utilization of the only easy canal route through the Appalachian Highlands became a reality in 1825. Statesmen had known of this mountain break to the Lake Country and what is now the Corn Belt as early as the Revolutionary period; but profitable trade waited for half a century. The opening of the canal, and the consequent expansion of trade gave great impetus to rapid

urban development in New York City (see Fig. 6–2).

In May 1954, the St. Lawrence Waterway Bill became a law. The long delay in passage was influenced by strong pressure groups who feared loss of trade resulting from the completion of the route. Buffalo, which profits by the movement of commodities from the Middle West to the Eastern Seaboard through that city, opposed the waterway. Railway labor feared that it would divert rail traffic to ships on the Great Lakes–St. Lawrence route. The coal-mining industry objected on the ground that the waterway would enable foreign countries to send coal by ship to North Central United States at a lower price than Pennsylvanian producers could send it by rail. Maritime New England believed that the opening of seaports in the Middle West would harm Boston, the northernmost of the large Atlantic ports of the United States. The Mississippi Valley Association opposed the project for fear that goods now transported to the sea south along the Mississippi would move east through the Great Lakes. Louisiana and Texas were against the change because of the possibility that New Orleans and Houston might lose some of their trade to Great Lakes ports.

Land forms and water bodies are significant transport influences in the examples cited, and one sees the importance of earth surface features upon the course and character of trade. Another example taken from the United States will show how topography may influence transport and the kind of trade characteristic of a region. In inaccessible parts of the Appalachian Mountains, moonshiners distill whiskey illegally (Fig. 18–5). Corn, which is their chief crop, cannot be taken to the lowland market cheaply for lack of good roads. Whiskey is only one thirtieth as bulky as the corn from which it is made. Cost of transport is thus reduced so that the mountaineer can market this product in the lowlands at a profit. This trade formerly was much more important than it is today, for the coming of motor vehicles and good roads has minimized its advantages except in extremely isolated areas.

Mountain and plateau topography throughout central Asia has limited transport and the overland trade depending upon adequate trans-

Fig. 18–4   World Travel Time is Shrinking. Man's inventions in all kinds of transportation—ships and harbor facilities; trains, railroads, and terminals; motor vehicles and roads; airplanes and various types of equipment—all these and many more are economizing on travel time and expense. Thus with isolation disappearing and travel becoming easy, the world seems smaller than a century ago. (*E. I. du Pont de Nemours & Co., Inc.*)

Fig. 18–5   Hillside Still in the Tennessee Mountains. All materials must be carried to and from the still, whose chief locational advantage is seclusion. During much of the year, dense foliage of broadleaf deciduous trees effectively screens operations from both ground and air; but from November to April, when trees are almost bare of leaves, chances of discovery are greater. (*Courtesy Tennessee Alcohol Tax Division*)

Fig. 18-6   The Gatun Locks. The Gatun Locks on the Atlantic side of the Panama Canal lie close together, and a ship is lifted about 28 feet over each of the three barriers. On the Pacific side, the two Miraflores Locks are separated from the Pedro Miguel lock by Miraflores Lake, about a mile in length. The separation was necessary because sufficient hard rock footing was not available to place the three Pacific entrance locks together. Between 1953 and 1963, commercial cargo through the canal rose from 36,095,349 tons to 62,247,094 tons, and ship transits rose from 7,410 to 11,017. In 1951 only 10 commercial vessels of 18,000 gross register tons or over passed through the Canal; in 1961 there were 336. The increase in ship size makes it more difficult to reach the optimum scheduling and dispatching of cargo; and as a result of the increase in size of vessel and in number of transits, the demand is growing for another larger and deeper canal. (*Courtesy G. Alexandersson and G. Norstrom,* World Shipping, *John Wiley & Sons, 1964, (Official Panama Canal Photograph 1961)*)

port even among neighboring countries. Other factors, such as small surpluses and somewhat similar commodities, have handicapped the India-China trade, for example; but not the least of the drawbacks has been the great Himalayan mountain and plateau complex that forms such a barrier boundary between these great civilizations. Asian trade shows further disadvantages from transport in the general regularity of the continent's coastline; such regularity is in striking contrast to the irregularity found among the many peninsulas of Europe. Coastal indentations easy for ship transportation are also few along the regular shores of South America and Africa.

Rivers may contribute favorable influences upon trade, especially in the continents of Africa and South America, where railroads are inadequate to handle the movement of commodities. Even in western Europe, where a dense rail net

crosses the land, the Rhine and its tributaries carry an enormous tonnage. The Rhine flows in the right direction for the best movement of trade—from a raw-materials-producing area, where bulky goods can move downstream, to a highly industrialized area from which less bulky goods can move upstream. Direction of flow is not as favorable upon the Danube as upon the Rhine. The Danube flows from highly industrialized western Europe through the Balkan countries with their lower stage of industrial development. Thus, when trade between these two sections is permitted by government sanction, eastern bulky raw materials will move upstream and lighter-weight industrial goods will move east with the current— not the ideal situation for trade.

Distance exerts an influence upon commerce. The narrow North Atlantic between the United States and Europe is easier to cross than the broad Pacific that separates America and eastern Asia. Our rapidly growing trade with Mexico and Canada is strongly favored by location of the countries along the United States boundary line; and boundary lines to these nations are far easier to cross than those already described between India and China. United States proximity to Caribbean lands favors commerce with Middle America far more than with distant Argentina and Chile, also parts of Latin America.

Canal building has lessened distances between Chile and eastern United States and serves as another example to show the importance of transport upon trade development. United States commerce with west-coast South American countries increased significantly after

1914, the year in which the Panama Canal was opened (Figs. 18–6 and 18–7). The strategic waterway also aided trade between the Atlantic and Pacific coasts of the United States and brought down east-west rail rates at the same time that it shortened east-west sea distances. Similar trade advantages resulted from the building of the Suez Canal in 1869.

Attention also should be called to the comparative advantages and disadvantages of both ocean and land carriers in the shipping of world commodities. Both means of transport were examined in some detail in Chapter 7, p. 126, and there ocean transportation shows up favorably in many characteristics when compared with that of land.

Ships that carry world commerce belong to

The Panama Canal

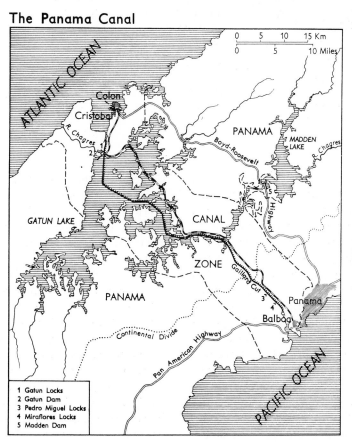

Fig. 18–7   The Panama Canal. The builders of the Panama Canal took advantage of a break in the mountains to construct the famous waterway. Gold Hill, through which Gaillard Cut was made, is the highest point on the canal route, and rises only 662 feet above sea level. The narrow isthmus in the vicinity of the canal stretches north towards South America and south towards North America; and the canal entrance on the Pacific side is about 15 miles east of the Atlantic entrance. (*Courtesy G. Alexandersson and G. Nostrom,* World Shipping, *John Wiley & Sons, 1964*)

Fig. 18–8   Coffee Pack Train Moving over Mountain Trails. Some of the world's commercial coffee still travels part of the way to market on the backs of domestic animals. Since it is a crop with good keeping qualities and high value per unit of weight, it can stand slow and relatively expensive muleback transport. (*Courtesy Pan American Coffee Bureau*)

two major classes—vessels that run on a regular schedule and what may be called tramp steamers. The timing and route of tramp steamers are governed by the availability of cargo at a specific time and place. For example, a corporation owning a tramp steamer may bargain to carry a cargo of pine lumber for shipment out of Seattle to Thailand; there, arrangements may be made to carry a load of rice to India; the ship may move back to Malaysia for a cargo of natural rubber for England; at Swansea, coal may be loaded for Spain; in southern Spain cork may move to the eastern seaboard of the United States; here contracts may be signed to carry special manufactured goods to Seattle. Thus it is possible for a tramp steamer to keep moving with different cargoes entirely around the world. The main idea is to move as few miles as possible without a load of commodities; strict schedules are likely to be secondary.

As previously suggested, many of the world's commodities are carried on inland waterways.

Some of the most important include the Great Lakes and the Ohio and Mississippi rivers in North America; the Rhine, Elbe, Oder, Volga, Vistula, and Danube in Europe; the Yangtze in Asia; the Nile in Africa; and the Amazon in South America. Inland waterways share certain advantages of the ocean highway as carriers of commerce. In the United States, government subsidy for improvement of inland waterways costs millions of dollars and incurs great criticism from competing railroads.

The movement of commodities by trucks is constantly becoming of greater importance. Competition with rail traffic has increased remarkably. Truck movement shows greater flexibility in schedule and destination than rail traffic and has been favored in many places by a lower tax load.

Animals carry several commodities on part of their journey to world markets. Coffee (Fig. 18–8) reaches rail and water transport in Colombia by donkey-back; and dates may move by camel caravan from a few Saharan oases. But commodity totals transported by animals are minor in comparison to those moved by rail, truck, river boat, and the great ships on the ocean (Fig. 18–9).

How will airplanes compete with ships and railroads as carriers of commerce? Air shipments become important when speed and high value per unit of weight are involved. Again, the plane is used for trade when no means of overland transport is available, as in Alaskan and Canadian isolated mining centers and in faraway mountain and desert sections of South America, Africa, and Australia. Planes do not yet compete for bulky, low-priced goods over routes now serviced by trains, trucks, and ships. In time, plane competition for this commerce may become significant (Fig. 18–10). Some predict bulk handling of wheat, minerals, and so forth, by air. Costs are too high for carrying such bulky commodities on today's commercial planes.

Government Restrictions upon Trade. One of the best examples of the lifting of government restrictions on trade began in Europe in the early 1950's. In the spring of 1950, a French foreign minister, Robert Schuman, proposed a European Coal and Steel Community, which became known as the Schuman Plan. Before the successful inauguration of the Plan in 1951, French iron ore at the pit cost a foreigner twice as much as a Frenchman; and Germans paid $9 per ton for Ruhr coal, which cost non-Germans $14 per ton. France needed cheaper German coal and Germany wanted a lower price on Lorraine iron ore. After several months of hard bargaining, West Germany, France, and four other West European countries, Belgium, Italy, Luxembourg, and the Netherlands agreed to eliminate major trade restrictions on coal, iron, and steel.

The Schuman Plan was only a start toward

Fig. 18–9   Large Modern Oil Tanker. The Asa V. Call is docked at Richmond, California's Long Wharf on San Francisco Bay. A small tanker for bunkering other ships lies across the wharf; and a T-2 tanker and freighter are docked in the background. The Call, built in Sweden, is 825 feet long, has a rating of about 70,000 deadweight tons, and possesses a cargo capacity of 528,300 barrels of oil (a barrel of oil is 42 gallons). Japanese shipyards boast construction of the Nissho Maru, 131,000 tons and have on order other tankers of 150,000 tons. (*Courtesy Standard Oil, California*)

Fig. 18–10   Air Cargo Increases in the Jet Age. Shipments, especially those demanding speed, range from orchids to heavy machinery and from baby chicks to auto parts and race horses. For dealers in fashion goods, the speed of air cargo means lower inventories. Ton-mile costs have declined from about 18 cents for the old DC-3's to about 5 cents on the jets. Although 1964 business is about ten times that of 1949, airlines carry less than 1 per cent of the 1.5 billion ton miles of freight shipped annually in the United States. (*Courtesy American Airlines*)

an expanding international trade; for in 1955 the six countries arranged to form the Organization for European Economic Cooperation, popularly known as the O.E.E.C. or the Common Market. Negotiations were started in 1956; and in March 1957 the Treaty of Rome launching the European Common Market was signed with pomp and ceremony in Rome's ancient city hall.

At the time Britain refused an invitation from the six nations to join. Instead the British formed a loosely knit European Free Trade Association, popularly known as the Outer Seven; besides Britain this group included Austria, Denmark, Norway, Portugal, Sweden, and Switzerland. Formation of the Outer Seven was really a British gesture of self-defense and a potential bargaining counter to the Common Market.

In 1962 progress and potential of the Common Market were so significant that Britain, lead by Prime Minister MacMillan made a determined effort to join but was barred from

membership by France. Greece has accepted an associate membership; Turkey, with a mere foothold in Europe applied; and most other European nations outside the Iron Curtain explored full or associate membership.

All of this lowering of trade barriers among the European countries brought repercussions throughout the world. British Commonwealth nations worried about the loss of a free market in the mother country if Britain should attain common market membership. The United States rushed through a trade act giving presidential power to adjust tariffs for trade advantages in the Common Market. Latin America and Africa with a surplus of raw materials worry about trade restrictions against their products. Iron Curtain and Bamboo Curtain countries are disturbed by the expansion and possible future growth of the O.E.E.C. Thus, the Common Market is an excellent example of what government trade manipulation can do to national and international trade.

Discoveries and Inventions Influence Trade. Discoveries and inventions have influenced trade throughout recorded history. Vasco da Gama's voyage around Africa ruined the monopoly of certain trading centers in the Mediterranean that had depended almost entirely upon overland trade; and the discovery of the new trade route to Asia via ocean transport expanded world commerce in general. Eli Whitney's invention of the cotton gin not only increased production of cotton enormously but also stimulated trade in the commodity in the same proportion. However, the invention of the combine[1] created an economic crisis in Yucatan; this area's sisal had supplied heavy shipments of binder twine to world markets for decades. Finally, the advent of the automobile, radio, television, airplane, and rocket—these and many other inventions have influenced local, national, and international trade in many ways.

War and Commerce. War changes the pattern of trade not only for the duration of the conflict but for long periods thereafter. A relatively modern example came with the start of the Japanese-United States war at Pearl Harbor. The disaster marked the real beginning of the synthetic-rubber industry in the United States. Supplies of natural rubber were cut off, and the government was forced into a production and trade pattern for rubber that has had many commercial repercussions. The present low price of rubber shows definite relationship to the growth of the manufactured product. During the same World War and the one previous, Germany tried to cut off Britain's sea trade in food products and to starve the island nation into surrender. Carefully guarded convoys whipped the submarine menace, but not before it damaged trade and trade routes throughout the world. In 1962 during the United States-Cuban friction, trade between the two countries was curtailed severely; and the United States at-

tempted to persuade other countries to stop their Cuban trade.

Religion and Trade. Religion has increased and decreased trade in several cases. Trade in pork products is limited in Moslem and Jewish countries because of religious restrictions against eating the flesh of swine. Fast days for meat increase fish trade among Roman Catholic countries of western Europe and among Roman Catholics in other lands. Interruption of trade between Israel and Egypt is probably influenced slightly because of differences arising out of religion; and no oil flows through the Iraq pipe line at Haifa because of conflicts between Moslems and Jews.

Advertising and Trade. Advertising has increased trade by making people conscious of and familiar with new products and by stressing desirable features resulting from their use. Moreover, the millions of pages of advertising printed each week also create an expansion of commerce in wood pulp and paper products. Other trade-expansion influences of advertising could be noted.

Port Activities and Trade. One of the world's best entrepôt ports has been losing trade because of a deplorable man-made factor. This city has a physical background for ocean trade among the best in the world. Its harbor has (1) islands to protect it from wind and waves; (2) good depth of water in channels and close to shore; (3) abundant anchorage room; (4) good wharfage and dock accommodations; (5) tidal scour that lessens dredging; (6) freedom from ice and a minimum number of days with fog; and (7) easy lines of communication to a rich hinterland. In the past this physical background has helped make New York one of the world's greatest ports. But New York loses some trade not because of depreciation of physical factors, but because groups of organized gangs steal and extort from shippers who use this fine port of entry to the United States. Here is a man-made handicap to trade active in New York and also in certain other major world ports (Fig. 18–11).

Trade, National Economy, and Power. The economic life and power of nations are strengthened by healthy trade. Throughout history nations have risen and declined with their rise and decline influenced many times by the state of

---

[1]Prior to this invention, such small grain as wheat, oats, and barley was cut and tied with sisal-made twine into bundles by a machine called a grain binder. Afterwards the bundles were arranged by hand into piles called shocks. Within a few days a threshing machine was used to thresh the grain—remove it from the stalk and the husk. The combine eliminated the necessity for binding and shocking because it cut and threshed the grain in one operation. The consequent elimination of the binding process cost Yucatan a huge world market for binder twine made from sisal, its major agricultural crop.

'FOULED UP'

Fig. 18–11 Fouled Up. Man-made conditions associated with New York's shipping trade have probably improved since this cartoon appeared in the 1950's; but there is still room for further improvement. (*Courtesy Loring in the Providence Bulletin*)

their trade. The city states of Venice and Genoa prospered as long as goods moved overland from eastern lands to be sold in their markets. When the Portuguese found a sailing-ship route to the East, Portugal prospered with the eastern trade and the Italian city states declined. Spanish trade with western hemisphere lands brought American gold and other valuable products to Spain and national economy and power reached great heights during this period of early Spanish American colonization. Spain also traded with the Orient through parts of her American Empire; from 1565 to 1815 Spanish Mexico's Manila galleons carried trade between Mexico and the Philippine Islands for the longest regular commercial travel ever followed by any shipping organization. It was through this trade that Urdaneta discovered the best sailing ship-route between America and Asia. Early Spanish discovery and trading ships were also responsible for the discovery of the best sailing-ship route

between America and Europe.

France and England pirated much of Spanish American sea trade, and both established trading colonies of their own on western hemisphere lands. The North American mainland fur trade spread French claims so far and with so little defensive facilities that stronger England was able to wrest most French territory away. Russian conquest of Siberia is also related to fur trade which extended Russian claims until they reached the Pacific. United States trade in furs and other goods extended national control of the land between the thirteen colonies and the Pacific.

Just as in years gone by, nations seeking to strengthen economy and national power must trade to accomplish these purposes. England must continue overseas commerce in order to get food enough to live. British attitude toward Russian trade is different from that in the United States because the latter country is more nearly self-sufficient; in fact foreign trade amounts to less than 10 per cent of the United States national income. Thus, Americans suffer little from abandoning much east European trade because of ideological differences.

Holland lost a strong advantage in East Indies trade with the formation of the Indonesia Republic; and Belgian economy was weakened by loss of the raw-materials-rich Congo. France held on to a large African colonial empire until the 1960's partly because these nearby colonies gave a definite help to French international trade. Italy lost African colonies in World War II, but they were of little trading value.

Russia, like the United States, is so nearly self-sufficient that foreign trade is not so vital as it is to England for example. Nevertheless, both Russia and the United States need several important raw materials which do not lie within national boundaries; and in a profit economy like that of the United States, it is much better for the nation's economic health if certain local commercial surpluses can be traded for needed foreign goods. These surpluses weigh on home markets sufficiently to weaken them and to bring lower prices; falling prices can weaken business, and weakened business spreads financial trouble through the entire national economy.

United States International Trade: (Fig. 18–12 and Table 18–1) Foreign trade of the

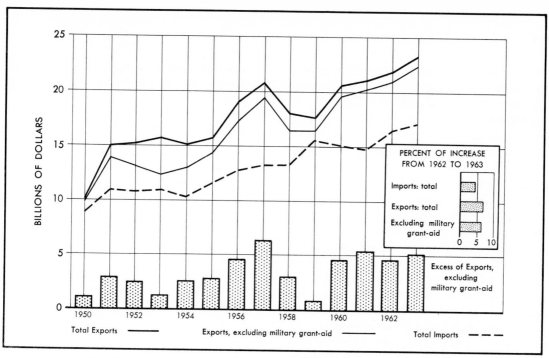

Fig. 18–12   U.S. Merchandise Trade, 1950–1963. Notice that both exports and imports show an upward trend and that the country has a favorable balance of trade—an excess of exports over imports. (*After Drawing in* Overseas Business Reports, *May, 1964, United States Department of Commerce*)

Table 18–1   Value of United States Exports, by Economic Classes, 1963

CLASS	MILLIONS OF DOLLARS
Total	22,922
Excluding military grant-aid	22,002
Agricultural	5,585
Nonagricultural	17,336
Excluding military grant-aid	16,416
Crude materials	2,577
Agricultural	1,765
Crude foodstuffs	2,273
Manufactured foodstuffs	1,497
Semimanufactures	3,284
Finished manufactures	13,291
Excluding military grant-aid	12,371

Value of United States Imports by Economic Classes, 1963

CLASS	MILLIONS OF DOLLARS
Total	17,005
Agricultural	4,017
Nonagricultural	12,988
Crude materials	3,288
Agricultural	832
Crude foodstuffs	1,725
Manufactured foodstuffs	1,998
Semimanufactures	3,605
Finished manufactures	6,389

Source—Overseas Business Reports, May 1964, U.S. Department of Commerce.

United States has changed significantly since the 1880's. Near the end of the nineteenth century agricultural commodities accounted for four fifths of total exports. By 1910 the proportion had dropped to 50 per cent; and at present farm-crop-overseas shipments are less than one third of the United States total. Several crops contribute to this trade with wheat, cotton, and tobacco the most important.

During the three-quarters-of-a-century decline in agricultural exports, the United States has become a highly industrialized nation. As a result of greater industrialization, more agricultural commodities have been used in the home market and more manufactured goods are shipped abroad. Manufactures now comprise over half the export total. These include aircraft, construction machinery, metal manufactures, motor trucks and buses, auto parts, radios, and televisions.

On the import side of United States trade, agricultural commodities and other raw materials are significant. Complementary agricultural imports—trade based upon differences in natural resources—make up about one fourth of the incoming shipments; minerals comprise nearly one third; and machinery and vehicles, which are important United States exports, make up about one thirtieth of the country's imports. Thus import statistics offer more evidence of increasing United States industrialization. A careful analysis of United States foreign trade will show the working of many influences previously mentioned. Probably the most important among these are differences in natural resources and differences in stage of industrial development.

QUESTIONS, EXERCISES, AND PROBLEMS

1. Give examples of trade encouraged by differences in resources; by differences in stage of industrial development; by differences in race, national character, and custom.

2. Point out how transportation and trade may be affected by each of the following: animals, climate, minerals, soils, surface features, vegetation, rail routes, air routes, roads, and water routes.

3. How do government restrictions handicap trade? Comment on the following statement: differences in surpluses may bring little trade when contrasts in basic national philosophies, such as that between

communism and democracy, create international friction. Is there any relationship between trade and national power? Explain.

4. How may discoveries and inventions influence trade? How may wars affect commerce? Does religion influence trade? Comment. How may unfavorable port activities discourage trade?

5. Describe in some detail the trade of Africa; Australia; Britain; Canada; China; Common Market and other countries of western Europe; India; Japan; Latin America; Middle East; Russia and other Iron Curtain countries.

6. Identify the following: Cauca, Magdalena, caviar, Deccan, Singhbhum, Minas Geraes, Mohawk Gateway, opposition to St. Lawrence Waterway, moonshiner, Danube's wrong-way flow, tramp steamer, Vistula, Oder, Outer Seven, Schuman Plan, Bamboo Curtain, Vasco da Gama, combine, Pearl Harbor, Haifa, Manila Galleon.

SELECTED REFERENCES

Alexandersson G. Norström G., *World Shipping*, John Wiley and Sons, 1964.

Barron's, "No Bargain: In the Realm of Trade, the Soviets Have nothing to Offer," Oct. 5, 1959.

Chang, Kuei-Sheng, "The Changing Railroad Pattern in Mainland China," *Geographical Review*, Oct. 1961, pp. 534–48.

Draine, E. H., *Import Traffic of Chicago and its Hinterland*, University of Chicago Press, 1963.

Gemmill, Henry, "U.S. Trade Solution: We can Compete Abroad Only by Cutting Production Costs," *Wall Street Journal*, Dec. 8, 1961.

Grotewald, Andreas, "Some Aspects of the Geography of International Trade," *Economic Geography*, Oct. 1961, pp. 309–19; "What Geographers Require of International Trade Statistics," *Annals of the Association of American Geographers*, June 1963, pp. 247–52.

Hance, W. A., Kotschar, V., and Peterec, R. J., "Source Areas of Export Production in Tropical Africa," *Geographical Review*, Oct. 1961, pp. 487–99.

Hoy, D. H., "Trends in the Banana Export Industry of Tropical America," *Journal of Geography*, March 1964, pp. 108–16.

Ives, R. L., "The Manila Galleons," *Journal of Geography*, Jan. 1964, pp. 5–19.

Mathewson, J. D., "Antitrust Abroad: Tighter U.S. Laws Put American Companies at a Disadvantage in Overseas Trade," *Wall Street Journal*, May 2, 1963.

Nystrom, Warren, *The Common Market*, Searchlight Book, D. Van Nostrand, 1962.

Taaffe, E. J., Morrill, R. L., and Gould, P. R., "Transport Expansion in Underdeveloped Countries: A Comparative Analysis," *Geographical Review* Oct. 1963, pp. 503–29.

The Conference Board, 460 Park Ave., N.Y. 22, N.Y., *Road Maps of Industry*, No. 1367, March 9, 1962, "U.S. International Investment Position"; No. 1394, Sept. 14, 1962,

"Value of U.S. Direct Investments Abroad"; and many other graphs concerning world trade.

Thoman, R. S., and Patton, D. J., *Focus on Geographic Activity,* McGraw-Hill, 1964, Chapters 27–28, "A Modern Food Wholesaling Firm in New England" and "A Major American-Flag Ocean Shipping Concern."

U.S. Dept. of Agriculture, "West European Issue," *Foreign Agriculture,* Nov. 1962.

U.S. Dept. of Commerce, *International Commerce,* a weekly news magazine for international business, Govt. Printing Office; *Overseas Business Reports,* formerly *World Trade Information Service,* Govt. Printing Office.

Warntz, William, "Transatlantic Flights and Pressure Patterns," *Geographical Review,* April 1961, pp. 187–212.

Yates, Barbara A., "Railroads and Waterways of Africa," *Journal of Geography,* March 1961, pp. 120–35.

Chapter Nineteen

Population and Geography

In studying population as it is affected by and affects geography a few major headings stand out. These include (1) the influence of the physical environment and other factors upon density and distribution; (2) movements as affected by physical and man-made conditions; (3) physical and cultural characteristics of the population; and (4) growth, both actual and potential. These topics will be examined in sequence.

Physical Factors That Now Discourage Settlement

Climate. Climate has much to do with the present distribution and density of population. Few people now live on at least 12,000,000 square miles of the earth's land surface largely because of low temperatures (Fig. 19–1, 19–2, 19–3, and 19–4). Where are these 12,000,000 square miles? Antarctica (Fig. 19–5) with over five million square miles, almost twice the size of the 48 contiguous United States and much larger than Europe has no one living there more than a year or two at a time; in fact the continent received very little world attention until the Geophysical Year in the late 1950's. Greenland (Fig. 19–6), with nearly a million square miles, only a little smaller than India with its hundreds of millions of people, has a population of about 35,000. Two territories in Canada, the Yukon and Northwest Territory, have over 1.5 million square miles, a larger area than India, and not more than 30,000 people. The District of Franklin, made up of Canada's northeastern island realm, may comprise 500,000 square miles with less than 20,000 people. Besides Canadian areas already mentioned, the Labrador Peninsula, northern Ontario, and poleward parts of British Columbia, Alberta, and Saskatchewan, probably contain 500,000 square miles too cold to encourage continuous settlement except

in highly mineralized spots. A glance at population distribution in the U.S.S.R. will show enough poleward locations with less than two people per square mile to complete the total of 12,000,000 square miles. In this huge area the number of people is not larger than the number in the city of Tokyo.

How long low temperatures will continue to discourage settlement in many of the cold areas of the world is hard to predict. It is possible that new techniques in farming, new hybrids among the various crops, expanding world markets for food and feed, improvements in world distribution of foods from food surplus to food deficient areas, increased standards of living among a rapidly increasing population—all these factors and others may combine to extend agricultural development farther poleward than it is today. Furthermore, places such as the Laurentian, the Scandinavian, and the Siberian Shields are a storehouse of metallic minerals. World demand could increase to such an extent that mining and the processing of minerals may expand and thus support a significant expansion in population. Finally, looking into the far distant future, a melting of the polar ice caps could change world climates so that northern Canada and Eurasia may receive an increase in both temperature and precipitation. This would not only make the subpolar lands more productive for agriculture but also more attractive for human occupation.

Besides the nearly one-fourth of the earth's land surface now unattractive for settlement because of low temperature, there are at least twelve million square miles more which, at present, hold little attraction because of low precipitation (Fig. 19–7). Think of the following middle and low latitude deserts: the Mexican and United States deserts in North America; the Atacama, Patagonian, and Northwest Argentine dry lands of South America; the Great

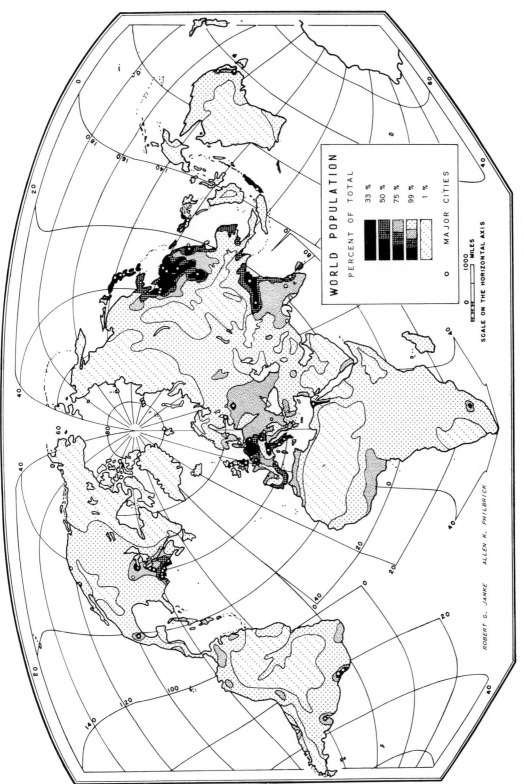

Fig. 19–1 World Population. (*Courtesy A. K. Philbrick, This Human World, John Wiley & Sons, 1963*)

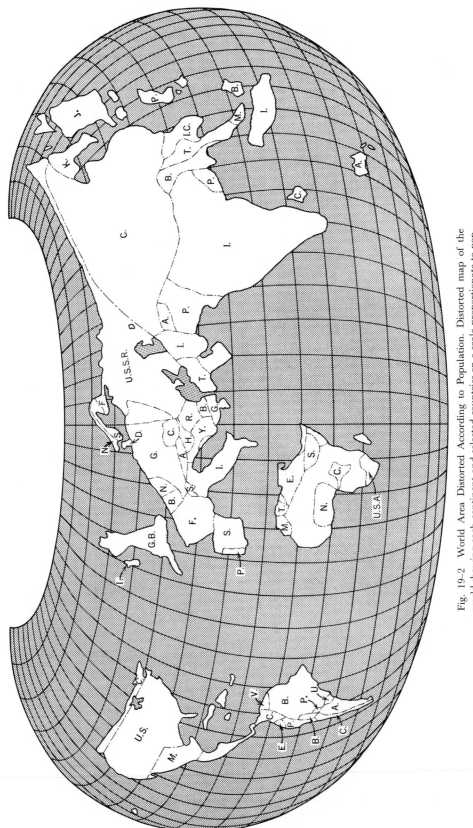

Fig. 19–2 World Area Distorted According to Population. Distorted map of the world showing each continent and selected countries on a scale proportionate to population. Uninhabited and sparsely populated areas of the Arctic and Antarctic do not appear. Europe, India, China, Japan, and Indonesia overshadow the thinly settled regions in Australia, Africa, and South America. Initials represent names of countries. *(Courtesy The Twentieth Century Fund)*

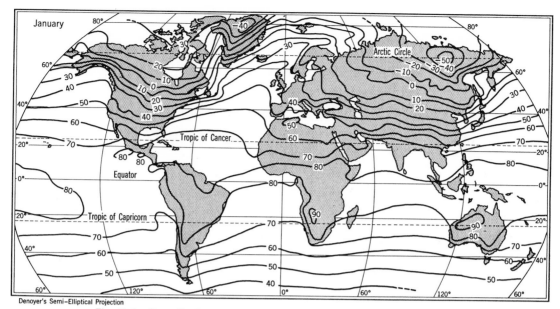

Fig. 19–3   Generalized Map of January Temperatures in Degrees Fahrenheit Reduced to Sea Level. (*Courtesy A. N. Strahler,* Physical Geography, *2d ed., John Wiley & Sons*)

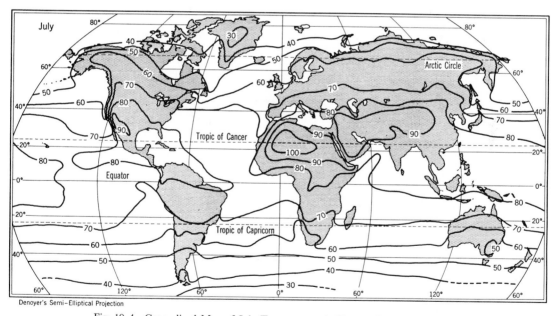

Fig. 19–4   Generalized Map of July Temperatures in Degrees Fahrenheit, reduced to Sea Level. (*Courtesy A. N. Strahler,* Physical Geography, *2d ed., John Wiley & Sons*)

Dead Heart of Australia; the Sahara (Fig. 19–8) and Kalahari deserts of Africa; and the Arabian, Syrian, Turkish, Iraqian, Iranian, Thar, Gobi, Ordos, Takla Makan, Kyzyl-Kum, and Kara-Kum barren regions of Asia—these and others total nearly another quarter of the earth's land surface.

Just as changing conditions may increase future population in the subpolar and polar areas, so changes may take place in the dry lands to

ANTARCTICA

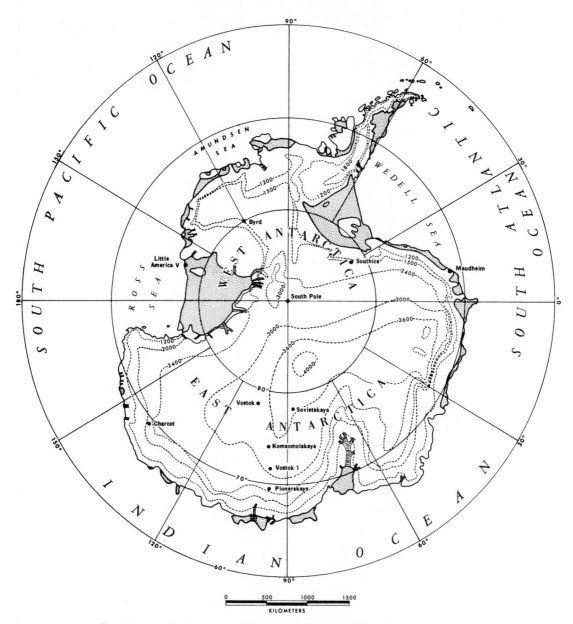

Fig. 19–5   Antarctica, Contour Map. Antarctica's high latitudes and altitudes (in meters) are not likely to attract large permanent settlement in the near future. (*Courtesy Paul C. Dalrymple*)

make them more interesting to man. Better control and utilization of water in such streams as the Nile and the Colorado may increase opportunities for agricultural and industrial expansion. More careful utilization of underground water seeping toward exotic desert streams may support more people. Cheaper removal of saline

deposits from ocean water bordering or not far distant from many of the world's deserts probably will soon provide water to irrigate thousands of square miles of desert. The attractiveness of the desert climate for health seekers, tourists, people approaching retirement, and those with wealth is already rapidly increasing settlement in desert sections of the United States. Increased exploration and exploitation of desert oil (see Fig. 3–2), natural gas, and metallic minerals will stimulate greater development of the dry lands. Furthermore, recent research by petroleum corporations has shown that food production may be increased by spraying soil after planting with a thin film of asphalt. This traps

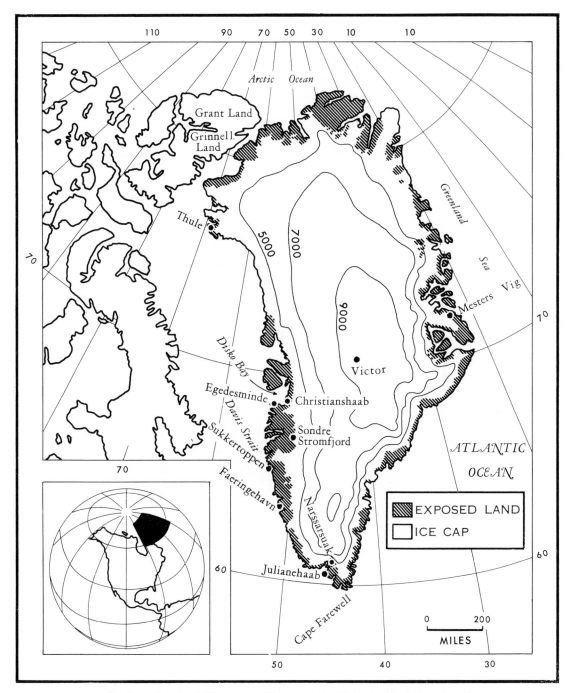

Fig. 19–6   Greenland. The icecap of Greenland, world's largest island, doesn't reach altitudes quite as high as those of Antarctica. Contours of 5,000, 7,000, and 9,000 feet are somewhat generalized. Ice cover and high latitude discourage dense settlement.

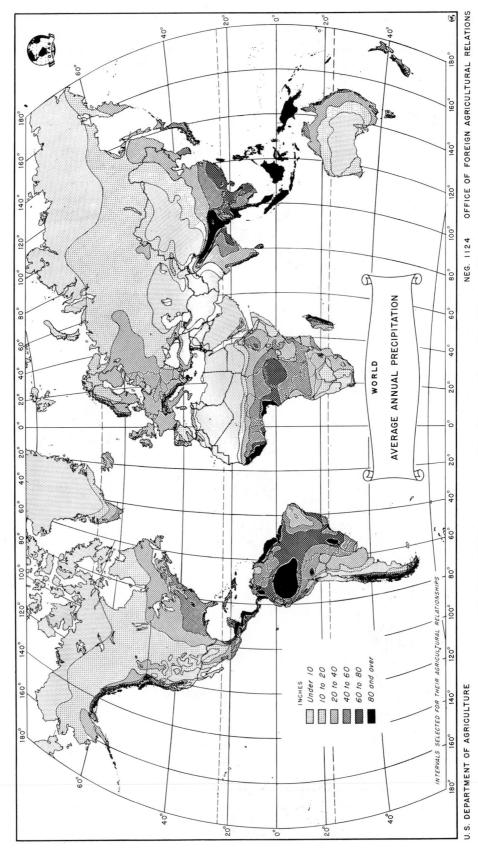

U. S. DEPARTMENT OF AGRICULTURE

INTERVALS SELECTED FOR THEIR AGRICULTURAL RELATIONSHIPS

WORLD

AVERAGE ANNUAL PRECIPITATION

INCHES
Under 10
10 to 20
20 to 40
40 to 60
60 to 80
80 and over

NEG. 1124   OFFICE OF FOREIGN AGRICULTURAL RELATIONS

Fig. 19–7   World, Average Annual Precipitation. (*Courtesy U.S. Department of Agriculture, Office of Agricultural Relations*)

the moisture in arid lands and promotes plant growth.

Finally, it may be well to recall that early explorers of the United States Great Plains, Coronado, Zebulon M. Pike, John Bradbury, Major S. H. Long and many others considered these plains a part of the Great American Desert. Moreover, frontiersmen moving west from the humid eastern part of the United States said that "Any land that won't grow trees won't grow crops." In fact, up to the time of the Civil War, the views of explorers and frontiersmen found expression in all good American textbooks which mapped the Great Plains as a part of the Great American Desert. Now, one hundred years later, these Plains are one of the world's great producers of cereals and meat. All the above comments suggest that the sparsely populated desert lands of today may not necessarily be peopled so sparsely in the future.

The Amazon Basin (Fig. 19–9) of South America, an area of about two million square miles, is another sparsely populated land. Some may say that climate is responsible for the few people in Amazonia, but this is not the complete answer. Climatic conditions along the Amazon are no worse than in some more densely populated sections of the Congo Basin, where settlement has been stimulated by the discovery and exploitation of copper, uranium, and other mineral deposits. Again, temperatures and precipitation should be no more of a handicap to a dense population in the Brazilian wet tropics than these elements are in the densely populated low latitudes of Southeast Asia. Just because the Brazilians haven't seen fit to populate the Amazon Basin doesn't mean that all mankind will refuse to settle there. In fact, today there are at least four Japanese agricultural colonies along the Amazon which produce most of their own food, together with a surplus of such crops as black pepper and jute for sale on the world

Fig. 19–8 Sahara Sand Dunes. These dunes located 400 miles south of Tripoli, Libya—the locale of the highest official shade temperature ever recorded—suggest little attraction for man's permanent settlement. (*Courtesy Standard Oil, New Jersey*)

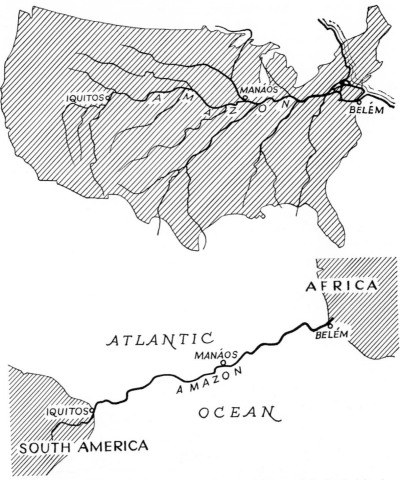

Fig. 19–9   The Amazon Superimposed on the United States and the South Atlantic. If the Amazon were laid on the United States, the basin would cover almost the entire area. If the stream could be laid between South America and Africa, the part navigable by ocean stea ners would span the South Atlantic. (*Courtesy Foreign Policy Association.*)

market. It may be that Brazilian prejudice against settlement and development of the humid tropics is one of the major obstacles to a relatively dense peopling of the Amazon Basin (see Fig. 3–3).

Highlands. High mountains limit settlement in many parts of the world both because of altitude induced cold and because of rugged topography; such areas may account for more than a million square miles on the earth's land surface (Fig. 19–10). The Himalayas, the Western Sierra Madre of Mexico, parts of the Caucasus, the Pamirs, the Armenian Knot, the High Andes—these and other high mountains hold

few of the world's people.

Not all mountains are sparsely populated. For example, highland Bolivia, with an average altitude of over 10,000 feet has more people than the eastern Bolivian lowlands; and highland basins in Ecuador and Peru are densely populated parts of those countries. This situation is not hard to explain. Most people in these South American Andes republics prefer the upland environment to that of the equatorial lowlands in spite of the fact that the lowlands are more productive for many types of agriculture. Highlanders don't like the hot lowland temperatures and heavy precipitation; they fear the greater disease hazards and more numerous lowland insects; and the lowlands are relatively inaccessible for them. Even the lower eastern slopes of the Bolivian Andes, with moderate temperatures and precipitation, sometimes called the Yungas region, are much more attractive farming country than that on the highlands. But most of the Bolivians still live on the uplands, where both temperatures and precipitation limit agriculture to the raising of such crops as hardy vegetables and cereals and to the grazing of livestock.

Of course in the highland tropics, at a mile or a mile and a half above sea level, people can enjoy mid-day shade temperatures of 60 to 65° F, while lowland inhabitants may swelter under an oppressive heat of 80° F or more. Moreover, nights are always cool at high elevations because the lower absolute humidity permits rapid outgoing earth radiation; and in the daytime the sun's rays may penetrate the atmosphere for the same reason. Thus if one wishes to be warm he may stand or sit in the highland tropical sunlight. Furthermore, as far as temperature is concerned, he can always get a good night's sleep,[1] whereas this boon to good health is not so consistently assured in the lowlands without air

[1]The thin air of places like La Paz, Bolivia, at 12,000 feet, may give the lowland native sleeping difficulties until he becomes acclimated to such a high altitude.

Fig. 19–10   Emperor Falls and Mt. Robson in the Canadian Rockies. Permanent settlement in country with such rugged terrain will be attracted only by the scenery, the hydroelectric power potential, or the possibility of mineral resources. (*Courtesy Canadian National Railways*)

conditioning. It should also be stressed that dense settlement in highland basins of Bolivia, Ecuador, and Peru has probably been influenced as much by the presence of valuable minerals as by the cooler temperatures.

Many Latin American capitals are located among the mountains. Good examples are Mexico City, 7,400 feet; San José, Costa Rica, 3700 feet; Caracas, Venezuela, 3000 feet; and Bogotá, Colombia, 8700 feet. Several geographic factors encouraged a relatively dense Indian population to occupy these sites even before the Europeans took control. The higher elevations gave cooler temperatures and more immunity from malaria and other diseases. All four capitals are situated in mountain basins with productive soil and adequate precipitation for agriculture. Useful metallic minerals were present in the mountains close to Mexico City and Bogotá. All these geographic advantages that interested Indian settlers also attracted their Spanish conquerors. Furthermore, Spaniards were pleased to find large Indian groups in these locations because they could enslave the Indians for a much-needed labor supply. Another important reason for the Spanish choice of these highland locations is the fact that they were much easier to protect than coastal cities during a period when pirates were extremely active in the Caribbean Sea and the Gulf of Mexico.

Mountains in high latitudes discourage settlement not only because of their terrain, but also because of cold resulting from both altitude and latitude. The Scandinavian Highlands, the mountains of northeast Siberia, the Rocky Mountain extension into Alaska—all are examples of sparsely populated high-latitude mountains.

Soils. Soils now discourage dense settlement in many sections, especially in the rainy lowland tropics, where primitive natives practice milpa agriculture; here they need large acreages to practice their migratory farming. This is one of several reasons why many parts of Borneo, Celebes, New Guinea, and Sumatra support low population densities. But these areas need not remain sparsely populated because of infertile soils. When fertilization and other modern farming techniques are used on tropical soils, they can be improved remarkably; and such improvement will support a much larger farming population.

From the preceding paragraphs, one can see that, at present, the physical environment exerts an important influence in discouraging settlement on nearly half of the world's land surface. Nevertheless, there are other discouraging factors such as (1) the prejudices of some nationalities against settlement in certain environments; and (2) the delays in the stage of technical advance in making some areas, now sparsely populated, more attractive for human occupance. The two latter conditions will probably change, and settlement may expand considerably in several of the land areas now touched but little by the hand of man.

Physical Factors Which Encourage Settlement

Plains. Within latitudes and at altitudes where climate permits or encourages agricultural production, where people live may be influenced significantly by the character of the topography (Fig. 19–11). It is a well known fact that the major fraction of the world's population gain their living by farming and that most people live on level, nearly level, or gently rolling terrain. These plains may lie close to the equator, like the nearly level West Indies island of Barbados, 13° North, with a population density of over a thousand per square mile; they may be in the subtropics like the Nile Delta at 30° North, with nearly two thousand people per square mile; or they may be found in the higher middle latitudes like the Scottish Lowland at 55° North, with its dense farming and industrial settlement.

The geologic origin of the plain usually makes little difference in the land utilization. Obviously a glacial-scoured plain with bare rock outcrops would be useless for agriculture. But most river, coastal, and lake plains provide opportunity for agriculture and other occupations. In Asia, China's Hwang Ho plain has about 100 million people, the Yangtze plain even more, and India's Ganges lowland supports approximately the same number as the Yangtze. In Europe, Italy's Po plain is one of the continent's most densely populated lands; in South America, that part of the Argentine Pampa near the La Plata estuary has millions of people; in Africa, Egypt's valley of the Nile supports more than 20 million people on approximately 3 per cent

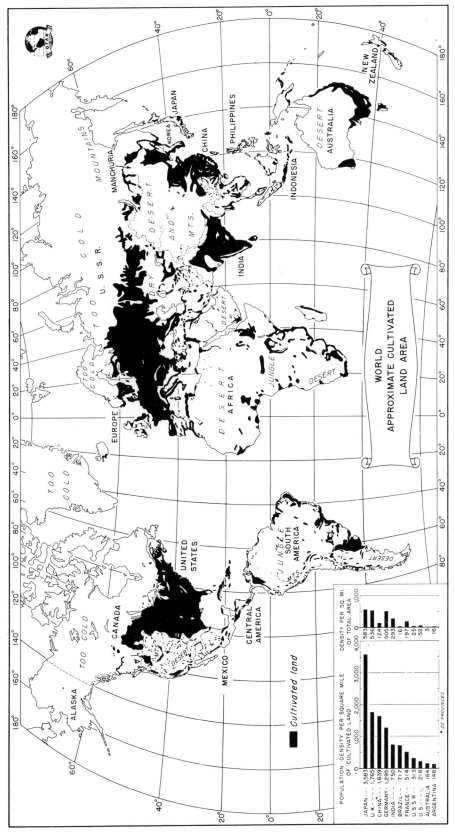

Fig. 19-11 World, Approximate Cultivated Land Area. Only a small per cent of the total land surface is cultivated. About two-thirds of the cultivated area lies in the middle latitudes; the remainder in the tropics. At present most of the uncultivated area lies in jungles, mountains, and lands of cold and drought. The map is highly generalized since crop yields, potential productivity, and pattern and intensity of agricultural land use are not shown. (*Courtesy U.S. Department of Agriculture, Office of Foreign Agricultural Relations*)

of the nation's nearly 400,000 square miles; in North America, the Mohawk valley is not only one of the greatest east-west transport routes, but it is thickly settled as well; and in Australia, the Murray-Darling Valley contains a large percentage of the continent's people. Of course the topography of these and other river valleys is not the only factor responsible for dense populations. Fertile soils are important; and, in desert areas like western Pakistan and Egypt, availability of water is extremely significant. Moreover, one must never forget that man makes the final choice of where he will live; and it has already been pointed out that one of the largest river plains in the world, the Amazon, is sparsely populated largely because Brazilians have not chosen to develop its wide expanse of plains topography.

The Hwang Ho, Yangtze, Ganges, and Nile mentioned above, as well as many other major streams, possess deltas which may also be classified as parts of the coastal plain. Several of these deltaic areas are densely populated; but others are not. Since all of them lie near sea level and are subject to flood, dikes may be necessary to protect farms, villages, and cities from inundation. Where lands are swampy, ill-drained, and too expensive to change for the better, man may leave them undeveloped and sparsely peopled. Two good examples of this situation are Venezuela's Orinoco delta and parts of that of the Mississippi. On the other hand, deltas of the two main rivers of China, India's largest river, and that of Egypt are all relatively well protected.

More extensive than any delta are the broad coastal plains of the United States bordering the Gulf of Mexico and the Atlantic Ocean. Look at a map (see Fig. 5–3), and note the contrast between the wide lowlands of eastern and southern United States and the extremely narrow, and in many places missing, coastal plain touching the Pacific on the west. Much of the eastern United States coastal plain is densely populated; and the northern portion, extending from Boston to Washington D.C., together with nearby adjoining lands has been described as Megalopolis—a large city—by Jean Gottman in the July 1957 issue of *Economic Geography*. However, the Gulf of Mexico coastal plain belonging to the United States is not as densely populated as the Atlantic coastal area; and the Gulf and Caribbean coasts

of Mexico and Central America are much more sparsely populated. This sparsity is not because the plain lacks level topography, but rather a result of climatic, drainage, and insect conditions, as well as a large number of cultural factors; the combination has influenced man's decision not to congregate in large numbers on the Atlantic coast of both Central America and Mexico.

The Atlantic coast of Middle Latitude Europe possesses a significant area of plain in northwest France, Belgium, the Netherlands, Denmark, southern Sweden, and Germany all of which support a dense population. Proportionately, coastal plains form a lesser percentage of the continents of Asia, Africa, Australia, and South America than they do of Europe and North America.

The land bordering the Great Lakes of the latter continent, in Canada and the United States, comprises the largest area of lake plains in the world; and it is all densely populated. However, not all of the level topography surrounding the large lakes of the earth is densely peopled. For example, a dry climate on the north and east of the Caspian Sea, really a large lake in spite of the name, helps keep the population sparse. On the other hand, heavy precipitation along the southern shores encourages a profitable agriculture that supports most of the population of Iran, a generally arid country.

One of the best examples to show the importance of plains in encouraging settlement may be seen in the present distribution of population in eastern United States. Compare a railroad map with the topographic map of the region (see Figs. 6–8 and 5–3), and note the contrast in rail pattern between plains lands and the sparsely populated rugged parts of the Appalachians, and the Ozarks, an outlier of the Appalachian mountain system.

Four maps (see Figs. 5–3, 19–1, 19–7, and 19–11) will help explain the present sparse population of a large portion of western United States—those of relief, precipitation, and population. With these maps, one can see how the rugged terrain in the Rockies, Cascades, Sierra Nevada, and the Intermontane plateaus, plus a rainfall averaging less than 20 inches, are major factors in discouraging a generally dense population.

Plateaus. Relatively dense settlement is found on some of the world's well known plateaus, whereas others, as indicated before, may be sparsely peopled. The upland area in the immediate vicinity of Mexico City, sometimes called the Central Plateau of Mexico, lying within the tropics at over a mile elevation, is one of the most densely populated parts of the country; and Mexico ranks next to Brazil for total population in Latin America. Altitude, relatively level terrain, climate, soils, and minerals, combined with man-made factors, have made the region attractive to settlers for centuries. Atmospheric conditions, sometimes described as resembling eternal spring, lack only variability to provide one of the world's most energizing climates. Soils left in the bed of an old lake or lakes and enriched by volcanic action aid climate in the encouragement of profitable agriculture; and vulcanism brought mineralization to nearby mountains and added diversity to the plateau's economic pattern. Is it any wonder that man has chosen to make the Central Plateau the most densely populated part of Mexico?

In South America, Brazil's East Central Plateau stands out as the most highly developed part of that country. Millions of people occupy this tropical upland. Here they grow most of the world's coffee and most of Brazil's cotton; and not far from coffee and cotton lands are mineral deposits containing one of the world's richest iron resources. Altitude brings energizing temperatures; these with gently rolling topography and well-distributed adequate rainfall encourage commercial agriculture; the presence of minerals and other raw materials stimulates mining and manufacturing. Brazilians consider all these geographic factors favorable for economic progress and have made the East Central Plateau the most densely populated part of the nation. Note the contrast in population density between this area and the neglected Amazon Basin.

A somewhat similar physical environment occurs on many plateau sections of Africa's east central highlands including the countries of Rwanda, Burundi, Uganda, Tanganyika, and Kenya. Although all areas support a relatively dense population, racial problems, prior to the early 1960's have retarded both economic and political progress. Now that the Negroes have gained control they will need both time and experience before they discover the best ways to make the generally favorable geographic background produce what it should for its native population.

Another large African plateau, the Ethiopian, has a geologic origin, dominantly volcanic, similar to that of three other large, but widely separated plateaus—the Deccan of India, the Paraná of southern Brazil, and the Columbia in northwest United States and adjoining Canada. The first two are located in the tropics, the third borders the tropics, and the fourth lies in the middle latitudes. The Deccan is the most densely populated and has maintained a dominantly agricultural economy for centuries. Farming is also a leading occupation in the three other uplands, but far different in each. Columbian agriculture is the most modern; Ethiopian the most primitive; and that of the Paraná in between. Most of these economic differences, as well as others of social and political character, result largely from cultural contrasts among the peoples who inhabit the four volcanic highlands.

Areas of Dense Population (See Figs. 19–1 and 19–2)

Three major areas of dense population may be noted easily by a glance at the world population map. These are southeastern Asia, western Europe, and eastern United States. It may be a mere coincidence that dense populations occur in the world's greatest rice growing and manufacturing areas. On the other hand, there may be some relationship in these situations (see Fig. A–2, p. 382).

Rice is a cereal crop with high food value and good keeping qualities for tropical latitudes. In the production of 90 per cent of the world's crop, southeast Asia's warm temperatures and monsoon rains permit two and sometimes three high-yielding crops annually. With its high food value, high yields, multiple cropping, and ease of preservation, rice furnishes most of the food for a major part of Asia's more than a billion people (Fig. 19–12).

It should be noted, however that southeast Asia is not the only place in the world with conditions favorable for rice production. For example, many of the wet tropical lowlands of

Fig. 19–12   Paddy Rice Production, Bandung, Java. Rice forms the principal diet of many densely populated countries in southeast Asia. About sixty million people live on the 51,000 square miles of Java and its satellite island of Madura. This photograph of paddy rice fields emphasizes the intensive nature of Javanese rice production and the way millions of farmers cultivate every foot of productive land. (*Courtesy Standard Oil, New Jersey*)

Latin America have a physical environment well suited to rice culture, but there's no such dense settlement in Latin America's potential rice country as in Oriental Asia. Thus rice should be considered as only one of several factors accounting for southeast Asia's millions.

Asia's position in manufacturing is not as high as in the production of rice, and the big continent gives away to Europe and North America in industrial leadership. Many factors, some geographic and others of a different character account for this high rating, especially in the United States, bordering parts of Canada and western Europe. These include (1) abundance of power—Appalachian Welsh, Westphalian, and Saar coal; oil, gas and water power from United States and Canada and increasing amounts from western Europe; (2) significant iron resources—Lake Superior; Birmingham, Alabama; Labrador; Lorraine; and Kiruna ores; (3) an energizing climate; (4) food crops, livestock, forests, textile crops, and other raw materials for manufacture; (5) people with inventiveness and manufacturing ability; (6) well-developed transport facilities; (7) large numbers of skilled and unskilled workers; (8) high living standards providing a broad home market; (9) large amounts of risk capital and labor with laws insuring adequate reward; (10) the start of the industrial revolution in Europe; (11) the industrial stimulation brought about by preparation and conduct of two world wars;

(12) the recent economic lift of Marshall plan aid; (13) lifting of trade barriers in many European countries; (14) extreme competition for earthly and space leadership between communist countries of Europe and the noncommunist groups of Europe and North America; and many other geographic and nongeographic influences.

In the future, continents other than those of Europe and North America may show greater manufacturing growth than that of today. In Asia, China's Great Leap Forward of the early 1960's started out auspiciously and brought transfer of many peasants into industry for a while. However that manufacturing venture soon fizzled, and most of the transferred workers moved back into agriculture to lessen famine conditions. India's various hopeful plans to raise living standards by increases in industry have depended on foreign aid, and so far show little real success. In the southern hemisphere, Australian physical factors have long been relatively favorable for manufacturing with adequate coal, iron, etc; but it took two world wars and the consequent isolation of the island continent from Britain to get a good start toward local industrial self sufficiency. In Latin America, adequate coal of good quality is lacking, but man more than the shortage of power and raw materials may have retarded industrial advance and the growth in population usually associated with it. Latin American wealthy classes have long placed a higher value on land ownership and the professions than upon any participation in industry. Of course such an attitude retarded manufacturing development.

The long delay in exploring and exploiting African power resources, the limited availability of industrial raw materials, and the general economic backwardness of the native population—all these and many other factors have combined to delay manufacturing in most of the continent. However, Egypt and South Africa are showing significant signs of progress in the early 1960's. Nevertheless, neither Africa, nor Asia, nor Australia, nor South America has yet achieved an efficiency over a broad area comparable to that of the United States and western Europe.

Looking at population distribution from the standpoint of world hemispheres, the northern or land hemisphere is by far the most populous (see Figs. 19–1 and 19–2). In 1960, more than 90 per cent of the earth's people lived north of the equator; about 70 per cent north of the line in the Americas and nearly 95 per cent north of the equator in Europe, Asia, and Africa. Moreover, within the northern hemisphere most of the people of the middle latitudes live within a few hundred miles of the coast. In fact, Europe is the only one with a densely populated interior. Important reasons for European interior as well as coastal density may be (1) the small size of Europe, next to the smallest of the continents; (2) the few severely cold areas; and (3) the lack of any true desert lands.

Migration

Voluntary. Movements of population can be divided into voluntary, forced, and periodic migrations (Fig. 19–13). Climate is probably responsible for many voluntary migrations in ancient and medieval time. W. B. Fisher describes the start of such an invasion as follows:

The steppes are the home of pastoral nomadism. . . . For a few weeks each year the steppe presents an amazing picture of luxuriant, almost lush vegetation; but with the approach of summer, only hardier bushes and thorns remain above the ground, and vast expanses of bare earth appear, upon which are strewn the withered remains of earlier plant growth . . . an extra week of rain (i.e. prolonged latter rains), will mean a more than corresponding lengthening of the spring pasture season, with great increase of flocks and herds during the ensuing year; an early cessation of rainfall means a long summer, with much hardship until the next spring. Under such conditions, even a small climatic fluctuation can have a disproportionately large affect upon human activity, and a few seasons of deficient rainfall may lead to widespread movements within the steppes, culminating in the invasion of adjoining lands, with vast consequences for human societies as a whole. Such great events as the Indo-Aryan invasions of Europe and the Middle East during the second millennium B.C., the Israelitish occupation of Palestine, and the rise of Islam in the seventh century A.D. can all be traced to slight changes in environmental conditions within the steppe lands of Eurasia.

In describing one of these invasions, Fisher states:

The early part of the second millennium B.C. was marked by a number of incursions by pastoral peoples

Fig. 19–13   The Great Wall of China. The Chinese built a thick, high, and lengthy wall to prevent migrations from bordering lands characterized by lower and less dependable precipitation. The huge barrier, extending for more than 1,000 miles, marks the approximate boundary between (1) the dry steppe and desert lands to the north and west, and (2) the more humid country to the south and east.

from the north. The Hyksos or Shepherd Kings invaded Egypt from eastern Syria, whilst the Kassites entered lower Mesopotamia. Two other peoples, the Mitanni and the Hittites, became settled respectively in northeast Syria between the Tigris and the Euphrates, and in Anatolia. These pastoral communities, though originally of lower cultural development than the agriculturalists they had conquered, quickly absorbed existing ideas, and also made important new contributions to the life of the Middle East. To them are due the introduction of the horse and the chariot; and to the Hittites in particular, the invention of iron, which was first developed as a curiosity in about 1300 B.C., and later replaced bronze as the chief metal of every day use.[2]

The discovery of new lands such as the Americas gave impetus to large migrations of people, most of whom thought that they could do better in the new environment. Between the start of the 17th century and World War II, nearly fifty million Europeans left their old world homes

for North America; and from 1820 to 1930, a little over a hundred years, more than sixty million Europeans moved to the Americas, South Africa, and Australia.

At the present time, fewer movements of this type are in progress for several reasons. Most of the new worlds are in outer space with limited transportation and great doubts about the suitability for human settlement; and within the known world, various nations have set up restrictions on immigration. For example, several of the Latin American countries are seeking only farmers for their undeveloped lands; and Australia, in fear of lowering living standards, has ingenious entrance devices to limit most immigrants to the white race.

Changes in ownership of lands has stimulated migrations. Two of these situations involve Puerto Rico and the Virgin Islands, which became a part of the United States within the last century. The change from Spanish to United States control has made it easy for Puerto Ricans to enter continental United States; this has brought problems to New York City, where most Puerto Ricans migrate. Migration is just

[2] W. B. Fisher, *The Middle East,* A Physical, Social, and Regional Geography, E. P. Dutton & Co., New York, 1950. pp. 73 and 126.

as easily arranged for people from the United States Virgin Islands, formerly under Danish ownership. Emigrants from St. Thomas, St. Croix, and St. John, the three major Virgin Islands, also prefer New York as their home.

The settlement of Manchuria by the Chinese came as a result of the overthrow of the Manchu government. From time to time the Manchus had restricted northward migration for the Chinese; but with a change of rulers, people from North China flocked into Manchuria by the millions.

One of the greatest migrations in modern history started in Europe during the middle of the nineteenth century when people began to move from agricultural lands to the growing industrial centers. Probably 40 or 50 million people participated in this movement. Such a migration is not confined to Europe; for in the United States the same kind of a population change involving about 50 million people has taken place since 1920. Similar migratory movements, possibly more slowly, are taking place in other countries throughout the world.

Minerals have been a strong magnet which attract migrations of peoples. Early Spanish exploration and settlement of the new world followed the banner of the three G's—Gold, God, and Glory. The forty-niners seeking gold in California totaled well into the thousands of people migrating to the western part of the United States. In Canada, present government policies offer rewards to people who will move to the northern areas to develop mineral deposits in that portion of the Laurentian Shield. Chinese by the hundreds have moved into Malaya to work in the tin mines; and emigrants from India have migrated to British Guiana to labor in the bauxite fields and sugar plantations. Many other examples can be cited about the influence of minerals upon population movements.

While minerals may be a magnet to attract migrants, the depletion of metals is responsible for many ghost towns in western United States as well as in other parts of the country and in other nations. Even the exhaustion of non-precious metals such as iron may account for movements of population. A case in point is that of the nearly depleted Mesabi iron range west of Lake Superior; although the depletion of the rich ore is a major cause for an incipient migra-

tion, new developments in mining low grade Lake Superior iron ore are partly responsible for declining and rising towns in the iron country. In short the enrichment and pelletising of taconite gives strong competition to the exploitation of what is left of the Mesabi iron. Taconite may be more expensive to mine and pelletise than Mesabi iron ore is to mine and put directly into the furnace, but the pelletized taconite provides a final product that is cheaper and better than that resulting from the processed Mesabi ore.

One of the most recent migrations stimulated by features of the physical environment came from Tristan da Cunha, a British island in the South Atlantic. Local volcanic eruptions made the island unsafe for habitation, and most of the islanders were removed to Britain. However, several of the migrants have gone back to their original home, now that vulcanism has subsided; they say they prefer the discomforts and relative isolation of Tristan de Cunha to the modern life of Great Britain.

Forced Migrations. One of the best known of the forced migrations during the last few centuries is the cruel transfer of approximately 15 million African slaves into Latin America and southern United States. More recently, within the last few decades, Russia has utilized thousands of political undesirables and World War II prisoners to hasten development of largely untapped resources in Siberia and Arctic lands. Two well known examples are the Vorkuta coal fields northwest of the Urals and the Alden and Kolyma gold regions in northeastern Siberia.

The Russians and other nations behind the Iron Curtain also expelled many million Germans from former German territories after World War II. This seemed a calamity to the migrants and to West Germany, the recipient country, at the time; but the population shift has proved a boon to Germans and West Germany since the great post-war economic revival of the Bonn republic. Another Russian-forced migration came with the resettlement of Finnish expatriates from territory lost to the Soviet Union. This movement resulted in putting idle Finnish land into production by the development of the so-called cold farms.

The founding of the state of Israel brought thousands of European Jews to Palestine and created settlement problems for thousands of Arab refugees. Before World War II, agitation for Jewish exodus from Germany was sponsored by many organizations. One of the places suggested for settlement was southern British Guiana.[3] Examination of the region, however, showed it unadapted to such prospective migrations.

Great population movements took place in China during World War II. The Chinese moved their capital from Nanking to Chungking, in the heart of the Szechwan Basin. Before the failure of the German siege of Moscow, the Russians moved their capital to Kuibyshev, hundreds of miles east of the Kremlin. When Britain relinquished control on India, among the many changes which occurred was the abandonment of a summer capital. The new Indian dominion could not afford the extravagance of a summer and winter capital. The summer capital city remains, but the economy is now supported by tourists and not by government employees.

At the end of World War I, Turkey and Greece arranged an exchange of nationals with people involved running into the millions. Nearly 2 million Greeks left Turkey and 350,000 Turks moved from Greece to Turkey. This transfer brought hardships to many people and changed the population patterns of both countries.

Since 1950 the world has witnessed many other forced movements of population. These include Korea, Vietnam, and Tibet. Moreover Hindus have been expelled from Pakistan, Moslems from India, the Dutch from the East Indies, the Belgians from the former Belgian Congo, and the French from former French Indo China and Algeria. These and numerous other migrations have been brought about by the rapidly changing political scene.

Periodic Migrations

The term "periodic migrations" taken in its broadest meaning could include a great many subheadings, even daily commuters, tourists, and religious pilgrims, as well as people moving

[3] For a detailed description of the proposed Jewish haven see Earl B. Shaw, "The Rupununi Savannahs of British Guiana," *Journal of Geography* March 1940, pp. 89–104.

seasonally or for a somewhat longer period. In this study, however, mention will be made only of those migrating for the duration of a season or longer.

Thousands of Mexicans move across the United States boundary to work on the agricultural lands of Texas, New Mexico, Arizona, and California. American labor strongly opposes this migration and may force an end to the movement of foreign labor into the United States. Workers also move from Puerto Rico and other West Indies islands to help on farms, mostly in the summer, in many of the Atlantic Coast states.

In middle latitude mountain and valley country such as the Alps of Europe, the Wasatch of the United States, and several mountain groups of Asia, herders move with cattle, sheep, and other livestock to highland pastures during the warm season and back to the lowland feeding grounds in the winter. During the cold period, pasture is unavailable in the highlands, but the higher sun of summer melts the upland snow cover and makes the grasses available during the warm months.

Blanchard, a French geographer well known in the 1930's, applied the term transhumance to such seasonal migrations; but he emphasized that a movement of the entire pastoral group with flocks and herds, whether seasonally between highland and lowland or a more or less constant migration over areas of little topographic difference should be called nomadism. Thus the distinction he stressed between transhumance and nomadism was whether all the community accompanied the animals or only the necessary workers. This may be a useful interpretation.

Nomadism involves huge areas of desert and steppe land in the low and middle latitudes and in the tundra or cold deserts of the polar regions. However, the numbers of people and animals making such migrations are relatively few and the end products small when compared to animal husbandry in humid areas of the United States and Europe. Nomadism is not usually an aimless wandering. Where pasture is plentiful, nomads may stay several days or more in one place; where it is poor, they will search for better grass. Experience teaches them to be weather wise, and they move flocks and herds to take advantage of the infrequent and widely scattered desert showers. Since all equipment is carried on the backs of animals it must be light and unbreakable. In parts of the Middle East, the family may sit down to a meal of sour milk, soup, or meat placed in a nonbreakable wooden container. The shelter is one that can be taken down readily and carried easily. Thus a tent is admirably adapted to such purposes, and the black tents of the Middle East Bedouins, made of goat hair, conform nicely to these requirements.

Nomadic migrations and numbers of people involved are steadily declining. Oil development in the Middle East has given work to many migratory Bedouins; widespread increases in irrigated land entice some nomads to sedentary agriculture; and work in the taiga forests, the subarctic and arctic mines, and at military installations is attracting more European Lapps and North American Eskimos.

Annual migrations of laborers to Alaska take place to aid in the salmon fisheries. Nevertheless, this movement may decline with the increased use of modern fishing boats equipped for processing as well as catching fish.

Mining is also an industry in which labor has been moved considerable distances for definite time periods. The South African Rand has always been short of local workers to operate the mines. First, an attempt was made to utilize demobilized European soldiers for unskilled labor. Later, in 1904, Chinese laborers were engaged, and the immigration reached a total of more than 50,000 before repatriation took place in 1910. Since then Africans are hired for a few months or longer, some coming from regions many miles distant from the South African gold and diamond mines. All this influx of temporary workers creates great social problems, both for the mining section and for the recruiting grounds left by the migrants.

Winter encourages a significant seasonal migration, largely of older people, between northern and southern sections of the United States. Thousands of older citizens and people in poor health leave states near the Canadian border and spend the winter months in California, Florida, and other low latitude sections. The above are only a few of the many illustrations of periodic migrations which can be cited.

Physical and Cultural Characteristics

Race. The physical attributes of population may be studied under many headings, but here only four will be emphasized, race, sex, age, and health.

There is much disagreement among scientists about the number and choice of criteria to be used in separating men into racial groups. Nevertheless human types are distinguishable from one another by such physical characteristics as color, hair type, and by an epicanthic fold in the eyes characteristic of Orientals. There is also little agreement as to the origin of these physical differences. It is not desirable or possible in a text of this kind to examine all these varying viewpoints, but it may be useful to glance briefly at a few geographic theories to explain certain human features.

In a world with greatly contrasting regions of surface features, vegetation, and climates, man existed for hundreds of thousands of years with an extremely primitive culture. Massive migrations over long distances were impossible or extremely difficult, and segregation of many groups could have occurred over long periods of time.

Moreover, it seems possible that different segregated groups, exposed to contrasting earth conditions could develop differing physical characteristics. To illustrate what might be the influence of long segregation in a specific environment, one may examine certain features of the so-called yellow race. At the close of the last glacial period, the Pleistocene, east central Asia was very cold and dry. For thousands of years, winter winds blowing out from the continent and laden with dust deposited enough sediment to form what is now called the Loess Plateau in the Chinese provinces of Shensi and Shansi. People who survived this dry cold and dust best would need protection for their eyes, their noses, and their sinuses. A heavy padding of fat around the eyes and sockets longer than those for round-eyed people would lessen eye damage from cold, wind, and dust; and noses and sinuses would suffer less if nasal passages were short and slanted back sharply. Thus the slant eyes, broad face, and snub nose of the typical Chinese, according to a geographic theory, may have developed through a survival of the fittest for the windy, cold, dusty air of Post-Pleistocene time.

Again, during the glacial period and for some time afterwards, what is now the Sahara Desert was a much more humid area; even primitive man could move across it with relative climatic safety. However, with a change in climate and the coming of a dessicated Sahara, it became a real barrier between primitive people living around the Mediterranean Sea and those in Central Africa. Thus, isolated from the rest of mankind for thousands of years, central African Negroes might have conserved and intensified the pigmentation of their skin, their broad noses, and their tightly curled hair. All these racial characteristics, according to the geographic theory, could have some relationship to climate. The tightly curled hair could provide better shade for the scalp in strong sunlight and yet would permit evaporation of moisture from the sweat glands. The expansion of the nose would offer no handicap for sinuses needing little protection from wind and dust in the calm, warm, moist air of the tropical rainforest. And the progressive blackening of the skin might insure better survival in the equatorial sunlight. Thus primitive man in Central Africa may have accentuated his negroid characteristics when he became isolated by the dessication of the Sahara.

Finally, the so-called white race may also be partly indebted to climate for the color of its skin. In the West Coast Marine climate of Northwest Europe, there is too little sunlight, not too much as in Central Africa. Although an abundance of ultra-violet light may be harmful to human beings, an optimum is needed for every climate to assure proper growth. In the cloudy skies of Northwest Europe, a dark skin might have filtered out so much sunlight that children would have been more susceptible to various growth-retarding diseases; and thus the surviving fittest would be those individuals who possessed the lighter colored skins.

Although there is no general agreement as to where to draw the line for racial groups—some anthropologists list as few as two and others as high as two hundred—it may be useful to give some United Nations figures for the groupings of the world's population according to color. In the early 1960's these totaled about 240 million for the black; 900 million for the brown-red; 930 million for the white; and 930 million for the yellow.

Sex. Wars have been a strong factor influencing the imbalance of the sexes in several nations, making women far more numerous than men. For example the five-year war, 1865 to 1870, between Argentina, Brazil, and Uruguay on the one side—the Triple Alliance—and Paraguay on the other lowered the number of people in the latter country from about 1,300,000 to approximately 250,000 of whom less than 29,000 were males. A more recent illustration of the effect of war upon sex ratio in a country's population is that of Russia during World War II, 1939 to 1945.

The heavy cost of this great war to the U.S.S.R. was apparent in figures of the 1959 census in two ways: (1) in the sharply lower population than there would have been without war; and (2) in the heavy surplus of women over men. As to (1), an estimate of 30 million people is the human cost of World War II, in terms of lives lost prematurely and babies unborn.

In regard to (2) the census shows that there are now about 20 million more Soviet women than men; and that virtually the entire excess of females is concentrated among Russian citizens 32 years old and older. In contrast to the 1959 census figures, the 1939 census showed an excess of women over men of approximately 7 million, a sex difference resulting partly from Russian loss of life in World War I, 1914 to 1919.

The great imbalance in the sex ratio of the adult Russian population since World War II may partly explain the fact that much of the hardest and dirtiest work in that country during the last decade or more has been done by women.

In both primitive and highly industrialized societies women take an active part in making a living. Karl Pelzer[4] states that "the collection of vegetable matter is almost exclusively the woman's task in the gathering economy" but that "among primitive cultivators men either assist women in the cultivation of plants or entirely take over this activity whenever hunting and fishing become less important than soil tillage." Furthermore, "during untold centuries in which they collected plant matter, women acquired an intimate knowledge of plant life.

[4] Karl J. Pelzer, *Pioneer Settlement in the Asiatic Tropics,* p. 5, American Geographical Society Special Publication No. 29, 1945.

Edward Hahn and others have therefore reasoned that women were the inventors of the cultivation of plants and therefore were the first food producers."

On the other hand in highly developed commercial and industrial countries such as those of western Europe and Anglo-America, where men have held a dominant role in commerce and industry for a long while, women are increasing their share of the industrial burden significantly.

However, religious barriers, such as those in Moslem countries have kept to a minimum the number of women taking an active part in commercial and industrial life. It is well to remember that religion is not only important in the economic life of a nation, but also in the political and social events as well. In fact, many actual practices and customs as favored or forbidden by religions are significant in determining growth rates of population. Such growth rates may also be affected by national policy. Pre-World War II Germany, Italy, and Japan offered bounties for large families in order to assure continued growth in the reproductive group, and to maintain man-power for labor and military service.

Age. Students of demography usually represent the population of a country with what may be called a population pyramid graph. In short, the number of people in each age group, nor-

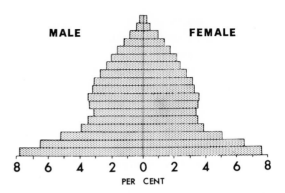

Fig. 19–15   Population Pyramid: United States. The United States, a well developed country, shows a relatively large proportion of the people in the higher age groups. (*Courtesy Norman J. G. Pounds,* Political Geography, *McGraw-Hill Book Company, Inc. 1963*) In a per cent pyramid, the total length of all bars in the graph—each representing the percentage of a certain age group in the country's entire population—should equal 100 per cent.

mally for five year periods, may be shown graphically with a sequence of horizontal bars. Bars are placed in position according to age, with the one at the bottom representing the youngest division, and the one at the top the oldest group; bars between bottom and top represent age groups between the very young and the very old.

The pyramid may also show sex ratio with the length of one side of the bar representing the number of males and the length of the other side the number of females.

The graphic pyramid includes a great deal of information about the population pattern of a country. For example, if the base of the structure is broad and the top narrow, the nation's population is expanding rapidly. In the Philippines (Fig. 19–14), Brazil, India, and Mexico, where population has increased rapidly in the 1950's and 1960's, children under 15 years of age make up about 40 per cent of the total population. The large number of persons in this age group will mean a high ratio in the reproductive age of the next generation.

If the pyramid base is narrower than the bar for the age group of say twenty to twenty-five, the graph suggests that the population is declining through a lowered birth rate. Again, in the better developed countries (Fig. 19–15), where life expectancy is greater, a larger proportion of the population appears in the higher age

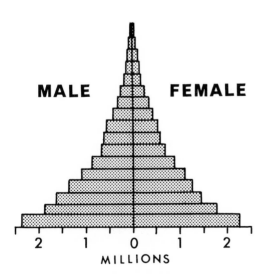

Fig. 19–14   Population Pyramid: Philippines. The Philippines, an underdeveloped nation shows a large proportion of the people in the younger age groups. (*Courtesy Norman J. G. Pounds,* Political Geography, *McGraw-Hill Book Company, Inc. 1963*)

groups. As a general rule, when a nation matures industrially, its population lives longer. For an illustration, the ratio of old people to total population is much greater in England, France, and the United States than in the Philippines, Brazil, India, and Mexico.

In the well-developed countries, the length of working life is longer than that of the underdeveloped areas. In the former lands, the generally accepted limits of the economically active people is between the middle or upper teens to the middle or upper sixties. In the underdeveloped nations, with a larger percentage of economic tasks consisting of hard manual labor in field or forest, the age limits begin younger and end earlier in life. For example in most Asian, African, and Latin American countries, well over half of the workers toil in agriculture, whereas in the United States and the United Kingdom less than 10 per cent of the labor force is used on farms.

On the other hand more than half of the labor force in the latter countries is employed in the so-called unproductive industries such as teaching, entertainment, trade, commerce, and government work, whereas the Philippines and India have less than 10 per cent in the same occupations.

Population Growth, Actual and Potential

Population of the world today, 1965, may be estimated at more than 3¼ billion, which is a distinct contrast to the two hundred and fifty million estimate at the start of the Christian era. About fifteen centuries later, between the time of Columbus' voyage and the landing of the Pilgrims, world population had doubled with a total of a half a billion. From that time on the increase became progressively more rapid. Shortly before the Civil War, in about 1850, the figure reached a billion.

It took man thousands of years, in fact from the beginning of human history, to increase his numbers to the first billion. But less than a century elapsed, between 1850 and 1930 or eighty years, before world population had doubled the 1850 figure. And only 30 years later, 1960, man's numbers had grown to 3 billion. In 15 years more, 1975, the earth's population will reach 4 billion, and more billions will come in constantly diminishing time unless something is done to stop what has been called the population explosion.

Birth rates in Africa, Asia minus Russia, and Latin America approach nearly 40 per thousand. During the last decade, 3 out of every 5 people added to world population live in Asia; another 1 of every 5 lives in Latin America and Africa. In the rest of the world—Europe, all of the Soviet Union, Anglo-America and Oceania—the birthrate is little more than half as high, under 25 per thousand. The death rate for people in the former regions, although higher than that in the latter areas is rapidly approaching the mark for people of European origin. As a result of this situation, population growth will be most rapid in Latin America, Africa, and Asia for some time.

Man's progress in the control of two most important factors that retarded population growth for centuries—pestilence and famine—partly accounts for the rapidity of recent increase and the potential future additions. However, man has made little advance in eliminating the third major retarding factor—that of war. Although he has decreased death rates by improvements in sanitation, by the prevention and control of disease and by enormously increased food production, he has developed simultaneously methods of expanding the effectiveness of war as a deterrent to population increase. In fact, he has expanded this effective deterrent so much that he could eliminate a large proportion, if not all, of the human race. And he could do this in less than a year.

Possible Solutions to the Population Explosion

Some demographers are more worried about the population explosion than they are about war. Others are not worried about either and they base their lack of concern about overpopulation upon factors such as the following:

1. Far from lagging behind the number of mouths to feed, as the alarmists assert, the supply of food in Western countries has been running ahead of the population increase for years. It must also be noted that in the United States the growing of crops is under strict control; and crop production with all the new hybrids and other yield-increasing crop techniques can be doubled and trebled if needed. Why can't such methods be put into practice elsewhere?

2. There are effective birth control measures. Man knows of these effective methods and can keep world population in balance with available and potential food supply by the use of birth control.

3. Massive redistribution of people is another remedy for overpopulation. There could be a removal of surplus population in overpopulated lands to the underpopulated countries. In the 1950's, Dudley Stamp and other well known geographers stated that the United States alone can absorb a half to three-quarters of a billion people without serious dislocation. Gazing into the future, it may be that the greatest benefit the space effort will confer upon the human race will be to enable man to migrate to other planets. Theoretically atmosphere can be created on planets where it is nonexistent or very thin. Perhaps this can be done by seeding new worlds with a catalytic substance to release oxygen now locked up there in compounds like carbon dioxide. Maybe the space effort can colonize other earths and relieve overpopulation in the world.

4. The lowering of trade barriers throughout the earth may help. The author believes that every geographer should subscribe to a policy of free trade. Each country should be permitted to produce to the limit the commodities whose production is best suited to that nation's environment; and surpluses should be allowed to move without tariffs, blocked currency, and other trade restrictions throughout the entire world. In short, maybe it is the bad economic, political, and social systems that peril mankind, not overpopulation.

QUESTIONS, EXERCISES, AND PROBLEMS

1. Point out how physical factors may discourage population settlement; stress each of the following: low temperatures, lack of moisture, too much heat, high mountains, soils, and vegetation. Does the fact that lands are sparsely populated today determine that they will be thinly settled in the future? Comment.

2. Describe how physical factors may encourage population settlement; stress each of the following: plains topography, mountains, plateaus, and soils. What two major reasons account for the highland location of many Middle American capitals?

3. Describe in some detail the causes and results of voluntary, forced, and periodic population movements.

4. Where are the world's great population regions? Why? Do rice growing and manufacturing have any influence upon population density? Comment. What hemisphere has the most people? Comment.

5. Comment upon the physical and cultural characteristics of population under the topics of race, sex, age, and health. Does the physical environment have anything to do with racial characteristics? Explain. How has war influenced the sex ratio in Russia? In what world regions do children form a very large proportion of the population? Name and describe several tropical diseases. What disease is an important handicap to work in the middle latitudes? Comment. Describe a population pyramid.

6. Where are the areas of greatest potential for population growth? What reasons are given by one group of demographers for their lack of worry about the population explosion? Give the total population, as well as the density, for each of the continents; the United States, Russia, Great Britain, France, Germany, Italy, Japan, China, India, Brazil, Mexico, Argentina, Chile, Central America, Indonesian Republic, and the West Indies.

7. Identify the following: District of Franklin, Gobi, Ordos, Thar, Takla Makan, Kyzyl-Kum, Kara-Kum, Pamirs, Armenian Knot, Tegucigalpa, Caracas, Bogotá, Celebes, New Guinea, Borneo, Irrawaddy, Rwanda, Burundi, Paraná Plateau, Deccan, Rupununi, Chungking, Kuibyshev, World Island, Three G's, pelletising, Tristan da Cunha, Vorkuta, Alden, Kolyma, transhumance, Triple Alliance, anopheles, nematode, bilharziasis, population explosion, FAO.

SELECTED REFERENCES

Ahmad, Enayat, "The Rural Population of Bihar, India," *Geographical Review* April 1961, pp. 253–76.

American Geographical Society, "The Alliance for Progress," *Focus* April 1964.

Barron's, "Standing Room Only? Bad Economics, Not Overpopulation Perils Mankind," Dec. 7, 1959.

Coon, Carleton, *The Origin of the Races,* Alfred A. Knopf, 1962.

Dorn, Harold F., "World Population Growth: An International Dilemma," *Science,* Jan. 26, 1962, pp. 283–90.

Gibbs, J. P., "Growth of Individual Metropolitan Areas: A Global View," *Annals of the Association of American Geographers,* Dec. 1961, pp. 380–91.

Gottmann, Jean, *Megalopolis,* The Twentieth Century Fund, 1961.

Gregor, H. F., "Spatial Disharmonies in California Population Growth," *Geographical Review,* Jan. 1963, pp. 100–122.

Hauser, P. M. and Duncan, O. D. editors, *The Study of Popula-*

tion, University of Chicago Press, 1959.

Hayes, Marion, "A Century of Change: Negroes in the U. S. Economy, 1860–1960," *Monthly Labor Review,* Dec. 1962, pp. 1359–65.

Klove, R. C., "The Growing Population of the United States," *Journal of Geography,* May 1961, pp. 203–12.

Lowenthal, David and Comitas, Lambros, "Emigration and Depopulation, Some Neglected Aspects of Population Geography," *Geographical Review* April 1962, pp. 195–210.

Martin, G. J., "The Law of Primate Cities Re-examined, *Journal of Geography,* April 1961, pp. 165–72.

Nelson, H. J., "Townscapes of Mexico: An Example of Regional Variation of Townscapes," *Economic Geography,* Jan. 1963, pp. 74–83.

Simpson, G. G., "The Nonprevalence of Humanoids: We Can Learn More About Life from Terrestrial Forms than we can from Hypothetical Extraterrestrial Forms, *Science,* Feb. 21, 1964, pp. 769–75.

Sopher, D. E., "Population Dislocation in the Chittagong Hills, East Pakistan," *Geographical Review,* July 1963, pp. 337–62.

The Conference Board, 440 Park Ave., N. Y. 22, N. Y., *Road Maps of Industry,* No. 1299, "The Fifty Largest U. S. Cities," Nov. 18, 1960; No. 1336, "World Population," Aug. 4, 1961; No. 1337, "A Nation of City Dwellers," Aug. 11, 1961; No. 1407, "Population by States, 1962," Dec. 14, 1962; No. 1459 "Economic Experience of the American Population," Dec. 13, 1963; No. 1472, "Population Projections to 1985," March 13, 1964; and other graphs on population.

Thorarinsson, Sigurdur, "Population Changes in Iceland," *Geographical Review* Oct. 1961, p. 519–33.

Walker, H. J., "Overpopulation in Mauritius: A Survey," *Geographical Review,* April 1964, pp. 243–48.

Warntz, William, "A New Map of the Surface of Population Potentials for the United States, 1960," *Geographical Review,* April 1964, pp. 170–84.

Zelinsky, Wilbur, *A Bibliographic Guide to Population Geography,* University of Chicago Press, 1962; "Changes in the Geographic Pattern of Rural Population in the United States," *Geographical Review,* Oct. 1962, pp. 492–524; "The Population Prospect in Monsoon Asia," *Journal of Geography,* Oct. 1961, pp. 312–21.

Part Three

Introduction to Political Geography

Chapter Twenty

Political Geography

Teachers of political geography, like other teachers, differ among themselves in their definitions and concepts of the subject. Among these definitions one may read that (a) political geography consists of the description and analysis of the politically organized area; (b) it is a study of the contribution of geography to world affairs; (c) it examines inter-relationships between earth and state; (d) it considers differences which exist among political regions and emphasizes geography's role in these differences; and (e) it stresses relationships occurring between man's political activities and the geographic environment both physical and cultural. Maybe the proper concept contains elements of all these definitions.

Important items of study may include, (1) location, area, and shape of the state;[1] (2) boundaries of various types, together with territorial claims of the state and those against it; (3) political relationships between states and water bodies, including oceans, seas, rivers, and lakes; (4) the number, structure, competence, skills, loyalty, and cohesiveness of the nation's[1] population; (5) the country's[1] resources including minerals, forests, power, food, and other raw materials as well as the manufacturing equipment and stage of technical advance necessary in processing natural resources; (6) transport

and communication facilities, both natural and developed; (7) the amount and character of internal and international trade; (8) the core area and capital or capitals of the state; (9) the country's alliances, colonies or the lack of them, military bases and military operations; and finally (10) the political pattern of the world. Most of the items listed above will receive emphasis in the following pages.

THE STATE'S LOCATION, SIZE, AND SHAPE

Where a state is located may be one of the most important factors in its political geography; and there are many ways to indicate place location, including latitude and longitude, physical position, location with reference to other countries, strategic situation etc. It may be useful to cite specific examples to show location relationships to political activities.

The location of France on the border of Germany (Fig. 20–1), long an aggressive neighbor, has had significant political results, particularly between 1870 and the 1940's. Iron mines and other French properties in Lorraine changed hands several times during the various wars of that period; and these changes were influenced, partly at least, by the vicinal location of France. Again, the position of the relatively weak countries of Finland, Poland, Czechoslovakia, Hungary, Rumania, and Bulgaria along the western borders of the Soviet, a great world power, has strongly influenced their government policies, especially since World War II.

Two good examples that illustrate the importance of strategically located countries are Egypt and Panama. Egypt controls the narrow constriction between Africa and Asia, the Isthmus of Suez. Panama includes a constricted isthmus that joins the Americas. Canals impor-

---

[1]The terms *state, nation,* and *country* were used interchangeably to avoid repetition; and this may be proper in popular usage. But used in a restricted sense, each term carries a somewhat different meaning to the political geographer. State may be defined as a region made up of area, people, and an effective mechanism of government with important attributes of sovereignty, boundaries, and a capital or capitals. On the other hand nation refers to a group of people with common descent, territory, political entity, customs, traditions, religion, and sometimes the fear of a common foe. Finally when the term country is used in the strict sense, it may refer to a group of people under the same government, but major emphasis is upon the physical environment occupied by the people.

Fig. 20–1 French Alsace and Lorraine Lie Close to Germany. Lorraine iron ore is a valuable economic resource. In the past its proximity to Germany has tempted that nation several times to annex the area. Alsace has important deposits of potash, but these are not as attractive as Lorraine iron ore.

tant to most of the world have been dug through both of these narrow pieces of land.

The importance of the Suez Canal in world power strategy may be seen in the willingness of France and Britain to launch a military attack against Egypt in 1954; this attack might have precipitated World War III. Both England and France withdrew, however, after the United States joined Russia and other members of the United Nations in frowning upon the British-French invasion.

Again, an important element of American World War II strategy was the defense of the Panama Canal. Even before the United States entry into the conflict, President Franklin D. Roosevelt traded Winston Churchill, Prime Minister of Britain, 40 old destroyers in exchange for island bases, many of which were strategically located for the defense of the Panama Canal.

Strategic locations rise and fall in their attractiveness to world powers with major economic and technical changes. For decades, in the age of coal dominance as a fuel, Britain maintained strategic coaling stations throughout the world to power her commercial and naval fleets. Most of these stations have long ago declined in importance. In contrast, note the

change in the strategic significance of the North Polar region. Now the Arctic has become important as a warning area against over-the-pole airplane and missile attacks. Vast sums have been spent upon the DEW Line (Distant Early Warning Service) which extends from Alaska across northern Canada to Greenland.

Prior to the age of air power and nuclear weapons, the shape of a state made a significant difference in its problems of defense (Fig. 20–2). A compactly-shaped country with a minimum length of international boundary was easier to protect against surface attack by land or sea than an attenuated-shaped state with national boundaries of maximum dimensions. For example, the length of compact Uruguay's boundary is only 105 per cent of the minimum length needed for its area; on the other hand sword-shaped Chile's boundary is 310 per cent of the minimum required for a compact state with an area equalling Chilean square mileage.

Shape has other political influences besides that for defense. It may affect administrative and social problems when it causes difficulties in transportation. Consider the situation of Pakistan, a divided state with about 900 miles of India separating the western and eastern parts of the Moslem country. And note the transport difficulties of the more than 20 states made up either entirely of islands, or of a continental mainland with fringing or widely separated isles. Contacts among various parts of a sea state may be costly to operate and susceptible to interruption; and these difficulties may create political hardships unheard of in a compact state.

Outlying portions of noncompact nations may not only create problems for the state itself, but also for states which it borders. Alaska's Panhandle cuts off parts of British Columbia and the Canadian Yukon from the Pacific ocean; and this condition has created more than one political controversy between the United States and Canada. Barriers within, as well as without a state may also cause a lack of national unity. Although Ecuador's shape is rather compact, the north-south trending Andes divide the country into three physical regions. These not only differ in terrain, climate, soils, and vegetation, but also in race, language, culture, and economic development. Such contrasts do not contribute to political cohesion.

The size of large states may also create difficulties in cohesion. Brazil has an area of more than three million square miles, nearly one-half that of South America. The country also contains approximately one-half of the continent's population made up of a mixture of many races. There are aboriginal Indians; descendants of Portuguese who began Brazilian settlement in the 16th century; Negroes who trace their ancestry to African slaves brought in to work tropical plantations centuries ago; and finally more recent immigrants from Europe and Asia. The Brazilian government and Brazilians in general do not frown on a mixing of the races and this fact encourages cohesion. However, more than 90 per cent of the total population live within 300 miles of the Atlantic coast; and the backlands are sparsely peopled by indigenous Indians having few contacts with the three populous regions—the coastal area, the East Central Plateau, and the southern Panhandle.

The government is trying to forge closer ties between the interior open spaces and the larger settlements of the East. In the early 1960's Brazil built a new capital, Brasilia, in southeastern Goiás, nearly 600 miles inland from the former federal capital of Rio de Janeiro by the sea. This new construction is only one of many bits of evidence that Brazil wishes to gain more cohesiveness for a country in which huge size creates a legion of economic, social, and political problems (Fig. 20–3).

A question is sometimes asked as to whether a country must be large to maintain independence and to become a great power. Huge size usually gives a country a wide variety of resources. The United States has almost every type of climate, soil, vegetation, mineral, power, and domesticated plants and animals. Russia lacks low latitude climates, soil, vegetation, and animal life, but her total natural resources are varied and numerous. China is also a large country with a diversity of physical features and natural resources; but the huge population, nearly one fourth that of the world, limits the effectiveness of these advantages.

In spite of the fact that Russia had almost as large an area (Fig. 20–4) as at present in the early years of the twentieth century, Japan, a nation only about the size of California, defeated the Russians in the war of 1904–1905. Moreover, for many years prior to the rise of Chinese Communist power in the 1940's, China

wasn't able to prevent several European powers, as well as Japan, from occupying and annexing parts of that huge country. However, within the last few decades, these two countries have reached great power status. Size may have helped; but the attainment of the goal depended more upon a people with a high percentage of military age, with an improving educational background, with a significant advance in technical efficiency, and with a national will to become a great power—a will that has been strengthened by a belief in Communism that is almost a national religion.

Another factor related to the size of states is how they grow. In general, countries expand in four ways, by cession of territory from other countries due to war; by purchase of lands; by occupation of land; and by addition of area through physical processes. A few examples will illustrate. In 1848, as a result of a United States victory over Mexico, Mexico relinquished control of a large part of what is now southwestern United States, including the states of California

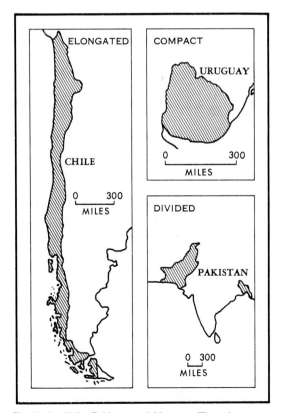

Fig. 20–2 Chile, Pakistan, and Uruguay. These three countries show great contrasts in shape.

Fig. 20–3 Brasilia is more centrally located than the former capital of Rio de Janeiro; but still it is about three times as far from the Peruvian border as it is from the coast. (*Courtesy J. P. Augelli and* Journal of Geography, *Sept. 1963*)

and New Mexico. In 1803, the United States gained an enormous amount of territory by the Louisiana Purchase from France; and expanded still farther in 1867 by a purchase from Russia of what is now the state of Alaska. Centuries before these purchases, European settlers occupied land along what is now the Eastern Seaboard of the United States, taking it away from the indigenous Indians. And finally, each year, the United States shows a small natural expansion through river deposition of silt at the mouth of the Mississippi river and the consequent enlargement of its delta. Many additional examples of national expansion by cession, purchase, occupation, and physical causes can be cited.

Finally, the size of some states in the past has been influenced by a belief of both people and government that the country's boundaries should conform to what may be called a physical unit. The cry of Manifest Destiny in the United States was largely a result of a national feeling that the United States had a God-given right to the natural middle-latitude North American region lying between the Atlantic and Pacific oceans.

A similar philosophy also inspired India's Nehru to denounce the creation of the state of Pakistan because the huge subcontinent of India was a natural unit bounded by the Kirthar, Sulaiman, and Himalayan mountains and the bordering seas. However, this denunciation did not prevent the formation of two states in the Indian peninsula—a division based largely on religious differences. At present the political trend is to make the state conform to the nation and not with some physical unit of the earth's surface.

Boundaries

Boundaries are dividing lines, in some cases zones, which separate the sovereignty of one state from that of another. These lines may follow natural surface features of various types or man may construct fences or walls to mark the limits of sovereign power possessed by each of the bordering nations.

Boundary concepts and values have followed a changing pattern among various peoples and during different historical periods. In certain primitive societies, spheres of sovereignty were separated from one another by zones, such as swamps, forests or deserts, rather than by definite lines. Even during the days of European feudalism, rulers were not so much concerned with carefully marking the limits of their king-

doms as they were with maintaining control over their serfs and soldiers. As a result, precise boundaries existed in but few places.

At present, much more thought and care is given to all phases of boundary making than in the past; and the trend toward greater precision may be noted in both delimitation—the definition of the boundary in the border agreement or treaty—and in demarcation—the interpretation of the treaty by those who mark the actual boundary in place.

Another noticeable trend is the lessening emphasis upon the choice of physical boundaries that may divide differing earth regions but fail to divide cultural groups of people. In fact, many mountains and rivers tend to unite rather than divide human society.

Finally, during the decade of the 1960's there is probably less concern over boundaries among member nations of the Communist World and among the countries of the noncommunist powers than there is over the deviation of any separate state from the group idealism or philosophy. However, boundaries between Communist and non-Communist states are fully as important as ever, possibly more so, as shown for

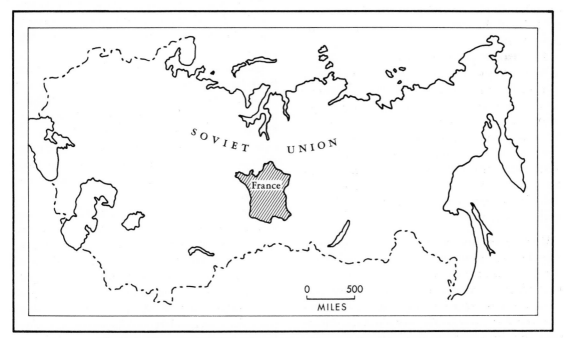

Fig. 20–4 France and the Soviet Union: A Contrast in Size. Russia's area of 8,603,-000 square miles is more than 40 times the area of France's 213,000 square miles; yet the French record for independence is probably just as good as that of the Soviet.

example by the many political implications of the boundary wall between East and West Berlin.

Several methods can be used to classify boundaries. Two which seem logical are (1) the morphological approach which includes rivers, lakes, seas, and so forth; mountains and hills; forests, swamps, and deserts; and geometrical lines; and (2) a classification based on whether the boundary is made through (a) an unpopulated area or (b) a populated one. Divisions of the second classification may be named antecedent, subsequent, and superimposed boundaries.

Antecedent, Subsequent, and Superimposed Boundaries. It may be useful to give examples of and comments upon various types of boundaries, many of them belonging to the two classifications mentioned above. The Canadian-Alaskan boundary, agreed upon between Canada and Russia in treaties of 1825 and 1827, qualifies as an antecedent one because it separated parts of a region with no settlers at all. Again, the Pakistan-Indian boundary of the late 1940's (1947) is an illustration of a subsequent type because it was established after the cultural pattern was formed. This pattern was one of two distinct religious groups, one Moslem, the other Hindu; and religion was the base used in dividing the Indian subcontinent into two separate states.

The superimposed boundary resembles the subsequent type in being drawn after settlement of a region, but differs from the latter in being forced upon the area with no regard to cultural or ethnic characteristics. Most African colonial boundaries were superimposed upon the continent by various European powers during the latter part of the 19th century. Such a superimposed division largely remained until the formation of numerous independent states during the middle of the 20th century.

Boundaries by Oceans, Gulfs, and Seas. The 48 contiguous states of the United States are bordered on the east by the Atlantic Ocean; the Gulf of Mexico and the Gulf of Lower California comprise approximately half of the southern boundary; and on the west the huge Pacific separates America from Asia's restless millions. Besides the Pacific, which lies to the south and west of Alaska; and the Arctic lying to the north, various seas, sounds, and straits separate our forty-ninth state from Siberia to the west. Our fiftieth state, Hawaii, is completely surrounded by the Pacific.

For centuries, the ocean was a great protection against enemy surface attacks. But now in the age of missiles, planes, and satellites, the large expanse of water is no protective shield from the air, a most common area of conflict. Furthermore, there is no general agreement among nations as to how far national sovereignty extends over the bordering seas. Hundreds of years ago, when the most powerful guns would shoot only a few miles, the three mile limit was almost universally accepted as a portion of international law. Today, in the 1960's, no such acceptance exists. Some nations want the three mile limit continued, but others wish to maintain national power over as many as 200 miles from their shores.

Inland Waters. Inland waters form parts of the northern and southern boundaries of the United States—Lake of the Woods, Rainy River, Rainy Lake, Lake Superior, the Saint Mary's River, Lake Huron, the St. Clair River, Lake St. Clair, Lake Erie, Niagara River, Lake Ontario, and the St. Lawrence, St. John, and St. Croix rivers all lie on the United States northern fringe; and the Colorado and Rio Grande Rivers border the country on the south (Fig. 20–5).

Inland waters also provide all or parts of the boundaries for more than half of the contiguous 48 states. Boundary rivers include the Chatahoochee, Colorado, Columbia, Connecticut, Delaware, Mississippi, Missouri, Ohio, Potomac, Red, Rio Grande, Savannah, and Snake. Numbered among the bordering lakes are Lake Champlain, each of the Great Lakes, and Lake Tahoe.

Whether a stream makes a stable boundary for a state or a nation depends upon its geologic age. Geologists classify streams according to their youth, maturity, or old age. Valleys of youthful streams are likely to be narrow and V-shaped. Many youthful rivers have deep and steep walled canyons which may be difficult to cross. Such canyonlike valleys give little chance for the stream to change its course, and boundary problems based upon the stability of the original stream course are kept at a minimum.

When a river reaches a mature stage, valleys become broad, slopes gentle, and the stream begins to meander (flow in great curves). During periods of heavy precipitation and flooding, the meandering river may take a short cut and break through the loop of the meander creating what is called an oxbow lake; and if such a mature stream forms a state or national boundary, the altered water route can cause serious political trouble.

The Rio Grande in its approximately 2000 mile course forms both a state and a national boundary. Along the border between the United States and Mexico, the stream varies in age from early youth, where it flows through mountain and plateau topography within steep canyon walls, to late maturity, where it meanders across a featureless plain. In the early youth section of Big Bend National Park (Fig. 20–6), there have been no boundary difficulties because the almost perpendicular valley walls keep the river in the same course through periods of flood and drought. But the situation is entirely different where a mature section of the Rio Grande meanders between almost imperceptible banks across the nearly level plain lying within and bordering the city of El Paso, Texas. A careful

observer driving over this plain can see almost forgotten channels far from the present course of the river. Maps since 1850, when the earliest American surveys were made, show a confusing maze of looping and intersecting lines that represent the dim ghosts of Rio Grandes of 25, 50, 75, and 100 years ago (Fig. 20–7).

As the river has been the boundary, since 1850, between Texas, and a small section of New Mexico, and since 1835, between Texas and Mexico, the wanderings of the river in and around El Paso have caused constant inter-governmental disputes and have played havoc with property titles. In the upper valley, the problems have been domestic, between Texas and New Mexico. Innumerable law suits between property owners were caused by the river's erratic changes; and it was not until the United States Supreme Court handed down a decision in 1928, that numerous residents in El Paso's upper valley knew what state they were living in. For many miles, the boundary fixed by the court does not follow the Rio Grande of today, but lies to the west along what was determined to be the river bed of 1850.

Straightening out the international boundary south of El Paso has been a difficult task. The

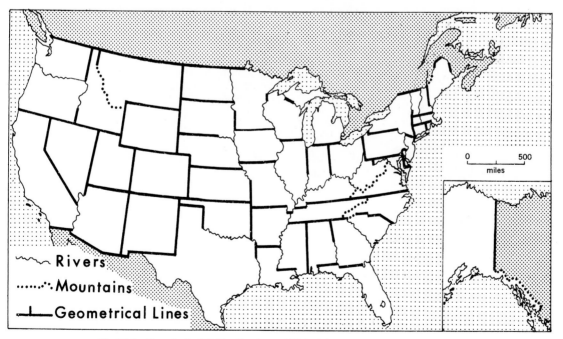

Fig. 20–5   Boundaries Within Continental United States. Various types of boundaries set apart the states of Continental United States. (*Courtesy Norman J. G. Pounds, Political Geography, McGraw-Hill Book Company, Inc., 1963*)

Fig. 20–6   The Gorge of the Youthful Rio Grande. The steep walls of the young Rio Grande in Big Bend National Park are far different from the low shifting banks of the mature stream flowing through the El Paso region. (*Courtesy National Park Service and George A. Grant, photgrapher*)

trouble comes in using a meandering river as an international boundary. If the original Mexican-U.S. border treaty had specified the course of the meandering river at treaty time as the permanent boundary, whatever changes the river made afterwards would have caused little political difficulty. The main trouble came in the lack of precision in boundary description in the treaty and in the same lack in actual marking out of the international boundary. Because this was not done, international problems came into being every time the Rio Grande cut across one or more of its many meanders; and thus bits of Texas were suddenly placed in Mexico; and fragments of Mexico placed in Texas.

On July 18, 1963 an historic decision was made by the presidents of the United States and Mexico over the Rio Grande boundary in and around El Paso. This arrangement should settle a long international dispute. The Chamizal Settlement as it is called, named for a type of vegetation originally covering much of the con-

tested region, makes concessions to both parties. One clause most interesting to the geographer is that the "Rio Grande will be relocated . . . and the new channel will be concrete lined." This puts man in control of the river's course by using a straight-jacket method; and if the concrete straight-jacket is kept in good condtion throughout future years, the meanders and cutoffs of the Rio Grande in the El Paso area should cause no more political trouble.

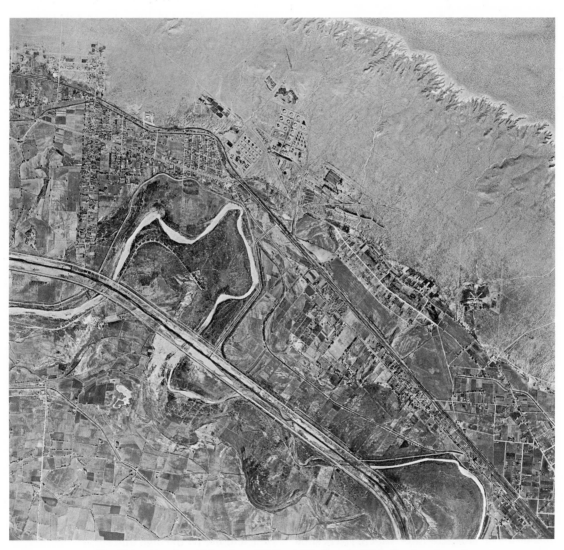

Fig. 20–7   Abandoned Meanders of El Paso's Rio Grande. While the river channel was straightened and meanders cut off by man in 1897, the stream has made meanders and cut them off many times and in many places during the last centuries. Moreover, stream action in cutting off meanders in the 1850's and 1860's created the Chamizal problem, long a sore spot in United States-Mexican relations. An amicable agreement was reached in 1963. (*Courtesy the National Archives*)

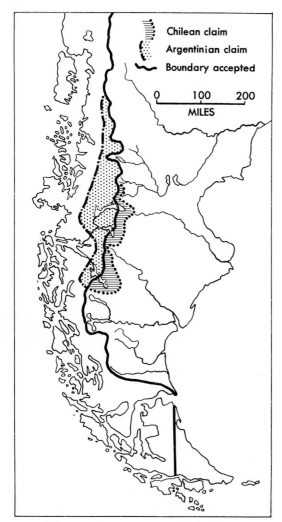

Fig. 20–8   The Boundary Between Chile and Argentina in the Southern Andes. Research on a boundary dispute between the two Latin American countries showed (1) no crest line in the Andes and (2) no conformation between the water parting and the higher ranges. Thus, descriptions of the crest line and conformation of the water parting with the higher ranges—descriptions appearing in the Treaty of 1881—simply did not correspond to the actual surface features. The dispute was settled peacefully in 1902. Settlement is commemorated by the statue, Christ of the Andes, erected along the Uspallata Pass, which constitutes part of the boundary. (*Courtesy Norman J. G. Pounds,* Political Geography, *McGraw-Hill, 1963*)

Mountains. Mountains make stable boundaries because a mountain ridge doesn't develop the meander characteristics which rivers show upon relatively flat plains. Nevertheless, political controversy arises over mountain borders as well as over the international limits of streams. This happens because of man's failure to describe the mountain boundary in sufficient and careful detail when the treaty between countries is made. Among other things, treaty makers should take pains to indicate whether the national limits follow the ridge crests or drainage divide because the two topographic features are seldom, if ever, the same. A brief description of the boundary dispute between Chile and Argentina will emphasize this point (Fig. 20–8).

The Chileans claimed the drainage divide as the boundary while the Argentines claimed the border to be the crestline of the Andes mountains. These opposing views were made possible by the vague wording of the boundary description in the Treaty of 1881. There is no true crest line, but there is a drainage divide that lies east of the highest ridges. Its eastern position may be explained as follows. Even before the last Andean glacial period, rivers on the western side of the mountains had cut headward across the Andean Cordillera until they had shifted the continental divide to the edge of the Pre-Andean Depression, a fault valley lying between the Patagonian Plateau on the east and the Andes mountains on the west. Glacial action gouged out the river-cut canyons through the Andes and made west-flowing drainage easier after the melting of the great ice sheet. Thus many preglacial and postglacial west-flowing streams extended their sources far to the east of the high Andes upon land claimed by Argentina.

The controversy was settled without war. Both countries agreed that Britain should settle the dispute. After a map of the disputed territory had been drawn, and the population distribution studied, the award was made; the settlement gave Argentina much of the controversial lake country in the north and Chile a wide stretch of country east of the mountains to the south—even a small section of east coast along the Strait of Magellan.

Until recent years, mountains have been barriers against enemy attack, except that by air, because crossings are difficult for all surface transport; and for the same reasons they limit commerce. India and China provide a useful illustration. These countries are separated from one another by the high and rugged Himalayas; and until the 1962 Chinese attack upon India, the great highland barrier discouraged large scale army movements. It is likely that the Himalayas will continue to limit international trade as they have in the past.

A similar situation has existed for a long time between France and Spain, separated from one another by the Pyrenees. Little commerce passes between the two countries; and a significant per cent of what does pass has been handled by smugglers—traders whose illegal dealings are favored by the mountainous terrain. Desert and swamp boundaries between states also may provide a barrier to trade as well as to enemy surface attack.

Geometrical Boundaries. Geometrical boundaries have been chosen many times in the past when clearly defined physical features were unknown or unsuitable. They include parallels, meridians, straight lines, and oblique lines. A meridian boundary was used in 1493 by Pope Alexander VI, who drew the line dividing unexplored parts of the world between Spain and Portugal. Illustrations of parallel boundaries are numerous. The 38th parallel was established in 1945 as the border between North and South Korea; and in 1954 the 17th parallel was defined as the boundary between North and South Viet Nam; the 49th parallel forming the northern boundary of the United States west of Lake of the Woods was accepted in 1818.

This 49th parallel boundary crosses plains, mountains and rivers regardless of the natural features. In many places it is almost as easy to cross the Canadian-U.S. border as it is to travel within either country. Fortunately, friendship due to similarity in race, language, and ideals, has led Canada and the United States to agree never to fortify the boundary or make any preparation for military activity along its course. This agreement is carried out rigidly, although a few small disturbances have occurred. During the U.S. Civil War, Canadian sympathizers with the Confederacy tried to organize an armed expedition to invade the northern states from Canada. Early in World War I, half a century later, German sympathizers from the United States crossed the boundary and tried to injure Canada by blowing up the Welland Canal. In later years the ease with which the Canadian border can be crossed was one of the greatest obstacles to the enforcement of prohibition and immigration laws of the United States.

The boundary of the United States Gadsden Purchase from Mexico, made in the early 1850's was described in the 1853 treaty as "a straight line" from a point at 31° 20′ N and 111° W to "a point on the Colorado River twenty English miles below the junction of the Gila and Colorado River." The southwestern boundary of the state of Nevada is an oblique line as are many national boundaries in Africa.

Fortified Boundaries. In the past fortified boundaries were probably more common than they are today. The Great Wall of China extends for about 1500 miles across that huge country. It was built centuries ago to protect the areas of sedentary agriculture from the nomads of the interior dry lands. The enormous work of building the barrier may be understood by noting some of its dimensions: 20 feet high and 20 feet thick, with towers 50 feet high every few hundred yards (see Fig. 19–13).

About fifty years ago the French thought that they could protect themselves from the Germans with the help of the Maginot Line.[2] History proved their thinking false. And in very recent time, 1961, the Russians built The Wall between East and West Berlin to stop persistent large migrations of East Berliners to the West.

Disputed and Unrecognized Boundaries. Bolivia and Paraguay fought the Chaco War of the 1930's over a zone or uncertain boundary in the Chaco region lying among Argentina, Bolivia, and Paraguay. Honduras and Nicaragua, until recently, had differing views of the boundary location between the two countries and a zone of disagreement existed for decades. Ecuador, Colombia, and Peru fought many skirmishes over the Oriente region along the borders of the three countries. A boundary settlement came after a Peruvian invasion during the 1940's, but Ecuador is far from satisfied with the present boundary. Much of the trouble in all three of these cases came from the lack of good maps, the support of differing maps by the con-

[2] The enormous loss of life incurred by France in World War I, and the failure of the 1918 Peace Treaty to give the French the security they desired probably were important conditions that encouraged French construction of one of the strongest defensive walls of recent time, the Maginot Line, which was intended to make her eastern border invulnerable from Switzerland to Belgium. Concentration on this one kind of defense kept the French from preparing for mobile warfare and gave them a false sense of security. The fall of the Maginot Line in 1940 clearly demonstrated the folly of relying completely upon fortification for defense.

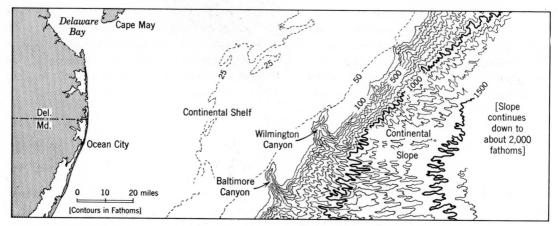

Fig. 20–9   Continental Shelf off Delaware and Maryland. Note that the shelf extends for scores of miles beyond the coast. (*Courtesy A. N. Strahler,* Physical Geography, *2d ed., John Wiley & Sons, 1962*)

testants, and careless descriptions of national limits by early surveys. And finally, the United States has never recognized the 1940 Russian take-over of Latvia, Lithuania, and Estonia.

Freedom, Control, and Jurisdiction of the Sea. The world's oceans and seas not only have political implications as boundaries, but they also are responsible for many other international problems—problems which involve international freedom of navigation; national jurisdiction over certain ocean resources; and complete national control of a limited extent of coastal waters.

It is almost universally agreed that use of the bulk of the ocean, the high seas, should be free to all nations for all legitimate activities. On this huge area, accounting for more than half of the earth's surface, every state has the right to move ships, to fly planes, and to lay cables on the ocean bottom. Where seas and oceans approach national shorelines, however, complete international freedom of usage is not guaranteed. In fact most countries accept the principle that each ocean-bordered country should have complete control over the open ocean for a distance of a *few* miles from shore. But there is no general agreement on the definition of *few*. The 1958 Geneva Law-of-the-Sea convention sought such an interpretation, but on this the conference reached no unanimity. As a result, *few* may mean 3 miles from shore for the United States

and up to 200 miles for some of the Latin American nations.

In 1945, President Truman issued a proclamation claiming jurisdiction over the natural resources, primarily petroleum and metallic minerals, on or beneath the floor of the continental shelf [1] adjoining the United States (Fig. 20–9).

Several other countries followed his proclamation of limited control with some carrying much broader jurisdictional claims. For example, Mexico claimed the entire continental shelf fringing its shores and every one of its natural resources. The 1958 Geneva Law-of-the-Sea convention defined depth limits of the continental shelf as 200 meters. Formerly the generally accepted depth definition was 100 fathoms or 600 feet. Under the recent ruling the world's continental shelf occupies over 10,500,000 square miles, and underlies more than 7½ per cent of the ocean.

[1] Each coastal state now has sovereign rights over the adjoining seabed and subsoil out to wherever the sea is 200 meters deep; and beyond that limit, for as much farther as it can exploit the natural resources of the undersea area. To a depth of 200 meters the right is exclusive; no other state can stake a claim within this limit. At greater depths possession goes with ability to exploit. These rights apply only to the land beneath the sea, not to the waters and not to the airspace above. The 1958 International Conference on the Law of the Sea drew up these rights, but they went into effect only recently, upon ratification by the necessary number of states. See "The Continental Shelf" *Science,* April 2, 1965, p. 25.

In 1958, Iceland and England almost reached a diplomatic break over fishing rights within 12 miles of the former country's shore line. Fish and fish products make up over 90 per cent of Iceland's exports and the island nation complained that foreign fishermen were depleting nearby fishing banks. For a time Britain guarded her fishing fleets with gun boats when they fished in the 6000 square miles of bordering ocean over which Iceland claimed jurisdiction. Shots were exchanged on more than one occasion; but later England accepted the Icelandic claim of control upon fishing within 12 miles of the island coast.

Finally, the right to search for smuggled goods on vessels within a few miles of a nation's shore is claimed by many states. As an illustration, the law of 1790 gave the United States this right; and the early law was used many times after the prohibition amendment, the 18th, was passed in 1919, more than a century later.

Inland Waters and International Relations

Like oceans and seas, the earth's inland waters create national and international problems other than those related to boundaries. Of course, rivers, lakes, and canals which lie entirely within any country and belong to that state may remain under national control. But when these water bodies form boundaries between states or flow through more than one nation, numerous international difficulties may develop. Important among these are (1) problems associated with navigation. The stream may need deepening; locks may be necessary around rapids or waterfalls; or ice breakers may be required to lengthen the navigation season in middle and high latitudes. Again, (2) agreement between countries sharing parts of a stream system may be advisable to determine each nation's share of stream flow for mutual purposes of irrigation and human consumption; and this agreement may well contain stipulations concerning the safeguarding of water from pollution by wastes from industrial plants or other sources of contamination. Finally, (3) international rivers almost always suggest problems of flood control, hydroelectric power, and possibilities of unifying the entire river basin into a functional unit.

Many of these problems, as well as others, are faced by nations sharing control of the Rhine with its source in Switzerland, its mouth in Holland, and its middle course waters touching France, Germany, and Luxembourg. These nations have been more successful in agreements on international use of the Rhine than Germany, Austria, Yugoslavia, Hungary, Czechoslovakia, Romania, Bulgaria, and Russia have with problems of the bordering or through-flowing Danube.

In Africa, the Nile (Fig. 20–10), probably the world's longest river, causes many political difficulties for five states which share its waters, Republic of the Congo, Uganda, Ethiopia, Sudan, and Egypt. In Asia, Pakistan and India have quarrelled for years over the waters of the Indus, so vital for irrigation of northwest India and all of West Pakistan. The river rises in Tibet, but flows through the province of Kashmir, claimed, fought over, and partly held by both countries.

In North America, the United States and Canada are cooperating on both navigation and power development of the Great Lakes-St. Lawrence Seaway composed of rivers and lakes shared by both countries. Farther south, the United States and Mexico signed an historic document in 1945 allocating waters of the Colorado and Rio Grande, rivers bordering or shared by both countries. This water is vital for irrigation and human consumption in both nations. The timing of the water agreement was especially auspicious; for the Mexican-United States treaty showed the many nations meeting at San Francisco, to form the United Nations, that the host country was willing to be cooperative, a spirit so necessary for world peace. These problems, and those of additional rivers, especially the Columbia, Paraná, Uruguay, Jordan, and Scheldt, should be studied in more detail. Time devoted to such study should give a more complete understanding of the political geography of international inland waters.

Population and Political Geography

Several characteristics of a country's population may be more significant than others when considered from the standpoint of political geography. Some have already received consideration in Chapter Nineteen. There, the topics of population structure, stressing sex and age; population growth, actual and potential; population

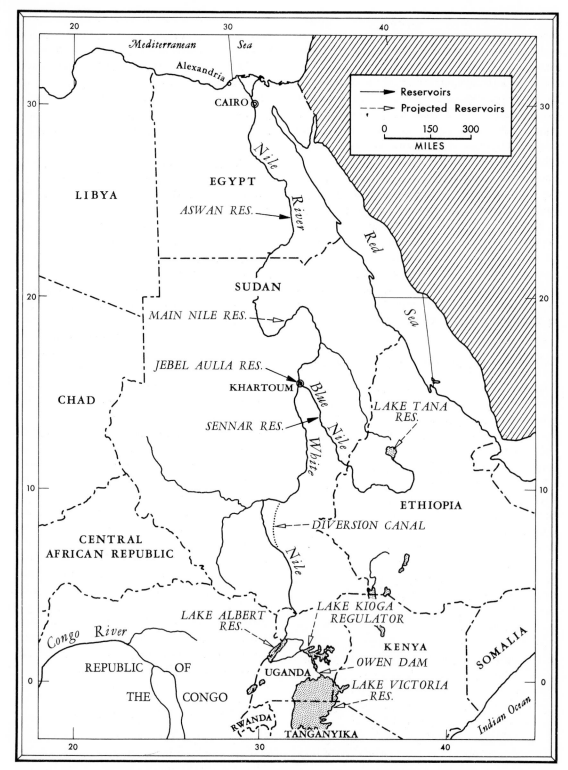

Fig. 20–10   The Nile Crosses Several Political Boundaries. The Nile flows through many different countries, all of which are interested in what happens to its waters. However, these waters are probably more vital to the economic life of Egypt than to any of the other countries. It has been said many times that "Egypt is the Nile." Some work is progressing on the projected Nile water storage, but the diversion canal across the Sudanese Sudd is still in the planning stage.

exchange and migration, all received some attention. Here, the question may be asked as to whether total national population figures are a true measure of a state's power. This is an "iffy" question, as former President Franklin Delano Roosevelt used to respond when needled by reporters. The answer is yes if there is a large percentage made up of males of military age; if there is a strong central government; if the country stands at a high stage of technical and industrial development; if there is unity, cohesiveness, and loyalty among the people; and if there are large natural resources. At least four countries of the world, China, India, Russia, and the United States have about or more than 200 million people. China, with the largest total, probably may be considered a great power although the state lacks a high stage of technical and industrial development and is dangerously lacking in food self-sufficiency and certain other natural resources.

India, second in total population among the nations, is not a great power. That state lacks dependable food supply; a widespread system of modern technology and industry; a large well-trained army; and certain other necessary bases of national power. In the early 1960's, India called upon Russia, Britain, and the United States for aid in the border war with China. All responded to India's call. Few will dispute the statement that at present, 1965, both Russia and the United States have far greater power than either India or China; and this suggests, as previously mentioned, that large natural resources together with the proper structure, competence, skills, loyalty, and cohesiveness of the nation's population may be fully as important, or more so, than the possession of a huge population lacking several, or nearly all, of the above listed power advantages.

It is suggested that the student study the populations of each of the present great powers, and those before World War II, with reference to all the above mentioned desirable characteristics. Such an examination will yield much information about actual and potential power and will strengthen student background in political geography.

Natural Resources

The possession of natural resources, food, minerals, manufacturing, transportation, and so forth, in great quantity and variety contributes significantly to a state's power. An account of world distribution of several important resources has been given already—food in the regional Chapters Twelve to Sixteen inclusive; minerals in Chapter Eleven; and manufacturing in Chapter Seventeen. Thus, it seems unnecessary to examine them again. However, it may be useful to look briefly at the transportation of two world powers, Russia and the United States, generally conceded to be most nearly self-sufficient in total natural resources of all the earth's nations.

In any assessment of transportation in Russia, mention should be made of the country's huge size, the dominance of middle and high latitude location, and the relatively cold climates. All these affect transport problems. Great distances make long hauls between widely spaced large cities; Moscow and Vladivostok are 5600 miles apart, and movement of freight by rail takes at least two weeks. Cold climates produce permafrost over half of the total area; and permafrost adds to the cost, the maintenance expense, and the difficulties of surface transport either by rail or road.

In 1959 over 90 per cent of Russian freight moved by rail. In the same year trains handled 40 per cent of that moved in the United States. At the same time 95 per cent of Russian long distance passenger travel rode the trains. In the United States 4 per cent of inter-city passenger movement was carried on railroads. Length of the Russian rail system, about 80,000 miles is approximately one third that of the United States; but the amount of traffic moving over each mile of track in the U.S.S.R. is 5 times that of U.S.

Although Russia has invested much in waterways, they have failed to relieve heavily burdened railways. Moreover, movement by water is slower than that by rail. Miles of Russia's all-weather roads number approximately 150,000, far fewer than the figure for the United States. Furthermore, the U.S. spends about $7 billion a year on roads, whereas Russian expenditures are but a minute fraction of that amount. Again, Russian truck traffic is far less than that of the United States, where trucks carry more cargo than the rails; and in Russia, the number of motor vehicles registered per 1000 persons in 1962 was 2.7; in the United States the number registered in the same year was 339.1 per 1000. All these facts emphasize the great dependence of Russia on one type of transport, the railroads. Such a lack of transportation flexibility points up a power weakness in this natural resource both during peace time and in time of war.

Political Geography and Foreign Trade

Various geographic aspects of trade were examined in Chapter Eighteen, which included one section devoted to "Trade, National Economy, and Power," and another calling attention to "United States International Trade." However, it may be worthwhile to add a description of the Communist-Free World wheat trade of the early 1960's in order to give further emphasis on the numerous political implications of foreign trade.

In the 1950's, Russia's Premier Khrushchev decided to expand grain production on a large scale in what became known as the Virgin Lands Experiment. Most of this new wheat country lies in Siberia east of the Ural Mountains, and near the heart of the huge land mass of Eurasia. For a few years after the Siberian steppe country was first plowed, crops were good with the biggest yield of all harvested in 1958. After that year, however, crop failure followed crop failure until something like a crop disaster occurred in 1963. The farming debacle was partly a result of a cold spring and a long summer drought, not unusual for a location with such a high latitude and lying so far from any ocean source of moisture. At the same time Russia's Virgin Lands were disappointing farmers, China's undependable monsoons dealt the Chinese a series of crop failures.

Of course, man-made conditions such as too much emphasis upon heavy industry and too little upon agriculture; the lack of incentive for farmers to produce good crops; a deficiency in fertilizer; too little attention to supplementary irrigation; and insufficient farm machinery and repairs—all these aided and abetted the bad weather in lowering crop yields. As a result, the Communist World had to call on the Free World for wheat.

China was the first to make purchases, and the Chinese bought grain from Canada and Australia before 1963. Russia followed with purchases from the same two surplus grain producers. And then, the Soviets let it be known that they were willing to buy grain from the United States. The news provoked controversy in the United States Congress and throughout the entire country. Some legislators felt that any sale of food to Russia was an aid to Communism. Others looked at the humanitarian aspect and stressed the favorable world propaganda value of help for hungry people. Still others stressed that our Allies were selling to Communists and that the former would continue to supply them if we didn't. Most Great Plains wheat farmers were in favor of the sale. On the contrary, elevator interests reaping good rentals from surplus grain storage were against the sale to Communists. Owners of ocean shipping sensed an opportunity to employ their idle ships, and exerted pressure for the grain deal. In fact political pressure came upon the administration from all sides. Finally a total of about 80 million bushels of United States wheat was shipped to Russia and other eastern European countries between July 1963 and March 1964. Russia received a little over half of the total. The wheat transaction is only one of a legion of foreign trades which illustrate the many influences of geography upon international relations.

Core Areas and Capitals

Most of the older states, including the great powers or former great powers, originated with and grew from a nucleus or core area. Usually nature endowed the core with an advantage or advantages encouraging national growth. The soil may have been unusually fertile, and together with level topography and mild climate may have supported a dense farm population; it even may have yielded enough to provide food for commercial and industrial workers. Or the core region may have possessed qualities favoring easy military defense; or the state's origin may have taken place where there is an intersection of important trade routes. One or all of these geographic qualities may foster integration of a nation. Illustrations are numerous.

Early Chinese civilization grew and flourished in the valley of the Hwang Ho and its tributaries. Here the fertile loessial soil was well suited to ancient agricultural practices; and here were located the earliest Chinese capitals.

If it had not been for the invasion of what is now European Russia by the Tartar horsemen of the eastern steppe, the Ukraine might be the core region and Kiev the capital of the present Soviet state. However, forests clothed the region to the north around Moscow, and they proved a good defense against cavalry charges of the Tartars; thus Moscow became the nucleus and capital of a nation with more than one seventh of the world's land area.

When the St. Gotthard Pass was opened for north-south trade early in the thirteenth century, the mountaineers of the four Swiss Forest Cantons bordering this steep Alpine opening sold their services to early traders. Thus a location near an ancient commercial highway through the Alps gave the nucleus for the original Swiss Republic. Indeed, it has been said with truth that Switzerland is a product of the St. Gotthard Pass just as Egypt is a creation of the Nile.

Switzerland may be used to illustrate another phase of the political geography of core areas and capitals. When the rugged Forest Cantons lost the economic leadership of the state to the more productive plateau region—an area topographically better for agriculture and for building cities, factories, and railroads—there was also a shift of the Swiss nuclear core as well as the capital. Bern became the new and permanent capital, and the plateau area roundabout Bern developed into a new core area.

England's core region was the lower Thames valley with London located at the first easy interior crossing of the river. France originated within the Paris Basin, and the country's very beginning came on the Ile de France, the early site of Paris. The significant position and geographic quality of the Ganges Basin made it the original nucleus of India; and Delhi, strategically located on the Jumna tributary was the capital for the highland invaders, for oversea conquerors, and nearby New Delhi for the present Dominion.

Many other topics on core areas and capitals remain for examination: (1) states with two nuclear cores such as Germany with Brandenburg and the Rhine Valley; Canada with Quebec and Ontario; and Ecuador with Guayaquil and Quito; (2) states with capitals outside the core area like Canberra in Australia and Madrid in Spain; (3) nations with more than one capital—The Hague and Amsterdam in The Netherlands; Bolivia's Sucre and La Paz; and South Africa's Capetown, Bloemfontein, and Pretoria; (4) states which have moved capitals during war time through necessity or to gain strength in depth as China's move from Nanking to Chungking and Russia's change from Moscow to Kuybyshev; (5) nations moving capitals to gain more national unity as the Turkish move from Istanbul to Ankara; and finally (6) the site, size, and function of capitals. Even a short study of the list above and other aspects of the main subject would take more space than is available in a one-chapter treatment of political geography; consequently the interested student must seek added information from consultation of the references at the end of the chapter.

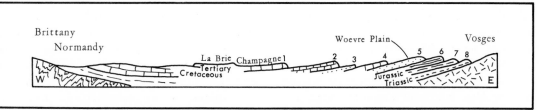

Fig. 20–11   Cuestas of the Paris Basin. The Paris Basin contains at least eight east-facing uplands which alternate with lowlands between Paris and the Vosges Mountains. Notice that the uplands, shown as steep escarpments in the drawing, are numbered from 1 to 8; the French have given each a local name. These cuestas are developed on rocks of differing geologic ages including Tertiary, Cretaceous, Jurassic, and Triassic. Uplands and lowlands are a result of differential erosion among weak and strong rocks in close contact with one another. Prior to the air age, they were a great natural defense for the French capital. (*The sketch and descriptive material are based on a portion of A. K. Lobeck's* Geologic Map of Europe)

Geography and Military Activities

Since geography is known to affect results of military activities, a few illustrations of environmental influences are mentioned below. One of the classic examples of topographic influences upon army movements was the German advance across the Belgian Plain during the early days of World War I (Fig. 20–11). There were many shorter routes than the one chosen by the German command in the drive against France. (1) The route straight west to Paris would have necessitated crossing the Vosges mountain barrier. (2) The roads north or south of the Vosges through the Lorraine or Belfort gateways were easy for the French to defend. And once these gateways were conquered by the Germans, they would still face the many limestone cuestas between the Vosges and Paris, cuestas which have been called the natural defenses of the French capital. (3) The route to Paris from the north and northeast through the narrow valleys of the Meuse and the Moselle was discarded because of the advantages for French defense. (4) Only the longer route by way of the Belgian Plain gave the topographic advantage that the Germans sought for a quick strike against Paris. In defense of this choice German generals state that "Belgian neutrality had to be violated on strategic grounds."

A significant climatic influence upon military activities occurred in the U-2 incident of May 1960. The advent of long spring and summer days after a winter of short periods of daylight was an important element in the decision to send a U-2 reconnaissance plane over the Soviet Union, May 1, just prior to the projected Communist-Free World summit conference.

Examples of minerals and power resources creating friction and military activity among the nations are legion. Winston Churchill in speaking of the progress of World War II stated that the Allies rode to victory on a sea of oil. Middle East petroleum is a major reason why great and small world powers have been interested in that region and why the Have-not Arab states are jealous and covetous of the Haves. The French-Algerian War probably lasted longer than it would have had no oil been discovered in the Algerian Sahara. Moreover, the Algerian-Morocco border fight of 1963 was influenced by the actual or potential presence of petroleum and iron in the disputed area.

Finally, political geographers have been studying global military strategy for centuries with a variety of approaches. Among the best known are H. J. Mackinder's treatise on the power potential of the Heartland of Eurasia; A. T. Mahan's books stressing the influence of sea power upon history; and N. J. Spykman's studies emphasizing that the Rimland of Eurasia is more important than the Heartland. These and most other historical views of world strategy may have had merit at the time they were presented, but they probably have little value in the present age of intercontinental missiles.

International Organizations

Closely allied to military activities are several international groups such as the North Atlantic Treaty Organization, NATO, formed in 1949; the Southeast Asia Collective Defense Treaty Organization, SEATO, organized in 1954; and the Central Treaty Organization, launched in 1955 by several Middle East powers primarily for the defense of Turkey and Iran against Russian attack. Treaties of all these international groups contain at least one clause resolving to unite efforts for collective defense. Even the United Nations, one of the world's largest political groupings, puts strong emphasis upon keeping the peace among the many of its numerous activities. This body, with 111 members in 1963 and only about 20 short of the world total, has supervised armies in the Congo, the Gaza Strip, and Yemen.

Certain other international organizations have aims primarily economic in nature. One of these, formed in the late 1940's was the outgrowth of the Marshall Plan to rebuild agriculture, manufacturing, mining, commerce, and so forth, in European nations whose economy had been ruined by World War II. Originally it was called the Organization for European Economic Cooperation, OEEC, but in 1960 the name was changed to Organization for Economic Cooperation and Development, OECD. The change in name and purpose was to broaden the scope of the group so as to include aid for the underdeveloped nations and to broaden multilateral world trade.

Other economic groups include the European Coal and Steel Community, OCSC, formed in 1952; the European Economic Community, EEC, better known as the Common Market, created by the Treaty of Rome in 1958; and the European Free Trade Association, EFTA, organized in 1959 and commonly called the Outer Seven. All these have been described in Chapter Eighteen, and no further comment is necessary. However, mention may be made of the Council of Economic Mutual Assistance started in 1949 by Communist Russia and its satellite states. The CEMA treaty differs from the three others in that the CEMA governments maintain control over agriculture, commerce, manufacturing, and mining in the respective states.

A third type of international organization emphasizes political-cultural activities. Prominent in this very general classification are the Organization of American States, formed in 1948 as an outgrowth of the Pan American Union; the Arab League, born in 1945, and at present well unified only in a major religion; and finally the British Commonwealth, an informal and very successful group of states. Several of the entirely independent members of the Commonwealth were either occupied by or were colonies of Great Britain; and it may be well at this point to comment briefly on the present status of colonialism.

The days of Great Power collection of colonial appendages are over. Among the reasons for making such collections were for economic advantage, exclusive control of scarce materials, outlets for surplus population, and establishing missions. All of these have been proven far less than successful. Although old time colonialism is dead or dying and colonies now make up less than 2 per cent of the world's total population, millions of people are still deprived of their elementary freedoms and possess no true democratic means of expression. In short, colonialism of history may be gone, but its historical characteristics remain widespread throughout the world.

Geopolitics

N. J. Spykman explained geopolitics as "the planning of the security policy of a country in terms of its geographic factors." Karl Haushofer, a prominent German geographer of World War II said that, "Political geography views the state from the standpoint of space, while geopolitics views space from the standpoint of the state." The word geopolitics gained considerable ill repute during the period between World Wars I and II. At that time several German scientists published what was supposed to be geographic research under the name of geopolitics. Most of their studies distorted geographic facts for the purpose of political aggrandizement. Possibly some day the term will gain a better reputation by establishing a discipline parallel to and intermediate between political geography and political science.

The World's Independent States[3]

The year 1964 started with 122 states generally accepted as independent; that is possessing statehood without foreign jurisdiction. At the start of World War I, there were 63; at the beginning of World War II, 71.

The world's states vary greatly in area from several with continental proportions to two—Monaco and Vatican City—which should be measured in acres rather than square miles. There are also broad differences in population from over 700 million in China to about 1000 in Vatican City. The number of independent states by continents is 14 in North America; 10 in South America; 31 in Europe; 29 in Asia; 35 in Africa; and 3 in Oceania.

The 122 states listed in *Status of the World's Nations*, U.S. Department of State Geographic Bulletin No. 2 are given below alphabetically by name; together with the most recent available figures on population, area, and capital. Population is given in 1000's; and area in thousands of square miles unless parentheses are used to indicate actual size. Membership in the United Nations is indicated by an (*) asterisk.

---

[3] The material in this section is based upon *Status of the World's Nations*, by G. Etzel Pearcy, Geographic Bulletin No. 2, revised March 1964, U.S. Department of State. It is suggested that each student obtain this 22 page bulletin from the Supt. of Documents for 25 cents.

Populations, Areas, Capitals, and U.N. Membership for All Independent States

STATE	POPULATION	AREA	CAPITAL
*Afghanistan	13,800	251	Kabul
*Albania	1,736	11	Tirana
*Algeria	11,300	920	Algiers
Andorra	10	(175)	Andorra
*Argentina	21,297	1,072	Buenos Aires
*Australia	10,916	2,971	Canberra
*Austria	7,151	32	Vienna
*Belgium	9,251	12	Brussels
Bhutan	600	19	Thimbu (a)
*Bolivia	3,596	424	La Paz (b)
*Brazil	75,271	3,287	Brasilia
*Bulgaria	8,045	43	Sofia
*Burma	23,664	262	Rangoon
*Burundi	2,600	11	Bujumbura
*Cambodia	5,749	67	Phnom Penh
*Cameroon	4,864	184	Yaoundé
*Canada	18,928	3,846	Ottawa
*Central African			
Republic	1,250	242	Bangui
*Ceylon	10,645	25	Colombo
*Chad	2,798	495	Fort-Làmy
*Chile	8,098	286	Santiago
*China	724,543	3,911	Taipei (c), Taiwan (provisional)
*Colombia	15,098	440	Bogotá
*Congo, Republic of	865	135	Brazzaville
*Congo, Republic of the	14,797	905	Léopoldville
*Costa Rica	1,325	20	San José
*Cuba	7,203	44	Havana
*Cyprus	589	4	Nicosia
*Czechoslovakia	13,902	49	Prague
*Dahomey	2,050	45	Porto Novo (d)
*Denmark	4,654	17	Copenhagen
*Dominican Republic	3,334	19	Santo Domingo
*Ecuador	4,690	106	Quito
*El Salvador	2,654	8	San Salvador
*Ethiopia	21,000	455	Addis Ababa
*Finland	4,555	130	Helsinki
*France	47,840	213	Paris
*Gabon	450	102	Libreville

(a) Thimbu is the official capital; Paro is the administrative capital and the summer capital.

(b) Although La Paz is the administrative capital, Sucre is the legal capital and seat of the judiciary.

(c) The United States does not recognize Red China with its capital at Peking. Of the total area of mainland China and Taiwan, 3,897,000 square miles and 712,000,000 people are on the mainland.

(d) Cotonou is scheduled to become the official capital.

STATE	POPULATION	AREA	CAPITAL
Germany, Federal Republic of	55,543	96	Bonn (provisional) (e)
*Ghana	7,244	92	Accra
*Greece	8,469	51	Athens
*Guatemala	4,095	42	Guatemala
*Guinea	3,357	95	Conakry
*Haiti	4,448	11	Port-au-Prince
*Honduras	2,008	43	Tegucigalpa
*Hungary	10,102	36	Budapest
*Iceland	183	40	Reykjavik
*India	458,677	1,180	New Delhi
*Indonesia	99,580	736	Djakarta
*Iran	22,182	636	Tehran
*Iraq	7,000	172	Baghdad
*Ireland	2,841	27	Dublin
*Israel	2,428	8	Jerusalem (de facto)
*Italy	50,421	116	Rome
*Ivory Coast	3,410	125	Abidjan
*Jamaica	1,684	4	Kingston
*Japan	96,150	148	Tokyo
*Jordan	1,752	37	Amman
*Kenya	8,676	225	Nairobi
Korea	37,700	85	Seoul
*Kuwait	322	6	Kuwait
*Laos	2,500	86	Vientiane (f)
*Lebanon	1,864	4	Beirut
*Liberia	1,310	43	Monrovia
*Libya	1,244	679	Benghazi; Tripoli (g)
Liechtenstein	18	(61)	Vaduz
*Luxembourg	324	1	Luxembourg
*Madagascar	5,803	230	Tananarive
*Malaysia	10,521	129	Kuala Lumpur
*Mali	4,303	465	Bamako
*Mauritania	850	419	Nouakchott
*Mexico	38,416	760	México, D.F.
Monaco	21	(0.6)	Monaco
*Morocco	12,300	174	Rabat
Muscat and Oman	565	82	Muscat
*Nepal	9,560	55	Katmandu
*Netherlands	11,998	12	Amsterdam (h)

(e) Population figure excludes West Berlin, which had an estimated population of 2,179,000 on August 30, 1963.

(f) Vientiane is the administrative capital; Luang Prabang is the royal capital.

(g) Benghazi and Tripoli are co-capitals. In addition a federal administrative center is being established at Baida.

(h) Amsterdam is the capital; The Hague is the seat of the government.

STATE	POPULATION	AREA	CAPITAL
*New Zealand	2,533	104	Wellington
*Nicaragua	1,524	57	Managua
*Niger	3,200	489	Niamey
*Nigeria	55,654	357	Lagos
*Norway	3,655	125	Oslo
*Pakistan	98,612	365	Rawalpindi (*i*)
*Panama	1,139	29	Panamá (City)
*Paraguay	1,862	157	Asunción
*Peru	11,511	482	Lima
*Philippines	30,758	116	Manila (*j*)
*Poland	30,806	120	Warsaw
*Portugal	9,073	36	Lisbon
*Rumania	18,681	92	Bucharest
*Rwanda	2,780	10	Kigali
San Marino	17	(24)	San Marino
*Saudi Arabia	4,500	618	Riyadh
*Senegal	3,000	76	Dakar
*Sierra Leone	2,183	28	Freetown
*Somalia	2,250	246	Mogadiscio
*South Africa, Republic of	16,640	472	Pretoria (*k*)
*Soviet Union	223,122	8,603	Moscow
*Spain	31,077	195	Madrid
*Sudan	12,650	967	Khartoum
*Sweden	7,581	174	Stockholm
Switzerland	5,870	16	Bern
*Syria	4,824	72	Damascus
*Tanganyika	9,726	362	Dar es Salaam
*Thailand	29,000	198	Bangkok
*Togo	1,559	22	Lomé
*Trinidad and Tobago	880	2	Port-of-Spain
*Tunisia	4,295	63	Tunis
*Turkey	30,256	296	Ankara
*Uganda	7,186	94	Kampala
*United Arab Republic	27,968	386	Cairo
*United Kingdom	54,210	95	London (*l*)
*United States	191,000	3,615	Washington
*Upper Volta	4,500	106	Ouagadougou
*Uruguay	2,556	72	Montevideo

(*i*) Rawalpindi in West Pakistan is the seat of the executive branch of the government pending the construction of the capital city of Islamabad. The new constitution (1962) designated Dacca in East Pakistan as the second capital of the country and seat of the legislative branch.

(*j*) A new capital, Quezon City, has been officially established near Manila; but the transfer of administration awaits construction of adequate facilities.

(*k*) Pretoria in Transvaal Province is the official capital and seat of the executive branch of the government; Capetown in Cape Province, is the seat of the legislative branch, while Bloemfontein, in Orange Free State, is the seat of the Supreme Court. Natal Province is reimbursed for not having any national governmental honors.

(*l*) Belfast, Edinburgh, and Cardiff serve to some extent as administrative centers for Northern Ireland, Scotland, and Wales, respectively.

STATE	POPULATION	AREA	CAPITAL
Vatican City	1	(0.2)	Vatican City
*Venezuela	8,276	352	Caracas
Viet-Nam	32,501	126	Saigon
Western Samoa	117	1	Apia
*Yemen	4,500	75	San'a
*Yugoslavia	19,113	99	Belgrade
*Zanzibar	320	1	Zanzibar (City)

States That Were Scheduled for Independence in 1964

Malawi (Nyasaland)	2,980	37	Zomba, July 6, 1964
Malta	328	(122)	Valletta, May 31, 1964
Zambia (Northern Rhodesia)	3,500	288	Lusaka, Oct. 24, 1964

QUESTIONS, EXERCISES, AND PROBLEMS

1. Give several definitions for political geography. Comment upon the subtopics that may be included in its study. Define state, nation, and country.

2. What different methods may be used to locate a state? Tell how location influenced the political geography of France, Egypt, Panamá, and other states. How may an area lose its strategic location and another increase in strategic significance?

3. Explain, with an illustration, how the shape of a country may influence its political activities. Does the size of a nation have anything to do with gaining and maintaining independence? How does a state grow?

4. Indicate at least two ways by which boundaries may be classified, and explain each classification. Has concern over national boundaries increased or decreased in the last century? Explain.

5. Describe with examples the history and utilization of oceans, gulfs, and seas as political boundaries; do the same for inland waters. How does the age of a stream influence its effectiveness as a stable boundary? Comment upon the Rio Grande as a boundary between states and nations. Do mountains make stable boundaries? Describe the Andean boundary between Chile and Argentina; the Himalayan boundary between China and India; the Pyrenees boundary between France and Spain.

6. Give several examples of boundaries marked by latitude and longitude; comment upon their effectiveness. Why did the Chinese build the Great Wall? Comment upon the Maginot Line and the Berlin Wall. Give a half dozen examples of disputed or unrecognized boundaries.

7. Tell of present thinking upon freedom, control, and jurisdiction of the sea. How may international relations be affected by inland waters? Give several illustrations to stress points made.

8. What characteristics of a country's population are most significant from the standpoint of political geography? Apply these characteristics to each of the present and former great powers. Compare the natural resources of the United States and Russia. Show relationships between political geography and foreign trade. Use specific examples to illustrate.

9. Describe the core areas and capitals of China, Russia, Switzerland, England, France, and India. Give examples of states with more than one capital; with more than one core area. Why did the Germans violate Belgian neutrality in World War I? Give other illustrations of the influence of the geographic environment upon military activities.

10. Identify the following: Gila, meander, mature stream, youthful stream, Panhandle, demarcation, delimitation, Sulaiman, Kirthar, Virgin Islands, U-2 incident, H. J. Mackinder, A. T. Mahan, N. J. Spykman, geopolitics, Karl Haushofer, DEW line, Brasilia, Manifest Destiny, Law-of-the-sea conference, Chaco War, Chamizal Settlement, crest line, drainage divide, Pre-Andean Depression, 49th parallel, 38th parallel, 17th parallel, New Delhi, NATO, SEATO, OEEC, OECD, Outer Seven, OCSC, EFTA, CEMA, Arab League, Pan American Union, St. Gotthard Pass.

SELECTED REFERENCES

Alexander, L. M., *World Political Patterns,* Rand McNally, 1963 or latest revision.

American Geographical Society, *Focus;* starting in the 1950's and continuing, this little magazine features a brief readable survey of country, region, or resource. The maps are especially useful for political geography.

Annals of the Association of American Geographers, *Issue on Political Geography,* Sept. 1959; "Boundary Concepts in the Setting of Place and Time," S. B. Jones; "The Nature of Frontiers and Boundaries," L. K. D. Kristof; "A Free Secure Access to the Sea," N. J. G. Pounds; "The Function and Methods of Electoral Geography," J. R. V. Prescott; "Exclaves," G. W. S. Robinson.

Augelli, J. P., "Brasilia: The Emergence of a National Capital," *Journal of Geography,* Sept. 1963, pp. 241–52.

Brown, R. H., *Historical Geography of the United States,* Harcourt, Brace, & World, 1948.

Carlson, Lucile, *Political Geography,* Prentice-Hall, latest revision.

Chang, Sen Dou, "Some Aspects of the Urban Geography of the Chinese Hsien Capital," *Annals of the Association of American Geographers,* March 1961, pp. 23–45.

Douglas, E. M., *Boundaries, Areas, Geographic Centers and Altitudes of the United States and Several States,* Geological Survey Bulletin 817, Govt. Printing Office, 1939.

Fair, T. J. D. and Shaffer, N. M., "Population Patterns and Policies in South Africa 1951–1960," *Economic Geography,* July 1964, pp. 261–74.

Gregory, Gladys, *The Chamizal Settlement, A View from El Paso,* Southwestern Studies, Summer 1963, Texas Western College Press.

Hamdan, G., "The Political Map of the New Africa," *Geographical Review,* July 1963, pp. 418–39; "Capitals of the New Africa," *Economic Geography,* July 1964, pp. 239–53.

Hippocrates, *Influences of Atmosphere, Water and Situation,* Ch. 16.

Hoffman, G. W. and Pearcy, G. E., editors, *Searchlight Books,* of various dates and by various authors and including the following and other titles, all published in the 1960's: "A New Soviet Heartland"; "Canada in the American Community"; "Central America"; "Divided Germany and Berlin"; "Environment and Policies in West Africa"; "Indonesia"; "Japan"; "Pacific Island Bastions of the United States"; "Pakistan"; "Poland Between East and West"; "Puerto Rico"; "Space"; "Spain in the World"; "The Balkans"; "The Changing Map of Africa"; "The Global Sea"; "The Himalayan Kingdoms"; "The Lower Mekong"; "The Philippines"; "The Russo-Chinese Borderlands"; "The Soviet Union"; "Transportation and Politics."

Jackson, W. A. D., editor, *Politics and Geographic Relationships: Readings in the Nature of Political Geography,* Prentice-Hall, 1964.

Jones, S. B., *Boundary Making, A Handbook for Statesmen,* Carnegie Endowment for International Peace, 1945.

Karan, Pradyumna, P. "Dividing the Water: A Problem in Political Geography," *Professional Geographer,* Vol. 12, No. 1, 1961, pp. 6–10; "The Sino-Soviet Boundary Dispute," *Journal of Geography,* May 1964, pp. 216–22.

Kimble, G. H. T., "A U.S. of Africa—Not Very Likely," *New York Times Magazine,* Sunday, March 29, 1964; "A Handicap for New Nations: Climate," *New York Times Magazine,* Sunday, Sept. 29, 1963; *Tropical Africa,* 2 volumes, The Twentieth Century Fund, 1960.

Lattimore, Owen, "Origins of the Great Wall of China," *Geographical Review,* Vol. 27, 1937, pp. 529–49.

Linge, G. J. R., "Canberra After Fifty Years," *Geographical Review,* Oct. 1963, pp. 467–86.

Morrison, John A., "Russia and Warm Water," *U.S. Naval Institute Proceedings,* 1952, pp. 1169–79.

Nel, A., "Geographical Aspects of Apartheid in South Africa," *Tijdschrift Voor Econ. En Soc. Geographie,* Oct. 1962, pp. 197–209.

Nelson, H. J., "Walled Cities of the United States," *Annals of the Association of American Geographers,* March 1961, pp. 1–22.

Nicholson, N. L., *The Boundaries of Canada, Its Provinces and Territories,* Geographical Branch Memoir 2, Dept. of Mines and Technical Surveys, Ottawa, 1954.

Pearcy, G. Etzel, *Boundary Concepts and Definitions,* Geographic Report, No. 1, April 28, 1961, U.S. Department of State; *Status of the World's Nations,* Geographic Bulletin, No. 2, U.S. Department of State, March 1964; *United States and Outlying Areas,* Geographic Report No. 4, revised, U.S. Department of State, Feb. 7, 1963.

Pounds, N. J. G., *Political Geography,* McGraw-Hill, 1963.

Robinson, K. W., "Sixty Years of Federation in Australia," *Geographical Review,* Jan. 1961, pp. 1–20.

Shaudys, V. K. "The External Aspects of the Political Geography of Five Diminutive European States," *Journal of Geography,* Jan. 1962, pp. 20–31.

Toynbee, A. J., *Greek Historical Thought from Homer to the Age of Heraclitus,* J. M. Dent tnd Sons, 1924.

United States Census Bureau, *State Origins and Boundaries,* United States Summary, Number of Inhabitants, Final Report, PC (1) 1A, U.S. Census of Population, 1960.

Appendix

World Agricultural Production Maps

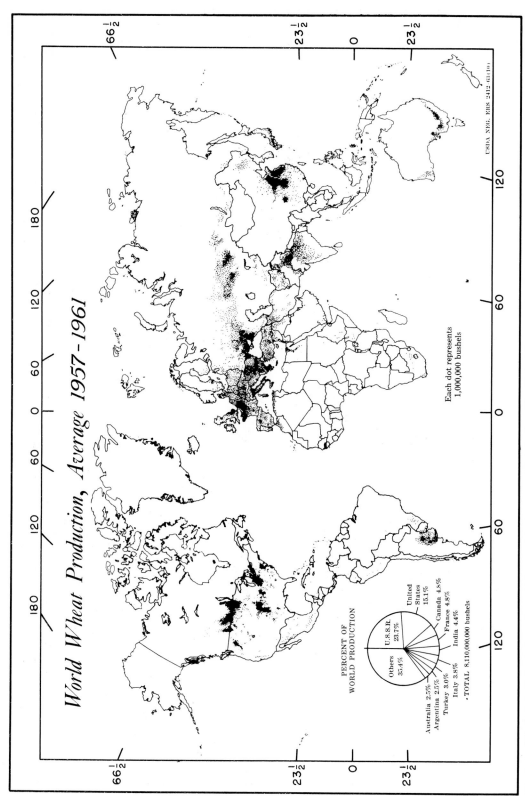

Fig. A–1 What kind of wheat, the spring or winter variety, is grown along the Canadian-United States border; in Argentina; in Russian Siberia; in other important wheat-growing lands? Explain. The United States with less than one-third as much land in wheat as the Soviet Union harvested nearly two-thirds as much grain in 1957–1961. Explain. (*Courtesy U.S. Department of Agriculture*)

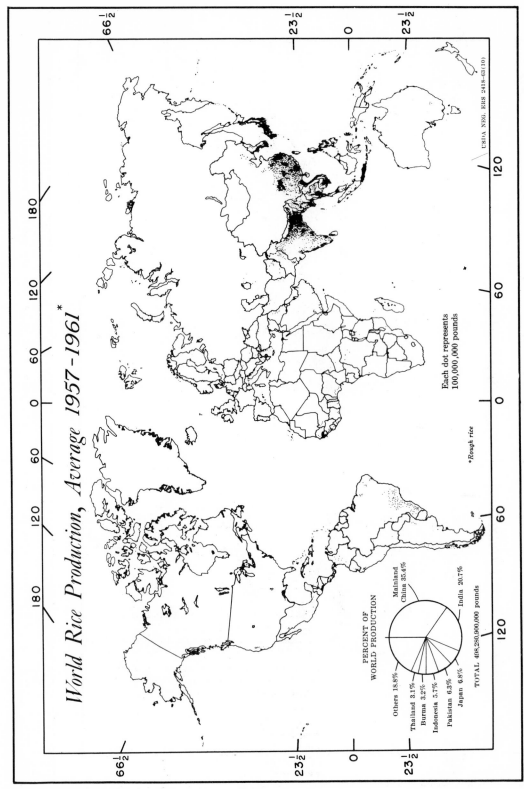

*World Rice Production, Average 1957-1961**

Each dot represents
100,000,000 pounds

**Rough rice*

PERCENT OF
WORLD PRODUCTION

Mainland
China 35.4%

India 20.7%

Japan 6.8%

Pakistan 6.3%

Indonesia 5.7%

Burma 3.2%

Thailand 3.1%

Others 18.8%

TOTAL 408,280,000,000 pounds

USDA NEG. ERS 2418-63(10)

Fig. A-2 Account for the dominance of Southeast Asia in world rice production. How can the United States produce rice for export to Southeast Asia? Why was it necessary for Communist China, normally a rice exporter, to import 6 million tons of the grain in 1963? Explain the production of rice in the United Arab Republic. (*Courtesy U.S. Department of Agriculture*)

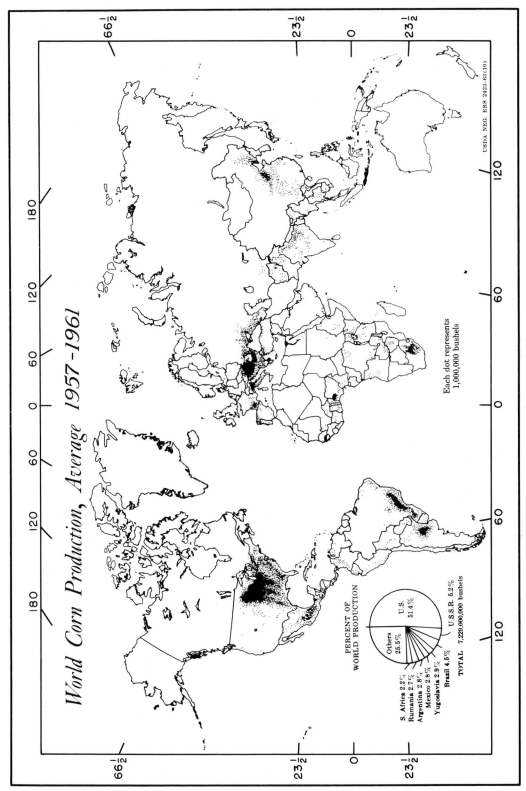

World Corn Production, *Average 1957–1961*

PERCENT OF
WORLD PRODUCTION

Others
25.5%

U.S.
51.4%

S. Africa 2.2%
Rumania 2.7%
Argentina 2.8%
Mexico 2.8%
Yugoslavia 2.9%
Brazil 4.5%

U.S.S.R. 5.2%

TOTAL 7,229,000,000 bushels

Each dot represents
1,000,000 bushels

USDA NEG. ERS 2423–63(10)

Fig. A–3 Corn is a cosmopolitan crop. The United States grows nearly half of the world crop in the middle latitudes on a little more than one fourth of the world's corn acreage; and yet corn is an important crop of tropical Mexico, Brazil, Nigeria, Java, and the Philippines. World export amounted to only 8 per cent of production in 1961–1962; most of this export went to the livestock industry of Western Europe. (*Courtesy U.S. Department of Agriculture*)

383

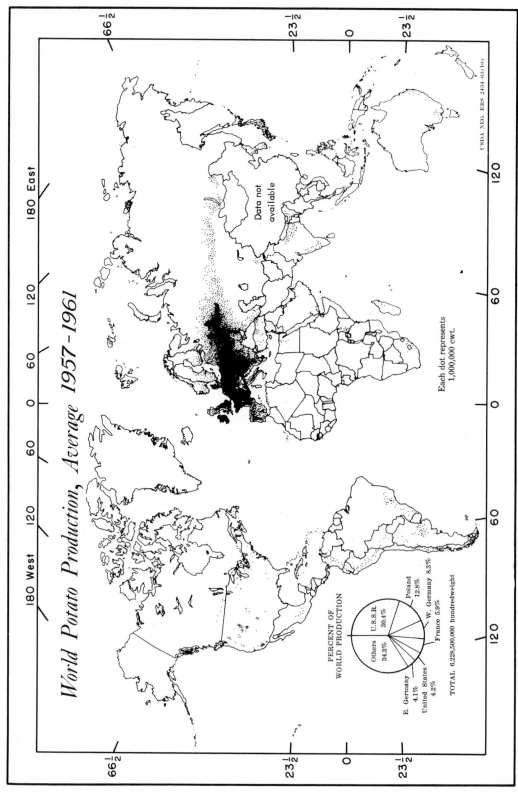

Fig. A-4 The bulk of the world potato crop is grown in the middle latitudes of low-altitude European lands although the plant was brought there originally from tropical Latin American highlands. Potatoes now grown in the tropics are produced largely in the highlands. Only about one per cent of the potato crop enters world trade, and most of this commerce is within the European continent. (*Courtesy U.S. Department of Agriculture*)

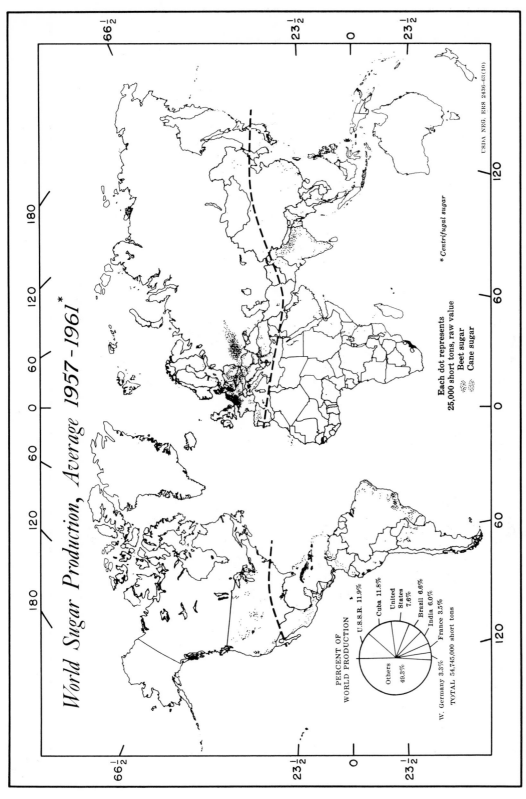

Fig. A–5 Cane sugar, along with coffee, cacao, and tea, ranks high as an export crop but little. Except for eastern Europe, the beet sugar producing regions are all net importers of sugar. Note that the sugar beet is a crop of the middle latitudes, whereas sugar cane is confined to the tropics and subtropics. The dashed line marks the boundary between cane sugar to the south and beet sugar to the north. (*Courtesy U.S. Department of Agriculture*)

World Sugar Production, Average 1957–1961

Each dot represents
25,000 short tons, raw value
Beet sugar
Cane sugar

* *Centrifugal sugar*

USDA NEG. ERS 2436–63(10)

PERCENT OF
WORLD PRODUCTION

U.S.S.R. 11.9%
Cuba 11.8%
United States 7.6%
Brazil 6.6%
India 6.0%
France 3.5%
W. Germany 3.3%
Others 49.3%

TOTAL 54,745,000 short tons

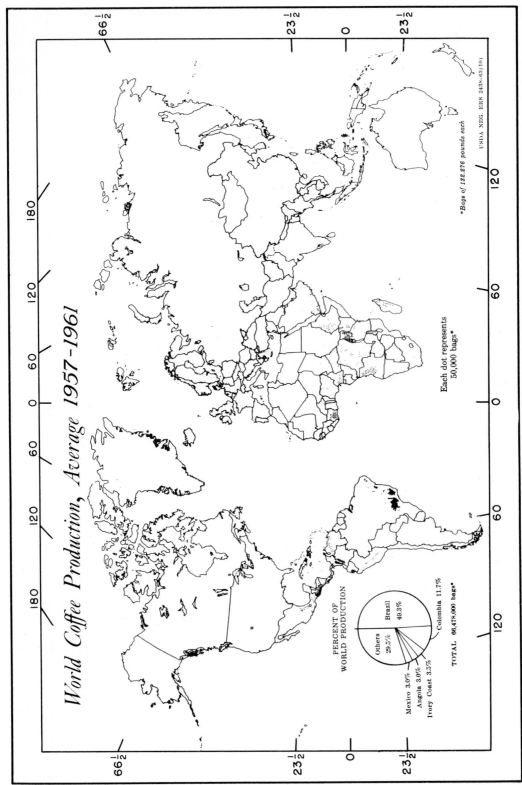

Fig. A–6 Coffee growing is confined to the tropics because the tree is vulnerable to frost damage. The crop is grown largely for export. Although production has expanded rapidly in the humid tropics of Africa, Brazil and the northern countries of Latin America account for the major part of world production. (*Courtesy U.S. Department of Agriculture*)

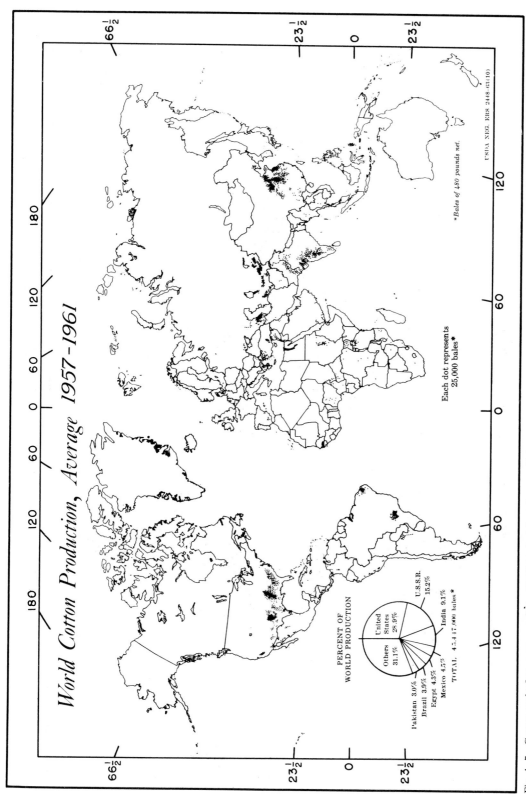

World Cotton Production, Average 1957–1961

66½

23½

0

23½

*Bales of 480 pounds net.

USDA NEG. ERS 2448-63 (10)

180

120

60

Each dot represents
25,000 bales*

0

120

60

PERCENT OF
WORLD PRODUCTION

Others
31.1%

United
States
28.9%

U.S.S.R.
15.2%

India 9.1%

Pakistan 3.0%
Brazil 3.9%
Egypt 4.3%
Mexico 4.5%

TOTAL 45,417,000 bales*

120

60

66½

23½

0

23½

Fig. A-7   Cotton ranks first among world textile fibers in value of output. It is produced chiefly as a rain-grown crop, but it also grows under irrigation in such dry areas as the southern part of the Soviet Union, United Arab Republic, Mexico, and western United States. Growth is limited to the tropics or subtropics because the plant needs a growing season of approximately 200 days for best results. (*Courtesy U.S. Department of Agriculture*)

387

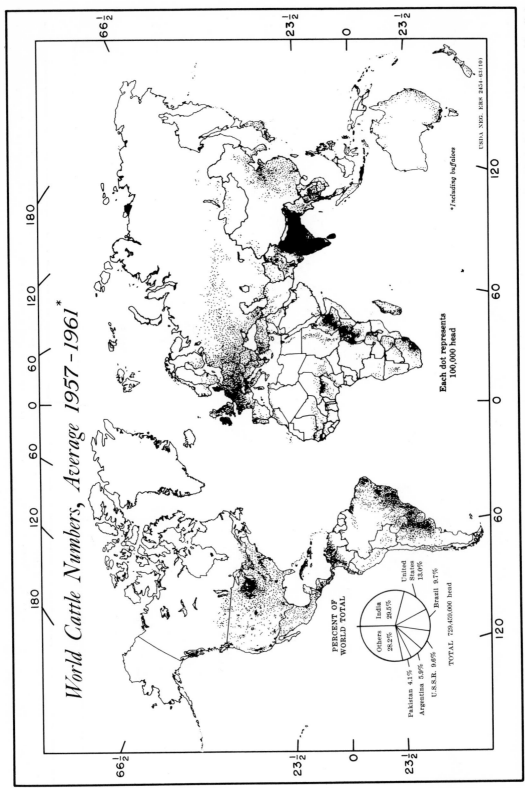

World Cattle Numbers, Average 1957–1961[*]

Each dot represents
100,000 head

PERCENT OF
WORLD TOTAL

India 29.5%

United
States
13.0%

Brazil 9.7%

U.S.S.R. 9.6%

Argentina 5.9%

Pakistan 4.1%

Others
28.2%

TOTAL 729,459,000 head

*Including buffaloes

USDA NEG. ERS 2434-63(10)

Fig. A–8 India contains more than twice as many cattle (including water buffaloes) as the United States. However, in India cattle furnish draft power and are used but little for milk or meat. In Latin America they are raised chiefly for meat; but dairy breeds predominate in Europe. Both beef and dairy cattle are important in the United States. Explain these differences. (*Courtesy U.S. Department of Agriculture*)

388

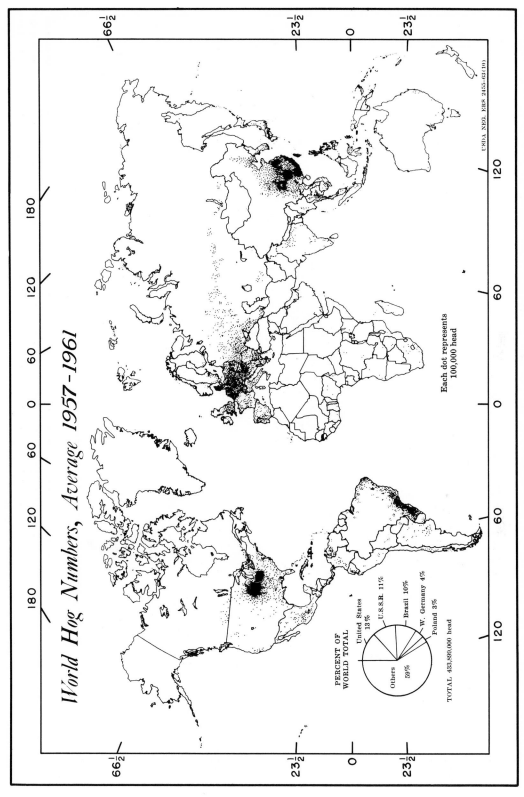

World Hog Numbers, Average 1957–1961

Each dot represents
100,000 head

PERCENT OF
WORLD TOTAL

Others
59%

United States
13%

U.S.S.R. 11%

Brazil 10%

W. Germany 4%

Poland 3%

TOTAL 433,890,000 head

USDA NEG. ERS 2455–63(10)

Fig. A–9 Note the general correlation between hogs and corn in the United States Corn Belt (see Fig. A–3). Here the animals are fattened on corn, but hogs are not particular about what they eat. In Denmark they feed on dairy by-products; in Spain on acorns; on refuse in China; on grass and grain in Brazil; and on table scraps around many of the world's cities. (*Courtesy U.S. Department of Agriculture*)

389

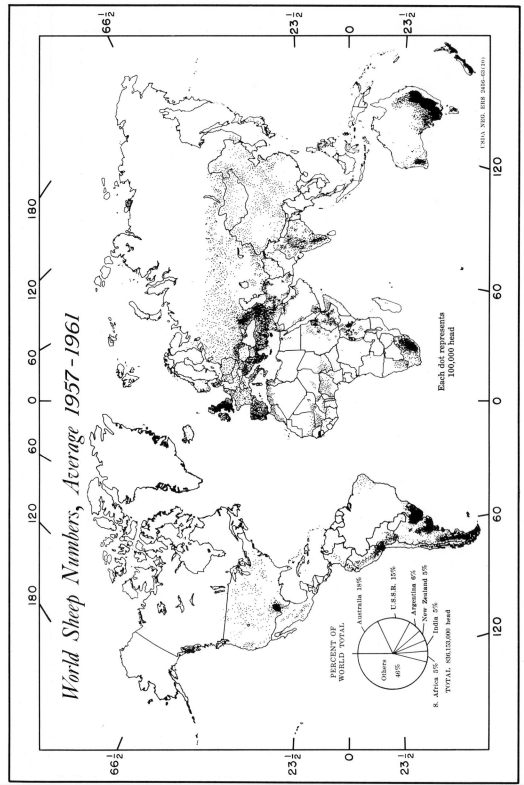

Fig. A–10   Explain the concentration of sheep in the Mediterranean lands, the British Isles, Texas, and the highlands and southern parts of the Southern Hemisphere. Australian sheep are raised primarily for wool. In most other advanced countries, breeding has emphasized both meat and wool. In many underdeveloped nations, sheep and goats are a principal source of meat and milk. *(Courtesy U.S. Department of Agriculture)*

List of Maps

List of Climatic Charts

Index

Denotes map or illustration.